ALLIES:
PEARL HARBOR TO D-DAY

John S. D. Eisenhower

ALLIES:

PEARL HARBOR TO D-DAY

DOUBLEDAY & COMPANY, INC., GARDEN CITY, NEW YORK

1982

ISBN: 0-385-11479-6
Library of Congress Catalog Card Number 77–16914

BOOK DESIGN BY BENTE HAMANN

Printed in the United States of America

First Edition

To Fox Conner

Give me allies to fight against.
　　　　　　—NAPOLEON

There is only one thing worse
than fighting with allies,
and that is fighting without them.
　　　—SIR WINSTON CHURCHILL

CONTENTS

LIST OF ILLUSTRATIONS

PHOTOS FOLLOWING PAGE 140

FRANKLIN DELANO ROOSEVELT (1882–1945)
HARRY L. HOPKINS (1890–1946)
WILLIAM D. LEAHY (1875–1959)
WINSTON LEONARD SPENCER CHURCHILL (1874–1965)
JAN CHRISTIAAN SMUTS (1870–1950)
SIR HASTINGS LIONEL ISMAY (1887–1965)
GEORGE C. MARSHALL (1880–1959)
ERNEST J. KING (1878–1956)
HENRY H. ARNOLD (1886–1950)
SIR ALAN F. BROOKE (1883–1963)
SIR (ALFRED) DUDLEY POUND (1877–1943)
SIR CHARLES F. A. PORTAL (1893–1971)
SIR JOHN G. DILL (1881–1944)
CORDELL HULL (1871–1955)
ANTHONY EDEN (1897–1977)
W. AVERELL HARRIMAN (1891–)
VYACHESLAV M. MOLOTOV (1890–)
DWIGHT D. EISENHOWER (1890–1969)
SIR HAROLD R. L. ALEXANDER (1891–1969)
SIR ARCHIBALD WAVELL (1883–1950)
SIR ANDREW B. CUNNINGHAM (1883–1963)
SIR ARTHUR TEDDER (1890–1967)
GEORGE S. PATTON, JR. (1885–1945)

LIST OF MAPS

Maps by Rafael Palacios

ACKNOWLEDGMENTS

I am greatly indebted to the efforts of Mrs. Wayne H. (Carol) Utecht, of Brokaw, Wisconsin. Her functions began in 1977 as a researcher into minor sources, some of which, after she had perused them, turned out to be major. Possessed of great reading speed and retention—and with a keen interest in the subject—she eventually proved her value as a double-check in nearly all phases of the manuscript.

This effort was also dependent on the work of my two secretaries, Mrs. Thomas M. (Judith Horvath) Hedberg, who has now played a major role in all three of my books, and in the earlier stages Mrs. Harold (Arlene) Himes.

The polishing of the later drafts was made much more comfortable by the courtesy of Major General W. W. Stromberg, USA (Retd.), who devoted a whole week in early 1979 to conducting me on a tour of Casablanca, Marrakech, Port Lyautey (now Kenitra), Fedala, Algiers, and Cherchel. Assisting him in the small odyssey were his associates, John and Paul Canton, Mr. and Mrs. John Beam of the American Embassy, Algiers, and the late M. René Valteau. How much the text of the first draft was affected by seeing these places firsthand is problematical, but the confidence I attained from the experience was invaluable.

Many individuals contributed information and help. Because of space I can mention (alphabetically) only Professor Stephen E. Ambrose; Ambassador Charles E. Bohlen; General Marshall S. Carter; Captain Charles O. Cook, USN (Retd.); Professor Arthur Layton Funk; Ambassador John I. Getz; the late Michael Hamblin; Governor W. Averell Harriman; General John W. Huston, Chief of Air Force History; General Lyman L.

Lemnitzer; General Frank McCarthy; the late Ambassador Robert D. Murphy; and Captain Victor Tyson (U. S. Merchant Marine Academy).

I am also much indebted to Mr. William H. Cunliffe, Assistant Chief, Modern Military Branch, U. S. Archives, for providing me with minutes of important meetings and to Mrs. Viola Destafano, Mrs. Flora Edgington, Mrs. Marilou Oakes, and Mrs. Audrey Green of the Defense Department for providing many of the photographs. Mrs. Kristin Gronbeck, Photo Researcher, Doubleday & Company, was invaluable in procuring photos not available from the Department of Defense. And thanks to Steve Ambrose for the quotations cited at the beginning.

Rafael Palacios, who created the maps for my father's *Crusade in Europe* more than thirty years ago, was the cartographer for this book. Rafe's keen knowledge of the war in the Mediterranean was a great assistance in the planning of these new maps. He did, in fact, come up with several ideas on how to condense and clarify the military information.

PREFACE

More than a dozen years ago as of this writing (1981), my curiosity became aroused regarding a subject which I had always taken much for granted: the creation, nurturing, and maintenance of the Anglo-American military alliance of World War II. My interest in this informal but binding relationship had been stimulated when I wrote a book, *The Bitter Woods,* which dealt with Adolf Hitler's Ardennes attack of late 1944, popularly referred to as "The Battle of the Bulge."

This offensive, a last-ditch attempt to destroy the powerful British and American forces then threatening the survival of the Third Reich, depended for success on creating a rupture in the Allied command structure. But despite spectacular, even frightening tactical success—and much concern in the press—Hitler's hope of splitting the Allies never came close. The alliance had been a truly solid coalition. And further thought led me to conclude that such an amalgamation between the efforts of two proud, independent countries could not have occurred by chance. It must have been methodically created and progressively nurtured. How had it come about?

While I was pondering these matters my father, General Dwight D. Eisenhower, had begun work on an informal manuscript describing his wartime relationships with Prime Minister Winston S. Churchill and General George C. Marshall, two men with whom his association had been close. Churchill, as British Prime Minister (and Defense Minister), and Marshall, as U. S. Army Chief of Staff, represented the two governments from whom my father, as Supreme Allied Commander, derived his authority. He obviously admired both men extravagantly.

The manuscript Dad was working on came to over a hundred pages. It was useful in providing insights but it was not ready for publication—too long for an article, too short for a book. Furthermore, it briefly touched on matters that tantalized one's interest, then left the reader dangling. Unwilling, at the age of seventy-seven, to take on another major writing chore—and aware of my growing interest in the alliance—Dad cheerfully handed me the manuscript and bowed out of the picture. He hoped, he said, that I would incorporate such of his material as I desired in a more ambitious project of my own. Thus was I launched on a work which might very well have been called *How They Put It Together*.

Progress on the new manuscript was stopped almost as soon as it was started. First came an unexpected thirty-month stint as U. S. Ambassador to Belgium, where writing was out of the question. On my return home in October of 1971 it was further delayed while I satisfied an urge to record my modest public life in a memoir, *Strictly Personal* (published in 1974). *Letters to Mamie* (1978) also intervened. And then, when I finally returned to the Western Alliance, I discovered the whole subject to be so complex that Dad's manuscript became almost incidental. Hence the long lapse from inception to this published product.

*

The Anglo-American alliance came into being before the United States entered World War II. By the time President Roosevelt had provided fifty American destroyers to the British in September 1940—and certainly by the time of the Lend-Lease Act of early 1941—the Americans were committed to the British cause. The alliance served well throughout World War II, and a "special understanding" has survived a rocky path even to the present day. When, therefore, should a book on this long-term relationship begin and end?

The start was easy: at Pearl Harbor in December 1941, when the alliance became a reality, accepted by all Americans. The cutoff was more difficult to pinpoint, as the story would be long and repetitious. To solve this I arbitrarily chose D-Day, June 1944, with the alliance fully established. This story, therefore, closes at the wedding, passing over the later stages of the marriage, which continued to be tested through the closing months of the war but never reached the point of divorce.

*

Now that I have studied this subject to my reasonable satisfaction, I have been left with two closely related impressions. First, the formation of the alliance, which included agreeing on a common strategy for defeating Germany, Italy, and Japan, proved to be a more difficult task than I had realized. As a cadet and young officer during World War II, I had never stopped to consider the differences between the American war aims and those of the British. The final Allied strategy—closing a ring around Europe and subsequently invading the Continent—appeared utterly logical. In fact it represented a compromise between the American preference for a direct blow against Hitler's Europe and the more cautious, indirect British approach which visualized a later assault against an isolated and worn-down Wehrmacht.

More than logic alone dictated this divergence, for the generals and admirals of Britain and the United States were the products of different military traditions. The Americans in 1941 thought basically as "continentals" who, with their own Civil War and the winning of the West still vivid in the psyche, reacted primarily as land animals, inclined to solve their problems of peace and war on large masses of territory. The British, on the other hand, had achieved world-wide power through maritime prowess; historically, their land battles had been the culmination of seaborne expeditions. (For the six years between 1809 and 1815, for example, no British soldier had set foot on Napoleon's European continent except in Spain.) This British orientation had stemmed from a logical use of available resources—long on industry, short on manpower. The Americans and British simply approached war from different directions.

My second, related conclusion was that this alliance, even once established, still recognized the independence of the two partners. Neither nation gave up any great amount of sovereignty. British units fought in British armies and American units nearly always in American. And while national viewpoints were remarkably submerged in Supreme Headquarters, lower formations remained national in character. British-American rivalries in the field were strong.

Winston Churchill, as an individual, turned out to be less "Allied" in his attitudes than his carefully constructed public image would suggest. For good reason Americans held him in great affection; but behind the scenes his thought processes were couched in terms of "we" and "they." He and Eisenhower, for example, became warm friends personally, but Churchill never ceased, it appears, to think of Eisenhower as one of "them." One must understand and even admire Churchill's British chauvinism, but Americans should not be taken in by his eloquent reminders that his mother had been American. It has been said that Churchill was half American and all British.

Still the alliance in World War II, despite its imperfections, became without question the most successful in modern history. During World War I the French, British, and American armies on the Western Front fought as virtually separate entities despite the appointment, in early 1918, of Marshal Ferdinand Foch as the over-all commander. (His General Headquarters remained completely French.) And another major coalition, that against Napoleon, was so ineffective as to cause my father to write after the war: "Even Napoleon's reputation . . . suffered when students . . . came to realize that he always fought against coalitions. . . ."

The two armies of Wellington and Blücher at Waterloo, for example, were completely separate and between them represented only a third of the total allied strength supposedly under the supreme command of the Austrian Von Schwarzenberg, who was hundreds of miles away. The Anglo-Americans of World War II, on the other hand, used all their common resources—and together. Every British division was committed to battle shortly after D-Day; and by the end of the war not one trained combat division remained in the United States. Nearly all the combat forces of both nations were thus involved against the common enemies.

*

Through nearly six years of the war the personal relationship between Churchill and Roosevelt, established in 1939, set the tone for inter-Allied cooperation at all levels. It stands as a monument to Roosevelt's perception that he initiated a private correspondence with Churchill as early as September of that year, when Churchill had just been appointed First Lord of the Admiralty. Roosevelt's rationale for the correspondence was that the two had occupied "similar positions" in World War I,[1] but his gesture leaves no doubt that he recognized in Churchill the future leader of Britain. On the latter's elevation to the post of Prime Minister on May 10, 1940, he lost no time in writing, "Although I have changed my office, I am sure you would not wish me to discontinue our intimate, private correspondence." The exchange, of course, grew, and with the passage of time Roosevelt and Churchill became more familiar with each other's viewpoints and attitudes.

Before Pearl Harbor Roosevelt and Churchill met once as heads of government, at Argentia Bay, Newfoundland, in August 1941. For three days they conferred on political and military matters. One result was a political declaration, the Atlantic Charter, which set forth commonly held war aims expressed in broad terms. The conference also developed a more closely coordinated military approach to the day when the United States would enter the war.

By Pearl Harbor Roosevelt and Churchill had therefore become cordial though perhaps not yet warm friends. The warmth did, however, develop later and lasted, at least on the surface, throughout the remainder of

[1] Roosevelt had exaggerated the comparison a bit. As First Lord, Churchill had profoundly influenced strategy; Roosevelt, as Assistant Secretary of the Navy, had been an administrator. Nevertheless the coincidence had provided an excellent excuse to begin the exchange of views.

Roosevelt's lifetime. The increasing dominance of Roosevelt and the Americans in the alliance did later rankle Churchill in private, but no rift ever became public.

Though Churchill and Roosevelt were always able to maintain a courteous façade, the same cannot necessarily be said of the uniformed military. As late as November 1943, for example, the Combined Chiefs of Staff could still meet below the Pyramids of Egypt in an atmosphere so acrimonious that one witness was not ruling out a fist fight, even hoping for it. This two years and six meetings after Pearl Harbor! For these were strong men, trained to directness in speech; they were also under great pressure, responsible for vast armies, fleets, and air forces. Happily they put their professional differences aside when they mingled in person outside the conference room.

*

As to this book itself, I cheerfully anticipate certain foreseeable criticisms. The accusation may be made, for example, that I have placed my father, a field commander, in too prominent a role. Actually I originally intended to keep the spotlight shining almost exclusively on the original architects of the alliance—Roosevelt, Churchill, Marshall, Brooke, and others—but as I continued to study I discovered that my father became too important to be relegated to the background. As the senior Allied Commander he grew with time to become not only the implementor of Allied strategy but the symbol of unity as well, the one high leader whose position as Supreme Commander carried no national label. When issues became deadlocked along national lines, therefore, the deciding vote tended to fall to him.

And I freely admit other limitations. Some may object to my unabashed neglect of the war in the Pacific and the Russian front. If I were telling the full story of the entire war, the lopsided view I have portrayed would be misleading. But both the Pacific and the Russian front were largely one-nation shows, and I have dealt with them only as they affected the formation of the Anglo-American alliance.

In a book dealing with high-level personalities one must cope with the danger of portraying war as a chess game, played in an exciting, heady atmosphere. I have tried to combat this tendency by describing some of the hardships endured by top leaders, emphasizing the long, hazardous, and extremely uncomfortable airplane trips, for example. I have also tried to prevent the inevitable humor of many situations from getting out of perspective. Churchill's personal foibles, Alan Brooke's frustrations, and the phlegmatic "Britishness" of Harold Macmillan are amusing to Americans.

Humorous moments, as Churchill himself insisted, made the burdens of responsibility bearable, and I considered it well to mention a few.

*

With the passage of time and with world problems appearing ever more difficult, we sometimes develop nostalgia for the last war we were determined to win, to forget the grim atmosphere in which even the Americans lived during World War II. It is easy now, nearly forty years after the war, to see the successful outcome as a foregone conclusion. As a matter of fact, the Allies had no guarantee of victory until the very end. What if the Germans had been first to develop the atomic bomb? We knew they had done some scientific work along these lines.

And personal tragedy was common. Two of the principal characters of this story, Marshall and Hopkins, lost sons in combat (Marshall's was a stepson but one he had raised). They were among some 292,000 Americans who died. And though this figure is smaller than the corresponding numbers for the American Civil War—and vastly smaller than the proportional losses of the British and Russians—that number of deaths should give pause to anyone tempted to refer to World War II as the "last good war." But again this book deals with a limited aspect of that conflict, and it can include little by way of combat stories. For a real exposure to the horrors and madness of war the reader must look elsewhere.

In closing I would like to add a word about the role of President Franklin D. Roosevelt. He is not covered in this book in so much detail as Churchill and Marshall. The reasons are not difficult to understand. For one, his records are sketchy compared to those of other prominent figures. Churchill's activities are recorded in almost excruciating detail in his extensive six-volume account. Eisenhower, Arnold, Alexander, and Montgomery also wrote memoirs; Forrest Pogue has produced three fine volumes on Marshall based on War Department records and lengthy interviews; Brooke allowed his personal diary to be published by Arthur Bryant. But Roosevelt seemed little inclined to produce memoranda and showed no noticeable interest in maintaining his own historical record—and he did not survive the war to write memoirs.

Equally important, however, was the difference between the respective roles played by Roosevelt and Churchill. In Britain Churchill had little to contend with in maintaining public interest in the war; for the bombs that rained from above, delivered by airplanes in the early days and V-bombs in the later, served as constant, violent reminders of the struggle the British were in. And Churchill fancied himself as a strategist, the Minister of Defense, surrounded by beribboned generals and admirals.

Roosevelt, on the other hand, though a lover of the sea and interested in naval techniques, had no desire to play the warlord. His overriding responsibility lay in keeping the American population (and a critical Congress) motivated to exert a maximum war effort, tolerant of if not enthusiastic about the Europe-first war priority. These home-front preoccupations are not the subjects of this book.

Nevertheless, one is impressed with Roosevelt's ultimate domination of even the strategic direction of the war. When critical decisions came to a head, it was Roosevelt who almost instinctively directed the course. His pragmatism, his instinct for the art of the possible, eventually exerted its pre-eminence in nearly all crucial situations.

ALLIES:

PEARL HARBOR TO D-DAY

Part One

CHAPTER I

A DAY OF INFAMY

O n the evening of December 7, 1941, Prime Minister Winston S. Churchill was entertaining dinner guests at Chequers, his official country residence about an hour's drive northwest of London. Chequers was a peaceful place, and Churchill made it a habit to spend nearly every weekend there. The country setting normally provided him a certain rest, but the Prime Minister's habit of sitting up to all hours of the night partly offset its restorative effect. This Sunday evening Churchill seemed fatigued.

That fatigue could not have been the result of recent bad news. Events, in fact, had been generally favorable. A battle between the British Eighth Army and German General Erwin Rommel's panzer forces was in progress near Tobruk, Libya. Rommel was reported to have suffered heavy tank losses. And the previous day the American Secretary of the Navy, Frank Knox, had declared the U. S. Navy "superior to any in the world." His annual report had cited 323 new ships and over 2,000 planes commissioned during the year. The Americans now had their Navy on a war footing. Knox said in public that the international situation demanded that the United States arm as rapidly as possible. Words like this from a nation technically at peace were agreeable to Churchill's ears.

The most encouraging news of the day came from the Russian front, where the Nazi attack toward Moscow appeared to be stalling.[1] The London *Times* on Saturday and the New York *Times* that morning had carried the same stories. NAZIS REPORTED IN DISORDERLY RETREAT ON

[1] Actually the Germans had given up the attack on Moscow the day before, but there was no way that Churchill could know.

TWO SALIENTS IN FRONT BEFORE MOSCOW, the New York *Times* headlines blared. Heavy snow was falling in Moscow with the temperature far below zero. Russian counterattacks were being executed along the Moscow–Volga Canal north of the city. Successes were also occurring in other parts of the line. At Taganrog, where the Russian right flank met the northern point of the Sea of Azov, a sizable German force was reported cut off. Russian Marshal Semyon Timoshenko's forces, spearheaded by armor and Cossack cavalry, were driving west toward the major town of Mariupol, and a force had turned south behind Taganrog. Reports said that Timoshenko's spearheads had reached the sea.

But all these stories were relegated to the background by the current crisis between the Americans and the Japanese. Relations between the two powers had been degenerating ever since the Japanese invasion of the Chinese mainland nearly a decade before. Tensions had increased since the United States had begun trying to stem Japanese expansionism by economic means in 1939. The previous July, after Japanese forces had occupied French Indochina and had rejected Roosevelt's proposal to "neutralize" the region, the United States Government had frozen Japanese assets in American banks. Now, six months later, it appeared likely that the Japanese, massed on the Thai border, were going to invade yet another neutral country.

Roosevelt had earlier sent a message through diplomatic channels asking the Japanese Government for assurances that they had no intention of invading Thailand. The Japanese had been evasive, simply reiterating their wish to avoid war with the United States. Two Japanese emissaries, Ambassador Kichisaburo Nomura and Saburo Kurusu, had been in Washington for some time, ostensibly trying to work out a *modus vivendi*. Secretary of State Cordell Hull had lost patience with the two and President Roosevelt had broken precedent by sending a personal appeal to Emperor Hirohito. American attempts to keep track of the Japanese fleet were meeting with little luck.

*

Churchill's guests at dinner included members of his official household, his daughter-in-law Pamela, and three Americans: U. S. Ambassador John G. Winant; W. Averell Harriman, "expediter" of American Lend-Lease in London; and Harriman's daughter Kathleen. The company was congenial and comfortable, and Churchill felt no compulsion to be entertaining. He had little to say throughout dinner.

Shortly after 9:00 P.M. was the time for Churchill's ritual of listening to the news. He picked up the British Broadcasting Corporation (BBC) on the small portable radio on the dining-room table. A few moments late, he missed some of the details of a British-Axis tank battle in Libya, but then the announcer turned to a flash:

"The news has just been given that Japanese aircraft have raided Pearl Harbor, the American naval base in Hawaii. The announcement of the attack was made in a brief statement by President Roosevelt. Naval and military targets on the principal Hawaiian island of Oahu have also been attacked. No further details are yet available."[2]

As the group around the table tried to absorb this bombshell, a phone call came from the Admiralty confirming the BBC report. Churchill, with Winant's assistance, thereupon placed a call to Roosevelt. The President could not give details over the phone, but the news was true. Roosevelt had decided to go to Congress to ask for a declaration of war the next morning. Churchill reiterated his promise, made a month earlier, of a declaration "within the hour." The Crown would make the declaration and notification would be given in the House of Commons. Later that night Churchill learned that the Japanese had landed in Malaya.[3]

*

This moment had been long in coming, and in a real sense it represented a personal triumph for Churchill. As a relatively young man (forty-one) in World War I, Churchill had been First Lord of the Admiralty, the British Cabinet position which corresponds to the American Secretary of the Navy. Blamed for the disastrous British Dardanelles campaign against Turkey, he had been forced to resign and then had served briefly in front-line duty as a lieutenant colonel of infantry at Ypres. Eventually he had been recalled to a lesser position in the Lloyd George Cabinet, and after the war had been Chancellor of the Exchequer. When Britain's Conservative Prime Minister Stanley Baldwin was replaced by socialist leader Ramsay MacDonald in the election of May 1929, Churchill had remained with the Conservative "shadow cabinet."

Once out of office, with no direct responsibilities, however, he began to fall out with the leader of the Conservatives over the role the party should assume with regard to the British Empire. Churchill felt that the Conservative opposition should "strongly confront the Labour Government on all great Imperial and national issues, should identify itself to the Majesty of Britain as under Lord Beaconsfield and Lord Salisbury. . . ." Baldwin disagreed, citing "changing times." When the question of India came up, Baldwin and other Conservatives advocated freedom. After the conference in London (in which Mahatma Gandhi held center stage) a dissatisfied Churchill resigned from the shadow government and went into

[2] The announcer was Alvar Liddell of BBC. Quoted in Harriman and Abel, *Special Envoy to Churchill and Stalin*, p. 112.
[3] The accounts of this sequence of events—Churchill, Winant, Harriman—are hopelessly at odds on details. This account largely follows Harriman.

retirement (except for his position as member of Parliament), which was to last for nearly a decade. He would support himself through his literary efforts.

During the 1930s Winston Churchill, M.P., had been a voice crying for greater military strength and stronger national will. Hitler had come to power in Germany in 1933 and Churchill had then watched in horror as Germany violated the Versailles and Locarno treaties by occupying the Rhineland in 1936, Austria in 1938, and Czechoslovakia (in two stages). He was vociferous and eloquent in his protestation against Western appeasement of Hitler, especially at the notorious Munich conference of September 1938. Though unable materially to affect policies during these years, he nevertheless had come to be associated with British might and with the will to stop Hitler.

In early September 1939 Churchill had been called back to public service. With Britain at war, Prime Minister Neville Chamberlain once more appointed him First Lord of the Admiralty. (His office, as he re-entered it, had scarcely been changed.) At this time, with Chamberlain's permission, he accepted President Franklin D. Roosevelt's invitation to correspond on "naval matters."

Despite the failure of Neville Chamberlain's peace policy, which had reached its climax in the Munich agreement, the British people had been willing for a while to continue with his wartime leadership. However, when Hitler invaded Denmark and Norway in April 1940, they had had enough. They turned to the voice that had been shouting warnings through all these years and Winston Churchill became Prime Minister.

Churchill was no victim of false modesty. Upon becoming Prime Minister on May 10, 1940, he had expressed his feelings:

> In my long political experience I had held most of the great offices of State but . . . the post which had now fallen to me was the one I liked the best. Power, for the sake of lording it over fellow-creatures or adding to personal pomp, is rightly judged base. But power in a national crisis, when a man believes he knows what orders should be given, is a blessing.[4]

Churchill had been allowed little time to congratulate himself. The day he took office the German Blitzkrieg was launched in France; he had thus been saddled with the unenviable role of presiding over the evacuation of the British Expeditionary Force at Dunkirk. And on the night of the French surrender, June 17, 1940, he had launched a series of broadcasts destined to inspire the British and the entire free world:

[4] Churchill, *The Second World War,* Vol. II, *Their Finest Hour,* p. 15.

"I grieve for the gallant French people who have fallen into this terrible misfortune. Nothing will alter our feelings towards them. . . . We shall defend our island home, and with the British Empire we shall fight on unconquerable until the curse of Hitler is lifted from the brows of mankind."[5]

That same morning Churchill had arranged for the escape of a relatively unknown French brigadier general, Charles de Gaulle. Outspoken, proud, and anti-Nazi, De Gaulle had become enough of a public figure that his life would be in danger if he were captured. Recognizing his worth as a symbol of France, Churchill had seen to it that he should escape by British aircraft. "De Gaulle," Churchill later wrote, "carried with him . . . the honor of France."[6]

Though Churchill's courage and eloquence had made him a hero to the populace, not all his actions could be lofty and idealistic. On July 3, 1940, barely two weeks after the fall of France, he had taken one of the most painful steps of his career. At Mers-el-Kebir (the port of Oran), at Alexandria, at Dakar, and at Algiers he had sent British naval squadrons to destroy those portions of the French fleet that had escaped from France to North Africa. Many Frenchmen were killed. In Oran three French battleships were sunk; the one at Alexandria was dismantled; the two battleships in Portsmouth were seized and the one battleship at Dakar was put out of action. Many smaller ships were sunk. Only one battle cruiser, the *Strasbourg*, escaped to Toulon, where the remainder of the French fleet lay protected. Sympathetic as Churchill was to his French friends, he saw the action as essential. He received plaudits for the moment but he would pay for it dearly with the French later.

From there on Churchill had struggled through nineteen months of bleak stewardship. His words and personal leadership might prolong British survival but could not give tangible promise of real victory. Roosevelt could and did increase American aid even at the risk of full participation, but the American people were not ready to shed blood. They might never be ready. And until they were, the British would sustain reverses and the final outcome would remain very much in doubt.

And the reverses came. In March 1941 Hitler moved through the Balkans into Greece. In May his forces seized Crete by airborne assault. And the Italians in Libya invaded Egypt.

Only in North Africa, the scene of a series of seesaw battles and pursuits, did the British enjoy any degree of success. At one point the British under Wavell had driven some five hundred miles across Cyrenaica to El Agheila only to be roundly defeated and driven back to the Egyptian bor-

[5] Ibid., 217.
[6] Ibid.

der. Now, in December 1941, the line of battle was deep into Libya. But
North Africa was a sideshow and even there the British military were
worried.

Allied future had brightened with Hitler's assault to the east (Operation
BARBAROSSA) in June 1941. And yet even the power of Russia could
not ensure Allied survival without the United States. No wonder Churchill
that evening of December 7, 1941, enjoyed "the sleep of the saved and
thankful."[7]

*

President Roosevelt received word of the Pearl Harbor attack while
having an informal bite of lunch with his friend and confidant Harry
Hopkins in his Oval Study.[8] At 1:40 P.M., Secretary of the Navy Knox
called. A radio message, Knox advised, had come in stating that Rear Admiral Husband Kimmel, the naval commander in Hawaii, was advising all
stations that an air raid attack was on. And THIS WAS NO DRILL.
Roosevelt gasped, "Oh, no!" but he was inclined to believe it, as this was
the kind of thing to expect of the Japanese. He was ready for a Japanese
attack; in fact when briefed the evening before on an intercepted part of a
Japanese message, he had said, "This means war." Only the audacity of
the Japanese in venturing so far east in the Pacific surprised him; all the
Americans were looking toward the Philippines or Southeast Asia as the
point of likely attack.

Churchill's first reaction on receiving the news was to call Roosevelt,
but the reverse was not true. Secretary of State Cordell Hull, Roosevelt
knew, was waiting to receive Nomura and Kurusu at 2:00 P.M. Thus the
first thing that Roosevelt did was to call Hull. When the two emissaries
arrived twenty minutes late,[9] Hull knew of the attack and had already
read the text of the message that Nomura was bringing. In order to conceal the fact that the United States had broken the Japanese code, Hull
had to go through the motions of reading the document. He then fixed
angrily on Nomura:

> "In all my fifty years of public service I have never seen a docu-
> ment . . . more crowded with infamous falsehoods and distortions
> . . . on a scale so huge that I never imagined until today that any
> government on this planet was capable of uttering them."[10]

[7] Churchill, Vol. III, *The Grand Alliance*, p. 608.
[8] The room referred to here is the oval-shaped room on the second floor of the
White House, above the Blue Room. The office today commonly referred to as the
"Oval Office" is a copy located in the west wing, built by Theodore Roosevelt. To
make distinction in these pages, I shall call this room in the Mansion the "Oval
Study" or the "Study."
[9] The Americans had deciphered the Japanese message long before the Washington-
based Japanese themselves did.
[10] *The Memoirs of Cordell Hull*, Vol. II, p. 1096.

Nomura mumbled something, but Hull waved him off and nodded toward the door. Two shaken men, deceived by their own government, walked out with their heads down.

At 2:28 P.M., forty-eight minutes after Knox's first call, Roosevelt received real confirmation of the attack. Admiral Harold ("Betty") Stark, Chief of Naval Operations, called to advise that the damage had been severe. The President thereupon ordered that the previously prepared orders to the Army and Navy be put into execution. Two minutes later he called Steve Early, his press secretary, and dictated a news release. A half hour later he sent out another.

At 3:00 P.M., Roosevelt's top officials came into the Study. Besides Hull and Hopkins there were the Secretary of War, Henry L. Stimson, seventy-four years old, who had been Secretary of State under Hoover from 1929 to 1933; and Frank Knox, Secretary of the Navy, who had been Alf Landon's running mate for Vice-President in 1936. (Both were Republicans.) On the military side were General George C. Marshall, Army Chief of Staff, a tall, spare, reserved individual whom Churchill would later dub the "architect of victory," and Admiral Stark, the mild-mannered Chief of Naval Operations.

The conference was not so tense as might have been expected. Possible war had been on the minds of all for weeks, even months. And while the group had to acknowledge the seriousness of this latest development, they had not yet received word of the extent of damage to the fleet. At first they seemed to feel that Hirohito had done a favor by providing the United States an excuse to enter into the war. Germany, not Japan, was the primary enemy. Nobody held any illusions, however, regarding the seriousness and the length of the coming struggle.

During the conference messages continued to come in, each one more shocking than the last. The President's secretary, Grace Tully, found generals and admirals both leaning over her shoulder as she transcribed the shorthand of the messages coming in from the Navy Department. Between messages Hull reviewed his interview with the Japanese and only after the conference had been under way for some time did the call come through from Churchill. The timing was good, for by now Roosevelt knew that the reports were true and was able to assure Churchill, "We are all in the same boat now."

Immediate moves, previously prepared as contingency plans, were put into effect. Protection of Japanese citizens and the Japanese Embassy, for example, was first on the list. General Marshall was anxious to get a message to General MacArthur[11] in the Philippines warning him to alert his forces. And the War Department, the Navy Department, and the White

---

[11] Hopkins, in his notes, referred to "McCarthy."

House had to be guarded. Finally the President discussed the general tenor of a message to Congress to be delivered the next day.

Harry Hopkins was, as always, sure in his mind what the President must do. Roosevelt should, he advised, hold two more conferences that evening. First, he should see the Cabinet (Roosevelt called it for 8:30 P.M.). And since Congress, not the President, declares war, another meeting should be held to advise the leadership of the House and Senate. The group would not be large because Representative Hamilton Fish, whom Roosevelt would not have in the White House, could not be included: the cutoff point for the invitees should come just above his name.[12] Fish, ranking minority member of the House Foreign Relations Committee, had fought against Roosevelt's Lend-Lease Act to aid Britain earlier in the year as well as any amendments to the hand-tying Neutrality Act of 1936. So bitter had been Fish's resistance that Roosevelt could not forgive him, even in crisis.

At 5:00 P.M. Roosevelt called in Grace Tully and dictated his speech for the next day. Hull brought over a State Department draft which read like a lawyer's brief. Roosevelt stuck to his own, under five hundred words. That evening, after the Cabinet meeting, the congressional leaders arrived. The President gave the group a rundown of all the information available. He tactfully asked the congregated solons what time the next day would be convenient for him to address a joint session. The time was agreed at 12:30 P.M. Though there could have been little doubt in anyone's mind, the President never said that he would be asking for a declaration of war. He did, in fact, say he had not decided. Roosevelt was too consummate a politician to trust such secrets to any congressional group this size. He would not be upstaged by the press.

That evening people on the streets were gathering around the White House some five deep behind the iron railings. When the congressional leaders left at 11:00 P.M., the crowd was beginning to thin out. Across the White House lawn small groups sang "God Bless America." Roosevelt, fatigued but still aroused, kept a long-standing appointment. He and two friends[13] had sandwiches and beer before turning in for the night.

*

The next morning, December 8, 1941, President Franklin Roosevelt drove to the Capitol and stood before a joint session of Congress at

[12] Henry Wallace, Vice-President; Senators Alben W. Barkley (Majority Leader); Charles McNary (Minority Leader); Chairman Tom Connally and Hiram W. Johnson of the Foreign Relations Committee; Warren R. Austin of the Military Affairs Committee; Speaker Sam Rayburn; House Minority Leader Joseph W. Martin; Chairman Sol Bloom and Representative Charles A. Eaton of the Foreign Affairs Committee; and Representative Jere Cooper, Acting Majority Leader.
[13] Edward R. Murrow of the Columbia Broadcasting System and Colonel William J. ("Wild Bill") Donovan.

12:30 P.M.: "Yesterday, December 7, 1941—a date which will live in infamy . . ."

At 4:10 P.M., December 8, 1941, he signed the declaration of war, which had existed since the previous morning between Japan and the United States.

CHAPTER II

THE FLOATING
TEN DOWNING STREET

On Friday, December 12, 1941, Prime Minister Churchill and his party secretly proceeded to Greenock, Scotland, boarding the battleship H.M.S. *Duke of York* bound for Washington by way of Norfolk, Virginia. Their route would take them southward through the Firth of Clyde, the Irish Sea, the Bay of Biscay, then across the North Atlantic.

The trip had been arranged quickly. Churchill's first reaction on hearing of Pearl Harbor was that he should go to Washington, but he slept on it before taking action. On arising the next morning, he concluded that the time was right and set the wheels in motion. He encountered no resistance in securing rubber-stamp permission from his War Cabinet and then addressed the appropriate letter to King George VI. "Sir: I have formed the conviction that it is my duty to visit Washington without delay. . . ." The King readily agreed.

In Washington President Roosevelt had been slightly hesitant when on December 9 Churchill proposed his visit. Roosevelt was concerned, he cabled, for the safety of Churchill's person, particularly during a return voyage.[1] Churchill persisted, politely belittling this fear. Finally on Wednesday, December 10, Roosevelt cabled, "Delighted to have you here at the White House. . . . Naval situation and other matters of strategy will have to be discussed. . . . News is bad but will be better. . . ."

Churchill, having already made preparations, was ready to leave almost immediately.

[1] Roosevelt's actual message has not been found, but it is referred to in Churchill's cable of December 10.

*

During the five days between December 7 and December 12 Churchill had been receiving one gloomy report after another. The damage inflicted by the Japanese at Pearl Harbor had not yet been determined, but the American losses were obviously heavy. Even the press[2] conceded 3,000 American casualties, a surprising half of them dead or presumed dead in the sunken ships. But still the figures were vastly underplayed. The New York *Times* reported "one old battleship" capsized. Even the Japanese, more nearly accurate, failed to recognize fully the extent of their success, claiming only the battleship *Arizona* sunk, three more battleships damaged; four cruisers sunk; and one hundred planes destroyed. The actual figures were 7 (out of 8) battleships sunk or out of action for months; 347 (out of 394) aircraft damaged or destroyed; 3,581 casualties (2,403 dead).[3]

Elsewhere, five Japanese landings had been made in the Philippines; Guam, Hong Kong, Wake Island, and Malaya had also been attacked. Thailand had been occupied in one day by Japanese troops poised on the border while the diplomatic talks had been going on.

The big shock for Churchill, however, came on December 10, the same day that his trip to Washington was confirmed. Word came in that two capital ships, the dreadnoughts H.M.S. *Prince of Wales* and H.M.S. *Repulse,* had been sunk by Japanese aircraft near Kuantan about two hundred miles north of Singapore on the east coast of Malaya. The event carried unusual emotional impact for Churchill, who had lived on the *Prince of Wales* while attending the historic Atlantic Conference with Roosevelt at Argentia, Newfoundland, the previous August. He personally knew many of the men lost, including the commander of the British Far East Fleet, Admiral Tom Phillips. Sadly Churchill went in person to report the disaster to Parliament.

One relief, on the other hand, was the declaration of war by Hitler and Mussolini on December 11. Up to then the United States had been engaged formally in hostilities only against Japan, not yet against the two European nations. Conceivably America could have remained at war only with Japan while Britain faced all three. The Axis leaders, however, had now made it easy. For once they had honored a treaty, the one with their Japanese ally.

*

No voyage through the rough North Atlantic in December would be a pleasure cruise. From the time the *Duke of York* pulled away from the protection of the river Clyde and headed out the Firth toward the tip of

2 Charles Hurd, New York *Times,* December 9, 1941.
3 *The West Point Atlas of American Wars.*

Ireland, the seas were heavy. The skies became dark and great waves battered against the sides of the ship and over the prow. Danger from enemy action was ever present, for the path of the battleship was to cross the routes normally used by the German U-boats. The First Sea Lord, Admiral of the Fleet Sir Dudley Pound, had assumed direct command of the ship's course and at first had specified that the *Duke of York* should crawl along at six knots to stay with its great convoy. At this speed it would take about forty-eight hours to round the southern coast of Ireland.

But then a second danger lurked, that of attack from land-based aircraft. Probably with the fate of the *Prince of Wales* and the *Repulse* on his mind, Churchill noted that the convoy was passing about four hundred miles from the German air base at Brest. The skies were clearing and the convoy was approaching the maximum range of air cover from British bases. Churchill and Pound conferred, concluding that the threat from the air was now greater than from the U-boats. (The chance of ramming a U-boat, Pound observed, was greater than that of being hit by a torpedo.) Forthwith, with Churchill's concurrence, Pound changed the instructions and the *Duke of York* proceeded with all possible speed, leaving the convoy behind.[4]

*

As this was to be a military conference the members of Churchill's party consisted of men directly concerned with military operations and supply. The Foreign Secretary, Anthony Eden, for example, had gone through with his long-planned visit to Moscow. The military services were represented by Admiral Pound, Field Marshal Sir John Dill, and Air Chief Marshal Sir Charles ("Peter") Portal. Pound and Portal were members of the British Chiefs of Staff Committee (BCOS).[5] Pound, sixty-four years of age, had been First Sea Lord since 1939. His health was not of the best and his outlook perhaps a bit constricted to naval matters; nevertheless, he enjoyed Churchill's confidence. Field Marshal Sir John Dill, until a month before Chief of the Imperial General Staff (CIGS), had been in that position since May 1940. Finally exhausted by trying to keep up with Churchill's schedule, Dill had left as CIGS with no prejudice against him, being replaced by General Sir Alan Brooke. Brooke was back in London learning his new duties while Dill's longer experience with the Imperial General Staff would make him of more value for this conference. Chief of the Air Staff "Peter" Portal had been in his position since 1940, even though only forty-eight years of age. Though a strong advocate of the air arm in general and long-range bombardment in partic-

4 Churchill, III, 626–27.
5 The term BCOS will be used here to differentiate the committee of British service chiefs from the American Joint Chiefs of Staff (JCS).

ular, Portal's view was broad. He was in every respect an influential, full-fledged member of the BCOS.

Also with Churchill to attend this ARCADIA meeting, as the Prime Minister himself had designated it, were W. Averell Harriman, who had been at Chequers the night of Pearl Harbor, and the colorful Lord Max Beaverbrook. Beaverbrook, age sixty-two, was a self-made millionaire, Canadian by birth, the head of a press empire, and known as a "political gadfly." Though he owed his position to Churchill, he was obviously a man of great ability. As Minister of Supply, his role would be crucial in the forthcoming talks. But powerful as Beaverbrook was in his own element, he was in a state of discomfort on this voyage. He lived on his nerves and feared readily for his life. Worse than that, perhaps, was his enforced role as a member of the audience when the Prime Minister would hold forth on all subjects. Beaverbrook was accustomed to occupying center stage in his own world, and he hated being a satellite to anyone else. But Churchill seemed not to notice.

Despite the heavy seas, the confinement, and the danger, the Prime Minister's work went on almost as usual. The ship carried powerful radio equipment, which with a team of competent cryptographers made it easy to communicate readily with both London and Washington. Thus Churchill kept the air waves popping with messages, beginning with instructions to Eden en route to Moscow and Lord Privy Seal Clement Attlee[6] in London. Through London he sent messages to India, Hong Kong, South Africa, and Singapore.

*

The President, after his initial hesitation, was cheerful over the prospect of the meeting. He had actually been contemplating something like this for months, and he had his own reasons for welcoming his guest. As an icebreaker he could assure Churchill that American Lend-Lease, temporarily frozen as of Pearl Harbor, would be resumed and increased.[7] Further, he looked forward to becoming more intimately acquainted. The three days at the Atlantic Conference the previous August had been cordial, but the atmosphere had been less than intimate. Each leader had stayed with his party on his own warship, visiting back and forth. Now Churchill was to be a guest at the White House and the two would be afforded the opportunity to truly come to know each other. Since each intended to be master in his own house on military matters—Churchill already was—it was of utmost importance that they become personal friends.

[6] In this coalition government, organized to prosecute the war, Clement Attlee, leader of the Labour Party, was Deputy Prime Minister, with the title of Lord Privy Seal, to the Conservative Churchill.
[7] Harry Hopkins had already notified Churchill of this informally.

And though he said little about it, the President was contemplating a formal "declaration of war aims," to be signed by the twenty-four nations who had individually declared war against the Axis[8]—the "Associated Powers," as they were then referred to. This pronouncement, he visualized, would be couched in general terms, but it would serve notice to the world that the Associated Powers were in this war together to the end.

The ARCADIA Conference, therefore, was being held because the two political leaders wanted it. Roosevelt had acceded to Churchill's proposal in the knowledge that his military chiefs were reluctant to meet with the British at this moment. The situation in the Pacific was degenerating every day; the Japanese invasion of the Philippines had been under way since December 11, and the West Coast was gripped in the fear of a Japanese invasion. The staffs were working around the clock juggling shortages among very immediate problems, and they would have liked to defer discussions of grand strategy until the first of the year. So they presented their position to the President.

But what concerned the American military most about the forthcoming conference, far more than the fact that the staffs were busy with other things, was their lack of preparation to face the British chiefs in discussions of world strategy. At ABC-1 Conference[9] and at Argentia, Marshall and Stark had been alerted to a British tendency, even intention, to employ American forces in support of British strategic objectives which had little to do with the winning of the war. One bone of contention in those talks, for example, had been the necessity of holding Singapore, a top priority for the British. To Marshall the idea of diverting American troops to help defend that British base was anathema. Now the BCOS, the Americans feared, would again push such issues and support them with arguments long since agreed and polished among themselves. In debate the British would hold the advantage of a united front.

General Marshall, as Army Chief of Staff, felt a special responsibility for representing the American military viewpoint, as he was the officer who commanded the bulk of the nation's armed forces. Further, he had held his position longer than any of his associates. Marshall could expect Roosevelt to hold his own fairly well against Churchill in private discussions of naval matters, but he would be less effective when talks turned to the employment of land and air forces in global strategy. Thus Marshall believed that American interests would have to prevail in the military

[8] The Axis here refers to Germany and Italy. The Soviet Union was not at war with Japan.

[9] A conference held between the British and American military planners between January 29 and March 29, 1941. It eventually resulted in an emergency action plan called RAINBOW 5, which was actually put into effect immediately at the beginning of hostilities.

discussions. It was necessary to settle arguments in that arena and avoid passing split decisions to the political leaders. He personally would have to take what leadership would be possible among the American military chiefs.

Nobody would contest that the American military team at this point was weak. The antiquated War Board, set up before World War I, represented the only mechanism in existence to coordinate the efforts of the Army and Navy. It was operating at this time without even a secretariat. Of its members Admiral Harold Stark, Chief of Naval Operations, was known to be on the way out as the President had found a man in whom he had more confidence, Admiral Ernest J. King. King's position at the moment was anomalous; he bore the title of Commander-in-Chief, United States Fleet, with a theoretical line of direct communication with the President himself, but under the "supervision" of Stark. King, obviously heir apparent to the ultimate position of Chief of Naval Operations (CNO), was a first-class sailor, expert in both naval aviation and submarines. But nobody was quite sure who was in charge of the Navy just then, and King had little background in the kind of global planning that would culminate in large-scale land operations.

Further, the Americans lacked an independent air chief to correspond to Air Chief Marshal Portal. Unlike the British, the Americans had not made the air arm a separate service between wars and it was too late to do so now. The position of Lieutenant General Henry H. ("Hap") Arnold, as Commanding General, U. S. Army Air Force, therefore, was subordinate to that of General Marshall. To rectify this imbalance, General Marshall, beginning with Argentia, had treated Arnold as an equal when dealing with the British. But Arnold was still one grade junior to his colleagues, and he was inclined to remain silent on matters of strategic interest, confining himself largely to technical matters pertaining to the air forces. On questions involving ground and naval forces he would not be able to provide a counterweight to the astute Portal.

Finally, Marshall's own staff was in a state of change. He had lost some confidence, for example, in the Chief of War Plans, Brigadier General Leonard T. Gerow, whom Marshall could not entirely absolve from some responsibility for the Army's lack of alertness at Pearl Harbor. And Gerow, a meticulous man, was doing too much of the War Plans job himself, showing signs of fatigue.

To supplement his staff, Gerow had asked General Marshall to call Brigadier General Dwight D. Eisenhower from San Antonio, where he was Chief of Staff, Third Army. Marshall had met Eisenhower only once or twice before, although the young (fifty-one) officer's reputation in the Army was high. (He had been included in the little book of potential leaders that Marshall had kept through the years.) Eisenhower possessed firsthand knowledge of General Douglas MacArthur's defense plans for the Philippines, having returned from his position on MacArthur's staff in Manila at Christmas 1939. Eisenhower had reported to Marshall the morning of December 14, and Marshall put him to the test by demanding a plan for the defense of the Pacific, to be submitted within a couple of hours. Eisenhower gulped and went to work. The result convinced Marshall that Eisenhower's methods and views were remarkably similar to his own. Almost on the spot he made Eisenhower Chief Operations Officer for the Pacific under Gerow. But Eisenhower would have been on the job only a week when Churchill and his party were due to arrive and his position, theoretically, had little to do with the subjects to be discussed.

A factor which boded ill for the future of Anglo-American cooperation was the remarkable dislike for everything British held by many of the senior American officers. Some of it doubtless originated in resentment of the condescension exhibited by the British military toward Americans in general. This national dislike, so prevalent west of the Alleghenies, was exacerbated by a feeling of professional inferiority, a realization that the British chiefs had been lieutenant generals when most of the Americans had been lieutenant colonels. The British military were conscious that they had been fighting Hitler for over two years. Whatever the causes, such hostility was widespread and virulent. Harry Hopkins, a man who missed little, became aware of this sentiment and cabled Churchill pleading that he "tread easy." Churchill promised the impossible. "Treading easy" was not in his make-up.

Fortunately General Marshall, a moderate man, did not share this animosity. But he harbored a real fear concerning the influence of Winston Churchill over Franklin Roosevelt. For Roosevelt hardly knew his own military advisers, and they had met infrequently. The Americans had therefore developed no "official" position. With nothing concrete to guide him, the President would be placed at a disadvantage when confronting a man who, as the symbol of British heroism from the days of 1940, had been meeting daily with the BCOS for a long time. Marshall groaned on learning that Churchill would be Roosevelt's personal house guest, occupying the Queen's Room on the second floor of the White House, within a few feet of the President's own bedroom.

*

If Marshall overestimated Churchill's ability to influence Roosevelt, he was correct in assuming that Churchill would make every effort to do so. And Churchill was confident when he contemplated his power to manipulate the Americans. On the morning after Pearl Harbor, someone in a BCOS meeting had assumed that Churchill would continue his former ingratiating attitude toward America. "Oh!" he had said. "That is the way we talked to her while we were wooing her; now that she is in the harem we talk to her quite differently!"[10]

One fundamental issue, however, was giving Churchill considerable concern as he contemplated the American attitude. He, Roosevelt, and the British/American planners at ABC-1 and Argentia had agreed that the first priority for military action should be Europe, not the Pacific. Now the United States was united as never before, but the public was inflamed not toward Hitler but toward Hirohito. American thirst for revenge against the Japanese could endanger the previous joint planning, which had assumed that Nazi Germany should be regarded as the primary antagonist. If Churchill could ensure that the Americans would continue to adhere to this basic principle, he was prepared to make almost any reasonable concessions.

As the *Duke of York* approached the end of the journey, therefore, Churchill worked on three messages concerning his own thoughts, which not surprisingly paralleled the views of the BCOS.

The first message presented an argument for the Allies to occupy, with French cooperation if possible, the coastline of North Africa from Dakar on the Atlantic, northward through Morocco, and eastward through the Mediterranean to include Algeria, Tunisia, Libya, Egypt, and Palestine, to the Turkish border. This venture should be the main Allied effort in 1942.

The second message outlined a series of measures for regaining control of the Pacific. Unfortunately it was based on inadequate appreciation of the damage suffered by the American fleet at Pearl Harbor. (He expected to begin regaining control of the vast reaches of the ocean as early as May 2.)

Finally Churchill recommended as the ultimate objective an invasion of the European continent in 1943, though he avoided specifying the route. These three, when put together, spelled out "Europe First," with initial emphasis on the Mediterranean but with a continental invasion planned for 1943. Only the third was completed while Churchill was still at sea, and he sent it ahead to Washington.

When Marshall and Stark received this third message on December 18, they proceeded at once to the White House to secure the President's approval. Contrary to Churchill's fears, the American military still saw Nazi Germany as the primary enemy and the one most vulnerable to Allied action in the first stages of the global counteroffensive. War in the Pacific would depend on a powerful fleet; and rebuilding it would take time. Fur-

[10] Bryant, *The Turn of the Tide*, p. 225.

thermore, Europe was the place where all three Allies—United States, Britain, and Russia—could concentrate in one region.

Thus, even before Churchill landed at Norfolk on December 22, he had achieved his main objective—to ensure that the "Europe First" policy should remain the basic tenet of Allied strategy.

CHAPTER III

ARCADIA

B y the time H.M.S. *Duke of York* arrived at Hampton Roads, Norfolk, Prime Minister Churchill had become impatient. The trip across the Atlantic had taken longer than he had anticipated—it was now the evening of December 22—and he was itching to get to Washington right away. Churchill therefore canceled the original plan to proceed up the Chesapeake and Potomac by boat. He took a plane which happened to be waiting. Roosevelt, notified of the switch, took Hopkins with him out to Washington National Airport. There, after dark, Churchill and his party arrived.[1] Soon Roosevelt, Churchill, Beaverbrook, Hopkins, and others were meeting.

Without delay Churchill began boring in on his objectives, summarizing essentially the three messages on strategy that he had composed on the voyage over. He began with his plan for the occupation of North Africa, which he hoped could be executed soon. Roosevelt had not received Churchill's message on that subject because it had not been sent from the *Duke of York*. He had a good idea of the nature of the plan, however, because Churchill had written on the subject on October 20. His letter, Churchill knew, had made an impression on the President. The plan entailed landing a British corps in North Africa to join with the British Eighth Army coming west from Cairo. It necessitated sending some three

[1] Arrangements had been made for boat travel because flying was not taken for granted in 1941. President Roosevelt, at this time, had only once been up in a plane. Other guests were Hull, Undersecretary of State Sumner Welles, Secretary of War Henry L. Stimson, and the British ambassador, Lord Halifax.

U.S. divisions to Northern Ireland to relieve the British forces earmarked for North Africa.[2]

Churchill found Roosevelt still receptive to this idea, at least that evening at dinner. The next day, therefore, the Prime Minister reported to the War Cabinet:

> The President said that he was anxious that American land forces should give their support as quickly as possible wherever they could be most helpful, and favoured the idea of a plan to move into North Africa being prepared for either event, i.e., with or without invitation [from the French]. . . .
>
> In the course of conversation the President mentioned that he would propose at forthcoming conference that United States should relieve our troops in Northern Ireland, and spoke of sending three or four divisions there.[3]

Elated, Churchill observed, ". . . we cut deeply into business."

The first plenary meeting of ARCADIA took place in the President's Oval Study the next afternoon, December 23.[4] Present at the meeting were Roosevelt, Churchill, Secretary of War Henry Stimson, Secretary of the Navy Frank Knox, Lord Beaverbrook, the British Chiefs of Staff (BCOS), the American Joint Chiefs (JCS). As host, Roosevelt sat behind his desk with Churchill on his left. The advisers, mostly military, arranged themselves in a semicircle in front of the desk, the two sets of Chiefs huddling together at any mention of a disputed question. This configuration was followed through the rest of the war.

The matter of grand strategy came up first. But the discussion was confused because the British, though they confirmed their intention to launch an assault on the Continent in 1943, were really more interested in selling certain "corollaries" to be executed first:

(1) a buildup of armaments, which meant maintaining the security of the areas of war industry,

(2) maintenance of essential communications between the United States and Britain, more commonly thought of as the Battle of the Atlantic,

(3) closing and tightening a ring around Germany from Archangel to the Black Sea, Turkey, the Mediterranean, and the Atlantic,

(4) wearing down German resistance by bombardment, blockade and subversion and,

---

[2] For full letter see Churchill, III, 544–48.
[3] Ibid., p. 665.
[4] "Plenary," as used here, will mean "political leaders with advisers."

(5) maintaining only such positions in the Far East as to safeguard
    vital interests while the Americans, British, and Soviets concen-
    trated on defeat of Germany.[5]

Of these five points the key one was (3) the "closing and tightening" of a
"ring" around Europe. This could mean anything, particularly when the
Mediterranean—and even the Balkans—were mentioned as a "prelude"
to the assault on Germany.[6] No preferred location for the final assault
was suggested; indeed Western Europe was listed last. But for the foreseeable future the "ring" would form the main basis for American-British di-
vergences.

At this first plenary meeting Churchill tried to follow up on his dinner
conversation of the night before, starting with the deployment of U.S.
troops to Northern Ireland and now Iceland (Operation MAGNET).
Only secondly did he mention the operation to occupy Northwest Africa
(code name GYMNAST). The two, MAGNET and GYMNAST, were
part of a single design.

Roosevelt readily agreed on the first proposal, to send American troops
to Ireland. However, he hedged on the invasion of North Africa. Churchill sensed quickly that Roosevelt had been advised by Marshall that
morning to back off.

The American military were open-minded from the very start about
sending troops to Ireland and Iceland, as that move would foreshadow the
build-up of trained divisions in Europe. On North Africa (GYMNAST),
however, Marshall and his staff were dubious. Aside from the enormous
risks, such an invasion represented to American eyes a diversion in the interests of the British Empire, not of defeating Hitler. They did not relish
fighting for the British "life line" to India.

This was not the first time a landing in North Africa had been considered by the Army staff. Even before December 7 the War Board had contemplated an American attack on Dakar, Senegal, where a Vichy French
submarine base stuck into the Western Hemisphere. Marshall's planners
had rejected such an invasion as too risky.

MAGNET and GYMNAST ran into trouble, however, not so much
through American reluctance as through cold figures on shipping, which
was scarce. The question became whether the Allies possessed enough
ships to execute both operations while simultaneously bolstering MacArthur's forces in the Far East.[7]

[5] Matloff and Snell, *Strategic Planning for Coalition Warfare: 1941–1942*, p. 100.
[6] Ibid., p. 101.
[7] *Crusade in Europe*, p. 22. At least one officer felt they could not. Brigadier General Dwight Eisenhower, at the time preoccupied with the Pacific, wrote himself a
memorandum: "I've been insisting that the Far East is critical—and no sideshows
should be undertaken until air and ground there are in a satisfactory state. Instead
we are taking on Magnet, Gymnast, etc."

As a result of this plenary meeting the British and Americans set up a subcommittee, headed by Brigadier General Brehon B. Somervell, Marshall's G-4 (Logistics), who later reported that a great part of the capacity necessary to transport a 200,000-man armada was already committed to reinforcing the Pacific.[8]

MAGNET and GYMNAST were now reduced to an either/or status and with remarkable timing an urgent cable came in from General MacArthur asking Washington to do something. The Japanese radio was correctly reminding the Filipinos that the U. S. Navy was "missing." The message from the Far East drove home the fact that shipping to that region could not be further reduced.

The end result was that the invasion of North Africa was put off indefinitely, with neither Roosevelt nor Churchill reconciled. Some American troops were soon deployed to Iceland and Northern Ireland, but North Africa was put on the shelf—permanently, it appeared.

The next morning, December 24, the American and British military chiefs met alone in the new Federal Reserve Building across Constitution Avenue from the dilapidated Munitions Building, which housed the Army Staff. Strangely, the British needed to be reassured on the most fundamental issue of all: Europe First. For some reason the confusion surrounding the plenary session the previous afternoon had obscured the American promise to exercise only a holding action in the Far East. At the beginning of this meeting, therefore, Marshall and Stark reassured Dill, Pound, and Portal that Germany was still the primary enemy and that the defeat of Germany was the key to victory.

This simple formula represented the most far-reaching strategic decision of World War II; and the proponents of General MacArthur's views have never ceased to denounce it. Mistakenly, they blame Churchill and his influence over Roosevelt; in fact it was heartily endorsed, and pushed, by both the War and Navy Departments.

*

Prime Minister Winston Churchill was finding his surroundings on the second floor of the White House agreeable. He was comfortable in the

[8] From the outset the Americans and British visualized GYMNAST differently. The British believed Northwest Africa could be occupied by using only 100,000 men, of whom they had 55,000 ready to go. The Americans, on the other hand, estimated that even if the landings were to be confined to a limited triangle in Morocco and Algeria (Casablanca, Agadir, Oran), 200,000 men would be necessary. And if the operation were to go deeper into the Mediterranean by adding a landing in Algiers, the Americans visualized 300,000. Matloff and Snell, p. 106.

pink Queen's Room, and in odd moments the historian and amateur artist could enjoy the numerous paintings of the American Presidents, most of whom were familiar ("those whose pictures are on the walls," he later called them). And he had at his disposal all that he needed to conduct business. To the distress of not only Marshall, but Stimson and Hull as well, the Prime Minister had brought along his own portable command post, the maps of which he installed, to the President's delight, on the walls of the Monroe Room, across from the Queen's Room. British officers and secretaries came and went with their impressive red brief cases while American officials, especially the Joint Chiefs, were banished to their offices on Constitution Avenue.[9]

Informality was the order of the day. From the outset Roosevelt and Churchill enjoyed each other and began wandering down the hall into each other's rooms (as Ismay described a later meeting) like "two subalterns." Both were in the habit of spending a good deal of time working in bed, and Roosevelt extended his evening working hours to accommodate his guest.[10] Churchill enjoyed wheeling Roosevelt around the second floor and made certain to do an unaccustomed amount of listening at meals. Roosevelt was one man Churchill liked to listen to.

But with it all, Churchill was undergoing a difficult time. Having had no vacation since 1939, he was tired, and he had not been sparing himself on the trip across the ocean. To add to his discomfort, he was somewhat taken aback when he learned of the ceremonial occasions he would be faced with. On Christmas Eve he and the President were to participate jointly in lighting the traditional National Christmas Tree. And then he was invited to address a joint session of Congress on Friday, December 26, an invitation not to be refused. Churchill was concerned about this joint session, aware that some American legislators, representing Irish and German constituencies, had in the past been less than friendly to the British. Picturing the rough-and-tumble debates in the House of Commons, Churchill feared possible demonstrations.

Churchill's personal physician, Lord Moran, was one of the few who realized that beneath Churchill's eloquence and apparent self-confidence he was subject to the same tensions as other humans before performing in public. And here he would be working under a severe handicap. Normally Churchill would closet himself for some forty-eight hours before he was scheduled to speak—and his staff would approach him with trepidation.

[9] President Roosevelt was so intrigued by Churchill's map room that he later set up a similar arrangement for himself on the ground floor of the White House.
[10] Churchill probably did not realize what a burden his habitual late hours put on Roosevelt. See Churchill, III, 663; Eleanor Roosevelt, *This I Remember*, pp. 242–43.

But now his preparation had to be interspersed with conferences, informal chats, and the usual business of directing the war.[11]

The first ceremonial event, the lighting of the National Christmas Tree, came on December 24, a warm day, reaching an astonishing sixty degrees. The weather encouraged nearly thirty thousand people to assemble that evening. From the balcony over the South Portico of the White House, President Roosevelt flicked the switch to light the tree. He seemed to keep his Christmas greeting unusually simple in order to allow his guest to steal the show, and he was not disappointed. Churchill's remarks were stirring, ending with a summary: "Let the children have their night of fun and laughter. Let gifts of Father Christmas delight their play. Let us grownups share to the full in our unstinted pleasures before we turn again to the stern task and the formidable years that lie before us. . . ."[12] The episode was dramatic, and coming from the hero of Britain, the talk provided the American people with the perspective to enjoy this one evening.

Afterward even the Prime Minister was shaken. "It has all been very moving," he murmured when the ceremony was over. "This is a new war, with Russia victorious, Japan in, and America in up to the neck." He then asked his doctor to take his pulse.

Churchill was known for his oratory, but few of his admirers realized how much work he put into each public appearance. Thus the challenge of a momentous address before the joint session of Congress to be delivered on December 26, 1941, hung over him in all his Christmas activities.

At dinner the night before the talk, he was noticeably unable to enjoy an otherwise festive affair in the State Dining Room that included all the British guests and many Roosevelts (though none of the five children or their families). He excused himself from the movie and retired to his room to work until about two o'clock in the morning.

On the day the speech was to be delivered Churchill was still editing until he was warned that he would be late. Leaving hurriedly from the South Entrance, his car dashed down Pennsylvania Avenue with sirens wailing, two security men on each running board. At the Capitol he was ushered into a small but comfortable waiting room. Lord Moran was with him. Pacing the floor, Churchill suddenly turned on the doctor and, "his eyes popping," demanded, "Do you realize we are making history?"[13]

[11] Prime Minister Curtin of Australia, for example, was now looking to the United States as his principal ally. Further he "refused" to accept the dictum that the Pacific struggle must be ". . . a subordinate segment of the general conflict." Churchill, Vol. IV, *The Hinge of Fate*, p. 8.
[12] Moran, *Churchill: The Struggle for Survival, 1940–1965*, p. 12.
[13] Ibid., p. 16.

If Churchill had been worried about the mood of Congress, it turned out that he had no cause. The shock of Pearl Harbor had amalgamated nearly all Americans, regardless of their ethnic backgrounds or previous isolationist convictions. In fact they were vying with each other to show support for the war. And here before them was the man who more than anyone else symbolized the Allied cause. The atmosphere was warm, and Churchill was deft in making the most of his American mother:

> "I cannot help reflecting that if my father had been American and my mother British, instead of the other way around, I might have got here on my own."

The congressmen, flattered, laughed heartily. But then Churchill turned serious:

> "What sort of people do they think we are? Is it possible they do not realize that we shall never cease to persevere against them until they have been taught a lesson which they and the world will never forget? He must indeed have a blind soul who cannot see that some great purpose and design is being worked out here below, of which we have the honor to be the faithful servants. . . . The best tidings of all is that the United States, united as never before, have drawn the sword of freedom and cast away the scabbard."

The cheers reverberated.

*

Though the worst pressure was over, the residual effects of the strain on Churchill were not. That night, while trying to open a window in his bedroom, he suffered chest pains which felt suspiciously like a minor heart attack. Unable to reach Lord Moran, who was staying elsewhere, Churchill lay in the dark alone. The next morning Moran arrived at the White House for his daily call, and despite the dull pain that Churchill described, he could find little to alarm him. His patient had apparently suffered a case of coronary insufficiency, for which normal treatment would be six weeks in bed.

Moran realized that he would have to make a judgment, possibly incurring some medical risk. Judging that no one but Churchill could handle the challenge of bringing the Americans properly into the war, Moran made an audacious decision and held back.

"Well, is my heart all right?" Churchill demanded.

"There is nothing serious," Moran answered. "You have been overdoing things."[14]

---

[14] Ibid., pp. 17, 18. Churchill, III, 691, places this incident the night of January 5, 1942. The author's judgment is that Moran's diary is more likely to be accurate.

*

Christmas, Thursday, could be regarded as the day on which the conferees of the ARCADIA shifted gears. The "Fundamental Basis of Joint Strategy," a joint political-military exercise, had been agreed. From then on the political and military worked separately. Roosevelt and Churchill occupied themselves largely with Roosevelt's Joint Declaration of the Associated Powers while the military chiefs concentrated on creating mechanisms for the military direction of the war. During the six plenary sessions held during the three-week span, Roosevelt and Churchill played their roles as commanders-in-chief; however, the military were not involved in the creation of the Joint Declaration.

Work on the Declaration actually began a little before Christmas. Roosevelt had brought up the idea some time earlier and he and Churchill had each undertaken to draft his own version. By Christmas Eve each had produced his draft, and the two met with their advisers. All were surprised at how parallel the texts were, and with ease they blended the drafts into one, which they sent to Lord Privy Seal Attlee in London. The essence of the Declaration was that the Associated Powers (at this time including only the United States, Britain, U.S.S.R., China, the Commonwealth, and occupied European countries),

> Being convinced that . . . complete . . . victory over their enemies is essential to defend life, liberty, independence and religious freedom, and to preserve human rights and justice in their own lands as well as in other lands, and that they are now engaged in a common struggle against savage and brutal forces seeking to subjugate the world, DECLARE:
>
> (1) Each Government pledges itself to employ its full resources, military or economic, against those members of the Tripartite Pact and its adherents with which such Government is at war.
>
> (2) Each Government pledges itself to cooperate with the Governments signatory hereto, and not to make a separate armistice or peace with the enemies.[15]

By the next day, Christmas, Attlee's answer on behalf of the War Cabinet came in. Apparently minor problems were important. For example, the precedence of the signatory nations became a matter of some disagreement. In all drafts the United States was the first signatory and Britain was second—no problem there. But in the early versions the nations of the British Commonwealth were grouped under Great Britain. And India, not recognized by the British as a full-fledged nation, was included along with the others. The War Cabinet therefore recommended that

15 Churchill, III, 684. See also Sherwood, *Roosevelt and Hopkins*, p. 447.

India be deleted from the list of sovereign nations, even in the Commonwealth.

There were other matters to be ironed out. Harry Hopkins, in a note written on December 27, suggested some mention of "religious freedom." Maxim Litvinov, Soviet Ambassador to the United States, objected that he needed the approval of Stalin. However, Roosevelt assured the Bolshevik that "religious freedom" meant freedom to have no religion at all; Litvinov gave in.[16] Roosevelt was proud of this triumph. Churchill promised to name him Archbishop of Canterbury if he lost the next election.

Another issue was a British request to include the term "social security." But Roosevelt, acutely conscious of his need for support from conservatives in the Senate, demurred. It sounded too "New Dealish," he feared.

The first response of the War Cabinet had been sent without the views of Anthony Eden. When Eden returned from Moscow, therefore, he immediately sent a special message. He would like to (1) lump the British Commonwealth nations together, (2) include De Gaulle's Free French as an independent nation, (3) retain "social security," and (4) exclude India. The message arrived on December 29, and Roosevelt arbitrarily— Churchill had gone to Ottawa on the evening of the twenty-eighth—did pretty much what he pleased. He ignored the Free French and left out "social security." As to the signatories, he placed the five members of the British Commonwealth—Canada, Australia, New Zealand, South Africa, *and* India—in alphabetical order, not lumped under the United Kingdom.

Prime Minister Churchill returned to the White House on New Year's Day to find the changes a *fait accompli,* which he took in good part. And President Roosevelt, on inspiration, had decided that the name "Associated Powers" should be changed to the "United Nations."

When Roosevelt was wheeled into Churchill's room to discuss the final draft and Roosevelt's changes, an exuberant Prime Minister showed him a reference to "United Nations" in Byron's *Childe Harold.* Later Soviet Ambassador Litvinov and Chinese Ambassador T. V. Soong arrived and were ushered to the President's Oval Study. Roosevelt, Churchill, Harry Hopkins, Litvinov, and Soong then went over the final wording of the text. When ready to sign, the President sent for Mrs. Roosevelt and a few of her guests to witness. "Maybe I should have signed as Commander-in-Chief," murmured Roosevelt.

" 'President' ought to do," said Hopkins.

In a day before all were considered equal, the representatives of twenty-two other governments, including India, signed the United Nations Declaration on the ground floor of the White House with the State Department supervising.

[16] Burns, *Roosevelt: The Soldier of Freedom,* p. 184.

As T. V. Soong was affixing the fourth signature in the Oval Study, Churchill was thinking out loud: "Four fifths of the human race!"

*

With the grand strategy agreed, the attention of the British and American military chiefs turned to "procedural" matters, concrete issues of paramount importance. First they chose to consider a plan for the coordination of efforts between British and American land, sea, and air forces. The concept of a unified command, the placing of all these forces in a region under one man, came as the result of a proposal by General Marshall, who became the driving force behind it.

The Western Allies had established a rudimentary unified command late in World War I, when the three governments gave French Marshal Ferdinand Foch command of all French, British, and American forces on the Western Front. Foch's function as a coordinator had been useful, but he had been given very little actual authority over the respective national armies.

Marshall's intellectual conviction regarding the value of such an arrangement was given emotional impetus on Christmas morning. The evening before, after the speeches on the White House balcony, Roosevelt and Churchill had apparently discussed what to do if the Americans found it impossible to get reinforcements through to the Philippines. Perhaps those forces previously earmarked for MacArthur could then be turned over to the British. To the Americans, this concept could mean writing off the Philippines in favor of Singapore.

As soon as the news reached Chief of Staff Marshall, he summoned both Arnold and Eisenhower. The three went almost at a run to the office of the Secretary of War. Stimson, an elder statesman who was prone to a certain pedantry in dealing with his Commander-in-Chief, became furious. He picked up the telephone and told Harry Hopkins at the White House that if the President was going to persist with "this kind of foolishness" he would have to get a new Secretary of War.

The intensity of the War Department reaction apparently came as a surprise to Churchill and Roosevelt, and both denied that any such contingency plan had been agreed upon. Later, apparently smarting at Stimson's defiance, the President made a snide remark about "incorrect rumors" passing around. In response, Stimson produced an extract from the record made by a British secretary. Cornered but undaunted, the President elected simply to rise above the subject. The episode was minor, but its timing was perfect to motivate Marshall.

Marshall brought up the idea of a single command, American-British-Dutch-Australian (ABDA), to his colleagues that same afternoon, but it was not pursued to any great length, since the high point of the day was the Christmas dinner hosted by Marshall at Quarters No. 1, Fort Myer, for all his colleagues. More important for the moment was the fact that Christmas happened to be Sir John Dill's birthday, and the group enjoyed noting that the American and British flags on his cake bore the stamp "Made in Japan." The big news had to do with a development more diplomatic than military. General Charles de Gaulle's Free French had just seized two small Vichy-controlled islands off the mouth of the St. Lawrence, St. Pierre and Miquelon. The forces involved were small, the main prize being only a radio station. But De Gaulle's arrogance in flouting a previous agreement to lay off ensured his exclusion as a signatory to the U. N. Declaration.

The next morning Marshall made his ABDA proposal more formally, drawing heavily on the Allied experience of World War I. Admiral Stark was non-committal, and the British Chiefs stalled. At the end of the meeting Marshall realized that he needed something more concrete than a concept expressed orally. He therefore directed General Eisenhower, still the planner for the Far East, to draw up a "letter of instructions" to a proposed Supreme Commander of the Pacific. This directive was to spell out the commander's mission and authority as well as to specify safeguards against his possible abuse of national interests. Marshall mentioned the idea later that day to Stimson and to Assistant Secretary John J. McCloy. He had already set his mind on giving the command, if its establishment were approved, to General Archibald Wavell, now commanding in India. Placing U.S. forces under a British officer might make the whole notion more attractive.

Stimson was enthusiastic about the concept and on Saturday morning, December 27, he asked Marshall and Arnold to accompany him to the White House. The President approved tentatively but rather typically put the responsibility on Stimson to sell the idea to the Navy. By noon Marshall was closeted with his counterparts in Admiral Stark's office. This time Marshall had better luck. The concept of service unity was easier for the Navy to swallow than the idea of giving the ABDA command to a British Army officer. Finally, however, Admiral King agreed that in no other way could the idea be sold to the British. Hardly had King spoken than everyone else fell in line, including Stark. Ernie King had obviously taken over the Navy, in fact if not in name.

But Marshall's work that day was not yet done. With the President and the Navy now behind him, he resumed his plea to his British counterparts. Admiral Pound was wary about putting the Royal Navy in harness, even under a British Army officer. But Marshall kept working. Suddenly, as one man, the British shifted over and began criticizing Marshall's plan as being too *restrictive*. Marshall, astonished, was glad to concede. As the meeting broke up, a British naval officer rushed to the door to shake

hands; both he and Dill actually put an arm around Marshall to congratulate him.

The Chief of Staff still faced one big obstacle: the Prime Minister himself. When Churchill and Roosevelt met that evening Churchill would
have none of the whole idea. No analogy existed between Foch's command on the Western Front in World War I, he contended, and the vast
area of the Southwest Pacific. Foch had commanded one continuous line
between the Vosges Mountains and the English Channel, but in the Far
East independent Allied forces involving three services of four different
countries would be separated by hundreds of miles. These forces should
remain independent and report only to a supreme command in Washington.

But as Churchill talked, his canny friend Beaverbrook observed him.
Detecting a lack of certainty, probably indiscernible to the Americans, he
passed a note to Harry Hopkins: "You should work on Churchill. He is
being advised. He is open-minded and needs discussion." Encouraged,
Hopkins managed an opportunity to plead with Churchill to talk directly
with Marshall. Churchill agreed, and the next morning, December 28,
Marshall found himself in Churchill's bedroom in a face-to-face confrontation.

The scene of the meeting was bizarre: here was the Prime Minister of
Great Britain propped up in the high four-poster bed glaring at the erect,
immaculately pressed, beribboned Chief of Staff, who paced the floor and
minced few words.

Churchill jumped off to the attack, demanding what an Army officer
could know about handling a ship. From his position of advantage above,
Marshall shot down, "And what the devil does a naval officer know about
handling a tank? I'm not interested in Drake and Frobisher, but only in
creating a united front against Japan. If the Allies don't do something
right away," he concluded, they are "finished in the war."[17]

Churchill knew that he would have to yield, as the weight of opinion
was arrayed against him. But he would not do so supinely. He broke the
conversation off, disappeared into the bathroom, reappeared with a wet
towel around his waist, waved Marshall off, and sent for his military
chiefs. Next evening Churchill cabled the War Cabinet informing them
that he had approved. They must back him up by January 1, as he wanted
his answer when he returned to Washington from Ottawa.

But Churchill's approval was given with a heavy heart, not from fear of
the unified-command principle but because of the hopelessness of Wa-

[17] Interview with General George C. Marshall by Forrest Pogue, October 5, 1956,
quoted in Pogue, *George C. Marshall*, Vol. II, *Ordeal and Hope*, p. 280. This book
is the major source of this account of the establishment of ABDA.

vell's task in trying to stem the Japanese. Before leaving Washington he drafted a message to Wavell personally:

> The President and his military and naval advisers have impressed upon me the urgent need for unified command in Southwest Pacific, and it is unanimously desired, pressed particularly by President and General Marshall, that you should become Supreme Commander of Allied forces by land, air, and sea assigned to that theatre. . . .
>
> You are the only man who has the experience of handling so many different theatres at once. . . . Everyone knows how dark and difficult the situation is. President will announce that your appointment has been made by his desire.

Churchill later commented that the offer was one "which only the highest sense of duty could induce [Wavell] to accept . . . as he would have to bear a load of defeat in a scene of confusion."[18]

Two days later the War Cabinet approved. And an abiding principle, that of unity of command in each region, had been established.

*

In London, General Sir Alan Brooke, newly appointed Chief of the Imperial General Staff (CIGS), was undergoing the pangs of frustration. Neither an optimistic nor a modest man, Brooke felt severe misgivings when he read the dispatches from Washington.

Actually Brooke was content, in a way, at being left behind, for personally he enjoyed his association with Deputy Prime Minister Clement Attlee, in charge during Churchill's absence. Attlee was very different from Churchill. He looked mousy and ineffective, with a bald head and a brush mustache. But this appearance belied the actual strength of one who had risen to the political top through the Labour Party. With no ambition to emulate Churchill's flamboyance and rhetoric, Attlee was careful, precise, and orderly. Brooke enjoyed this three-week respite from Churchill; he could learn his new job in relative peace.

But the world situation, as Brooke saw it, was distressing. At Hong Kong the British had been driven from the mainland to the island (it fell on Christmas); the Japanese invasion of the Philippines was progressing; Borneo, with its oil fields, had been invaded; Padang, on the west coast of Malaya, had been taken; and finally word had come in that the *Queen Elizabeth* and the *Valiant* had been crippled in Alexandria Harbor on December 19 by Italian frogmen. In the course of one month the British and Americans together had lost fifteen capital ships, that is, half their combined strength. Except for Malta, the British now had between Gibraltar

18 Churchill, III, 677.

and Alexandria only three cruisers and a handful of destroyers and sub-marines.

And though Churchill in Washington was exuding optimism about a link-up between Auchinleck's Eighth Army in Libya[19] and an invasion from the northwest coast of Africa, Brooke was pondering the facts grimly. "The more I look at the situation," he wrote in his diary on De-cember 20, "the more I dislike it. From now on the Far East will make ever-increasing inroads into our resources."[20] To Brooke an Anglo-American landing in French Africa was premature and unrealistic.

When the Prime Minister's message regarding ABDA reached London the evening of December 28, Brooke was unhappier than ever. "The whole [ABDA] scheme," he scribbled, "is wild and half-baked . . . only catering for one area of action, namely the Western Pacific . . . and no central control. . . ."[21] And Brooke's attitude toward the new American allies was made no more sanguine by a pessimistic letter he received from Sir John Dill:

> This country is the most highly organized for peace you can imag-ine. Everything is done on a grand scale. I have never seen so many motor cars, but I have not seen a military vehicle. . . . And yet amid all this unpreparedness the ordinary American firmly believes that they can finish off the war quite quickly—and without too much dis-turbance. . . . Never have I seen a country so utterly unprepared for war and so soft.[22]

There was one significant difference between Dill's make-up and Brooke's: in the coming months Dill would become America's friend; Brooke never would.

*

On returning to Washington on New Year's Prime Minister Churchill (having signed the Joint Declaration) immediately plunged into the usual round of conferences. But the wear and tear on him was beginning to show even to his American hosts, and they urged him to take a rest. To accommodate him, Edward R. Stettinius, Jr., a member of the White House staff, offered the use of his home near Palm Beach, Florida. Chur-chill accepted gratefully and left on January 5 in Marshall's plane. At his request, General Marshall made the trip down with him, as Churchill wanted to become better acquainted. In Florida the Prime Minister lounged on the beach, in the shade, and in the water.

[19] General Sir Claude Auchinleck was actually Commander, Middle East. Eighth Army was commanded, under Auchinleck, by General Sir Neil Ritchie.
[20] Diary, quoted in Bryant, *Turn of the Tide*, p. 229.
[21] Ibid., p. 236.
[22] Dill to Brooke, December 28, 1941, quoted in ibid., p. 233.

The respite was a godsend. In addition to the few days' rest, Churchill was able to pull his thoughts together in a quiet atmosphere. It was impossible for him to set the war aside, however, and his mind continued to dwell on it as actively as ever.

Hardly had Churchill arrived when the news of the *Queen Elizabeth* and the *Valiant* came in.[23] Immediately he sent orders to London directing that strong air reinforcements, especially torpedo planes, be sent to the Mediterranean, even at the expense of the bomber offensive against Germany. Always thoughtful of his favorite commanders, Churchill inquired after the state of mind of Admiral Sir Andrew Cunningham, the naval commander. And his mind passed from Alexandria immediately to Scapa Flow, where the harbor might be subject to the same type of action: "Are we in fact patrolling the entrance with depth charges every twenty minutes? No doubt the strong currents would give far greater protection than the calm water of Alexandria. How does the matter stand?"[24]

Churchill's attention was never confined to the news of the day. At the same time he was also thinking about the political situation in India, where he blamed the Congress Party and the Hindu priesthood for the current unrest. He was happy, however, that the American public was unconcerned with India, as the Americans were preoccupied with the war.

And perhaps the brightened prospects for victory prompted Churchill to think way ahead to the future boundaries of the Soviet Union. The Russians were fighting bravely, he recognized—but only for their own homeland. Churchill could not forget that the Russians had been indifferent to the British plight until they themselves had been attacked the previous June. In a memorandum to Anthony Eden, Churchill projected himself to the end of the war, optimistically hoping that the Russians would need the Anglo-Americans worse than vice versa.

To fill in what time was left, Churchill sent General Sir Hastings Ismay, his personal military assistant, a military evaluation of the future of the war, with a copy to Roosevelt in Washington. On the evening of January 9, after only four days, Churchill left by train for Washington. He arrived on the eleventh.

*

Meanwhile, work in Washington had proceeded unabated despite Mr. Churchill's absences. The problem now at hand was to set up a mechanism for the military direction of the war, a global arrangement to correspond on a world-wide basis to the regional unified command. Somehow, with the ABDA principle established, agreement on the establishment of

---

[23] Churchill, III, 692. It is difficult to believe that the word took seventeen days, from December 19 to January 5, to reach him. Nevertheless, Churchill refers to his own account on p. 576 in the same book.
[24] Ibid., p. 693.

an "appropriate joint body" came much easier. Here President Roosevelt, rather than Marshall, took the lead, particularly regarding the authority vested in the proposed supreme military authority, the Combined Chiefs of Staff (CCS). The Combined Chiefs, as the name implies, would be composed of the BCOS (British) and JCS (American) sitting together as one unit. This body would be complete at such times as the two sets of chiefs could meet personally, but some means had to be devised for functioning on a day-by-day basis. The British BCOS could not, after all, live in Washington. To solve this problem the American and British military had originally recommended that the British establish a three-man "standing committee" in Washington. Then, when a theater commander should need direction, he would send two messages, one to the American JCS in Washington and the other to the BCOS in London. The British Chiefs would then notify their Washington representatives on what position to take.

To Roosevelt this compromise seemed too weak: the prestige body in Washington would, he discerned, be watered down if the theater commanders reported simultaneously to both capitals. Accordingly he practically dictated that the Combined Chiefs in Washington should receive all direct messages from the theater commanders. Thereupon the British members of the CCS would solicit the views of the British Chiefs (BCOS) in London and then act accordingly. A small point, technically, but psychologically important.

At the outset the British balked, for requiring theater commanders to report only to Washington meant that on a daily basis the war would be run from there. In the due course, however, they gave way; and on his return from Florida Churchill accepted the change.

To Alan Brooke, in London, news of this Combined Chiefs arrangement came as another body blow. It was almost unthinkable, he fumed, to subordinate the "hard won knowledge, organization, and battle experience of the British high command" to the American leaders, who were "still only beginners." "Selling our birthright for a plate of porridge," as he put it.[25]

Not so Churchill. "We are no longer single," he observed, "but married."

Fortunately for the entire CCS concept, the officer designated to represent the British in Washington, Field Marshal Sir John Dill, was a man of the highest prestige, ability, and understanding. And though Dill's career had seemed to be over, it turned out that his most significant contribution to the war effort still lay ahead of him. He and Marshall became warm

[25] Bryant, *Turn of the Tide,* p. 237.

friends, a fact which helped make the Combined Chiefs a viable arrangement.

*

At 3:30 P.M., January 14, 1942, came the final meeting of the ARCADIA Conference. A pressing need existed for a mechanism to direct the allocation of munitions, shipping, and raw materials among British, American, and other United Nations forces.

This problem had long been a subject of debate and the British had for months been concerned over the haphazard machinery employed by the United States. Marshall and Stark, aware of this deficiency, had attempted to get a "munitions board" established. Beaverbrook, in London, had advocated a "supreme command" over supplies.[26]

In establishing a joint American-British Munitions Allocation Committee, little disagreement was encountered as to who should head it up: Beaverbrook as the British Minister of Supply and Harry Hopkins.[27] But the status of the committee was something else. When it was first discussed, the British had come up with a scheme for two separate allocation boards, one in London and one in Washington. The British, they proposed, should distribute munitions (produced in America) to their so-called "protégé" nations: the British Commonwealth, France, the Netherlands, Egypt, and Turkey. The United States would be relegated to allocating what was left to Latin America and China. American reaction was understandably violent. The idea got nowhere.

Just before this late afternoon meeting, President Roosevelt sent for Marshall and Hopkins to read his latest version of the plan in which a single new board would have two heads, Hopkins and Beaverbrook. These two co-equal officials would each report to his own head of government on a level with the Combined Chiefs of Staff. Thus any disagreements would have to be settled by Roosevelt and Churchill themselves. Marshall could never accept relegating the power to control the means of waging war to Hopkins and Beaverbrook, capable as they were. If the Combined Chiefs did not ultimately control allocation of munitions, they could not fight a war, he declared, and he personally could not carry his own responsibility, meaning that his own job would be vacant.

[26] After Pearl Harbor Roosevelt had established an *ad hoc* committee called the Strategic Munitions Board, consisting of Marshall, Stark, and Hopkins. But with events moving so rapidly, the committee had not met before the arrival of the Churchill party.

[27] In fact, Roosevelt had earlier been urged to appoint Hopkins as a sort of munitions "czar," but he had consistently demurred in the light of possible opposition from Congress. As Administrator of the Works Progress Administration during the New Deal, Hopkins had made enemies that were to trail him throughout his life.

President Roosevelt was a flexible man, prone to loft trial balloons. But this was the second time during the conference that a top official of the War Department had threatened to resign. An impasse was possible. To Marshall's surprise and relief, however, Hopkins came to the rescue. He himself, he said, could not serve as the head of a Munitions Allocation Board unless that Board were considered a subcommittee of the Combined Chiefs.

The American position was now consolidated and the British were backed to the wall. Since the munitions in question were produced in the United States, the Americans could, if they insisted, send their tonnage anywhere without reference to the British.

The best that Churchill and Beaverbrook could do under the circumstances was to agree. They saved face by calling their agreement "on a trial basis," one month at a time. Washington would now be the headquarters for every aspect of the conduct of the war, and Roosevelt plainly was established as *de facto* first among equals. The new member of the harem had not behaved according to expectations.

One of Winston Churchill's claims to greatness—not recognized generally—was his ability to rise above disappointments, even humiliations. He never let these considerations becloud the goal of victory. Furthermore he could point to two important developments: (1) American adherence to the "Europe First" strategy and (2) the astronomical amounts of equipment that President Roosevelt had called upon the American nation to produce.[28]

Thus Roosevelt, Churchill, and Hopkins sat down to a congenial dinner the evening of Churchill's departure. Basking in what had been accomplished, the three lingered for an hour past the time they were scheduled to leave. They then drove down New York Avenue to a siding on Sixth Street N.W., where a special train was waiting to take Churchill and his party to Norfolk.

*

At Norfolk a large, luxurious Boeing flying boat waited. And at Bermuda, the *Duke of York* and its escort were prepared to carry on from there. In the air, however, Churchill asked Pound and Portal if they were amenable to taking the Boeing on to London. After all, the President himself had expressed concern about Churchill's safety on the way home, and twenty U-boats were known to be clustered in the path of the *Duke*

[28] In his State of the Union message, January 6, Roosevelt had called for production of 45,000 operational aircraft in 1942 and 100,000 in 1943; 45,000 tanks were to run off the line in 1942 and 75,000 the next year. The other figures were similarly breathtaking.

of York. The situation in Malaya demanded the Prime Minister's personal attention. Pound and Portal reluctantly came around. They spent the next day, however, in Bermuda.

On the final morning in Bermuda, Churchill woke up uneasy. He would be just as happy, he admitted to himself, if the weather should be reported bad for flying. He received no such relief: a reduced contingent of passengers were off the ground by 1:00 P.M. January 16, soon flying through fog at 7,000 feet. Churchill went to bed and slept.

Churchill never appreciated the dangers of this flight. The American pilot became lost, and had not Portal changed course, the lone plane would have crossed over Brest. Only after landing at Plymouth did Churchill learn that six British Hurricanes had been ordered to shoot them down, as they were unidentified. The Hurricanes had failed only because they had lost their target. Undaunted, the Prime Minister dispatched a short telegram to Roosevelt mentioning nothing of his close call and was soon off to face the grim realities of the impending military disasters that were bound to come.

CHAPTER IV

"A HELL OF A BEATING"

G eneral Sir Archibald P. Wavell, Commander-in-Chief, India, received Churchill's notification of his new appointment at his headquarters in New Delhi. Like the Prime Minister, he quickly realized that his task with the newly formed American-British-Dutch-Australian Command was well-nigh hopeless. The ABDA covered a vast area, mostly water, where military disasters had already occurred or were impending: the fall of Hong Kong on Christmas; Japanese landings in Malaya; Japanese crossings from Indochina into Siam (Thailand). On the Malay Peninsula, the area of his primary concern, Japanese forces were halfway down the coast.

The Philippines were also included in his command. There the Japanese Fourteenth Army (General Masabaru Homma) had made its major landing in the Lingayan Gulf on the northwest coast of Luzon and had pushed southward toward Manila; the Americans there were retreating southward toward the Bataan Peninsula. A secondary Japanese landing southeast of Manila was about to take the city.

This was a command that no soldier would have asked for, but Wavell had no choice. Traveling by way of Singapore, he would, as directed, establish his new headquarters at Bandung, Java, Dutch East Indies.

*

Wavell, fifty-eight years of age at the time, was one of Britain's foremost soldiers. Stocky, rugged, blind in one eye since the Battle of Ypres, he personified the British field commander at his best. Reticent and abrupt, he was a respected military thinker. His former adversary Erwin Rommel carried with him a copy of Wavell's book *Generals and*

Generalship. As a diversion, Wavell was a prolific writer of doggerel po-
etry.

Wavell had already undergone hard knocks in this war. In 1939 as
Commander-in-Chief, Middle East, he had been charged with building up
the British forces along the border between Egypt and Libya. Then,
shortly after Mussolini had entered the war in June 1940, Italian General
Graziani had driven eastward fifty miles into Egypt. There Wavell had
held him and in December had launched a counteroffensive over five hundred miles into Cyrenaica (Libya). Wavell had become the foremost military hero of Britain overnight.

But Wavell's luck had run out. In early spring of 1941 German General
Erwin Rommel, with his Afrika Korps, had taken over from Graziani
while Wavell had been ordered to send the bulk of his troops to Greece
and then Crete. His supply lines stretched and his forces depleted, Wavell
had been driven back to the Egyptian border. The line had been stabilized
by the end of May 1941, but in mid-June, beset with the worries of three
divergent campaigns (Syria and Iraq had been added), Wavell had un-
successfully attacked Rommel at Salum, a mishandled battle in Churchill's eyes.

During these months Wavell's relations with Whitehall had become increasingly strained; observers noticed his weariness. Churchill therefore
had decided to replace him with General Sir Claude Auchinleck, who
Churchill hoped could bring a "fresh eye and fresh hand" to the
beleaguered Middle East. Wavell, relieved but not discredited, had been
moved to Auchinleck's former position as Commander-in-Chief, India.
There he could regain his strength for some other crisis. Now that crisis
had come.

*

Minister of State Sir Alfred Duff Cooper, diplomat and sometime author, had a feeling that his temporary posting to Singapore was about to
end. He had completed a fact-finding mission in the Far East and, with
his wife, had been relaxing in Singapore. The two had been on hand to
greet an old friend, Admiral Sir Tom Phillips, when he, commanding the
Prince of Wales and *Repulse,* arrived from Australia. Phillips had called
socially in a lighthearted, Britannia-Rule-the-Waves atmosphere. That
had been last November, 1941. For some reason Cooper had not been
surprised when told at 3:00 A.M., December 8, of Japanese landings on
the northeast coast of Malaya. And three days later the Prime Minister
had appointed him "Resident Cabinet Minister," a position in which he,
as a member of the government, was to coordinate the British war effort
in Southeast Asia.

That day, while he was visiting General Sir Robert Brooke-Popham, the Commander-in-Chief, Far East, the news came in that the *Prince of Wales* and the *Repulse* had been sunk; Tom Phillips was missing.[1]

Duff Cooper was satisfied with the job he had done in securing cooperation between the military and the local government, and he had been too busy to worry over the distressing daily dispatches from the fighting in the north. But basing his report on that grim situation, he recommended to Churchill that no serious defense be attempted above Johore, about fifty miles north of the city. The Prime Minister had approved while at sea on the way to ARCADIA.

But now the circumstances had changed. General Wavell had been appointed Supreme Commander for the entire Far East, and Cooper surmised that this position would supersede his. He was right; on January 7 a telegram came in: ". . . Wavell's appointment as Supreme Commander . . . necessarily brings your mission to an end. . . ." Relieved, Duff Cooper met Wavell when he arrived from New Delhi that same evening, and they dined in a portentous atmosphere before he and his wife departed.

*

General Wavell, now functioning in his role of Supreme Commander, ABDA, stayed over in Singapore for a couple of days in order to study the situation. It was bad. Total Commonwealth ground forces consisted of three divisions, two Indian and one Australian,[2] scattered along a six-hundred-mile peninsula, deployed not tactically but to protect airfields. The Japanese enjoyed complete control of the air and the seas. And despite a Western tendency to underestimate the Oriental as a soldier, the Japanese ground forces performed superbly in jungle warfare. Lightly equipped and highly trained for this task, they outfought the Commonwealth troops, British included, at every turn.

On arrival in Singapore Wavell reported by cable to the Prime Minister when Churchill was on the sands of Palm Beach. On the day he headed back for Washington, the Prime Minister approved Wavell's withdrawing all outposts to the planned main defense line protecting Johore. But despite the fact that he had been kept well informed, Churchill could not instantaneously absorb the extent of the disaster. Though Wavell had tried to explain the non-existence of British naval power, he still could not reconcile himself to this unthinkable development.

*

The over-all Japanese plan for conquests in the Pacific was actually limited (see map, p. 54–55). Their objective was to occupy, develop, and

[1] Phillips had insisted on going down with the *Prince of Wales*.
[2] The 9th and 11th British-Indian and the 8th Australian. Later reinforced by the 18th—just in time for the ultimate disaster.

exploit a well-defined area including the Dutch East Indies and Southeast Asia. Before Pearl Harbor the Japanese had already occupied Manchuria, Korea, the coast of China, Formosa, and French Indochina. To complete the "Co-Prosperity Sphere," all the Imperial Forces now needed to do was take Siam, Burma, Malaya, and the Dutch East Indies.

To protect this wealthy empire, however, the Japanese high command considered it necessary to expand farther east into the Pacific: their ultimate planned defensive perimeter included the Philippines, the northern half of New Guinea, the Bismarck Archipelago, part of the Solomon Islands, the Gilbert Islands, the Marshall Islands, and Wake.[3] But even these objectives were scattered and could not be attacked all at once; therefore the immediate targets after Pearl Harbor were the Philippine Islands and Malaya (including Singapore).

Naval supremacy in the Objective Area gave the Japanese the same overriding advantage strategically that they enjoyed tactically in Malaya: they could concentrate at any point they chose. But the ground forces employed were remarkably modest, consisting of only ten divisions and four separate brigades,[4] allocated to four armies, directed by Headquarters, Southern Command, at Saigon. The Fourteenth Army was assigned to the Philippines; the Twenty-fifth to Malaya and Singapore; the Fifteenth to Burma; and the Sixteenth to the Dutch East Indies. Of these the task of the Sixteenth Army was the most far-reaching. It would hop from island to island, its spearhead pointed toward Bandung, on Java, the capture of which would split the Philippines from Singapore.[5] But the force employed was adequate. The plan was well conceived and thoroughly executed, prompting Churchill to growl about the "hideously efficient Japanese war machine."

The Philippines represented the eastern sector of Wavell's theater. On its main island, Luzon, the front lines had stabilized between the day of Wavell's appointment and his arrival in Bandung. Manila had fallen the day after New Year's, but General Douglas MacArthur had succeeded in eluding the Japanese trap which attempted to split the two wings of his forces (Wainwright in Pampanga to the north and Parker to the south). He had now established a strong position on the Bataan Peninsula, about twenty miles long and thirty miles deep. Below it in the mouth of Manila Bay lay the island fortress of Corregidor.

[3] By August 1942 that was precisely the area the Japanese occupied. They had no intention of going farther.
[4] Total available:. fifty-one divisions and fifty-nine separate brigades, most of which were retained in Japan and China.
[5] *West Point Atlas,* Vol. II, is the source of this operation summary.

The establishment of a strong, last-ditch position on the Bataan Peninsula conformed to the long-standing American plan. The peninsula was a
natural; it was rugged and narrow. So long as Bataan could be held, Corregidor would be impregnable. Together they controlled the mouth of
Manila Bay. Manila, the "Pearl of the Orient," was as important to the
Philippines as Paris is to France. But withdrawing to the Bataan position
as a concept was one thing; squeezing two retreating forces through the
bottleneck between the Zambales Mountains and the bay was another.
MacArthur had been at his best.

When MacArthur was first informed that he would be subordinate to
General Wavell, he had responded with a magnanimous pledge. But in
practice he never acted as if Wavell existed; nearly all his com-
munications were with Washington. Therein lay the true weakness of the
ABDA Theater. From Bandung, two thousand miles away, Wavell was in
no position to direct the detailed day-by-day operations of MacArthur.
And Wavell could offer nothing by way of reinforcements or supply.
Small wonder that Wavell focused on Malaya and Singapore while the
Philippine operation remained an independent American concern.

Douglas MacArthur was an enigmatic figure, whose legend has engulfed
the man. His public image excited strong emotions, ranging from near-
worship to hatred. His personal make-up was unusually complex, including a brilliant mind, an "old-time religion" type of patriotism, a flair for
the dramatic, great moral and physical courage, and extraordinary personal charm. These virtues, unfortunately, were at least partly offset by an
overweening ego and a messianic faith in himself which sometimes
beclouded his judgment. These qualities enabled him to spellbind the
most hardheaded critic or, when he chose, to patronize anyone, Presidents
of the United States not excepted. (Even Roosevelt, it was observed,
treated MacArthur with "kid gloves."[6]

But personality had little to do with the situation facing MacArthur's
troops. On the tenth of January 1942 MacArthur wired Washington that
he had now placed his troops on half rations and that the men were
becoming exhausted. Bataan Peninsula, he pointed out, was inadequate to
provide any source of food. The force was completely dependent on communications by sea.

MacArthur remained convinced that the Japanese were spread thin and
that their naval blockade was so lightly manned as to allow medium-sized
ships to pass through without unacceptable risk. Unaware of the desperate
efforts in Washington to find ways to assist him—and possibly unaware

[6] Interview with W. Averell Harriman, September 30, 1975.

also of the extent of the losses suffered by the Navy—he was frustrated by what he termed a "lack of will to win" in Washington.[7]

On the day of MacArthur's desperate wire to Washington, General Masabaru Homma, commanding the Japanese Fourteenth Army, sent him a message:

> Sir, you are well aware that you are doomed. The end is near. The question is how long you will be able to resist. You have already cut rations in half. I appreciate the fighting spirit of yourself and your troops who have been fighting with courage. Your prestige and honor have been upheld.
>
> However, in order to avoid needless bloodshed and to save the remnants of your divisions and your auxiliary troops, you are advised to surrender . . . .

MacArthur declined to answer the message, and soon the American lines were receiving propaganda leaflets. The broken English tended to raise rather than lower morale:

> The outcome of the present combat has already decided and you are cornered to the doom. But, however, being unable to realize the present situation, blinded General MacArthur has stupidly refused our proposal and continues futile struggle at the cost of your precious lives.
>
> Dear Filipino Soldiers!
>
> There are still one way left for you. That is to give up all your weapons at once and surrender to the Japanese force before it is too late, then we shall fully protect you.
>
> We repeat for the last!
>
> Surrender at once and build your new Philippines for and by Filipinos.[8]

MacArthur's headquarters was actually located on Corregidor, a tadpole-shaped island once part of a long-dead volcano. The head of the tadpole, pointing west, was higher than the tail and therefore called "Topside." The tail was appropriately designated "Bottomside." The two

[7] MacArthur's wrath was not confined to those back home. Admiral Thomas Hart, commander of the Asiatic Fleet, had been appointed naval commander under Wavell and was directing some actions in the Dutch East Indies. MacArthur, therefore, had no control over Hart, and the latter prudently refused to risk his pitiful force of small carriers, a few destroyers and old submarines to fight the Japanese blockade. When Hart's forces were withdrawn to the East Indies by Christmas, MacArthur had taken over all naval facilities in the Philippines.

[8] MacArthur, *Reminiscences,* pp. 129, 130.

sections were separated by an impressive hill through which had been drilled the elaborate Malinta Tunnel, whose branching corridors provided space for ammunition storage, hospitals, and offices.

Originally MacArthur had located his headquarters on Topside, ostentatiously exposed. A heavy three-hour Japanese air raid one afternoon had destroyed it. MacArthur subsequently moved into the Malinta Tunnel.

To do what he could for sagging morale, MacArthur created a personal image for himself designed to divert his troops on the Bataan front. This he did with relish, sporting the unique uniform that was to become his trademark: scrambled-egg khaki cap, outsized corncob pipe, open-neck shirt, sometimes sunglasses. This Hollywood version of an Army uniform fitted his role of hero at home, though his friend Manuel Quezon, President of the Philippines, admonished him from Corregidor to avoid making himself a conspicuous target on the front.

One discouraging note, a possible threat to the morale of the Filipino soldiers, was a radio broadcast by General Emilio Aguinaldo. Aguinaldo, whose capture in 1901 had ended the Philippine Insurrection, had long since become America's friend, but he now pleaded publicly with MacArthur to give up the struggle. This action cut MacArthur, but he could only ignore it. Marshall, in Washington, agreed.

Day by day the situation of U.S. and Filipino forces on Bataan continued to degenerate. MacArthur's own description of those days reveals much about the condition of his troops and of himself:

> Our troops were now approaching exhaustion. The guerrilla movement was going well, but on Bataan and Corregidor the clouds were growing darker. My heart ached as I saw my men slowly wasting away. Their clothes hung on them like tattered rags. Their bare feet stuck out in silent protest. Their long bedraggled hair framed gaunt bloodless faces. Their hoarse, wild laughter greeted the constant stream of obscene and ribald jokes issuing from their parched, dry throats. They cursed the enemy and in the same breath cursed and reviled the United States; they spat when they jeered at the Navy. But their eyes would light up and they would cheer when they saw my battered, and much reviled in America, "scrambled egg" cap. They would gather round and pat me on the back and "Mabuhay Macarsar" me. They would grin—that ghastly skeleton-like grin of the dying—as they would roar in unison, "We are the battling bastards of Bataan—no papa, no mama, no Uncle Sam."[9]

9 Ibid., pp. 135–36. "Mabuhay" corresponds to "aloha," or "long live." Two accounts have stated that MacArthur visited Bataan only once in the seventy-seven days he was on Corregidor. See Wainwright, *General Wainwright's Story*, pp. 49–50, and Manchester, *American Caesar*, pp. 235–38.

*

From Wavell's headquarters in Bandung the campaign in Malaya over-rode all others. Singapore not only provided a base capable of supporting large fleets; it was located close to the center of the Japanese Objective Area, about halfway down Sumatra toward Java. Wavell needed no copy of the Japanese war plans to point out that Singapore would be their single most important objective.

And the capture of "impregnable" Singapore would have world-wide repercussions, as that bastion had come to symbolize British power. After establishing his command post, therefore, Wavell flew back after four days to take another look. Still in the habit of corresponding with Churchill rather than the Combined Chiefs, Wavell reported that the enemy's advance southward had been more rapid than expected. The battle for Singapore would be a "close run thing,"[10] he wrote optimistically, and delivery of sufficient reinforcements by sea might become difficult. The heavy rain was assisting the British convoys into Singapore, however. Wavell reported morale high.

The next day, as Churchill was arriving back in London from Washington, he was already expecting the loss of the Malay mainland. Before leaving he had cabled permission to withdraw all British troops to Singapore Island and had received a shocking reply:

16 Jan 42

. . . Until quite recently all plans were based on repulsing seaborne attacks on island and holding land attack in Johore or farther north, *and little or nothing was done to construct defences on north side of island to prevent crossing Johore Straits.* The fortress cannon . . . have all-round traverse, but their flat trajectory makes them unsuitable for counter-battery work.[11]

The Prime Minister sank into self-recrimination. How could the British have neglected the possibility of defending Singapore from the peninsula to the north? Why had he, the Prime Minister, not been told? Why had he not asked? In desperation he wrote back to Wavell, exhorting him to defend "every inch of ground." But then, somewhat inconsistently, he directed the destruction of all abandoned material. ". . . no question of surrender," he concluded, ". . . [may be] entertained until after protracted fighting among the ruins of Singapore City."[12]

The doom of Singapore was approaching by the moment. On January 15 a large convoy discharged two fresh Japanese divisions in the north.

[10] A term used by Wellington to describe Waterloo—with different results, however.
[11] Quoted in Churchill, IV, 48. Italics supplied.
[12] Ibid., p. 53.

Ten days later the British lost their last twenty-three planes trying to prevent a Japanese landing on the east coast just north of Johore. The next day the hopeless effort to hold Johore was abandoned.

*

In London, Alan Brooke saw that January 30 as one of the "dark days of the war." In North Africa, Rommel had routed Auchinleck. And at Singapore the defense was retiring that night into the island. "I doubt whether the island can hold out very long," he wrote. But at least the bulk of Commonwealth troops made their way safely across the single causeway from Johore onto the island of Singapore.

On Singapore, Lieutenant General A. W. Percival, commander in Malaya, disposed his troops as best he could. The island is diamond-shaped with the long axis running east–west. The front facing north was about twenty-five miles long and the island from north to south is about fifteen miles deep. Percival defended this front most heavily on the right (east) with two divisions, holding the left half with only three brigades. Singapore town was located on the south of the island and the naval base, on the north, was on the Johore Strait. Both were far enough east that the enemy could be conceded a landing on the west without immediate threat to town or naval installation.

The Japanese, enjoying freedom of movement, were able to concentrate in any area they chose. Accordingly on the evening of February 8 they stacked three divisions on a small front and crossed the strait on the lightly held western end. Within a day they had rolled up the British left flank.

Up to this time the Prime Minister had been exhorting the garrison at Singapore to fight to the end. As late as February 10 he had written that the newly arrived 18th Division had a chance to "make its name in history"; commanders should die with their troops. Wavell viewed the situation in the same light, or at least pretended to, never letting up the pressure on Percival.

On February 14, however, even Churchill realized that the situation was hopeless. An attempt was made to evacuate all technical and specialist troops. Few reached safety. When the governor reported that "the streets were full of dead and dying and within twenty-four hours the million inhabitants and the 70,000 defenders would be without water,"[13] Churchill decided to relent. He called Brooke from Chequers that Saturday afternoon with instructions giving Wavell authority to capitulate. General Percival surrendered Commonwealth forces unconditionally at

13 Bryant, *Turn of the Tide*, p. 244.

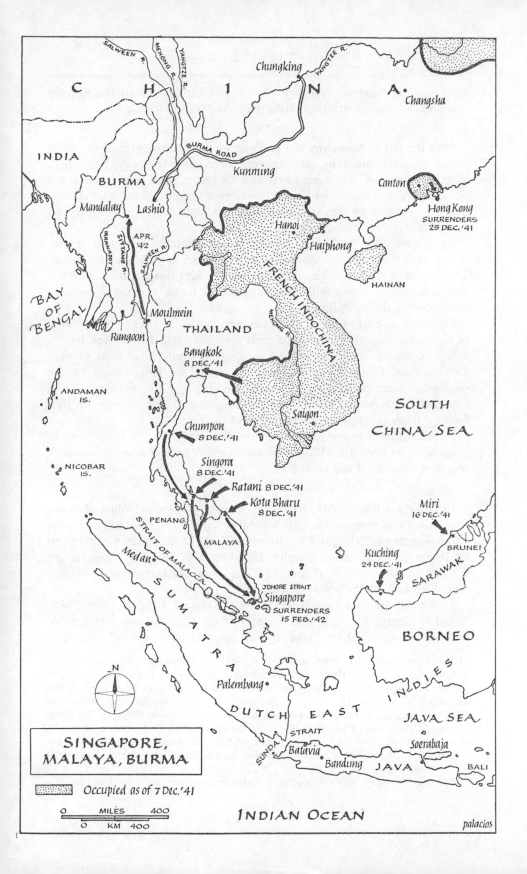

CHINA

Chungking

Changsha

SALWEEN R.
MEKONG R.
YANGTZE R.

BURMA ROAD

Kunming

Canton

Hong Kong
SURRENDERS
25 DEC. '41

INDIA

BURMA

Mandalay   Lashio

Hanoi

Haiphong

APR. '42

IRRAWADDY R.
SITTANG R.
SALWEEN R.

Moulmein

BAY
OF
BENGAL

Rangoon

THAILAND

Bangkok
8 DEC. '41

ANDAMAN
IS.

FRENCH INDOCHINA

MEKONG R.

Saigon

SOUTH
CHINA SEA

HAINAN

Chumpon
8 DEC. '41

NICOBAR
IS.

Singora
8 DEC. '41

Ratani 8 DEC. '41

Kota Bharu
8 DEC. '41

Miri
16 DEC. '41

PENANG

MALAYA

STRAIT OF MALACCA

Medan

Kuching
24 DEC. '41

BRUNEI

SARAWAK

JOHORE STRAIT
Singapore
SURRENDERS
15 FEB. '42

BORNEO

SUMATRA

Palembang

DUTCH   EAST   INDIES

JAVA SEA

Soerabaja

N

SINGAPORE,
MALAYA, BURMA

Occupied as of 7 Dec. '41

SUNDA STRAIT

Batavia

Bandung   JAVA

BALI

0   MILES   400

0   KM   400

INDIAN OCEAN

palacios

8:30 P.M. on Sunday, February 15, 1942. Churchill called the episode "the greatest disaster to British arms which our history affords."[14]

*

With the fall of Singapore the collapse of the entire Dutch East Indies began to accelerate. The six Japanese divisions previously fighting in Malaya, with their supporting naval and air forces, were now free for use elsewhere. The Japanese had not, in fact, even waited for the final surrender. On February 14 they landed on Sumatra and four days later they hit Java from the east. Borneo was already taken.

By February 20, 1942, both Roosevelt and Churchill had become convinced that the ABDA command was no longer a viable arrangement. The Southeast Asia area was therefore broken into two portions, with the British retaining responsibility for Burma and India, and the Americans concentrating on the Philippines and Australia.[15]

Churchill, as part of the move, instructed Wavell to resume his position as Commander-in-Chief, India. Wavell inevitably felt that he had let the two governments down but the Prime Minister would have none of that. Commanders, Churchill always insisted, should be judged only by the quality of their performance, not the results. On the evening of the twenty-fifth, therefore, Wavell left Bandung for Ceylon, thence to New Delhi. ABDA Headquarters was a thing of the past.

Alan Brooke therefore received one compensation for the bitter news of Singapore. At least the ABDA command, which he had heartily opposed, was now discredited and abolished.

*

In Nigeria a tough, wiry, hawk-faced man, who looked older than his fifty-nine years, peered through his wire-rimmed GI spectacles to read about Singapore. "Vinegar Joe" Stilwell did not have to play a role to live up to his name; it came naturally. His disgust at this defeat showed no concern for the verdicts of history: "Singapore has surrendered—60,000 men. Christ. What the hell is the matter?"[16]

Lieutenant General Joseph W. Stilwell, Class of 1904 at West Point, friend of George Marshall, and the nearest the United States Army could boast to a true expert on China, was en route to take over an assignment

[14] The Commonwealth forces had started out the campaign with an estimated 106,000 troops, about half of them British and Australians. These had been reinforced. The Japanese, on the other hand, never had that many in all of Malaya and Singapore. (Churchill, IV, 100.) In the course of the campaign the British lost 138,708 casualties (mostly prisoners of war) while Japanese General Tomoyuki Yamashita's loss totaled less than 10,000. (*West Point Atlas,* Map 118.)
[15] General MacArthur had not yet been ordered to leave the Philippines, but Roosevelt and Churchill were contemplating his eventually commanding American forces from Australia.
[16] *The Stilwell Papers,* p. 40. The account had grossly understated the actual loss.

nearly as hopeless as had been Wavell's in Java. He was headed for Chungking, where he would hold three positions at one time: (1) Chief of Staff to Generalissimo Chiang Kai-shek, (2) Commander of American forces in China and Burma, and (3) Administrator of Lend-Lease to Chiang's Nationalist Government. Nigeria was a stopover point on the long, circuitous route from Washington to Chungking—from Lagos he would cross Africa to Khartoum, then north to Cairo, east to Iraq, and to China by way of India.

Stilwell had received this thankless but important assignment by default. The Secretary of War, who took an intense personal interest in this task, had preferred another officer, Lieutenant General Hugh H. Drum. Drum, once considered the most prominent officer of the Army, had been the leading contender for the post of Chief of Staff in 1939. But nobody held Drum in higher esteem than did Drum himself. Visualizing himself as the "Pershing of the next war," Drum saw the task as beneath him and had discussed it with Stimson in a condescending, offensive manner. Stimson had decided to put Drum on the shelf and Stilwell had been sent instead. This switch gave pleasure to George Marshall, who had always preferred Stilwell.

Stilwell was far more than a China expert. He was a first-rate combat soldier, a veteran of World War I who had impaired vision in one eye to show for it. He had served under Marshall on the faculty of the Infantry School at Fort Benning, Georgia, and at the time of Pearl Harbor he was a corps commander, in charge of American defenses in California. When Operation GYMNAST was considered a possibility at ARCADIA, Stilwell was the officer Marshall had in mind as the prospective commander.

But Stilwell was known in the Army for more than his professional competence. Indeed, his military virtues were almost overshadowed by his penchant for speaking his mind, a habit which all too frequently manifested utter contempt for incompetence in peer and superior alike. Unfortunately, Stilwell's future role with Chiang Kai-shek would demand a great deal of tact. As an organizer and combat leader of Chiang's armies, Stilwell would be a master; as a diplomat in pretentious New Delhi or corrupt Chungking, he would be a misfit.

Having served ten years in China in the course of three tours of duty, Stilwell was no stranger to Generalissimo Chiang Kai-shek. His regard for Chiang was not high, and his nickname for the President of China, "Peanut," had reached Chiang's ears. This had done nothing to warm relations between the two.[17]

[17] The nickname tells as much about Stilwell as it does about Chiang. For Stilwell had a sarcastic nickname—sometimes several—for many: "Big Boy" for Roosevelt, "Glamour Boy" for Mountbatten, and "Little Willie, the Country Boy," for himself. Men like Generals George Marshall and Sir William Slim could feel complimented that Stilwell had no special names for them.

In this Stilwell was not completely fair, and he never seemed quite able to appreciate the awkward position Chiang occupied. His titles, "Supreme Commander, China," and "President of China," recognized in world capitals, meant little to the three hundred warlords or so-called division commanders, whose loyalties Chiang would keep only by greasing their palms at the expense of American Lend-Lease. And like many other American generals, Stilwell underestimated the formidable Chinese Communist forces under Mao Tse-tung in Hunan Province. Though Mao had formally agreed to join in the war effort against Japan, he and his followers still bore no loyalty to Chiang himself. As a result the Generalissimo had consciously chosen to be cautious with his own forces. He could not, he felt, risk destruction of his army in fighting the Japanese; he must preserve its strength for the future.

These political matters, of course, were technically outside Stilwell's area of concern, as he was charged with prosecuting the war against Japan. But political considerations would weigh heavily in calculating the strength that Chiang could—or would—put in the field.

Actually Burma, rather than China, was the next Japanese target in the spring of 1942. This peculiar country was valuable to the British in India and to Chiang in China, but for different reasons. Cut off from the world on the east, north, and west by formidable mountains, Burma's terrain consists of a series of hills and valleys running from north to south. Lateral east-west communications were practically non-existent in early 1942. Therefore the British saw Burma as a barrier, the importance of which lay in the protection its mountains afforded India.

To Chiang (and therefore Stilwell), however, the country constituted a life line. Since the Japanese occupied the coast, the only route by which supplies could be delivered inland to China was the Burma Road, a snakelike artery which wound for 700 miles through high mountain ranges from Lashio in Burma to Kunming in China. But Lashio, the terminus of the Burma Road, was 550 miles north of the port of Rangoon, where supplies came in. Tonnage therefore went from Rangoon by railroad and the Irrawaddy River to Mandalay, after which the river ceased to be navigable. From there they had to be delivered the last 150 miles to Lashio exclusively by rail. At Kunming in China supplies could be distributed to the thirty Chinese divisions recognized by the United States (except for those distributed to the three hundred that comprised Chiang's network of fiefdoms). Mandalay was the hub of this route, but the route itself could be cut anywhere.

When Stilwell arrived in Chungking on March 6, 1942, the invasion of Burma was already well under way. At the outset the British had expected the Japanese to wait until the fall of Singapore, but by December the Fifteenth Army had crossed the Siamese-Burmese border and had occupied Moulmein and the province of Tenasserim. In February the Japanese had continued across the Sittang River. They occupied the vital port of Rangoon on the day after Stilwell's arrival.

Wavell, as Commander-in-Chief, India, had appointed General Sir Harold R. L. Alexander as commander of the Burmese Army. Alexander, an experienced officer whose corps two years earlier had covered the Dunkirk evacuation, could be expected to hold Burma if anyone could. But the situation was desperate, and Wavell asked Chiang to send two Chinese armies over the mountains to assist in the defense. This was a humiliating move for him to have to make. At a conference just after Pearl Harbor he had turned down Chiang's offer to provide those armies. This had been done on the basis that (1) Burma lacked the resources to feed them, (2) the Chinese armies would be operating in a territory where the population was hostile, and (3) so long as Indian reinforcements were coming (a false assumption), he preferred to protect India with troops of the British Empire.

Wavell's previous refusal had infuriated Chiang, and when Stilwell reported to him in Chungking, Chiang devoted most of the time venting his rage against the British, for whom he bore no love anyway. The Chinese historically had resented the chain of events which had followed the Opium War of 1839–42, and Chiang now had a new humiliation to resent. To make matters worse, the British had recently confiscated certain American supplies earmarked for Chungking on the docks at Rangoon. Rarely have two allies fighting in a common cause disliked each other so heartily.

But Burma, with its railroad to Mandalay and its navigable Irrawaddy River, was so important to Chiang's supply situation that he relented and promised to send the Fifth and Sixth Chinese Armies on the condition that they remain under Stilwell's command. This created a temporary impasse, since Wavell insisted that Alexander command all forces in Burma regardless of nationality. Stilwell broke the log jam by agreeing to serve under Alexander. Somehow Stilwell convinced Chiang that he personally would actually be in control of the Chinese forces.

As matters turned out, it was academic who theoretically commanded the two Chinese armies, as both reported directly back to Chiang. The two Chinese generals obeyed only those orders from Stilwell that suited their convenience.[18]

The 1942 Burma campaign was uncomplicated. It consisted of a steady

[18] It is possible but unlikely that Stilwell would have been given more support by Chiang if he had not been theoretically serving under Alexander.

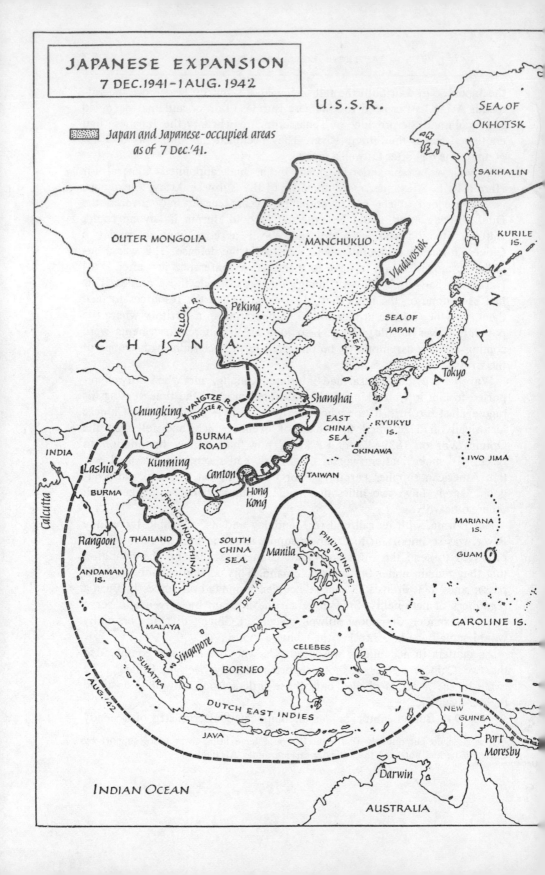

JAPANESE EXPANSION
7 DEC. 1941 – 1 AUG. 1942

Japan and Japanese-occupied areas as of 7 Dec. '41.

U.S.S.R.

SEA OF OKHOTSK

SAKHALIN

OUTER MONGOLIA

MANCHUKUO

KURILE IS.

YELLOW R.

Peking

KOREA

SEA OF JAPAN

Vladivostok

C H I N A

J A P A N

Tokyo

Chungking

YANGTZE R.

YANGTZE R.

Shanghai

EAST CHINA SEA

RYUKYU IS.

OKINAWA

IWO JIMA

BURMA ROAD

INDIA

Lashio

Kunming

Canton

TAIWAN

Calcutta

BURMA

Hong Kong

FRENCH INDOCHINA

MARIANA IS.

GUAM

Rangoon

THAILAND

SOUTH CHINA SEA

Manila

PHILIPPINE IS.

ANDAMAN IS.

7 DEC. '41

CAROLINE IS.

MALAYA

Singapore

CELEBES

SUMATRA

BORNEO

1 AUG. '42

DUTCH EAST INDIES

NEW GUINEA

JAVA

Port Moresby

INDIAN OCEAN

Darwin

AUSTRALIA

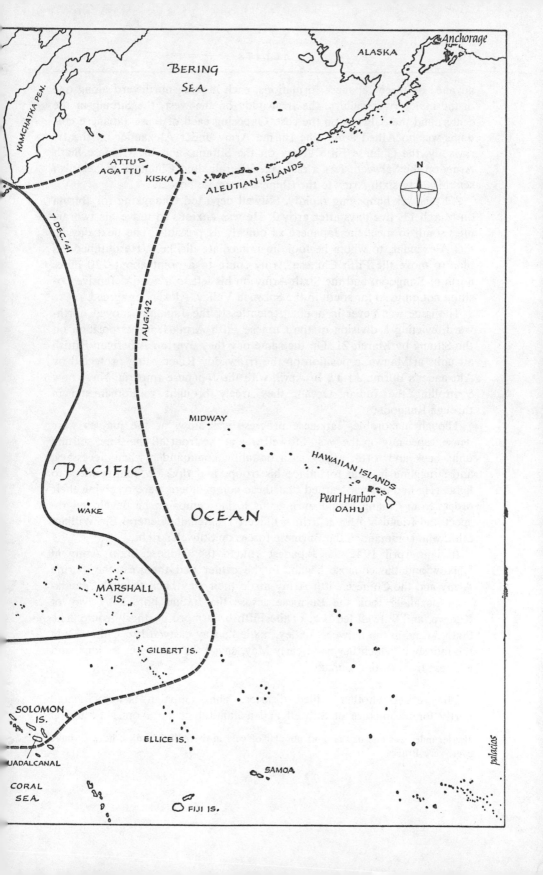

advance by three Japanese formations, each moving northward along one of the major river valleys, the Irrawaddy on the west, the Sittang in the center, and the Salween on the east. Opposing each of these Japanese columns was an Allied army: the Burma Army under Alexander on the Irrawaddy, the Chinese Fifth Army on the Sittang, and the Chinese Sixth Army on the Salween. (As a reserve, Generalissimo Chiang Kai-shek also sent his Sixty-sixth Army to the Chinese-Burmese border.)

All this was happening rapidly. Stilwell departed Chungking for Burma on March 11, five days after arrival. He was anxious to move his two armies south to meet the Japanese as quickly as possible. The next day he met Alexander, to whom he took an immediate dislike.[19] He outlined his plan to move the Fifth Chinese Army south to a point about 120 miles north of Rangoon, and the Sixth Army on his left to a good defensive position not quite so far south in the Salween Valley. Alexander agreed.

The issue was never in doubt. Relentlessly the Japanese moved northward, evicting a division of the Chinese Fifth Army from its position on the Sittang by March 21. On the same day they overran American-British air units at Magwe, a position on the Irrawaddy River being protected by Alexander's Burma Army. In April, with the Japanese Imperial Navy now controlling the Indian Ocean, they freely brought reinforcements in through Rangoon.

Though inexorable, Japanese progress was slow, as the jungles were dense, especially on the west. Stilwell was at the front all the time, shifting units back and forth, acting as a battalion commander when necessary, and struggling in vain to induce his troops and division commanders to fight. (He had not yet learned that these commanders were receiving their orders from Chiang.) And during this losing campaign he developed respect and friendship for a British officer, Lieutenant General Sir William Slim, who commanded the Burmese forces on Stilwell's right.

In late April 1942 the Japanese routed the Chinese Sixth Army at Loikow and the collapse began. In the center and the west the Burma Army and the Chinese Fifth Army made their way back through Mandalay. Alexander took the Burmese across the Indian border by way of Kalewa, and Stilwell led part of the Fifth on a more northerly route. The Sixth Army, in the Salween Valley, made its way eastward to China. Only the monsoon, which begins in early May, saved the Burmese, Indians, and Chinese from further pursuit.

Thus ended another Allied disaster. The campaign is remembered partly for the picture of Stilwell and a handful of survivors sloshing on

[19] Alexander was one of the most popular officers in the Allied armies; he was, however, very British.

foot up the shallow river toward India. But even more, it is remembered for Stilwell's frank remarks to the press:

"I claim we took a hell of a beating. We got run out of Burma and it is humiliating as hell. I think we ought to find out what caused it, go back, and retake it."

Part Two

Part Two

CHAPTER V

ATTACK IN 1942!

A rmy Chief of Staff George C. Marshall was feeling uneasy, even discouraged, as he prepared to face one of the most uncomfortable moments he would experience during World War II. Rarely did Marshall expose his inner feelings to another, even to a close friend like Secretary of War Henry Stimson. But on this twenty-fourth of March 1942 he did.

It was not the word of disasters from around the globe that was causing Marshall's malaise, although tidings were uniformly bad. He and Stimson were prepared to face the grim facts that American forces on Bataan were about to surrender; that the fall of Corregidor would follow soon; that the Dutch and British East Indies, Singapore, and Malaya had fallen to the Japanese; and that the entire Indian Ocean was open to the enemy. What was haunting the Chief of Staff, as he and Stimson conferred, was the task to be performed the next day. Marshall was to brief the President on the War Department's strategy for employment of forces as they should become available.

Diversionary pressures were formidable. In Australia Prime Minister John Curtin and General Douglas MacArthur[1] were pushing their demands for more troops and planes to stem the southward Japanese advance; Admiral Ernest King was constantly calling for more Army divisions to bolster strength in the central Pacific;[2] and most worrisome of all,

[1] MacArthur had been ordered to Australia from Corregidor in early March 1942.
[2] One hundred and thirty-two thousand American troops had been shipped from American shores since New Year's of 1942, and all of these, except for 20,000 who had gone to Northern Ireland and Iceland, were in the Pacific.

Marshall feared that President Roosevelt, influenced by Churchill, would direct what Marshall called a "piecemeal scattering and stopping-up of urgent ratholes" which would benefit only the future British Empire. Roosevelt himself, Marshall mused, might add to the confusion by producing a series of his own alternate schemes. Marshall, however, had no really exciting prospect to offer; he was not prepared for the confrontation the next day and he knew it.

In the broadest terms Marshall believed in his own basic strategy: to build up forces in the United Kingdom and eventually attack across the English Channel, but the major crossing into France would require time and preparation. Needing a plan for the immediate future, one to prevent dissipation of his forces, Marshall had directed Eisenhower, now elevated to chief of the newly formed Operations Division (OPD),[3] to codify his ideas into a single memorandum. Eisenhower had been quick to respond. "The first question," he wrote, was to decide "the region or theater in which the first major effort of the United Powers must take place." The principal target of Allied efforts would "govern training and production problems and . . . constitute a basis on which subsidiary decisions [will] be made."

This formal language meant: give priority to one region, Europe or the Pacific, and gear training and production accordingly. Bowing to all conflicting demands rather than concentrating the national effort would have to cease.

The memorandum then went on to answer its implied rhetorical question as to theater priorities by listing basic strategic objectives: "the security of England, the retention of Russia in the war as an active ally, and the defense of the Middle East. . . ." All other operations, it concluded, including the Pacific, were to be placed in the "highly desirable" rather than the "mandatory" class. These considerations meant that "the principal target for our first major offensive should be Germany, to be attacked through western Europe.[4]

Eisenhower was, of course, mirroring Marshall's views. The memorandum reflected that Stimson, Marshall, and the War Department staff were thinking forward to victory despite the current global debacle they were witnessing.

Foremost in Marshall's mind the next day, as he rode from Constitution Avenue up Seventeenth Street to the White House, was a plan he called BOLERO, which simply meant a top-priority build-up of American

[3] By this time Gerow had left the War Department to command the 29th Division as a major general. War Plans had been renamed Operations Division (OPD) with Eisenhower as its head.
[4] Alfred E. Chandler, Jr., ed., *The Papers of Dwight D. Eisenhower*, I, 205–6. (Hereafter referred to as "Chandler.")

forces in the United Kingdom. Concentrating American forces in Britain was the key, Marshall believed, to guiding the Allies in the direction of Germany. The concentration of forces in Britain would preclude their employment in other regions.

Eisenhower's memo had likewise given extensive arguments to support BOLERO: (1) an eventual attack on Germany from Britain involved the shortest possible sea routes from the United States; (2) on the Atlantic sea route naval escort would be concentrated; (3) an Allied build-up in Britain would provide a threat which, it was hoped, would prevent Germany from concentrating all forces against Russia; (4) land and/or amphibious operation from Britain could be well supported by plentiful airfields; (5) only from the United Kingdom could the major portion of British combat power be employed; and (6) it would attack the principal enemy (Hitler) while he was engaged on the Russian front. The War Department's position had logic behind it—but other pressures would militate against it.

*

Marshall presented these arguments to the President at lunch that day in the presence of Stimson, Knox, Arnold, King, and Hopkins and soon confirmed that his previous uneasiness had been justified. The President was still attracted to the idea of an operation against North Africa, and he added to Marshall's discomfort by employing what the Chief of Staff privately referred to as his "cigarette holder gesture," an upward tilt which implied a certain jaunty disregard for unpleasant details. Nevertheless, Marshall made his case methodically; his reward was tentative approval and an instruction to "put it in shape, if possible, over this weekend."

A week later Marshall was again at the White House, this time outlining a more ambitious and dramatic plan which put meaning into the general BOLERO concept. Since BOLERO signified only a build-up of U.S. forces in the United Kingdom and did not define a concrete objective for the use of all that power, Marshall now visualized an invasion of Europe across the English Channel at its narrowest point, the Pas de Calais (Strait of Dover), to be launched in the spring of the next year. The ultimate invasion of Europe had been mentioned at ARCADIA, but only in general terms; Marshall's new plan, however, was specific: a force of eighteen British and thirty American divisions (a million American troops), supported by powerful British and American air forces. Once ashore, this force would be built up to provide the base for liberating all of France and subsequently invading Germany. The code name was ROUNDUP.

Aside from ROUNDUP, however, was the problem of Russia. During the early spring of 1942, Russia's survival to 1943 was by no means certain. The Nazi spearheads had been stalled during the winter of 1941, but Hitler was still capable of powerful new offensives and if the Russian situation should become desperate, the only way in which the Western Allies could help her would be to launch some sort of invasion on the Continent in 1942, even a premature one.

Such an attack would be risky, but Marshall still felt it necessary to present some sort of proposal, even a sacrifice operation. Accordingly he presented a second contingency for the exploitation of BOLERO, code-named SLEDGEHAMMER. This second plan, like ROUNDUP, also involved an attack across the Pas de Calais. But SLEDGEHAMMER would be executed in September 1942, only five months away. If the bridgehead could be held, it would provide the base for ROUNDUP in 1943.

SLEDGEHAMMER had definite weaknesses. First of all, the Americans and British together had fewer divisions on hand in Britain than the Germans already had in France, and this landing might be crushed without need for transfers from the Russian front. Further, Allied air power was still too weak to support an invasion. Finally, few American troops had arrived in Britain, which meant that SLEDGEHAMMER, if executed in 1942, would be an almost exclusively British operation.

In the end, however, Marshall carried his point, or so it seemed. Roosevelt tentatively approved BOLERO and its two associated plans provided that Marshall could secure the concurrence of Churchill. To put the task directly on Marshall's shoulders, the President ordered all those present to say nothing of this plan to Sir John Dill, whose duty it would be to report it to London. Marshall and Hopkins were to go to London and outline the scheme in person.

*

On Saturday morning, April 4, George Marshall and Harry Hopkins took off from Baltimore. On the way to Bermuda their flying boat developed engine trouble, necessitating a pleasant delay over Easter Sunday. The interlude in the balmy breezes afforded a respite from the hectic Washington routine and gave the members of the party a chance to compare notes. The engine repaired, they left Bermuda the morning of April 7 and flew directly to Lough Erne, Northern Ireland. By the next morning they were in London.

It was fortunate for the Americans that they had been afforded a rest, for they would have none in London. There to meet them at Hendon Airport was the Prime Minister himself, who announced forthwith that he would meet them at No. 10 Downing Street that afternoon and dine with them that evening.

At the appointed time Marshall and Hopkins pulled up to the curb of the narrow little street off Whitehall and entered the unimpressive building, No. 10, where the Prime Minister lived and worked. In the Cabinet Room, which served as conference room and also as the Prime Minister's office, British hosts and American guests took their places around the long table.

Here the Americans were in for their first surprise. The SLEDGE-HAMMER idea had originated with the British, but the Americans assumed that it had been forgotten. Mr. Churchill, however, exuberantly seized the initiative, informing Marshall and Hopkins that the British had long been considering such a limited plan; they were prepared to go ahead with it, even without the Americans. Churchill admitted that the BCOS held reservations; but in spite of all the difficulties, he as Prime Minister and Minister of Defense was prepared to order it.

Marshall, unfamiliar with Churchill's way of conducting business, was quick to take this statement seriously, and left the afternoon meeting optimistic, for Churchill's morose review of the situation in the Indian Ocean was less dramatic by far than his apparent acceptance of a cross-Channel attack in 1943 or even 1942.

Perhaps an objective observer could have pointed out that, despite Churchill's declaration, the Americans and British were being guided by different preoccupations. The Americans listened to Churchill's words of encouragement about an invasion across the Channel; at the same time, however, the minds of Churchill and the BCOS were really focusing on the Indian Ocean and the Middle East. Japan's unhampered drive to the south and her successes in Burma had transfixed British eyes on the Philippines, East Indies, Indian Ocean, and even Ceylon. In the course of the two hours Churchill expounded on the difficulties he was having with General Auchinleck in North Africa and the "Singapore business." But the Americans heard only the words about the English Channel.

Marshall was feeling his responsibility keenly. As Army Chief of Staff and as an adviser to President Roosevelt, he had long been influential, but from the background. Now for the first time he found himself the main character in a major negotiation—and with the Western world's most prestigious and persuasive figure at that! Dealing with Churchill on his own represented something of a new experience.

From the outset Marshall found Churchill formidable. As others had discovered, he learned that the Prime Minister in debate could use every persuasive weapon, "winning charm, cold persuasion, rude insistence, eloquent flow of language, flashes of anger, and sentiment close to tears."[5] Marshall also quickly learned that the only way to deal with a man of this force and cunning was to be dogged, difficult as the obstinate role was. Further, on the automobile trip into the center of London that morning

5 Pogue, II, 313.

Marshall had viewed for the first time the destruction that London had suffered in the Battle of Britain. The sight of what the British had gone through was jarring, even to a veteran of the First World War. What a contrast to the atmosphere of Washington where, despite the attack on Pearl Harbor, life was going on very much as usual!

But Marshall was basing his arguments on strong convictions. From study of the First War he had developed a suspicion of what he considered a British inclination to fight around peripheries. He had always regarded the ill-fated expedition against the Dardanelles in 1915 (engineered by Mr. Churchill himself) as "well-deserved retribution for an unjustifiable strategic gamble." And now the purpose of this very mission was to prevent the Allies from repeating that mistake. Holding the line on this issue, Marshall could tell, would constitute a test of his will.

That afternoon meeting of April 8, 1942, and the dinner that evening consisted of little more than sparring. The evening conversation was primarily social, with Churchill talking little business, preferring to relax with a discourse on the American Civil War and World War I. Brooke would have liked to address SLEDGEHAMMER in order to dampen the impression of Churchill's enthusiasm. However, his effort was to no avail.

*

The next morning Sir Alan Brooke confronted his American counterpart alone for the first time. The atmosphere in Brooke's office was cordial enough, but the two generals viewed each other critically. To Marshall, Brooke was "icy and condescending." Conscious of his experience as a corps commander as far back as the 1940 campaign in France, Brooke obviously considered himself superior to all others in the practical art of war and in the grasp of grand strategy. His unimpressive figure, with narrow shoulders and spindly legs, belied his active life outdoors as an avid hunter and bird watcher. Professionally he was precise and methodical, universally respected among the British. To Marshall he possessed one attribute that might be useful: among the British military, Brooke seemed uniquely able to stand up to the Prime Minister.

Brooke's evaluation of Marshall was less charitable. He saw his colleague as "overfilled with his own importance,"[6] but possessing a certain amount of charm.

Neither regarded the other as particularly bright.

While Marshall was calling on Brooke, Churchill was meeting with Hopkins, with whom he had come to feel comfortable. Hopkins, informal and political-minded, represented to Churchill the views of President

6 Bryant, *Turn of the Tide*, p. 285.

Roosevelt himself, and was therefore on a level unofficially above the military.

Alone with Hopkins, Churchill once more dwelt on his preoccupations with India and the naval situation in the Indian Ocean. The British fleet was obviously outgunned and, worse, the enemy apparently enjoyed air superiority across the vast expanse between Burma and Africa. Two cruisers had recently been sunk by a force of some sixty Japanese fighters. As a result, the commander of the British fleet was currently planning to withdraw his main force to the East African ports. Ceylon, just off the tip of India, had been attacked by Japanese aircraft and Churchill feared for its future safety. As if to dramatize the point, their conversation was interrupted by a message that the *Hermes,* a small British aircraft carrier, had been sunk by Japanese aircraft just off Ceylon.

The Prime Minister went on. Coordination between American and British actions in the Southwest Pacific was inadequate; Rommel's Afrika Korps was advancing in Libya; Auchinleck was procrastinating in taking positive action against his vaunted foe. As a result it was late before the subject of any cross-Channel assault came up. When Churchill finally turned to ROUNDUP and SLEDGEHAMMER, Hopkins was ready. He jumped in and emphasized that the United States was prepared to commit all available resources to SLEDGEHAMMER that year. Marshall, he explained, was worried for fear that the large army he had created would be immobilized, a force without an enemy to fight. There the talk ended.

*

After the preliminary conversations, the Prime Minister invited the Americans to spend the weekend at Chequers. The April weather was beautiful, and the unscarred English countryside with its quaint houses struck a welcome contrast to the depressing surroundings in London. The change had a noticeable effect on everyone's spirits, and on arrival Marshall called his staff in Washington with the good news that Churchill had virtually agreed to all the American proposals. Hopkins likewise cabled Roosevelt.

The house at Chequers was an ideal conference place. Standing alone in the green pasture land, it was large enough to accommodate a sizable group. Parts of it were four hundred years old, once owned by relatives of Cromwell. In 1917 it had been presented to the British Government by a Viscount Arthur Hamilton Lee on the condition that nothing should ever be changed—the name, the house, the grounds, or the art. The British Government had so far managed to observe these stringent requirements.

The main feature of the house was its great hall, around which all else was constructed. The ceiling of the hall was the roof of the building, and the bedrooms were tucked away behind the second-floor balcony, which

overlooked the main hall on three sides. The fourth wall, stone, boasted a
great fireplace, where a dozen people could sit in a comfortable semicircle. The space behind the front row of sofas and easy chairs could accommodate almost any number of lesser guests.

Having arrived, the Prime Minister seemed to let down. Up to this time
he had maintained an optimistic and cheerful front, but now his spirits
sagged. Small wonder that they should. Churchill was, Hopkins observed,
suffering from "general exhaustion." The strain of absorbing one military
defeat after another was telling on him; and the presence of an American
party exerting pressure to accept a risky concept did nothing to help. His
fatigue, however, could not prevent Churchill from sitting up till all
hours, as was his wont, with the convivial Harry Hopkins.

Late Saturday night, or more accurately at 3:00 A.M. Sunday morning,
an aide interrupted to deliver a cable from President Roosevelt. The subject was India. In the midst of military defeat, Britain was undergoing the
first stage of the disintegration of her empire. In an effort to cope with the
rise of nationalism in that country, Churchill had recently sent a member
of the War Cabinet, Sir Stafford Cripps, to confer with Gandhi in New
Delhi. Cripps, a crusty Labourite, was seeking to work out a new status
for India without breaking ties. An influential visiting American, Louis
Johnson,[7] had apparently inserted himself in the talks without authority
from the British. The resulting three-sided argument—British, Indian, and
now American—had angered the British Governor General. Partly as a
result of this confusion Cripps had met with a solid rebuff. And President
Roosevelt was unabashedly offering advice. "The feeling is held universally," the cable said, "that the deadlock [between Cripps and Gandhi]
has been due to the British Government's unwillingness to concede the
right of self-government to India's people. . . . Should the current negotiations be allowed to collapse . . . and should India subsequently be invaded successfully by Japan . . . it would be hard to overestimate the
prejudicial reaction of American public opinion."

Churchill reacted strongly and assailed Hopkins in a manner that he
probably would not have used with Roosevelt. He refused to be responsible, he said, for a policy that would throw the whole subcontinent of
India into confusion, with the invader at the gates. A national Indian government, such as Roosevelt was pressing, would probably mean the
withdrawal of all Indian troops from the Middle East; it could possibly
mean India's allowing the Japanese to cross its territory. Emotionally,
Churchill declared that he, personally, would retire to private life if
American public opinion so demanded. But to hold fast in India was the
course he was bound to follow.

[7] Later U. S. Secretary of Defense under President Truman.

Later in the day Hopkins telephoned Roosevelt and told him that Cripps had already left India.

On Monday morning Churchill and his guests returned to London for further conferences. On arrival, Hopkins and Marshall were invited to a meeting of the British War Cabinet. The next morning an optimistic Hopkins cabled the President again that he expected the American mission to be a success. As always, however, the sky was clouded with the multitude of other worrisome matters. To the desperate situation in the Indian Ocean were added gloomy reports regarding the attitude of Chiang Kai-shek. And a prospective visit to London and later Washington by Soviet Foreign Minister Vyacheslav Molotov was now being arranged. The problem of briefing Molotov about Allied plans could not be brushed aside.

During the day Marshall attended a meeting of the BCOS and went to dinner with Brooke. Brooke was mellowing, ever so slightly: "The more I see of him," he wrote in his diary, "the more I like him."

*

The climax of the American visit occurred that Tuesday evening, April 14, at a meeting of the Defense Committee, an arm of the War Cabinet, to which Marshall and Hopkins again were invited.[8] As in other military meetings, the interests of the two nationalities appeared ironically to be reversed. The British, whose island was located just off the continent of Europe, were most concerned by the war against Japan and the Indian Ocean. The Americans, with their Philippine garrison about to surrender —and with public opinion railing against Japan—were urging a cross-Channel invasion through France and Germany.

Everyone spoke his mind freely. Marshall once again outlined his plans for BOLERO, ROUNDUP, and (if necessary) SLEDGEHAMMER. Churchill, as before, agreed in principle but for the benefit of all urged that the Allies not neglect the Indian Ocean. Brooke, the land soldier, painted a dramatic picture regarding the consequences of further defeat in the Indian Ocean. If Japan's advance westward through southern Asia were not halted, he projected, three quarters of a million fighting men in the Middle East would be cut off. Japan and Germany might join hands, exchange raw materials, surround Turkey and threaten Russian oil supplies in the Caucasus, and the Russians would be forced to surrender. Then

[8] This Defense Committee consisted of the Prime Minister (who was also the Defense Minister), Deputy Prime Minister Clement Attlee, Foreign Minister Anthony Eden, Oliver Lyttelton (Minister of Production), A. V. Alexander (First Lord of the Admiralty), Sir James Grigg (Secretary of State for War), Sir Archibald Sinclair (Secretary of State for Air), and the military chiefs—Pound, Brooke, Portal, Ismay, and Mountbatten.

no cross-Channel assault on Germany would be possible.[9] A "domino theory" carried to the extreme.

Hopkins conceded that American public opinion generally favored an all-out effort against Japan. He expected also that the feeling would become more acute when Wainwright would be forced to surrender Corregidor.[10] Priority to the Far East, of course, was contrary to both British and American governmental strategy, but in one respect American military and public opinion were agreed: our men must fight. "Americans," Hopkins concluded, "do not want their men to be sent across oceans merely for the purposes of sightseeing: they want to engage the enemy and finish the war."[11]

The meeting ended with a general feeling of euphoria. Churchill uttered one of his oft-quoted phrases, referring to "our two nations marching together, shoulder to shoulder, in a noble brotherhood of arms." He described the meeting as "memorable."

All seemed settled; only Brooke and Marshall still had reservations. Brooke, though he claimed to recognize the need for an eventual cross-Channel invasion, saw that operation as the last, rather than the first, stage of the war. Marshall, recovering from his first optimism, now noted to himself that the British had agreed to BOLERO and its related operations only *in principle,* not in detail. Nevertheless Marshall cabled Stimson that evening that the Prime Minister had declared his complete agreement with the American plan.

Brooke and Marshall spent the morning after the "memorable meeting" together once again. By now the two were becoming more frank with each other. Marshall was describing Admiral Ernest King's continuing efforts to drain more and more American soldiers to the Pacific. (No news, really, to Brooke.) He went on to tell of the pressures that MacArthur was generating from the Far East.

Brooke was coming to like the American more, but he was unwilling to change his mind regarding Marshall's strategic understanding. Conscious that concepts such as ROUNDUP dealt only with the first phase of a land invasion, Brooke had wearily concluded that he was the only person who recognized this fact; he would therefore have to carry the burden of "balance wheel." In that role, he feared, he would have two major problems

[9] Bryant, *Turn of the Tide,* pp. 286–87. For some reason Brooke gave Eisenhower credit for having seen the need for defending the Indian Ocean more clearly than Marshall. Doubtless he was impressed by the rather lengthy memorandum written by Eisenhower to Marshall on February 28, 1942.

[10] Lieutenant General Jonathan Wainwright, left in command when MacArthur was ordered to Australia.

[11] Sherwood, p. 538.

on his hands: (1) the Prime Minister and (2) the War Department, personified by George Marshall. In both sectors, Brooke would repeatedly have to quell premature enthusiasm.

While Marshall was making his final call on Brooke, Hopkins went by to see Churchill. Despite all the bad news, Hopkins noted, Churchill was still buoyed by the results of the previous day's meetings. He did, however, transmit a request: could the Americans supply more planes to India and send the U.S.S. *North Carolina*[12] to Scapa Flow? The Royal Navy in the north needed help.

*

Marshall, Hopkins, and their party flew from London to Londonderry, Ireland, on the morning of April 17, nine days after their arrival. The first American troops to disembark in the European Theater had been located in that vicinity and Marshall was eager to see them. But before they could leave for home, a cable came in from the President:

> This morning we have received reports indicating that Pétain [in Vichy France] has resigned. . . . Welles and I both feel that there is some chance that orders from Laval will not be accepted by the French in North Africa. . . . *I ask that you discuss this whole subject with him* [Churchill] *although I do not suggest revival of GYMNAST.*[13]

This message gave Hopkins pause. It was quite apparent that, although Roosevelt had approved the BOLERO-ROUNDUP concept, he still retained a yearning to invade North Africa. Immediately, therefore, he contacted the President for instructions. Should he and Marshall return to London? The President replied that they should not. On April 18 the party left for Washington.

*

On arrival home, Marshall and Hopkins noticed the ambiance visibly changed. By the very fact of their own well-publicized trip, plus the exhilarating news that Lieutenant Colonel Jimmy Doolittle had just raided Tokyo, Americans everywhere were beginning to feel that the tide had turned. The optimism was premature.

[12] The U.S.S. *North Carolina* was America's newest battleship. It had not been with the fleet at the time of Pearl Harbor.

[13] Roosevelt to Hopkins, quoted in Sherwood, pp. 540–41. Italics supplied. Pierre Laval would inherit none of Pétain's prestige in North Africa.

CHAPTER VI

SECOND THOUGHTS
ON A SECOND FRONT

Churchill's agreement to BOLERO and SLEDGEHAMMER at the "memorable meeting" of April 14 appeared definite. The lofty principle would logically form the basis on which to draw up firm, detailed guidelines for the future conduct of the war. "Two nations marching together, shoulder to shoulder," was heady wine. But hardly had Marshall and Hopkins set foot in the United States than the hangover set in on both sides of the Atlantic.

In London, Alan Brooke, who never supported a Channel crossing in 1943, let alone 1942, had now begun to fix his attention on one hard practicality: the availability of landing craft. These vessels, from the small landing craft, infantry (LCI), to the seaworthy landing ship, tank (LST), were indispensable for amphibious invasions over enemy-held beaches. And adequate numbers were simply not there. Without them the small invasion force that the Allies could put ashore led Brooke to remark that such a weak beachhead could only end in the "death, capture or ignominious reimbarkation of the entire force. . . ."[1] And landing craft were tenth priority on the American shipbuilding list.

To add to Brooke's vexation, a new strategic plan had caught the interest of the Prime Minister. His eye was now wandering to northern Norway. An invasion there, as Churchill saw it, would "unroll the Nazi map of Europe from the top," although a more practical aim would be to ease the problems of delivering supplies to the northern parts of Russia. To execute this operation, which he had named JUPITER, Churchill was willing to incur heavy losses, up to one fifth of the transports and landing

[1] Bryant, *Turn of the Tide*, p. 301.

craft. This new project startled Brooke, who was complacently presuming that Churchill's zeal for continuing small actions had been sated by three recent commando raids on the French coast, one on the submarine base at St. Nazaire. But sated the Prime Minister was not. "The process of trying to control the Prime Minister's actions," Brooke wrote his friend Wavell, "is fraught with difficulty and uncertainties."[2]

*

Back in Washington, General Marshall was encountering his own headaches as he strove to protect the integrity of BOLERO against thieves in the night. One misunderstanding was typical. On April 29 President Roosevelt made a remark that was interpreted as a directive to raise the number of Army planes in Australia to 1,000 and the troop level to 100,000.[3] Marshall reacted quickly. Uncharacteristically his memo to the President complained of the difficult time he had experienced on his April trip to London in facing the skepticism of the British regarding the troop build-up. Three days later he wrote that "if the BOLERO project is not to be our primary consideration, I would recommend its complete abandonment. . . ."

The President replied immediately. He had been misinterpreted: "I do not want BOLERO slowed down."[4]

Problems involving interservice and inter-Allied cooperation were also vital to future ground action in Europe. One involved the nature of Allied air power. Roosevelt and the JCS were impatient to get Americans into the European conflict, but for the moment they could fight only in the air. So Roosevelt, on April 28, predicted that American "Flying Fortresses" would soon be "fighting for the liberation of the darkened Continent of Europe." This statement, innocuous on the surface, implied a warning to the British that the Americans were going to develop their own air forces under U.S. command. The JCS sent General Arnold and Admiral John H. Towers to Britain to discuss how soon these separate American air operations could become reality.[5] When the two officers reached Britain, however, they found RAF Chief Sir Charles Portal still demanding American bombers without crews, contending that hard-won experience enabled the British in the short haul to make better use of the aircraft than could the Americans. For the moment Portal's views held sway and the

[2] Brooke to Wavell, May 5, 1942, quoted in ibid., pp. 229, 300.
[3] Memo, McCrea for JCS, 1 May 1942, Subject Aircraft in Transport for Australia, quoted in Matloff and Snell, p. 217.
[4] Memo, FDR for Marshall, 6 May 1942, quoted in ibid., p. 219.
[5] When President Roosevelt explained that the Americans wanted to begin participating in the fight, Prime Minister Churchill understood: "God knows, we have no right," he wrote, "to claim undue priority in the ranks of honour. Let us each do our utmost. . . ."

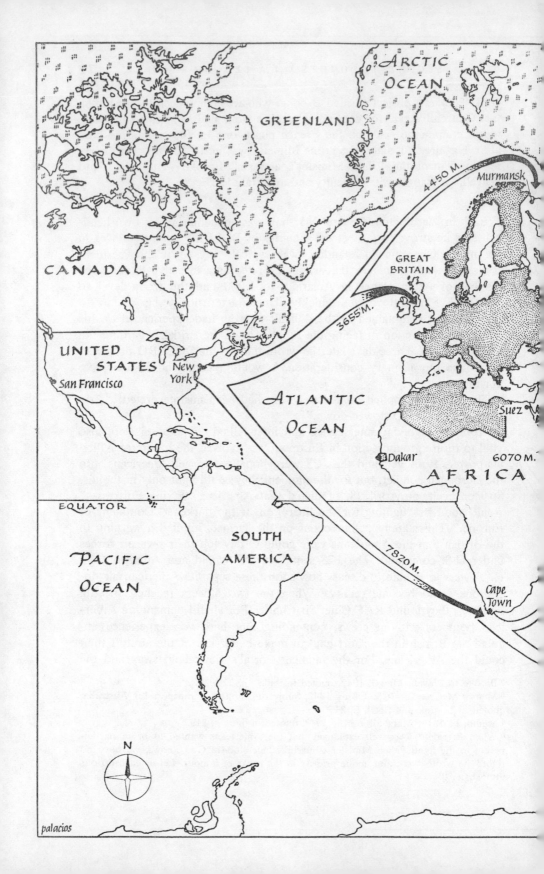

ARCTIC
OCEAN

GREENLAND

CANADA

4450 M.

Murmansk

GREAT
BRITAIN

3655 M.

UNITED
STATES

New
York

San Francisco

ATLANTIC

OCEAN

Suez

Dakar

6070 M.

AFRICA

EQUATOR

SOUTH
AMERICA

PACIFIC

OCEAN

7820 M.

Cape
Town

N

palacios

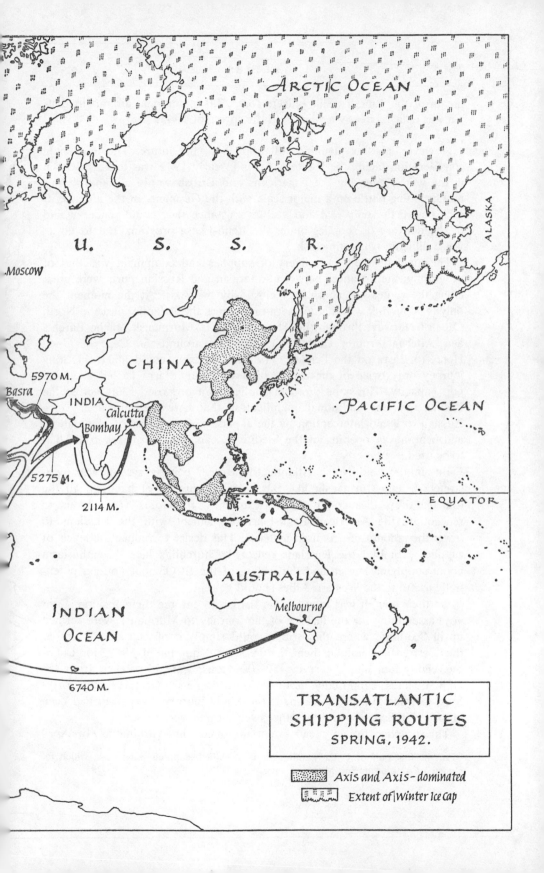

ARCTIC OCEAN

U. S. S. R.

Moscow

ALASKA

CHINA

JAPAN

PACIFIC OCEAN

5970 M.

Basra

INDIA

Calcutta

Bombay

5275 M.

2114 M.

EQUATOR

AUSTRALIA

Melbourne

INDIAN
OCEAN

6740 M.

TRANSATLANTIC
SHIPPING ROUTES
SPRING, 1942.

Axis and Axis-dominated
Extent of Winter Ice Cap

dream of the American air officers for 3,500 operational aircraft in Britain was delayed nearly a year, until the spring of 1943.

However, all this planning still applied to the future. The immediate consideration facing the Western Allies in early 1942 was to keep Russia in the war. Preferably the Americans and British would accomplish this best by doing battle on a major scale with the Germans. In the absence of such action the only real and visible assistance they could render would be the delivery of supplies under the Lend-Lease program. But to do so was a difficult, frustrating task.

The main problem in delivery of supplies and equipment was that of geography; the distances between American and Russian ports were great along the routes not completely closed by the Axis. At the moment the only feasible link was the northern one across the Atlantic, past the North Cape of Norway, through the Arctic Ocean to Murmansk on the Barents Sea. Alternate routes existed, such as that around the Cape of Good Hope, to Basra on the Persian Gulf. But one ship could make this long journey only twice in the course of a year, and Basra lacked adequate port capacity. The same problem applied to a proposed route across the Pacific, with the additional complication that here the ships had to be Russian to avoid interception by the Japanese. By process of elimination, and pending an opening of the Mediterranean, the Murmansk route had to be used.

But in the cold North Atlantic the British convoy system was over-stretched, and Murmansk, like Basra, was incapable of handling all the tonnage the Allies could deliver. Churchill, therefore, was anxious to renegotiate the American Lend-Lease agreement with the Russians to lower the amount of promised material. This desire to reduce the levels of supplies promised the Russians reflected Churchill's lack of enthusiasm about supplying Russia and the feeling of the BCOS that nothing potentially useful to the Western Allies should be sent.

On their own, it was easy for the British to enforce their position. Convoys assembling for the last leg of the journey to Murmansk were formed up in Scotland, where the British could simply confiscate such ships as they desired and unload them. In the second quarter of 1942, for example, eighty-four ships, carrying 522,000 tons, were dispatched from the United States, supposedly destined for Murmansk. Of these only forty-four, carrying 300,000 tons, made the whole journey. Seventeen had been unloaded in Scotland and the other twenty-three were sunk.[6]

This practice by no means went unnoticed in Washington. In April

[6] For the first half of 1942, 4 million tons of Allied shipping were sunk, which included 1.5 million during May and June.

Harry Hopkins cabled Churchill citing the President's concern. This off-loading in Scotland, Roosevelt warned, might have "disquieting" effects in Russia. Churchill, however, despite pressure from both the Americans and the Russians, stood his ground. Blaming the off-loading practice on the strained capacity of the Royal Navy, he answered, "What you suggest is beyond our power to fulfill."[7]

*

Cadet Midshipman Victor E. Tyson knew that his ship, the S.S. *Wacosta,* was in danger. It was summer, 1942, and this 8,000-ton rust bucket was nearing Bear Island, north of Norway, destined for Murmansk. On the previous day a Norwegian-based Focke-Wulf had discovered the sixty-ship convoy and all crewmen now knew they would be the target of a Nazi search-and-destroy mission. Submarines, aircraft, and three known pocket battleships would be looking for them. And though the day was gray with high clouds, visibility was unlimited.

Tyson, a cadet midshipman from the U. S. Merchant Marine Academy at Kings Point, Long Island, found his life agreeable. It afforded better pay than the armed services, and it spared one the drudgery of basic training. And being at sea was interesting. All was not a bed of roses, of course. The food could have been better. (A couple of the cooks had previously been undertakers.) And the stretches at sea were long. Still, men in regular service could be away from home for years.

The fifty-seven-man crew of the *Wacosta* were tough birds, old sailors who were not inclined to accept the discipline of the Navy. On the other hand, they were no cowards. The ship had left Philadelphia two months earlier and had stopped in at New York, Halifax, Scotland, and Iceland. But even when they had learned that the next leg of the voyage would be to Murmansk, none of the men had jumped ship, even though they knew that the previous convoy had been virtually wiped out.

Everyone in the convoy knew what kinds of attack to expect. The least dangerous threat, strangely, was the conventional German submarine, and bombs from high-flying aircraft had little effect. The parachute-dropped torpedoes were more dangerous; once in the water, they were programmed to circle in ever diminishing radii. But most dangerous were the torpedo bombers, capable of coming in low under the radar of the escorts. Defense against them was non-existent. The *Wacosta,* in the second line —that is, with one cargo ship south of her—mounted one five-inch gun on the stern, useless against airplanes. The two 20-millimeter A.A. guns were better. In extremis the crew had a couple of shoulder-fired .45-caliber Lewis machine guns, which reminded Tyson of the gangster weapons of

[7] Sherwood, p. 545.

Edward G. Robinson. These things were fit to be carried in violin cases, but hardly constituted anti-aircraft protection.

It was not lost on Tyson that just before the convoy left port Prime Minister Churchill announced on the radio that the British would "carry things through." Most of the cargo vessels—formed up in six lines, ten abreast, ships four hundred yards apart—were American or Russian. A very few were British, such as the cruiser H.M.S. *Scylla,* the minesweeper, and the six or seven destroyers.

Captain J. Jensen, in command of the *Wacosta,* was an experienced old seaman who had worked his way up through the ranks. He drank a bit, as did his men, but he was respected. One measure that Jensen had developed for passive protection of his crew was a source of comfort: all the men not on watch—except for the deck officers, including Tyson— had been placed in the lifeboats on the protected (north) side. These lifeboats, nearly full, were lowered to a level just above the wave line, ready to be dropped if the order came to abandon ship.

All of a sudden, at 4:50 P.M., the attack came. A German Heinkel penetrated the sporadic fire of the right (south) lane and homed in on the *Wacosta.* Stupefied, the officers and men on the deck watched helplessly as the aircraft skimmed the water, loosed its two torpedoes, and made a steep bank in front of the bow. On the bridge Tyson could clearly see the triumphant grin on the pilot's face as, waving, he passed by. Immediately the two torpedoes smashed into the starboard side. Deafening explosions shook the deck. Tyson tightened, knowing that the *Wacosta* was carrying ammunition which, if hit, would blow the whole ship into small pieces. The torpedoes, however, missed the lethal area, one striking a consignment of boots (all left-footed to avoid pilferage) and the other plunging into a space containing tons of butter.[8] Massive globs flew over the bridge, and a sizable hunk hit the captain squarely in the face. Momentarily unable to speak or to see, Jensen regained his composure enough to pull the emergency rope. A bell and whistle gave the signal to abandon ship.

The order sounded and lifeboats splashed into the water. The seven officers on the deck could now slide down the ropes into the boats. Rope burns were a minor thought. Captain Jensen brought up the rear, and his last act as skipper was to toss a box of secret documents and the ship's log into one of the lifeboats. The log, unfortunately, included records of individual fines, and somehow the box slipped into the sea. The captain groaned; some five to ten thousand dollars in greenbacks had gone to the bottom.

Tyson, as the only officer in his lifeboat, was in charge, saddled with

[8] Exactly why the United States was sending butter to the Soviet Union was questionable, but there was no doubt what it was.

the responsibility of deciding which half-frozen bodies in the water should be pulled aboard. Only those showing a chance of survival could be considered, as it took four men to pull one in while the rest of the occupants leaned to the opposite side to balance. And the imperiled seamen had to keep the bow pointed into the waves to avoid being swamped. As it turned out, Tyson was able to rescue every man his boat found.

Tyson looked back: within fifteen minutes of the attack, the *Wacosta* was vertical, its propellers in the air. Now the British minesweeper came swooping down at fifteen knots, fast enough to evade any torpedoes. Quickly it picked up all the crewmen in Tyson's lifeboat. It could not, however, slow down to pick up any doomed strays in the water as it went from ship to ship.

Eventually the minesweeper pulled alongside the cruiser *Scylla*. The four-foot waves of the Arctic waters permitted no time for hesitation, so if a seaman fell between the bulkheads he would be crushed and drowned. Tyson felt a twinge when a British marine jammed a machine gun in his back and shouted, "Jump!" Tyson made it. So did almost all the others. Once aboard the *Scylla* four hundred survivors of the attack were herded below. Though huddled up, they had space to relax, glad to be alive even though locked in the hold of a cruiser.

Throughout the rest of the day German air attacks continued; but the *Scylla* remained unscathed. To spare his charges more anxiety than necessary, the captain of the *Scylla* broadcast periodic briefings. Occasionally the loudspeaker would warn that a dive bomber was coming and tell the men to lie down. The human cargo were grateful to know what was going on.

Five days later the *Scylla* delivered Tyson and his comrades back to Scotland. Tyson was sent on to Glasgow and eventually repatriated, ready to re-embark on other missions. Thirty-two of the sixty ships in his convoy had gone down in a thirty-minute attack. The *Wacosta,* thanks to Captain Jensen, was the only one that did not lose a man.[9]

*

Given the difficulties which beset Allied efforts in the Arctic Ocean and Barents Sea, it is understandable that the Allied leaders found it impossible to put aside the events in North Africa and the Mediterranean. And of immediate concern there was the plight of Malta. This small archipelago, with an area of only 122 square miles, is about two hundred miles east of Tunis and about fifty miles south of Sicily. As the only British presence between Gibraltar and Alexandria, it was of critical strategic value, the only base from which British aircraft could interdict supplies from Italy to Rommel. But it was also very vulnerable.

[9] Interview, Captain Victor Tyson, Kings Point, New York, August 19, 1975. Subsequent correspondence and conversations.

The major danger to the retention of Malta was the threat of starvation. In April 1942 British ground forces in North Africa were still about five hundred miles away and resupply convoys were subjected to unacceptable losses in traversing that length of enemy-controlled water. Efforts were made to no avail.

Thus it was doubly difficult for Churchill to countenance what he considered General Auchinleck's unjustifiable delay in mounting an attack on Rommel despite recent reinforcements in armor and supply. When Auchinleck recommended sending some of his equipment to India, Brooke and others were hard put to restrain Churchill from replacing his commander on the spot.

Closely related to the military situation of the British in the eastern end of the Mediterranean was the attitude of the North African French, who, though subject to the puppet Pétain regime, maintained some element of independence in North Africa and controlled Tunisia, Algeria, and Morocco. Assessing the future of French Northwest Africa was doubly confusing because of the divided loyalties of the French Army officers. Most of these, accepting defeat by Hitler, had remained on duty under Pétain's collaborationist government. To others, therefore, these regular Army men were actually tools of Hitler. And the British had universally antagonized the French by destroying most of the French fleet in July 1940. Then, in early May 1942, the British were taking possession of the French-dominated island of Madagascar, whose governor, loyal to Vichy, resisted for some months, another source of animosity.

President Roosevelt kept a close eye on all these developments. So receptive was he to news of affairs in the Mediterranean that Secretary of War Henry Stimson still regarded the invasion of Africa, GYMNAST, as the President's "great secret baby." Roosevelt said nothing; he simply kept abreast.

But the American public, especially the inhabitants of the West Coast, were little concerned about France or North Africa. In Los Angeles and San Francisco the fear was still rampant that the Japanese could attack even the United States. General Jonathan M. Wainwright's surrender on Corregidor as recently as May 6 was still fresh in everyone's mind. And Admiral King added his voice to those who were calling for greater defenses on the Pacific shoreline.

General Marshall was thus forced to send anti-aircraft, barrage balloons, and pursuit planes, earmarked for BOLERO, to the West Coast. He managed, however, to turn a deaf ear to King's professed needs for reinforcements in Fiji and Australia. And on May 29, 1942, he was afforded a highly visible platform from which to reaffirm his "Europe First" strategy. At the U. S. Military Academy, West Point, Marshall's graduation speech to the Class of 1942 pounded on his support of BOLERO.

The significance of Marshall's text was lost on the young cadets, who were interested primarily in their own immediate futures and who saw only a remarkably calm, composed Chief of Staff,[10] but his words regarding Allied strategy were not lost on those in Washington and London.

*

On that same May 29, 1942, the Japanese Combined Fleet, the most powerful naval force ever assembled, was passing to the north of Kyushu, from the Inland Sea. Its destination was Midway Island, some nine hundred miles northwest of Oahu, and its mission, vaguely put, was to seize this American outpost. A secondary objective, more important than Midway, was to lure Admiral Chester W. Nimitz's main American battle fleet into open combat.

This Japanese armada was commanded by Admiral Isoroku Yamamoto, aboard the new 63,000-ton superbattleship *Namoto,* and all told it consisted of eleven battleships, eight carriers, twenty-three cruisers, sixty-five destroyers, and ninety-five auxiliaries. Its cutting edge was the Carrier Striking Force, known as the *Kido Butai,* commanded by Vice-Admiral Chuichi Nagumo. This *Kido Butai* was a balanced fleet in itself, comprising four carriers, two battleships, eleven destroyers, and one light cruiser. The Midway Invasion Force, the part of the fleet assigned the role of making the actual landing, consisted largely of transports.

At first there had been some doubt among the Japanese naval command as to the feasibility of this Midway invasion. It was an ambitious undertaking a long way from home. And the Combined Fleet was in need of refitting and rest. Enjoying almost complete success since Pearl Harbor, it had executed all its missions with largely the same team of commanders, men, and ships. Therefore, as of the beginning of May the mission was in doubt. On May 7, however, the Carrier Striking Force, supporting a land invasion of Port Moresby, New Guinea, had engaged an American formation in the Coral Sea. In the course of the battle it had sunk the carrier U.S.S. *Lexington* and had badly damaged the U.S.S. *Yorktown.* (The Japanese believed it sank.) The mission had been turned back from its objective, but the supposed sinking of two American aircraft carriers by the least experienced air squadron in the fleet, the 5th, convinced the high command, as they reveled in exaggerated press accounts, that they were invincible. Along with the euphoria came a decision to go ahead with Operation MIDWAY.

On the American side, Admiral Chester Nimitz was aware, as it left port, that the Japanese fleet was on the seas. The Japanese code had been broken, and Nimitz had been informed of enemy activities. Intercepted messages had even prompted him to intercept the Port Moresby force.

---

[10] Marshall made a hit by happily joining in conveying special congratulations to the class "goat," the last man to graduate. The author was a cadet in the audience.

Only one piece of information was missing: the identity of the actual Japanese objective. It was referred to in messages simply as "AF." Though analysts in Washington read "AF" as meaning Oahu, Nimitz and his intelligence unit read it as Midway. Willing to bet on his interpretation, Nimitz flew in person to Midway and decided to reinforce with more planes, men, and anti-aircraft. He then composed a message complaining about a breakdown in the island's distillation plant. When his intercept a couple of days later reported that "AF" was out of water, Nimitz had the last piece in his jigsaw puzzle.

To meet the threat, Nimitz had only two operational task forces. One, Task Force 16, commanded by Rear Admiral Raymond Spruance, consisted of two carriers, the U.S.S. *Enterprise* and the U.S.S. *Hornet,* six cruisers, and eleven destroyers. The second, commanded by Rear Admiral Frank Jack Fletcher, consisted of only the carrier *Yorktown,* two cruisers, and six destroyers.[11] Fletcher was placed in command of the two formations.

Aboard the *Akagi,* flagship of the Carrier Striking Force, Admiral Nagumo was still somewhat confused as to his exact mission. He had been told to (1) assist the Midway Invasion Force in seizing the island, (2) destroy the American fleet sent out to intercept them, and (3) destroy the aircraft on Midway which could attack the carriers. He decided to emphasize two tasks: to destroy the air forces on Midway that could hurt his carriers and to destroy what American naval forces he could. Assisting in the invasion would be lower priority.

Though a Catalina PBY flying boat had sighted part of the fleet as early as June 2, real contact was not made until the early morning hours of June 4, at which time the Japanese Striking Force was 240 miles northwest of Midway and (unbeknownst to Nagumo) Spruance was 200 miles due north of Oahu. Knowing that they had been sighted, Nagumo launched his torpedo planes at 4:30 A.M., headed for Midway. A little over an hour later the American planes took off from the island—ten torpedo planes (six Navy and four Army) with twenty-five Marine fighters—toward the task force. All ten torpedo planes were shot down without scoring a hit; fifteen of the fighters, completely outclassed by the Japanese Zeros, were lost. However, since Midway still had a capability, Nagumo decided to hit it again. Planes were sent by elevator below to have their torpedoes replaced by bombs.

Admiral Spruance was, in the early morning hours, faced with an important decision. He knew that he was more than a hundred miles from the Japanese force, the distance normally considered the prudent limit. However, in order to catch the Striking Force by surprise, he decided to

---

[11] This force was delayed awhile after Task Force 16 had left in order to allow fourteen hundred workmen to put the *Yorktown* back into fighting condition. They accomplished this feat, estimated to take three months, in two days.

risk a premature launching. At 7:02 A.M., therefore, he launched sixty-seven dive bombers, twenty fighters, and twenty-nine torpedo planes. Fletcher, behind him, launched about one third that number two hours later.

At 10:20 A.M. the first flight of twenty-seven American dive bombers caught two of the Japanese carriers preparing to launch their planes (after the switch to bombs). Both the *Akagi* and the *Kaga* were hit and burst into flames. Moments later another flight of seventeen dive bombers discovered the other two carriers, the *Hiryu* and the *Soryu*. The *Soryu* was in flames thirty minutes later. At ten-forty the *Hiryu* was also attacked but not before it had launched six fighters and eighteen dive bombers. These planes found Task Force 17 and scored hits on the *Yorktown*. By 3:00 P.M. the *Yorktown,* veteran of the first two carrier battles of World War II, was abandoned. The *Hiryu* was not excessively damaged until sunset, when twenty-four dive bombers from a second strike came in from the southwest and she was set hopelessly afire.

By evening all four Japanese carriers were sunk, two of them, the *Akagi* and the *Hiryu,* scuttled. The battle was essentially over, although American planes caught and sank a heavy cruiser from the Midway Invasion Force as late as June 6. The evening of June 4 the Japanese offered battle on the surface, but Spruance wisely withdrew. His surface force was no match for the Japanese battleships. The mission a failure, Admiral Yamamoto ordered a withdrawal of the Combined Fleet. He preferred to save his remaining power to fight other battles.

At a party for the German and Italian Embassies in Tokyo, an Army officer whispered to Prime Minister Tojo that the Navy had made a great mistake and lost four carriers at Midway.

Tojo, while gloating that the Army had advised against Operation Midway, warned, "The news must not leak out. Keep it a complete secret."[12]

But the Japanese could not keep the results of Midway from the Americans, particularly Marshall and King, who each chose to treat the stunning victory in his own fashion. Marshall now felt free to recall the units he had been forced to send to the West Coast. King and MacArthur, on the other hand, saw Midway as an opportunity for further offensives in the Pacific. So the diverted Army matériel was removed by authority of Secretary Stimson, and Admiral King went on with more ambitious planning.

*

From the time that Marshall and Hopkins returned from London in mid-April, little seemed to transpire in preparation for a September inva-

12 This account is taken primarily from John Toland's excellent book, *The Rising Sun,* pp. 267–390, and "Six Minutes to Victory" by Martha H. Byrd, *American History Illustrated,* May 1975.

sion of the Continent—almost as if the subject was being avoided. It was brought back to center stage in late May, however, with the visit of Soviet Foreign Minister Vyacheslav M. Molotov to London and Washington. Next to Stalin, Molotov was probably the most prestigious individual in Russia, and he was making this perilous journey over Nazi-held Europe with hard negotiating on his mind. This was no mere social call.

The initiative for the Molotov visit to Washington seemed to come from Roosevelt, who had cabled Stalin on April 11 that since he was unable at the time to meet the Soviet leader face to face he would, in the interim, like Molotov to visit him in the very near future. Actually the urgency of this invitation stemmed from Roosevelt's knowledge of a pending twenty-year treaty of alliance which the British planned to sign with the Soviets. As part of the treaty, Roosevelt understood the British planned to recognize Russian absorption of the three small Baltic states, Latvia, Estonia, and Lithuania, which they had occupied at the time of the French surrender in June 1940. Roosevelt objected to giving that military occupation any sort of official blessing, but Churchill felt no such compunction. And indeed, on April 8, as Marshall and Hopkins were arriving in London, Churchill's message had gone to Molotov asking him to come to London to sign. Roosevelt, in his desire to forestall this bilateral pact, apparently hoped that the prospect of coming to Washington might dissuade Molotov from accepting the invitation to London.

Stalin, in Moscow, had two primary objectives. One, of course, was recognition of the Baltic occupation, to which he knew Roosevelt would object; the other was a promise for an Allied second front on the European continent in hopes of drawing off some forty divisions from Russia, a ROUNDUP-in-1942. Russian priority between the two was not clear in early April, as the war on the Russian front seemed to be going well. On April 20, however, Stalin decided to send Molotov to both London and Washington (London first) to see what could be attained. This was not what the President had hoped for, but the arrangement was preferable to being left out while Churchill and Molotov conferred on an exclusive basis.

*

Molotov reached Britain late on May 20. For some reason he and his party elected to be housed at Chequers and drive into London for conferences. Churchill was quite willing; but his guests comported themselves in a bizarre fashion. Not only did they demand all the keys to their bedrooms, but they posted heavy details of Soviet police guards around the clock. These security people inspected every room in detail before occupation. Beds had to be made by Russian chambermaids. Only after a goodly portion of Molotov's nine-day stay in Britain did the Soviet police become even halfway friendly with the household staff.

By the time of Molotov's arrival the military situation in Russia had degenerated. The Second Front was becoming uppermost in Stalin's mind, now taking on far greater importance than recognition of frontiers.[13] Apparently reflecting this switch in emphasis, and aware that he had the British and Americans competing against each other, Stalin had now instructed Molotov to add the Curzon Line, in Poland,[14] to the frontiers to be recognized in a treaty. Now even the British, who had entered the war against Hitler because of Poland, would not be able to agree. Perhaps Churchill would be embarrassed by this apparent backing down on his part and just might then be disposed to give in on the issue of the Second Front. On the other hand, the Soviet ambassador in London, Ivan M. Maisky, had advised Stalin that the British were opposed to any cross-Channel invasion.[15]

Thus Britain and the United States might each veto one of the two Soviet desiderata, but Molotov had a chance to achieve one of them, or at least embarrass Roosevelt and Churchill so as to give the Soviets some psychological advantage in future dealings.

Conversations between Molotov and Churchill in London began on Friday morning, May 22, with the focus on the Second Front. Molotov came right to the point, asking about Allied plans for an invasion that year. Churchill, though now disenchanted, did not want to admit it. He therefore delivered a lecture on "difficulties." He no longer regarded the entire European coastline from Norway to the Bay of Biscay as one long landing beach. Now he emphasized the limitations of amphibious operations: fighter aircraft, necessary to modern invasions, had limited ranges, tied, like balls on a string, to their bases. The Germans, Churchill went on, could switch their bases easily from point to point on the European coast. An invasion of Europe from the British Isles could then be confined to landing places between the Pas de Calais and Normandy; Brest at the extreme limit. To stress the importance of air power to an invasion, Churchill cited the situation in June 1940, when Hitler had declined to attempt an invasion against an unarmed Britain because he had been unable to get command of the air.[16]

Molotov in his turn said he believed that the British genuinely wanted

13 The Germans had invaded the Crimea and were about to occupy all of it. A great Russian offensive at Kharkov in the Ukraine had been roundly defeated.
14 A temporary demarcation line from 1919, which limited the Soviet occupation of Poland in 1939.
15 Maisky, *Memoirs*, p. 268, quoted in Stoler, "The Politics of the Second Front," p. 123. The BCOS had in fact turned thumbs down on SLEDGEHAMMER May 8.
16 Churchill, IV, 332–35.

the Red Army to survive the summer. Then, appearing to play on Churchill's ego, he asked for—and received—an estimate of the Red Army's chances of survival for the summer. Churchill hedged, saying only that prospects looked better in 1942 than they had in 1941. He conceded that a collapse of the Red Army would expose the West to the "gravest danger" and that the fortunes of the West were "bound up with the resistance of the Soviet Army." But if worst came to worst, Churchill contended that Western Allies would fight on and ultimately would prevail.

The next day Molotov and Anthony Eden began the negotiation of the twenty-year treaty of alliance. Molotov, conscious of American objections to recognizing the Russian version of their future frontiers—and aware that Churchill could never recognize Russian occupation of Poland up to the Curzon Line—settled for a treaty which made no reference to postwar matters. He was thinking almost exclusively about a second front and was now looking to Washington for his concessions.[17]

Twice during the period of Molotov's visit Churchill himself went to Chequers to spend the night. Here, with Russian Ambassador Maisky interpreting, Churchill used maps to try to explain in more detail the limitation of amphibious operations and the tenuous nature of the Allied life line across the Atlantic. By the end Churchill began to sense that he had been able to transmit a glimmer of understanding to Molotov's mind.

When Molotov left for Washington on Thursday, May 28, Churchill telegraphed Roosevelt. He had really promised nothing, he said, but had told Molotov that he would have "something ready for him" when he returned to London on the way home to Moscow. Churchill added, moreover, that Lord Louis Mountbatten would arrive in Washington shortly to explain some "difficulties" to Roosevelt. For the first time Churchill mentioned a landing in the north of Norway. And he added a sentence: "We must never let GYMNAST pass from our minds. . . ." This message was apparently the first serious indication to Roosevelt that Churchill was beginning to weaken on SLEDGEHAMMER,[18] the emergency cross-Channel assault.

*

Molotov arrived in Washington on Friday, May 29, equipped for any contingency: a pistol to defend himself and a loaf of black bread and sausage in case of siege.[19] He was whisked immediately to a four o'clock

[17] The evening of May 24 U. S. Ambassador John Winant had come by Chequers and said that Roosevelt was interested in a second front, a new Lend-Lease agreement, and postwar aid. Stoler, p. 127.
[18] Sherwood, p. 556.
[19] The pistol and food were in his suitcase. Eleanor Roosevelt, *This I Remember*, p. 250.

meeting at the White House. The conference was informal and broad, covering the general situation in the South Pacific, Nazi treatment of POWs, prospects for bringing Turkey into the war, and the idea of ferrying supplies from the United States to Russia by way of Siberia. Roosevelt, Harry Hopkins observed, seemed ill at ease. The President was at home with most of the greats in the world, but his previous exposure to prominent leaders had been largely with people of polish. The square-headed, mustached "Hammer," with the jutting jaw and expressionless eyes behind his pince-nez glasses, was something new. Between wars Winston Churchill had gained exposure to dictators and tyrants when he, as a private individual, had tried to penetrate the circle around Hitler. Roosevelt, on the other hand, was encountering a leading figure in a dictatorship for the first time. However, far from shrinking from the challenge, he rose to it with relish. And as the Molotov visit went on, the atmosphere became warmer. Molotov even decided to spend that night, Friday, in the White House.

But when it came to business, Molotov pressed his points hard. In the meeting with Roosevelt, Hopkins, Marshall, King, and others on the morning after his arrival, he was direct. Comparing the situation then existing with the specter of a bleak 1943, he emphasized that in 1942 the Red Army was still holding its own, despite the failure at Kharkov, but the Nazi summer offensive was nearing, and the Russians might not be able to withstand Hitler's armor and artillery. If the Nazis should become master of all Europe in 1943, then that year would be "difficult" for the Western Allies. Foodstuffs and raw materials of the Ukraine—and the oil wells of the Caucasus—would be Hitler's.

Molotov summarized: Could the Western Allies take action to draw off forty German divisions in 1942? "If you postpone your decision," he warned, "you will have eventually to bear the brunt of the war."[20]

Roosevelt left it largely to Marshall to answer Molotov's military questions. Normally wary of promising too much, Marshall did say that the United States was making every effort to create a second front for 1942. He had been encouraged, Marshall said, by the Russian performance against the Germans that year. The fact that they had even attempted a counterattack was a good sign. To help, the United States had troops, munitions, aviation, and armored divisions ready for invasion. Particularly because of the Atlantic convoys, however, sea transport was still a problem.

Then Marshall, speaking for Roosevelt, promised that a second front of some sort would be launched before the end of the year. He did not define the term, although the Americans were thinking of five to ten divisions and Molotov was thinking of forty.

20 Bryant, *Turn of the Tide*, p. 314.

President Roosevelt and Admiral King outlined the difficulty in sending Atlantic convoys to Murmansk via the North Cape. German surface vessels such as the *Von Tirpitz, Scharnhorst,* and *Gneisenau* were lurking in the path, as were Nazi U-boats. German air units based at Narvik, Trondheim, and other places in Norway were taking their toll. Molotov listened without a show of emotion.

Luncheon at the White House that day was more relaxed than the atmosphere at the conference, as it included a broader group of guests, such as Vice-President Wallace, noted for his friendship with the Soviet Union. Members of Congress were also invited. Molotov entertained the group by describing his former dealings with Hitler and Ribbentrop, whom he ironically described as "disagreeable" people. He then gave a rundown of the abortive Soviet offensive at Kharkov. That afternoon the President gave Molotov a list of 8 million tons of Lend-Lease material which would be available during the year beginning July 1, 1942. But he specified that because of shipping limitations the United States could ship only 4.1 million tons, just over half.

The last meeting occurred on June 1 and centered around the amount of Lend-Lease that should be sent to the Soviet Union during the next fiscal year. The President, having received more protests from the British, now tried to reduce Lend-Lease commitment from the 4.1 million tons he had mentioned two days earlier to 2.3 million. This would allow a larger number of ships to be sent to England for the Second Front. Molotov dug in, insisting that a second front would be stronger if the First Front (Russia) still stood. Molotov's attitude somehow seemed more belligerent that morning, possibly because Soviet Ambassador Litvinov was there to watch him.[21]

Finally Molotov asked Roosevelt once again for a simple answer to take back to Moscow. The President repeated that (1) the United States expected to establish a second front and (2) that the United States could "proceed toward its creation with the more speed if the Soviet Government would make it possible for us to put more ships into the English service."[22]

That afternoon Roosevelt and Hopkins flew to Hyde Park. Molotov remained in Washington and during that time sent Roosevelt a final list of supplies the Soviets needed soon. They could not all be provided, but the President approved an urgent demand for 3,000 trucks a month.

*

Molotov then returned to London. A message from Roosevelt had put the Prime Minister in a state of upset, as Roosevelt was now stronger than

[21] This was the impression of Professor Samuel H. Cross, the notetaker.
[22] Sherwood, p. 575.

ever on SLEDGEHAMMER, the cross-Channel invasion. And against Marshall's advice, Roosevelt had arbitrarily moved the timing up to August, only two months away. Churchill's mind now set, he sent Molotov back to Moscow with only an aide-mémoire; the critical words were that he could "give no promise."[23]

[23] Churchill, IV, 342.

CHAPTER VII

DECISION FOR AFRICA

L ieutenant General H. H. Arnold was a guest at Chequers the evening of May 30, 1942, the night Sir Arthur Harris' Bomber Command made its historic first "thousand-plane raid" on Cologne. What was later termed "Air Offensive Europe" had begun. Arnold was happy with the success of the raid although he sensed that it had been made with very much of an eye to public opinion. Psychologically he had been set back in his arguments for a separate American air effort, which he was trying to sell to the Prime Minister. But the good-humored "Hap" Arnold took it in his stride. And for the trip home to Washington on June 1, he enjoyed the company of Lord Mountbatten in his plane.

Lord Louis Mountbatten, "Dickie" to his friends, was on a delicate mission. He was ideal for it. Young (forty-one), tall, handsome, and aristocratic, he had earned a valid fighting reputation as commander of a destroyer flotilla, an aura which overcame the worst in Yankee prejudice toward such a British Britisher.[1] Further, as the Director of Combined Operations, charged with the development of amphibious techniques,

---

[1] Eisenhower later wrote of his visit to London at this time:

The first question . . . was, "And who would you name as commander of this expedition?"

. . . I replied, "In America I have heard much of a man who has been intensively studying amphibious operations for many months. I understand that . . . his name is Admiral Mountbatten. . . . I have heard that [he] is vigorous, intelligent, and courageous, and if the operation is to be staged initially with British forces predominating I assume he could do the job."

My remarks were greeted with an amazed silence. Then General Brooke said, "General, possibly you have not met Admiral Mountbatten. This is he sitting directly across the table from you." (*Crusade*, p. 67.)

Mountbatten's interests coincided with those of the American Army as well as of the Navy. He had a foot in both doors.

On the day that Arnold and Mountbatten arrived in Washington, June 2, the latter met with the American Joint Chiefs. Ostensibly the purpose of his trip—possibly a cover—was to discuss production and crews of landing craft.

This matter was nothing trivial. The President himself was so interested that a couple of days earlier he had sketched his own personal design. In mid-April he had raised the priority on the shipbuilding list. The Navy was now planning to complete six hundred landing craft within three months to accommodate a SLEDGEHAMMER in early September. But even this impetus should have come earlier, as it took six months to do this type of work,[2] and Admiral King was a difficult man to interest in the subject. In his determination to concentrate on ships such as carriers and cruisers, he appeared to be a law unto himself.

Mountbatten gave King a new thought. As a fellow naval officer, able to talk on a professional basis, he told an unreceptive King that crews must be trained. An eventual cross-Channel invasion was inevitable, he said, and ships and crews would be needed. If the Navy failed to train them, the Army would. The Navy would then have sold its "birthright" if the Army could deliver itself. King quickly asked what he could do to ex- pedite a solution.[3]

But however valuable the discussions of landing craft, the more important purpose of Mountbatten's trip came out later. Having finished his short session with Marshall and King, he left them and proceeded at once to join Roosevelt and Hopkins at Hyde Park. Roosevelt, Hopkins, and Mountbatten dined alone.

Lord Louis knew what points he wanted to make and he made them, sending a memorandum to the President a week later summarizing his version of the discussion: (1) American desire to get troops into the fight as soon as possible, (2) agreement that no Allied landing made in France during 1942 could draw off German divisions, since Hitler had twenty-five already there, and (3) Roosevelt's interest in Churchill's recent sentence, "Do not lose sight of GYMNAST."

Seeds planted, Mountbatten returned immediately to London without seeing Marshall and King again. They learned what had transpired only when their BCOS counterparts gave them copies of Mountbatten's cable. Perhaps the British Chiefs were unaware of Churchill's little game.

*

Roosevelt did not, however, seem to relent in his support for SLEDGE-HAMMER. His promise to Molotov was still on his mind, and his June 4

[2] Sherwood, p. 544.
[3] Pogue, II, 331.

message to Churchill (sent while Mountbatten was on the way home) urged an August SLEDGEHAMMER. But the GYMNAST idea for North Africa had not been allowed to die in Roosevelt's mind.

In London, Churchill was receiving new data to support his objections to SLEDGEHAMMER. Current computations indicated that landing craft on hand limited an assault on the French coast to a force of something like five thousand men, a pitiful handful against the twenty-five Nazi divisions in France. By June 11, therefore, Churchill asked the British Cabinet to agree that (1) no landing in France should be made until the Allies were prepared to remain, and (2) none could be possible in 1942 unless the Germans became suddenly and unexpectedly demoralized by actions on the Eastern Front. The British requirement had been switched from a Russian demoralization to a German demoralization.

The issue was now dead with the British, however, and it was Churchill's task, as he saw it, to convince Roosevelt. This would not be easy: Major General Eisenhower, already selected to command U.S. forces in Europe, was soon to leave for London with a mission to plan for SLEDGE-HAMMER that summer. Churchill therefore convinced Roosevelt that they should confer again in Washington.

No sooner had they agreed to meet than Churchill received bad news from North Africa. While Auchinleck had been planning an offensive, Rommel had hit him. By June 13 the British Eighth Army was in full retreat toward Egypt. To make matters worse, news came in that two naval convoys intended for Malta had been heavily attacked, only two of the seventeen ships completing the trip. The position of Malta was now more precarious than ever.

*

On June 17, 1942, Churchill, Brooke, and Ismay left London by Churchill's private train to Stranraer Loch in Scotland, knowing that the Eighth Army was in full retreat. Brooke, who had stayed home for the ARCADIA conference, was flying the Atlantic for the first time. Though the Americans had been flying back and forth for the last few months, the regular transatlantic ferry service had been instituted less than two years. Churchill, however, seemed oblivious to the dangers of the trip. He was engrossed in his own thoughts and walked up and down humming a little ditty to himself, "We're here because we're here." The song seemed appropriate, as Brooke tended to wonder why the two of them were going to Washington, how they should get there, what they should achieve, and whether they would ever get back.[4] They deferred leaving until 11:30 P.M. in order to avoid any stray German Focke-Wulfs.

The long trip on the flying boat was comfortable but required an es-

4 Bryant, *Turn of the Tide*, p. 332.

timated twenty-seven hours' flying time; and the Prime Minister insisted that "his clock was his stomach," demanding to be fed every four hours. This presented Brooke with a new problem. Courtesy required that Brooke join in, but he found it a little strenuous to join his chief in champagne and brandy at every meal.

During the next day Brooke was able to enjoy the scenery as the clipper flew southwestward over Newfoundland, Nova Scotia, and down the U.S. eastern seaboard. The party approached Washington at 8:00 P.M. in hazy light. To Brooke, seeing Washington for the first time, the scene was pleasing—and something of a relief. "Our arrival in Washington," he wrote, "is one more of those episodes which remains almost as clear in my mind as if it had been only yesterday. The sight of this beautifully laid-out town in the hazy light of the evening; the Potomac looked like a small silver ribbon running through the middle of it. The large Clipper slid down on to the water like a great swan. . . . I found it hard to realise that in one hop I had moved through space from Stranraer Loch to the Potomac."[5]

On hand at National Airport were General Marshall, Field Marshal Dill, and others. Churchill stayed overnight at the British Embassy, and Brooke was soon at Dill's home for the evening. He was not, however, spared attending dinner at the embassy. He found it worthy of note that they went to bed at 1:45 A.M., the equivalent of 7:45 A.M. by English time.

The next morning the Prime Minister flew to Hyde Park, where the President awaited him.

*

The military, American and British, were still deeply concerned by these unchaperoned, face-to-face conferences between Roosevelt and Churchill. For Brooke was as leery of Churchill's agile imagination as was Marshall, and unlike the first Washington conference the British military, like the American, were now excluded.

This fact may have been of some comfort to Marshall, but not much. Brooke, though he would push the British position, was a known quantity, but Churchill and Roosevelt together could come up with surprises. A couple of days before, June 17, Stimson, Marshall, King, and others, fearing that Roosevelt was weakening on SLEDGEHAMMER, had urged him not to abandon it. They were not encouraged. As Stimson wrote,

> The President sprung on us a proposition which worried me very much. . . . He wants to take up the case of GYMNAST again, thinking that he can bring additional pressure to save Russia. . . . I think he may be doing it in his foxy way to forestall trouble that is

[5] Ibid., p. 324.

now on the ocean coming towards us in the shape of a new British visitor. . . . Altogether it was a disappointing afternoon.[6]

Later that day Stimson drew up a strong written argument. To cover all tracks, Marshall secured the agreement of Arnold and Eisenhower to back up his own concurrence and wrote a letter to accompany Stimson's. These documents, dated June 19, were sent to Hyde Park for Roosevelt to read almost simultaneously with Churchill's arrival.

When Prime Minister Churchill arrived, he found the President unwilling to begin substantive discussions until the next day. He was, according to Churchill, awaiting some "more information from Washington," which meant the Stimson letter. Nevertheless, the two enjoyed the pleasant surroundings and the next day after lunch they settled in the small room on the ground floor that Roosevelt used for an office. Hopkins stood in the background. Churchill, unaccustomed to the intense heat, observed that it did not seem to bother the Americans.

Two momentous problems were foremost on their minds. The first involved the Allied development of a superbomb, based on the energy released by splitting the atom. This so-called "atom bomb" was still in the theoretical stages, and the problem was to decide whether to gamble a couple of billion dollars on a project which had as evidence nothing more than the assurances of a handful of scientists. Both Britain and the United States had been working on atomic fission and knew enough about the subject to have inklings that the Germans also were trying to make military use of it. But it was not the billions that concerned the two; they were wary of draining off so much scientific brain power from other efforts.

However, they soon realized that, whether the gamble would pay off or not, the prospect of being behind in the development of this kind of weapon was too frightening; the West had no choice but to push its development.

The second question was the one the American military had been dreading. Churchill presented his argument against SLEDGEHAMMER, which boiled down to (1) an insistence that no substantial landing in France should be made unless the Allies were determined to stay, (2) a recognition that no plan existed for an invasion of France, and (3) a recommendation, in the absence of an invasion of France, that North Africa be studied.[7]

---

[6] Stimson diary, June 17, 1942, quoted in Stimson and Bundy, *On Active Service in Peace and War*, p. 419.

[7] We are bound to persevere in the preparation for "Bolero." . . .

Arrangements are being made for a landing of six or eight divisions on the coast of Northern France early in September. However, the British Government do not favour an operation that was certain to lead to disaster. . . . *We*

Roosevelt continued the discussion. He sent a message to Marshall and King in Washington asking various questions as if the issue had not been hashed over for weeks.

By the end of the day Roosevelt seemed convinced that Churchill was determined to veto SLEDGEHAMMER, which he could do because its execution would depend almost entirely on the British. So the two, agreeing to talk no more strategy without their military advisers, changed their plans and took the presidential train. This was Saturday night, June 20. They would arrive in Washington early the next morning.

*

Meanwhile Marshall and Brooke were sweltering in the Washington heat. They both worried over what the "two great diversionists," as Stimson called them, were cooking up at Hyde Park. In the meantime they kept a fairly leisurely pace, however. Brooke visited with Dill on the morning of June 19 and then joined the rest of the Combined Chiefs at twelve-thirty. They met as a body again the next morning and then, to the relief of the wool-clad British, General Marshall invited them for lunch at Fort Myer. There the breezes were cool and they could enjoy the panoramic view of Washington in relative comfort.

After lunch Brooke was driven over to the home of Robert E. Lee in Arlington Cemetery, only about a mile away. Here the view of Washington was as magnificent as that from the Chief of Staff's quarters but the place held added significance to Brooke because in this stately, pillared home Lee had pondered his fateful decision in 1861 to leave the Union and draw his sword for his state of Virginia. "I was thrilled with [the Lee Memorial]," Brooke wrote, "and could easily transfer myself back to

hold strongly to the view that there should be no substantial landing in France this year unless we are going to stay.

No responsible British military authority has so far been able to make a plan for September, 1942, which had any chance of success unless the Germans become utterly demoralized, of which there is no likelihood. Have the American Staffs a plan? At what points would they strike? What landing craft and shipping are available? Who is the officer prepared to command the enterprise? What British forces and assistance are required? If a plan can be found which offers a reasonable prospect of success, His Majesty's Government will cordially welcome it, and will share to the full with their American comrades the risk and sacrifices. This remains our settled and agreed policy.

But in case no plan can be made . . . and consequently no engagement on a substantial scale in France is possible in September, 1942, what else are we going to do? Can we afford to stand idle in the Atlantic theatre during the whole of 1942? _It is in this setting and on this background that the French Northwest Africa operation should be studied._

Churchill, IV, 381–82. Italics mine.

the days he was there. I could almost see him going through the crisis of his life deciding on which side he would fight."[8] Later that afternoon the Combined Chiefs gathered for a sherry party and became even better acquainted, with Brooke meeting Stimson for the first time.

Despite the casual pace, the Chiefs of Staff had time to indulge in some straight talk. In many ways Brooke and Marshall were now thinking alike. Each, concerned with his chief's propensity to indulge in unnecessary sideshows, was dedicated to BOLERO—but for different reasons.[9] And they were set against both Operation JUPITER in Norway and GYM-NAST in North Africa.

The issue on which the two men differed was SLEDGEHAMMER. Marshall was determined that American troops should fight somewhere in 1942 whereas Brooke was perfectly willing to let the winter go by without action, simply building up the American presence in the British Isles. No meeting of the minds could be reached.

On Sunday morning, June 21, Brooke and Dill donned their "old clothes" and were headed for a relaxing few hours which would include a visit to Mount Vernon. Before they got under way, Brooke received a telephone call. The morning's plans were shattered; the Prime Minister and the President had arrived in Washington at 8:00 A.M. Brooke was wanted at the British Embassy immediately.

Without taking time to change clothes, Brooke reported to Churchill, who was angry to learn that the military had agreed to recommend against operations in either Norway or North Africa. Once the Chief of the Imperial General Staff had soothed the irate Prime Minister, the two headed for the White House.

On arrival, the Prime Minister, Brooke, and Ismay were ushered to the President's Oval Study on the second floor. As at ARCADIA, the President sat behind his huge desk, framed by a scene of the White House fountains, the Ellipse, and the point where Mr. Roosevelt would soon dedicate the Jefferson Memorial. Brooke felt ill at ease in his slovenly clothes, but in this, his first meeting, he was charmed by the President's informality. Roosevelt even insisted that Brooke remove his coat and be comfortable.

---

[8] Bryant, *Turn of the Tide*, p. 325.
[9] Though Marshall viewed BOLERO as the base for ROUNDUP or SLEDGE-HAMMER, Brooke had certain other motives. His interest was in saving Egypt, and he wanted to get American troops into Europe (in contrast to the Pacific). Further, in his view, if the Russian front should collapse in 1942, then the Germans would in all likelihood turn westward against Britain again. The presence of American troops in Britain would be a strong deterrent to even the remote possibility of a German attack across the Channel.

Not much was left of the morning and soon the group, which included Roosevelt, Churchill, Hopkins, Brooke, Marshall, Ismay, and others, went to lunch, where they were joined by Mrs. Roosevelt. In the course of the conversation Roosevelt further disarmed the Irish soldier by his memory of a visit many years previous by Brooke's father to Hyde Park.

Luncheon completed, the party returned to the Oval Study and the conferences on BOLERO, ROUNDUP, SLEDGEHAMMER, JUPITER, and GYMNAST reconvened. In midafternoon a pink slip of paper was delivered by an aide. On it was appalling news. Tobruk, the "impregnable" British position in Libya, the symbol of British indomitability, had surrendered with a garrison of 25,000.[10] Ismay, in the background, reflected sadly that today, June 21, was the birthday of Claude Auchinleck—and incidentally his own.

After a stunned silence Roosevelt turned to Churchill and asked, "What can we do to help?" The answer was obvious: the British Eighth Army needed tanks. Marshall, who would provide the equipment, was at first inclined to adhere to his policy of keeping American units intact and to send an armored division. The 2nd Armored, commanded by Major General George S. Patton, Jr., could very quickly be shipped around the Cape. On reflection, however, all could see that a whole division with infantry, artillery, and service troops would take too long to deliver. The British needed the shipping space for tanks. Finally Marshall decided to send three hundred Shermans aboard six fast American freighters, though he knew he would have difficulty when he told his subordinates that he had denuded an American division of its tanks to send them to the British.

The instant response to give equipment so badly needed for training U.S. units was not lost on the British. Both Churchill and Ismay wrote later in emotional terms of this generous impulse of both Roosevelt and Marshall. And Brooke also was touched: "I always feel that the Tobruk episode in the President's study did a great deal towards laying the foundation of friendship and understanding . . . between the President and Marshall on the one hand and Churchill and myself on the other."[11]

Four meetings were held that twenty-first of June in the White House. Though gratitude rightly had no effect on British determination in bargaining, the news from North Africa shifted the thinking of the group from northwestern France to the Mediterranean. By the time the evening was over, North Africa was being mentioned in the combined meetings for the first time. And as the day broke up, President Roosevelt signaled General Marshall to stay behind. What, he asked, did Marshall think of creating a major U.S. force to control the area between Alexandria and

10 Thirty-three thousand, it turned out. Churchill, IV, 383.
11 Bryant, *Turn of the Tide,* p. 329.

Teheran? By this time, weary with discussions—and utterly defeated by this latest diversion from his beloved BOLERO—George Marshall's soldierly discipline almost broke down. He did not allow himself to answer and could not for a couple of days thereafter.[12]

*

On that same twenty-first of June, Major General Dwight D. Eisenhower sat on the front porch of his comfortable quarters at Fort Myer, only a stone's throw from Quarters ⚹1. He was saying good-by to his family before departing for London to be Commanding General, U. S. Forces in Europe. He had known of his assignment for only a short time. On his return from an inspection trip to London on about the first of the month, he had given General Marshall his views on what needed doing in the growing European command. They also discussed their own plan for SLEDGEHAMMER. "Do you agree with every part of this plan?" Marshall asked.

"Yes, sir, I do," answered Eisenhower.

"Well, that's good," said Marshall, "because you are going to command it."[13]

There were no dramatics in Eisenhower's family farewell, but even the gloom of the fall of Tobruk was overshadowed for a while by a sense of family separation. The paths of father and son were now parting even more drastically than on that day a year before when one reported to Fort Sam Houston and the other to West Point. After this rather subdued get-together, Eisenhower's cadet son left; his wife prepared to move their household belongings from their quarters at Fort Myer to the Wardman Park Hotel[14] on Connecticut Avenue.

The next morning Eisenhower and Major General Mark W. Clark went by the White House to pay a courtesy call on the President and the Prime Minister before leaving for London. It was the first time that Eisenhower had met Churchill, who, as was his custom, received his visitor in bed. Nothing of substance was said.

*

On the night of June 23, Churchill and his party boarded a special train that Marshall had arranged. Marshall was particularly keen about this outing, an opportunity to show off some U.S. troops in training. Fort Jackson, South Carolina, is hot in the summertime, but all were game. The temperatures reminded Churchill of his days in India, and he

12 Stimson diary, June 22, 1942, quoted in Pogue, II, 334.
13 Eisenhower had recommended Deputy Chief of Staff Joseph T. McNarney to be the theater commander. He had also recommended Mark W. Clark to be the senior U.S. corps commander.
14 Now the Sheraton Park.

enjoyed himself. During the day Churchill, Dill, Brooke, Stimson, and Marshall witnessed demonstrations by elements of three infantry divisions and a parachute drop. Though the British were impressed by the efficiency of the battalion of parachutists, they were less impressed with the demonstrations put on by the rest. Brooke termed the exercise "disappointing" and even Ismay, when asked by Churchill, said that it would be "murder" to send these green Americans into battle against "Continentals." Nevertheless, the diversion provided considerable relief for the Prime Minister, a cavalryman in the Boer War. He was boyish when asked to speak into a "walky-talky" radio, and he recognized, perhaps magnanimously, that these still raw Americans were excellent basic material.

But in a way the day hardened the British resolve. Planning for 1942 had never addressed the readiness of American troops. The limitation was always shipping. Thus the Prime Minister left from Washington the evening of June 25 more convinced than ever that GYMNAST was the proper operation for 1942.

*

Special Agent Michael F. Reilly, head of the President's Secret Service detail, was feeling uneasy as he rode in the right front seat of the car taking Prime Minister Churchill to the airport at Baltimore. A few days before, the President himself had called Reilly to his office and asked him to be extra cautious when Churchill left on June 27. The President was always concerned about the safety of his foreign guests, but at this time he seemed to be having some sort of premonition.

Mike Reilly had done the best he could. The safest way to get Churchill out of town would be to run him across the Potomac to the Naval Air Station at Anacostia, only a few minutes from the White House. There the Boeing flying boat could be waiting. But the British Embassy would have none of this. "That sort of thing isn't necessary," he was told politely. "There is a British Overseas Airways base at Baltimore, and if he flew from there it would be quite good for the workers' morale, you know." Nothing Reilly could say would change the situation; the Embassy had full confidence in the British subjects who ran the base, and all the Americans had been checked out by the Canadian Mounties.

Roosevelt this evening had ridden with Churchill only through the tunnel under the Treasury Department across from the White House. He went, he said lightly, "only to make sure that you don't steal any of Henry Morgenthau's gold." Then the President had returned to the White House and left Churchill in the hands of Harry Hopkins, the naval aide, and Reilly.

On arrival at the BOAC base, Reilly asked the Prime Minister to stay in the car a moment while he checked things out. At the dock where the flying boat was moored Reilly saw one of his agents, Howard Chandler, scuffling with one of the BOAC guards. By the time Reilly arrived Chandler had disarmed the man and had him subdued. "This jerk wants to kill Churchill," Chandler reported laconically.

The guard, who had been unwise enough to announce his intentions in advance, was hustled into another waiting car. Reilly returned to Churchill and Hopkins. "Everything's fine, sir," he reported.[15]

*

As he flew back to London, Winston Churchill realized that accounting to Parliament for the fall of Tobruk would be unpleasant. Before the trip to Fort Jackson, he had described himself as "the unhappiest Englishman in America since Burgoyne."[16] And in saying good-by to Harry Hopkins he said wistfully, "Now for England and home and—a beautiful row."

Churchill knew what he was talking about. Under attack from the British newspapers—and even some in America—he faced a vote of confidence in the House of Commons. His Conservative Party[17] had suffered sufficient losses in recent by-elections that a serious setback in the vote of confidence could result in general elections.

The discontent regarding Churchill's conduct of the war was intense. Proposals ranged from the severe (relieving the Prime Minister of the conduct of the war and appointing a professional soldier or sailor) to the ridiculous (remove all British generals and replace them with Czechs, Poles, and Frenchmen).[18]

As it turned out, however, these proposals represented the carpings of fringe groups. Churchill's prestige carried the day without serious threat. On July 2 he won a vote by a count of 475 in favor and 25 against. But this lopsided vote applied to whether or not Churchill should stay in office. Public opinion on the government's conduct of the war—in contrast to finding someone to replace Churchill—was polled at only 40 percent favorable.[19] And Churchill was not happy with any dissension regarding the government's running of the war, even if the House of Commons overwhelmingly desired he be retained.

After Tobruk Churchill could stand no more disasters. His survival as Prime Minister depended, he was convinced, completely on a victory—at the very least no more defeats—in the field.[20]

The situation was even worse on the military side than on the political.

[15] *Reilly of the White House,* pp. 127–28. The man, an American, was later judged insane. Churchill never learned of the incident.
[16] British general who surrendered at Saratoga in 1777.
[17] The wartime government was a coalition, but dominated by Conservatives.
[18] Ismay, *Memoirs,* p. 257.
[19] Grigg, *1943—The Victory That Never Was,* pp. 36, 47–48.
[20] Moran, p. 51, describes Churchill's determination never to suffer another setback as the "backcloth to every scene."

General Ritchie's Eighth Army, having lost most of its armor in the recent fiascos, made an unsuccessful stand at Mersa Matruh, about one hundred miles east into the Egyptian border; it had been forced to fall back on El Alamein, another hundred miles, with the loss of another 6,000 men. Admiral Harcourt's Mediterranean Fleet had now retreated from Alexandria and had taken refuge in the Red Sea behind the Suez. On the Russian front the Germans had broken through the Russian lines and were driving to the Volga and the Caucasus. And in a single week Britain and America had lost 400,000 tons of shipping in the Atlantic.

Within a couple of days, however, both the military and the political situations began to stabilize. At El Alamein Rommel's supply lines were badly stretched and the Eighth Army was in a strong position with the Qattara Depression on the south limiting the length of the British front to something like forty miles. Churchill, his battle in the Parliament won, was now contemplating a personal visit to the Middle East. Brendan Bracken, the Minister of Information, joined with Brooke in discouraging him. For aside from the physical danger, Brooke in particular dreaded what would happen if the Prime Minister himself should arrive to direct the current battle personally.[21] For this moment, Churchill set the idea aside.

Brooke, however, had not totally lost his sense of humor. Though aware that the British Embassy in Cairo was burning all documents, he could observe wryly that Auchinleck was fighting in what he described as "the British Army's spiritual home, the last ditch." At any rate, Auchinleck, who had removed Ritchie as Eighth Army commander and had assumed that position himself, seemed to be holding out well on his new front. Now, Brooke mused, his own immediate task would be to prevent Churchill from demanding a premature counterattack.

*

In the United States the military situation appeared bleaker than it did to the British. On June 30 Roosevelt at Hyde Park queried Marshall as to what would happen if the Nile Delta were evacuated. Could the Suez Canal be blocked? So desperate did he and Hopkins see the situation that they were talking in terms of Turkey's swinging to the Axis. Could Basra in Iraq and the Black Sea area be defended? Marshall answered that the British could indeed block the Suez Canal. At worst they would probably have to withdraw to the Upper Nile. Marshall held out against trying to defend Syria and Turkey. These, he insisted, would bleed us white.

Assistance to the British in the Middle East now came from an unexpected quarter. On July 4 Churchill cabled Roosevelt asking for forty-eight A-20 bombers approaching Basra, headed for Russia. Roosevelt

21 Bryant, *Turn of the Tide,* p. 338.

asked Stalin if the Soviets would be willing to give up these bombers. Amazingly, Stalin agreed.

But Marshall was momentarily discouraged for reasons other than the immediate military situation. He could see that the British were backing off from BOLERO, let alone SLEDGEHAMMER. Backed up by King, he began seriously to consider abandoning the "Europe First" concept. Somehow the word reached President Roosevelt, whose concept of "Europe First" included North Africa as well as the English Channel. Angered, Roosevelt compared Marshall's consideration of an about-face toward the Pacific as petulant and childish. He further considered the Chief of Staff's attitude a bluff.

In this Roosevelt was correct; Marshall later admitted that he had indeed been bluffing, out of exasperation.[22] However, his frustration soon let up.

*

On June 23, 1942, after their farewell call at the White House, Generals Dwight D. ("Ike") Eisenhower and Mark W. (Wayne) Clark[23] took off for London. It was an informal event, with no ceremonies at either end. Immediately the two set up headquarters in a building on Grosvenor Square near the famed Marble Arch of Hyde Park.

Eisenhower's instructions as Commanding General, United States Forces, European Theater, were simply to "prepare for and carry on military operations in the European Theater against the Axis Forces and their allies." Eisenhower was aware that conflicts had been assailing the minds of his superiors, but he had not been privy to the conversations in recent days. He therefore assumed that his mission was simply to prepare for SLEDGEHAMMER. Clark was to command the single participating American corps.

If Eisenhower's arrival went unnoticed publicly, however, he was very much under the observation of one influential British officer, General Sir Hastings Ismay, Chief of Staff to the Prime Minister. At first Ismay was perplexed that such a young, junior officer should command American forces; he soon began to see why. Eisenhower, according to Ismay's description, was alert, sure of himself, exhibiting "no trace of conceit or pomposity." He was frank, sincere, and friendly but "master in his own house," and capable of being "firm to the point of ruthlessness."[24]

One of Eisenhower's first moves—and one which impressed Ismay— was to give careful thought to relations between American soldiers and British civilians. The Americans, Eisenhower feared, might consider

22 Pogue, II, 340–41.
23 Clark was known as Wayne in the Army, as Mark in the press.
24 Ismay, p. 258.

themselves crusaders coming to save Europe. The British, on the other hand, having carried on the war for so long, might resent the further burden on their domestic life presented by the arrival of the Yanks. Eisenhower consulted Ismay and on his advice went to see Information Minister Brendan Bracken. Apparently not conscious of the modest civilian backgrounds of many of the American generals, Ismay was rather astonished that a soldier would be so concerned with the feelings of a host civilian population.

One day, not long after the United States Forces Headquarters had been set up, Ismay came to see Eisenhower with a complaint. One high-ranking U. S. Army officer, he said, was inclined when drinking to boast that the Americans would show the British how to fight. To Ismay's surprise, a livid Eisenhower sent for the officer to report the next morning. "I'll make the son of a bitch swim back to America," Eisenhower growled.

Ismay now tried vainly to smooth the matter over. Eisenhower even turned on Ismay himself: "If we are not going to be frank with each other, however delicate the topic, we will never win this war."[25]

The Prime Minister also began at once to establish a rapport. He set up a regular schedule: on Tuesdays he and Eisenhower would lunch together and on Fridays they would dine, usually accompanied by one or more other American officers. There was something about the chemistry of the two men that gave them a mutual affinity from the start. Their personal habits were very different, but both were strong, vital, intelligent men with a single purpose: victory. Neither took differences in judgment personally, and each treated the position of the other with respect. As time went on, they would develop a mutual affection based on a sharing of victory and sometimes defeat. But though that comradeship would have to grow, they were comfortable with each other from the start.

*

Within two weeks of arrival Eisenhower received informal word from Churchill that the British would no longer consider a cross-Channel invasion during 1942. Naturally he reported this news to General Marshall. Marshall, in turn, passed the word to Secretary of War Henry Stimson, who then proceeded to write one of his letters of advice to the President. Marshall protested, not because he disagreed with Stimson but because he felt that in strategic matters he was the one responsible, that he was shirking his duty by allowing his civilian boss to carry the brunt of the argument.

As a result Stimson, King, and Marshall met with the President on July 15. The disagreement was bitter, as both Roosevelt and Marshall said to

[25] Ibid., pp. 258–59.

each other what had been on their minds in private. Marshall repeated his alternative: perhaps the Americans should turn all efforts toward the Pacific in order to place the maximum number of fighting men in action by the end of the year. This would be preferable to North Africa. Roosevelt retorted to Marshall that the idea was a "red herring," tantamount to taking one's "dolls and dishes home."

Roosevelt was in a better position than the War Department to appreciate Churchill's uncomfortable political position. Roosevelt could well see that a sacrifice military operation would be impossible for Churchill to tolerate at this moment, and he had probably given up on crossing the Channel before this. To avoid overriding the Chief of Staff, therefore, the President resorted to the same device that he had used the previous April. Once more he sent Marshall and Hopkins to London, leaving the next day, so that Marshall could again talk to the Prime Minister in person. Admiral King was also sent this time.

The heart of the directive from the President carried by the American party on July 16, 1942, was as follows:

> In regard to 1942, you will carefully investigate the possibility of executing SLEDGEHAMMER. Such an operation would definitely sustain Russia this year. It might be the turning point which would save Russia this year. SLEDGEHAMMER is of such grave importance that every reason calls for accomplishment of it. You should strongly urge immediate all-out preparations for it, that it be pushed with utmost vigor, and that it be executed whether or not Russian collapse becomes imminent. In the event Russian collapse becomes probable SLEDGEHAMMER becomes not merely advisable but imperative. The principal objective of SLEDGEHAMMER is the positive diversion of German Air Forces from the Russian Front.
>
> Only if you are completely convinced that SLEDGEHAMMER is impossible of execution with reasonable chances of serving its intended purpose, inform me.[26]

But directives or no directives, the three representatives being sent by Roosevelt were all inclined in different directions. Upon learning who was coming, Alan Brooke in London could note with amusement, "It will be a queer party, as Harry Hopkins is for operating in Africa, Marshall wants to operate in Europe, and King is determined to stick to the Pacific."[27]

Sir John Dill, in Washington, decided to do his best to minimize the feelings when the Americans should arrive. Virtually as the party was

[26] Sherwood, p. 604.
[27] Brooke diary, July 15, 1942. Quoted in Bryant, *Turn of the Tide,* p. 341.

climbing aboard the flying boat Dill cabled Brooke. Marshall, he wrote, was about at the end of his patience and the British must convince him they were determined to defeat the Germans on the Continent as soon as possible, only 1942 was not the year. (Doubtless Dill was aware of Marshall's thoughts regarding a possible shift in emphasis to the Pacific.) Brooke received Dill's cable with equanimity.

The Americans landed in Scotland on the morning of Saturday, July 18. Since the weather was unfavorable for flying to London, the Prime Minister's personal train was on hand to meet them, together with an invitation to spend the weekend at Chequers.

As the train sped on its way southward, Marshall made an uncharacteristic gesture: he directed the train to keep going to London. For some strange reason the engineer of the Prime Minister's train complied. The Americans went directly to Claridge's Hotel to meet with Eisenhower, Admiral Stark,[28] and Major General Carl Spaatz (USAAF). This move on Marshall's part can only be explained by the intensity of his feelings. Though direct by nature, he was a courteous man, and always a stickler for the subordination of military to civilian authority. But for now Marshall had to regard Churchill as an antagonist; he was not willing to allow Churchill to make use of his position to help sway an argument vital to the conduct of the war.

The gesture was not lost on the Prime Minister, who put on a violent display of temper, perhaps partly for effect. Sincere or not, Hopkins was convinced that he should go to Chequers. Thus Hopkins stayed with the American military Saturday night and spent Sunday night and Monday evening at Chequers.

In London Marshall and King met with Eisenhower. Together they devised a modification they hoped might make SLEDGEHAMMER palatable to the British. Instead of the Pas de Calais, their new plan visualized crossing the Channel at a wider point to the west. A bridgehead in Normandy would constitute a reduced risk, Eisenhower believed, though its greater distance from Germany would make it less desirable for conversion to ROUNDUP. The revision, admittedly, would be a forlorn effort to secure British agreement.

Meanwhile Churchill at Chequers had sent for his own military chiefs —Brooke, Pound, Portal, Ismay, and Mountbatten. They conferred until 2:45 A.M., Sunday morning. The Americans, they finally concluded, should be told categorically that GYMNAST was the only feasible opera-

[28] Admiral Harold Stark, after leaving Washington, had been designated as Commander, U. S. Naval Force, Europe. He was, however, not part of Eisenhower's command.

tion for 1942. Even Brooke gave in, reversing his strong opposition of a month earlier.

Harry Hopkins arrived that Sunday and succeeded in calming the Prime Minister's hurt and anger. The British Chiefs, though present, were excluded when Churchill, Hopkins, and Eden began to talk confidentially.

On Monday, July 20, Churchill and Hopkins returned to London. For a long-drawn-out three days, Monday through Wednesday, the American and British military in London argued virtues and shortcomings of the new SLEDGEHAMMER. For a while it appeared as if the British might relent. By Wednesday, however, even Hopkins recognized that the British had established a solid front. The divided Americans were simply not going to talk them into a cross-Channel venture. By Wednesday afternoon Hopkins was scribbling on a pad, "I feel damn depressed."

That evening Brooke presented his views strongly to the British War Cabinet, and SLEDGEHAMMER was voted down unanimously. Marshall and Hopkins so informed President Roosevelt.

The next day President Roosevelt answered. The cheerful tone of his reply implied that he had expected a failure all along, and he directed Marshall and Hopkins to immediately find some other way in which U.S. forces could be employed against the Germans in 1942.

At lunch that day, Alan Brooke received a message to report to No. 10 Downing Street by 3:00 P.M. There he was happy to learn of Roosevelt's message. That evening Brooke entertained Marshall at dinner; Marshall seemed to be in excellent spirits, perhaps relieved, perhaps just resigned.

The die was cast. The decision had been made, and though the Americans had lost, no rancor resulted. Brooke, for one, went out of his way to ensure that the British War Cabinet, having won this all-important argument, should resist the temptation to press the Americans further.

The next two days, therefore, were devoted to discussions of the African invasion, SLEDGEHAMMER forgotten and BOLERO deferred. In private all realized that the North African venture would certainly rule out ROUNDUP in 1943. To give the new operation an American complexion—and partly to assuage American feelings—Churchill suggested that the commander of the new operation should be an American.

*

If Roosevelt accepted the British view regarding SLEDGEHAMMER with alacrity—and if Marshall accepted his defeat gracefully—one individual who took the news hard was newly appointed American commander Lieutenant General Dwight Eisenhower. It was not his own future that bothered Eisenhower; he could personally expect a major role in whatever happened. But he had been working with conviction on the cross-Channel concept since the previous February, when he had written the original memorandum advocating it. He believed in SLEDGE-HAMMER—and particularly its parent BOLERO—and he feared, as did Marshall, the tendency toward diversionism. "Well, I hardly know where to start the day," Eisenhower said as he sat down at breakfast on Thursday, July 23. "I'm right back to December 15th [1941]. Wednesday, July 22, 1942," he confided to his naval aide, "could well go down as the blackest day in history."[29]

Eisenhower had no time to mull over his disappointment, for during the afternoon General Marshall asked for a broad plan to initiate the attack against North Africa. The former GYMNAST was now TORCH, renamed by the Prime Minister.

On Saturday, July 25, Marshall and his party left London for Washington. Just before leaving, Marshall sent for Eisenhower to come for a last visit in Claridge's Hotel. While scrubbing away in a bathtub Marshall brought him up to date.[30] Eisenhower, Marshall said briefly, would be designated to direct planning for TORCH. And he, supported by King, would recommend that Eisenhower command the operation. Marshall expected the appointment to be accepted in a couple of weeks.

That evening the train carrying the American party to Scotland stopped off at Chequers. There they enjoyed a pleasant, informal dinner, with Lady Churchill included as one of the guests. All were weary. Though glad to have carried the day, Brooke wrote, he was even more glad that the week was over.

*

The decision to execute TORCH rather than SLEDGEHAMMER represented the great decision of the European war, the one instance where Roosevelt's instincts forced him to override the judgment of George Marshall. From a strictly military point of view (especially if the Soviet Union were in a state of collapse), SLEDGEHAMMER might very well have been the more desirable operation to mount. It might, if reasonably successful, have shortened the war. But political considerations prevailed. Roosevelt, by the American Constitution, could have survived the resounding unpopularity which was all too likely with the failure of SLEDGEHAMMER. Churchill, on the other hand, could not, and Roosevelt understood Churchill's position better than could Marshall. The President was adamant on only one point: that American troops engage the enemy in Europe or North Africa during 1942. The War Department agreed.

[29] Eisenhower later wrote that the decision to execute GYMNAST/TORCH in 1942 was probably the correct one. It was not, however, his feeling at the time.
[30] Eisenhower, Unpublished Manuscript.

In hindsight, therefore, the conclusion was inevitable: American troops had to fight in 1942 and the British could not go across the Channel that year. An operation had therefore to be launched in (a) the Pacific, (b) Norway, (c) the Middle East, or (d) North Africa. North Africa was clearly preferable.

Even the American military have since admitted as much.

CHAPTER VIII

MISSION TO MOSCOW

General Sir Alan Brooke had been anxious to visit General Auchinleck in Cairo for some time, but his trip had been held up by the intense British-American discussions just finished. Brooke had never ceased to hope that, once he had headed off the American scheme of crossing the Channel in 1942, this trip would be his next order of business. Even before he accompanied the Prime Minister to the United States in June, he had been laying the groundwork, and he finally secured Churchill's approval. He fully intended to go alone, and it appeared for a while that he would be allowed to do so. One reason for seeing Auchinleck would be to do what he could to maintain the integrity of the military. Brooke knew that Churchill had been dissatisfied with Auchinleck's performance and was likely to remove him without the benefit of Brooke's advice. As CIGS Brooke could make recommendations only after evaluating the situation himself.

Now in late July 1942 the situation had been somewhat clarified. At least SLEDGEHAMMER was off. So, on the departure of Marshall, King, and Hopkins from London, Brooke began to put his plans in concrete form.

Unfortunately from Brooke's point of view, the Prime Minister shared the same inclination and also began resurrecting the trip he had been considering in early July. This would be a good time to go. Planning for TORCH under General Eisenhower was just beginning. General Sir Harold Alexander, resting up in Ireland after the Burma campaign, had been appointed to command the British forces in the new operation. That accomplished, Churchill felt he could contribute little in London for the

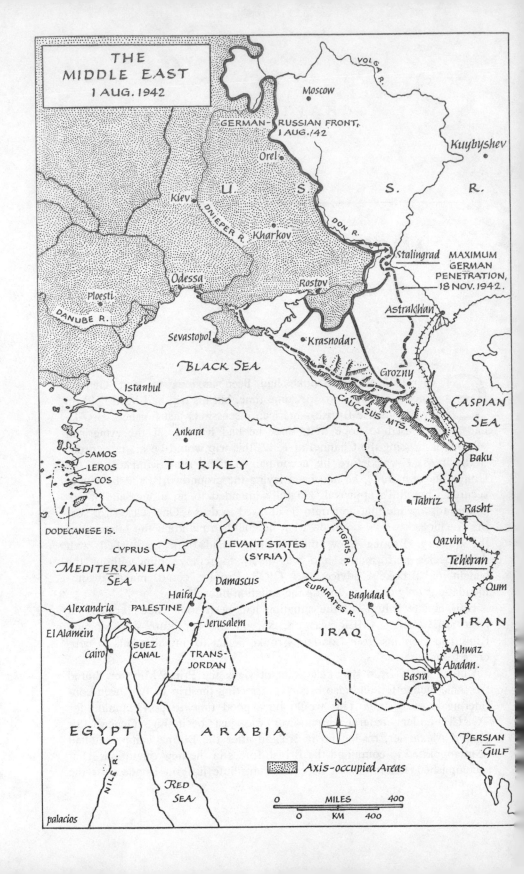

THE
MIDDLE EAST
1 AUG. 1942

GERMAN-RUSSIAN FRONT,
1 AUG. '42

VOLGA R.

Moscow

Kuybyshev

Orel

U.   S.   S.   R.

Kiev

DNIEPER R.

Kharkov

DON R.

Stalingrad   MAXIMUM
GERMAN
PENETRATION,
18 NOV. 1942.

Odessa

Rostov

Astrakhan

Ploesti

DANUBE R.

Krasnodar

Sevastopol

BLACK SEA

Grozny

CASPIAN
SEA

Istanbul

CAUCASUS MTS.

Baku

Ankara

SAMOS
LEROS
COS

TURKEY

Tabriz

Rasht

DODECANESE IS.

CYPRUS

LEVANT STATES
(SYRIA)

TIGRIS R.

Qazvin

Tehran

MEDITERRANEAN
SEA

Damascus

EUPHRATES R.

Baghdad

Qum

Haifa

PALESTINE

Alexandria

Jerusalem

IRAQ

IRAN

El Alamein

Cairo

SUEZ
CANAL

TRANS-
JORDAN

Ahwaz

Abadan.

Basra

EGYPT

ARABIA

N

PERSIAN
GULF

NILE R.

RED
SEA

Axis-occupied Areas

0   MILES   400

0   KM   400

palacios

time being, and the need to explain the choice of TORCH to Stalin was urgent. Thus Churchill had two objects to be gained in one trip. First of all he, like Brooke, wanted to check on the command situation in the Middle East, including that of the Eighth Army. From there he could continue, if Stalin agreed, to Moscow.

Most of the members of the British War Cabinet objected to this proposed trip, but the Prime Minister had no intention of being denied. Catching King George off his guard at a social event—as Brooke had done with him—Churchill secured permission. He was soon haggling with his doctor and others.

The War Cabinet had good reasons for questioning Churchill's trip. Axis aircraft roaming at will over the Mediterranean made a direct flight between Gibraltar and Cairo prohibitive. This meant that the only route considered safe would have to go across Black Africa, a region so ridden with disease as to require strong inoculations. Lord Moran was concerned about the effect of these. Yellow fever shots, absolutely necessary in this part of the world, were not yet proven safe, and Churchill was sixty-seven years old.

It so happened, however, that Churchill ran across a young American, Captain William Vanderkloot, U. S. Army Air Corps, who before entering service had logged a million miles. Vanderkloot had just crossed the Atlantic in an American B-24 Liberator and exhibited great confidence. The trip to Cairo could very well be made in one hop from Gibraltar. His plane (the *Commando*) could start across the Mediterranean at dusk and pass over Spanish Morocco and Vichy-held North Africa during darkness, arriving at the Nile by dawn. Thus the entire trip from England would require only two days. This was Churchill's answer. No bother about yellow fever shots!

So Brooke's dream of visiting Auchinleck without Churchill was burst. While adjusting to the disappointment he and Moran wondered unhappily why Churchill should have to depend on an American pilot, a *captain* at that, to make the trip. But Vanderkloot had provided Churchill an easy way to get to Cairo—and nobody else had. "The PM gets his own way with everyone with hardly a murmur," Moran groaned.

But Cairo represented only the first part of the journey. Churchill on July 30 therefore sent a message to Stalin: "I am willing, if you invite me, to come myself to meet you in . . . the Caucasus or similar convenient meeting place." Stalin answered the next day that Churchill would be most welcome in Moscow, the timing and duration of the stay to be completely at Churchill's own pleasure. Accordingly Churchill and Vanderkloot took off early on August 2. Brooke went separately in another American Liberator by way of Malta. The parties were to meet in Cairo on Monday, August 3.

Brooke's stop in Malta was by no means wasted. The governor was his former chief, Lord Gort, who had commanded British Expeditionary Forces on the Continent in 1940. The island was in a shambles; the destruction was worse, as Brooke saw it, than he had observed at Ypres and Arras in World War I. Rations had been drastically reduced, and a German-Italian invasion was a real possibility. Personally, Gort was in a low state of mind, not only because of his surroundings but also because he felt that he had been left out on a limb, his career finished in the British Army. Brooke's news about the forthcoming invasion of North Africa and the dramatic build-up of Auchinleck's Eighth Army put Gort's mind somewhat at rest.

Churchill, despite his advanced years, seemed to weather these hazardous, sometimes uncomfortable journeys better than his younger companions. He took delight in the fact that they were able to go in darkness across Spanish and Vichy French territory. In the early morning of August 3 he was, as was often his habit, ensconced in the co-pilot seat of the Liberator beside Vanderkloot, peering at the sight of a silver streak, the Upper Nile, as it gradually appeared in the first break of light. Shortly the Liberator set down at Cairo Airfield, northwest of the Pyramids. Now Churchill was "on the spot," present personally. His friend and trusted adviser Field Marshal Jan Christiaan Smuts of South Africa was waiting at the British Embassy and would be at his side through every decision of the next few days.

Churchill got down to business immediately. First priority was to find a commander for the Eighth Army, as in Churchill's opinion Auchinleck could not personally command both the Middle East and a field army. Churchill's jumping between personalities seemed almost willy-nilly. At first he offered the Eighth Army to Brooke, who would presumably serve under Auchinleck. Brooke declined, feeling that for the moment he should remain with Churchill in London. Churchill then turned to Lieutenant General W. H. E. ("Strafer") Gott, who had commanded a corps in the Desert for three years and who was reputed to be the idol of the Army. Brooke felt otherwise; in his view, this long term of service must have worn Gott down. To Churchill, however, Gott would be the man if he could find the residual energy. Churchill would have to see for himself.

At El Alamein, about a hundred and fifty miles northwest of Cairo, Gott's personal attitude toward the prospect of the Eighth Army command was somewhat ambivalent. The general had, as he had confided to Brooke, used up most of his ideas on fighting Rommel, and he was totally willing for someone else to be appointed over his head. He had, after all, been away from home for three years. However, on being confronted by the Prime Minister, Gott said that he would be willing to take over. Calm, with confident blue eyes, he seemed to have enough in him to do the job. When Churchill and Brooke returned to Cairo, therefore, Brooke accepted Churchill's decision that Gott would be the man.

But at least the Prime Minister and his CIGS were agreed almost from the start that Auchinleck had been spent. He should be replaced as Commander, Middle East. Once again Churchill offered this command to Brooke; once again Brooke refused it on the same basis that he had refused Eighth Army. The next logical choice, then, would be General Sir Harold Alexander, presently scheduled to command British forces in TORCH, whose combat performance in both Europe and Burma had earned the admiration of all.

It would not be pleasant to inform Auchinleck that his relief was imminent. "The Auk" was a man highly admired by all of the British hierarchy. He had done his best, his principal shortcoming being his unfortunate selection of subordinates, which had prompted him to try to do too much of the job himself. To minimize the pain of Auchinleck's wound Churchill devised a scheme, not illogical, to divide the former Middle East Command into a Near East Theater, comprising the Mediterranean and North Africa, and a true Middle East Theater, including Iran and Iraq, where vital oil supplies existed. The Nazis were presently driving into the Caucasus in Russia, and if they continued into Iran they would threaten the oil fields at Basra and Abadan at the head of the Persian Gulf. This part of the world logically deserved a British military command of its own.

On August 6, therefore, Churchill sent a recommendation to the War Cabinet that the heretofore Middle East Command should be designated as the Near East and that a new Middle East Command, comprising Iran and Iraq, should be established as a separate entity. In the same telegram Churchill mentioned Auchinleck's replacement by Alexander and Gott's assumption of the Eighth Army. After some discussion the War Cabinet agreed. Some members had doubts about the Middle East Command but they had little choice.

The propensity of the British to transfer generals without prejudice was contrary to American practice. However, since the British had been fighting the Germans for three years, they had come to realize that a commander could hold a position of great strain for only a reasonable amount of time, after which he would need a rest. Thus, following Churchill's tenet (which he had applied to Wavell and Alexander) of "performance only, not results," the relief of a British commander did not necessarily mean failure. The Americans, having been spared facing one defeat after another, were less inclined to be charitable.

But despite the fact that Churchill offered the command of the new Middle East area to Auchinleck, the removal could still not be made pleasant. Lord Moran chanced to be in the garden of the embassy in downtown Cairo when Brooke was talking to Auchinleck alone. The latter had already received the news by way of a letter from the Prime Minister. He was now absorbing the impact, seated on a stool, elbows on his knees, head hung over. Bearing no responsibility for this personal tragedy but feeling its impact, Moran found the episode almost too much to witness. But the decision was a necessary and courageous one for the Prime Minister.

The change in the Middle East Command and the appointment of Gott as commander of the British Eighth Army were now agreed between Churchill and Brooke. Fate took its hand, however, only two days after Churchill had talked to Gott. On the way to Cairo, Gott's plane was caught by a lone German pilot and shot down.

Churchill eventually was forced to contact London and summon General Sir Bernard Law Montgomery, whose name had been under serious consideration all the time. (See p. 149 below.) Even from this distance he could visualize the feelings of General Eisenhower, who had experienced two changes in British command for TORCH in as many days. But it had to be. General Auchinleck refused the offer of the Middle East Command and chose instead to retire.[1]

*

On August 7, 1942, W. Averell Harriman arrived in Cairo at the request of Prime Minister Churchill, who had now picked a departure date to leave for Moscow. Churchill had been anxious to have an American representative on hand when he would be forced to tell Stalin the unpleasant news of no second front during 1942. Harriman, who had earned the confidence of both Roosevelt and Churchill as the President's London representative for Lend-Lease affairs, could credibly participate for the American Government.

Harriman was particularly useful on this trip because as a lifelong railroad executive he could render advice regarding the railroad line now operating from the Persian Gulf to the Caspian Sea. If the line became really effective, it might provide the Anglo-American Allies a way to supplement the costly northern convoys to Murmansk and Archangel. Since the military situation in Cairo was of no direct concern to Harriman, he went ahead of Churchill to Teheran, following the route of the railroad to observe progress of construction and effectiveness of operation. In Teheran he talked to the American officers involved. From this reconnaissance Harriman concluded that under the current British management the railroad was carrying at best only about 3,300 tons of supplies daily. If

---

[1] Auchinleck later returned to command in India and eventually was promoted to field marshal.

Americans could run the line with their own equipment, the capacity, he estimated, could be raised to some 6,000 tons a day. When they met in Teheran, therefore, Harriman recommended to Churchill that the Americans take over this responsibility. He could use many of his own people from the Union Pacific. Churchill for the moment declined to answer.

On the night of August 10, 1942, Churchill, Harriman, and Moran left Teheran for Moscow, flying along the east shore of the Caspian Sea to avoid the battle zone where the Germans and Russians were struggling in the Caucasus.

Not so fortunate was Churchill's military party, which followed in the other Liberator. A short way out of Teheran the plane carrying Brooke's party, which included General Wavell, Air Chief Marshal Sir Arthur Tedder, and Lord Alexander Cadogan of the Foreign Office, lost an engine and had to turn back. On landing, Brooke's party found that the damage to their Liberator was severe; the plane could not be repaired immediately. They were fortunate, however, to find a Soviet Douglas DC-3 transport (the American C-47, Lend-Lease) and just by chance it was prepared to take the party on by way of stops at Baku and Kuibyshev for refueling. The Douglas was a comfortable aircraft, equipped with armchairs and couches for passengers, in striking contrast to the frigid, uncomfortable Liberators. The pilot and crew were congenial, the pilot a little bit too much so:

> Our Russian pilot was a grand specimen of manhood, about 6 ft. 6 in. tall and proportionately built of fine physique. A perpetual lighthearted smile on his face. We were also to discover that as a pilot he was equally light-hearted. His method of take-off was to fly low to the end of the runway, then to turn with a terrific bank, the inside wing almost cutting the daisies. He then headed back to where we had taken off and made the plane do a flip-flop as a goodbye to his friends.[2]

Because Baku and Kuibyshev were located on the western, dangerous coast of the Caspian Sea, Brooke's party flew the whole distance along the coast at an altitude of two hundred feet, crossing the Russian rear-area defenses. These, according to Brooke, were almost non-existent, an evidence that all was not under control in the Red Army.

At the end of the journey to Baku Brooke's pilot engaged in one more burst of exuberance. He leveled the plane straight for the hangar on the airfield, in the last instant pulling it into a nearly vertical climb. Passen-

[2] Bryant, *Turn of the Tide*, pp. 369–70.

gers in the plane, unwarned, were tossed hither and yon. They did, however, arrive at each base without serious injury.

*

As his party approached Moscow, Winston Churchill was pensive. Once, years before, he had been noted as the foremost enemy of the Soviet system. This had been just after World War I. He later recalled the moment:

> I pondered on my mission to this sullen, sinister Bolshevik State I had once tried so hard to strangle at its birth, and which, until Hitler appeared, I had regarded as the mortal foe of civilised freedom. What was it my duty to say to them now? . . . It was like carrying a large lump of ice to the North Pole. Still, I was sure it was my duty to tell them the facts personally and have it all out face to face with Stalin. . . .[3]

On hand to meet the Churchill party in Moscow was Molotov, with a sizable contingent of dignitaries. After a precision honor guard, short speeches, and the national anthems of the Big Three, Churchill and Moran were conveyed to a sumptuous villa in the Lenin Hills across the Moscow River, some eight miles from the Kremlin. (Harriman was to stay in the American Embassy.) Molotov was host. During the car trip Churchill, on winding down the window, discovered that the glass was two inches thick! The interpreter explained quietly, "The Minister thinks it is more prudent."

On arrival at State Villa No. 7, Churchill was intrigued by his new surroundings. Always one to appreciate creature comforts, he was quick to indulge in a luxurious hot bath. His large, resplendent military aide seemed to come from some princely czarist family. But Churchill would have little chance to partake of the liquors, wines, caviar, and other delicacies which had been amply provided. He had asked Molotov for a meeting with Stalin that evening, and Molotov had set the time for 7:00 P.M. Since they had landed at 5:00 P.M., the caviar and vodka would have to wait for another time.

At the appointed hour Churchill and Harriman were meeting with Joseph Stalin in circumstances far simpler than those at the villa. And the talk was direct.

The first hours of the meeting were downright uncomfortable, as Churchill had previously decided to let Stalin absorb all the bad news first before going on to the alternate Allied plan (TORCH). As this was his first meeting with Stalin, Churchill eyed the Marshal closely. He found the man impressive; soft-spoken, acute, and hard.

[3] Churchill, IV, 475.

The Prime Minister began by outlining the reasons why the Western Allies could not mount an invasion of northwestern France (SLEDGE-HAMMER) in 1942. The Americans and British would be willing, he said, to risk losing heavily, even 150,000 men, if such a sacrifice would take the pressure off the Soviets; but the Western leaders believed that such an expedition would be defeated by the Nazi forces already in France without need of reinforcement. At every point Stalin disagreed, finally conceding that he had no power to countermand the decisions of the Western Allies.

Churchill then outlined plans for bombing Germany. Stalin brightened a bit and recommended that the Allies bomb houses as well as factories. Churchill conceded only that destruction of houses would be an adjunct to misses on factories. Finally Churchill discerned a certain relaxation in the tension. (It had so far taken two hours.) Then—and only then—did he mention alternate Anglo-American plans.

As Churchill began describing TORCH, Stalin became interested. It was a sensible military operation, he conceded, but he had doubts about many of the political aspects—particuarly the assumption of French cooperation with an "American" invasion force. Stalin confessed dislike for De Gaulle, but he thought that De Gaulle's Free French would have more luck politically in North Africa than would the Anglo-Americans. As the conversation began to come to a close, Churchill was rewarded. Stalin leaned forward and summarized the benefits which could accrue:

First, [the invasion] would hit Rommel in the back; Second, it would overawe Spain; Third, it would produce fighting between Germans and Frenchmen in France; and, Fourth, it would expose Italy to the whole brunt of the war.[4]

Churchill then added a fifth to Stalin's list: the opening of the Mediterranean would shorten the length of time required to supply the Russians by way of the Persian Gulf Railroad. And given the bad situation of the Murmansk convoys, this railroad line would take on added significance in the Lend-Lease picture.

Churchill left the meeting at the Kremlin that night much encouraged, feeling that real progress had been made. Nevertheless, the next morning he was thinking of Stalin's attitude in a more sober vein. When they got together at noon, he said to Molotov that it would be "very unwise" for Stalin "to treat us roughly when we have come so far." Molotov answered non-committally that Stalin was a wise man.

*

During the evening of August 13, 1942, the military contingent of Churchill's party arrived, after having been subjected to some more of

4 Ibid., p. 482.

their pilot's acrobatics over the Moscow Airport. The entire British-American delegation met with Stalin at 11:00 P.M.

Churchill's previous uneasiness was now proving well founded. The tensions that had seemed to relax at the end of the previous evening's encounter were now restored. At the long table in a bare room, which resembled a "waiting station"—only a single picture of Lenin graced the wall—Stalin produced an intransigent memorandum which insisted once again that a second front was possible and necessary in 1942 and that the Allies had agreed to it.

Churchill refrained from answering this memo point by point. Instead he took it with the promise that he would answer it later in writing.

In the course of the evening Stalin gave vent to his criticism of the Western Allies, particularly the British, whom he accused of being afraid to fight the Germans on the ground. (If they really tried it, he added, they would find that it was not so bad.) Finally the Prime Minister's ire was aroused. He crashed his fist down on the table and held forth in what Brooke described as one of his greatest orations. He would excuse Stalin's remarks, he said bluntly, only because of the bravery of the Russian soldier.

Churchill talked too rapidly for his interpreter. From time to time he would stop and ask, "Did you tell him this? Did you tell him that?" Finally Stalin interrupted: "I don't understand what you're saying but by God I like your sentiment." From that time on the situation improved.

Churchill was somewhat bewildered by Stalin's turn of attitude, but Lord Cadogan was able to give him some reassurance. When Eden had been in Moscow the previous December (while Churchill was at the AR-CADIA Conference) they had encountered the same experience: Stalin was congenial the first evening and then changed course abruptly during the next.

Despite Cadogan's reassurance, Churchill was still ready to concede the conference as a failure and leave. When Stalin invited him for dinner the next evening, Churchill reluctantly accepted but specified that he would leave Moscow on the morning of the fifteenth. Stalin seemed taken aback. The evening ended with the future schedule still in doubt.

The next day Churchill was in low spirits, unable to visualize his mission as anything but a failure. While the military chiefs got together and discussed a new type of Soviet mortar (nothing came of a Soviet promise to send the details), Churchill brooded.

That evening at the Gelum Palace in the Kremlin, Stalin hosted his guests. The atmosphere was less lavish than customary, observers noted, despite the nineteen-course meal. Conversation between Stalin and Churchill was lively and frank but not always cordial. Stalin told of his encounter with Lady Nancy Astor and George Bernard Shaw some years earlier. Lady Astor had tried to excuse Lloyd George for the 1918 "intervention" in Russia on the basis that he had been misled by Churchill. Churchill admitted his own role and asked if Stalin had forgiven him. "All that is in the past," said Stalin. "And the past belongs to God."

Excusing himself early from the dinner—"early" meaning 1:30 A.M.— Churchill walked determinedly down the hall toward the exit. He found himself accompanied by an anxious Soviet Premier, who obviously did not want this visit to be a complete disaster.

On the evening of August 15 Churchill appeared at Stalin's office for a final conference. He found his host in a mellower mood. After an hour of useful talk, Stalin asked Churchill to come by his small apartment in the Kremlin for some drinks. Churchill responded that he was in principle always in favor of such a policy, and the two walked across the yard of the Kremlin—the entire enclosure covers only about fifty acres—and arrived at Stalin's apartment. There Stalin's daughter, Svetlana, gave her father a dutiful kiss and retired. Molotov joined them.

This evening, which finally lasted for seven hours, was friendly, marred only at one point by Stalin's criticism of the Royal Navy. Churchill reminded Stalin that he himself had some knowledge of naval warfare, to which Stalin retorted sarcastically that this remark meant that he knew nothing of it. In low key, Churchill explained that the Russian is a land animal and the Britisher is a sea animal. Stalin accepted the compromise. The talk was frank; Stalin even admitted at one point that the war was a small problem compared to collectivizing the Ukraine farms in the 1930s.

Churchill left at 2:30 A.M. Polish General Władysław Anders, who had been waiting at the guesthouse to discuss postwar Poland, was disappointed. But Churchill was satisfied.[5]

Without sleep, Churchill left straight for the airport. His whole party went non-stop to Teheran, where the comforts of the British Embassy did much to defray their exhaustion. From there they returned to Cairo, for visits to both Alexander and Montgomery. Churchill arrived back in London aboard Vanderkloot's *Commando* on the evening of Monday, August 24, 1942.

Winston Churchill had carried the hod for the Western Allies by undertaking a dangerous and often highly unpleasant trip to give the news on the Second Front directly to Soviet Marshal Stalin. He had also, in his own mind, established a "relationship."

[5] General Anders later turned up in Cairo at Churchill's request.

CHAPTER IX

THE MOST ANXIOUS MONTHS

Lieutenant General Dwight D. Eisenhower, while not yet officially appointed as Allied Commander for TORCH, was nevertheless charged with its planning. He therefore found himself faced with a challenge almost without precedent in warfare, an experiment to prove that the Allied concept would work. Whether or not he personally would eventually be given the command, Eisenhower did know that he would serve as the deputy. Therefore he set about doing what he would have expected any future commander to do: establishing a headquarters composed of both British and Americans. His own position could be defined later.

Since Churchill had proposed that the Allied Commander should be an American, the decision as to whether that officer would be Eisenhower was up to Roosevelt. Confirmation of Eisenhower's appointment came informally on August 6 to Churchill in Cairo. In the meantime the British staffs, simply presuming that Eisenhower was "it," at least for now, had acted accordingly.

*

In Washington General Marshall and Secretary of War Stimson were still unable to bring themselves to accept the London decision as final. Marshall conceded that SLEDGEHAMMER was canceled, but he could not reconcile himself to the suspension of BOLERO in favor of TORCH, which would render any cross-Channel invasion in 1943 impossible. He would, in fact, have preferred no American military action in 1942, to allow concentration on BOLERO. Word of Marshall's attitude reached

Roosevelt, who then declared firmly that he, "as Commander-in-Chief, had made the decision: TORCH would be undertaken at the earliest date." Marshall now gave up for good. Meanwhile Eisenhower, though aware of his chief's lingering doubts, had to assume that TORCH was going to be executed, and he went about his chores with renewed energy.

To begin the job of organizing a truly allied effort, Eisenhower's first problem was to create an integrated command team. While U.S. and British combat formations would usually fight independently, the supreme headquarters, which was to direct the subordinate national formations, would have to be manned about equally between Americans and British and its members indoctrinated to rise above national viewpoints. In contrast to Foch's *"famille militaire"* of World War I, composed almost entirely of Frenchmen, Eisenhower set about sandwiching personnel in authority so that no staff section would be dominated by either nationality.

He specified two exceptions to this principle. First of all, Major General Mark W. Clark, who had come to Britain to command II Corps, was now appointed as Eisenhower's deputy, with responsibilities for planning. An American was necessary, Eisenhower believed, to take over in case something should happen to him personally. In addition, Eisenhower wanted an American chief of staff. Since that key officer would often be acting for the commander, easy understanding and confidence could not wait to be developed. Eisenhower therefore prevailed on Marshall to release Brigadier General Walter Bedell Smith, currently Secretary of the War Department General Staff, to come to London to take the position. Valuable as Smith was to Marshall, the Chief of Staff gave him up.

Smith, a hard-driving, meticulous man, would be the perfect counterbalance to the more gregarious Eisenhower. Eisenhower could be harsh, as Ismay had noted, but he generally preferred to depend on persuasion. Smith's tough exterior and abrupt manner would serve as a constant reminder that the iron fist was always there.

But assignment of personnel at all other levels was only part of the task; the indoctrination in "allied" thinking would take time to develop and vigilance to maintain. Cooperation was not automatic; officers in different uniforms at first approached each other, Eisenhower wrote later, like "a bulldog meeting a tomcat."[1] And, not surprisingly, the burden of a conciliatory attitude had at first to be borne by the Americans, as Eisenhower's control of them was absolute and immediate. Fortunately, the story soon circulated of how Eisenhower made an example of an indiscreet American officer by sending him home for calling one of his counterparts a "British son of a bitch." The "SOB" term didn't bother him much—but the "British" did. This story may have grown out of the episode that

[1] Eisenhower, *Crusade*, p. 76.

Ismay witnessed earlier when Eisenhower was an American, not yet Allied, commander. Its truth was immaterial, however, so long as the members of headquarters believed it. They apparently did believe it—or considered it typical—for they soon tended to lose themselves in the problems at hand, rising above narrow nationalistic interests. This growing teamwork was heartening to all, especially to Eisenhower himself.

Organization of the British First Army was not Eisenhower's responsibility. But as Allied Commander he naturally held a keen interest in the personality of the senior British officer, especially since First Army, whose strength hardly justified the designation, would lead the initial attack from Algeria to Tunis. Thus Churchill was deeply chagrined that it was necessary, on August 6, to transfer General Montgomery from TORCH to Cairo when "Strafer" Gott was killed. The British First Army commander would now be Lieutenant General Sir Kenneth A. N. Anderson. Eisenhower had no complaints about Anderson—indeed he later considered him to be one of Britain's underrated soldiers. But when Ismay gave the news of a second change of First Army commanders in as many days, Eisenhower asked sadly, "Are the British really serious about TORCH?" The British understood Eisenhower's viewpoint—and they were indeed serious about TORCH.

On August 21, 1942, Admiral Mountbatten came into Eisenhower's office to discuss a dismal report on a recent raid, long planned by his Office of Combined Operations. A force, largely Canadian, had landed at Dieppe, a town about halfway between Normandy and the Pas de Calais in northwestern France. Of the five thousand Canadians and thousand British commandos who conducted this "reconnaissance in force," almost three thousand had been lost—six hundred were dead and nearly two thousand taken prisoner. In spite of the price the objective had not been reached. The public, kept in the dark as to the actual facts, was exhilarated by any news of action, but those charged with future landings realized that current techniques had a long way to go. The Allies learned lessons that partially justified the startling cost.

This was not the kind of landing that British and American planners expected to make in North Africa, especially since they hoped the French would not resist. The episode did, however, illustrate the difficulties that would have faced any major cross-Channel attack in 1942. In Cairo Brooke felt that his persistent opposition to SLEDGEHAMMER was vindicated.

Planning for TORCH did not, of course, wait for the return of Churchill from Moscow and Cairo, and the British and American military chiefs began considering the objectives of the attack. Four landing areas were selected for consideration. Three were within the Mediterranean: (1) Bône, about a hundred miles west of the ultimate objective of Tunisia; (2) Algiers, about halfway between Tunisia and Morocco; and (3) Oran, just within Algeria to the west. A fourth was Casablanca, on the Atlantic coast of French Morocco.

But since the Allies possessed forces adequate to land in only two or three of these places, the Combined Chiefs disagreed on which sites to select. And Eisenhower, not yet established with the authority he was later to enjoy, found his recommendations providing only the basis for discussion.

Eisenhower's inclination was to land as far east as possible; this meant including a landing at Bône or nearby Philippeville. By August 23, however, he had reached some conclusions that compelled him to warn the Combined Chiefs of prospective hazards. The strength of the expedition as planned lacked the power to seize Tunisia quickly. Determined French resistance would make reaching Tunisia ahead of the Germans and Italians impossible. Furthermore, Gibraltar itself was weak, and if the Spanish should enter the war—or allow the Germans to go through their territory —Gibraltar could be rendered useless. The Allied landing force in the Mediterranean would be cut off from the Atlantic.

Finally, Eisenhower concluded, his experts had convinced him that naval forces earmarked for the operation were insufficient. In the light of all this, he reluctantly concluded that Casablanca, on the Atlantic coast, should be included as one objective. Casablanca was one terminal of a railroad leading south of Spanish Morocco to Oran, and its possession could ensure a line of supply and retreat even if the Strait of Gibraltar should be closed.

The next day Eisenhower went to Whitehall to discuss this matter with the British Chiefs of Staff. He felt himself in "a hell of a pickle." The British, though respecting his arguments, were now advocating landings at both Casablanca and Philippeville, a thousand miles apart. Admiral Pound was also complaining about the paucity of the forces provided by the U. S. Navy. The British were concentrating all their efforts on the Murmansk run and on TORCH, even pulling two aircraft carriers out of the sensitive Indian Ocean. Pound thought the Americans could do better.

In a low frame of mind, fearful that his warnings could be construed as undue pessimism, Eisenhower returned to his office at 20 Grosvenor Square to prepare a dispatch to Marshall advising that the British Chiefs had agreed to include Casablanca. But the emphasis of the message lay in a plea for Marshall to approach King in hopes of securing more ships from the Pacific. If more U.S. naval forces could be provided, Eisenhower was willing to postpone the landings until November 7. Immediately Marshall answered: No, the Navy could spare no more ships from the Pacific.

*

Winston Churchill returned from his odyssey to Moscow and Cairo on the same day that Eisenhower was meeting with the BCOS. As soon as he had sent a report to Roosevelt covering his trip to Moscow, therefore, Churchill turned his entire energies toward TORCH. Thus began what he later described as the two "most anxious months of the war," with projected offensives in both Egypt and Northwest Africa, against the backdrop of a possibility that his government could be brought down at any time. The evening after his return he invited Eisenhower to dinner. Word had just come in that the American Joint Chiefs were now proposing to limit the entire TORCH operation to landings at Casablanca and Oran, eliminating Algiers. Eliminating Bône was bad enough, the two agreed, but such a retreat would be disastrous. Algiers was, after all, the center of pro-Allied sentiment in North Africa and closer to Tunisia. Churchill therefore cabled these views to Roosevelt, citing Eisenhower's support. Eisenhower likewise warned Marshall that abandonment of the landing at Algiers would eliminate any chance of reaching Tunisia before the Germans and Italians.

This was the period of the war in which Churchill and Eisenhower began their close relationship. Churchill continued inviting Eisenhower to lunch every Tuesday and to dinner every Friday, and he sought to build Eisenhower's position as Allied Commander. At one point in the backing and filling across the Atlantic he sent Roosevelt a message proposing to give Eisenhower complete latitude regarding landing sites in the Mediterranean. "You will start TORCH on October 14th, attacking with such troops as are available and at such places as you deem fit," he suggested. The time had not yet come when the Americans would be ready to give Eisenhower that much latitude.

The impasse regarding Casablanca versus Algiers continued for about a week. The evening after the dinner with Churchill, Eisenhower and Clark were keenly anticipating an American meal in Clark's room at the Dorchester Hotel. The treat that evening was to be the sausage that Sergeant Chaney, Clark's orderly, prided himself on. As he was about to leave 20 Grosvenor Square for the four-block walk, however, Eisenhower received word that the Prime Minister would like to see him. The disagreements had become so severe that Churchill was now contemplating another visit to Washington and he would like Eisenhower to accompany him. Eisenhower, of course, was willing, but as it turned out the trip never transpired. The two sides reached a compromise: somehow they would manage three landings: Casablanca, Oran, and Algiers.

At the end of August Roosevelt made a new proposal. In view of the antagonism of the Vichy French toward the British, perhaps the landing phase of the operation should be given an entirely American complexion. All the assault units would be American, even though many of them would be delivered in British vessels. Churchill was perfectly willing for the Americans to accept the political and military onus of the landings, though he doubted that the French could be fooled for long. Further, Churchill noted, this arrangement would render the British unable to do their part until the reinforcement phase. However, once the two agreed in principle to make the assault phase exclusively American, Churchill became enthusiastic. He even offered to put British troops in American uniforms. Soon, however, he dropped that idea.

In the strategic discussions across the Atlantic Eisenhower's views tended to parallel those of the British, probably because he was on the ground, working with the people who were going to do the job. He would have been astonished to realize that some of his colleagues in Washington were beginning to feel that he was being overly influenced by British viewpoints, particularly those of the Prime Minister.

Only one issue now remained to be settled at the political level. In early September 1942 Roosevelt sent Churchill the American view of troop strengths for the three assault landings:

- Casablanca, 58,000 US troops. (34,000 in the assault and 24,000 in follow-up.)

- Oran, 45,000 US troops. (25,000 in the assault and 20,000 in follow-up.)

- Algiers, 10,000 US troops in assault, followed within an hour by British troops, the size of follow-up to be determined by General Eisenhower.[2]

Churchill regarded this proposal as a step backward. To him the imbalance between the forces allocated for the Casablanca landing and those designated for Algiers indicated that the Americans had not yet accepted Algiers as vital. Immediately Churchill sent for Brooke, who was soon conferring with Eisenhower, Clark, and the British naval commander, Admiral Sir Bertram Ramsay. Together they concluded that the proposed Casablanca landings should be cut by 10,000 men and the Algiers landing

[2] Roosevelt to Churchill, September 2, 1942.

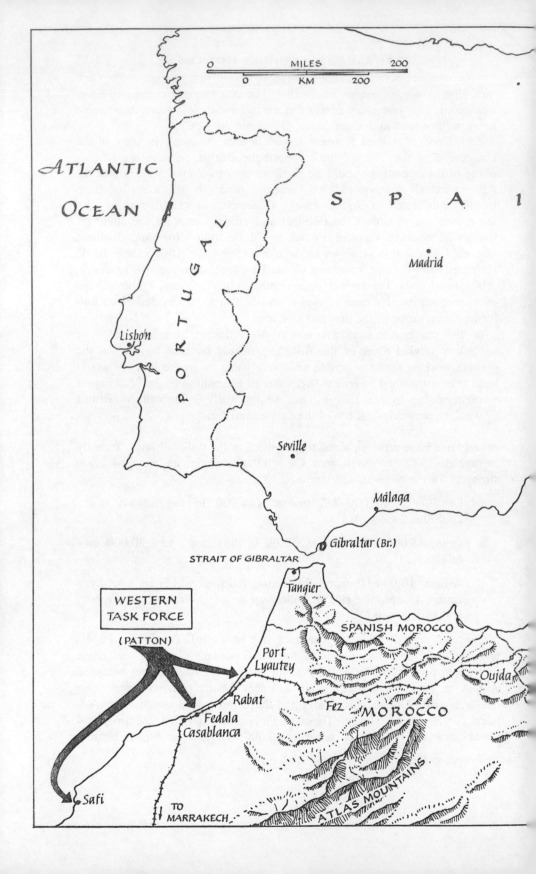

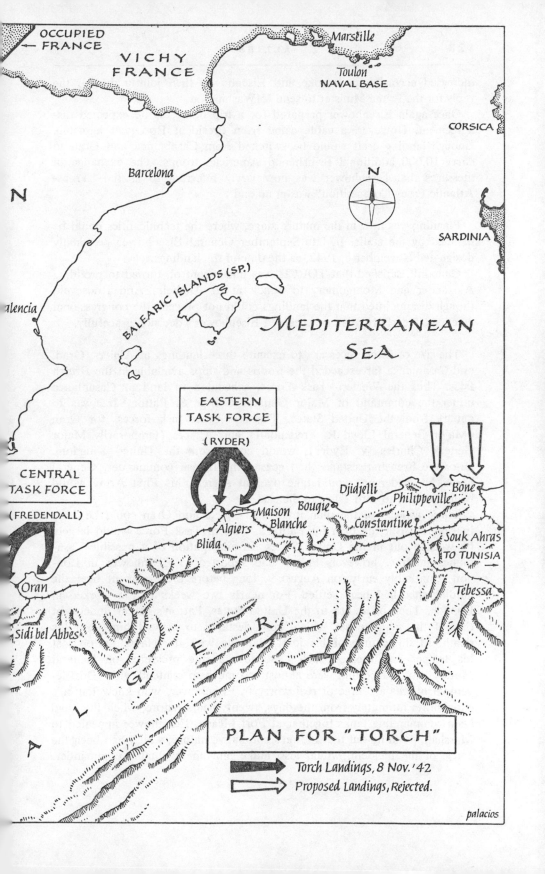

OCCUPIED
FRANCE

VICHY
FRANCE

Marseille

Toulon
NAVAL BASE

CORSICA

Barcelona

SARDINIA

N

Balearic Islands (SP.)

Valencia

MEDITERRANEAN
SEA

EASTERN
TASK FORCE

(RYDER)

CENTRAL
TASK FORCE

(FREDENDALL)

Djidjelli

Bône
Philippeville

Bougie
Maison
Blanche
Constantine

Souk Ahras
TO TUNISIA

Algiers
Blida

Oran

Tébessa

Sidi bel Abbes

A   L   G   E   R   I   A

PLAN FOR "TORCH"

Torch Landings, 8 Nov. '42
Proposed Landings, Rejected.

palacios

increased accordingly. Brooke and Eisenhower then jointly drafted the reply for the Prime Minister to send to Washington.

Once again Eisenhower prepared for a trip home, as he expected disagreement. However, a cable came from President Roosevelt agreeing. Enough landing craft would be switched from Casablanca and Oran to carry 10,000 additional British and American troops. The exchange of messages that Eisenhower was now wryly referring to as the "Trans-Atlantic Essay Competition" was at an end.

Planning was now in the mature stage, where the technicalities could be handled by the staffs. In late September General Eisenhower personally designated November 8, 1942, as the date of the landings.

Churchill, satisfied that TORCH was under control, turned to prodding Alexander and Montgomery to attack at El Alamein. And Roosevelt, though disappointed that the landings could not precede the congressional elections in early November, accepted Eisenhower's decision gracefully.

The size of force necessary to execute three landings at Algiers, Oran, and Casablanca far exceeded the troops and ships available in the British Isles. Thus the Western Task Force, scheduled to land at Casablanca under the command of Major General George S. Patton, Jr., was to debark from the United States. The two other task forces, for Oran (Major General Lloyd R. Fredendall) and Algiers (temporarily Major General Charles W. Ryder), would come from the United Kingdom. Once the French resistance had ceased the British commander, General K. A. N. Anderson, would take over at Algiers; his First Army would begin the race toward Tunis to the east.

Those aspects of the plan involving Algiers and Oran could be done in London. But the plan for Patton's Western Task Force would largely be worked out in the United States. In anticipation of a possible Casablanca landing, however, Patton had reported to Eisenhower in London remarkably early, on August 9, long before the argument over the landing sites had been settled. For nearly two weeks Patton worked in London. Then on return to the United States, Patton's career underwent one of the many crises which were destined to bedevil him until his death. In the course of his joint planning with the Navy, Patton lost his temper and created such a scene that the pressures on General Marshall to replace him were almost too much to contend with. This development was a source of real worry to Eisenhower, who knew Patton's capabilities intimately from the days, twenty years before, when they had been commanding tanks together at Fort Meade. Eisenhower appealed to Marshall, pointing out that Patton's combative nature, which had been the cause of the incident, would also make him an invaluable commander.

He suggested that "Georgie" be sent out of Washington so he could be with his troops. His chief of staff could deal with the Navy.[3]

Marshall, who likewise appreciated Patton's worth, barely succeeded in preserving his command, much to Eisenhower's relief.

*

Robert D. Murphy, U.S. consul general in Algiers, received unexpected instructions to report to Washington early in September 1942, about the time that Roosevelt and Churchill were agreeing on the broad landing plan for TORCH. Murphy was not the picture of a typical American diplomat. A tall, informal Irishman with thinning red hair, he had a face with a built-in, beaming smile. And the smile was genuine, for he liked people. On his other side Murphy had a native adroitness in manipulating difficult situations. His problem, such as it was, was that his liking for people sometimes overrode his adroitness.

He had served in Paris for some years before the war broke out. After the French surrender in June 1940 he had been chargé d'affaires in the Vichy embassy on that July day of 1940 when the Royal Navy seized the French vessels in England and Egypt and destroyed those at Mers-el-Kebir. Two months later Murphy had been summoned to Washington and transferred from Paris to North Africa as one of those "personal representatives" whom Roosevelt habitually sent out, men who reported directly to him. Thus his official title of "Consul General" was a cover; he was doing more important things. And though Murphy had originally regarded this job as temporary, he was still there two years later.

Starting in December 1940, Murphy had been able to work closely with a single French authority, the much-admired General Maxime Weygand. So prestigious was Weygand personally that, despite France's humiliation and the autocratic nature of the Vichy government, his position as Delegate General in North Africa was somehow treated as semi-autonomous. With Weygand's help, Murphy had begun to develop for the first time an appreciation for North Africa. Progressively he acquired the confidence of the various French leaders while at the same time coming to appreciate their power and potential usefulness.[4]

[3] Ismay described Patton's attitude: "Since the Americans had not as yet had any practical experience of amphibious operations, they asked us to lend them a couple of planning experts. Our officers found, on arrival, that the Admiral's [Hewitt] and General's [Patton] headquarters were miles apart and suggested that everyone working on plans which had to be so closely interlocked should be under the same roof. On this General Patton exploded. 'Go anywhere near that bunch of rattlesnakes? Not I!' " Ismay, pp. 264–65.

[4] "The more I learned the more I realized what a potentially explosive area this was and the more I was impressed with the skill with which French Administrators had retained control over these diverse and often hostile communities, even during years

Murphy was breaking new ground. One of his first tasks in early 1941 was to negotiate an aid pact between the United States and Vichy governments, which seemed on the face of it to be an unlikely thing. No legal bar stood to interfere with such an agreement, however, as both the United States and Vichy France were theoretically neutrals in a war between Britain and Germany. The United States hoped that rendering aid to North Africa might cause the authorities there to loosen ties with Vichy. The payment for the aid was to be provided from French funds impounded by the United States when the Nazis occupied the major part of France in June 1940.

This Murphy-Weygand Accord, signed in March 1941, ran into trouble from the beginning, and it was never effectively implemented, due largely to Churchill. The British Government actually had no quarrel with the pact in principle; but the Prime Minister's suspicion and contempt for Pétain, and any French military leaders who would serve under him, led him to oppose any American aid to North Africa without examination of each shipment by British inspectors. Since the British naval blockade was effective, the pact could not be implemented against their desires. On the other hand the North Africans wanted no British inspectors in their ports. The end result was an impasse, serving only to exacerbate the already bitter resentment against the British among the French North Africans.

Eventually the Nazis, spurred by the annoyingly independent attitude of Weygand, forced Pétain to remove him from his position as Delegate General. When Weygand retired in November 1941 it became impossible for Murphy to deal with a single authority, as Weygand's former semi-autonomous position was abolished.

The situation at Vichy was also cloudy. In 1940 Marshal Henri Philippe Pétain, then eighty-four years of age, had been arbitrarily installed by the Nazis as ruler of France. Though a revered French hero of World War I, Pétain was now considered nothing but a partially senile puppet, and he had never been in full control of the government. Power struggles among his entourage were an accepted characteristic of Vichy, and the more the American public learned of what was going on, the stronger feeling grew against all the participants, particularly against the blatantly collaborationist Pierre Laval.

At the time of Pearl Harbor Laval had been replaced as Pétain's deputy by one Admiral Jean François Darlan, a controversial character but not

---

of French defeat and occupation. What would these mixed up people do if French Africa should become a battleground? The answer, it seemed to me, was that only French Administrators already familiar with the complexities of variegated local situations could possibly maintain the order in French Africa." Murphy, *Diplomat Among Warriors*, pp. 97–98.

hated quite so strongly as Laval. Convinced, like Laval, that an eventual Allied victory in World War II was out of the question, Darlan had done what he could to negotiate the best possible bargains for what he considered a permanently subjugated France, at the same time furthering his own individual position with the Nazis.

In April 1942, however—as Marshall and Hopkins were stopping in Ireland en route home from London—word came that Darlan had been replaced and Laval was back in power.[5] At this point the U.S. ambassador, retired Admiral William D. Leahy, denounced the French action and recommended his own recall. Roosevelt agreed, and Leahy returned home to become the President's personal chief of staff in the White House.

Despite his ouster as Pétain's deputy, Admiral Darlan was appointed Commander-in-Chief of the Vichy Armed Forces. His control over the not-to-be-overlooked remainder of the French fleet was absolute. For, with all his drawbacks, Darlan had developed a secure reputation with the French Navy through his years of peacetime effort to modernize it. More recently he had secured the release of some 60,000 French sailors imprisoned by Hitler. The admiral was a force to be reckoned with.

Progressively, perhaps because of the influence of De Gaulle, American impatience with the Vichy regime grew despite Secretary of State Cordell Hull's so-called Vichy policy. And Murphy, convinced that American interests lay with Vichy officers, especially in North Africa, continued to plead with the American Government to avoid letting antagonism go too far. Just before Pearl Harbor he urgently cabled Roosevelt recommending that the United States not "slam the door in the face of the French." Murphy was thereafter typecast as a Vichy advocate in Washington.

Thus, on being summoned home in early fall of 1942, Murphy was not displeased. He could, he felt, espouse the cause of moderation better in person than at the end of a cable.

Murphy was greeted in Washington by his former associate Admiral Leahy, who was cheerful, anticipating that the long months the two had spent in building up French contacts would soon pay off. But before Leahy could go into the details of TORCH, President Roosevelt himself summoned Murphy to Hyde Park. An Army plane was waiting.

At Hyde Park Roosevelt and Hopkins, in shirt sleeves, greeted Murphy in the library of Roosevelt's family home. Though Murphy by now had a strong inkling that he was to set up a "fifth column" for an Allied invasion, Roosevelt had reserved to himself the pleasure of outlining the task.

In the course of the conversation Roosevelt emphasized his policy, which he consistently followed through the war, that the United States

[5] See p. 71 above.

had no right to decide on the composition of a future French Government. He refused to recognize any French group, including the Vichy regime, until the people could freely elect their own government. He realized that this position was anathema to General de Gaulle, whose preoccupation was and always would be to secure recognition for himself, but De Gaulle's anger was of little concern. More important in the short term was that present dealings with Frenchmen had to be confined to those willing to step aside once the war was won.

Roosevelt was enjoying this kind of intrigue, and he instructed Murphy to withhold all details even from the Secretary of State. Murphy's concern as a professional Foreign Service officer was dispelled only partially by Roosevelt's blithe assurance: "Don't worry; I'll take care of Cordell."

This novel *modus operandi* of reporting directly to the President and to an Army general (Eisenhower)—but not to the Secretary of State—was weird, necessitated by the need for secrecy. (Roosevelt had described the State Department as a "sieve.") But Murphy had no choice. He would play the game according to the President's rules or refuse the mission. Refusal, of course, was unthinkable.

After his brief meeting at Hyde Park, Murphy returned to Washington. General Marshall, Murphy found, had not yet overcome his basic resistance to the whole idea of TORCH; and he was carrying out this strategy only as a good soldier. And Marshall was strongly skeptical about the usefulness of Murphy's African contacts, unwittingly complicating Murphy's task by forbidding him from taking even the most trusted Frenchmen into his confidence. Since those helping Murphy were to be kept in the dark, their ability to assist the Anglo-Americans would be severely restricted. Marshall, however, remained adamant. On one thing the two agreed: Murphy should visit General Eisenhower in London, as he was now really part of the TORCH team.

A certain practical problem presented itself in arranging Murphy's trip to London: his face was now well known to Axis intelligence. If he were to be recognized with Eisenhower by French and German agents, the enemy would be alerted that something was brewing in North Africa. Marshall had an answer: Robert D. Murphy, Esquire, was now designated Lieutenant Colonel McGowan, USA, and decked out in Army uniform. "After all," Marshall snorted, "nobody notices a lieutenant colonel."

*

From Washington Murphy flew to London. He arrived a little earlier than expected, and his appearance on the scene caused some confusion for Eisenhower and his staff. The commanding general's naval aide, Harry C. Butcher, was interrupted at a pleasant luncheon and dispatched to pick up General Clark, whom he was to drive down to Eisenhower's rented hideaway south of London. Eisenhower would head for Telegraph Cottage, as it was known, while Bedell Smith met Murphy at the airport. A small group would have an informal dinner at the cottage, after which they would be joined by Ambassador John G. Winant and Special Representative W. Averell Harriman.

When Butcher arrived at Telegraph Cottage late that afternoon he found his boss and Murphy, who looked self-conscious in his ill-fitting uniform, sitting out in the rose garden, talking intensely, oblivious to the beauties of the mild September day. Though guests came and went, the essentially two-sided conversation went on until the early morning hours.

Eisenhower, Murphy found, was as unhappy with the prospects of TORCH as was Marshall. Like the Chief of Staff, Eisenhower disliked mounting an operation which was essentially a diversion and at the same time full of inponderables. During this brief period, however, Murphy was able to supply a great deal of information which Eisenhower needed, whether it gave him comfort or not.[6] As of then, for example, Murphy believed that substantial French resistance to an Anglo-American landing was very possible. And making contact with various powerful figures was difficult. But whom could the Allies look to as one capable of preventing or halting French resistance to the landing? The ones most likely, Murphy believed, were General Auguste Noguès, French Commander-in-Chief, Casablanca (who also held the position of Moroccan Foreign Minister); General Henri Honoré Giraud; and Admiral Jean François Darlan. Of these three, Giraud seemed to offer most promise as a temporary leader of the North African French.

General Giraud was a prominent soldier whose appearance, dignity, and valor made him almost the prototype of the ideal French soldier. He had, in his career, escaped from the Germans twice, first as a captain in World War I. As commander of the French Ninth Army in 1940 he had been taken prisoner along with many other French generals. This time the French Intelligence Service helped him escape from the German prison camp of Königstein, and though the armistice of 1940 had theoretically

[6] "That African venture was probably more unpalatable to Eisenhower than any other assignment in his distinguished career. The General disliked almost everything about the expedition: its diversion from the central campaign in Europe; its obvious risks in vast untried territory; its dependence upon local forces who were doubtful at best and perhaps treacherous; its bewildering complexities involving deadly quarrels among French factions, and Spanish, Italian, Arab, Berber, German and Russian politics. Eisenhower listened with a kind of horrified intenseness to my description of the possible complications. Perhaps some of the things I said were as incomprehensible to him as military mapping and logistics would have been to me. The General seemed to sense that this first campaign would present him with problems running the entire geopolitical gamut—it certainly did." Murphy, p. 104.

made non-occupied France a sanctuary, Giraud was finding it prudent to live clandestinely in Lyon. This escape was doubly significant; it established him as a symbol of French defiance and it also left him independent of Vichy and the Nazis. Other French generals had secured release by signing pledges not to bear arms against their conquerors; not so Giraud.[7] Finally, the general showed no interest in politics. By all logic, Giraud seemed to be the man behind whom the French in North Africa could rally—if only he could be produced.

At the time of Murphy's visit to Washington and London, however, the name of Admiral Jean François Darlan was also being discussed. Darlan's convictions regarding Nazi invincibility had been shaken, and he seemed to be making feelers toward the Allies. He had an emissary, one Admiral Raymond Fenard, who had contacted Murphy the previous May, just after Darlan's ouster as Pétain's deputy. Fenard had assured Murphy that, contrary to American belief, Darlan did indeed control all the French armed forces, not just the Navy. Murphy had reported this encounter to Washington, but it had been ignored.

But while Darlan was not tarred with the same brush as Pierre Laval, he was still regarded in London and Washington as at least a somewhat unsavory opportunist. The fact that he had, as Pétain's former deputy, sent Rommel 1,000 trucks, 100,000 tons of wheat, and 4 million gallons of gasoline had not been forgotten.[8] Given an alternative, the Allies would have preferred to deal with someone else.

After a brief stay in Washington Murphy flew to Casablanca by way of Lisbon, arriving in mid-October. He then resumed his double life, outwardly passive (as a consul general) but clandestinely at top speed. Within hours of landing at Casablanca he was in contact with General Noguès, describing a vast American force which would land in North Africa to cooperate with the French. As Murphy had feared, however, Noguès was uncooperative. His command, he exclaimed, would resist the invaders with all forces available. Murphy could understand. He knew that Noguès had gone through the same soul searching in June 1940 as had the rest of the French generals. Like many of them, he had finally elected to obey his civilian superiors and stay on duty, a decision which he had found extremely difficult. Having made the choice, however, Noguès had resolved to honor his pledge, perhaps more stubbornly than if it had been easy.[9]

With Noguès now eliminated from consideration as a possible supporter among the French, Murphy could at least look to General Emile Marie

[7] Grigg, p. 42, says Giraud eventually did sign such a pledge. However, this is what the Americans believed, and Giraud acted as a completely free man.
[8] Pendar, *Adventure in Diplomacy*, p. 66.
[9] See Murphy, pp. 111–12.

Béthouart, the divisional commander at Casablanca, who had been an Allied friend from the beginning. The attitude of Béthouart was exactly opposite to that of Noguès; he had, in fact, resolved that when the Allies landed he would attempt to make Noguès a prisoner.

Murphy spent the rest of his time at Casablanca making contact with M. Jacques Lemaigre-Dubreuil, a man who because of his commercial interests was permitted to travel freely from Dakar to Dunkirk. Lemaigre-Dubreuil could reach Giraud and he agreed to make a special trip to do so. Then, on about October 16, Murphy arrived back in Algiers and immediately contacted General Charles E. Mast, deputy commander of the French XIX Corps and considered Giraud's representative. Through Mast and Lemaigre-Dubreuil Murphy might get some idea of Giraud's attitude. Time was running short as Darlan, the other possibility, was becoming more active in probing his future should an Allied expedition materialize.

Thus Murphy began a barrage of messages to Eisenhower and, through the War Department, to Roosevelt. The main themes throughout these messages were (1) that the North African situation was not simple, (2) that Darlan was making overtures to join the Allied cause, and (3) that he, Murphy, needed help from General Eisenhower's headquarters. Mast and Giraud were demanding reassurances from the highest authority.

*

Major General Mark Wayne Clark, Deputy Allied Force Commander, had set a policy for his own office that all personnel should come in late (10:00 A.M.) on Sunday mornings. Therefore on Sunday, October 18, he followed his own dictum and arrived at Norfolk House too late to peruse the text of an intriguing message from Marshall to Eisenhower. For as he sat down at his desk the phone was ringing. Eisenhower wanted him at 20 Grosvenor Square.

The telegram that Clark had glanced at was only one of the many traversing the Atlantic that day. First was a report from Murphy of Darlan's offer (through representatives) to deliver the French fleet "under certain circumstances." Another was a report on Murphy's conversations with Mast. But the message that excited Clark was one requesting a high-level officer to meet with Murphy and French officials in North Africa the night of Wednesday, October 21, only three days away. Though fully aware of the heavy risks involved, Clark had determined, while riding the two miles across town to Grosvenor Square, that this was a job he wanted to do.

Wayne Clark would be ideal for such a mission. Young (forty-six years old), tough, ambitious, shrewd, and thoroughly knowledgeable, he could represent Eisenhower (and through him both governments) with authority. He had also earned the confidence of Churchill. Since Eisenhower himself could not go, Clark decided instantly that he was the man.

On his arrival in Eisenhower's office, Clark practically pre-empted the decision as to who would be selected. He merely asked, "When do I go?"

"Probably right away."

Eisenhower and Clark had no need to discuss the importance of this task, for the question of the French attitude was the greatest imponderable in the whole risky TORCH venture. Supplies could be procured; troops could be processed and delivered; landing places could be selected on the basis of fairly concrete facts; but the resistance to be expected from the French still had to be explored. Accordingly, the Prime Minister would have to know right away.

Time was too short for Eisenhower to observe amenities of protocol. Churchill was spending his usual weekend at Chequers, but Eisenhower felt it necessary to interrupt. Clark soon had Ismay on the line. "A message," Clark said, "has arrived from Washington. It's too hot to talk about over the telephone." Ismay passed the telephone to Churchill and Eisenhower came on at Grosvenor Square. At first an irritated Prime Minister balked and insisted that Eisenhower could talk, as the telephone was "secret." Eisenhower refused to disclose his subject and insisted that he and Clark were too busy to run up to Chequers.

Finally Churchill grunted, "All right, I'll meet you at No. 10 this afternoon."

Eisenhower and Clark spent the rest of the morning and early afternoon studying the messages from General Marshall and sending back their own. It was urgent to obtain the American Government's view on some of the questions that had been bothering Murphy. Addressing the problem of the Giraud-Darlan relationship, Eisenhower had come up with a compromise:

> Giraud to be recognized as our principal collaborator on the French side, with the proposal that he accept the position immediately of French Governor of all French North Africa. . . . Giraud to be requested to make proper contacts with Darlan and to accept him as Commander-in-Chief of French military and/or naval forces in North Africa or in some similar position that will be attractive to Darlan.

But since Giraud had demanded that he personally be designated as supreme commander for the entire Allied expedition, Eisenhower said:

> In order to satisfy these French leaders as to ultimate Allied intentions, we intend further to propose that eventually the entire military

command of all North Africa pass to the French . . . which it is calculated will require a sufficient length of time (certainly several
months). . . .

In this message Eisenhower also advised Marshall of the pending after-
noon meeting with Churchill, at which time he would attempt to obtain
British approval on these proposals. Finally he wrote that he was sending
Clark, with four assistants, to depart by way of Gibraltar that evening.[10]

The two Americans entered 10 Downing Street that afternoon to find
Churchill full of enthusiasm. Arrayed along his side were an entourage
which included Attlee, Mountbatten, Pound, Brooke, and Anthony Eden.
As Eisenhower summarized the prospects held out by the Murphy message, Churchill broke into a big grin behind his cigar. "This is great!" he
kept repeating.

Being a man who loved adventure, the Prime Minister tended to become absorbed at times in the dramatic physical details of the mission.
But Eisenhower kept pressing him on one specific point: how much would
Clark be allowed to tell the French about TORCH? The answer was
about the same as the Americans had agreed on, that discussions should
be centered around the *principle* of the operation, not the details. No
French generals were reliable enough to be trusted with information as to
timing. French antagonisms were so strong that no individual's exact loyalties could be counted on.

When the question of Darlan came up, Churchill was open-minded, as
he, along with Roosevelt, was yearning for control of the French fleet. "If
I could meet Darlan, much as I hate him," Churchill exclaimed, "I would
cheerfully crawl on my hands and knees for a mile if by doing so I could
get him to bring that fleet of his into the circle of Allied forces."[11] Churchill and the Americans grossly underestimated the intensity of anti-
Darlan feelings in both Britain and United States. There was, as Murphy
later recorded, "no thought in the minds of American War Planners that a
'Darlan Deal' would not be acceptable in Washington."[12]

At the end of the meeting Churchill turned to Clark: "The entire resources of the British Commonwealth are at your disposal," he said. "I
want to assure you once more how important it will be to get this infor-

[10] Those in Clark's party included Brigadier General Lyman L. Lemnitzer, head of
Allied Force Plans Section; Colonel A. L. Hamblen, a shipping supply expert; Captain Jerauld Wright, U. S. Navy liaison officer; and Colonel Julius C. Holmes, a
State Department officer in uniform. Eisenhower to Marshall, Cable ⚓3711, 17 October 1942.
[11] Eisenhower, *Crusade,* p. 105.
[12] Murphy, p. 118.

mation and to cut down French resistance. . . . Keep in mind that we will back you up in whatever you do."[13]

*

The cables from Washington had set the rendezvous point on the night of October 21 at an isolated villa at Messelmoun on the African coast, some fifteen miles west of Cherchel (in turn about sixty miles west of Algiers). To reach it would require a tight schedule with precious little time to make preparations. Fortunately, security would be no problem as Clark was supposed to accompany Eisenhower to Scotland. By staying behind, ostensibly to follow Eisenhower later, Clark would not draw undue attention. Thus, when Clark and his party departed for Polbrook Air Base that Sunday evening they caused no speculation. As the trip was going to be dangerous, and the unpleasant possibility of capture always present, Clark penned a short note to his wife for delivery in case he should fail to return.

The Flying Fortresses were unable to get off the ground at dusk because of foul weather, but early in the morning of October 19 the weather cleared. They were off by 6:30 A.M. The two bombers flew most of the way over heavy clouds, and as they approached Gibraltar their occupants were relieved to see British Spitfires scrambling. These were the first B-17s ever to land on the short Gibraltar air strip but they got in safely. Once on the ground, the Americans were required to leave their coats and caps on the plane. The Spanish border was only three hundred yards away, close enough for the always present Nazi agents to recognize the rank insignia. And the novel Fortresses would undoubtedly attract attention. The curtains in the car were pulled to hide the visitors' faces.

While at Gibraltar, Clark assessed the situation with concern. The delay in getting off at Polbrook had made it problematical that H.M.S. Seraph, a small, slow British submarine, could ever cover the four hundred miles to Cherchel by the evening of October 21, only forty-eight hours away. He derived no comfort either from the pessimistic attitude of the local British officers, particularly the governor, Lieutenant General Sir F. N. Mason-MacFarlane. Clark had no authority to call off the mission, but he did cable Washington to request that the conferees return to the appointed spot the night of October 22 if the party should fail to arrive on the twenty-first.

With these gloomy prospects, therefore, Clark was relieved when he talked to Lieutenant Norman A. A. ("Bill") Jewell, the youthful commander of the Seraph. "I am sure we can get you in there and get you off

[13] Clark, *Calculated Risk,* p. 72.

again," Jewell assured him. His confidence was a relief after the skeptical generals and admirals. They boarded the *Seraph* and left without delay.

The quarters on the *Seraph* were cramped, especially for a tall man, but the hospitable British crew refreshed the American party's spirits. They had no knowledge of the purpose of the trip, of course, except that it was a "screwy mission with some Americans." Jewell had calculated that in order to make the trip in time they would have to go part of the way on the surface, which would allow them to clock some ten or twelve knots in contrast to two or three submerged. Traveling in this fashion was dangerous and rough—but necessary.

The journey, though uncomfortable, was relatively uneventful. For part of Tuesday, the twentieth, Jewell had to keep the *Seraph* submerged, as the craft was running close to the African coast. The passengers amused themselves by playing bridge, and at one point were instructed by the three British commandos, who were part of the crew for this purpose, in techniques of embarkation on the small canvas kayaks that they would later use.

Thanks to Jewell's precise calculations, the *Seraph* came within sight of the proposed rendezvous point during the early morning hours of October 21. Jewell and Clark could spot a light from a building—the identification of the rendezvous point—but they dared not risk a landing. After such a long trip across the western end of the Mediterranean the most experienced navigator could easily miss the target by a mile or so; furthermore, dawn was near at hand. The party was therefore forced to spend the entire day submerged. The air was foul. One of the crewmen lit a match; the flame went out for lack of oxygen. Lyman Lemnitzer coined the phrase "The Longest Day" long before Erwin Rommel in Normandy.

The *Seraph* lay far enough out from shore, however, to permit communications with Gibraltar. After some confusion a message came to the effect that Murphy and the French would occupy the house on the nights of both October 21 and 22, thus giving Clark and his party two tries. And while he sat in the discomfort of the submerged submarine, Clark was well aware that some of the units under General Patton had that day embarked from the United States, bound for Casablanca.

When evening fell, it began to look as if the plans for that night had fallen through. Disconsolate, Clark gave up and tried to get some sleep. At midnight he was aroused. The house on the shore had turned on its seaward light. Jewell pulled the *Seraph* up to within a couple of hundred yards of the shore, and the Americans, assisted by the three commandos, made it to the beach. Once ashore, they rushed through the blackness to the bluffs, carrying their gear and their kayaks with them.

From the darkness they heard a voice: "Welcome to North Africa," said Robert Murphy, alias Lieutenant Colonel McGowan. "Damn glad we made it," said Clark.

The villa on the bluff has been described as "typical of the region." It was built of solid materials around a courtyard, roomy and with a full second floor. Its owner, M. Henri Tessier, was edgy. He had found a pretext to send his Arab servants away, but they could return without warning. After the landing boats were locked up in a room off the courtyard, however, the American visitors found places to collapse for a couple of hours. The three commandos were hidden on the top floor. Even the French conferees should not see them for fear of destroying the carefully nurtured impression that only Americans were involved in this whole enterprise.

General Mast arrived on schedule at 5:00 A.M. after the seventy-five-mile drive from Algiers. Murphy aroused Clark, and the three conferred over a continental breakfast. Clark was ill at ease since he was unable to be frank with Mast on the timing of the expedition, and he did not enjoy being restricted to presenting the concept only in hypothetical terms. To make the prospect attractive, however, he deliberately gave an exaggerated figure of half a million Allied troops, including two thousand planes.[14]

Clark was encouraged that Mast's recommendations regarding the most favorable landing spots corresponded roughly to Allied plans, except for Mast's inclusion of one in southern France. Further, Mast affirmed that, if the Germans should become suspicious and try to invade North Africa before the Americans, the French would resist with all they had.

On the gloomy side, however, Mast continued to reiterate Giraud's insistence on the appointment of a French supreme commander, which he regarded as necessary to the honor and prestige of the nation. To this Clark could only stall, saying truthfully that the Allies hoped to turn complete military control of the area over to the French as soon as possible.

When it came to the subject of Darlan, Mast claimed that Giraud wanted no affiliation with the admiral. Thus, for Murphy, this hazardous meeting solved very little except to reassure each side that the other meant business. To the military planners, however, the information on French troop dispositions, installations, and gas dumps obtained was invaluable. Best of all, however, was Mast's confirmation that the basic Allied plan was sound.[15]

---

[14] Actually only 112,000 Americans and British came ashore at the first landings. Later, naturally, the force did build up.

[15]

    a. In our planning of TORCH our intelligence information was practically nil —both the US and British had very little or no military intelligence of French North Africa. Accordingly, we had to plan the invasion practically in the dark.

FRANKLIN DELANO ROOSEVELT (1882–1945) President of the United States, serving an unprecedented third term in office. Inaugurated in 1933, his preoccupation during the first two terms had been the fight against the Great Depression. Since 1940 his attention had been devoted to America's role in preserving Western civilization from Nazi tyranny. WIDE WORLD PHOTOS

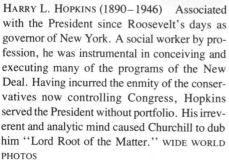

HARRY L. HOPKINS (1890–1946) Associated with the President since Roosevelt's days as governor of New York. A social worker by profession, he was instrumental in conceiving and executing many of the programs of the New Deal. Having incurred the enmity of the conservatives now controlling Congress, Hopkins served the President without portfolio. His irreverent and analytic mind caused Churchill to dub him ''Lord Root of the Matter.'' WIDE WORLD PHOTOS

WILLIAM D. LEAHY (1875–1959) A retired four-star admiral, Leahy was appointed American ambassador to the Vichy government in 1940 in the forlorn hope that his military background would give him special rapport with the aging Marshal Pétain. His mission finished shortly after the beginning of this narrative, Leahy served as chief of staff to the President, ex-officio chairman of the Joint Chiefs. U.P.I.

WINSTON LEONARD SPENCER CHURCHILL (1874–1965) British Prime Minister since May 1940, taking office just as Hitler's panzers were overrunning France. As First Lord of the Admiralty in World War I and as the foremost advocate of resistance to Hitler between wars, Churchill had come to embody the best militant qualities of Britain. His days of greatest personal acclaim were behind him by the time this narrative begins, but his grasp of military affairs and his hold on the British populace rendered him still indispensable to the British and the Allied cause. (Photo taken December 30, 1941.) © KARSH, OTTAWA, WOODFIN CAMP

JAN CHRISTIAAN SMUTS (1870–1950) Field Marshal and Prime Minister of the Union of South Africa, Jan Christiaan Smuts once, during the Boer War, enjoyed the distinction of holding Winston Churchill prisoner. Since then the two had become fast friends, and Churchill rarely made a major decision without consulting his onetime enemy. © KARSH, OTTAWA, WOODFIN CAMP

SIR HASTINGS LIONEL ISMAY (1887–1965) General Sir Hastings Ismay was never mentioned in headlines because his value as military assistant to the Prime Minister made him irreplaceable in that role. Perhaps this was well, for as a field commander "Pug" Ismay might have been too genial. But as a "bridge" to the Americans his contributions to the Allied cause were far greater than those of more lustrous fame. WIDE WORLD PHOTOS

GEORGE C. MARSHALL (1880–1959)
Appointed Chief of Staff, U. S. Army, in 1939,
General George C. Marshall found himself in a
position of leadership among the Americans at
the time of Pearl Harbor. This he had reached
not only because of his rank but because he controlled the largest single fighting formation of
the Western Allies. Aloof and rigidly self-disci-
plined, Marshall exercised his leadership with
diplomacy and tact. Churchill once referred to
Marshall as the "noblest Roman of them all."
More significant was the label "Architect of
Victory." U. S. ARMY

ERNEST J. KING (1878–1956) A true
"sailor's sailor," Admiral "Ernie" King had
no serious rivals as the best-qualified admiral in
the U. S. Navy. His expertise extended from
submariner to line officer to naval aviator. His
temper and toughness were legendary: Roosevelt said jokingly that he shaved every morning
with a blowtorch. Affable, even charming in private; his preoccupations were undisguisedly
directed toward defeat of Japan in the Pacific,
where he waged what was sometimes referred to
as his "own private war." U. S. ARMY

HENRY H. ARNOLD (1886–1950) Lieutenant
General Henry H. ("Hap") Arnold was a pio-
neer and proponent of long-range strategic air
power. Genial, as his nickname implies, Arnold
was somewhat hampered in his role as a member
of the Joint Chiefs by his subordination to Marshall. Under his command, the Army Air Forces
grew more rapidly than any other single formation in the war. The overwhelming air power
that made OVERLORD possible was due in no
small measure to this unpretentious man's
efforts. U. S. ARMY

SIR ALAN F. BROOKE (1883–1963) General
Sir Alan Brooke, Chief of the Imperial General
Staff (CIGS), was new in this position when the
narrative begins. A superb commander, but
sharp-tongued and impatient of anyone who disagreed with his views, Brooke was certain to
clash with the American naval chief Ernest
King. But Brooke served well as a professional
balance wheel for his mercurial and imaginative
Prime Minister. Those who knew him well considered him the most capable of all British generals. U.P.I.

SIR (ALFRED) DUDLEY POUND (1877–1943)
Appointed Admiral of the Fleet and First Sea
Lord in 1939, Admiral Sir Dudley Pound exercised direct, detailed control over the Royal
Navy throughout four years of World War II. By
the time of Pearl Harbor, he was beginning to
tire, and the position of chairman of the British
Chiefs of Staff Committee passed to the newly
appointed CIGS, Brooke, without prejudice to
Pound. As the victor in the Battle of the Atlantic, however, his position remained secure until
his untimely resignation and subsequent death.
U. S. ARMY

SIR CHARLES F. A. PORTAL (1893–1971)
Chief of the Air Staff at the age of forty-seven,
former head of British Bomber Command,
"Peter" Portal was one of the most capable of
the high-ranking Allied officers. Personally, he
was bookish and reserved, even mysterious.
Open-minded toward new ideas, Portal modified his preference for strategic air operations
when necessary to support land operations. Like
Ismay, Portal was popular with the Americans,
and he could present the British viewpoint
lucidly but without causing offense. U. S. ARMY

SIR JOHN G. DILL (1881–1944) Somewhat
older than his colleagues on the BCOS, Field
Marshal Sir John Dill had succeeded General
Ironside as CIGS in May 1940. His realism pro-
voked conflict with Churchill, who at that stage
of the war felt forced to carry on through hope
alone. Furthermore, Dill found that coping with
Churchill's nighttime hours was beginning to
damage his health, and he was relieved as CIGS,
without prejudice, in December 1941. Assigned
to represent the BCOS in Washington, Dill's
years of greatest service were still ahead of him
when this story begins. U. S. ARMY

CORDELL HULL (1871–1955) Perhaps owing to his Tennessee mountain background, Hull was the temperamental opposite of the President he served as Secretary of State from 1933. In 1940 Hull adhered to a policy of cooperation with the Pétain regime in Vichy France, and he summarily dismissed the pretensions of Charles de Gaulle. Hull remained in office though he gradually lost Roosevelt's confidence, as the President grew to rely more on other men. © KARSH, OTTAWA, WOODFIN CAMP

ANTHONY EDEN (1897–1977) Young, energetic, handsome, Anthony Eden quickly became a symbol of Britain's Conservative Party and of resistance to Nazism. In 1938 he electrified the British by resigning as Foreign Secretary under Neville Chamberlain over the notorious Munich agreement with Hitler. Brought back when Churchill became Prime Minister, Eden enjoyed Churchill's full confidence. Churchill hated to make any important decision without Eden's advice. © KARSH, OTTAWA, WOODFIN CAMP

W. AVERELL HARRIMAN (1891–) A converted Democrat and chairman of the board of Union Pacific Railroad, Averell Harriman had been regarded as a link between the New Deal and business. In 1941 the President sent him to London as administrator of the new Lend-Lease program, during which time, in September 1941, he visited Moscow with Lord Beaverbrook. Roosevelt often counted on Harriman as one who could represent him faithfully as an emissary to Churchill or Stalin. U. S. ARMY

VYACHESLAV M. MOLOTOV (1890–) An old-line Bolshevik; Molotov's brusque manner earned him the nickname "The Hammer." His signing of the Molotov-Ribbentrop Pact in 1939, which made possible the Nazi invasion of Poland, was of course Stalin's policy, but it was associated with Molotov's name. A survivor, Molotov remained in his post as Foreign Minister until well into the 1950s. U.P.I.

DWIGHT D. EISENHOWER (1890–1969) Young for his fast-growing responsibilities, Dwight Eisenhower had, up to the age of fifty-one, followed a seemingly routine Army career; he was promoted to the grade of colonel only nine months before Pearl Harbor. Though his Army record was nearly impeccable, he had been denied much peacetime command. During World War I he had remained in the United States. As assistant to General Douglas MacArthur in the Philippines during the 1930s, Eisenhower had a detailed knowledge of defense plans and was brought, much against his will, into War Plans a week after Pearl Harbor. U. S. ARMY

SIR HAROLD R. L. ALEXANDER (1891–1969) A man of wide experiences from the time of World War I and the expeditionary forces sent to Siberia, General Sir Harold R. L. Alexander faced defeat or victory with equanimity. Defeat at first seemed the rule: after Dunkirk he commanded the ill-fated defense of Burma. In both cases he performed so well that he became a favorite of Churchill's. His modest manner helped him to get along well with Americans, who would have vastly preferred him over Montgomery as British commander on D-Day. U. S. ARMY

SIR ARCHIBALD WAVELL (1883–1950) General Sir Archibald Wavell was an unlucky man, but one who never lost the respect of peers and superiors because of his stoicism in the face of impossible situations. As Commander-in-Chief, Middle East, Wavell's initial success against the Italians was thwarted after the arrival in North Africa of a German force under Erwin Rommel. Wavell was at his post in New Delhi when Pearl Harbor was attacked. But his days of performing impossible tasks were not yet over. U.P.I.

SIR ANDREW B. CUNNINGHAM (1883–1963) A courageous, fighting admiral, Cunningham was also a pleasant man and an effective diplomat in difficult situations. During the dark days of 1940, while parts of the French fleet were sinking in Oran Harbor, Cunningham, utilizing the arts of persuasion, was taking over the remainder of the fleet in Alexandria. Eisenhower, one of his many admirers, later wrote: "He was the Nelsonian type of admiral. He believed that ships went to sea in order to find and destroy the enemy. He thought always in terms of attack, never of defense." WIDE WORLD PHOTOS

SIR ARTHUR TEDDER (1890–1967) Quiet, personally unassuming, Air Chief Marshal Sir Arthur Tedder did not suffer fools easily. But Churchill took his matter-of-fact ways as cynicism, and Auchinleck was barely able to rescue Tedder's command in the Middle East in late 1941. A year later, however, Tedder had gained air supremacy, making victory at El Alamein possible. A severe critic of Bernard L. Montgomery, Tedder frankly named his postwar memoir *With Prejudice*. U.P.I.

GEORGE S. PATTON, JR. (1885–1945) The personification of flamboyance, Major General George Patton was an effective field commander whose high-strung nature accounted for his most dashing exploits and his periodic disgraces. His great personal wealth had allowed him to view the Army throughout his career as an intriguing hobby. Because of his zest for the pursuit role of cavalry, Patton was considered irreplaceable by his superiors. Only that would save him from losing his command on several occasions. U. S. ARMY

LUCIAN K. TRUSCOTT, JR. (1895–1965) Tough and aggressive, but of modest demeanor, Brigadier General Lucian K. Truscott represented the best of the U. S. Army officer corps. Though he lacked the contacts which come with a West Point diploma, Truscott was known in peacetime as one of the Army's finest polo players. But at Fort Lewis, Washington, in 1941, his remarkable professional competence came to the attention of Dwight Eisenhower, who concluded that Truscott was up to any job that could be given him. His responsibilities would grow accordingly. U. S. ARMY

SIR BERNARD L. MONTGOMERY (1887–1976) General Sir Bernard L. Montgomery, the British officer the Americans loved to hate, was nevertheless a competent commander. As a division commander under Brooke during Dunkirk, "Monty" so impressed the future CIGS that Brooke never lost an opportunity to further Montgomery's personal career. Egocentric and tactless to the point of cruelty, Montgomery's self-assurance, when he came to the fore, was welcomed by the war-weary British. Alexander would later write: "Personally, I owe Monty a lot—as we all do." WIDE WORLD PHOTOS

HENRI PHILIPPE PÉTAIN (1856–1951) The hero of Verdun and later Commander-in-Chief of the French Army in World War I, Pétain was venerated by a generation of Frenchmen. Because he believed that France should accommodate to permanent Nazi domination, he was willing, at the age of eighty-four, to form a puppet government at Vichy after the fall of France. U.P.I.

PIERRE LAVAL (1883–1945) Though the Allies considered him the personification of evil, Pierre Laval looked on himself as a French patriot serving (and manipulating) Henri Pétain. But his collaboration was so autocratic and pro-Nazi that his name became the ultimate symbol of treason. When he was out of favor with Pétain, the Allies relaxed a bit. At the time of Pearl Harbor Laval was indeed temporarily out—but not for long. STEDMAN JONES, LIFE MAGAZINE © 1940 TIME INC.

JEAN FRANÇOIS DARLAN (1881–1942) The rival of Pierre Laval for Pétain's favor, Admiral Jean François Darlan was a political moderate by comparison. Though definitely a collaborator in the Pétain style, the little admiral had a basis for claiming some respect. He had built the French fleet between wars, and he had negotiated the release of thousands of French sailors being held prisoner by Hitler. Churchill once regarded Darlan as ''one of those good Frenchmen who hate England.'' But much had happened since that judgment in 1939, and Darlan's service under Pétain could never be forgiven. U. S. ARMY

HENRI HONORÉ GIRAUD (1879–1949) A true French military hero, General (five-star) Henri Honoré Giraud embodied the pride of the French Army. He had escaped from the Germans in both World War I (as a captain) and World War II (with some help from the French underground). Uninterested in politics, Giraud appeared to be the man to rally the French during the war and then step aside afterward. Despite American support, however, he was not equipped to survive politically when faced with a rival of de Gaulle's caliber. U.P.I.

CHARLES DE GAULLE (1890–1970) A professional soldier with strong political ambitions, Charles de Gaulle had reached a position of some influence in France before her surrender in 1940, when he was rescued by Churchill and brought to England as a symbol of the "honor of France." With no resources except Churchill's wavering support, de Gaulle quickly established himself as the leader of the "Fighting French," or "Free French" as the Americans preferred to call them. Between wars, de Gaulle wrote an intriguing book, *The Edge of the Sword,* of which perhaps the most revealing chapter was entitled "Prestige." U.P.I.

ROBERT D. MURPHY (1894–1978) Murphy was a career diplomat, formerly stationed at the U.S. embassies at Paris and later at Vichy, when he was selected as one of President Roosevelt's personal "eyes and ears." Gregarious and disarming, Murphy would fight an uphill battle to further U.S. policies regarding the wartime French. U. S. ARMY

HAROLD MACMILLAN (1894–   ) Like Churchill, Harold Macmillan was "half American and all British." He was a Member of Parliament and Minister of State when he was sent by Churchill to Algiers as a personal representative to the Allied commander. Macmillan, like Ismay, proved to be one of the invaluable "bridges" between two nationalities, and he would later enjoy a tremendously successful career in British politics. U. S. ARMY

BENITO MUSSOLINI (1883–1945) With his seizure of power in Italy in 1924, his organization of the Italian state, and his 1935 invasion of Ethiopia, Mussolini was truly Hitler's teacher. Greatly surpassed by his pupil by late 1941, Il Duce's power was already on the wane. His soldiers had no stomach for the war or for his bombast any longer. U.P.I.

ERWIN ROMMEL (1891–1944) A superb commander from platoon level up, General Erwin Rommel, highly decorated in World War I, caught Hitler's eye as a division commander in France in 1940. Sent to Africa with his Afrika Korps, he stopped Wavell's first offensive and subsequently created a legend, an obsession with the British from Churchill on down. THE BETTMANN ARCHIVE

VICTOR EMMANUEL III (1869–1947) Still on his throne throughout the regime of the dictator Mussolini, King Victor Emmanuel III had been powerless to prevent Italy's entry into the war, though he opposed it. It would require the failure of Mussolini's North African power before the King reasserted his authority at the age of seventy-four. WIDE WORLD PHOTOS

PIETRO BADOGLIO (1871–1956) An active soldier since the Italian campaign against Ethiopia in 1896, Field Marshal Badoglio had been prominent in World War I and the occupation of Ethiopia in 1935. After resigning over the disgraceful Italian performance in the Greek campaign of 1940, Badoglio had opposed Mussolini ever since. He was still in retirement when the United States entered the war. WIDE WORLD PHOTOS

PRESIDENT ROOSEVENT SIGNS THE DECLARATION OF WAR AGAINST JAPAN, December 8, 1941. HISTORICAL PICTURES SERVICE, CHICAGO

CHURCHILL BEFORE THE U. S. CONGRESS, December 26, 1941. U.P.I.

PRIME MINISTER CHURCHILL AND GENERAL MARSHALL AT FORT JACKSON, June 1942.
Left to right: Marshall, Dill, Churchill, Stimson, Major General Robert L. Eichelberger,
Brooke. U. S. ARMY

GENERAL MARSHALL AT WEST POINT, presenting the diploma to Cadet Alan R. Scullen,
May 29, 1942. AUTHOR'S COLLECTION

AMERICAN TROOPS ABOARD SHIP. En route to French Morocco, November 1942. U. S. ARMY

GENERAL EISENHOWER MEETS WITH ADMIRAL DARLAN. Left to right: Eisenhower, Darlan, Clark, Murphy. November 13, 1942. U. S. ARMY

PRESIDENT ROOSEVELT AND PRIME MINISTER CHURCHILL IN ROOSEVELT'S VILLA, ANFA, CASABLANCA. Seated, left to right: Arnold, King, Churchill, Roosevelt, Brooke, Pound, Marshall. Standing, left to right: Brigadier Vivian Dykes, Ismay, Mountbatten, Major General John R. Deane, Dill, Portal, Hopkins. January 1943. U. S. ARMY

HOTEL ANFA, CASABLANCA. U. S. ARMY

Prime Minister Churchill at Anfa with Major General George S. Patton, Jr., and Sir Hastings Ismay, January 1943. U. S. ARMY

Harry Hopkins, Patton, Major General Ernest Harmon at Rabat, January 1943. U. S. ARMY

"Bride and Groom" Meet the Press at Roosevelt's Villa, Anfa. Left to right: Giraud, Roosevelt, de Gaulle, Churchill, January 24, 1943. U. S. ARMY

The Shotgun Marriage. The same cast of characters a few moments later. U. S. ARMY

As Mast was taking a considerable risk to his own life by being at this meeting, he decided by about noon to return to Algiers before his absence from headquarters would be noticed. He had, however, stayed for about seven hours of discussion.

Though the important part of the meeting was now over, the American party would have to remain under cover, as embarkation during daylight would be suicide. Thus the party spent the early afternoon relaxing and conferring in small groups with the Frenchmen who had stayed behind— the commandos were still out of sight upstairs. Then came word that the police were on their way. The Frenchmen disappeared instantaneously, and soon only Tessier, Murphy, and Murphy's assistant, Mr. Ridgway Knight, remained with Clark. Tessier motioned Clark and his group to a large, dark wine cellar, where they remained quiet. As they nervously fingered their carbines, Clark mumbled, "How the hell do you work this thing?" Without Tessier's knowledge, one of the commandos went out to communicate with Jewell. Plans had to be changed if the submarine were to wait longer. The faithful Jewell would.

Murphy, understandably, was less concerned than Clark, for he soon discovered—but could not pass the word—that the police were searching for smugglers, not conspirators. Tessier's servants had suspected that some illicit activity was going on, and they had notified the police in

---

Most of our terrain, communications, and other critical data had to be obtained from maps—and very poor ones at that. The Cherchel meeting confirmed that we had generally selected the best landing beaches and gave us important information on alternative beaches in the Algiers, Oran and Casablanca areas if we needed them.

b. We obtained much important information on the best routes to use after landing and where we would likely meet the strongest resistance from Vichy French military forces, etc.

c. We also obtained much useful information (not previously available to us) as to the location of the headquarters, motor pools, ammunition depots of the Vichy French forces we would come up against.

d. Aviation and motor gasoline were critical items of supply after we landed. Information on the location of substantial stocks of aviation gasoline at Maison Blanche (Algiers) Airfield was especially valuable. It provided the fuel for Spitfire aircraft to operate from that airfield long before we could have landed aviation fuel there from our convoys. This gave us valuable air cover much earlier since the Spitfire could scarcely make it on a one-way flight from Gibraltar to Algiers before running out of fuel.

e. We obtained firm up-to-date information on the Vichy French forces in North Africa which was previously unavailable to us—their combat capability, training, leadership, equipment, where they were located, etc.

f. Finally, and the most important, the information we received from General Mast and his staff confirmed that our invasion plans were sound and workable. This was very reassuring to us and improved our morale considerably.

Letter, General Lyman L. Lemnitzer to author, March 1, 1976.

hopes of receiving a reward. Smuggling searches were not uncommon, however, and the police were fairly casual.

In the living room above the cellar Murphy and Knight played their parts well. Murphy made no secret of the fact that he was the American consul in Algiers; but he played the inebriated host and, implying that a slightly irregular party involving women had been interrupted, he asked if the police could refrain from looking upstairs. Eventually the intruders, perhaps disarmed by Murphy's wine, departed. Murphy called to the basement and warned the occupants that they had better clear out. Clark and his party immediately hauled the boats down the bluff to the beach and stayed out of sight. Over the sound of the waves they could hear the sounds of a second police search.

From this time on things became, in Clark's words, "pretty frantic." Tessier, now realizing the extent of his own personal jeopardy, fell victim to a case of jitters. Worse, the Americans were finding it impossible to launch their small boats into the roaring surf. At one point, in an effort to get off, Clark stripped himself of all his clothing except his shirt and undershorts, meanwhile unloading hundreds of dollars' worth of gold coins. This attempt to launch failed, however, and it was hours before Captain Wright found a place somewhat sheltered from the surf. With Murphy, Knight, Lemnitzer, and Tessier pushing, Clark and his party, all frozen, hungry, and bleeding, made it out. Each boat capsized at least once in the effort.

The occupants of the three boats then had a long way to paddle through the blackness. Miraculously, by 4:00 A.M. all reached a point where the infrared flashlights carried by the commandos guided them to the waiting *Seraph*. The escape had been remarkably successful except for the fact that Holmes's canvas boat and his bag were lost in the waves. Jewell submerged and headed for Gibraltar. Later a worried Clark asked Jewell to surface long enough to allow him to send a message to warn Murphy to scour the beach. Holmes's bag contained secret papers, including reports from Murphy to President Roosevelt that could give away everything. Neither the boat nor Holmes's bag was ever found.

Twenty-four hours later a Catalina Flying Boat provided by the Prime Minister made contact with the *Seraph* and picked up the American party. Once aloft, Clark sent a message to Eisenhower giving the details of his adventure. Aside from the bare-bones account, with only the slightest touch of humor,[16] the message contained one sentence that portended trouble: "All questions were settled satisfactorily except for the time the French would assume supreme command. My view on this question was submitted to Giraud, through Mast, for his consideration with the definite understanding that my proposal must yet be confirmed by you."

16 Clark mentioned hiding out in "empty *repeat empty* wine cellar."

*

While General Clark was on his perilous mission to Africa, General Eisenhower was being kept surprisingly well informed of what was happening. Fortunately for his anxiety, he was busy with final preparations. Besides the innumerable decisions confronting the commander of such a complex operation, his schedule involved inspection trips to various participating units. He discovered many problems, some of which could not be solved in anything like the time left. One of his concerns, for example, was the weakness of American leadership below the rank of lieutenant colonel, which could only be corrected by time and untiring effort.

One procedural matter vital to the future of the Allied effort was solved with remarkable ease: the degree of authority Eisenhower would exercise over British forces under his command. One day the BCOS sent Eisenhower a draft of the instructions they were issuing to General Anderson. When he read it over he grabbed a stub pencil and began to scratch furiously. He handed the paper back to the two British colonels who had brought it. "No one could be an Allied commander-in-chief with such negative terms of reference," he growled.[17] Somewhat to his surprise and relief, Eisenhower discovered that the British Chiefs were not only receptive to his comments but almost apologetic. The error had come about, they said, because they had carelessly reprinted the instructions formerly issued to General Haig in the spring of 1918 and to Lord Gort in 1940, the text of which allowed the commander of the British Expeditionary Force to appeal to Whitehall should he receive an order he considered dangerous to his command. In essence this "escape clause" negated the authority of the Allied chief.

When the British Chiefs rewrote the directive, they now instructed General Anderson that he could appeal to the British Government only if an objectionable order—the possibility of which they specifically described as "unlikely"—endangered some part of the *Allied* command. Further, he was to notify Eisenhower *before* sending his appeal. This was as far as any nation could go in placing its forces under a foreign commander. Eisenhower observed gratefully that the British were probably becoming more sold on the Allied concept than even the Americans.[18]

*

In the meantime President Roosevelt and Prime Minister Churchill were working on messages to be transmitted simultaneously with the landing of Allied troops. They were to go from Roosevelt to Pétain and other heads of government who might be frightened by the prospect of Anglo-

[17] Letter, Lyman L. Lemnitzer to author, February 26, 1976.
[18] The incident came to the attention of General Ismay, who also thought it highly significant. See Ismay, p. 264.

Americans in North Africa.[19] In only one draft did the two heads of government diverge. Always anxious to make use of personal relationships, Roosevelt wrote a friendly letter to Pétain.

> My dear old friend [it started out], I am sending this message to you not only as the *Chef d'Etat* of the United States to the *Chef d'Etat* of the Republic of France, but also as one of your friends and comrades of the great days of 1918. May we both live to see France victorious again against the ancient enemy.
>
> When your government concluded, of necessity, the Armistice Convention of 1940, it was impossible for any of us to foresee the program of systematic plunder which the German Reich would inflict. . . .

The letter then continued on for two pages, warning of the dangers of Axis invasion of North Africa and explaining our own friendly spirit. It did, of course, appeal for French cooperation.

Roosevelt cabled the text to Churchill. The Prime Minister replied instantly. The tone was "much too kind," he complained. Pétain's great reputation enabled him to inflict greater harm to the Allied cause than could a "lesser man." The President promptly obliged. Pétain was now addressed by his name rather than as the "dear old friend," and all references to "great days of 1918," as well as the words "of necessity," were deleted.[20] The letter was set aside for use at the proper time.

*

Throughout the planning stage of TORCH, tension in the various Allied headquarters was understandably high. In the face of enemy submarine and air threats, the Western Allies were to send a convoy of 600 vessels, with an assault force of 90,000 men (with another 200,000 follow-up). The distance by sea would be 1,500 miles from Britain and 3,000 from the United States. In the target area the Allies held not a single port or airfield; and the region was guarded by some 200,000 French troops supported by an air force of 500 planes. The French Navy, if disposed to be hostile, was of considerable strength. Only two British carriers were available to provide air cover inside the Mediterranean, and the small, overcrowded strip at Gibraltar was five hundred miles from Algiers. To take the airfields, parachute troops from Britain would have to cross more than twelve hundred miles of occupied France full of enemy bases.[21] The venture was less risky than a cross-Channel invasion but infinitely more complicated.

[19] Franco, General Antonio Carmona (President of Portugal), the Governor General of Algeria, the Sultan of Morocco, and the Bey of Tunis.
[20] Sherwood, pp. 644–46.
[21] Bryant, *Turn of the Tide,* p. 404.

One incident was enough to cause concern over possible loss of surprise. In late September a flying boat had been lost between Lisbon and Gibraltar, and the bodies of the crew and passengers had been washed up on a Spanish beach. Inside a pocket of Captain R. N. Turner, one of the victims, was a letter from Bedell Smith to the Governor of Gibraltar regarding Eisenhower's future headquarters. The Spanish, being neutral, returned the body; and the British found the letter, still sealed, inside the coat pocket. There was no evidence that German agents had read the letter, but the Allies could never be certain.

Commander Harry Butcher was finding himself in a small quandary. Though a peacetime journalist himself—he had been a vice-president of the Columbia Broadcasting System—he gave priority to his military duty, but a close second in his mind was to maintain his cordial status with his journalistic contemporaries. Thus, when the American public relations officer, Colonel Morrow Krum, asked him about rumors that Eisenhower was being sent back to Washington, Butcher got himself off the spot by arranging for him to see Bedell Smith. Butcher knew that Eisenhower and Clark had paid a farewell call on the King the day before (October 29) but Krum had been kept in the dark.[22]

Butcher sat spellbound as Smith told Krum of his disappointment that the Eisenhower-to-Washington story was out, as it was supposed to be secret. The position of headquarters, Smith concluded, was simply "No comment."

The next day AP reported that Eisenhower was going home, and Butcher was hounded for confirmation. With a straight face Butcher simply quoted Smith, thus keeping faith, of sorts, with both camps.

*

In Algiers, Robert Murphy was receiving one piece of alarming news after another. After the Cherchel talk, Murphy had contacted Lemaigre-Dubreuil and asked him once again to go to Lyon to see General Giraud. Four days later Lemaigre-Dubreuil returned with a letter demanding that (1) Giraud be placed in command of TORCH within forty-eight hours of landing and (2) that the landings include southern France. Obviously the general's position had stiffened, if anything, since Cherchel. Disturbed, Murphy contacted Eisenhower on October 28 requesting permission to tell General Mast that the expedition would arrive early in November. With qualms Eisenhower agreed.

Murphy had not expected the violent reaction that he received from Mast. The Frenchman complained bitterly about the lack of confidence the Americans had demonstrated toward him and toward Giraud. For a

[22] It is a strange but necessary practice in war to spare the public relations officer from knowing sensitive secrets. The PRO is considered almost one of the press.

while Murphy was concerned that Mast, in his emotional state, might leak the crucial information. Mast soon calmed down, however, and Murphy relaxed a bit.

On November 1 another blow fell. General Giraud now insisted that leaving France would be impossible before November 20. Whether this posture resulted from necessity or pique was academic: French cooperation was so necessary, Murphy believed, that the expedition must be put off at least two weeks, from November 7 to November 21. He so recommended to Marshall.

In London Eisenhower received a copy of Murphy's message and lost no time in firing off his own:

> It is inconceivable that McGowan [as Eisenhower then thought of Murphy] can recommend such a delay. . . . It is likewise inconceivable that our mere failure to concede to such demands would result in having the French North African Army meet us with serious opposition. Recommend the President advise McGowan immediately that his suggested action is utterly impossible and that we will proceed to execute this operation with more determination than ever.[23]

Further, Eisenhower advised, the submarine earmarked to pick up Giraud (again the *Seraph*) would remain on hand.[24]

In Washington, Murphy's recommendations were received with similar alarm. Given the complications of this vast military undertaking—Patton had departed from the United States ten days earlier—there was nothing President Roosevelt could do. Thus the next day, November 2, Admiral Leahy cabled Murphy: "The decision of the President is that the operation will be carried out as now planned and that you will do your utmost to secure the understanding and cooperation of the French officials with whom you are now in contact."

Thus it was up to Murphy to do whatever he thought best. That same day he asked Lemaigre-Dubreuil to return to Lyon a final time. In a conciliatory letter Murphy once again assured the increasingly agitated Giraud that the United States Government, considering the French as allies, intended to put the military command of the region in their hands as soon as possible after the first phases, which involved the landings and the

[23] Eisenhower to Marshall, R4373, November 1, 1942. Murphy later claimed that he had been ignorant of the details of the operation.
[24] The *Seraph* was still commanded by Jewell. Since Giraud had insisted that it be an "American" submarine, Captain Jerauld Wright, though no submariner, was sent along as the titular "commander." The conning tower of the *Seraph* is now a monument at the Citadel in Charleston, South Carolina, put there when General Clark was Superintendent.

consolidation. Until then the American organization would have to remain unchanged. The *Seraph* was dispatched to the Gulf of Lion.

*

By now there was little left for Eisenhower to do in London. He dropped a note of thanks to U. S. Ambassador John Winant, had a farewell luncheon with Churchill, locked up his desk, and prepared to depart for Gibraltar. That night of Monday, November 2, Eisenhower, Clark, and various staff members boarded a train for Hurn Airport at Bournemouth. They arrived the next morning, however, to be told that weather permitted no flying—and the train should not remain during the day. Wearily, Eisenhower returned to London and instructed his staff to stay home, away from the office.

Back in Bournemouth again early Thursday morning, Eisenhower found the weather marginal at the very best. The pilot,[25] who had flown Clark to Gibraltar two weeks earlier, was wary of flying under these conditions. But now the trip was vital, as D-Day was almost upon them. For the only time in his military career, therefore, Eisenhower insisted over the pilot's misgivings. The six Flying Fortresses, supposedly destined for Washington, took off through the rain and fog and headed south toward Gibraltar. Whatever lay ahead, the "most anxious months" were over.

[25] Major Paul Tibbets, who was later to be the pilot of the B-29 which dropped the first atomic bomb on Japan.

CHAPTER X

TURNING POINT
AT EL ALAMEIN

G eneral Sir Harold R. L. Alexander, newly appointed Commander-in-Chief, Near East, arrived at the British Embassy in Cairo in time for breakfast on Sunday morning, August 9, 1942 (nearly three months before Eisenhower's departure for Gibraltar). Prime Minister Churchill and General Sir Alan Brooke, on their way to their historic meeting with Stalin in Moscow, were also on hand. (See pp. 112–14.) On hearing that Alexander had arrived, Churchill and Brooke each tried to reach him before he would see the other.

The Prime Minister and the CIGS had developed a difference of opinion regarding the nature of Alexander's new command, and each wanted to solicit his support before the three would meet. Churchill, after the death of "Strafer" Gott, was becoming doubtful that a separate commander for Eighth Army was necessary. Alexander, he believed, could command both the Near East and the Eighth Army simultaneously, as had Auchinleck after the removal of Ritchie. The Iran-Iraq area was no longer, after all, a diversion from the Near East command. Brooke, seeing the Near East as still too broad for this arrangement, held out for two positions. The theater commander was necessary, he felt, to manage logistics, civil affairs, and other matters while his subordinate Eighth Army Commander would direct the battle.

Both points of view had their merits. Churchill had a logical point in assuming that Alexander could concentrate adequately on the Eighth Army, and the alternative might bring trouble. An insufficiently occupied theater commander, who might tend to supervise Eighth Army too closely, could clash with a strong-minded Desert Army commander. And things had to go right with the Eighth Army; in fact Churchill tended at this time to brush aside everything except the defeat of Rommel—indeed he would pace the floor shouting the German's name over and over again.

And for good reason. Churchill's political position in Britain was becoming increasingly vulnerable. Gone were the days of 1940, when Britain was immediately endangered and Churchill symbolized her defiance. Very conscious of the poll which showed only 40 percent of the population approving of the government's handling of the war, Churchill considered his fate as leader tied in with that of the Eighth Army.[1] The battle now pending some sixty miles west of Alexandria must receive all the attention of the best-qualified soldier in the British Army, who in Churchill's mind was Alexander.

Brooke, on the other hand, was tenacious in clinging to a division of responsibilities between the Near East Command and the Eighth Army. Exactly why is not clear; but it may have stemmed from his partiality for General Montgomery. Throughout the war Brooke boosted the fortunes of Montgomery, and it may be that some professional jealousy of Alexander was behind it. Be that as it may, Brooke was finally able to sell his point of view, and the Alexander-Montgomery team was formed.

Brooke's concept eventually worked, however, only because Alexander and Montgomery each defined his own role and respected that of the other. The arrangement probably would not have been successful with Auchinleck as Near East Commander, for his temperament could never fit with that of Montgomery. But Alexander, despite the fact that his tactical qualifications and experience excelled those of his subordinate, decided consciously to restrict his activities to running the Near East Command and to allow Montgomery to fight his own tactical battle.

After the breakfast meeting on August 9 a full day elapsed before Alexander met with Churchill again, this time to receive his formal instructions, written longhand on a piece of embassy stationery. They read as follows:

1. Your prime and main duty will be to take or destroy at the earliest opportunity the German-Italian Army commanded by Field Marshal Rommel together with all its supplies and establishments in Egypt and Libya.

2. You will discharge or cause to be discharged such other duties as pertain to your command without prejudice to the task described in paragraph I, which must be considered paramount in His Majesty's interests.

The document was remarkable in two respects. First, it mentioned the commander of the enemy by name; second, it restricted Alexander's sphere of operations to Egypt and Libya, probably in deference to

[1] Grigg, pp. 36, 47–48.

TORCH, which was expected to seize Tunisia early. No mention was made of any coordination between the two converging theaters, but the intent of the order was clear: Churchill wanted Rommel beaten.

Alexander, now at loose ends until his assumption of command on August 15, had time to examine the situation himself, both in Cairo and up at the Eighth Army positions at El Alamein.

Harold Rupert Leofric George Alexander, at age fifty, was one of the most experienced of the British generals. He had served in the trenches during World War I; he had later seen small combat in India; he had commanded the 1st British Division and later the entire rear guard during the evacuation from Dunkirk in 1940. Like MacArthur's in the Philippines, his handling of the hopeless situation in Burma had increased rather than detracted from his stature among British generals.

After resting up for a month in Delhi, an exhausted Alexander had returned to the United Kingdom in early July 1942, still several pounds underweight. Hardly had he arrived in his native Ireland for a rest with his wife, however, than he had received word to report back to the War Office for "very important business," command of the British First Army in the forthcoming invasion of Northwest Africa. Alexander and Eisenhower had met for the first time on August 4. The two made favorable impressions on each other, auspicious for the future of TORCH. Two days later Alexander had been ordered to Cairo.

As Alexander passed his few days without direct responsibility, he drove through the streets of Cairo, noting symptoms of conditions that needed his attention. For one thing, even though his car carried the flag of the new commander-in-chief, nobody bothered to salute it. Alexander saw this breach of military custom as an indication of low morale. Correction would have to be gradual, however, encouraged by a general uplift throughout the command.

One action Alexander decided to take was to move his main headquarters out of Cairo. While temporarily exercising command of the Eighth Army as well as the whole Middle East, Auchinleck had maintained two separate staffs, one at El Alamein and one in Cairo. For himself he had established a small "tactical" Middle East headquarters at Mena, just west of Giza, literally in the shadow of the Great Pyramid of Cheops. This spot, while still a hundred and fifty miles from the battlefront, was located on the Desert Road which ran northwest to Alexandria on the coast. Its location was near enough to Cairo but free of the congestion of a crowded city.

This was the place to which Alexander planned to move his "main" headquarters. City living in Cairo was cutting into the efficiency of the headquarters troops, and the comfortable conditions had served to remind visiting front-line soldiers of the maldistribution of hardships between those exposed to battle and those directing their fortunes. If nothing else, the more rugged living conditions in the desert sands of Mena would help to make headquarters troops feel more at one with those fighting to the west.

Alexander was arriving at a propitious time. To the casual observer it would seem that the fortunes of the British Eighth Army were at a low ebb. Rommel's reputation was at its zenith after his victories in June despite Auchinleck's skillful counterattacks in the First Battle of El Alamein in July. Rommel still believed he had a slim—very slim—chance of delivering a knockout blow to the Nile Delta and Cairo. If such a drive could be linked up with a successful Nazi push through the Caucasus, Iran, Iraq, and Palestine, the plight of the Allies would be dire indeed.

Alexander's spirits, however, were high. He was receiving messages daily through radio intercept (ULTRA)[2] that despite the appearance of success Rommel's real situation was growing more precarious every day. And Alexander also knew that large quantities of supplies and equipment were coming to him up the Red Sea. The Near East Command would soon receive some 400 tanks (many of them the new American Shermans promised by Marshall in the White House), 500 guns, 7,000 vehicles, and 75,000 tons of supplies during the month of August alone. And he could also see the end of the plight of Malta. This heroic garrison, once so undersupplied as to make surrender an imminent possibility, was now in the process of being resupplied. Soon it could even make a contribution to Alexander's operations by support from the air.[3] What an excellent moment to take command!

With time on his side, Alexander knew that if he could hold the Prime Minister at bay long enough to train his troops in the new equipment and become used to the Desert his prospects would be bright indeed. He

[2] A secret, high-level radio intercept based on the breaking of the German *Enigma*. It sometimes provided information not otherwise attainable. Winterbotham, *The Ultra Secret*, p. 95.

[3] On August 10, 1942, a convoy of fourteen cargo ships left Gibraltar destined for Malta. They were escorted by a convoy which included three carriers, two battleships, seven cruisers, and twenty-four destroyers. This Operation PEDESTAL proved costly: one carrier, the *Eagle*, was sunk and the other two, the *Victorious* and the *Indomitable*, were severely damaged; two cruisers were lost. Only five of the fourteen merchant ships reached Malta, but the supplies they were able to deliver, 47,000 tons, assured Malta the ability to hold out until December and to operate the fighter planes previously immobilized. Churchill, IV, 505–6.

For the dramatic saga of the tanker *Ohio*, see Shankland and Hunter, *Malta Convoy*. The *Ohio*, with a British crew, was the most important ship in the convoy. It was abandoned twice in the voyage but finally, almost carried into Malta, it delivered 10,000 tons of fuel oil.

would, to be sure, be required to launch a major attack some time before TORCH (although in early August the date of November 8 had not yet been decided), but, unlike Auchinleck, he had Churchill's confidence. Drawing on that, Alexander would finally be permitted to defer his attack at El Alamein until the last week in October. Ironically, Auchinleck had been relieved for specifying a date one month earlier than Alexander's.

*

Lieutenant General Sir Bernard Law Montgomery, recently Commander-in-Chief of Home Forces in Britain, and for a couple of days Commander, First British Army, probably realized what a stroke of good fortune this new assignment was to him personally. For instead of commanding a relatively small British force under an American commander in TORCH, Montgomery was now going to head the largest British Army thus far assembled. And his army would fight alone, all British and Commonwealth troops, in a pending battle which Prime Minister Churchill had determined would be the last great all-British victory of the war.

Whether or not Montgomery appreciated his personal good fortune, he certainly approached his task with ample confidence. Undoubtedly he was aware, as was Alexander, of the tremendous build-up coming to the Eighth Army through the Red Sea. A story which Churchill enjoyed described Montgomery's feelings as he rode to the airport with General Ismay; he was thinking of his future adversary Rommel in terms of sympathy.[4]

Montgomery was a man who, though exhibiting no remarkable intellect, possessed a quality that compelled his superiors to be unusually tolerant of his idiosyncrasies: his self-assurance. He made the most of this mystique, and for his own reasons often seemed to go out of his way to be difficult. Only when faced with the inevitable would he give up. Such was acknowledged by Alexander.[5]

In person Montgomery was a loner, at home with subordinates and su-

---

[4] "A story—alas, not authenticated—has been told of this conversation. Montgomery spoke of the trials and hazards of a soldier's career. He gave his whole life to his profession, and lived long years of study and self-restraint. Presently fortune smiled, there came a gleam of success, he gained advancement, opportunity presented itself, he had a great command. He won a victory, he became world-famous, his name was on every lip. Then the luck changed. At one stroke all his life's work flashed away, perhaps through no fault of his own, and he was flung into the endless catalogue of military failures. 'But,' expostulated Ismay, 'you ought not to take it so badly as all that. A very fine army is gathering in the Middle East. It may well be that you are not going to disaster.' 'What!' cried Montgomery, sitting up in the car. 'What do you mean? I was talking about Rommel!' " Churchill, IV, 465. Unfortunately Montgomery, in *Memoirs*, pp. 72–73, denies the story.

[5] Alexander, *The Alexander Memoirs*, p. 16.

periors but uncomfortable with contemporaries. The death of his wife in 1936 had left him a solitary man, devoted strictly to his profession and to the raising of his only son, David. Convinced of his future as a man of destiny, Montgomery was utterly ruthless in his handling of subordinates whose incompetence would threaten the fulfillment of that destiny. He was also obsessed with physical fitness, a complete teetotaler and non-smoker—and intolerant of those who indulged. His egocentricity made him often oblivious to what was going on around him. He could appear interested in a conversation, never hearing a word. And yet Montgomery possessed a keen insight into the psychology of the British soldier, and he was a master at building morale around his own image.

In short, Montgomery possessed many admirable military qualities. His critics, including many British contemporaries and nearly all his American colleagues, contended that he grossly overdid them.

Early on Wednesday, August 12, Montgomery arrived at the airfield near Mena House, the palatial hotel near Auchinleck's tactical head-quarters at Mena. Because Auchinleck was still in command—and would be for the next three days—Montgomery left immediately for his main office in downtown Cairo. Monty wanted to pay his respects but to waste no time.

The session was far from pleasant. Auchinleck, always the gentleman, continued to cover his personal pain with a front of professional dignity. However, he quickly became resentful of a couple of Montgomery's pointed questions regarding the tactical dispositions at El Alamein, and directed him to go to El Alamein the next day. But since Auchinleck in-tended to remain the commander to the end, he specified that any crisis which might arise between that moment and August 15 would be handled by himself (Auchinleck) and W. H. Ramsden, acting Eighth Army Com-mander. None of this exchange was pleasant to Montgomery; he left as soon as he "decently" could.[6]

Montgomery had learned little from this encounter. On the contrary, he wittingly or unwittingly left with a grossly erroneous impression that Auchinleck was actively considering a retreat from the El Alamein posi-tion to take up defense on the Cairo Delta should Rommel attack. Noth-ing in the official estimate drawn up two weeks earlier by Auchinleck's staff would indicate such an intention; actually such a retreat was now no longer being considered. But Montgomery somehow received—or in-terpreted—the opposite impression. At any rate, he always unjustly claimed that Auchinleck had been planning a retreat.[7]

[6] Montgomery, p. 87.
[7] Ibid.

That, however, was Montgomery at his worst. For the rest of the day (August 12) Montgomery was at his best. After leaving Auchinleck he went to see Alexander, who was biding his time. There Montgomery explained the idea he had been considering on the trip from London, that of creating an armored striking force in the Eighth Army comparable to Rommel's Afrika Korps (which comprised only a fraction of his whole command, the Panzergruppe Afrika). The formation of such a *corps de chasse* should be possible with the arrival of new units every day. Immediately the two men sent for Major General Sir John Harding, Auchinleck's deputy chief of staff. Having outlined the plan, Montgomery and Alexander asked Harding to work out concrete plans for this armored corps by the late afternoon.

Then Alexander, who had already been over the prospective El Alamein battlefield, began discussing other matters. Under no circumstances, the two agreed, could the Eighth Army ever withdraw from El Alamein. If it could not hold such a strong position—a forty-mile front with both flanks protected—then the Allied cause might be hopeless. And the determination to hold to the last at El Alamein would have to be understood by all ranks. From his observations, Alexander had received the impression that the troops, ignorant of the plans of the staff, believed that the Army would retreat if necessary in order to "remain intact."[8] The "no retreat" policy must be made clear to all, lest this misunderstanding persist.

Alexander and Montgomery then studied the tactical situation at the front. The Eighth Army occupied a secure line, not too long, with one flank protected by the Mediterranean (north), the other by the impassable Qattara Depression (south). Almost exactly in the center lay a prominent east–west ridge known as Ruweisat; and less than ten miles to the southeast of Ruweisat Ridge was a smaller one, Alam Nayil. Extending from the eastern end of the Alam Nayil Ridge slightly northward to the rear was the long Alam Halfa Ridge.

Anywhere else these ridges—which rose only some fifty to a hundred feet above the flat Desert—would not be considered impressive terrain features. But in that clear air they provided observation for miles, dominating the territory. Thus three ridges, their western edges forming a blunt angle to the south—Ruweisat to the northwest, Alam Nayil to the south, and Alam Halfa to the northeast—constituted a natural fortress against any movement against the left (south) flank.

On this terrain Auchinleck had placed four infantry divisions on the front facing west.[9] That left a gap of some thirty miles between the Alam

---

[8] Alexander, p. 18.

[9] From north to south, the 9th Australian, the 1st South African, the 5th Indian (on the Ruweisat Ridge), and the 2nd New Zealand with southern boundary on Alam Nayil.

Nayil and the Qattara Depression, where Rommel, according to desert practice (substantiated by intelligence), was expected to envelop the main position from the south. This gap, according to Auchinleck's plan, was to be filled by the 7th Armoured Division,[10] fighting a mobile battle. When forced back by Rommel's main body, this 7th Armoured Division would then withdraw to the north to fill the gap between the 2nd New Zealand Division on Alam Nayil and the Alam Halfa Ridge. On the latter, however, Auchinleck had placed only one infantry brigade.

All in all, Auchinleck's plan was excellent, perhaps even obvious; the key lay in presenting a strong southern flank along the two critical ridges. Both Auchinleck and Alexander after him presumed that Rommel would have to turn north against the ridges before continuing eastward, for if he should decide to by-pass them in an all-out drive toward Cairo, he would be taking an unacceptable risk; his rear would be left open to an intact Eighth Army through only a narrow corridor.

Alexander and Montgomery, therefore, made no change in Auchinleck's basic concept. They would simply reinforce the southern ridges with the new divisions coming in. In reserve behind the XXX Corps, which consisted of the three northernmost divisions, Alexander and Montgomery were able to station the newly arrived 10th Armoured. And now the 44th Division and an armored brigade were available to place on the critical Alam Halfa Ridge on the east part of the southern flank. In addition, they planned to deepen the mine fields between Alam Nayil and the Qattara Depression. These changes were not the result of any brilliant new scheme but rather a reflection of the fact that more troops and munitions had become available.

After having approved these new tactical plans, Alexander, knowing Montgomery's personality, "released" him to fight the forthcoming battle his own way. Alexander would provide everything possible that Montgomery requested—reserve troops from the Delta, all possible supplies, and anything else. In addition, of course, Alexander would be keeping his eye on other developments in the Near East. So they agreed that morning in Cairo.

With that understanding, the two officers went their ways until late that afternoon. At 6:00 P.M., August 12, they met once again with General Harding, who presented his scheme for constituting the armored reserve. This force, according to Harding's plan, would be designated X Corps and would consist of three armored divisions, the 1st, 8th, and 10th, each of which would include an armored brigade, an infantry brigade, and divisional troops. This X Corps would presumably also include the pow-

---

[10] The spelling "Armoured" is British usage.

erful New Zealand Division, with a strength of two infantry brigades and one armored brigade.

As conceived, this mobile striking force would be a match for Rommel's elite Afrika Korps, which it resembled.

At 5:00 A.M., August 13, Montgomery left the British Embassy for the ninety-mile drive up the Desert Road to a crossing just west of Alexandria. There Brigadier Francis ("Freddie") de Guingand, Auchinleck's Brigadier General Staff, was waiting for him. Together the two rode the remaining sixty miles along the Coast Road to the Eighth Army position.

Freddie de Guingand was in an awkward position. He had no idea what his own future was—in fact he expected to be sent elsewhere—but he gave Montgomery a frank rundown of the tactical situation as he saw it. He felt a strong loyalty to his outgoing commander, Auchinleck, but in some quarters has been accused of exaggerating what Montgomery wanted to hear: Auchinleck's purported plans for withdrawal. Probably De Guingand said nothing untoward—it was not his nature—but as he was talking Montgomery was eying the truck columns lined up pointing to the rear. Montgomery detected that he had found a device to dramatize the "no retreat" decision that Alexander and he had already agreed on. Though possessing no authority, Montgomery ordered these trucks removed.

On this trip Montgomery was evaluating De Guingand. Despite the difference in their ages (fourteen years) they had been close friends at one time but had been out of contact since. Montgomery recognized De Guingand as his own opposite in personality. In contrast to the Spartan Montgomery, De Guingand enjoyed his reputation as a *bon vivant* who enjoyed eating, drinking wine, and gambling.[11] On the other hand, Mont-

---

[11] De Guingand later wrote regarding his earlier transfer from a comfortable berth in Cairo to the Eighth Army:

> When the front had finally been stabilized, and Eighth Army had its flanks securely protected by the sea and the Qattara Depression, I decided that it was about time for me to return to my Headquarters in Cairo, where a lot of work was awaiting my attention. . . .
>
> That evening, as I sat eating a delicious dinner with friends at the Mohamed Ali Club, little did I know what was in store for me and how the whole pattern of my existence for the rest of the war was shortly to be changed.
>
> The following morning I arrived at the usual time in my office. . . .
>
> On my table lay a signal for "deGuingand's eyes only," and after sitting down in my comfortable chair, I ripped open the envelope and before I had read very far my eyes were literally popping out of my head.
>
> It read something like this:
>
> Request you hand over duties of D.M.I. to your Deputy and leave immediately for Headquarters Eighth Army to take up appointment of B.G.S.

gomery reasoned, this contrast was not too bad. De Guingand could smooth over some of the rough spots in Montgomery's personality, which Montgomery had no intention of correcting, and the two would be performing their duties in different locations anyway. Montgomery always liked to be alone in his own small tactical headquarters, away from his staff. De Guingand, with Main Headquarters, could run the show. And Montgomery decided that De Guingand, instead of being designated merely as the Brigadier General Staff, would now be elevated to Chief of Staff, a prestigious position of authority which the Eighth Army had not previously recognized. De Guingand would have the authority to speak for Montgomery himself.

It proved a fortunate choice. De Guingand would indeed be Montgomery's perfect supplement—and he would even save Montgomery's command and position on at least one occasion during the war.[12]

On arrival at Eighth Army Headquarters Montgomery was met by Lieutenant General W. H. Ramsden, commander of XXX Corps and acting commander of the Eighth Army. Montgomery brushed Ramsden to one side, the first public insult to the departing Auchinleck.

Eighth Army Headquarters was located on the eastern (rear) edge of Ruweisat Ridge in the center of the main line. On arrival there Montgomery was displeased with what he saw. Though ascetic in his personal habits, he always strove to assure reasonable comfort for his staff. Apparently trying to set an example for the deprived front-line troops, Eighth Army Headquarters was overdoing its own hardships. Officers, including Auchinleck, slept on the ground; the mess was abominable, swarming with flies. At once Montgomery directed the headquarters to move to the vicinity of Burg-el-Arab on the coast. Here his staff could work efficiently while he lived elsewhere. Desert Air Force Headquarters was already there.

During the day Montgomery inspected the southern end of the Army's position from the Ruweisat Ridge to the Alam Nayil and around the corner to Alam Halfa, confirming that this last, easternmost position was critical. He had decided earlier that by the time Rommel's attack would be launched in late August the Eighth Army should easily handle it. But it would not have the power, especially in trained tank personnel, to strike

---

I rang the bell and showed it to my faithful Personal Assistant, Christopher Gowan. I think he was as shaken as I had been myself.

I remarked, "The Auk must be round the bend."

De Guingand, *Generals at War,* pp. 64–65.

[12] See ibid., pp. 106–15, and John S. D. Eisenhower, *The Bitter Woods,* pp. 382–85, for an account of De Guingand's role as intermediary between Montgomery and Eisenhower during the Battle of the Bulge.

back. Therefore, Montgomery reasoned, he would settle for a strictly defensive victory. The general commanding the 7th Armoured Division was
startled to learn that Montgomery was planning to use his tanks in a passive role, as dug-in pillboxes. This was so foreign to Auchinleck's previous concepts—and to the accepted principles of armored warfare—that
the unwary officer protested. His future under Montgomery was automatically doomed.

In the early afternoon that same day Montgomery decided to assume
command of the Eighth Army, despite Auchinleck's orders to the contrary. He sent General Ramsden back to XXX Corps and signed a message as "Commander" at 2:00 P.M. He then returned to headquarters and
directed De Guingand to gather the principal staff officers. When they met
he announced his directive that no withdrawal from El Alamein would be
considered. The Eighth Army would fight in its present position as had
the Spartans at Thermopylae. He outlined his plans for the creation of a
new X Armoured Corps. He announced that the new headquarters was to
be moved to a location on the sea at Burg-el-Arab. Finally he explained
his own method of doing business: Chief of Staff de Guingand would act
with full authority in dealing with the staff, as he himself would be off
away from the paper work. In one day Montgomery had made his presence felt.

That evening of August 13 Montgomery sent a message to Cairo outlining what he had done. He signed it as "Commander" but pointedly made
no requests which might be refused—or call attention to his actions. He
also planned to remain unavailable for the whole next day, Auchinleck's
last. He retired for the evening with an "insubordinate smile," having
taken charge two days early.[13] Perhaps fortunately, Montgomery's report
never reached Auchinleck personally, and Montgomery did indeed stay
out of contact with GHQ throughout August 14.

For the next couple of weeks Montgomery went about his job methodically and skillfully. He requested that the 44th and 51st Divisions be
released from the Delta to the Eighth Army.[14] (Alexander complied without a murmur.) He readjusted and strengthened the dispositions of the
three infantry divisions on the northern half of the line, meanwhile reducing the number of troops in reserve. He made drastic changes in command personnel. Above all, he concerned himself with what was then
considered the weakest aspect of the Eighth Army, its morale.

The Eighth Army in August 1942 was not a collection of recruits.
Tough, almost blackened by the sun, the rank and file tended to give

13 Montgomery, p. 94.
14 These divisions came in addition to the *corps de chasse* which he and Alexander
had arranged on August 12.

newly arrived British officers, even Montgomery, a twinge of self-con-
sciousness about their own "pink knees." The Eighth Army had gone back
and forth across Tripoli (and part of Egypt) twice. They had fought well.
But somehow or other each victory had ended in defeat. The successful
stand called the First Battle of El Alamein, in which Auchinleck had
skillfully stopped Rommel, had not compensated for previous disappointments. Therefore Montgomery quickly decided that three things were
necessary to restore morale. First, he would establish himself as a personality—a "mascot," he later termed it—who could be recognized by the
troops wherever he went. This he effected by disdaining the regular British officer's cap and adopting instead an Australian bush hat covered with
insignia, trading it soon thereafter for a black tanker's beret.[15] Second, he
made a policy of speaking to officers and men at all echelons, making
them feel that they were a part of what he proposed to do. Third, he laid
down the law that there would be no more "bellyaching." He had detected—perhaps with reason—that officers of all ranks had been prone to
regard orders as negotiable. Orders from Montgomery were to be obeyed
and not questioned.

Montgomery, along with Alexander, had decided that the primary need
for the Eighth Army was a victory over Rommel—not necessarily a
victory of annihilation, just a victory. A defensive success would be
enough, but to win that would call for World War I tactics. This approach
was not universally admired but it filled his needs, and he shrugged off
adverse comments.

Finally, Montgomery decided he needed new commanders and again he
drew on the support of Alexander. One by one he sent for men who had
served under him, men who were capable and loyal to him personally.
Each was to command one of Montgomery's three corps. To X Armoured
Corps Montgomery sent Lieutenant General Sir Miles Dempsey. To command the XXX Corps, holding the northern portion of the front line,
Montgomery replaced Ramsden with Lieutenant General Sir Oliver
Leese.[16] And finally, to command the XIII Corps on the south, where the
attack was expected, he sent to England for Lieutenant General Sir Brian
Horrocks, who only days before had been serving under him as a division
commander in England.

*

On August 19 Prime Minister Churchill, on the way home to London
from Moscow, visited the new Eighth Army Headquarters at Burg-el-

[15] This distinctive hat was a technique Montgomery had suggested years before,
when he was a major lecturing at the Staff College. Grigg, p. 46.
[16] Montgomery's attitude was well illustrated by the tactless way in which he
dismissed Ramsden: "You're not exactly on the crest of a wave, Ramsden." Thompson, *Churchill and the Montgomery Myth*, p. 80.

Arab. In contrast to his harsh treatment of those who were down, Montgomery was the soul of hospitality to his superiors. His briefing on the Eighth Army situation was impressive. He assiduously kept the press away while Churchill swam in the Mediterranean. And finally, Montgomery arranged for good food, wine, and brandy to liven the Prime Minister's dinner. He was rewarded the next day by Mr. Churchill's tacit recognition of his assumption of command on August 13, which date, as the anniversary of the Battle of Blenheim, caught his imagination. As if to put the seal of approval on Montgomery's actions, Churchill wrote in his guest book:

> May the anniversary of Blenheim which marks the opening of the new Command bring to the Commander in Chief of the Eighth Army and his troops the fame and fortune they will surely deserve. August 20, 1942, Winston S. Churchill.

*

Lieutenant General Sir Brian Horrocks, commanding the 9th Armoured Division in England, received a telephone call during the early evening of August 15, 1942. At the other end of the line a voice from the War Office said, "You are to travel down to London tonight and you will be going on a journey almost immediately."

Unable to discuss details over the telephone, Horrocks stretched security procedures: "Cold or warm?"

"Warm, and you will be moving one up."

Horrocks now knew that he was going to command a corps, probably under Montgomery in the Eighth Army. Professionally, this was an assignment that any young (forty-seven) general would welcome. But being no Montgomery, Horrocks was a little worried, only hoping that he could meet expectations. Within thirty-six hours Horrocks was flying in a B-24 Liberator to Cairo. By Tuesday, August 18, he was in Alexander's headquarters, soon on his way up to Burg-el-Arab. En route he passed the 44th Home County Division on its way to Alam Halfa. This was a cheering sight for a man whose confidence could use bolstering; he had commanded this division back in England, and many of the faces would be familiar.

Soon Horrocks was in conference with Montgomery, who was giving him a concise summary of the situation. Two corps were in the line, Montgomery explained, XXX Corps on the right (north) and XIII Corps on the left (south). XXX Corps was strongly held, but XIII Corps was the one which would bear the brunt of the flanking movement which Rommel would doubtless attempt around the British left.

Then, either consciously or unconsciously mispronouncing Horrocks' name, Montgomery turned on him: "You, Jorrocks, are to take over command of this corps—XIII—and you will defeat Rommel and repel his at-

tack *without getting unduly mauled in the process.* . . . I don't much like
the existing plan on XIII Corps front. Go up and alter it as you see fit,
but keep me informed of what you propose to do and I will come and see
you at any time. In my opinion the key to the battle on your front is the
Alam Halfa Ridge, which is now occupied by the 44th Division."[17]

On arrival at his new headquarters on Alam Halfa Horrocks was
pleased by the nature of the terrain; it was what he considered a "tanker's
paradise." The ground was too hard to permit digging foxholes readily.
Observation was superb, and concealment for the individual infantryman
was nearly non-existent. The surface permitted tanks to travel almost anywhere at will. Shortly Horrocks was conferring with his chief of staff and
his intelligence officer.

Rommel, they agreed, would attack the XIII Corps position with the
entire Afrika Korps (21st Panzer, 15th Panzer, 90th Light Infantry Divisions) south of the Alam Nayil Ridge (the New Zealand Division) and
through the gap between that and Alam Halfa. At that point Rommel
would have the choice of continuing toward Cairo or turning northward
across the Alam Halfa Ridge. The staff of XIII Corps, like Alexander and
Montgomery, believed that in all likelihood he would turn north across
the very ground they were standing on.

Horrocks looked around. The 44th Division was in place on Alam
Halfa, but certain areas needed special reinforcement, especially a little
knob on the western end of the ridge, Hill 102. Horrocks had a unit available, the 22nd Armoured Brigade, equipped with sixty new American
tanks. Since at the moment these were the only tanks in the Eighth Army
capable of matching Rommel's, they were known as "Egypt's Last Hope"
(ELH).[18] Horrocks decided to dig them in on Hill 102, knowing that doing so was completely consistent with Montgomery's admonition, "Don't
get mauled." Until the 10th Armoured Division should arrive with sixty-
six more American tanks, Horrocks planned to leave the corridor open
south of Alam Halfa.

Horrocks' original concern at having been given this challenging assignment was not eased overnight. He was another "new boy with pink knees"
and was hardly in a position to establish himself with strong, immediate
action, as had Montgomery. His malaise lingered, and his morale sank
even lower when the Prime Minister made his celebrated visit to Montgomery's headquarters on the nineteenth of August. Horrocks had arrived
only the day before, but Churchill, always eager to attack, seemed to
blame him personally for planning a defensive battle on XIII Corps's
front. Horrocks explained that if Rommel tried to go to Cairo his XIII
Corps would pounce on his rear like a dog eating a rabbit. Churchill was

[17] Horrocks, *Escape to Action,* p. 108. Italics supplied.
[18] The tanks were M3 Grants, soon to be superseded by the even better M4 Shermans.

not placated. For the rest of the day he kept mumbling to himself, "Dog eat rabbit!"[19]

Montgomery later called Horrocks in. Sensitive to the browbeating that his lieutenant had received at the hands of the Prime Minister, he gave encouragement. With this support from his chief, plus the build-up in force—the 22nd Armoured Brigade now had ninety-two tanks—Horrocks looked to the future with more optimism. He busied himself rehearsing maneuvers in which the tanks would move up to their dug-in positions at the outset of battle.

*

On the morning of Friday, August 28, 1942, Field Marshal Erwin Rommel was facing one of the most difficult decisions of his career, whether or not to go ahead with his planned attack around the south end of the British Eighth Army. The date could be delayed no longer since the moon, so necessary for a night operation, was on the wane. After August 30 it would be too late.

Rommel had reasons not to make the attack. Most of the odds were stacked against him, one of which was his own physical condition. He was a sick man at the time, sick enough to ask Hitler to replace him with General Heinz Guderian. His faintness and stomach ailments were probably the result of weariness; he was one of the few German officers over forty years old who had lasted in Africa for such a length of time. Further, he had a head cold, a sore throat, and low blood pressure. The previous week he had been too weak to write, and his physician, Professor Horster, reported him "not in a condition to command the forthcoming offensive." Rommel, Horster concluded, should be treated at home, although he could still make it "temporarily" in Africa.[20] By the next week Rommel was somewhat better, and although his performance at this time was perhaps not so brilliant (or lucky) as in previous months, he seemed to have recovered enough to go on the attack.

A more serious situation, from a practical point of view, was the fact that Rommel's army was now inferior in strength to that of Montgomery. He was, according to one source, 16,000 men below strength, and disease was reaching epidemic proportions. His Panzer Army was short over 200 tanks and nearly 200 troop carriers. At this point Rommel could field only 203 battle tanks in contrast to the 765 available to the British.[21] Rommel could not have known the exact details of British strength, but

---

[19] Horrocks later learned that Churchill had recommended that Montgomery replace him. Montgomery reportedly suggested that he and the Prime Minister should each stick to his own sphere.

[20] Thompson, *Churchill and the Montgomery Myth*, p. 97.

[21] Irving, *The Trail of the Fox*, p. 206. The term "British" is used here to cover all Empire and Commonwealth troops.

he realized that with the steady build-up from Allied convoys around the Cape, time was against him.

He was also short of gasoline and oil. Ten days earlier, on August 18, Marshal Ugo Cavellero, Chief of the Italian High Command, had assured him that 6,000 tons of gasoline would arrive by the thirtieth, to come in six ships. But by August 27, the day before Rommel was facing his final decision, he knew that four of the six had been sunk.

Under these conditions he would certainly have called off his attack except for the fact that the day before, on August 27, Field Marshal Albert Kesselring had arrived from Italy and assured him of 700 tons of gasoline to be air-lifted by the thirtieth "if all else failed." Seven hundred tons was a dramatic shortfall from the promised 6,000, but at least it was something.

This situation did not come about completely through luck on the part of the Allies. The fact is that British Intelligence was at this moment far superior to Rommel's, and information picked up by ULTRA on August 23 was at least partly responsible for the sinking of the six promised shiploads of gasoline. ULTRA, in fact, was telling Montgomery of Rommel's state of health as well as the date he would launch his attack, if at all. (Not even ULTRA, of course, could pick up what final decision Rommel would make unless he reported back to Hitler.)

There were reasons, however, why Rommel felt that the attack must go ahead. This being a now-or-never situation, he had at least a fighting chance of turning the British position, disrupting the Eighth Army, and capturing a British gas dump. Capture of British gas and oil might permit him to head east, past a defeated Eighth Army. Rommel's previous victories had almost always been achieved with inferior forces, and maybe he could emerge once more victorious, taking Cairo. Unaware of the strength of the British mine fields south of the Ruweisat Ridge, he decided on the morning of August 29 to go ahead.

In a proclamation Rommel expressed his confidence:

> "Today our army sets out once more to attack and destroy the enemy, this time for keeps. I expect every soldier in my army to do his utmost in these decisive days! Long live Fascist Italy! Long live the Greater German Reich! Long live our great leaders!"[22]

*

Sir Brian Horrocks knew that this night, August 30, was the one on which Intelligence had said Rommel would attack. But, since all the defenses of XIII Corps were set, he did that evening what generals like most: he visited the front-line troops. He elected to go to the 2nd New

22 Ibid., p. 207.

Zealand Division on Ruweisat Ridge, where the Maoris[23] were scheduled
to carry out a large raid on Rommel's position.

As Horrocks was leaving to return to his headquarters the whole southern flank on Alam Halfa seemed to go up in flames. Rommel's attack was
coming off according to schedule. It was 11:00 P.M.

Horrocks found his operations staff busy; there was nothing he could
do personally to affect the battle. His men were in position and their defensive plan was good, so it would be morning before he could take any
action. Horrocks therefore forced himself to get a good night's sleep. He
would be refreshed the next day, and somehow it seemed necessary to
show confidence in his plan by disappearing from the view of his staff.
Montgomery had done the same, retiring at nine.

*

No such luxury fell to Montgomery's adversary to the west. After midnight, now the morning of August 31, the ailing Erwin Rommel moved
his headquarters to Jebel Klakh, behind his forward troops. He believed
that the enemy sector was weakly mined and defended in this area, and
this was the spot from which he could direct the exploitation after the
breakthrough. But he was in for an unpleasant surprise. Shortly after 8:00
A.M. he received reports that his troops were discovering dense mine
fields, defended heavily by British infantry, backed up by machine guns,
artillery, and mortars. The area of attack was illuminated by parachute
flares, and for the first time Rommel's troops were under air attack at
night. Afrika Korps Commander Walther Nehring was wounded, and
Rommel's chief of staff, Colonel Fritz Bayerlein, was taking direct command of the famed unit. To make matters worse, General Georg von Bismarck, commanding the 21st Panzer Division, had been killed.

At this point Rommel considered breaking off the battle, a sensible
move in view of the developments, but he allowed himself to listen to
Bayerlein, who knew how to hit Rommel emotionally: to break off the attack now, Bayerlein argued, would "make a mockery" of those who had
fought through the night to breach the mine field. Rommel went ahead. It
was obvious, however, that surprise was lost and that he could never
by-pass Alam Halfa Ridge. He would have to turn northward. British Intelligence could not have done better had they drawn up Rommel's plan
themselves.

*

That morning Brian Horrocks maintained his façade of casual certainty. He forced himself to move calmly as he shaved, dressed, and
walked (not ran) to the operations room. There to his delight he found
everything going as predicted. By 11:00 A.M. his staff had definitely

---

[23] New Zealand aborigine troops.

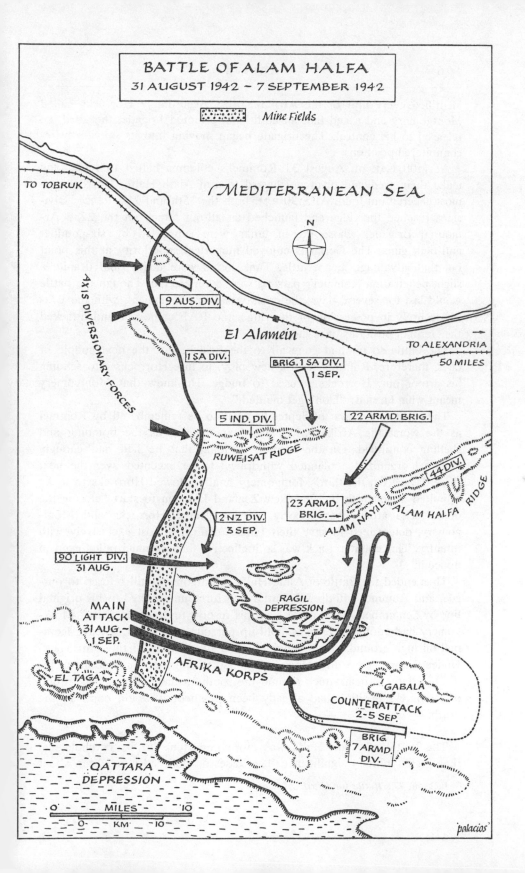

BATTLE OF ALAM HALFA
31 AUGUST 1942 – 7 SEPTEMBER 1942

Mine Fields

MEDITERRANEAN SEA

TO TOBRUK

AXIS DIVERSIONARY FORCES

9 AUS. DIV.

El Alamein

TO ALEXANDRIA

50 MILES

1 SA DIV.

BRIG. 1 SA DIV.
1 SEP.

22 ARMD. BRIG.

5 IND. DIV.

RUWEISAT RIDGE

44 DIV.

23 ARMD. BRIG.

ALAM NAYIL

ALAM HALFA RIDGE

2 NZ DIV.
3 SEP.

90 LIGHT DIV.
31 AUG.

RAGIL DEPRESSION

MAIN
ATTACK
31 AUG.–
1 SEP.

EL TAGA

AFRIKA KORPS

GABALA

COUNTERATTACK
2–5 SEP.

BRIG.
7 ARMD.
DIV.

QATTARA
DEPRESSION

0 — MILES — 10

0 — KM — 10

palacios

identified every unit of the Afrika Korps. Accordingly Horrocks called Montgomery and asked that an additional armored brigade, the 23rd, be released to his control. The brigade began moving into its previously reconnoitered positions.

At 1:00 P.M. on August 31 Rommel's columns halted to refuel and make their predicted pivot northward toward Alam Halfa. Horrocks almost cheered out loud. At 5:30 P.M. both the 15th and 21st Panzer Divisions reached the ridge and launched an all-out attack on the 22nd Armoured Brigade, whose dug-in tanks were supported by six-pounder anti-tank guns. The Germans enjoyed numerical superiority at this point but that advantage meant little. Tank losses were heavy; and despite a slight penetration Rommel's panzers were soon ejected. Though the battle would last for several days, the crisis was over. That night, with the British securely in possession of the ridge, the RAF came out and attacked the German positions once more.

The battle so far had gone all to the British. For the next couple of days, therefore, Rommel tried a new ploy, to lure Horrocks into sending his armor out. Horrocks refused to budge. He knew that Montgomery meant what he said: "Don't get mauled."

The night of the first of September was to be remembered by Rommel as the worst the Afrika Korps ever experienced, as the bombing and shelling continued. On the second, deciding that he had had enough, Rommel organized a planned withdrawal to be executed over the next three days.[24] On the third Montgomery finally allowed Horrocks to make a limited attack with the 2nd New Zealand Division to start "closing the door." The attack went poorly, partly because Horrocks and Montgomery, determined to save their tanks, made it almost exclusively with infantry. This counterattack was so ineffective that Rommel failed even to notice it.

Thus ended the Battle of Alam Halfa. Montgomery still refused to pursue, and Rommel withdrew his attacking force unmolested to his original line by September 7. But aside from his resolve to "take no risks," Montgomery had another reason to hold up pursuit: he wanted to leave Rommel on high ground, which provided good observation of the British left. Under Rommel's eye Montgomery planned to stage demonstrations to indicate a later British attack around the southern flank. But a penetration of Rommel's position had already been planned; it would come in the north.

The Battle of Alam Halfa was more important for its psychological than for its military significance. The losses on both sides had been about

24 Jackson, *The Battle for North Africa,* p. 274.

equal[25] (the British were better able to afford them), and no significant territorial changes occurred. But the Desert Army had won a victory! Rommel's illness, brought on at least partly by nerves, was highly intensified, while British confidence soared.

Alexander and Montgomery would now have six weeks to prepare for their own major offensive, which would be executed with a numerical advantage far greater than they enjoyed in late August. Alam Halfa had set the stage. All eyes were now turned toward the last week of October.

*

The date on which the Second Battle of El Alamein would be launched was practically dictated by the tactical plan. It would be a night attack, and since Rommel's flanks were protected, Montgomery planned a penetration of his main position, which in turn called for strong moonlight to permit the sappers to clear the mine fields. This meant a waxing rather than a waning moon, and that would occur only during the third week of September or October. The night of the full moon in September would come only two weeks after Alam Halfa. Therefore, when Churchill tried to hold Alexander to the original agreed date of the third week in September for the attack, Alexander pointed out that the Battle of Alam Halfa had intervened since the agreement, giving his conclusion that "the best date . . . to start would be minus 13 of TORCH." That would mean the next moon, October 23. The Prime Minister replied, "We are in your hands."[26]

The Eighth Army attack could be executed anywhere so long as it was made somewhere along Rommel's forty-five-mile front; therefore Montgomery could keep him in the dark as to the exact location(s). Two corridors were duly selected, both in the XXX Corps sector to the north. To keep Rommel guessing as to where these corridors would be, Montgomery early in October began placing dummy tanks, artillery positions, and dumps in great numbers all along the front. Through normal observation, even from the air, it was impossible for an enemy to distinguish the dummies from the real things. Thus under the cover of darkness the British could substitute the real equipment for the dummies at any desired point, and aerial photography would show no apparent changes. To further guard against compromise of plans Montgomery delayed informing participating commanders as long as possible. Those units along the line, whose troops were subject to capture, would be kept ignorant of plans until the last moment.

All circumstances were favorable. The Desert Air Force would enjoy complete air supremacy by the time of the attack; the British would have

[25] Jackson, ibid., gives the following figures: British losses, 1,750 men; 67 tanks; 68 aircraft. Rommel's losses, 1,859 Germans and 1,051 Italians; 49 tanks; 41 aircraft.
[26] Alexander, p. 53.

preponderance in all ground arms; and Rommel's supply line was badly stretched, vulnerable to air attack. Under these conditions a battle of attrition, if pursued relentlessly, would almost have to be successful. The plan was extremely conservative, in keeping with Montgomery's dictum of "no defeats." For even after the infantry had dug through the German position, at great loss, the tanks were still not to be risked by seeking out Rommel's armor. Instead the British tanks were to simply assume blocking positions as they did at Alam Halfa, once more to act as dug-in pillboxes to wear down Rommel's tank strength. In exchange for a sure-fire plan, Mongtomery, with Alexander's approval, was willing to exercise "surgical callousness" and pay heavily in lives.[27] The infantry "dogfight" would last for days.

After a tremendous artillery barrage the attack jumped off on schedule at 9:40 P.M. on October 23. Progress was made along the two corridors, but the gains were not nearly so deep as Montgomery had hoped. According to a previous contingency plan, therefore, Montgomery committed his X Armoured Corps before the mine fields were completely breached. The corps commander, Lieutenant General Herbert Lumsden, protested and was summarily relieved of his position for expressing disagreement with the infallible commander of the Eighth Army.

Though the Second Battle of El Alamein bore very little risk of actual defeat, it could, under a less willful and driving commander, have wound up in a stalemate. Montgomery showed flexibility in the middle of the battle by pulling the New Zealand Division from the south to exploit success in the north. And he exhibited a remarkable grasp when, with the attack apparently bogging down, he was visited by a worried Minister of State Hugh Casey and Near East Commander Alexander. Arguing that the battle was about to be won, Montgomery convinced them to let him continue his own way. (Brooke, in London, successfully kept the Prime Minister quiet.) Montgomery's judgment was vindicated: Rommel tried to break off the battle on November 2 but Hitler denied permission. Two days later Rommel's position collapsed.

El Alamein was not followed up with an aggressive pursuit. Although Rommel's army suffered heavy losses, the bulk escaped to fight another day. But attaining a major victory was important. And with TORCH about to land in Rommel's rear, Hitler's forces would never return to Egypt. Rommel's campaigns in Africa would degenerate to a long delaying action back to Tunisia.

The month of November 1942 witnessed the beginning of the end for

[27] Lewin, *Montgomery as Military Commander,* p. 103, places eventual Eighth Army casualties in four days at 6,140.

Hitler. His drive on Stalingrad stalled, and his forces suffered defeat in North Africa. In size the battle at Stalingrad dwarfed that at El Alamein. But by the calendar these two battles represented the high-water mark of Nazi advance of World War II.

Part Three

CHAPTER XI

TORCH I:
THE ALLIES LAND

In the dim past some anonymous commander first exclaimed, "God grant that I may win my first battle!" The reasoning is not difficult to appreciate; as in so many aspects of human activity, success seems to breed success. This axiom seems particularly important to the warrior's psyche. Thus success of the expedition to North Africa, code-named TORCH, was of unique importance to the Western Allies as the year 1942 drew to a close. The most anxious months were over and swift-moving events were about to occur.

*

Eisenhower, Clark, and the rest of their small party (minus one B-17 held up by engine trouble) arrived at Gibraltar late in the afternoon of November 5, 1942, after having made the trip at an altitude of a hundred feet to avoid detection by German radar on the French coast. They flew so low that the pilots were forced to climb to reach the traffic pattern. Air defenses of Gibraltar, unsure of their identity, were on "yellow alert," CAUTION. Fortunately the warning never turned red.

On Gibraltar General Eisenhower was given comfortable sleeping quarters in the governor's mansion, long called the Convent (which it had actually been many years earlier). His office, however, would be located in a tunnel drilled deep into the Rock. This eight-foot-square room was shared by Eisenhower and Clark and was later described by Eisenhower as the "most dismal setting" he occupied during the war. The long tunnel leading to it was dark, lighted only at intervals by single bulbs hanging from the ceiling. The dankness and stagnation seemed unresponsive to the clattering electric fans. General George Patton, visiting later, snorted at the safety of the place; but the outdoors-minded Eisenhower would vastly have preferred a more exposed—and less claustrophobic—location.

Eisenhower had personally selected Gibraltar as his command post for TORCH, though actually he had been afforded no choice. Gibraltar was the only base in British hands west of beleaguered Malta; furthermore it provided an adequate communications system capable of keeping in touch with the three landing forces whose destinations lay a thousand miles from end to end. Gibraltar was necessary as the headquarters for the start of the operation, but Eisenhower was impatient to transfer to North Africa.

After a routine but cordial welcome by the governor, Lieutenant General Mason-MacFarlane, Eisenhower stumbled down to his little cave to confer with his naval commander, Admiral Sir Andrew Cunningham, who had come earlier by fast cruiser. A meeting with Cunningham was always enough to lift one's spirits, for his courage, cheerfulness, and optimism were contagious. Together they went over weather reports and exchanged what meager knowledge each had picked up regarding the movements of convoys.

Mostly their information was negative—which was good. There was no news of disaster for the moment, and reports by ULTRA indicated that Field Marshal Albert Kesselring, commanding the Axis forces in the Mediterranean, was still ignorant of Allied intentions. Kesselring was expecting Allied landings, as ships had been sighted, but his messages to Hitler revealed no knowledge of where they were heading. North Africa, Sardinia, and Sicily were mentioned. Eisenhower was thus assured that plans for TORCH had not fallen into Axis hands.

But between his arrival at Gibraltar and the all-important night of November 7 the hours for the Allied Commander were long. He paced the floor, conferred, wrote in his diary, and dispatched lengthy letters to Marshall, the Combined Chiefs, and his family. To his son at 10:30 A.M. on November 7:

> Just how this particular venture is going to turn out no one knows. So a man has to learn to be patient—and keep himself from cracking under a constant realization that he can do nothing but wait while the developing situation slowly spells out either a victory or a disaster for his country. This period is far from an easy one—but I've only 24 more hours to go before I should have some idea.

He also dispatched a brief note to the Prime Minister, as he was touched by certain messages from London. Bedell Smith, left behind, had reported: "Prime Minister was hard to hold during your trip. He called me and everyone else at ten-minute intervals. . . . When your message finally arrived Pug [Ismay] took it in to him and he exclaimed 'Don't tell me he has drowned.' We replied that everything was okay on which he said, 'I never had the slightest idea that it would be otherwise.'" The next day a second message came from Churchill: "I feel that the Rock of Gibraltar will be safe in your hands."[1] This concern was flattering to Eisenhower personally, but nothing happened for a long time to relieve the tension.

The suspense was broken for a while by word that Lieutenant Bill Jewell's H.M.S. *Seraph* had succeeded in picking up General Giraud in the Gulf of Lion and that Giraud and Wright had been transferred to a flying boat. Finally they came in, unshaven and weary. Wright was obviously elated over the success of the rescue mission, and Giraud carried himself with impeccable military dignity despite his crumpled civilian clothes.

At this point began an interview—or rather a series of interviews—which brought to the surface the degree of misunderstanding which had always existed between Giraud and the Allies. Giraud sincerely expected to be named supreme commander of an exclusively Anglo-American force whose enemy, if it were to have one, would be French.

For three hours Eisenhower and Clark (Colonel Julius Holmes interpreting) tried to reach a meeting of the minds with Giraud. Eisenhower began by explaining Allied plans, which counted on a proclamation by Giraud, as French commander, saying, "I resume my place of combat among you."

But Giraud would have none of this. Stiffening, he said, "Now let's get this clear. As I understand it, when I land in North Africa I am to assume command of all Allied forces and become Supreme Allied Commander in North Africa."

Clark gasped, but he observed no outward reaction by Eisenhower, who simply said, "There must be some misunderstanding."

Both sides stood their ground until dinnertime. Giraud left, unconvinced, to join Mason-MacFarlane, and the two Americans went back to their messages and ate at their desks. The indications came that the surf at Casablanca, one of the most feared elements of risk, seemed to have calmed down.

That evening the talks with Giraud resumed. Still convinced that the honor of France precluded his assuming a subordinate role, Giraud stood

[1] G-76, Nov. 6, AFHQ Message Center Files, Reel 16B, Chandler, I, p. 653. G-95, Nov. 7, ibid.

Eisenhower was the only non-Britisher in modern times to command Gibraltar.

his ground to the point that Eisenhower, though sympathetic to Giraud personally, gave up for the moment and turned the discussion over to Clark. Even Clark's more earthy approach failed. Finally Giraud issued an ultimatum: "Then I shall return to France."

"Oh, no, you won't," Clark retorted. "That was a one-way submarine. You're not going back to France on it." The argument continued in direct, blunt terms, but neither side would give way. Clark was now coming to feel that Giraud was merely awaiting developments. Finally Eisenhower broke into the conversation again, saying that they were all tired and should get some sleep. But before retiring he went to the top of the Rock.

The night of November 7–8, as the hours were getting shorter, was the first of many suspenseful vigils Eisenhower would keep during the war. But before trying to rest, he had to finish a message to General Marshall that he had begun at 9:30 A.M. that day. The body of the letter was long though informal, a think piece as much as a report. At 4:00 P.M. he added a cheerful postscript:

> KINGPIN [Giraud] has just reached here. I will see him in twenty minutes. The boy [British submarine captain] that picked him off is the same one that carried Clark on his hazardous mission. I'd like to give him a Silver Star this evening!

At 10:00 P.M. he scribbled another postscript by hand:

> I've had a 4 hour struggle with KINGPIN. He—so far—says "Either I'm Allied C-in-C or I won't play!" He threatens to withdraw his blessing and wash his hands of the affair. I'm weary! But I'll send you a radio later tonight, after this thing is finished.[2]

And after midnight he wrote a long message to the Combined Chiefs:

> My impression, shared by the EAGLE[3] and Cunningham, is that KINGPIN is playing for time and that he is determined, knowing that there will be some French resistance, not to lay himself open to the charge of being in any way responsible for the shedding of French blood. . . . His method of gaining time is to insist upon a point which as a soldier he is well aware the Allies cannot accept at this moment. If we are generally successful tonight [in the landings] we will not be surprised to find him more conciliatory tomorrow morning. . . .
>
> EAGLE and I are bitterly disappointed, principally because of the

---

[2] Eisenhower to Marshall, Review ⚹1 (⚹93 EM Cable File), ibid., pp. 665–68.
[3] Code name for Clark.

help KINGPIN could have rendered except for his intense personal ambition and ego. . . .[4]

Of the three landings, Algiers, Oran, and Casablanca, the one that Eisenhower had most on his mind was that of Patton's Western Task Force, making an unprecedented landing on a foreign shore after crossing the Atlantic. He had good reasons to worry. French resistance in the Casablanca area was expected to be the strongest in the North African region, in contrast to Algiers, where pro-Allied sentiment was strong. And Murphy of course had reported his talk with the commander in Casablanca, General Noguès, who had said he would resist any Allied landings with all available forces. The French naval commander in the region, Admiral François Michelier, was likewise known to be adamant.

But the greatest imponderable in the Morocco landings, Casablanca in particular, was the surf. Pessimists had estimated that out of the year only twelve days enjoyed seas fit for landing of assault craft; the surf often rose as high as fifteen feet.[5] Eisenhower had been heartened by the news at dinner that the Atlantic was like a millpond and by his sporadic communications with Patton at sea. Previously Patton had announced that impossible landing beaches would only cause him to turn into the Mediterranean to attack Oran or Spain. Had Eisenhower not known "Georgie," his threat to land in Spain would have been a cause for panic. But to be assured that his friend had not lost his impishness gave the Allied Commander a lift.

George Patton's boasts, typically, were calculated for the benefit of his audience. By no means was he so sure of himself. With his own brand of religion, he was continually praying for strength. "I am the best there is," he would notify the Deity, "but that in itself is not enough."

And as the Western Task Force approached the North African shore, Patton's diary reflected the improvement in the weather:

November 5. Last night it was very rough, almost a storm. This morning it is still very rough, with a forty mile wind . . . things are bound to get better, as they could not get worse. I have done some extra praying. I hope that whatever comes up I shall be able to do my full duty. . . .

November 6. Things are looking up. It is calmer, and the wind has fallen to about twenty miles and it is northeast, which is OK. The

[4] Eisenhower to Combined Chiefs of Staff, Review #2 (#113 EM Cable File), Chandler, II, pp. 669–72.

[5] A visit by the author in January 1979 convinced him that such surf was the exception, not the rule.

forecast is for a possible landing condition. The [radio] intercepts indicate that the French will fight.

November 7. This morning it is very quiet and cool, almost too good
to be true. Thank God. I hope He stays on our side. . . . In fifteen
hours I should be ashore.[6]

Patton's force consisted of two reinforced divisions: the 3rd Infantry
Division was to land in the center at Casablanca under Patton's personal
supervision; the 60th Regimental Combat Team (RCT) was to land at
Port Lyautey (now Kenitra) on the left under Brigadier General Lucian
K. Truscott, Jr.;[7] and Combat Command B of the 2nd Armored Division,
reinforced with the 47th RCT, under Major General Ernest N. Harmon,
was to land at Safi on the right (south). The distance from Safi to Port
Lyautey was about two hundred miles. No landings were planned in between these three points.

*

Aboard the U.S. transport *Henry T. Allen,* Brigadier General Lucian
K. Truscott, Jr., commanding Sub Task Force GOALPOST, found himself alternately planning as a hardheaded professional and then indulging
the streak of the poet in him. As the transport plowed its way southward
toward the Cape of Good Hope and then turned northeastward toward
Morocco, Truscott found moments to admire the magnificence of a convoy at sea. He thought of stately swans gliding across a park lagoon, of
waterfowl flying in precise formation, or of the herds of cattle undulating
across Western plains. This convoy, for sheer grandeur, exceeded them
all. Ahead of the *Allen* went the battleship *Texas,* as if breaking the way;
on the flanks were destroyers, affording protection from the U-boat wolf
packs. A real sight.

On duty, however, Truscott was a true professional, who kept his men
constantly training, not only as a device to fight boredom and apprehension but also to familiarize many with their new weapons. To himself
he mulled over what would happen if a U-boat should make a couple of
kills among his landing force. Truscott's force consisted of the equivalent
of about four 800-man battalions, each carried by one transport. Thus, if
he were to lose one ship he would have to rethink his plan for the landing; if he lost two, he could not get ashore.

Best known in peacetime as one of the Army's finest polo players, Truscott came to Eisenhower's attention in 1941 when he was on the staff of
the IX Corps at Fort Lewis, Washington. Unimpressive in appearance, he
was of medium height, slightly stooped, with protruding eyes and a shock

---

[6] Blumenson, *The Patton Papers,* II, 99–102.
[7] An RCT consisted of an infantry regiment of approximately 3,000 men, with one
field artillery battalion (twelve pieces) attached.

of graying hair. His voice was a rasp. But Truscott was tough, and he had already seen some action in this war. Just before returning to the United States to join Patton's Western Task Force, he had been the U. S. Chief of Combined Operations in London, directly under Lord Louis Mountbatten. As such he had been present and had witnessed the entire debacle of the Dieppe landing three months before.

Port Lyautey was important for both its naval base and its airfield. The impressive Sebou River meandered past the small town, making a distinct upside-down "U" just before entering the Atlantic. Inside the "U" lay the airfield. The port itself, nine miles up the river on the south side, afforded a draft of thirteen feet at low tide and seventeen feet at high tide, enough to handle a heavy cruiser. The exits from the landing beaches on the ocean were restricted by a steep row of dunes which could be crossed only at certain points. The country in the region was dense scrub, hard going even for men on foot.

Truscott's plan, worked out in detail before leaving the United States, was logical. Two of his four battalions (2nd and 3rd Battalions, 60th Infantry) would land on either side of the mouth of the Sebou. If surprise were attained, one of these, probably the 2nd Battalion on the south bank, would seize the Kasbah[8] within an hour or so after landing. Another battalion, (1st Battalion, 60th Infantry) would land five miles south of the river, as close to the town as the dunes would permit, and drive toward the port itself. A composite battalion would land about five miles to the north and attempt to by-pass above the bend in the river and approach Port Lyautey from that direction.

One problem facing Commodore Gray, the naval commander in this operation, was to make sure he knew exactly where his convoy was. The officers aboard the *Allen* admitted frankly that even the charts they were using indicated a possible error of three miles in their depiction of the coastline. Gray had made provision for this danger by sending ahead a submarine to scout. Nevertheless, he was apprehensive that something could go wrong. A delay would make the landing exceedingly hazardous.

Truscott was well aware that the success of the entire TORCH operation was heavily dependent on French cooperation. To do what he could regarding the French attitude, Truscott had devised his own scheme, forlorn as the hope might be, to eliminate resistance. He drew up a letter addressed to the commander of the French forces, had it translated into French, and decorated the final product with a neat ribbon. He found two volunteers eager to deliver the letter, Colonel Demas T. Craw and Major Pierpont M. Hamilton. These two Air Corps officers, who had spent years on the Continent, were fluent in French, men of dignity and presence.

[8] A strong fortress on a promontory on the south bank, so located that it overlooked the entire river mouth.

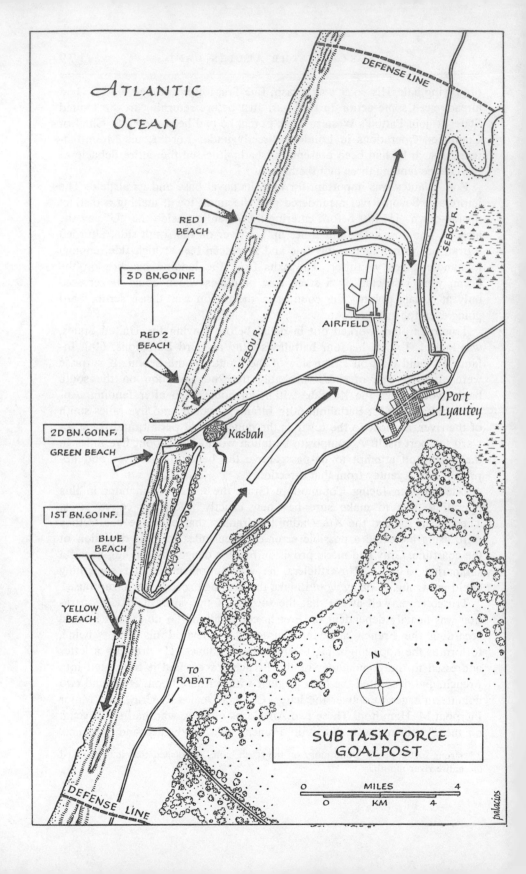

ATLANTIC
OCEAN

RED 1
BEACH

3D BN. 60 INF.

RED 2
BEACH

SEBOU R.

AIRFIELD

SEBOU R.

2D BN. 60 INF.

GREEN BEACH

Kasbah

Port
Lyautey

1ST BN. 60 INF.

BLUE
BEACH

YELLOW
BEACH

TO
RABAT

N

SUB TASK FORCE
GOALPOST

0   MILES   4

0   KM   4

DEFENSE LINE

DEFENSE
LINE

palacios

Major Hamilton had been the first to present himself, and Truscott had approved him immediately. He was more reluctant to accept Craw because of his responsibility as Truscott's air officer. However, the importance of the mission justified the risk. The two would go in with the lead troops, and if they were successful many lives and much valuable time might be saved.

On the morning of November 7 Truscott noticed that the convoys had now separated into three groups, each bound for its own landing area. Now the ocean seemed strangely empty. Around 10:00 P.M. lights began to appear on some unknown shore. Stars were out, and the ships proceeded silently in the calm, though the navigators of the ships were still unable to identify what towns the lights represented. Soon, however, the scouting submarine appeared, only to warn that the *Henry T. Allen* had been sailing too close to shore; the commodore would have to pull back out to sea to find the other ships.[9] Truscott was worried to note that GOALPOST was already one hour late.

Without waiting to make contact, the *Henry T. Allen* began lowering boats at 12:30 A.M., expecting to disembark an hour later. Since no craft from other ships had been reported, however, Truscott took his aide and proceeded in a small boat into the dark to identify each transport, one by one. Crews were reluctant to communicate with the unexpected figure appearing out of the dark, so Truscott had boarded each one of the four and reviewed last-minute plans with the troop commanders. He returned to the *Henry T. Allen* at 3:30 A.M. He hoped that, with luck, his troops could still reach shore before daylight.

On the *Allen* an excited chief of staff reported that General Eisenhower's message to the French people was coming over the radio. The President's proclamation had begun at 3:00 A.M., and this was a rebroadcast of Eisenhower's follow-up.

With a sinking heart Truscott realized that the task forces inside the Mediterranean had landed a little ahead of time and that the proclamation had been aired an hour early. It would be extremely fortunate if the French on the shore were not alert. He had little time to worry, however, for soon five brightly lighted French ships sailed out in column, through the GOALPOST fleet. One of them signaled in French (fortunately a young naval officer could read the message): "Be warned. They are alert on shore. Alert for 0500."

The French ships proceeded on, but Truscott knew that surprise had been lost.

*

In the White House President Roosevelt received a message from the man whom he had originally intended to address as "my dear old friend."

---

[9] By now all ships were blacked out, observing radio silence.

Pétain's answer to Roosevelt's cable, delivered while the landings were going on, was categorical:

> It is with stupor and sadness that I learned tonight of the aggression of your troops against North Africa.
>
> I have read your message. You invoke pretexts which nothing justifies. . . . France and her honor are at stake. We are attacked; we shall defend ourselves; this is the order I am giving.
>
> PÉTAIN

*

As the night of November 7 approached, Robert Murphy in Algiers was finding it difficult to maintain his outward composure and avoid disclosing the secret of the landing. Callers were coming and going, and many of them were fishing for information. The foremost Algerian nationalist, Ferhat Abbas, for one, came to Murphy, probably in all innocence, to discuss the attitude of the United States toward Algerian independence after the war. Murphy could only sidestep, saying that America, though sympathetic, was concentrating on the defeat of the Axis.

Much more difficult to deal with was an old acquaintance from Paris and Vichy, Pierre Etienne Flandin, a former French Premier and Foreign Minister. Flandin warned Murphy that if the Americans delayed too long in coming, say within a month, it would be too late. A spate of rumors about an imminent Axis invasion of Tunisia was flying about, he warned, and he emotionally urged American action. It would have been a pleasure for Murphy to tell his friend that the invasion was only hours away, but divulging the secret even this late was out of the question.

The secrecy restriction placed on Murphy was causing more than personal inconvenience. He had made contact with certain groups of Frenchmen who could assist the Allied landings given sufficient notice. One of these was a Colonel Van Hecke, who represented a corps of 30,000 youths. But Murphy well knew that the lack of warning would prevent Van Hecke from making his organization effective.

Most disturbing to Murphy's plans was the absence of General Giraud. Murphy had made all of his plans on the understanding that Giraud would be on hand in Algiers when the Allies would land. After a frantic exchange of telegrams, however, Murphy had learned that Giraud was headed for Gibraltar to confer with Eisenhower instead of coming to Algiers. Though Murphy could appreciate the value of such a meeting, Giraud's absence would exacerbate his problem.

As dusk fell the evening of Saturday, November 7, it was common knowledge among informed people in Algiers that a huge Allied convoy had passed through the Strait of Gibraltar into the Mediterranean. This fact in itself was not particularly dangerous, because it was presumed that this was simply another effort to resupply Malta. Shortly before midnight, however, the British Broadcasting Corporation in London (BBC) sent the coded message that all the clandestine radios were tuned in for: *"Allo, Robert. Franklin arrivé."*

On hearing this message Murphy immediately contacted his various resistance groups, and they flew into action. Soon they controlled many of the police and power stations, military headquarters, communications, and transportation centers. Murphy then proceeded to the hillside residence of General Alphonse Juin, the ranking Army officer in French North Africa. Now was the time when Murphy needed the absent Giraud.

Juin, despite his rank, had not been on the list of those given advance information. Though considered for a while as a possible French leader— Murphy was aware of Juin's hatred of the Nazis and Fascists—Juin was one of those who had been forced to pledge not to take up arms against the Nazis as condition for his release as a prisoner of war. Juin's pledge, rendered under duress, *could* be considered invalid. But in view of the high sense of honor characteristic of the French military hierarchy, he was considered a bad risk.

Juin's Senegalese guards allowed Murphy through the courtyard to the Villa des Oliviers, though it was well after midnight. Juin, in striped pajamas, sleepily answered the door. Instantly, however, he was wide awake and furious to learn what was happening without his knowledge. Murphy tried to placate him by stressing that the Americans were coming in by invitation of the French, represented by General Giraud. Juin, then, asked pointedly where Giraud was; Murphy had to admit that the general was not on hand.

Juin took some time to adjust himself to the new developments. When he finally recovered from his shock, he mentioned that Admiral Jean François Darlan, Commander-in-Chief of the French Armed Forces, was on hand at Admiral Fenard's house. Despite his personal pique, Juin finally admitted that he would be with the Allies were the decision in his hands. But with Darlan on the spot, he, Juin, held no authority. He was willing, however, to call Darlan with the word that Murphy was at his villa with important news. Soon Darlan was speeding through the narrow, winding streets to the Villa des Oliviers; he appeared within twenty minutes.

Murphy felt certain that he possessed full authority to deal with Darlan, despite the ambivalent feelings that many in Washington held about him. As late as October 17 Roosevelt had sent Murphy a personal message authorizing him to initiate any arrangements with Darlan that could be helpful. Now, by coincidence, the admiral had come to Algiers to be at the bedside of his son Alain, recently stricken with polio.[10]

When Darlan and Fenard joined Juin and Murphy, Darlan predictably became furious. "I have known for a long time that the British are stupid," he exclaimed. "But I'd have believed the Americans were more intelligent. Apparently you have the same genius as the British for making massive blunders."[11] Immediately the little admiral began pacing the floor; the stooped, towering Murphy paced along with him, trying to keep step.

Darlan continued with his tirade. If the Americans had only waited a few weeks, he exclaimed, they could have received effective cooperation, both in France itself and in Africa. Now he was worried about France. What would happen to the unoccupied portion in the light of this "premature unilateral attack"? Darlan seemed to be assuming that the "effective cooperation" would have been provided by him, based on the unrealistic presumption that the "Anglo-Saxons" would have preferred him over Giraud. But at least his tirade convincingly demonstrated that this was no calculated performance. Darlan had obviously been taken off balance. In turn Murphy could conclude that Darlan's presence in Algiers was indeed a matter of chance and that the secret had not leaked.

Murphy then tried another approach. Would Darlan cooperate, he asked, if armed with the authority of Pétain? Darlan, pausing for a moment, admitted that he would of course cooperate with the Allies if Pétain approved. He thereupon called in a junior French naval officer and dictated a message.

When the four men went out the door to head for Admiralty headquarters, they were confronted with a surprise. There, replacing Juin's Senegalese guards, was a group of forty French *aspirants* (officer candidates) who had been among those called to action when Murphy alerted the resistance groups. The *aspirants* had orders from somewhere and would allow nobody to pass except Murphy and the local vice-consul, Kenneth Pendar. Darlan would not believe that Murphy was as surprised as the others, but he consented to allow Murphy to dispatch Pendar down the mountain to the Admiralty to send Darlan's message to Vichy. It was never acknowledged.

With time on their hands now, Darlan, Fenard, Juin, and Murphy returned into the villa. Here they bided their time and, in a calmer atmosphere, discussed the political situation. Darlan gave Murphy one warning

[10] Many have conjectured that Darlan may have used his son's condition as an excuse to be in Algiers. If such is true, it is also true that his son's polio was very real. A coffin had even been ordered for him. Tompkins, *The Murder of Admiral Darlan*, p. 65.

[11] Murphy, p. 129.

regarding Giraud: "He is not your man; he is a good divisional commander." Murphy had no way, at the moment, of judging whether the admiral was correct or not, though the evaluation, given without rancor, appeared to stem from sober conviction.

In the early morning hours the *aspirants* guarding the villa were dispersed by the state police, whose loyalty belonged not to Murphy but to Juin. Now Murphy was the prisoner, and for a while he feared that the police might summarily shoot him as a Nazi agent. Darlan, however, declared himself personally responsible for Murphy's conduct. The group remained in Juin's house until word arrived that Major General Charles Ryder's Eastern Task Force had landed. It was now 6:30 A.M.

Darlan and Juin then left Murphy under guard in Juin's house and headed for Fort l'Empereur, military headquarters in Algiers. Fenard stayed behind, possibly to watch Murphy, and nothing could change his mind. Murphy was therefore sentenced to spend many more hours of suspense in the villa.

Darlan and Juin were gone through the morning. At 3:00 P.M., satisfied that Ryder's task force was indeed in control of the city, they returned. Darlan thereupon provided Murphy a chauffeur-driven car bearing a French flag and a white flag to take him into the American lines. Soon Murphy found himself in Ryder's temporary command post.

General Ryder, looking dazed, insisted on donning a fresh uniform before going to see Darlan. He also took time to send a dispatch to Gibraltar. It seemed to an impatient Murphy that it took Ryder hours to write a paragraph, but on learning that Ryder had gone days without sleep, Murphy understood; he was in much the same condition himself.

Ryder's message completed, the two Americans left in Murphy's borrowed car for Fort l'Empereur where Juin and Darlan were waiting. There, amid the distant sound of American bombs, Darlan issued an order for all Frenchmen to cease fire in the Algiers area.

By nightfall, November 8, 1942, all guns around Algiers were stilled. But this was only the beginning.

*

Cordell Hull, Secretary of State but hardly the man closest to the President he served, was feeling elated. To be sure, his widely criticized Vichy policy had been largely engineered and directed by the President himself, with Hull more of a follower than a prime mover. But Hull had been taking the brunt of a bad press, and now Vichy had come through despite the harpings of his many critics. Hull considered himself exonerated.

With the first news of the successful landing in Algiers, therefore, the Secretary called a hasty press conference. On November 9 he crowed to a temporarily silenced press corps extolling the genius of the Anglo-

American invasion, the groundwork laid to ensure its success, and the prominent role that the State Department had played. The press had no immediate comeback.

But unwittingly Hull was making himself the symbol of the "Darlan deal" in Algiers. His exuberance of the moment turned out to be premature.

CHAPTER XII

TORCH II:
DEATH OF THE
LITTLE FELLOW

B y Monday morning, November 9, 1942, General Mark W. Clark
prepared to leave Gibraltar for Algiers, where he would set up Advance Allied Force Headquarters. General Giraud, having agreed
to serve as French commander under Eisenhower, was also planning to
make his entrance into Algiers. Murphy had managed to secure a French
airplane, and early in the morning Giraud took off for Bida Airport, some
forty miles out of the city. Clark, with a small staff and the two old faithful B-17s, was scheduled to take off at the same time. For some reason,
however, the weather forced a postponement of Clark's flight. As a result
his party did not get off until about noon.

On the B-17 *Red Gremlin* Clark carried a letter from Eisenhower to
Murphy conveying congratulations for his fine job in setting up the cease-
fire at Algiers and welcoming him to his new position as Civil Affairs
Officer of Allied Force Headquarters. As the emphasis in North Africa
was shifting from the political to the military, Murphy was now part of
Eisenhower's organization.[1] Until Eisenhower could come to Algiers personally, Murphy would report to Clark.

Clark's late departure from Gibraltar gave Murphy a welcome opportunity to visit firsthand with Giraud. The general desired to stay in relative
seclusion for the time being, and on landing at Bida, he headed for the
house of Jacques Lemaigre-Dubreuil in the Arab quarter of Algiers.
Murphy arrived soon thereafter and, meeting Giraud for the first time,
was relieved at the Frenchman's calm demeanor. Murphy had been half
expecting Giraud to become agitated on learning of Darlan's presence on

[1] Chandler, I, 681.

the scene, for it augured a drastic change in the arrangements Murphy had been describing to him through Lemaigre-Dubreuil and Mast. To Murphy's relief, however, Giraud was calm and said he recognized that Darlan could have been working underground toward joint French-American action, as had he. Even when Murphy intimated that Juin and Darlan had accused him (Giraud) of "jumping the gun," the general still showed little surprise. Soon Murphy concluded that Giraud wanted to avoid political controversy, and his former determination in demanding a high position for himself had been only to ensure that due recognition would be given to the importance of the French.

After the short flight across the Mediterranean to Maison Blanche Airport General Clark found a hot reception waiting for him. At 5:00 P.M. a dozen German JU-88s came through the heavy Allied anti-aircraft fire. Their target, actually, was not the airfield but the crowded harbor nearby. From the direction of the harbor Clark could see solid ack-ack fire filling the sky full of orange balls. Americans and British cheered when they saw a Spitfire knock down a Junker. But the airfield was not out of the area of danger. Three bombs from one of the Junkers fell within a hundred feet of the tail of the *Red Gremlin,* and one German plane seemed to be heading straight for Clark and his party. Fortunately it exploded in the air, its derelict tail striking the ground a short distance away.[2]

After the air battle ended, a temporarily weak-kneed Clark, accompanied by General Ryder, headed through the narrow, winding streets up the hill to the St. George Hotel, a luxurious spot previously leased by Murphy to serve as Allied Force Headquarters. Murphy arrived at the St. George from his session with Giraud at about the same time. He was relieved that Clark had come, as he had done all he could alone and was ready to turn over the responsibility to someone else. He was downcast, however, when Clark wryly remarked that for a military "show of force" he could provide only three tanks or so.

Soon Murphy became concerned with Clark's impatience toward French "foot dragging," for Clark seemed in no mood to understand why the French would not simply give the Allies whatever they needed without question.[3] Hoping that the passage of a little time might calm Clark down, therefore, Murphy persuaded him to postpone his meeting with Darlan until the next morning. Clark, though he agreed out of deference to Murphy, was eager to begin the Allied drive eastward to capture Tunis; to him every hour counted.

In Murphy's eyes the situation was not that simple by any means. Clark, he felt, grossly underestimated the psychological trauma that the

[2] Many Arabs, in their frenzy and excitement, were killed and wounded by ack-ack fragments. From that time on, the Arabs learned to stay indoors during air raids.
[3] Murphy, p. 136.

French had sustained after their defeat in 1940, and to ignore the feelings of these officers who could help—or hinder—so much would do untold damage to the cause.

Clark, however, was in for more discouraging news. He was shocked to learn from Murphy—and from Giraud himself—that the French were according Giraud a cool reception. A series of visitors during the day had convinced even Giraud that it was Darlan, not himself, who had the following among the French North Africans. By many Giraud was considered almost a traitor. But since Eisenhower and the respective governments had committed Allied prestige to him, Clark groped for a compromise. As he viewed the situation, at that moment, Giraud had to be retained in some prominent position even if Darlan were to be recognized as number one man.

After the evening's business was done, Clark decided to get a good night's sleep. Outside his door Sergeant Chaney saw to it that nobody should disturb him—and nobody tried. Murphy, on the other hand, sat up most of the night conferring with Darlan. Thus Clark awoke the next morning refreshed while most of the other participants in the morning meeting were exhausted.

But Murphy had not completely wasted his time during the night. He had been able to follow the situation throughout North Africa and to become better acquainted with Darlan. He was now becoming convinced that Darlan would be cooperative if the Allies could only assure him that French sovereignty in Africa would be respected.

The cheerful atmosphere of the conference room at the St. George Hotel belied the seriousness of the proceedings. Outside was a peaceful garden with flowers and palm trees; the hotel balconies overlooked the picturesque harbor only a mile away. Inside the elaborate room was a long table lined with grim-faced Americans and Frenchmen. Clark took his place at the end of the table, Darlan on his left, Juin on his right, Murphy interpreting.[4]

Darlan made anything but a favorable first impression on Clark, to whom the admiral was a "little man with watery blue eyes and petulant lips." With something bordering on contempt, Clark noted how Darlan mopped his balding head, shifted in his chair, and fumbled with the papers in front of him. Darlan's short stature contributed to the disdain of the height-conscious Clark, who almost from the outset tacked the sobriquet "The Little Fellow" on the Frenchman.

Clark had now assumed all responsibility, and Murphy's overt function was primarily to act as interpreter, though outside the meetings he tried

[4] Besides Clark, Americans included Murphy, Colonel Julius Holmes, Captain Jerauld Wright, and others. French included Darlan, Juin, Fenard, Vice-Admiral d'Escadre Moreau, and five others. See Clark, p. 106.

informally to smooth the ruffled feelings of the French. Like them, Murphy was somewhat dismayed by Clark's overbearing attitude and table pounding. But Clark was actually playing a role that he didn't care for. He was a man who normally preferred not to raise his voice, exhibiting his strength primarily through a calm though direct demeanor. But on this day—and on the days following—he conducted himself on his conscious assumption that the only way to shake these confused, lethargic Frenchmen was to be visibly tough. At one point, in sincere exasperation, Clark even threatened to incarcerate all the French officials and initiate a military government. This prospect frightened Murphy more, he later wrote, than it did the French. For the French generals and admirals also held cards. The Americans, they realized, could never fight the Germans in Tunisia while at the same time trying to keep order among the twenty million Arabs and hundreds of thousands of Frenchmen in Algeria and Morocco. The Americans possessed neither the strength nor the experience to govern and fight at the same time.

At the outset Darlan stated a firm position. He could do nothing, he said, to help the Allied cause without the permission of the venerated Marshal Pétain. He had already, he said, sent a résumé of the situation to Laval; he expected a reply that day. But soliciting Pétain's cooperation was the last thing Clark had on his mind. To begin with, the delay in awaiting a reply from Vichy might be considerable, but worse, the chances were great that the Vichy reply would be unfavorable.

Despite his nervousness and his small stature, Darlan turned out to be a formidable opponent. Clark's threat to put him in protective custody seemed to impress him little; and when Clark suggested that General Giraud could sign a cease-fire document rather than Darlan, the latter doubted that Giraud's orders would be obeyed. Conscious that any order for the French to cooperate with the Americans would result in Nazi occupation of Vichy France, Darlan was unwilling to accept such a responsibility himself, especially from North Africa. He would, however, send another, more specific telegram to Pétain. This offer was not good enough for Clark.

When they finally reached an impasse, Darlan asked if he could meet alone with his staff and commanders—Giraud was conspicuously absent —and Clark grudgingly assented. Eventually Clark rejoined the Frenchmen and to his surprise Darlan produced an order which Clark found acceptable. All French land, sea, and air forces were to cease fire, return to their garrisons, and observe neutrality. French officers were to retain their military commands; and the political and administrative authority in Algeria and Morocco would remain unchanged. Darlan took full responsibility upon himself.

This order was all that Clark could ask for at the moment. Inserting the words "for the present," he warned Darlan that his agreement would stand only if Eisenhower approved. But the warning was for show; secretly Clark was delighted. On one issue Clark, though bewildered, gave in: he agreed that Béthouart in Casablanca and Mast in Algiers, despite their pro-American leanings, should be temporarily without commands. (Unbeknownst to Clark, General Noguès in Casablanca had put Béthouart in prison; Mast had gone into hiding.)

After the large, formal meeting was over and the order issued, Clark, Darlan, and Murphy stayed to discuss the French fleet in Toulon. Darlan was doubtful that he could produce it, although he would do his best. He did, however, promise what he had been insisting on for years: that the portion of the fleet still in Toulon would never fall into German hands.

After leaving Clark, Murphy escorted Darlan out to his car. Darlan turned. "Would you do me a favor? Please remind Major General Clark that I am a five-star admiral. He should cease shouting at me and treating me like a junior lieutenant." Murphy agreed. When he later mentioned Darlan's protest, Clark seemed a trifle surprised. Undaunted, however, he sent a cable to Eisenhower: "I now have two Kingpins."

With this much accomplished, Wayne Clark expected smoother sailing at a second meeting that afternoon, this time with General Giraud. Before it began, however, word came from Vichy that Marshal Pétain had rejected the North African armistice; in the process he had fired Darlan as commander of the armed forces, to be succeeded by Noguès. Darlan, surprisingly, was dejected. Clinging to the mystical devotion shared by all the French officers toward Pétain, he now tried to change his position. "There is nothing I can do now," he said, "but revoke the order that I signed this morning."

"You'll do nothing of the kind," Clark replied. "There will be no revocation of these orders." To make certain that his words would hold true, Clark placed Darlan in custody and stationed a platoon of American troops to guard him in Fenard's house. There Darlan would remain isolated from the outside.

That night of November 10 Clark and Murphy met with Giraud. The general now demonstrated that, of all the French military, he was the most detached. He realized, he said, that Darlan, not he, could unify the French in North Africa. This development effectively relieved him of political responsibility and caused him no anguish so long as he could serve as French military commander under Darlan. The sooner he could get out of the political mess the better.

However, Giraud had information from underground sources that was new to the Americans. The Germans, he said quietly, were at that moment on the verge of preparing to occupy Vichy France. He turned out to be right.

*

At Port Lyautey, Brigadier General Lucian Truscott was finding the situation more difficult than he had bargained for. Owing to the premature announcement of the Allied landings, the French troops in the Kasbah had indeed been alerted. The 2nd Battalion, 60th Infantry, at the mouth of the Sebou River had made little progress toward this formidable fortress; its guns were making it difficult for the Americans to move. Truscott had heard nothing from his two emissaries, Craw and Hamilton.

Truscott spent a miserable night, cold and alone, in the darkness at the command post he had set up on Blue Beach to the south. Men were all around, but it was too dark to see them. Finally Truscott violated his own order and lit a cigarette, secretly relieved to see other offenders doing the same. At one point a figure came out of the darkness and in an alien voice demanded one. Truscott wearily complied. Two officers then appeared out of the darkness and thrust machine guns in the man's side. Truscott's companion turned out to be Lee, the Chinese cook of C Company, 540th Engineer Battalion.[5]

Dawn was welcome. When he could see, Truscott headed south to visit the right limit of his beachhead, where a severe French counterattack had just been repulsed by an American armored force supported by naval gunfire. Four French tanks were burning, and bodies were sprawled around. The situation on the right now secure, Truscott returned to Green Beach at the mouth of the Sebou. Here he was told that the commander of the Kasbah had offered to surrender. Truscott shaved and dusted off his uniform. Then he and his staff waited for most of the morning for a parley which failed to transpire. False alarm.

In the early afternoon Truscott left to check on the 2nd Battalion, 60th Infantry. The regimental commander was present. The battalion had suffered heavy losses, he said; its companies—normally nearly two hundred men—were down to about forty or fifty each. This estimate made little sense to Truscott, as the fighting had not seemed heavy. Most of the losses, he quickly concluded, were due to straggling. Truscott turned on the regimental commander and ordered him to use the troops of his headquarters to search every house in the area. Eventually more than two hundred stragglers turned up, a sad commentary on the state of training of these green Americans.

[5] Based partly on this experience, Truscott later picked up Lee from C Company to be his own cook, only to have him stolen in turn by Patton.

That night of November 9, Truscott's second on shore, was not so difficult as the previous. Two French deserters brought news of Colonel Craw and Major Hamilton. Craw had been killed despite the flag of truce they carried. Major Hamilton had been taken prisoner but had not been released because of the French fear of the American reaction on learning about Craw.

As the fighting was obviously not over, Truscott sent a message to Patton. If he failed to take the Kasbah by the morning of November 10, he wrote, he would need reinforcements. All his troops were committed.

Gradually, however, Truscott's situation began to improve. The 2nd Battalion, 60th Infantry, scaled the steep slopes toward the Kasbah during the night and had reached the walls by morning. But since mortar and machine-gun fire had stopped them short of the walls, Truscott now gave up trying to take the Kasbah with minimum French casualties. He would reduce it by any means necessary, so he called for naval support. Guns opened up from the cruiser *Dallas*. More effective, however, was an attack of eight dive bombers directed by a young forward air controller with Truscott. The 2nd Battalion, withdrawn some distance for safety, prepared to assault the moment the bombing should cease. Meanwhile they watched, fascinated, as explosions in the Kasbah rocked the ground and sent clouds of smoke skyward. A few minutes later the bombers were gone and the naval fire ceased; the 2nd Battalion, with Truscott right behind it, reached the main gate, where French officers and native soldiers surrendered en masse. The battle for the Kasbah was practically over. Satisfied, Truscott went down the steep hill and turned his attention to the airfield.

The five miles between the Kasbah and the airfield were hard going, as the area was honeycombed with fortifications. The two battalions advancing south of the river were moving slowly. Late in the afternoon, however, Truscott learned that the 1st Battalion, from Blue Beach, had captured the local commander. Though the Frenchman desired to arrange an armistice, Truscott refused to speak to him until he released Major Hamilton. Shortly after dark Hamilton was in American hands at the airfield. The story of Craw's death turned out to be true. The Port Lyautey area was secure. Truscott now prepared to move southward to seize the airfield at Rabat, forty miles away.

Shortly after midnight several French officers arrived at Truscott's command post, having run a gantlet of American fire not unlike that which had greeted Craw and Hamilton. General Mathinet, the officers said, had arrived with instructions from Admiral Darlan to cease all opposition. Truscott sent the truce party back. He would meet Mathinet at eight the following morning.

Sub Task Force GOALPOST, the most difficult of the three landings in the Western Task Force, had accomplished its mission.

*

Major General George S. Patton, Jr., was awakened the morning of November 11 with the news of the French surrender at Port Lyautey. As Safi had fallen, only one area of French resistance remained: Casablanca. It appeared that General Noguès had decided not to comply with Darlan's order, and Patton was preparing a final assault. Major General Jonathan B. Anderson, commanding the U. S. 3rd Infantry Division, reported that he was ready and eager to attack at dawn. Patton, however, was not so sure that Anderson was sufficiently organized. He therefore delayed to give the 3rd Division a chance to doublecheck their positions by daylight. With everything in order—with naval air and gunfire ready to begin the bombardment of the city—word came in that the garrison was ready to surrender. Patton later wrote: "Anderson wanted to attack at dawn, but I chose 0730 so as to give him a chance to form up by daylight. Actually the French quit at 0640, so had we attacked at 0600 as planned, many needless lives would have been lost. Again the hand of God."[6]

When General Noguès and Admiral Michelier came to discuss surrender terms in the early afternoon, Patton had an honor guard drawn up. "No use kicking a man when he is down."[7] He even arranged a champagne celebration.

The terms Patton presented—which were agreed to—were generous, more so than those that Eisenhower's headquarters had issued for use. They included, for example, the right of the French to retain their arms. Though Patton exulted in his military victory, the end of hostilities had been brought about not by the weight of American might but by the decision of General Noguès finally to obey the orders of Admiral Darlan.

Such details could never dampen the spirits of George Patton, who was in an ebullient mood. "They drank $40 worth of champagne," he wrote, "but it was worth it."

*

At a dinner for the Lord Mayor of London on Tuesday, November 10, 1942, Prime Minister Winston Churchill made one of the most revealing speeches of his career. Delivered in a triumphal atmosphere, his words reveal a great deal about the man and his attitudes.

Churchill began by exulting over the Eighth Army's victory at El Alamein. He reminded his audience that he had never promised anything but blood, toil, tears, and sweat, but he then went on to describe a "new

[6] Blumenson, *The Patton Papers*, II, p. 110.
[7] Ibid.

experience." The British had had a victory, remarkable and definite: "The bright gleam has caught the helmets of our soldiers and warmed and cheered all their hearts." He mentioned General Alexander and his "brilliant comrade and lieutenant" General Montgomery by name and declared that Rommel's army had been "very largely destroyed as a fighting force."

"Now this is not the end. It is not even the beginning of the end. But it is, perhaps, the end of the beginning."

Churchill then turned to TORCH (without mentioning it by name). Here, consistent with the policy of giving the North African invasion an American complexion, he called the President of the United States "the author of this mighty undertaking. . . .

"In all of it," Churchill added, "I have been his active and ardent lieutenant."

The Prime Minister then declared his faith that France would rise again. He mentioned De Gaulle and Giraud on about equal terms and promised that, though the British desired to see Alsace-Lorraine restored to France, Britain held no ambitions in North Africa or anywhere else.

Churchill then turned to a subject which had been rankling him for some time. An "Open Letter to the People of England" had been published in *Life* magazine a month earlier, and Churchill was offended by remarks about India and imperialism. The article had ended with a warning that the United States was definitely not fighting for the preservation of the British Empire.

Churchill might have let that *Life* article pass, except for the publicity accorded to a statement made by the Republican presidential nominee of 1940, Wendell L. Willkie. Willkie, having just returned from a trip around the world under the auspices of the American Government, had gone on the radio to tell the American people that world leaders were resolved to do away with imperialism. And President Roosevelt, in an attempt to soften the effect of Willkie's truculent words, had held a press conference. In it he emphasized that Willkie's speech meant only that the Atlantic Charter applied to all humanity.

Unfortunately Roosevelt's statement gave authority to Willkie's words. In London it was said that Roosevelt had given "great force" to the Willkie speech.

This was obviously too much for Churchill, and he seized the occasion to warn the world:

"Let me, however, make this clear, in case there should be any mistake about it in any quarter: we mean to hold our own. I have not become the King's First Minister in order to preside over the liquidation of the British Empire. For that task, if ever it were prescribed, some one else would have to be found. . . ."

In the light of rapidly moving events Churchill's remarks were little noted, but the feelings he expressed were to guide his whole conduct of the war.

*

At Gibraltar General Eisenhower, sleeping in the comfortable Convent but still working in the tunnel, was becoming exasperated at the bewildering lack of detailed information he was receiving concerning Patton's Western Task Force. Elsewhere the news was good, especially the early fall of Algiers. And Eisenhower had been relieved to hear from Major General Lloyd Fredendall that the French garrison in Oran had capitulated to the Central Task Force on the morning of November 10. (Darlan's orders had not been obeyed in this case; only the sheer weight of American force had brought about the surrender.) Word was now becoming more certain that the Nazis had occupied France since Pétain's last-minute try at an accommodation with Hitler had come to naught. But Eisenhower learned that Hitler's violation of the 1940 peace treaty had convinced General Noguès to cease disregarding Darlan's orders and surrender Casablanca to Patton.

Eisenhower's main preoccupations at this moment were fourfold. First, he was anxious for General K. A. N. Anderson's British First Army to move out and seize Tunis before the Axis could reinforce. Second, the local French political situation had to be cleared up. Third, Eisenhower wanted to secure the French fleet in Toulon, Darlan's trump card.[8] Fourth, satisfactory communications with Patton at Casablanca had to be established.

Of these concerns, the fourth should have been no problem. Perhaps the code equipment of the two headquarters somehow failed to mesh; but a strong suspicion existed that the mischievous Patton was enjoying his temporary isolation, using the lack of communications, for example, as an excuse to rewrite Eisenhower's terms of surrender for Noguès and Michelier. After all, Patton had airplanes that he could easily dispatch to Gibraltar, and it was important to the planners in London to learn the condition of the harbor at Casablanca. Eisenhower could only fret.

The French political situation was obviously going to be more difficult than had been expected. From Clark in Algiers Eisenhower was receiving

---

[8] The French fleet was far from puny, consisting of 10 cruisers, 28 destroyers, and 14 submarines which, together with miscellaneous other vessels, came to a total of some 61 ships, totaling 225,000 tons. Churchill, IV, 628.

a stream of alternately hopeful and frustrated reports. As late as November 11, for example, when Darlan had attempted to rescind his order for Admiral Esteva in Tunis to resist the Axis occupation, Clark had threatened to incarcerate him and Juin aboard a U.S. warship. Clark had settled, however, for putting the two officers under house arrest. Then, when Noguès came to Algiers as Pétain's newly appointed French Commander-in-Chief, Clark refused to recognize him. Finally, on the afternoon of November 12, Clark induced the French to agree on some arrangement which would allow all Frenchmen to pull together. By that evening Clark reported that he saw a shaky promise of such an agreement, and on receiving this word Eisenhower determined, if at all possible, to go personally to Algiers the next day. Perhaps the presence of the Commander-in-Chief would spur the French into action.

The morning of November 13 Clark reported the situation in Algiers to be promising. Taking Admiral Cunningham and various aides along with him, therefore, Eisenhower left in a Flying Fortress escorted by three P-38 fighters, who weaved their way in and out of the clouds above. At exactly noon they landed at Maison Blanche, much to Clark's relief. Like Murphy before him, Clark had now carried his share of the responsibility on the spot long enough. As Clark and Eisenhower sat down for a quick lunch at the St. George Hotel, Murphy came in with the word that the French were about to reach an agreement.

Soon Darlan, Juin, Giraud, and Noguès were ushered into Eisenhower's suite. The Allied Commander shook hands with them all and congratulated them on their agreement which, incidentally, strongly resembled that which he himself had proposed weeks before.[9]

Here Eisenhower made one of his important decisions of the war. He recognized that entering into a formal arrangement with a former Vichy collaborator would bring protests in Washington and London, but he decided to assume the responsibility without referring back. From a military point of view Darlan was the only man who could maintain stability among the French, which the Allies needed, and a delay of days in recognizing his authority could not be tolerated. It was plainly necessary, in the Allied interest, to sign the Darlan agreement; the respective governments of Britain and the United States could later decide whether to support it, reverse it, or even relieve Eisenhower of his position.

After the short conference Eisenhower left in midafternoon for the return to Gibraltar. He would have preferred to stay in Algiers, but communications from there were stretched; he could not yet control the entire

[9] Darlan was to be the French political chief in North Africa, Giraud was to be the military commander under him, and Noguès was to be reinstated as Governor of Casablanca.

theater from the St. George. Along with him rode an exhausted Robert Murphy, who slept through the rough and dangerous flight.[10]

That night of Friday, November 13, 1942, after Eisenhower's return from Algiers, Admiral Darlan broadcast his assumption of political responsibility in North Africa. He ordered the French to cooperate and specified that General Noguès would continue as Commander-in-Chief, French Forces in Morocco. He neglected, however, to mention that Giraud would be in command of French military forces under him. (Eisenhower had ruefully given in on this point for the moment.) He did, however, mention General de Gaulle, in a negative way, emphasizing that De Gaulle was *not* included.

The next morning Eisenhower received a message from Bedell Smith in London advising him that resentment in British and American circles was becoming severe. By and large Eisenhower's actions had been approved by both governments—both Roosevelt and Churchill had sent him messages of congratulation—and up to this time the press had been so exuberant over the success of the military landings that the negotiations with Darlan had received little attention. But now, especially in Britain, Darlan was being attacked vociferously; the most strident criticisms were coming from sources connected with De Gaulle's Free French.

At first this news did not bother Eisenhower. He had already intended to report the situation and he simply informed Smith that an answer would be coming. Eisenhower then wrote the message to the Combined Chiefs outlining all the elements of the Darlan arrangement.

First of all the message expressed appreciation of the bewilderment in the two capitals brought on by the negotiations in Algiers. It emphasized, however, that sentiment in North Africa bore no resemblance to what had been expected during planning. The great fact, heretofore unrealized, was the tremendous influence of Pétain in the region. Based on this, local officials agreed that authority had to come from Pétain's "representative," Darlan.

The message went on to point out that the end of French resistance had come about from Darlan's orders, not by virtue of American military might.

Finally Eisenhower listed the consequences of repudiating Darlan:

a)   Loss of cooperation from the French

b)   French resistance

c)   No hope of seizing Tunisia quickly

d)   Loss of French military assistance

e)   Loss of last glimmer of hope to gain the Toulon fleet.

[10] Eisenhower later commented that probably the pilot had depended more on his rabbit's foot than on more scientific landing equipment. *Crusade,* p. 109.

The message recommended that if the two governments were still dissatisfied they should send a mission of representatives from home to study the situation on the ground.

*

Although they occupied the headlines, the French political maneuverings in Algiers served merely as a backdrop for the main effort of the North African campaign, the drive toward Tunisia. The occupation of French Northwest Africa from Algiers to Casablanca had been the minimum objective of the operation but could never have justified the risks inherent in TORCH. The real purpose of the whole effort was to reach Tunisia in time to cut off Rommel from the rear. And after the Eighth Army's victory at El Alamein, Allied possession of all North Africa now shone as a glittering, attainable prize. Rommel and his forces were important, but the greater objective of this particular campaign was to gain vital real estate.

In classic military terms, possession of ground as such is looked upon with some disdain; destruction of the enemy's armed forces is the primary objective. But this campaign was different, for possession of the North African shores would provide air bases to open the Mediterranean for Allied shipping. And an open Mediterranean meant the quickest, easiest, and safest route to send supplies to Russia. Allied possession of the North African shoreline would also provide them with the strategic advantage of forcing the Axis, especially Italy, to guard against an invasion of Europe from the south as well as from England.

In few campaigns has the mutual dependence of air and ground forces been so obvious. The ground forces, on their part, were unable to conduct major operations if exposed to the enemy's unchallenged fighter-bombers. On the other hand, in the light of the short range of fighter aircraft, air power was dependent on seizure of forward fields by the ground forces. Thus when the Allied planners were looking at the coast of North Africa they saw not only ports but also airfields.

In the race for Tunisia the Germans and Italians were heavily favored by the ease with which they could arrive from Sardinia, Sicily, and southern Italy. Those places also boasted airfields close enough to allow them to dominate the Tunisian area. It would take time for the Anglo-Americans to establish airfields to contest them. The Allies, on the other hand, were closing in from both east and west. Rommel was weakened, having lost at El Alamein (by Alexander's estimate) some 20,000 prisoners, 350 tanks, and 400 guns. And his supply routes across the Mediterranean were threatened from the air as far west as Tripoli. With time Rommel would be refitted partly, but the ultimate odds against him were great.

The main problem facing Eisenhower as he attempted to build forces in

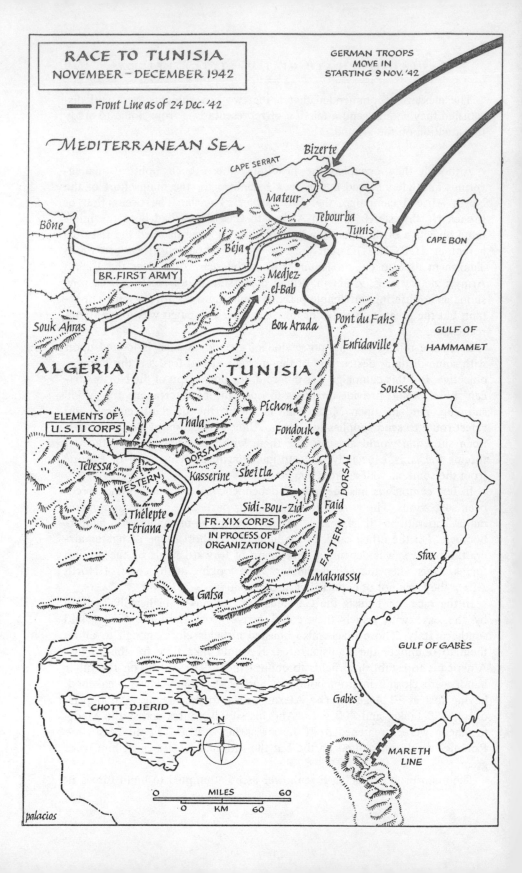

RACE TO TUNISIA
NOVEMBER – DECEMBER 1942

—— Front Line as of 24 Dec. '42

GERMAN TROOPS
MOVE IN
STARTING 9 NOV. '42

MEDITERRANEAN SEA

CAPE SERRAT

Bizerte

Mateur

Tebourba

Tunis

CAPE BON

Bône

Béja

BR. FIRST ARMY

Medjez-el-Bab

Souk Ahras

Bou Arada

Pont du Fahs

Enfidaville

GULF OF
HAMMAMET

ALGERIA

TUNISIA

Sousse

Pichon

Thala

ELEMENTS OF
U.S. II CORPS

Fondouk

DORSAL

Tebessa

WESTERN

Kasserine

Sbeitla

Sidi-Bou-Zid

Faid

EASTERN DORSAL

Thélepte
Fériana

FR. XIX CORPS
IN PROCESS OF
ORGANIZATION

Sfax

Maknassy

Gafsa

GULF OF GABÈS

CHOTT DJERID

Gabès

N

MARETH
LINE

0   MILES   60

0   KM   60

palacios

Tunisia was not a lack of total force in Morocco and Algeria; it was the inability to deliver that force from the rear to the fighting area where it was needed. A rickety, single-track railroad and a two-lane dirt road provided the only surface means by which to transfer troops and equipment across the four hundred miles from Algiers to Tunis. Had communication lines been anything resembling the quality of those in Western Europe, the Tunisian campaign might have amounted to little more than a skirmish.

According to original plans, when General Ryder landed his Eastern Task Force at Algiers, the British First Army under General Kenneth Anderson was waiting in floating reserve, ready for instant movement to the east. Thus the veneer of an "American" expedition was preserved while Anderson's troops, fresh for the eastward drive, would be unencumbered by residual problems of the landing.

As early as November 10, therefore, a portion of Anderson's force, the 36th Brigade of the British 78th Division, landed at Bougie, a hundred miles to the east of Algiers. The next day, as Eisenhower was receiving news of Noguès' surrender in Casablanca, Anderson boldly set off to capture Bizerte and Tunis. Despite the overwhelming obstacles that lay in his path, Anderson accepted Eisenhower's urgent orders without a murmur.

Eisenhower was well aware of what Anderson was up against, operating on a shoestring because of lack of shipping. Neither at Algiers nor Bougie could the strength necessary for a quick campaign be landed. Motor equipment was short. And the miserable weather rendered the pitiful coastal road and dirt air strips almost useless.

As feared, Axis reaction to the Allied landings was instantaneous. As early as Monday, November 9, even before the fall of Oran, Hitler had begun the occupation of Tunisia. At first the French commander-in-chief, Admiral Jean Pierre Esteva, was paralyzed. He had not yet received definite orders from Darlan, and he did nothing to resist. Fortunately for the Allies, however, the French ground commander in Tunisia, General Georges Barré, decided to take action on his own and began to withdraw French ground forces from Tunis into the mountains to the west. At this point the Axis still had inadequate strength to stop him.

Two days later Eisenhower received word that Axis forces had seized the El Aouina Airport at Tunis and had landed 100 planes and 500 troops from Sicily, Italy, and Sardinia. The next morning the Nazis were basing nineteen JU-52s at Catania, Sicily, and were towing transport gliders. At about noon, November 12, Anderson's British commandos and paratroopers seized Bône without opposition.[11] That day Axis aircraft made a

[11] Bône, it will be recalled, was one of the objectives considered in the initial planning of TORCH, but rejected because it was too far to the east for the tastes of the American Combined Chiefs.

heavy raid on the harbor at Bougie, unhampered by Allied fighter opposition. Four transport ships were sunk or badly damaged. Anderson moved overland to capture Djidjelli and its adjacent airdrome. And on the same day Allied aircraft from Algiers bombed the airfield at Tunis and destroyed at least ten German aircraft on the ground.

During the next few days this fluid situation consolidated. Tunis and Bizerte lie on a coastal plain about forty miles apart, Bizerte roughly to the northwest. But the plain is dominated by difficult country to the west. Rough hills begin only ten miles from Bizerte and about twenty-five from Tunis. Thus when Barré evacuated Tunis and Bizerte with his modest French forces, he had only a short distance to go before he reached an easily defended position, where he could about-face and defend. This he did and held out until, on November 17, he made contact with one of Anderson's parachute battalions coming from the west at Béja. This meeting place was some distance from the Tunis-Bizerte plain, but Barré still controlled the hills, and Anderson was able to move his own forces quickly to positions overlooking the plain. Barré's French troops fell in on Anderson's south (right) flank.

At the same time a battalion of the U. S. 509th Parachute Infantry Regiment landed near Tébessa, a hundred miles south of Bône, and moved sixty miles farther south to Gafsa. Possession of this communications center protected the south flank of the British adequately for the time being.

German forces, however, were rapidly building strength in Tunis. Aggressive parachute units followed on the heels of Barré and by November 23 a line of battle began to form in the mountains from Cape Serrat on the north to Medjez-el-Bab (on the plain) to Bou Arada in the higher ground to the south. French forces continued to patrol lightly between the main British battle line on the north and the small American task force far to the south at Gafsa.

At this point Anderson's force, though called an "army," consisted only of the 78th Division, two parachute battalions, a commando battalion, and a mobile, combined-arms team called "Blade Force." It would be generous to rate his strength at two divisions. In the light of the weather and the Axis domination of the air, Anderson concluded that he lacked the means at the moment to take Tunis. He therefore called for reinforcements and planned to resume the attack two days later, on November 25.

*

After his harrowing return flight from Algiers to Gibraltar on November 13, General Eisenhower had resolved to move Allied Force Headquarters to Africa as soon as possible. On November 23 he made good on this matter, accepting the fact that communications from Algiers were inferior to those from Gibraltar. Stopping at Oran on the way, Eisenhower received his first glimpse of the port. He was taken aback by the chaotic, clogged conditions, but he was even more jolted to witness firsthand the devastating potency of the mud. His B-17 was able to land on the hard-surfaced strip, but it was unable to taxi off for fear of sinking. Conditions such as these would cut the capacity of an air strip to a small fraction of its designed potential.

Later that day Eisenhower continued on to Algiers, where his aides had set him up temporarily in the St. George Hotel. By this time he was convinced that Anderson's First Army must be reinforced by American units, so he alerted Combat Command B (CCB) of the 1st Armored Division to be ready to move. American troops would be committed in increasing numbers, as rapidly as the inadequate communications line would permit.

*

In Casablanca George Patton was appalled by the news that American troops would be sent unit by unit to reinforce a British army. Possibly to share his frustration, he flew to Oran to talk to Lloyd Fredendall, from whose forces CCB had been taken. This imagined dissipation of American strength in support of the British was anathema to the chauvinist Patton, who appeared to regard the principle of keeping American forces intact as more important than fighting the Axis. Word of this concern, shared by other American officers, reached Eisenhower. He dismissed it with a scoff.

Eisenhower was not long in Algiers before he realized that his move from Gibraltar had been wise. On every hand were matters that needed the authority of the Commander-in-Chief. One of these was the problem of air defense and its relationship to the attitude of the populace. Every night Algiers was pounded by Axis air raids, directed at the harbor but causing casualties among the population. If the people wanted to give up, the British and Americans would probably be able to control them but at the expense of their ability to fight the Axis in Tunisia. Air defense had been hampered because the latest vectoring equipment had been held back in Britain. On Eisenhower's arrival it was dispatched forthwith.

Military decisions were also easier to make on the spot. Three days after his arrival in Algiers, for example, Eisenhower discovered that CCB, 1st Armored Division, had not yet departed to join Anderson because a staff officer had denied permission. Many of the vehicles in this combat command were half-tracks, the officer said, and the trip from Algiers to Tunisia would use up half their predicted life. Restraining himself in the face of this bureaucratic shortsightedness, Eisenhower personally ordered the commander of CCB to move out by road.

*

Anderson's attack had jumped off as planned on November 25, advancing along three axes, the main effort toward Mateur, an important road and railway center on the plain between Bizerte and Tunis, which controlled the major communications in the area. The British 6th Armoured Division, planned for the operation, failed to reach Anderson on time, however, and Mateur was not quite taken. Anderson was halted at Tebourba, only twenty miles from Tunis.

The main obstacle to this effort continued to be the weather. The mud was so severe that the B-17s, vital to the operation, had to be propped up under the wings when parked off hard strips. The advance airfields in Anderson's territory, where fighters and light bombers were based, were bogged down except at Bône. German ME-109s, on the other hand, were based on hard strips at Tunis and Bizerte. In the meantime, Admiral Cunningham, having lost almost all his shipping east of Bougie, had decided to send no more convoys to Bône until Allied air cover could be established.

*

On Friday, November 27, Eisenhower and Clark were preparing for a car trip to the Tunisian front the next day, despite the danger from enemy aircraft. That morning a staff officer came running into the outer office and demanded to be let in. The French fleet at Toulon, he panted, had just been scuttled.

Eisenhower called Cunningham. Certainly it was a disappointment to lose this powerful fleet. On the other hand, the outcome could have been far worse; the fleet could have fallen into German hands. The French ships in Alexandria Harbor had been scuttled at the same time, the two men learned, but here Cunningham felt sure that they could be readily repaired, as he had seen to it that they had been sitting in a draft of only six feet. It would take an entire year, Cunningham estimated, for the Germans to refurbish the scuttled portion of the fleet in Toulon. On balance, there was much more to be thankful for than mourned in Hitler's occupation of southern France. The move had triggered the surrender of Noguès at Casablanca and now the neutralization of a powerful naval force.

Eisenhower and Clark, accompanied by Sergeants McKeough and Chaney, left for Tunisia the next morning as planned. It was a difficult trip, marred along the way when a twelve-year-old Arab boy was killed by one of the lead vehicles. Though a French officer on the spot declared that the fault lay with the youngster, the incident did nothing to make the ride cheerful. The convoy arrived at Anderson's headquarters at midnight, but Anderson was not to be found. He had moved on ahead.

The fighting conditions in Tunisia were appalling. Eisenhower was touched by the spirit of these relatively untrained and inexperienced British soldiers, whose courage and stamina, as he later wrote, were un-

surpassed even by the oldest of veterans. The mud had confined all operations to the roads, which in places had disappeared. Further, the winter
cold was beginning to descend, and supply was short. By the time Eisenhower had located Anderson on the front lines, however, lead elements
had reached a point where the three officers could make out Tunis and
Bizerte in the distance on the plain.

Anderson, Eisenhower found, was accepting his situation stoically, far
more so than one outspoken American officer who declaimed that the
British were being "murdered." Though nobody present realized it,
Tebourba represented the farthest advance that Anderson's army would
make that winter.

By the night of Monday, November 29, Eisenhower and Clark arrived
back in Algiers, dog-tired and sore. Eisenhower was now suffering from a
severe case of flu (later diagnosed as walking pneumonia) and he was
confined to bed. But he was still determined that the attack in Tunisia
should go on at the first possible moment.

*

On receiving Eisenhower's cable of November 14, which explained the
Darlan situation, General Marshall sent a copy to the President. Its con-
tents came as a great relief to Roosevelt, who, like everyone else, had
been confused as to the reason for the arrangement. He read Eisenhower's
telegram aloud to Harry Hopkins, providing it all the emphasis and eloquence that he used in his fireside chats. By the time he was finished he
was convinced that the action taken had been not only the best thing but
probably the only thing.

Churchill, of course, had received his own copy but was more doubtful
than Roosevelt about dealing with Darlan. Since the days of 1939, when
Churchill had entertained Darlan at the Admiralty and had sized him up
as "one of those good Frenchmen who hate England,"[12] Churchill's
distaste for the Frenchman had grown in the light of his later activities at
Vichy. Nevertheless, Churchill now agreed with Roosevelt that dealing
with Darlan was necessary. The fact that Admiral Cunningham, one of his
own, was party to the arrangement made it more palatable.[13]

---

[12] Churchill, II, 229. In his toast Darlan had made the point that his great-grand-
father had been killed at Trafalgar.

[13]

We cannot say that our doubts or anxieties are removed by what is proposed
or that the solution will be permanent or healthy. Nevertheless, in view of the
dominating importance of speed and of the fact that the Allied Commander-in-
Chief's opinion is so strongly and ably expressed and that it is endorsed by our
officers, including Admiral Cunningham, who were with him on the spot, we feel
we have no choice but to accept General Eisenhower's arrangements for maintaining local and interim equilibrium and for securing the vital positions in
Tunis.

But even President Roosevelt could not simply make a decision and let it go at that. Public opinion had to be contended with. And in this case the reaction was far from instantaneous, because of the prevailing American ignorance of French politics. Actually, the Darlan incident was well reported in the United States; it was only that the public and the more "liberal" radio commentators took a little time to absorb the significance.

When Darlan's name was first mentioned in the American press, it was to announce that he was a prisoner of the Americans. A front-page article in the New York *Times,* dated November 10, 1942, appeared on November 11. It was written by David Anderson, who obviously had some background. He began by citing the release put out by Allied Force Headquarters in London: "Admiral François Darlan," he quoted, "Chief of Vichy's armed forces, is now in Allied hands at Algiers 'being entertained by one of our American generals [Clark] with the respect and dignity due an officer of his rank.' . . ." Then he went on: "No detail was given as to how and when Admiral Darlan got into his present situation." He described the admiral as "never one to carry resistance to extremes, especially when there is something to gain." He noted Darlan's "marked dislike of the British," which Anderson said accounted for "many of his actions in Vichy." It predicted that Darlan, like Giraud, would try to "reestablish his fortunes," but he deemed this unlikely, as Darlan was considered "too unreliable." The same issue of the *Times* mentioned the announcement of Hitler's occupation of Vichy France.

Not all the comments were as perceptive as Anderson's. The next day a meeting of the School of Politics of the Republican Women was reported as giving full support to Hull's Vichy policy. Undoubtedly mesmerized by the Secretary's press conference of November 9, Mrs. H. R. Callaway hailed Hull in exultant if somewhat vague terms. She observed that the "moves of our State Department have been tremendously strategic."

The next day, November 12, the emphasis focused on the French fleet in Toulon. Eisenhower's appeal to the fleet to "join us" was overshadowed by Darlan's role: ADMIRAL EXPECTED TO WIN PART OF [FRENCH] FLEET FOR UNITED NATIONS. This article, sent from London by Raymond Daniell, referred to Darlan as a "mystery." The Associated Press gave great play to Darlan's message to the French fleet, reminding the readers that Darlan was a "prisoner" of the Americans.

The real objections began to flow on November 14, when Darlan's proclamation assuming command reached the United States. Emphasizing American approval, James MacDonald accurately described Pétain's

---

2. We feel sure you will consult us on the long-term steps, pursuing always the aim of uniting all Frenchmen who will fight Hitler.

Churchill to Roosevelt, November 15, 1942, quoted in Churchill, IV, 631–32.

firing of Darlan in favor of Noguès, who had in turn passed authority
back to Darlan on that November 13 meeting in Algiers. MacDonald was
questioning the wisdom of this move: "Some quarters in London said that
armistice terms had to be made with Darlan but . . . an armistice would
not necessarily mean an alliance." A correspondent named only "Per-
tinak" reported to the North American Newspaper Alliance that Darlan
was believed to be seeking to "sidetrack" Giraud. Such scheming, Per-
tinak believed, was "doomed." Like others, he had noticed the omission
of Giraud's name in Darlan's proclamation.

Beginning with November 15, the Darlan issue seemed to be temporarily set aside in the American press. Eyes turned toward the campaign
in Tunisia, which at the moment seemed to promise a quick seizure of
Tunis and Bizerte. But in this respite Roosevelt concluded that a public
statement by him was necessary. Having officially approved General Eisenhower's actions regarding local political arrangements with a compli-
mentary personal note, he then composed a statement. He sent the text to
Churchill to read in a secret session of Parliament. He then issued the
statement at home:

> I have accepted General Eisenhower's political arrangements made
> for the time being in Northern and Western Africa.
>
> I thoroughly understand and approve the feeling in the United
> States and Great Britain and among all the other United Nations that
> in view of the history of the past two years no permanent arrange-
> ment should be made with Admiral Darlan. People in the United Na-
> tions likewise would never understand the recognition of a reconsti-
> tuting of the Vichy Government in France or in any French
> territory. . . .
>
> The future French Government will be established, not by any in-
> dividual in Metropolitan France or overseas, but by the French peo-
> ple themselves after they have been set free by the victory of the
> United Nations.
>
> The present temporary arrangement in North and West Africa is
> only a temporary expedient, justified solely by the stress of battle.

This statement, of course, gave Eisenhower full backing, and the "temporary expedient" designation was hailed by Gaullists in London. But at
the same time it weakened Darlan's position in Algiers. Actually the statement was consistent with Roosevelt's position all along: that the French
after the war, not the United States or Britain, would dictate the future
French Government.

In London, reaction in the press against the Darlan arrangement
seemed to grow even more slowly than in the United States. This was at-

tributable partly to the fact that TORCH, even in its highly dramatic landing stage, never approached Rommel's retreat across North Africa as top billing in the news. The London *Times* continued to report every skirmish involving the Eighth Army while it sniffingly mentioned only barebones highlights of TORCH. Darlan was not worth examining closely.

However, once the supporters of Charles de Gaulle recovered from their shock—De Gaulle was not informed of TORCH ahead of time— they began their counteroffensive in the press. From Ottawa on November 18 a M. Philip gave his support to De Gaulle with a warning, NO PARLEY WITH VICHY "TRAITORS." The thrust of Philip's statement was a warning to De Gaulle himself that he could negotiate with Giraud but "had no authority to deal with Darlan and his associates such as General Eisenhower had accomplished, because he received his mandate from the French Committee of Liberation." And Radio Maroc darkly mentioned that "American military authorities have presented the French authorities with demands not related to military necessity." The statement, from a station which advertised its independence from both United States and British control, later denied the allegation that the Allies were sympathetic to Vichy—but weakly. Its emphasis, it claimed, was on French independence. On November 28 De Gaulle proclaimed from London a moment of silence for the Frenchmen killed in scuttling the fleet in Toulon.

The matter came to a head on the same day when, in the House of Commons, the Labour Party came out with a statement: "The Labour Party deplores relations with Admiral Darlan as inconsistent with the ideals for which we are fighting."

*

In early December the hostile press and radio comment on the Darlan affair had not died down. Sensing something strange, President Roosevelt decided to send an emissary to North Africa. He chose Milton S. Eisenhower, deputy director of the Office of War Information. Eisenhower, who had risen through the ranks of the civil service in the Department of Agriculture, was a man who knew Washington thoroughly and had performed other tasks for Roosevelt including the administration of the move of the American Japanese from the West Coast.[14] He had been assigned to his present position to assist Elmer Davis, the chief, who was primarily a newspaperman.

The fact that Milton Eisenhower was Dwight Eisenhower's youngest brother led some to believe that his mission to Algiers was solely designed for the protection of his brother's reputation. Actually an investigation of

---

[14] Milton Eisenhower was always sensitive about that particular assignment, as he had not been a participant in the decision but was strictly a government administrator.

the virulent anti-Darlan broadcasts emanating from Radio Maroc had been partly Milton Eisenhower's idea, but he had recommended that Harry Hopkins be the one to go. Further, having decided to send Eisenhower, President Roosevelt gave him two additional tasks. He also wanted a report on the status and number of refugees emigrating to North Africa through Spain. Finally Eisenhower was directed to check up on the effectiveness of the local psychological warfare program, a normal function of the Office of War Information.

Milton Eisenhower made his way to Algeria by way of Bermuda and Gibraltar, arriving in Algiers ill from his many shots. After having moved into his brother's new Villa Dar el Ouard, near the St. George, he immediately began to look into the Darlan problem. As a starting point he went to Drew Middleton, a young foreign correspondent and a friend from Washington days. Middleton's observations astonished him. The commercial telegraph cable between Algiers and the United Kingdom, Middleton advised him, had been cut by a sunken ship, and the American correspondents in Algiers, even though they understood the Darlan situation, were unable to file reports. This left Radio Maroc, the powerful 50,000-watt station in Rabat, currently the only source of information to the outside world. It was, by some oversight, controlled by the Gaullists, some of whom hated the Vichyites worse than they hated the Nazis. Their poisonous daily dispatches about Darlan and every other appointment in North Africa were picked up in Britain, rewritten, and sent on. This was a bizarre situation which had somehow escaped the notice of General Eisenhower and even of Darlan.

Milton Eisenhower checked Middleton's story and found it correct. He informed his brother, who within minutes had arranged for him to see Darlan,[15] who, when he heard Eisenhower's story about the performance of Radio Maroc, picked up the telephone, spoke briefly and authoritatively for a few moments, and hung up. "Very well," he said. "Your men may take over tonight."

The conversation between the two men was relatively brief, but Eisenhower was closely observing this enigmatic and complex little man who had become the center of such a storm back home. His personality was a military one—stern, austere, accustomed to command. He seemed friendly enough but showed no evidence of any desire to make an impression. As to his own future, Darlan simply repeated what he had been saying ever since Roosevelt's statement emphasizing the temporary nature of his position. "I know what you Americans think of me," he said. "Your President thinks I'm a lemon to be held until all the juice has been

[15] Darlan, Eisenhower found, was a somewhat stern figure. As ever, he hated the British but seemed to find no sympathy for the Nazis. At any rate he was far from the ogre that he was being pictured in the press.

squeezed out. Then the rind will be discarded. That is all right with me; I am cooperating with you not for the benefit of the United States or Great Britain, but for the good of France."[16] Eisenhower had no reason not to believe him.

Now sorely in need of personnel to replace the Gaullist broadcasters ousted from Radio Maroc, Eisenhower contacted Elmer Davis, who provided a substitute team very rapidly. Robert Sherwood, head of the OWI Overseas Department, quickly pulled together a group of U.S. foreign correspondents to take over. This switch, however, proved unsatisfactory also, for the people available were primarily foreign correspondents whose leanings were nearly as anti-Darlan as those of the Gaullists. Milton Eisenhower discovered this quickly and cabled home once more. This time Davis sent over a new team headed by C. D. Jackson of *Time-Life*. Soon the transatlantic cables were repaired and a much improved atmosphere resulted.[17]

His work complete, Milton Eisenhower left Algiers by way of Accra on the Gold Coast, thence across the Atlantic. He spent Christmas on Ascension Island.

*

Admiral Jean François Darlan had been giving a great deal of thought to his own future, more than he had expressed to Milton Eisenhower. He was perceptive enough to realize that his role in the Allied invasion of North Africa was about finished and that he was daily becoming more of an embarrassment than an asset. He was keenly aware that there were at least four plots afoot to assassinate him personally.

[16] Milton Eisenhower, *The President Is Calling*, p. 141. Interviews with author, Baltimore, 1977–81.

[17] Even at this late date Dwight Eisenhower was astonished at his brother's accounts of the attitude toward Darlan in some quarters. It prompted him to write a letter to his son the evening of December 20:

From what I hear of what has been appearing in the newspapers, you are learning that it is easy enough for a man to be a newspaper hero one day and a bum the next. The answer is that just as one must not let his head get swelled too much by a bit of acclaim, he must not be too upset and irritated when the pack turns on him. Apparently, the people who have been creating the storm do not like Darlan. The answer to that one is "Who does?". The only thing that a soldier can use for a guide is to try to do what appears right and just at the moment of the crisis. If it turns out wrong—or if it even appears to turn out wrong —the reaction may be serious, but there is no other course to follow. That is one reason we train people all their lives to be soldiers, so that in a moment of emergency they can get down to the essentials of situations and not be too much disturbed about popularity or newspaper acclaim.

Letter, Dwight Eisenhower to John Eisenhower, December 20, 1942. Quoted in Chandler, II, 855. Original in author's possession.

None of this appeared to upset the admiral unduly. On December 23 he attended a luncheon with Murphy, Cunningham, and others in which he toasted a British victory. After the luncheon, in his office, Darlan gave Robert Murphy a list of nominees for his successor, one of whom, surprisingly, was Charles de Gaulle. And he offered to sign a letter of resignation which could be accepted any time that General Eisenhower so directed. Darlan would perhaps have preferred for that resignation to be honored soon, asking only that his wife and he be given an opportunity to go to the United States. One motivation for such a move, beyond his own personal safety, was that his son Alain was a guest of President Roosevelt at the Warm Springs Foundation for Infantile Paralysis. Roosevelt, as a victim himself, had a warm spot for anyone afflicted with that disease, and his kindness to Alain Darlan had probably contributed to the admiral's diligence in working for the Allied cause.

On Thursday, December 24, 1942, Admiral Darlan went to his office in downtown Algiers as usual. While he was there a young Frenchman named Bonnier de la Chapelle, a member of a pro-royalist Algiers family, made his way through Darlan's security guard and pumped a couple of bullets into the defenseless admiral. Darlan died on the operating table a few minutes before Clark and Murphy arrived at the hospital.

De la Chapelle was an unlikely assassin, and the identity of the person who had convinced him that he would be acclaimed a hero remained a mystery. For the head of Darlan's security, Air Force General Jean Marie Joseph Bergeret, embarrassed as well as grief-stricken, ordered the assassin executed the following morning. De la Chapelle's secret died with him, for the moment at least.[18]

*

General Eisenhower, having bidden farewell to his brother, was at Medjez-el-Bab with General Kenneth Anderson that Christmas Eve, 1942. The political situation back in Algiers had been an annoyance that had cost him more time than he would have liked and had taken him away from his main obsession, to take Tunisia before winter set in for good. He had driven—weather prohibited flying—to be with Anderson, who by now had about decided that the chance for instant success was gone. An attack was set for that day and Eisenhower was up front to witness it.

The condition of the troops in Tunisia, still mostly British, was worse than it had been on Eisenhower's previous visits. Furthermore, CCB, 1st U. S. Armored Division, had lost the bulk of its equipment during the

[18] Murphy, pp. 142–43. For information which later came to light, see Ambrose, *Ike's Spies*, pp. 49–56.

withdrawal from Mateur into the mountains. But always the overriding factor was the weather.

When Eisenhower and Anderson went out to check the front in the heavy rain, Eisenhower noticed an incident which, he later wrote, convinced him more than anything else of the hopelessness of an attack. About thirty feet off the road four soldiers were struggling to dig out a motorcycle, stuck in the mud. All they achieved was to become mired themselves; and by the time they gave up, the motorcycle was more deeply bogged down than when they had begun.

Eisenhower went back to Anderson's headquarters and directed that the attack toward Tunis be indefinitely postponed. His fondest hope had failed.

At this time he learned of the death of "The Little Fellow" back in Algiers.

CHAPTER XIII

CASABLANCA I:
THE TESTATOR'S MISTRESS

It was about mid-January 1943, and a pink, rotund, balding little man of sixty-eight years was enjoying the beach at Anfa, a suburb south of Casablanca in Morocco. The warm sunshine contrasted pleasantly with the penetrating chill of England in the winter. Prime Minister Winston Churchill, making the most of a couple of days of relative quiet, watched the surf come crashing up on the beach.

Churchill enjoyed wading in the ocean and the large waves made it all the more exciting. But his mind was seldom far from business, and this surf served as a reminder of the American landing under General George S. Patton which had been made near this spot only two months earlier. No wonder that so many landing craft and ships' boats had been turned over with all their men![1]

But Churchill was seldom alone as he trudged up and down the sands. High-ranking British officers—Army, Navy, and Air Force—came and went. For Churchill and his military advisers were not here on vacation; they were preparing for the beginning of the most dramatic meeting of the war, the Casablanca Conference. President Roosevelt and his entourage were scheduled to arrive in a couple of days, on January 14.

The Atlantic beach below the Anfa cliffs would appear to be an unlikely location for such serious business. But nothing that Churchill ever did paid very much homage to convention; and this meeting near

---

[1] Churchill, IV, 675. Patton, it will be recalled, actually landed on one of the better days.

Casablanca was only the latest of the unorthodox schemes that he and Roosevelt had cooked up in their nearly three years of association.

*

The idea of an overseas conference between heads of government began to germinate as early as November 1942, less than three weeks after the Allied forces had stormed ashore. At that time it was hoped, if not presumed, that North Africa would be cleared of Axis forces before mid-January, and the question of what the Allies should do next had not even been addressed. On November 26, therefore, Roosevelt cabled Churchill proposing a meeting of the British, Russian, and American military chiefs, to be held perhaps in Cairo or Moscow. Churchill turned down the idea in a message the same day, expressing doubt that any meaningful agreements could be reached with the Russians at a strictly military level, particularly if the meeting were to be held outside of the Soviet Union. The time required for the Russian emissaries to check every point with Stalin would be unacceptable.

The next day, it so happened, Harry Hopkins was at Mitchel Field, near New York City, to meet Madame Chiang Kai-shek. Although publicly her visit to the United States was purely for medical purposes, Madame Chiang nevertheless harangued an unreceptive Hopkins all the way to the Harkness Pavilion. The United States, she volunteered, should give top priority to the defeat of the Japanese, primarily through the Chinese theater. Having survived that ordeal without committing himself, Hopkins left for Hyde Park, where the President was waiting. Madame Chiang's visit would provide him with an excuse to reopen an idea he had been advocating for months, a joint meeting of Roosevelt, Churchill, and Stalin. By now Hopkins was sensing that the President was beginning to be convinced, and he used the visit of Madame Chiang to pound home that the time had come to review American-British strategy. The lady's advice had borne fruit. Only China would not be an issue.

Soon thereafter, on December 3, Roosevelt sent a cable to Churchill: "I have been giving a good deal of thought to our proposed joint conference with the Russians, and I agree with you that the only satisfactory way of coming to the vital strategic conclusions that the military situation requires is for you and me to meet personally with Stalin." Further, the President proposed that both he and the Prime Minister bring small groups, consisting primarily of their respective chiefs of staff. He was determined that this should be military in nature; and though he intended to bring Harry Hopkins and Averell Harriman, he specified that no one from the State Department would be there.

Further, Roosevelt proposed to begin the meeting about January 15 in "a secure place south of Algiers or in or near Khartoum," demurring at

Churchill's earlier idea of Iceland or Alaska, as both were too far north and probably too distant from Moscow. He preferred, he concluded, "a comfortable oasis to the raft at Tilsit."[2] Concurrently, Roosevelt sent an invitation to Stalin.

Churchill agreed enthusiastically with the idea of the high-level meeting, but he strongly desired to include Foreign Minister Anthony Eden. In the British Government, Churchill argued, Eden held a special status as a member of the War Cabinet. He functioned almost independently of the Prime Minister and in the British system enjoyed more prestige and responsibility than an American Secretary of State. Further, Churchill advocated a prior meeting between the British and American military chiefs before the official beginning of the three-power conference. Roosevelt objected to both of these proposals; Churchill gave in.

Stalin was not long in sending his regrets. Within four days he answered that, though he welcomed the idea of a meeting between the three heads of governments, he personally would be in no position to leave the Soviet Union. Operations of the winter campaign were proceeding at a high tempo, he explained, and would not be relaxed in January. He did, not surprisingly, add his usual nudge regarding an Allied second front in 1943.

At this point Roosevelt seemed to regress. He cabled his disappointment to Stalin and asked Churchill's opinion once again regarding a meeting of the military chiefs somewhere outside the Soviet Union. Churchill again refused a purely military meeting. Roosevelt went through the motions of pursuing the idea of a Big Three conference, deferring the date to a time around the first of March, when the Russian winter campaign would be over, though he held little hope that Stalin would be more receptive than before.

By December 11 Roosevelt was resigned to Stalin's lack of interest and was now beginning to think in terms of a meeting between himself and Churchill. Roosevelt's thinking was narrowing down to a site either south of Algiers or near Casablanca. Since both of these locations would allow him to meet with Allied military leaders, either would sit well with the American public.

Some people, especially those not well acquainted with the President, have long wondered why he was so keen on holding a conference outside the United States. But the answer may not be so mysterious. Harry Hopkins had his own theory: "I shall always feel that the reason the President wanted to meet Churchill in Africa was because he wanted to make a trip! He was tired of having other people—particularly myself—speak for him around the world. He wanted no more of Churchill in Washing-

[2] A reference to the meeting between Napoleon and Alexander I of Russia in 1807.

ton, for political reasons he could not go to England,[3] he wanted to see our troops, he was sick of people telling him that it was dangerous for him to ride in airplanes. He liked the drama of it. But above all, he wanted to make a trip!"[4]

Roosevelt would, of course, have to contend with some adverse public opinion regarding his flying over the seas—no president had ever flown before while in office nor had one ever left the United States during wartime—but he surmised that criticism would be minimized if the meeting became public knowledge only after he had safely returned. The people would gasp but accept. They might even be caught up by the drama of the thing.

On December 17 Stalin's anticipated regret arrived. He could not leave the Soviet Union even at the beginning of March, he wrote, suggesting that any problems between the Western Allies and the Russians be discussed by way of "correspondence." Stalin's refusal to be out of touch with the daily battle, while illogical to the British and Americans, was actually valid, as he had personally commanded all Russian troops in his capacity of "marshal" or "generalissimo."[5]

Finally, by December 21, Churchill and Roosevelt had agreed to meet at some spot in North Africa, not necessarily at Casablanca. An exuberant Churchill suggested the code name SYMBOL for the conference.

The exact location for the conference would have to be determined by existing facilities, and between December 23 and December 29 General Marshall in Washington and General Eisenhower in Algiers exchanged telegrams almost daily. A suitable site had to be found somewhere in Allied-occupied North Africa. Eisenhower, who viewed a high-level meeting in his theater as a great annoyance, had no choice but to send reconnaissance parties to Oran and Algiers as well as Fédala and Casablanca, the latter two on the coast of Morocco. Finally an assistant of Bedell Smith's recommended Anfa, a suburb a mile from the Atlantic Ocean on a hill just south of Casablanca. General Patton had already discovered it and was living comfortably there. The area included the fine Hotel Anfa, which would provide rooms for large meetings; around the hotel were excellent villas, detached, walled, and easily guarded. An airfield capable of

---

[3] A somewhat puzzling excuse since both King George VI and Churchill had visited the United States during the previous year.

[4] Hopkins' diary, dated Monday evening, January 11, 1943. Hopkins' role in convincing Roosevelt of the political inadvisability of going to England is problematical. However, even General Eisenhower had noted that Harry Hopkins hated Chequers "like the devil hates holy water."

[5] In the course of his usual reminder about a second front in the spring of 1943, Stalin gratuitously expressed approval of the way that General Eisenhower had handled the Darlan situation in North Africa.

handling large planes was nearby, and the proposed villa for President Roosevelt would be sufficiently level to minimize the President's ambulatory problems.

Once the location for SYMBOL was agreed upon, Roosevelt and Churchill reacted with the relish of two youngsters heading for a ball game. They delighted in selecting their own secret code names. Roosevelt chose "Admiral Q"; Churchill thereupon christened himself "Mr. P." so that the two could "watch their P's and Q's."

On New Year's Eve, 1942, President Roosevelt held his usual family party in the White House. The movie that evening starred Ingrid Bergman and Humphrey Bogart in *Casablanca*. Not many in the room could sense the significance of this title. And those who did dared not let on.

*

Just about a year had elapsed since the First Washington Conference (ARCADIA) that had established the Combined Chiefs of Staff (CCS) and the first unified command (ABDA). Much had happened during that year, at first all of it bad: the fall of the Philippines, Singapore, the Dutch East Indies, and Burma. As the year wore on, however, the situation had brightened. The Russians had stopped the German offensive in the Caucasus and had surrounded Von Paulus' Sixth Army at Stalingrad. The Western Allies, too, had tasted success with the British victory at El Alamein and the success of TORCH, which had at least consolidated Northwest Africa.

Since ARCADIA, Roosevelt and Churchill had met once, in Washington during the summer, and other significant high-level meetings had transpired: the Marshall-Hopkins visit to London in April; their second visit in July; and Churchill's perilous trip to Moscow in August.

During this year the top military leaders had remained the same, though the roles they played were evolving. On the American side President Roosevelt seemed more sure of himself and less vulnerable to Churchill's persuasions. He remained the consummate domestic leader, but he elected to be a less active war leader than Churchill. He saw his military chiefs of staff only rarely—perhaps only once a month[6]—and he did not fancy himself the reincarnation of a warrior ancestor as did Churchill.[7] He would be capable of making a broad decision when necessary, but he preferred for others, including Churchill, to perform the leg work.

Of the American military chiefs, General George C. Marshall was steadily forging into a position of greater leadership. True, Admiral

[6] In his diary of April 10, 1942, Brooke wrote: "He [Marshall] certainly had a much easier life of it with Roosevelt; he informed me that he frequently did not see him for a month or six weeks. I was fortunate if I did not see Winston for six hours." Bryant, *Turn of the Tide*, p. 242.

[7] Churchill was a descendant of the Duke of Marlborough.

William D. Leahy, as Roosevelt's personal "Chief of Staff," would preside when the JCS met. But Leahy commanded no fighting force—Army, Navy, or Air Force—and therefore lacked the solid power inherent in directing day-by-day operations.

Marshall had risen to his position of "first among equals" perhaps unconsciously, for though he was a personally confident man, he lived by a code that placed selflessness above any other professional attribute of a military officer. Though his naked power was vast, as the professional head of the U. S. Army, which would eventually include over 8 million men, he exercised his leadership through diplomacy, not through desk pounding. And his influence was enhanced by the fact that he possessed a broad global strategic concept for the employment of all United States forces. Though he was certain in his own mind that the decisive thrust of the war should be an invasion of Western Europe across the English Channel, some of his Army divisions fought in the Pacific as well as Europe. Both Eisenhower in Europe and MacArthur in the Far East were subordinate to him in their U. S. Army capacities.[8]

Marshall's counterpart, Admiral Ernest J. King, was also a man with influence. He nearly always sided with Marshall in matters pertaining to the European war, but his so doing constituted almost an abdication; his real interest was the war in the Pacific, which would benefit from an early victory in Europe. King tended to regard the Pacific as his own area of special influence, and Army divisions sent there he viewed largely as support forces for the Navy's efforts.

King retained the rough, tough style that had served him so well as a naval line officer. Colonel (later General) Albert Wedemeyer, somewhat of a "Young Turk" in the War Department's Operations Division, regarded King as the "strongest" of the American Chiefs. But such comparisons are idle. And while King freely displayed impatience and temper, especially with the British, he was not a man to hold personal rancor. Everyone who dealt with him, even the British, soon discovered that when he made a commitment he would deliver ahead of time.

The third member of the American Joint Chiefs, accorded this position to round out the body, was Lieutenant General Henry H. ("Hap") Arnold. Genial, as his nickname would imply, Arnold was much liked by both the British and American chiefs. In early 1943, Arnold still tended to confine his interest to questions pertaining to the Army Air Forces per se. His long-term ambition, shared by many of the aviators, was the attainment of Air Force autonomy; and he felt that he would have to exert all efforts to ensure that his airmen would be appreciated. In those terms,

[8] In their functions as Allied commanders, of course, both reported directly to the CCS, but through Marshall as "executive agent."

therefore, Arnold was an unreliable ally to Marshall. He sometimes appeared sympathetic with the developing British "periphery" strategy. For an air base in the Mediterranean tomorrow might be more interesting than an invasion a year hence. And maybe the war could be won by air power alone!

On the British side, the roles of the members had changed less, since the BCOS was already an efficient machine as of Pearl Harbor. Winston Churchill was still both Prime Minister and Minister of Defense and his personal influence had been strengthened when forcing the Allies to assault North Africa rather than attempt the cross-Channel attack. On his mission to Stalin during August 1942, he had represented the entire West. Churchill manifested no reticence when it came to telling his Chiefs of Staff how to do their jobs, be it flying an individual airplane or calculating the possibilities of a military venture.

Of the British Chiefs of Staff, General Sir Alan Brooke, CIGS, had been the official leader since March 1942. As such he was also the most positive of the three. He had survived the year well, and it was a monument to his fortitude that he physically and emotionally had withstood the pounding of the Prime Minister's ungodly personal schedule and fertile imagination. Brooke's personality, however, continued to irritate both his British colleagues and the Americans. He had not altered the low opinion in which he generally held the latter.

Admiral Sir Dudley Pound, First Sea Lord, resembled "Hap" Arnold in his tendency to stay largely in the background except when his own service, the Royal Navy, was involved. This reticence was due partly to Pound's gentlemanly character; but it may have resulted also from his degenerating health. Like Arnold, he was personally admired and liked by the other members of the Combined Chiefs.

Air Chief Marshal Sir Charles R. ("Peter") Portal was making a real contribution to harmony between the British and Americans. While conscious of the position of the air forces—and of British interests versus American—Peter Portal was a favorite of the Americans, as he possessed the breadth of vision to understand their point of view.

Among the three, Portal was definitely the British chief with whom George Marshall preferred to deal.[9]

Taken as a whole, the British delegation still overshadowed the American in effectiveness because they knew their goals whereas the Americans held different preoccupations: Marshall, the Europe-minded; King, who

[9] He and Marshall were two of the five men whom Dwight Eisenhower, in his contemplative years, would classify as "great."

tended always to look to the Pacific, who felt free to resist allocation of too much to European operations;[10] and Arnold, concerned more with developing the AAF than with strategy.

The blame for this American disarray must be laid at the feet of President Franklin D. Roosevelt, who seemed to have no strategy of his own. Before leaving for Casablanca Roosevelt held only one meeting, on January 7, the result of which could be summed up as "no conclusions." His "policy" was "wait and see."[11]

*

SYMBOL had many items to decide, some large and some small. The question of the Europe First priority in 1943 had to be reaffirmed, not only in principle, but as a matter of specifics. The Americans, for example, even Marshall, were anxious not to allow the Japanese to dig in too strongly in the Far East. And the British, though unanimous in the desire to concentrate exclusively on Europe, realized that in the final analysis they had to sell their views. For the Americans, while divided among themselves, might become stubborn and unite in resisting *any* British proposals just on general principle.

This possibility, however, did not dim the confidence of the British Chiefs. Even Portal, on January 14, wrote an astonishing memo:

> We are in the position of a testator who wishes to leave the bulk of his fortune to his mistress. He must, however, leave something to his wife, and his problem is to decide how little he can in decency leave apart for her.

This from the most pro-American of the British Chiefs, referring to American resources (the wife's) at that!

The next issue was the question of further Allied moves after the fall of Tunisia. Marshall, for one, was willing to propose nearly any alternative in order to see operations in the Mediterranean closed. In the course of the meeting on January 7 he had even proposed to invade the Brittany Peninsula during 1943 rather than go farther into the Mediterranean. The

[10] Colonel (later Brigadier General) Frank McCarthy later witnessed an amusing exchange between Churchill and King. Churchill had invited the British and American Chiefs of Staff, along with General Smuts, to accompany him on a train. The atmosphere was festive.

Admiral King, as usual, was looking glum, lost in his own thoughts. Churchill, noticing, turned to him and said, "Don't look so sour, Ernie. I'm not trying to take anything away from the American Navy just now." King was so shocked that he dropped his spoon in the soup and it splashed all over his immaculate uniform. Interview with Frank McCarthy, October 4, 1968.

[11] Robert Sherwood, in his monumental work *Roosevelt and Hopkins,* makes no mention of this meeting of January 7, 1943.

operation might not succeed, Marshall conceded, but it would be less expensive in shipping.

When word of Marshall's Brittany project reached London, Churchill and the BCOS could hardly take it seriously; it would be another SLEDGEHAMMER. So Churchill still pretended to hope that further operations in the Mediterranean would not prevent some sort of ROUNDUP in 1943—provided that Germany was on the verge of collapse.

Not all, however, had been sweetness and light in the British planning. The question remained as to the specific targets to be hit in the Mediterranean after the clearing of Tunisia. The British Planning Staff, supported by Lord Louis Mountbatten, favored Sardinia, closer to the heart of Italy than Sicily. Churchill would have none of it. "I shall not be fobbed off by a sardine [Sardinia]," he grunted. As usual he carried his point; the British position would be to attack Sicily within a very minimum time after the fall of Tunisia. The BCOS then came to Anfa proposing that the Allies' policy should be:

1) To exploit TORCH as vigorously as possible with a view to (a) Knocking Italy out of the war; (b) Bringing Turkey into the war; and (c) Giving the Axis no respite for recuperation.

2) Increased bombing of Germany.

3) Maintenance of supplies to Russia.

4) The build-up of BOLERO *on the greatest scale that the above operations admit,* in order . . . to re-enter the Continent with about twenty-one divisions in August or September, 1943, if the conditions are such that there is a good prospect of success.[12]

Other matters were to be discussed: operations in Burma; the question of the command in Tunisia when Eisenhower's and Alexander's forces should converge in that country; and, at the political level, some rapprochement between Giraud and De Gaulle. The French political situation was still messy; the British and Americans each appeared to have their own pet Frenchman.

Little wonder that Winston Churchill in writing his memoirs entitled one full chapter, "Our Need to Meet."

*

Kenneth Pendar, the young vice-consul who, with Robert Murphy, had been so involved in the drama the night of November 7, 1942, had returned to Morocco. Though assigned to Casablanca, he was free to travel

12 Churchill, IV, 671. Italics supplied.

in his line of work, and he had taken station in the attractive pink and orange Arab town of Marrakech, about a hundred and fifty miles inland.

Pendar was a rather unusual character, who described himself as a "very American American who deeply loved France." An archaeologist by training, he had worked in France for three years before 1940 and then on his return home had taken a job in the library at Harvard University. He was a venturesome sort by nature, however. In the spring of 1941, therefore, when a Navy friend told him that the armed services were recruiting a group of French-speaking "vice-consuls" he readily signed up. A dozen of these young men were to be stationed in an exciting place, French Northwest Africa.

Pendar and his group received almost no instruction at the State Department before proceeding to North Africa, but they soon learned that they would be doubling in brass: they would help Robert Murphy in administering the Murphy-Weygand Agreement, but they would also be intelligence agents. On arrival in Morocco, Pendar found anything but a bed of roses. He felt slightly uncomfortable living with the rather rigid procedures in the American Consulate; and the regular American officials in Casablanca, disliking the Murphy-Weygand Accord, tended to vent some of their disapproval on Pendar and his group. There were, however, compensating factors. Among these was his lovely villa in Marrakech, which Mrs. Moses Taylor, an American, had loaned to the U. S. Government.

On January 2, 1943, Pendar was instructed to meet a brigadier general of the Air Transport Command at Casablanca Airport. On arrival, however, he found himself accosted by two important-looking Army officers, one an American brigadier general named Alfred M. Gruenther, chief of staff to Lieutenant General Mark W. Clark, and the other a British colonel, William Sterling, an assistant to General Ismay in London. Within moments Pendar's instructions had changed; he was to take Gruenther and Sterling back to Marrakech. This task, he was assured, took priority over the other. Gruenther and Sterling spoke with authority and he complied.

The three flew back to Marrakech to inspect Mrs. Taylor's villa. Pendar was somewhat curious to hear Gruenther and Sterling each refer to two unknown individuals as "our number one man" and "your number one man." But Pendar, having now been in North Africa for nearly a year, was used to mystery, and he paid little attention. After all, Gruenther could easily be referring to Clark or Eisenhower—and Sterling could be talking about a corresponding British personage. After a certain period of time, however, the two apparently agreed between themselves that the villa, which boasted six master bedrooms and impressive servants' quarters, was adequate for their purpose. Then they let him in on their secret:

in about ten days' time the American and British heads of government were planning to meet in Morocco, at Anfa, near Casablanca, or right here in this villa. In any case, even if the meeting were to be held in Casablanca, the two principals would in all likelihood return to Marrakech to relax for a couple of days.

Knowing this, Pendar could now be of more help. Once the Taylor villa had been thoroughly screened, he conducted Gruenther and Sterling around Marrakech. Other possible villas abounded. And the sumptuous Hotel Mamounia, a couple of miles away, could comfortably house the staffs.[13]

As it turned out, the Anfa area was eventually selected for the actual conference, but Pendar would be provided with all the equipment the Army could give: barbed wire, "secret" telephones, generators, and transformers. He was to be ready to erect the wire fence on a few hours' notice and be prepared to take over the Hotel Mamounia. He should also find living space for the guests displaced from the hotel.

After a few days members of the Secret Service began arriving to inspect the villa. The head of the presidential detail, Special Agent Mike Reilly, scoured every corner of the building, expertly searching out spots where microphones might be hidden. Reilly, giving safety priority over beauty, placed the President in an inside bedroom with only one window looking on the courtyard. Anti-aircraft guns were placed in the open spaces around the dense foliage which enclosed the house, despite the fact that Marrakech was considered outside the range of any known German aircraft.

The prospect of being host to the two great men, however, was heady stuff, and Pendar looked forward to the event with relish. He was to be a firsthand witness to something that could be described in no terms other than "historic."

*

The American Joint Chiefs took off from National Airport, Washington, at 8:30 A.M., January 9, 1943. They flew in two C-54s, the first carrying General Marshall, General Arnold, and Field Marshal Dill. In the second plane rode Admiral King; Lieutenant General Brehon B. Somervell, head of the Services of Supply, Rear Admiral Charles M. Cooke; Colonel Wedemeyer; and others. The distribution was calculated to minimize the loss should any one plane fail to reach Casablanca. The route went from Washington to Miami, Puerto Rico, Belém and Natal in Brazil, across the Atlantic to Bathurst, Gambia. From there the trip north would be overland to Marrakech. It was not necessary to stop at Marrakech,

---

[13] The Hotel Mamounia had been the favorite retreat of Winston Churchill between the wars.

so close to Casablanca, but the comfortable surroundings at the villa would provide the weary travelers a night's rest. Besides, Marrakech could be counted on to provide good weather conditions, and the party could, if necessary, complete the trip to Casablanca by car.

General Marshall's C-54 landed a little ahead of Admiral King's and therefore he, Arnold, Dill, and Brigadier Dykes[14] arrived before the rest and were duly conducted through the courtyard amid the confusion of an excited household staff. Pendar had never seen any top military figures before, and he watched them keenly. He was struck in particular with the simplicity and thoughtfulness of Marshall, who first asked to see Dill's room. During the year that Dill had been the British representative on the Combined Chiefs, Marshall had become fond of him personally; and as Dill's host Marshall wanted to make sure before anything else that his guest would be comfortable.

Later in the afternoon the rest of the party joined up and all were offered tea on the terrace behind the building. As the various members were quietly helping themselves, Pendar noticed an older man sitting alone. The man was obviously a high-ranking admiral and, though Pendar had never seen a picture of King, he surmised that this would be he. He approached King and found him "definitely and gruffly uninterested in eating or drinking." Pendar, however, was not discouraged and he pulled up a chair in an attempt to strike up a conversation. The attempt failed. Then did the admiral wish to see his room? No. Finally King seemed to give up fending off his eager young host and took a cup of tea, and as he began to loosen up, he became friendly. Soon Pendar sensed that the two were being watched, some of the others possibly expecting an outburst of King's temper. But it never appeared, and Pendar always regarded the Chief of Naval Operations with a special warmth.

The visitors were all fascinated by the house and garden at the Taylor villa, especially the tower. Despite their long hard trip, some of the party decided to see the town and perhaps buy something in the *souks* of Marrakech. This prospect worried Pendar. The Arabs, he knew, were adept at discerning important people. Steering his visitors clear of the crowds, Pendar took them to the flat top of a hotel overlooking the marketplace. There, from only a hundred yards off, the Americans could watch the natives plying their trades: water salesmen, snake charmers, and countless souvenir vendors. The visitors, having seen the mobs, seemed satisfied to observe from where they were.

Dinner that evening was particularly genial, the tone being set by the

[14] Brigadier Vivian Dykes—British secretary to the Combined Chiefs of Staff in Washington—was unfortunately killed in an air crash en route to London after the Casablanca Conference.

good humor of Sir John Dill. The principals went to bed early while the younger members of the group stayed up awhile and relaxed among themselves.

The party left for the nearby airport in the dark at 8:00 A.M. the next day. As Pendar was preparing to drive off a little ahead, he yelled out of the window offering a ride to anyone. A quiet voice asked, "Would you have room for me?" Pendar welcomed his unknown visitor. It turned out to be General Marshall. As they passed the time pleasantly over the short distance, Marshall told of his first contact with Pendar's boss, Robert Murphy. Some months earlier Murphy's arrival in Washington had cost Marshall a weekend leave, the first holiday he had planned since the beginning of the war. No wonder that Murphy had received a cool reception at the War Department the previous October!

The military having left, Pendar hoped that unsuitable weather at Casablanca would force President Roosevelt also to stop over. Casablanca, however, remained clear and the President flew there directly.

Marshall, King, Arnold, Dill, and the rest were met at the Casablanca airport by General Wayne Clark. Soon they were settled in the nearby Hotel Anfa, warm, comfortable, with a beautiful view of the ocean in the distance. Marshall was disturbed, however, to learn that, in contrast to the small American delegation, the British group was huge. Further, a communications vessel, H.M.S. *Bulolo*,[15] was anchored in the nearby harbor. She would provide instant messages between the British delegation and their staffs in London. In the inevitable confrontations, the British Chiefs would be armed with plenty of facts and statistics.

*

On Tuesday night, January 12, while the American military party was resting in Marrakech, the British delegation left London under less comfortable circumstances. As secrecy was of the utmost importance, all members were instructed to meet in a small village in Wiltshire, rendezvous time 11:00 P.M. They were told nothing more. Sir Hastings Ismay, for one, had an early dinner at White's Restaurant in London and then left feeling like "a thief in the night." He found his way through the pouring rain but on arrival at the appointed village he found the narrow street clogged with traffic. A solitary policeman eventually straightened out the chaos, however, and the departure point turned out to be Lyneham Airfield, where all gathered in the officers' mess for final preparations.

Ismay had done his share of flying, but this journey was to be something new. First, all passengers were briefed on procedure in case of

15 Churchill had notified Roosevelt about this ship in their correspondence.

forced landings. After they struggled into their parachutes and "Mae Wests,"[16] they were each given French and Spanish currency and notes written in Arabic promising ransom for their safe return. Finally, each individual was given a gadget designed to catch the night dew and save one from dying of thirst in the desert—if, as Ismay observed, he was "clever enough to use it properly."[17]

Soon the party left the overheated mess and boarded their respective planes, crudely converted, unheated B-24 Liberators. They faced a cold ten-hour journey over the Atlantic, and Ismay never closed his eyes all night.

Not everyone was quite so miserable as Ismay, however. Sir Alan Brooke slept on the floor of a small cabin toward the rear of the plane, and his chief complaint lay with his sleeping companion, Admiral Mountbatten. Brooke's sense of humor seemed to hold up best under unpleasant conditions. As he later wrote, "I did not find . . . [Dickie Mountbatten] a pleasant bed companion, as every time he turned around he overlay me, and I had to use my knees and elbows to establish my rights to my allotted floor space!" However, Brooke was able to get at least some sleep.

These discomforts were shared by the Prime Minister himself. In his plane an effort had been made to provide some heat, which proved more dangerous than comforting. At about 2:00 A.M. Churchill awoke feeling that his toes were burning from a heater located near his feet. Concerned that the outlet might become red hot, the Prime Minister climbed out of his bunk and woke up Portal, Churchill's chief consultant on personal flight safety. The two men then clambered into the bomb bay of the Liberator, where they found two men hard at work trying to keep the central gasoline stove going. Preferring to freeze rather than to burn, Churchill ordered all heat turned off. From that point on he shivered with the rest in an unheated plane 8,000 feet above the Atlantic.

However, Churchill arrived at Casablanca refreshed, bouncy, and cheerful. Adventure and excitement always seemed to give him endurance exceeding that of far younger subordinates.

*

The air was warm; the sun was bright; and the heavy palm trees and bougainvillea cast dark clear shadows in the daytime. In this cheerful atmosphere the Allied leaders began their preparations for the forthcoming conference. All were comfortably housed. Solid, cool villas hidden from each other by walls and vegetation were within easy walking distance of each other. Four of these, almost in the shadow of the Hotel Anfa, were reserved for Churchill, Roosevelt, Giraud, and De Gaulle (should he

16 Inflatable life jackets named after the voluptuous movie actress.
17 Ismay, p. 284.

come). The military chiefs were also comfortable in the modern Anfa Hotel, constructed to resemble a huge ship's cabin. The Anfa site, being on the crest of a large round hill, provided vistas of the Atlantic Ocean on one side and the picturesque white city of Casablanca on the other. Time for enjoyment and for personal visits would be limited, however. Admiral King would be afforded a chance to inspect the damage done by his warships to the French battleship *Jean Bart* the night of the landings; but except for such quick escapades the uniformed chiefs would have their hands full.

The day of Wednesday, January 13, was devoted to preparatory military meetings of the respective chiefs, two teams running through their final practices. This opportunity for preparation was particularly welcome to the Americans who, busy back in Washington, had still not reconciled their respective positions. When they first met, Admiral King took the initiative, insisting that over-all global strategy be addressed first. Until the Allies could settle on the relative emphasis to be placed on the Pacific versus Europe, they could hardly discuss specific operations to be executed in any given region. Marshall agreed that Europe should continue to be top priority, but within that framework the allocation of resources should approximate something like 70 percent to Europe and 30 percent to the Pacific. King was delighted, remembering that up to now only 15 percent of American resources had gone to the Pacific. Within the European area Marshall still hoped for a small invasion of the Continent in 1943, but even before leaving Washington he had doubted his ability to prevent an invasion of Sicily. That move would almost automatically rule out any chance.

The Combined Chiefs met together for the first time the next morning, January 14. As always the group sat around a long table, speaking informally but sometimes intensely. This lack of format meant that those most interested in a given subject would do most of the talking; equal time for each member was no consideration. By and large Alan Brooke played the role of spokesman for the British, and on this morning, when the subject of global strategy was the first issue discussed, Admiral King by prearrangement spoke for the Americans.[18]

In the first discussions the lines of battle were drawn simply. The American ratio of 70 percent of U.S. resources to Europe and 30 percent to the Pacific was vehemently challenged by Brooke, who interpreted the term "priority to Europe" as meaning almost nothing for the Pacific. (With astonishing optimism, Brooke claimed it was at least possible for the Allies to win the war in Europe before the end of that very year

[18] Admiral Leahy had fallen sick and had been left behind in Trinidad. He was traveling with the President and would have missed this meeting anyhow.

1943.) He then laid out the proposed British strategy, which made the defeat of Italy and the entrance of Turkey the immediate objectives. The British balked severely at American plans for the Pacific and Burma, fearing that, if the Americans began a small invasion of Burma (RAVENOUS) or a major one (ANAKIM) in late 1943, those operations might well become full-scale and detract from the effort in Europe.

During the second meeting, held that afternoon, King continued to present American arguments in favor of the Pacific. On whom, he asked, would the burden fall to fight Japan once Germany had been knocked out? And why were the British so lukewarm about any operations even in the Indian Ocean? What King probably did not know was that the British resistance to major American operations in Burma was partly inspired by Churchill's concern for the future British Empire. Burma, Churchill felt, should be retaken by Empire forces. This the British Chiefs could not disclose.

Thus in the early conferences King and Brooke each presented positive plans, while Marshall was temporarily relegated to a negative role, trying only to prevent further commitment in the Mediterranean but lacking an alternative proposal. As a "patient friend to the wife," however, he came to the aid of King, more than once hinting that the United States might still re-evaluate the present policy of priority to Europe. For five days, through six full-scale meetings of the Combined Chiefs, this clash of views would continue to hold the center of the stage.

On the afternoon of January 14, as the Combined Chiefs of Staff were holding their first formal meetings, President Roosevelt and his entourage landed at Casablanca. They had taken a train from Washington the night of January 9, transferring to a Boeing flying boat at Miami, thence to Trinidad, Belém, and across the ocean to Bathurst, Gambia. There the President had transferred to a C-54 for the final leg to Casablanca. (The flying boat was deemed unsafe to land in the Casablanca surf.) The trip was novel to the President, who had never before slept on an airplane, and he seemed to relish it.

On arrival the President was immediately conducted to his villa, named Dar es Saada, where he learned that the military staffs had finished their stormy afternoon session and were having a cocktail across the street at the Anfa Hotel. He invited them to join him and Churchill for dinner. The trip had been sufficiently tiring that even the convivial Harry Hopkins left the gathering at midnight. The two political chiefs, however, sat up until 2:00 A.M.

The next few days would be relaxed, ideal for family reunions. Lieutenant Colonel Elliott Roosevelt, USAAF; Lieutenant Franklin D. Roosevelt, Jr., USNR; Captain Randolph Churchill of the Special Service Brigade; and Sergeant Robert Hopkins, a combat photographer in Tunisia, were all on hand at some time or other.

*

In Algiers General Eisenhower was now focusing on a threatening situation on the Tunisian battlefront. Rommel was known to be fortifying the Mareth Line on the Libyan border, and if he could hold Montgomery with small forces, he would have enough troops left over to create a threat to the thinly spread Americans. Certain that he would be asked to render a firsthand report at the Anfa meeting, Eisenhower had visited Tunisia, though still sick with "walking pneumonia." General Marshall's eventual summons came as no surprise, and Eisenhower left Algiers the morning of January 15 for Casablanca.

Friday, January 15, proved a long one for the harassed Allied Commander. A dilapidated B-17 Flying Fortress took him and his naval aide, Commander Harry Butcher, first to Oujda for a quick visit with General Clark. Neither paid much attention to the condition of the aircraft, although it was described as "battle fatigued," fit for passenger service but not for combat. After this brief meeting Eisenhower took off again across the Atlas Mountains.

Above the crest Eisenhower nudged Butcher and pointed out the window. One of the engines was spewing oil. By now it had quit and the pilot was obviously unable to feather the propeller. The strain on the fuselage caused by wind resistance was noticeable.

Immediately word came from the pilot for all passengers to strap on parachutes. Eisenhower and Butcher tried to help each other. In the process a strap caught one of the stars on Eisenhower's jacket and tore it off. When Butcher lunged to pick up the star to pin it back on again, his chief noticed his hands shaking. "What's the matter, Butch? You've often pinned stars on me. What's your trouble?"

"Yes, sir," Butcher answered. "But never when I had to put you in a parachute." Eisenhower put the star in his pocket.

As the two stood by the door, Eisenhower was debating whether he would actually go out even if the order came. He was unconcerned about the possibility of a parachute malfunction, but the trick knee that had plagued him throughout his twenty-eight years of service would never hold up in the rugged Atlas Mountains. He would be incapable of walking, Eisenhower reasoned, and he would probably perish before anyone could find him. While he pondered whether to stay with the plane, a second engine went out and a third began to give trouble, leaving only one of the plane's four engines operating fully.

Fortunately, they had now passed the peak of the mountains, and the pilot was able to head into a long glide toward the coastline; eventually one of the three offending engines began working again. Eisenhower, a qualified pilot himself, noted with satisfaction—and relief—that the plane made a fine landing.

General Patton was on hand to meet him, but the two had no time for talk. Eisenhower's main concern was to get the plane's engines fixed, as he intended to return to Algiers the next morning.

An hour and a half later, as Eisenhower was conferring in the Anfa Hotel, a messenger slipped him a piece of paper: "It is impossible to repair your airplane. It is being scrapped immediately. It will never fly again."[19]

Eisenhower stayed in session with Marshall and King for the rest of the morning and had lunch with General Marshall in his hotel room. That afternoon he was afforded, for the first time, an opportunity to describe the local situation to Roosevelt, Churchill, and Hopkins. He explained the details of the "Darlan deal" and was astonished at the lack of accurate information that had reached the White House. Roosevelt, for example, frankly admitted that he had never realized that Darlan had actually been an American prisoner.

After the conference Roosevelt remarked to Hopkins that Eisenhower appeared "jittery." Hopkins, however, understood and explained. He knew that Eisenhower had suffered from respiratory difficulties almost steadily since coming to Africa and had been in bed several days just before they arrived. Further, Eisenhower's hopes for a quick victory in Tunisia had been frustrated, and he was not happy to be caught in the middle of the bewildering French political mess. Conflicting instructions from Washington had not helped.[20]

Hopkins admired Eisenhower's courage and candor in explaining his positions on the Darlan issue to the President and the Prime Minister. And Eisenhower's philosophy that generals could be replaced (whereas governments could not) explained something that had bothered Roosevelt: Eisenhower's decision to deal with Darlan without consulting Washington. He had, it was now apparent, risked his own future with his eyes open.

Roosevelt, pleased, invited Eisenhower for dinner that night. The next day, at noon, with a new airplane supplied by General Ira Eaker,[21] the Allied Commander left Algiers.

[19] Eisenhower, At Ease, p. 259; Butcher, My Three Years With Eisenhower, p. 237.
[20] Eisenhower had received a veto from Undersecretary of State Sumner Welles on the appointment of one Marcel Peyrouton to become governor general in Algiers. However, Secretary of State Hull had overridden Welles and approved Peyrouton.
[21] Eaker had come from London to attend the conference.

*

It was well for Eisenhower's future role in the war that he had been afforded this opportunity to explain the local situation to the President, for Roosevelt, although impressed, still held some reservations toward him. These may have stemmed from his disappointment, shared certainly by Eisenhower most of all, that the initial rush to Tunisia had failed. And the Chief Executive, not always one to bother with harsh realities, may have felt that Eisenhower should have tried harder to execute the North African landings before the 1942 congressional elections. Whatever the reason, Roosevelt felt that Eisenhower had still to prove himself, and when Marshall, later in the conference, pressed him to promote Eisenhower to full general, Roosevelt at first refused until there was some "damn good reason." Roosevelt wanted a victory to justify a promotion; and Eisenhower's position vis-à-vis his higher-ranking British colleagues seemed less important to him than it did to Marshall.

Eisenhower was unaware of any such feelings on Roosevelt's part; in fact he had every reason to feel elated at the results of his visit. For soon Alexander's forces, pursuing Rommel, would be crossing the border into Tunisia from Libya, and the two forces combined would be almost three quarters British in composition. Despite this fact the British themselves had proposed that Eisenhower retain supreme command in Tunisia, with Alexander serving as his deputy and directing the day-to-day battle under him. Thus Eisenhower was given a stamp of approval for his handling of TORCH and Darlan. All the more remarkable since Alexander, Tedder, and Cunningham all ranked Eisenhower by one grade!

Eisenhower's retention of command was brought about by at least three factors: the unwavering support of George Marshall; the affection and respect in which he was held by his main British subordinates (especially Admiral Sir Andrew Cunningham); and the fact that Eisenhower's Allied Force Headquarters was a truly British-American organization whereas Alexander's was strictly British. The choice, while surprising on the surface, was logical, and both British and Americans were happy. The British had ensured, however, that land, sea, and air force commanders in the Mediterranean were all their own men.

*

The visit of General Eisenhower to Anfa, while beneficial, did little to affect the broad Allied plans for future strategy. The Combined Chiefs met again the same afternoon in which Eisenhower was closeted with Roosevelt; they continued every day. By the morning of Monday, January 18, the positions of the two sides appeared to have hardened and compromise of any kind was beginning to look impossible. General Marshall complained to Brooke that the British seemed content to engage the enemy solely in the Mediterranean, with the force in the United Kingdom barely large enough to exploit a German collapse. As an alternative, as Marshall saw it, Brooke would willingly leave a large force idle in Britain rather than fight in the Pacific. Coming from Marshall, this accusation alarmed Brooke: it sounded like King! In the heat of argument Brooke warned in return that if the Allies should try to defeat Japan first they would "lose the war."[22] The Allies had agreed to defeat Germany first: the question remained whether to go into northern France or to exploit the Mediterranean. Brooke favored the latter as the only way the Allies could maintain pressure in 1943.

To this Marshall denied proposing total inactivity in the Mediterranean or France, but the Allies could not afford idly to allow the Japanese to consolidate their gains in the Pacific. And he was tired of telling American forces in the Pacific to fight on a shoestring.

As time went on, moreover, Admiral King was becoming increasingly annoyed by Brooke's detailed examination of American operations in the Pacific. The British had been thrown out of the Far East by the Japanese and the Americans were carrying the entire burden. This being the case, too much unsolicited advice from Brooke was unwelcome. The United States, King insisted, planned only to gain positions to facilitate the final offensive later. Finally King and Marshall conceded that future action in the Far East would not be hurt if forces already in the Mediterranean were to conduct further operations so long as they were not reinforced from other areas. At this point Portal jumped in. The British, he said, would be satisfied if they could be assured that the Americans were worried *not* about operations but only about *a greater build-up* in the Mediterranean.

The arguments went back and forth. Reconquest of Burma, Marshall said, would bolster China; going from island to island in the Pacific was proving too expensive. King agreed that the same forces used against Rabaul could later take the Marshalls. He also wanted to take Truk, in the Carolines, during 1943.

Finally Marshall made a concession. He would stick to proposals to take the Gilbert, Marshall, and Caroline Islands (including Truk) but *"with resources available in the theater."*[23]

The conferees then recessed for lunch. As they walked out, Brooke turned to Dill. "It is of no use," he said. "We shall never get agreement with them."

"On the contrary," Dill answered, "you have already got agreement to most of the points."

22 Pogue, Vol. III, *Organizer of Victory,* p. 28.
23 Ibid., p. 29.

Dill, having served so long in Washington, D.C., understood the Americans. He suggested that the British meet after lunch. He also informed Air Marshal Sir John Slessor, Portal's assistant, of what he had said to Brooke. Slessor quickly drew up a possible agreement and presented it to Portal, who liked it.

The meeting between Dill and Brooke after the lunch bore fruit. Dill asked Brooke how far he would go in order to secure complete accord; Brooke refused to concede anything. They would then, Dill warned, be obligated to go to Roosevelt and Churchill. "You know," Dill pressed home, "what a mess they would make of it." This being Brooke's weakest point, the CIGS agreed to listen. Dill then outlined several concessions that Brooke might discuss with Marshall. Brooke gave in.

At that point Portal brought in Slessor's typed proposal and Dill took it to Marshall immediately. Between the two friends, Dill and Marshall, the way for a compromise was paved.[24]

Before the beginning of the afternoon session—actually in the conference room—Marshall and King checked over Slessor's paper together as the British watched. The Americans quickly decided that their basic positions had been met, and miraculously the Combined Chiefs approved the essence of future Allied strategy. What had appeared impossible just before lunch had fallen into line. The hero of the hour was Field Marshal Sir John Dill.

At 5:30 P.M. President Roosevelt invited the Combined Chiefs to join him and the Prime Minister at Villa Dar es Saada for the first plenary meeting—political and military together—of SYMBOL. He asked Brooke to sit on his right and promptly inquired as to who was chairman. Brooke answered that General Marshall was presiding.[25] Roosevelt turned to Marshall, who promptly deferred to Brooke for an outline of the CCS recommendations.

This was a tense moment. So much work and conflict had gone into these finely honed agreements! But Brooke described their essence, which consisted really of a trade-off. British proposals to attack Sicily as soon as possible after the fall of Tunisia had been accepted in exchange for British acquiescence in an attack in the South Pacific (and later that year in Burma). In neither case would the continued offensives involve allocation of additional resources.

Both the President and the Prime Minister approved the military agreements. Even Churchill, accustomed as he was to interfering in mili-

[24] This discussion is drawn largely from Pogue, III, 27–30, and Bryant, *Turn of the Tide*, pp. 449–50.
[25] General Marshall was the senior of the Combined Chiefs of Staff, having been in his job since 1939. Also, the Americans were acting as hosts.

tary affairs, said nothing. The Prime Minister had achieved what he wanted, a further exploitation of the expected victory in Tunisia, and he realized that the Americans had made a major concession. And, after all, the discussions had involved almost exclusively American resources.

Marshall now realized that the developments he had been fearing had come to pass. Any invasion across the English Channel in 1943 was now definitely out.

After the first plenary meeting of the evening of January 18 discussions went more smoothly within the CCS. On January 20 the Combined Chiefs confirmed once and for all that General Eisenhower should retain supreme command in the Mediterranean for the now agreed invasion of Sicily (HUSKY). The British were satisfied so long as Alexander, as Eisenhower's deputy, was directed to run the day-to-day land battle. Brooke in particular believed that the CCS had shoved Eisenhower up into the rarefied atmosphere where he could do little military harm.

A ripple among the more tranquil waters occurred the next day, however, when the British Joint Planners began resurrecting their arguments in favor of invading Sardinia rather than Sicily. Brooke was jolted, especially when he found that even Portal was wavering and Pound was indifferent. Brooke stood his ground. He would simply have nothing to do with a change in objectives, and he was concerned regarding his own personal relations with the Americans. Having fought for Sicily—and having attained agreement on that basis—Brooke could never bring himself to ask Marshall to scrap it all and start over again. Fortunately Churchill would consider no such idea. He still refused to be "fobbed off by a sardine."

Other matters of a peripheral but important nature were discussed, including the appointment of the controversial Frenchman Marcel Peyrouton as governor general of Algiers. More important than that, however, was the question for which Eisenhower had ordered Major General Ira Eaker to come from London.[26] The British, in order to unify British and American bombing efforts in the mounting air war against Germany, were attempting to set up a single air command. Eaker could agree only so long as a single command posed no threat to American development of daylight bombing. Churchill, possibly toying with Eaker, demanded to know why the Americans were not yet bombing Germany from Britain. The answer to that was simple: nearly all American aircraft had been sent from

[26] General Eisenhower still commanded the U.S. forces in the United Kingdom. He was relieved of the European command at this meeting on his own recommendation.

Britain to the Mediterranean. In that region even Churchill knew they were beginning to rival the British.

Finally the matter was settled by compromise. The British would exercise over-all strategic direction of the bombardment of Germany, and the Americans would continue to develop their daylight pinpoint bombing. Somewhat to Churchill's surprise Eaker later gave him credit for saving the daylight bombing. The Prime Minister thought he had been in the role of antagonist.

*

On the evening of January 23 the Chiefs of Staff made their final report to President Roosevelt and Prime Minister Churchill. It included much that had not been controversial. For example, it gave top priority to winning the battle against U-boats, assumed by the Chiefs all along as of primary importance. The strategic plan, as summarized, was as follows:

> The defeat of the U-boat must remain a first charge on the resources of the United Nations. The Soviet forces must be sustained by the greatest volume of supplies that can be transported to Russia.
>
> Operations in the European theatre will be conducted with the object of defeating Germany in 1943 with the maximum forces that can be brought to bear upon her by the United Nations.
>
> The main lines of offensive action will be:
>
> *In the Mediterranean:*
>
> (a) The occupation of Sicily with the object of:
>
>   (i)   Making the Mediterranean line of communications more secure.
>
>   (ii) Diverting German pressure from the Russian front.
>
>   (iii) Intensifying the pressure on Italy.
>
> (b) To create a situation in which Turkey can be enlisted as an active ally.
>
> *In the United Kingdom:*
>
> (c) The heaviest possible air offensive against German war effort.
>
> (d) Such limited offensive operations as may be practicable with the amphibious forces available.
>
> (e) The assembly of the strongest possible force in constant readiness to re-enter the continent as soon as German resistance is weakened to the required extent.

The agreement allowed pressure to be maintained on the Japanese but kept within such limits as would not jeopardize any opportunity for defeating Germany in 1943. It allowed plans for the recapture of Burma (ANAKIM) beginning in 1943 and for operations against the Marshalls and the Carolines (Truk) within resources allowed.

In addition, the President and Prime Minister emphasized:

(i)   The desirability of finding means of running the W.J. [Winston-Joe] Russian convoys even through the "Husky" period.

(ii) The urgency of sending air reinforcements to General Chenault's forces in China and of finding personnel to make them fully operative.

(iii) The importance of achieving the favourable June moon for Sicily and the grave detriment to our interest which will be incurred by an apparent suspension of activities during the summer months.

(iv) The need to build up more quickly the U.S. striking force in U.K., so as to be able to profit by favourable August weather for some form of "Sledgehammer."

Thus ended the military side of the conference. Though no one was totally satisfied, it had on the whole been successful. The British had carried most of the day. But then the British point of view made better sense anyway.

CHAPTER XIV

CASABLANCA II:
UNCONDITIONAL SURRENDER

T he Casablanca Conference lasted nearly two weeks. For the professional uniformed military it was an intense period, but it was less so for the heads of government. During the whole time Roosevelt and Churchill held only three plenary sessions: the all-important one on January 18 which set the immediate strategy for the conduct of the war; the interim gathering of the afternoon of January 20; and a final wind-up session late on January 23. In all three cases the recommendations had been agreed among the Combined Chiefs and were simply presented for joint approval at the political level.

Roosevelt and Churchill had, of course, been kept informed on a daily basis of how the military discussions were going, but they had remained in the background and avoided a direct confrontation at the times when agreement seemed out of reach. Neither had cause for distress over the outcome. Churchill had secured American assent to further operations in the Mediterranean; Roosevelt, not personally averse to Churchill's views, was spared the need to override his own military chiefs, who regarded the outcome as a defeat. The two political leaders, therefore, were afforded some opportunity to relax in the pleasant atmosphere of the palms and breezes and to enjoy the warmth of the sun. Nobody begrudged them this justified respite from the pressures back home.

In their own sphere, however, Roosevelt and Churchill had one specific problem they hoped to resolve: to develop a rapprochement between the two French military leaders, General Henri Giraud and General Charles de Gaulle. These two French generals, whom the Anglo-Americans tended to regard as temporary caretakers, were both patriotic Frenchmen, each in his own way dedicated to the good of France—each of them vying for the honor of being considered the leader of the French.

At the time of Casablanca Giraud seemed to be firmly established. Some 200,000 French troops in North Africa were all serving under his command, some of them fighting alongside British and Americans in Tunisia. Furthermore, in the hierarchy of the French Army, Giraud's rank of five-star general, attained in 1940 (when De Gaulle had been only a colonel), gave him towering prestige over his two-star rival. ("Petit De Gaulle," Giraud was prone to say.) By contrast with Giraud's unified army, De Gaulle controlled only some 100,000 Free (or "Fighting") French, dependent for their existence on the largess of the British Government and scattered around the world among London, Syria, Lebanon, and Equatorial Africa. And De Gaulle's organization was considered by the Allies as too political-minded and untrustworthy. The failure of the abortive British-Gaullist attack on Dakar in September 1940 had been blamed on "leaks" from De Gaulle's headquarters; since then he and his associates had been denied access to any serious secrets—including TORCH.

To ensure that the British political point of view be represented in Allied Force Headquarters, Churchill had recently assigned a member of Parliament, Harold Macmillan, to act as his personal representative in Algiers. Roosevelt had concurred. In recognition of the American complexion of TORCH—and of Eisenhower's ultimate responsiblity for its success—Churchill had designated Macmillan, though a "minister of government," as "Assistant to the Political Advisor to General Eisenhower."[1]

As senior British political representative, Macmillan would work co-equally with Murphy, and they quickly developed mutual respect and congeniality. Eisenhower therefore relied heavily on the two of them as a team in all matters pertaining to the Giraud–De Gaulle problem. So when they had proposed that the Allies consider Giraud and De Gaulle as co-equal in Northwest Africa, Eisenhower had agreed without a great deal of reservation. And so great was his confidence in Murphy and Macmillan that when he departed Anfa after his brief stay he was content for the two to jointly represent him when further political questions should arise. Despite Eisenhower's intentions, however, each reverted to his own national status and reported to his own head of government, Murphy to Roosevelt and Macmillan to Churchill. Hull and Eden might just as well have been present.

[1] Macmillan recalled his first meeting with Eisenhower as inauspicious: "The General made no attempt to conceal his feelings. 'Pleased to see you,' he said, 'but what have you come for?' I tried to explain that I thought my appointment had been arranged between the President and the Prime Minister. 'But I have been told nothing of it. You are a Minister, but what sort of a Minister are you?' 'Well, General,' I said, 'I am not a diplomatic Minister; I am something worse.' 'There is nothing worse,' he replied." Macmillan, *The Blast of War,* p. 173.

The concept of a joint authority between De Gaulle and Giraud in North Africa was appealing, especially to Churchill, who felt that this arrangement would represent a promotion for De Gaulle—and incidentally shift the expenses of the Free French from the British Government back to the economy of French North Africa. (His Majesty's Government had already supported De Gaulle to the tune of seventy million pounds.) Thus, within a couple of days after Roosevelt's arrival, he and Churchill decided that Giraud and De Gaulle should somehow meet under their own benign auspices.

Giraud, already in North Africa, came to Anfa without a murmur. In conferences with Roosevelt, however, he exhibited almost complete indifference to political questions, pressing only for reinforcements and more equipment for his forces in Tunisia. His mind seemed to wander on political affairs. Giraud's attitude puzzled Roosevelt, who later asked Murphy why he had selected such an apolitical character as over-all French head man. Murphy answered promptly that Giraud conformed to Roosevelt's consistent concept of French authority: that the Allies should do nothing to influence the political future of France. The very military-minded Giraud would be content to serve as strictly an interim French boss. Roosevelt, in no position to disagree, approved continued American support for Giraud.

Churchill, on the other hand, still felt a sense of responsibility toward De Gaulle. Difficult though he was, De Gaulle had elected to cast his lot with the British during the dark days of 1940. And the Francophile Churchill still grudgingly admired De Gaulle's arrogance. With each head of government holding some sort of a vested interest in his own French general, therefore, a compromise seemed to be the easiest way out. Giraud, however, was still regarded as the first among equals, at least in North Africa.

One element of this tidy arrangement was missing: the presence of De Gaulle himself, who for the moment had shown every intention of boycotting the entire scene. The task of bringing De Gaulle down from London to Casablanca naturally fell into the lap of Churchill, and he knew it would not be easy. De Gaulle, Churchill was aware, had been incensed that the Anglo-Americans had decided not to notify him before the TORCH landings, and his pride had been further wounded when Roosevelt canceled a previous invitation for him to visit Washington when Darlan was assassinated. In an effort to stay in the picture, then, De Gaulle had cabled Giraud and proposed that the two meet on French soil (North Africa) to discuss differences. But Giraud, convinced that De Gaulle had been involved in Darlan's assassination, had repeatedly spurned offers from De Gaulle to come to North Africa. After this series of rebuffs, De Gaulle was in no mood to come at the beckoning of Churchill to a meeting conducted under the auspices of the "Anglo-Saxons." Relationships between Frenchmen needed no supervision or guidance from these outsiders.

After Eisenhower's departure from Casablanca, Roosevelt and Churchill, on advice of Macmillan and Murphy, decided to put the pressure on De Gaulle. Roosevelt, always optimistic, sent a message to Cordell Hull in Washington assuming no problem:

> General Giraud arrives here tomorrow and Mr. Churchill and I have arranged that General de Gaulle shall be brought here on Monday [January 18] . . . it appears that we must get a civilian into the administrative picture here. Apparently Giraud lacks administrative ability and the French army officers will not recognize de Gaulle's authority.[2]

At the same time Churchill sent a message to Anthony Eden asking him to invite De Gaulle to Casablanca. When Eden called the next day, De Gaulle, as Eden put it, "expressed no pleasure."

Roosevelt's attitude toward De Gaulle's stubbornness seemed mixed. On one side Churchill's discomfiture amused him. Making light of the situation, he enjoyed bantering about the "bride" and "groom." On the other hand he was much concerned, as he did not relish returning to the United States without some public evidence of bringing the two French factions together. He thus allowed Churchill to include him in the ultimatum the Prime Minister sent on January 18:

> I am authorized to say that the invitation to you to come here was from the President of the United States of America as well as from me.
>
> I have not yet told General Giraud, who came attended only by two Staff officers, and is waiting here, of your refusal. The consequences of it, if persisted in, will in my opinion be unfavourable for you and your movement. First, we are about to make arrangements for North Africa, on which we should have been glad to consult you, but which must otherwise be made in your absence. The arrangements when concluded will have the support of Great Britain and the United States. . . .
>
> The position of His Majesty's Government towards your movement while you remain at its head will also require to be reviewed. If with your eyes open you reject this unique opportunity we shall endeavour to get on as well as we can without you.[3]

De Gaulle now had no choice, though his answer reflected his pique:

[2] Sherwood, p. 678.
[3] Churchill, IV, 680–81.

January 20, 1943

It appears from your second message that your presence there and that of President Roosevelt has, as its object, that of coming to some agreement with General Giraud over the future of French North Africa. You are kind enough to propose my taking part in the discussions, whilst at the same time adding that the agreements will be eventually concluded without my participation. . . .

I acknowledge, however . . . that the general situation of the war and the position in which France is situated . . . cannot allow me to refuse to meet the President of the United States and His Britannic Majesty's Prime Minister. I agree, therefore, to take part in your discussions.[4]

On the morning of January 22, 1943, General Charles de Gaulle landed at Fedala Airport, near Casablanca. His arrival was secret, and he was met only by an American brigadier general and a British civilian, representing Roosevelt and Churchill respectively. A French Colonel de Linares presented an invitation to join General Giraud at lunch. De Gaulle noted wryly that no troops were there to present honors, although the airport was well guarded by American soldiers. Several cars immediately drove up to the plane and De Gaulle stepped into the first one. But before they drove off, the American had dipped a rag in the mud and smeared the windows. De Gaulle's presence in Morocco was to be kept a secret even from his own followers.

On arrival at the Anfa compound, De Gaulle was taken aback to notice that a portion of the suburb had been fenced off with heavy barbed wire and that the owners of all the villas, mostly Frenchmen, had been moved elsewhere. De Gaulle was annoyed by the sight of American sentries posted both inside and outside the perimeter. Soldiers were even assigned to man the households.

To De Gaulle all this was captivity. He could have no objection if Roosevelt, Churchill, and their staffs should choose to impose such indignities upon themselves but to apply such measures to General de Gaulle, in French territory at that, was a "flagrant insult." He refused to enter his villa until assured that the owner was a Dane, not a Frenchman.

When De Gaulle arrived at Giraud's quarters for lunch, therefore, he vented his anger: "What's this?" he demanded. "I asked you for an interview four times over and we have to meet in a barbed-wire encampment among foreign powers!" Giraud, embarrassed, could reply only that he had not been free to act otherwise. In view of Giraud's sponsorship by the Americans, De Gaulle could understand, regrettably, why this was so.

[4] De Gaulle, *The Complete War Memoirs of Charles de Gaulle,* Vol. II, *Unity,* p. 128.

After the initial exchange, however, the luncheon became cordial, consisting largely of reminiscences. After the meal business began. Giraud defended the use of the "proconsuls"—Noguès, Boisson (Governor of Dakar), and the newly arrived Peyrouton. And, aside from declaring his determination to fight the Germans, Giraud volunteered nothing critical of Pétain and Vichy. In an obvious effort to convince De Gaulle of his own apolitical attitude, Giraud made himself look inept. He gave his attention, he said, solely to military matters. He did not wish to concern himself with political questions. And he never listened to anyone who tried to interest him in a theory or a program. He even avoided reading a newspaper or turning on the radio.[5] The conference resulted in nothing except an improved mutual evaluation.

For the rest of the afternoon De Gaulle remained in his quarters. He did, however, receive a visit from Harold Macmillan, who acquainted him with the formula the Anglo-Americans were trying to devise for French unity, a co-equal status between Giraud and De Gaulle. De Gaulle, while not immediately turning the idea down, explained that any such *entente* could be realized only between Frenchmen. With this exchange he agreed to walk down the street to visit the Prime Minister, striding into Churchill's villa with much the same attitude he had shown to Giraud earlier in the day. He would never, he immediately declaimed, have come to Casablanca had he known he was to be surrounded, on French territory, by American bayonets. Churchill answered sharply: "This is an occupied country!"

With the atmosphere cleared by this exchange of outbursts, Churchill and De Gaulle began to discuss the formula that Macmillan had outlined earlier. De Gaulle and Giraud, according to Churchill, would be established as joint presidents of a governing committee. All members would enjoy equal status. Giraud would execute supreme military command, however, because the United States, the source of all French Army equipment, would deal with no one else. As an additional idea, Churchill remarked that his friend General Alphonse Georges could constitute a third "president," thus creating a triumvirate to direct the committee. Noguès, Boisson, and Peyrouton would retain their positions and be members of the committee. Churchill insisted that the Americans had accepted these men and wanted them to be trusted.

De Gaulle reacted sharply. "This solution might appear adequate at the quite respectable level of American sergeant," he retorted, "but I never dreamed that you would take it seriously." But then he backed off, emphasizing his respect for both Churchill and Roosevelt personally. He stuck to his basic contention that no foreigner, no matter how powerful,

[5] Ibid., p. 389.

had any authority to deal with questions of sovereignty within the French Empire.

The Allies, he went on, had instituted the system now functioning in Algiers and, finding it only partially successful at best, were planning to swamp the Fighting French in it. But Fighting France, personified by him, would never play this game.

De Gaulle's position made sense on the assumption that he was actually speaking for France, but Churchill was unwilling to start at that point. (He could not, with the Americans supporting Giraud.) He therefore pressed home that if De Gaulle should fail to cooperate, His Majesty's Government would find someone else to lead the Free French. De Gaulle accepted this but not abjectly, leaving the meeting with head high. Churchill felt a flush of admiration, despite his anger, as he watched the Frenchman leave.

De Gaulle did not meet with Roosevelt formally until that evening. The President was worn out from a visit the previous day with American troops in Rabat, exhilarating though the day had been, and was conserving his strength the day De Gaulle arrived; he wanted to be at his best when the Sultan of Morocco arrived at his villa for dinner.[6]

That evening De Gaulle waited, unaware of what was going on, while Roosevelt entertained the Sultan. The dinner was a stiff affair, as the guest list included both Churchill and General Noguès, French Governor, who could not have enjoyed the President's blithe hints regarding his support for dismemberment of the French Empire after the war. The discomfort was, for Churchill, compounded by the President's deference to the Moslem's taboo against alcoholic beverages. Regardless of who suffered most, the dinner was enough of a strain that Roosevelt hoped to put off meeting De Gaulle until the morning. Harry Hopkins, however, insisted that Roosevelt offend De Gaulle no further and the President agreed to meet that evening.

De Gaulle remained icy at this, his first confrontation with Roosevelt. He was unimpressed, he said, by the agreements that Roosevelt and Churchill had drawn up for rearming the French Army. The meeting did, however, provide Roosevelt some insight into the De Gaulle mentality. When Roosevelt, for example, said that the French, in dire military straits, needed a general of "Napoleonic caliber," De Gaulle answered calmly that he himself was this man. Then, for every French leadership need that Roosevelt mentioned, De Gaulle volunteered that he filled it.

[6] Actually the night of January 21 was supposed to be the wind-up of the meeting, and a press conference was originally scheduled for Friday, January 22. However, the Combined Chiefs still had some polishing to do on their plans for 1943. And when he learned that De Gaulle would be arriving, Roosevelt told Hopkins to put off the press conference. Hopkins notified a happy Churchill of the delay.

France's bad financial state required a Colbert. Answer: *"Mais, je suis cet homme."* France, an amazed President went on, was so devitalized politically that she needed a Clemenceau. Again: *"Mais, je suis cet homme."* At the end of this interview Roosevelt had some inkling of the problem *Le Grand Charlie* was going to present.[7]

While Roosevelt and De Gaulle were talking, Harry Hopkins was looking around. The President's entire Secret Service detail, Hopkins noted, seemed to be behind the curtain and on the gallery above. One agent was holding a submachine gun. Hopkins excused himself for a moment and found that about a dozen agents were likewise armed. Hopkins thought that De Gaulle himself probably had no idea of the suspicion under which he was held. (Actually, De Gaulle was very much aware.) During his entire stay at Anfa he would always be in the sights of some Secret Service man.[8]

*

Brigadier General Alfred Gruenther, in charge of arrangements for the conference, was given an unpleasant task. On the morning after General de Gaulle's arrival at Anfa, the Combined Chiefs of Staff were scheduled to meet at the Anfa Hotel. Gruenther was given the job of preventing De Gaulle from attending. No guidance was provided as to what means Gruenther should employ.

Finally hitting on a scheme, he reported to De Gaulle's villa and asked if the general would like a tour of the Anfa compound. De Gaulle willing, they soon were walking past the various villas, circling around the Anfa Hotel, viewing the ocean on one side and Casablanca on the other. De Gaulle, unimpressed as usual, kept repeating *"Formidable"* sarcastically. After a short while his suspicion that he was being duped was firm. He demanded to return to the villa, strode through the door, and slammed it shut behind him.[9]

The rest of the day, however, was a busy one for De Gaulle. First he received a call from a magnanimous Giraud, who apparently interpreted De Gaulle's having lunch with him the previous day as satisfying protocol

[7] Pendar, pp. 143–44.
[8] Sherwood, p. 685.
[9] In the early 1950s General Gruenther was Chief of Staff and later Supreme Commander of the NATO forces in Europe. General de Gaulle was then in retirement, and Gruenther decided it would be proper to pay a call. It had been nearly a decade since Casablanca. When the two men first met, De Gaulle eyed Gruenther narrowly and asked where they had met before. Gruenther recounted the details. Both agreed that on that morning at Casablanca De Gaulle had every right, in Gruenther's words, to be "sore as hell." Interview, General Alfred M. Gruenther, Washington, D.C., December 24, 1978.

regarding their relative ranks. His proposal, similar to that of Churchill, brought only rebuff. Robert Murphy and Harold Macmillan then dropped in to outline their "co-equal" plan. Neither meeting bore fruit.

Having exhausted their own resources, Murphy and Macmillan then tried a long shot. They asked Brigadier General William H. Wilbur, a classmate of De Gaulle's at the Ecole Supérieure de Guerre, to call late in the afternoon. De Gaulle was probably not pleased by Wilbur's Congressional Medal of Honor, earned in action against Frenchmen some weeks before, but he did appreciate talking to another soldier, especially an old friend. And unlike most Americans, Wilbur spoke perfect French.

General Wilbur thus enjoyed a far better atmosphere with De Gaulle than had anyone else. He sensed that De Gaulle unbent. Before American arrival in Morocco, De Gaulle explained, his were the only forces fighting for the liberty of France. Therefore, no other elements represented the "true" France. He regretted what he termed the "mystery of the Marshal" (Pétain) which competed with the "mystery of the Fighting French" (De Gaulle). These two had become almost religions. Marshal Pétain, he said, was reportedly lucid for only a couple of hours a day. Personally Pétain was utterly ineffective—the real Marshal had died in 1925—but the symbolism of his name still served as an adhesive force for his followers.

Darlan, as De Gaulle put it, had represented those who, in Pétain's name, had collaborated with Hitler. Therefore the Free French could never have dealt with Darlan had he lived. Darlan had already been too long in office at the time of his assassination. Giraud likewise could never represent the true France, as he held his position by the assent of three Vichyite governors: Noguès in Casablanca, Boisson in Dakar, and Châtel in Algiers. De Gaulle had offered Giraud command of French troops under himself, he said, but Giraud could not himself "represent" France. Giraud should join the Fighting French rather than expect the Gaullists to subordinate their movement to a government headed by himself.

In the course of the conversation De Gaulle frankly admitted that, should England succumb to the position of the United States and deprive the Fighting French of supplies and equipment, he personally would be finished. But, even if Giraud succeeded in establishing himself temporarily in France, he would find the people against him. The beneficiaries would be the Communists.

For once De Gaulle seemed to be willing to listen. Wilbur expressed American sympathy for the French in their present plight, especially during this difficult winter. He knew that De Gaulle had the interests of the French at heart and must therefore be capable of withdrawing from extreme positions. When Wilbur mentioned De Gaulle's adherents in Morocco, many of whom he saw often, De Gaulle's interest was titillated. Wilbur promised to tell them that De Gaulle had conferred with Giraud to no avail but that De Gaulle would at least send a liaison officer from London to North Africa.

As the meeting ended, Wilbur emphasized the need for calm in Morocco, asking De Gaulle to instruct his adherents to avoid causing more trouble. The American effort needed their help. Surprisingly, De Gaulle agreed. He also asked for Wilbur's address in order to communicate further.[10]

Harry Hopkins was up early on Sunday, January 24, 1943, in order to hammer out the finishing touches on a communiqué and on a telegram to Stalin. In his room he breakfasted with Robert Murphy and Harold Macmillan, each of whom had already been with their respective French protégés. Giraud, Murphy told Hopkins, would be quite willing to "cooperate" with De Gaulle but would never work under him. De Gaulle, Macmillan reported, felt the same way about Giraud. De Gaulle had a curious way of associating himself with historical French figures—shades of children playing cowboys and Indians!—and he proposed that he (De Gaulle) be the Clemenceau and Giraud the Foch for this war! In other words, no progress had been made in any effort to induce either one to serve under the other. Even if the Frenchmen themselves would get together, Hopkins could never imagine Roosevelt's recognizing De Gaulle as French political leader. On the other hand, Hopkins observed, Roosevelt might agree to a joint leadership between De Gaulle and Giraud, with Giraud "running Africa" and De Gaulle "the rest of the show."[11]

Hopkins then left the room and went to Villa Dar es Saada to see President Roosevelt, who was at the point of severing relations with De Gaulle. At Hopkins' urging, however, Roosevelt agreed for the moment not to "disavow" De Gaulle completely. If any beating were to be done on De Gaulle, Hopkins insisted, it should be done by Churchill. Hopkins held a hope that the conference might produce some sort of joint statement by De Gaulle and Giraud; it might be possible even to get a picture of the two together.

Giraud arrived at Dar es Saada to visit the President at 11:30 A.M., while De Gaulle was in conference with Churchill. Giraud, as always, seemed amenable, and he willingly accepted Roosevelt's referring him to General Eisenhower for additional troop equipment. After this short conference Giraud departed and soon De Gaulle entered with some of his staff. Though De Gaulle's calm confidence impressed Hopkins, his position remained rigid. There could be no joint communiqué, he said at first,

10 Report of William H. Wilbur, January 23, 1943. Quoted in Sherwood, pp. 686–87.
11 Sherwood, p. 691.

and he repeated that Giraud must serve under him. Roosevelt reacted strongly and eventually he secured De Gaulle's agreement to a communiqué—which De Gaulle would write.

Events were moving swiftly, and Hopkins, on learning from the Secret Service that Churchill was outside saying good-by to Giraud, rushed out the door and followed Giraud down the street as Churchill walked into the villa. Soon Hopkins had returned with Giraud, and the four principals —Roosevelt, Churchill, Giraud, and De Gaulle—found themselves face to face, a bit confused. Even the poker-faced De Gaulle showed bewilderment. It was nearly time for the noon press conference, however, and the President and the Prime Minister began again urging the two Frenchmen to compose a joint statement. When De Gaulle demurred, Churchill turned and shook his finger in his face. "General," he declared in French, "you just cannot place obstacles in the way of winning the war!"

Perhaps because of Churchill's outburst, De Gaulle miraculously agreed to draw up a joint statement with Giraud later.

The President then homed in with another request: "Will you agree to being photographed beside me and the British Prime Minister, along with General Giraud?"

"Of course," De Gaulle answered, "for I have the highest regard for this great soldier."

"Will you go so far as to shake General Giraud's hand before the camera?"

"I shall do that for you," replied De Gaulle in slow English.[12]

That settled, De Gaulle and Giraud suddenly found themselves stepping out the door to a low porch in the small, enclosed garden. Photographers and correspondents were crowded in. The newsmen, who had just arrived the day before from Algiers, gasped in astonishment to see the President carried to his chair and the Prime Minister following in the bright sun.[13]

Once in place, the President asked De Gaulle and Giraud to stand up and shake hands. De Gaulle, keeping his cigarette, even managed a weak, almost imperceptible smile. Roosevelt and Churchill beamed. Thus the "shotgun marriage," so soon to end in divorce, was blazoned to the world as a triumph of French unity.

After the photograph of De Gaulle and Giraud was taken, the two French generals left and Roosevelt and Churchill visibly relaxed in the warm Moroccan atmosphere. Questions from the stunned members of the

12 De Gaulle, II, 399.
13 As the photos turned out, the four principals appeared to be seated in a spacious area. Actually the back yard of Roosevelt's villa was extremely confined. In 1979 the rented villa was still occupied by the U.S. consul when the author visited.

press began, and Roosevelt as host and head of state (a protocol matter that Churchill scrupulously observed) spoke first. Basking in the success of his coup, Roosevelt became ebullient. As his enthusiasm rose, so did his rhetoric, which reached its crescendo with the announcement that the Allies would accept no terms from the three Axis powers except "unconditional surrender." This statement came as a surprise to Churchill, who had not been consulted. In the interest of Allied unity, however, Churchill found it advisable to lend support, not only passively but positively.

These two instants at the press conference, the "shotgun marriage" handshake and the offhand statement by Roosevelt, immediately filled the headlines. "Unconditional surrender" had an impact on the Western world and the Axis as well.

The fact that Roosevelt's gratuitous announcement came as a surprise to Churchill has been the subject of curiosity among historians ever since. Roosevelt had his own explanation. He had just finished an unpleasant argument only moments before, he later explained, and getting these two French generals together, he thought, was like getting Lee together with Grant. As Roosevelt associated the name "Grant" with "unconditional surrender," the expression just popped out.[14]

But the term had come up before, as early as January 7, 1943, in the White House.[15] It had also been mentioned at lunch the day before.[16] And Churchill had exchanged telegrams on "unconditional surrender" with his War Cabinet.[17] Nevertheless, considering the flurry of ideas coming to Roosevelt's attention, the formula could have been mentioned and slipped his mind. None of these reports confronted Roosevelt in his lifetime. He always believed his inspiration that Sunday morning to be totally original.

Views on the effect of the "unconditional surrender" statement vary. Churchill believed that it made no impact, pointing out that Italy later did surrender under "conditional" terms. And Japan, two and a half years later, surrendered only on the condition that her Emperor be retained.

And Churchill has made another telling point. The passions of the war, as they existed at this uncertain time, were strong. Had Churchill been

[14] General Ulysses S. Grant had reportedly used the term first in 1862 at Forts Henry and Donelson. It has since been associated with his name.
[15] Wedemeyer, *Wedemeyer Reports!*, p. 186.
[16] Elliott Roosevelt, *As He Saw It*, p. 117. Churchill (IV, 685) does not deny the possibility.
[17] On January 20 Churchill had asked the War Cabinet to consider some declaration of "unconditional surrender" but pertaining only to Germany and Japan. The War Cabinet in London had insisted that Italy be included in such a declaration and Churchill had apparently dropped the matter. Churchill, IV, 686.

called upon to lay out a *specific* set of terms for Nazi surrender, he would have couched his ideas so harshly that the German people would have considered them even worse than the broad term "unconditional surrender."

This conjecture is fairly unimportant, but the effect of the pronouncement was not. It provided a psychological lift for the populations of both Britain and the United States. And it could not be lost on the absent member at the conference. In fact, Stalin may unconsciously have been the primary target.

*

The press conference over, both parties scattered all over the globe. Marshall, Arnold, and King left that same Sunday morning to visit Eisenhower in Algiers. Ismay and Pound joined the Americans in Algiers and then quickly returned to the United Kingdom. But Churchill, determined to get a couple of days' rest at his favorite oasis in Marrakech, prevailed on the President to accompany him to Mrs. Taylor's villa, where Kenneth Pendar was waiting for them. Together the two drove southward along the straight two-lane road, guarded by troops on either side and air cover above. In Marrakech they could luxuriate and enjoy a few hours of relaxation, accompanied only by the unobtrusive Alan Brooke. At one point Roosevelt gamely allowed himself to be carried the sixty steps to the top of the tower. The day was clear, and the rugged High Atlas Mountains stood out in the distance, clearer than the Rockies from Denver. Dinner that night was festive, with wine and song. Taking advantage of the informality, Kenneth Pendar ventured to ask Churchill about De Gaulle. Churchill turned slightly: "Oh, let's don't speak of him. We call him Jeanne d'Arc and we're looking for some bishops to burn him."[18]

That evening the two leaders of the Western world said good-by. The next morning, however, Roosevelt came by Churchill's room. Churchill jumped into his famous siren suit and donned a pair of bedroom slippers. Together they drove once more to the nearby airfield where the C-54 was waiting. Churchill planned to stay for another day.

As Roosevelt disappeared through the door of the plane, Churchill could not watch. "If anything should happen to that great man," he murmured to Pendar at his side, "I couldn't bear it. He is the greatest man in the world today. Come, Pendar, let's go home. I don't like to see them take off."[19]

[18] Pendar, p. 151.
[19] Ibid., p. 154.

CHAPTER XV

CASABLANCA III: FOLLOW-UP

After his return to Algiers from Casablanca, Lieutenant General Dwight Eisenhower put the conference out of his mind. But he took advantage of his ready access to the national leaders by trying to expedite the decison on the suitability of Marcel Peyrouton as governor of Algeria, a matter still being discussed at Anfa (see p. 234). Harry Hopkins at Anfa checked with the President and quickly secured approval.[1]

The most pressing concern to Eisenhower, however, remained the Tunisian battlefront, where the line now extended from the sea on the north some two hundred and fifty miles to the south. (See map p. 200.) The forward elements of the British on the north, the French in the center, and Americans on the south were spread along a range of hills called the Eastern Dorsal, overlooking the Tunisian coastal plain. At Pont du Fahs this Eastern Dorsal joined another range, the Western Dorsal. Together they formed an inverted "V" with the point being about seventy miles from the Mediterranean. At Gafsa, where the American south flank dangled, the Eastern Dorsal and the Western Dorsal were about eighty miles apart. Between them was flat country where some fine airfields had been constructed, the best being at Thélepte and nearby Fériana.

The weak southern end of the line was being held by Major General Lloyd R. Fredendall's American II Corps, with its command post at

[1] Murphy for some reason regarded the incumbent governor, Châtel, in a much better light than did Eisenhower. His views were exonerated by the fact that Peyrouton was soon attacked with the same virulence as Darlan had been previously. Murphy, pp. 156–60.

Tébessa back on the Western Dorsal. The corps, theoretically, consisted of three divisions: the 1st Armored, the 1st Infantry, and the 34th Infantry. At the moment only the 1st Armored (reinforced), under Major General Orlando Ward, was on hand.[2] The rest of the 1st Division, under Major General Terry de la M. Allen, was arriving piece by piece. The 34th, under Major General Charles W. Ryder, was still guarding lines of communication between Constantine and Algiers. Eisenhower was far from happy that this American force, protruding so far to the south, was so small. The logisticians, however, had calculated that nothing more could be supported across the tenuous life line from Algiers without reducing supplies to Anderson's First British Army, charged with the main effort toward Tunis and Bizerte. If Anderson's push could soon succeed, then whatever happened south at Gafsa would be immaterial, for Rommel's rear would be cut off, the main objective of the whole campaign.

Eisenhower was also worried about the command setup. The whole front should logically have been commanded by Anderson. But the center of the line was being held by the French XIX Corps, a sizable force, and the French commander, General Alphonse Juin, refused to serve under a British officer. Thus the lingering British-French antagonism resulted in danger to both their forces.

What immediately prompted Eisenhower's hurried trip forward on Monday, January 18, was the need to cancel an attack by Fredendall's corps from Gafsa eastward to Sfax on the Tunisian Gulf. Such a drive would separate General Jürgen von Arnim's forces in northern Tunisia from Rommel's, retreating from Libya, and it had made sense while Rommel's army had been farther east. At Anfa, however, Eisenhower had learned that Tripoli would soon fall to Montgomery and that the Eighth Army would be arriving on the border of southern Tunisia during the second week of March. Though this news was welcome, it meant that Rommel would be back in Tunisia sooner than expected and the Axis forces on the American II Corps front would be overpowering. In this new, unforeseen circumstance, Eisenhower planned to hold the Americans on the Dorsal in an "active defense." Fredendall should hold the critical passes with infantry, meanwhile building up a strong armored reserve.

At Tulergma Airfield Eisenhower was met by the recently promoted Major General Lucian K. Truscott, Jr. With the title of Deputy Chief of Staff, Truscott was running Eisenhower's small headquarters in an orphanage at Constantine, Algeria. He took Eisenhower and Spaatz to the command post where Anderson, Juin, and Fredendall waited.

[2] For convenience, the 1st Armored Division will be referred to as the "1st Armored"; the 1st Infantry Division will be referred to as the "1st Division."

The outwardly correct conduct of the conference, held in the presence of the Allied Commander, could not conceal potential sources of friction among the divergent personalities. Anderson, a Scot whom Eisenhower always considered a fine officer, was tall, handsome, and charming. But his obvious personal bravery was not always matched by tactical aggressiveness, despite his proprietary attitude regarding the prerogatives of his First Army. And unfortunately Anderson was reserved, even for a British officer, a characteristic which made him a hard man for Americans to understand. Fredendall, on the other hand, was small in stature, loud and rough in speech, outspoken in his criticisms of superior and subordinate alike. In contrast to Anderson, he was inclined to jump to conclusions, and his personality was abrasive. All in all Fredendall was not acceptable to, or accepting of, British officers. The French general, Alphonse Juin (who had spent the night of November 7 with Murphy and Darlan), suffered mostly from the poor condition of his troops. His unwillingness to serve under Anderson conformed to the feelings of all the French officers at that time.[3]

The other major members of the conference, Carl Spaatz and Lucian Truscott, presented no problems—indeed they were among Eisenhower's closest associates. Truscott, in particular, enjoyed Eisenhower's confidence, borne out by his handling of the landing at Port Lyautey. He could do much to bridge the differences between the three national ground commanders.

The purpose of the visit actually was to exchange information, as Eisenhower's decision to abandon the push toward Sfax had already been made. Anderson briefed Eisenhower on plans for counterattacking and restoring a local German penetration in the French line near Pont du Fahs. This plan seemed satisfactory, although it meant the employment of Combat Command B (CCB), the strongest single element of the 1st Armored. Eisenhower disliked even temporarily splitting the strength of the mobile reserve he was so determined to maintain.[4] He nevertheless approved.

Back in Algiers the next day General Eisenhower was feeling the pressure of problems on all sides. His diary entry was hardly cheerful:

> The past week has been a succession of disappointments. I'm just writing some down so as to forget them.
>
> a. The French began showing signs of complete collapse along the front as early as the 17th. Each day the tactical situation has gotten worse. We will be pushed to make a decent front covering Tunisia.

[3] See Truscott, *Command Missions*, p. 143.
[4] U. S. 1st Armored was organized into four combat commands (one improvised) of various sizes; CCB comprised almost half its strength.

b. The aggressive action and local attack I had so laboriously planned for the 24th [of January] and following days have had to be abandoned.

c. The newspapers want my scalp for "political censorship"—but there is *none*. Has not been for 2 weeks. Why the yell?[5]

d. Peyrotoun's appt. to succeed the worthless Châtel has been received with howls of anguish at home. Who *do* they want?? He is an experienced administrator and God knows it's hard to find many of them among the French in Africa.

e. We've had our r.r. temporarily interrupted twice. I'm getting weary of it, but can't move the troops (even if I had enough) to protect the lines.[6]

On the more cheerful side, Eisenhower received final confirmation that he would retain command in Tunisia after the arrival of Alexander when Marshall cabled from Anfa, "Alexander will be your man when British Army joins you after Tripoli."

But until Alexander should arrive, Eisenhower would still be concerned with the details of the Tunisian battlefield. Accordingly he scrawled a memorandum to his G-3 (Operations):

Tanks:=	where-when-replacements. Can't we beat the schedule Gale showed me for Anderson's re-equipping?
French Forces:=	How much can *we* give them? When? What can we expect in tactical [offering?]—Airplane replacement?
L/C:=	Are we improving? Is the system integrated? Do we have a definite objective toward which to work in this matter?
Defense reserves:	Can we not get a few mobile reserves established so that a minor attack by Bosche can be quickly prevented? Is our system working? When we need support we ought to be able to get all the air—coordinated in action and speedy on the uptake.
Art.=	What can we do for Anderson?

[5] In December, Eisenhower had imposed political censorship regarding the French situation in view of the strenuous efforts of pro-Gaullists to tear down the Darlan-Giraud arrangements. He had, as the memorandum indicates, lifted the censorship two weeks earlier. He later admitted that the censorship, while well intentioned, had been a mistake.

[6] Eisenhower diary, quoted in Chandler, II, 909–10.

Supplies:	Let's pile them in—dispersed but handy. When we start we want to go to town.
Camouflage and Concealment	We ought to get out something worthwhile on this subject. It is sadly neglected.
Alertness by all troops:	We must *stress* this
Training—all the time—all the time!![7]	

The next day a message came from Truscott reporting that the situation on the French front was even worse than originally imagined. The Germans were pushing their attack at Pont du Fahs and were now hitting at other points of the line. The French were showing increasing signs of demoralization all the way up through the command, thus casting doubt on the validity of Allied plans, which had assumed that Juin's four or five divisions would be able to hold four mountain passes—Pont du Fahs, Pichon, Fondouk, and Faid (from north to south). The French were short in anti-tank equipment, and roads, though sparse, could handle armor. (The Americans had mistakenly considered the front unsuitable for tanks.) Veteran Germans were attacking with infantry, artillery, and the largest tanks seen to date, the Mark VI Tiger. Eisenhower decided to return to the front again on January 21.

At Constantine once more, Eisenhower now concluded that Anderson, Fredendall, and Truscott were probably right: the French troops in their present condition could never hold even a portion of the front without British and American support. He therefore approved a series of southward attacks by Anderson and northward attacks by Fredendall to gradually pinch the French sector down. This could not be done overnight, however, and Eisenhower still insisted that Brigadier General Paul McD. Robinett's CCB, 1st Armored, be kept intact even though temporarily removed from the division. He further took steps to coordinate air support of ground troops by sending a trusted Air Corps officer to represent Spaatz at Constantine. On return to Algiers Eisenhower was still uneasy.

He now prepared himself for a personal conference with his future deputy, General Alexander, anticipating his taking personal charge in Tunisia as soon as possible. Alexander, on the way back from Casablanca, said he thought he could arrive permanently somewhere around the fourth or fifth of February, assuming that Tripoli could soon be cleared for use as a port. This prospect came as a considerable relief.

The day after Alexander's departure, however, Eisenhower received yet another disturbing message from Truscott. Von Arnim had attacked

[7] Ibid., pp. 912–13. Brackets in original.

French positions once again, and the French troops were now so demoralized that Fredendall, Anderson, and Truscott were urging that they be removed immediately, not gradually. General Marshall and Admiral King, Eisenhower knew, were arriving for a visit the next afternoon, but the Tunisian front commanded first priority, and Eisenhower arranged for an early morning flight to Tulergma Airfield to confer once again. To save time he met his subordinates at the airfield, Truscott spreading a map across the hood of a jeep. If the Americans and British planned to pinch out the French sector, Fredendall urged, the strength of his II Corps should be increased to include the entire 1st Division (under way), the 34th Division, still stretched along the life line, and the 9th Division back in Morocco. Eisenhower's operations officer (G-3)[8] concurred in the idea, especially since French units would no longer have to be supplied on a combat basis.

Eisenhower approved. However, even without French units in front-line positions, some sort of "French sector" would be essential for political reasons. This meant that Juin's XIX Corps would retain command of a part of the line without French units. But having made this concession to French pride, Eisenhower no longer felt it necessary to accommodate Juin's refusal to serve under Anderson. From here on, both U. S. II Corps and French XIX Corps would be attached to Anderson's First British Army. He further directed Anderson and Truscott together to inform Juin, who was absent, of the new arrangement. French troops now on the Eastern Dorsal would be pulled back for retraining. Those exceptional French units such as the "Constantine Division" which were considered combat-worthy would not necessarily be moved to Juin's corps; the Constantine Division, for example, would remain with Fredendall. Thus, though the major sectors on the front would carry national names, none except Anderson's British First Army would comprise a single nationality.

Back in Algiers that same afternoon Eisenhower greeted General Marshall, Admiral King, and their parties at Maison Blanche. He was happy to report that Juin had cheerfully agreed to the new arrangements, including subordination to Anderson. French combat units would undergo training back on the Western Dorsal, now being established as a second line of defense. Alexander's arrival in ten days would remedy the awkward situation caused by Anderson's command post being so far north.

The Tunisia battle was of course only one of the subjects discussed between Marshall, King, and Eisenhower, for much had transpired at Casablanca since Eisenhower's departure. The decision to seize Sicily soon after the fall of Tunisia, for example, was news. And as always, Eisenhower enjoyed the visit with his two immediate American bosses and

[8] General Lowell W. Rooks.

increasingly appreciated the value of their support. From what Marshall and King told him, Eisenhower was satisfied with the outcome of SYMBOL.[9]

During the visit General Marshall manifested fatherly concern for Eisenhower's health. Ten years Eisenhower's senior in age, Marshall charged Harry Butcher with ensuring that his chief get more rest and exercise. Without mentioning names, Marshall told of releasing Gerow about a year earlier as head of the War Plans Division. Gerow, Marshall said, had simply burned himself out with overwork, and he didn't want Eisenhower to do the same in Algiers. This lecture to Butcher may have sounded like a veiled threat, but Butcher's mind was eased when Marshall predicted that Eisenhower had further great responsibilities ahead of him, facing problems that would "make the Darlan episode seem minor."[10]

Admiral King left on the morning of January 25, after a single night's stay, but General Marshall stayed on two days. On the afternoon that King left, Marshall, Eisenhower, and General Somervell, head of the Army's Services of Supply, conferred on local logistical problems. The most serious shortage, Eisenhower said, lay in truck transport. Supplies in the United States could ease the situation, Somervell said. He could produce some 5,400 two-and-a-half-ton trucks immediately, enough to transport 75,000 men at one time, provided the Navy could furnish escorts for the cargo ships to transport them across the Atlantic. As Admiral King was believed to be in Casablanca, Eisenhower sent a message to Patton for transmittal. King, however, had flown straight to Dakar. Somehow King was located and Eisenhower's message delivered. King looked it over and sent back a simple message: "The answer is yes!" The trucks arrived within three weeks, destined to play a critical role in the campaign.

Hardly had General Marshall departed from Algiers than Eisenhower received word on Friday, January 29, that the Germans had hit a detachment from the French Constantine Division at Faid, a critical pass which controlled the main road from Tébessa to Sfax on the Gulf of Gabès. The

[9] To Thomas Troy Handy (OPD)   January 28, 1943

Dear Tom: The great meeting has passed into history and I hope that history will declare the decisions reached to be wise ones. Frankly, I do not see how the "big bosses" could have deviated very far from the general course of action they adopted. ROUNDUP, in its original conception, could not possibly be staged before August of 1944, because our original conceptions of the strength required were too low.

[10] Butcher, pp. 247–48.

unit had been nearly wiped out, and the pass was now in German hands. Fredendall's counterattack had been unsuccessful.[11]

Once again Eisenhower flew to Tulergma. Here Anderson, who had always taken a jaundiced view regarding overextension in the south, complained that Faid on the Eastern Dorsal and Gafsa (to the southwest of Faid) were too far away. If he could pull back from these exposed positions, Anderson said, he could better build the First Army for the final drive in the north.

Eisenhower generally agreed that Fredendall should stay as compact as possible, and again he directed the 1st Armored to be concentrated. But he was reluctant to give up the Thélepte and Fériana airfields, and he therefore insisted that some detachments be kept in Gafsa and Faid to protect them. They would, he reasoned, provide magnificent air support when Montgomery arrived.

*

After the strenuous time at Casablanca, Sir Alan Brooke was looking forward with relish to the stopover at Marrakech. He was tired from the day-to-day slugging matches across the conference table in the Anfa Hotel and was glad to arrive in this beautiful town, with a luxurious room in the Hotel Mamounia. His room overlooked a plantation of orange and palm trees, and the majestic, glistening High Atlas Mountains behind made a restful view. Brooke had been noting the bird life around the region, remarking on the variations in pattern between the species at Marrakech from those at Casablanca, only a hundred and thirty miles away. He had been on duty, as it were, as long as Roosevelt was in Marrakech, but as soon as the President had left, Brooke observed happily that Churchill had taken his paints to the tower of the Taylor villa. Now was the time to go for a full-day partridge shoot.

As Brooke was almost at the door of his car, ready to go, a shout brought him to the telephone. The Prime Minister wanted to see him.

On entering Churchill's bedroom, Brooke was struck by what he saw. Though accustomed to seeing the Prime Minister in bed, Brooke had never observed him quite so colorful—or so amusing. Churchill was propped up in Mrs. Taylor's master bedroom under a fresco of green, blue, and gold.

The head of the bed rested in an alcove of Moorish design with a religious light shining on either side; the bed was covered with a light blue silk covering with 6-in. wide lace *entre-deux* and the rest of the

[11] The French commander, a General Schwartz, had barely escaped down the road westward to the safety of Combat Command A (CCA), 1st Armored, located at Sbeitla. The action had brought French losses to 2,500 in recent weeks.

room in harmony with the Arabic ceiling. And there in the bed was
Winston in his green, red and gold dragon dressing-gown, his hair, or
what there is of it, standing on end, the religious lights shining on his
cheeks, and a large cigar in his face! I would have given anything to
have been able to take a coloured photograph of him.[12]

The news the Prime Minister had, however, was not welcome. They
would, he declared, be off at 6:00 P.M. that day, destination London or
Cairo. Brooke, seeing his outing disappear, began spouting a series of
vain arguments: Churchill had been longing to paint the scenery of
Marrakech for the last six years; inadequate time was available in which
to warn Cairo (if they should go in that direction); Ambassador Sir Miles
Lampson would never have time to get the embassy ready. All to no
avail. Brooke's partridge shoot had died a-borning. All he had left was a
short space of a few hours before departure.

Churchill's hurry to leave Marrakech had been prompted by his natural
impatience. After SYMBOL he was convinced that the promise of a continued Mediterranean strategy would enable him to persuade President
Ismet Inönü of Turkey to bring his country into the war. To this end
Churchill had telegraphed Attlee and Eden five days earlier saying that he
and President Roosevelt were agreed that the time was right. He also
asked Eden to request an invitation for Churchill to visit Turkey. The
next day had come a negative reply; Attlee and Eden opposed his going
even to Cairo. The time was not right for an approach to the Turks, and
Churchill would be courting either "a rebuff or a failure."

With Winston Churchill such a turndown represented only the beginning of an argument. The same day that he received this refusal he sent a
return message referring to the "golden opportunity." He had no intention, he said, of extorting a pledge from the Turks, but he wanted to explain ways in which the Allies could now help them into a "position of security." He was prepared to offer guarantees of Turkish borders,
substantial munitions aid, and pledges of reinforcements in the event the
Germans attacked. He would not feel the least rebuffed if the Turks
should be afraid to come in. Again the War Cabinet disapproved.

There the matter sat until after the Casablanca Conference. On that historic Sunday, January 24, Churchill resumed the exchange, this time using
President Roosevelt's backing to the fullest. Growing impatient with what
he considered the "obstruction" in London, he followed with another long
message written from his bed early in the morning before going with
Roosevelt to the airfield.[13]

As always, the War Cabinet finally crumbled, and at noon a message of

[12] Bryant, *Turn of the Tide,* pp. 460–62.
[13] Churchill, IV, 703.

assent arrived. Churchill sent his thanks and continued with his plans. In Cairo he would wait for an answer from the Turks as to whether to continue to Ankara.

Churchill and Brooke were off from Marrakech in the B-24 Commando by 6:30 P.M. En route the Prime Minister could not resist sending a jubilant message to Eden:

> We are just over the Atlas Mountains, which are gleaming with their sunlit snows. You can imagine how much I wish I were going to be with you tomorrow on the Bench [in the House of Commons], but duty calls.

The trip to Cairo was far safer than the one Churchill had taken with the same American plane and crew the previous August. Skirting south of the Tunisian battlefield, they flew over territory that was clear of all enemy, the danger of interception practically non-existent. The trip took about eight hours, still uncomfortable at 9,000 feet in an unheated airplane, but safe. As before, early dawn found Churchill in the co-pilot seat by his friend Bill Vanderkloot, peering for his first glimpse (this trip) of the Nile. Eventually it appeared.

Churchill landed at the Heliopolis Airfield, ten miles east of the Pyramids, and quickly hastened off to the British Embassy downtown. He was in one of his exuberant moods, and when the subject of breakfast was mentioned, he horrified the discreet Alan Brooke by announcing his plans without consulting the hostess: "We shall have breakfast now." Once at the table, Lady Lampson offered him a cup of tea: completely unsatisfactory. On demand he was provided with a glass of white wine. "Ah, that is good," he grunted, "but you know I have already had two whiskeys and soda and two cigars this morning." Despite the hour of the day, the uncomfortable flying conditions, and the libations, Churchill showed not a sign of fatigue.[14]

Churchill and Brooke spent the next three days in Cairo, busy but relaxing somewhat from the high pressures of the conference. Alexander was on hand and General Sir Henry Maitland ("Jumbo") Wilson came from Baghdad to discuss the situation in his Middle East Command.

On the morning of arrival a message arrived at the embassy confirming an invitation from the Turks to meet on their soil, the only problem being the location. Since Turkey was officially neutral, German agents were able to circulate freely within the country; therefore Ankara, the capital, was ruled out. Finally Churchill and Inönü agreed on Adana, near the Turkish-Syrian border.

On Saturday morning, January 30, the few days of resting, conferring,

---

[14] Bryant, *Turn of the Tide*, p. 464.

and sightseeing in Cairo were over. The party, consisting primarily of the Prime Minister and Generals Brooke, Alexander, and Wilson, prepared to leave. They were hardly an impressive-looking group, as the military members, not allowed to wear uniform, were required to borrow ill-fitting civilian clothes. Thus Brooke remarked that Jumbo Wilson, in a suit belonging to an even more corpulent Lampson, wore a jacket which looked something like a maternity garment. Brooke, on his part, had obtained some clothes from Lampson's aide, a gentleman eight inches taller than he. The trousers were held up by suspenders, but Brooke had to pull them so high that they caught in his armpits—and then he discovered that the top fly button appeared above the opening of the coat, half concealing his necktie. "We looked more like a third rate theatrical travelling company," he wrote, "than anything else."[15]

The bumpy flight of seven hundred miles took Churchill and his group up the coast of Palestine and Syria, passing over Haifa, Beirut, Gaza, and Tripoli (now Tarabulus), Lebanon. They were met at Adana by the Turkish Prime Minister and Foreign Minister. Their train, however, was late. When it finally arrived, the motley contingent boarded and enjoyed lunch as they headed westward to join President Inönü and Field Marshal Cakmak. After an awkward welcome—formal and protracted speeches— the political and military officials separated, each group to confer in its own sphere.

On the political side, Churchill opened up by presenting a lengthy memo to Inönü for later study. The main thrust of this document was that the Allies saw every advantage to Turkey if she would enter the war sometime in 1943. He promised that the British and Americans together would certainly send at least twenty-five air squadrons, along with tanks, anti-tank guns, and anti-aircraft guns. Both Churchill and Inönü recognized that the Turkish armed forces at present were inadequate to fight the Germans; their infantry and artillery were strong but they lacked modern equipment, even tanks. Churchill's objective, actually, was not to marshal and train the Turks as a threat to Germany but to obtain the use of their air bases to attack the vital oil fields at Ploesti, Rumania.

The conversation then turned to the postwar era, which Churchill visualized would be governed by a structure based on the United Nations Declaration signed in Washington on New Year's Day 1942. A lively discussion also involved future relations between Turkey and the Soviet Union, two countries which had a long history of bitterness between them. Churchill's mentioning the names of Roosevelt and Stalin together (as leaders urging Turkey's entry) stimulated Inönü's suspicions, and he observed that it would be necessary to be "very prudent." And Churchill's

[15] Ibid., p. 467.

picture of the strong international organization designed to enforce the peace was also not persuasive. All in all, Churchill found the discussions satisfactory; after all, he had left Marrakech not even certain that the Turks would receive him.

On his part, Brooke was less satisfied. The Turks, he discovered, were completely out of touch with planning for modern war, and it was difficult to talk to them in intelligent terms. In addition, Brooke was concerned about the security arrangements, as assassination attempts on Churchill would not be out of the question. Brooke's concern was intensified when Inönü announced how delighted the Turkish people were to know that Churchill was in their country. The conference was supposed to have been kept utterly secret, Inönü pointed out lightheartedly, but nothing could really be kept secret.

The danger, however, worked to Brooke's advantage. He was sick of the conference and wanted to leave, and he utilized the very real physical danger as a means of dissuading Churchill from staying an extra night. On a personal check around the two trains, standing side by side, he had noted that the Turkish sentries were more interested in hiding from the rain than in guarding the safety of the Prime Minister and the President. On hearing this, Churchill approved departure for Cairo the next morning.

On Sunday, January 31, 1943, Churchill and his party bade farewell to President Inönü, the Prime Minister, and Field Marshal Cakmak. Just before take-off, however, Churchill learned that the pilot had understood the destination to be Cyprus rather than Cairo. (Hardly surprising, as Churchill had been backing and filling for the last few days.) Churchill, therefore, said to go ahead to Cyprus, where British officials, accustomed to the Prime Minister's impulsiveness, were prepared. He was duly met on arrival at Nicosia, where the party spent a comfortable and pleasant day, Brooke inspecting the British defenses and Churchill reviewing the 4th Hussars, of which he was the colonel. The next afternoon they went on to Cairo.

Two days later Churchill and his party left Cairo for Tripoli, some twelve hundred miles away. After a good view of the El Alamein battlefield they crossed the Desert to land that afternoon at Castel Benito Airdrome, where Alexander and Montgomery were on hand. At Montgomery's headquarters Churchill was brought up to date on plans to assault the Mareth Line on the Tunisian border once the port of Tripoli had been made capable of unloading supplies.

To Churchill and Brooke this visit to the Eighth Army was a thrilling experience. On their last visit the Desert Army had been down in the mouth, Montgomery having taken over only a couple of days before. Now they could see it in its triumph after Alam Halfa, El Alamein, and the pursuit across the Desert. The 51st Highland Division, in particular, was a joy to see, as it had been just arriving, pink-kneed and inexperienced, the previous August. The troops were now confident, tanned, battle-seasoned veterans. In the course of the stay Brooke and Churchill also visited the harbor and reviewed the New Zealand Division, headed by General Bernard Freyberg. Neither Churchill nor Brooke felt any embarrassment over the tears that rolled down their cheeks. The next morning, again defying the protests of a helpless War Cabinet, Churchill's Commando took off westward from Tripoli, circled south around the battle area, thence some nine hundred miles to Algiers.

*

Few men ever held a greater personal affection for Winston Churchill than did Dwight Eisenhower. And few men were ever less happy at the prospect of greeting him as a visitor. On learning that Churchill was coming to stay a day at Algiers, Eisenhower exploded. Back in England, he exclaimed, the Prime Minister was worth at least two armies to the Allied cause; here he was a liability. Eisenhower was always nervous about the safety of important personages (although he took remarkably few precautions for his own); but the concern this time was made more acute by rumors of special German agents on the way. Churchill, aware that Eisenhower's concern was shared by the War Cabinet, telegraphed London that he would be staying in Admiral Cunningham's villa, in the same small compound with Eisenhower. Both were protected by a high wall, barbed wire, and heavy guard. Churchill was, in fact, partially telling the truth, as his danger was negligible except when motoring back and forth to the Maison Blanche Airport, which could not be reached except by way of narrow, hilly streets through city districts lined with substantial French buildings capable of hiding any number of assassins.

Eisenhower met Churchill with an armored car, windows smeared with oil and mud. The driver had orders to go to the compound by a carefully planned, roundabout route. He personally would stay behind to meet the second plane carrying Brooke. Churchill went on, and when Brooke arrived, the two generals drove directly and openly to Eisenhower's villa in his regular Buick. Even in that car a bodyguard cradled a submachine gun and Eisenhower held a revolver. Arabs on the streets may or may not have been deceived into thinking that the only visitor was Brooke.

Despite the long day—Churchill and Brooke had arisen at 3:00 A.M.—Churchill insisted on having luncheon with a specially picked group: Giraud, Noguès, Boisson, Peyrouton, Alexander, Cunningham, and Sir Alexander Cadogan. Brooke went his own way in order to discuss the Tunisian front with General Anderson, in the course of which he was startled to be told that Churchill had practically decided to stay another day. Back at the villa Brooke finally convinced his chief to go that night as planned, as his colleagues back in London, he insisted, were becoming impatient.

Churchill and Eisenhower had dinner and a long conversation that evening in Cunningham's villa, where Churchill had spent the day. Afterward their convoy left for Maison Blanche. All went well en route, but no sooner were all comfortably aboard the two planes than Captain Vanderkloot discovered a malfunctioning magneto in one engine. Churchill, delighted, was soon back in Cunningham's villa for the night. Lord Moran, however, was not so comfortable. He had taken a sleeping pill which proved too effective, and he slept unawares on the plane.[16]

Though the aircraft was repaired by morning, Churchill remained in Algiers for the day on the basis that the flight would be safer at night. This time he stuck to his plan and at 2:15 A.M. Sunday, February 7, 1943, Prime Minister Winston Churchill was finally off the ground bound non-stop for London, his three-week visit to Casablanca and the Mediterranean at an end. General Eisenhower heaved a sigh of relief.

*

One aspect of Churchill's visit made Eisenhower pause. It was a subtlety he detected in British thinking which could, if not challenged, be injurious to his own authority. Before the visit of Churchill and Brooke, Eisenhower had assumed that no publicity would be given to the functions of Cunningham, Tedder, and Alexander. But at Algiers Brooke had told Eisenhower that plans were being made for a public announcement in Britain on February 11.

Quite naturally Eisenhower had been pleased by his retention as Allied Commander in the Western Mediterranean and, being busy with the Tunisian fighting, he had not up to this time bothered to read the "fine print" of the arrangements. When he read the agreement carefully, however, he discovered that the language spelled out the specific duties of his three principal subordinates. Eisenhower's main concern was the description of Alexander's position, which the Combined Chiefs had described not only as Eisenhower's deputy but also as the tactical ground commander for Tunisia and for the later invasion of Sicily (HUSKY). The CCS had specified further that in Sicily Alexander would "cooperate" with Cunningham and Tedder and "coordinate" the actions of the three

16 The alacrity with which Churchill decided to stay led some to suspect that he had conspired with someone to destroy the magneto. The security at the airport made this unlikely, although when determined to get his way Mr. Churchill was cunning and resourceful.

armies—including Clark's U. S. Fifth Army in Morocco, not even scheduled for employment in Sicily.

Eisenhower was willing to concede that there was probably nothing malicious behind all this; rather he saw it as a reflection of conflicting national attitudes toward the position of a field commander, in which the British, in contrast to the Americans, tended to supervise from London in a manner the Americans would never consider. But this particular action seemed to be calculated beyond mere doctrine. Eisenhower began to suspect—realistically, as it turned out—that Brooke would agree to American supreme command in the Mediterranean only because three British officers, each in his own sphere—land, sea, air—were specifically appointed by the two governments. Eisenhower, as "generalissimo," would be ultimately—almost theoretically—in command. But he would be responsible for other matters such as administration, logistics, and French politics. Brooke's vision of keeping Eisenhower in the "rarefied atmosphere" had begun to show through.

On February 8, therefore, the day after Churchill and Brooke had left, Eisenhower sent two messages to Marshall. Though they dealt with other matters, they obviously reflected his preoccupation with the definition of his own authority. In the first message he dwelt on the matter of a public announcement. "Here even Brooke had expressed surprise that the arrangements were to be made public."[17] The British, he believed, considered the demonstration of Anglo-American unity more important than secrecy. But even if he had to live with the wording of the CCS command agreement—which obviously he did—Eisenhower still did not want these detailed duties spelled out in public. Any public announcement, he urged, should merely state that Alexander was his own deputy and should not identify him as commanding the newly formed 18 Army Group in Tunisia.

Later in the day Eisenhower sent Marshall a second message in an even stronger vein. Going beyond the public announcement, he mentioned the inevitable trend of the British mind toward "committee" rather than single command. Particularly he objected to a Combined Chiefs statement that "further details would naturally be left to the Air Commander-in-Chief." Confidentially he advised that in practice he would pay no attention to such a directive, since he personally would be held ultimately responsible. And further, he would have no difficulty with any of the personalities involved, as he admired Alexander, Tedder, and Cunningham tremendously. But his anger showed through when he uncharacteristically volunteered a snide remark: "Only a man of Portal's turn of mind would have

[17] Eisenhower had not discussed this matter with Marshall previously because it had not come up in Marshall's earlier visit.

thought of inserting such a statement."[18] Eisenhower would later have cause to feel differently toward Portal.

*

When Marshall received Eisenhower's message he brought it to Roosevelt's attention. The President, in turn, cabled Churchill the next day emphasizing that the Allies could best encourage French cooperation by continuing to stress the American supreme command. He considered it inadvisable, therefore, to release information regarding the detailed duties of Alexander or Tedder. Churchill agreed to comply with Roosevelt's view but warned that British criticism of the command arrangement could not be avoided without some definition of the duties of Alexander and Tedder. His government could withstand the criticism, but the Americans would then be irritated because of the "inevitable" comparisons the British press would make regarding the relative war experience of Eisenhower and his three British subordinates.

Churchill said he thought the public should be told that General Eisenhower was Allied Chief, that Alexander was commanding the forces of the United Nations fighting in Tunisia, and that Tedder was commanding the air forces. Having made his point, however, Churchill would comply with Roosevelt's desires. Churchill made good his promise when he spoke before the House of Commons two days later. After about a week, however, all duties were announced. It was unrealistic to try to keep them secret.

Eisenhower appreciated the generosity the British had demonstrated in retaining him as Allied Commander in the light of the preponderance of British forces serving under him. Quite possibly, however, he failed at first to link that generosity with the fact that his three principal commanders, all British, had been selected for him. He now resolved, either consciously or unconsciously, that he was not going to be kicked upstairs out of the military arena. He was going to keep his fingertips on the fighting—not in detail, but not as an aloof "chairman of the board" either. He was now alert to a title's being one thing and authority another. He would never forget that lesson.

[18] Chandler, II, 944.

CHAPTER XVI

DEFEAT AND VICTORY
IN TUNISIA

About the time that General Eisenhower was protesting the details of the command agreements at Casablanca, he received word that Alexander's arrival in Tunisia would be delayed until February 17; the clearing of the port of Tripoli and Montgomery's advance were behind schedule. This was a keen disappointment, as Eisenhower had expected Alexander to take over the day-by-day direction of the Tunisian front nearly two weeks earlier. Anderson, to be sure, was now in formal command of all forces; but in anticipation of Alexander's arrival he was still commanding from his old headquarters in the north. Further, Eisenhower was not prepared to let Anderson fight the battle without careful supervision since he was still somewhat of an unknown quantity. His lack of zeal in following Eisenhower's instructions to concentrate the 1st Armored was troublesome, and Juin's willingness to obey Anderson's orders fully was questionable. The personal antagonism between Anderson and Fredendall was obviously deepening. Alexander's assumption of command would eliminate these problems, but Eisenhower could not afford to lose touch in Tunisia in the meantime.

On February 11, 1943, Eisenhower received word, at first indirectly, of his promotion to four-star general, which put his rank on a par with that of his three principal subordinates. His delight at receiving the news was almost boyish, and he promoted every enlisted member of his household staff. He was annoyed, however, by the casual way in which the War Department handled the matter. Eisenhower heard nothing from Marshall until after Butcher had picked up the word over the radio—and after a telegram of congratulations had come in from his wife, Mamie. But there was little time to worry about such matters, as he would be off by car for his headquarters at Constantine early the next morning.

On arriving, Eisenhower spent the night conferring with Lucian Truscott, who outlined the situation as he saw it in some detail. Truscott believed that every advantage—ground, air, and sea—lay with the Allies. And Truscott could realize that Axis supply difficulties were at least as great as those of the Allies. On the other hand there was cause for short-term concern since the retreating Axis forces retained "the ability to concentrate superior means in local areas and to retain the initiative." Rommel and Von Arnim were operating from a central position against several converging, sometimes spread-out formations. Further, their subordinate leaders had greater experience. This factor, though an intangible, was important.

Truscott, however admitted to a certain amount of confusion. Intelligence in British First Army—and at Allied Force Headquarters—placed so much weight on information gathered from radio intercept (ULTRA) as to practically ignore almost all other forms of combat intelligence. All signs pointed to a strong attack by Von Arnim or Rommel through one of the four passes on the Eastern Dorsal; and with their local superiority in men and equipment—and the protection of the Mareth Line to the south—it seemed almost inevitable that such an attack would come. But where? Either Fondouk or Faid Pass would seem likely, but intelligence officers were certain, based on ULTRA alone, that the assault would come through Fondouk. They could be placing too much faith in one intelligence source.

Truscott had no reason, he said, to question the value of radio intelligence, but no other standard sources—prisoner interrogation, enemy air strikes, increased incoming artillery—confirmed Fondouk as the only prospective point of attack. With this in mind, Eisenhower and Truscott prepared to leave the next morning to look things over.

In the areas around Constantine—that is, the rear of the Tunisian battlefield—the danger from assassination was great, as agents could well be concealed among the teeming civilians. As a precaution, therefore, Truscott had detached a mechanized cavalry platoon for escort. The party traveled first to a British and then to an American air base at Youks les Bains, just west of Tébessa. Satisfied with what he could see of morale among the airmen, Eisenhower determined to go on to II Corps Headquarters.

At Tébessa Eisenhower was taken aback to hear the din of hammers and drills. Corps engineers were busy digging caves to protect the command post from air attack, even though all installations were hidden in a well-protected ravine at a distance of some hundred miles from the front. Truscott had alerted him that corps engineers were being wasted in this silly activity, but Eisenhower had to see it personally. His temper was further aroused by a gratuitous lesson in military organization by a condescending junior staff officer. When Eisenhower asked if the engineers had first helped prepare front-line positions, the young man exclaimed, "Oh, the front-line divisions have their own engineers for that!"[1]

Eisenhower was thus in a belligerent mood when he confronted Anderson and Fredendall. His anger worsened when he learned that Anderson had again, despite his own orders, failed to concentrate the U. S. 1st Armored. Major General Orlando Ward, whose headquarters was located a few miles northeast of Tébessa, had under his own control only one battalion of light tanks; the rest of the division was parceled out. Robinett's powerful CCB, for example, was still about fifteen miles behind the 1st Division near Fondouk. Brigadier General R. A. McQuillan's CCA was thirty miles south at Sidi-Bou-Zid, near Faid. And the other two task forces—they could hardly be dignified with the term "combat commands" —were scattered another eighty miles south to Gafsa.

Determined to see the front for himself, Eisenhower left II Corps just before dark, his convoy now stripped down to four vehicles. He dropped in at Ward's headquarters and drove past the airfields of Fériana and Thélepte. From there he went almost due east through Sbeitla to visit McQuillan's CCA. McQuillan's dispositions and reconnaissance seemed satisfactory, though he had little to fight with. He had two infantry battalions in position on the Eastern Dorsal, supported by one battalion of artillery. In reserve around Sidi-Bou-Zid McQuillan held an infantry and a tank battalion. Eisenhower was shaken, however, by the lethargy of American troops as they went about digging in. The Germans facing Anderson, he knew, could prepare a complete defensive position in the course of a couple of hours, but these Americans, having been on the ground for two days, were merely engaged in "making plans" for the next day. Eisenhower gave orders to start laying mines immediately, dark though the night was, and determined to have words with the higher commanders.

Truscott had called ahead and arranged for Eisenhower's old friend Paul Robinett to come down from Fondouk to McQuillan's command post. Robinett was not an officer who tried very hard to please anyone, but Eisenhower placed a great deal of faith in his judgment, and his observations reinforced Truscott's. Up at Fondouk, Robinett said, he could see no evidence of a German build-up, at least nothing to rule out an attack anywhere else. Eisenhower resolved to direct a re-evaluation of the current intelligence estimate as soon as he should return to II Corps.

Another visitor that evening was Colonel Thomas D. Drake, from one

[1] Each division had one combat (light) engineer battalion. The heavy construction units were controlled by corps, usually to perform difficult, high-priority work at the front.

of the infantry battalions up on the Dorsal. Drake had distinguished himself for gallantry a few days before, and Eisenhower took real pleasure in decorating him with the Distinguished Service Cross. Even in the blackness of the night the Allied chief was effusive: "Drake," he said, "I think you're going to go a long ways." How long a ways Drake would go within the next couple of days Eisenhower had no way of knowing.

Determined to enforce his will regarding the concentration of the 1st Armored, Eisenhower left Sidi-Bou-Zid through Sbeitla on the way back to Tébessa. The trip through the darkness was dangerous. At one point Eisenhower's driver fell asleep and the jeep slid into the ditch; and as the party approached Tébessa[2] sporadic firing broke out. Suspecting ambush or a raid on II Corps Headquarters, a couple of members of the small convoy went forward to check. The gunshots, it turned out, came from trigger-happy sentries.

Eisenhower and Truscott reached II Corps Command Post at dawn. Here they were met by word that German forces had broken through Faid Pass and taken Sidi-Bou-Zid, where Eisenhower had decorated Colonel Drake a couple of hours earlier.[3] The situation was still unclear; but a major attack seemed likely. Soon reports came in that another German penetration had been made south of Gafsa. The two were both apparently headed toward an important road junction at a pass on the Western Dorsal named Kasserine.

Eisenhower could do little to affect the tactical battle from II Corps Headquarters. He did, however, remain impatiently at Constantine pending the time that the situation should be clarified. While waiting he reported formally to the Combined Chiefs and more informally to General Marshall. Neither message showed undue concern, since these penetrations had been expected:

To: *Combined Chiefs of Staff:*   February 15, 1943.

. . . Our present tactical difficulties result from my attempt to do possibly too much coupled with the deterioration of the French resistance in the central mountainous area, which began about January 17. That deterioration has absorbed the bulk of the United States 1st and 34th Divisions, which formations had originally been pushed forward to provide general reserves and to permit us to attack from the line which we were then holding.

His message to Marshall consisted of a personal account of his visit to the front. He regarded the situation as grave but never doubted that it would

2 Truscott, p. 155. Eisenhower (*Crusade*, p. 142) gives a slightly different account, placing the incident at Sbeitla. Truscott's account, being written at a later date and based on more detailed notes, would seem more accurate, though the exact location is unimportant.

3 Eisenhower would later learn that Drake was made a prisoner of war.

be overcome. He wrote home to his wife remembering the anniversary of their engagement and ruminating on the responsibilities which were now his.

Shortly thereafter Eisenhower decided to remove his intelligence officer, in whom he had lost confidence. He requested a replacement from Brooke, as that position was one that Eisenhower felt should be held by a British officer. The slavish fixation on Fondouk Pass (caused by excessive faith in ULTRA) had been just too costly to afford any more such mistakes.

*

The blow that hit the Tunisian front at Faid early on February 14 is usually associated with the name of Field Marshal Erwin Rommel. In the first stages, however, the battle was commanded by General Jürgen von Arnim, Rommel's theoretical co-equal and fierce competitor. It was lucky for the Anglo-Americans that the Axis command chain was even more confused than their own.

Von Arnim, three years Rommel's senior, had commanded Axis forces in Tunisia ever since his arrival on December 9, 1942. His forces were approximately equal to Rommel's in theoretical strength—Von Arnim had 100,000 in contrast to Rommel's 70,000—but Von Arnim's 10th and 21st Panzer Divisions were far fresher than Rommel's Afrika Korps (now a combined German-Italian unit of approximately divisional size). Furthermore, Von Arnim's troops had been enjoying successes, as he had been seizing passes on the Eastern Dorsal and keeping the Americans off balance. They were limited actions, but they were still successes.

Von Arnim personally was a highly respected Silesian aristocrat, a graduate of all the right schools, a member of the "club," which Rommel was not. Despite the fact that Rommel was the most popular general in all Germany, Von Arnim tended to look down on him, encouraging his own officers to do likewise. Rommel, to Von Arnim, was an uncultured has-been. Rommel, nevertheless, was a field marshal and ranked Von Arnim by a grade, a fact which made his arrival doubly unwelcome.

When Rommel's army withdrew into Tunisia, his preoccupation remained in the direction of Montgomery at the Mareth Line. He was aware of the strength Montgomery had in that Army and he was concerned that the Mareth Line, an antiquated French defense that he was now occupying, would never compensate. Nevertheless the presence of the American II Corps on the Dorsal to his rear made him uncomfortable. The Americans, he knew, had one armored division with which they might drive to Sfax or Gabès on the Gulf (as Eisenhower had planned before his trip to Casablanca), and they might attempt to do just that in conjunction with an attack by Montgomery on Mareth. At this time Rommel had little regard for the Americans, untried and green as he knew they were. And the French and British prisoners were quite willing to curry favor with their German captors by making disparaging remarks about the Americans. ("Our Italians" was a popular term.) But a corps threatening his rear, a corps with armor, could not be ignored.

Rommel was still sick, convalescing from the intestinal and nervous disorders contracted the previous October at the time of El Alamein. The retreat across Cyrenaica and Tripolitania had left him depressed. Further, his conduct of the retreat had earned him the disfavor of the Italian *Commando Supremo,* under whom even Field Marshal Kesselring theoretically served. Rommel, they now believed, had conducted operations to the disadvantage of his Italian components. And from their berths in Italy they considered his retreat across Italian territory too hasty and his surrender of Tripoli premature.

Hitler knew of Rommel's condition and had decided to rescue him from North Africa as soon as possible and allow his army to be taken over by Italian General Giovanni Messe. But timing was a problem, for the German high command, wishing to avoid the appearance of relieving Rommel for cause, was leaving the date of departure up to him. Rommel, with a fierce loyalty to his "Africans"—the Germans of the Afrika Korps —was refusing to leave until ordered to do so; he would not appear to be deserting his men.

An impasse had resulted, and Rommel was still in Africa long after anyone desired. Kesselring, who seemed to alternate between antipathy toward Rommel and a tendency to placate him, told Von Arnim to bide his time. Rommel should have his last chance for glory in an attack on the Americans in the southern end of Tunisia, but he would not command all Axis forces. Von Arnim's Fifth Panzer Army and Rommel's Desert Army would therefore operate independently during the forthcoming offensive, which began that Sunday morning of February 14, 1943.

The essence of Kesselring's plan was for Von Arnim to keep his 10th and 21st Panzer Divisions to attack near Faid. On taking Sidi-Bou-Zid, Von Arnim would send a portion of his 21st Panzer south to reinforce Rommel's Afrika Korps along the route El Guettar–Gafsa, toward the Fériana–Thélepte plain. Von Arnim protested against giving any panzers to Rommel at all, even later, and Kesselring felt it necessary to come to Tunisia. On the ninth of February the three met at a Luftwaffe base near Gabès (on neutral ground between the commands) and Kesselring crammed his plan down Von Arnim's throat. Rommel, on his part, remained interested primarily in the condition of his 15th Panzer at the Mareth Line. At first he designated a deputy to command the Afrika Korps when it should move against the Americans at Gafsa.

On February 15 Rommel was still at Mareth when he learned of Von Arnim's success at Faid and Sidi-Bou-Zid: fifty-four American tanks destroyed on the fourteenth; a like number the next day. Now he could have the panzers! Shortly thereafter Rommel learned that the Americans had hastily evacuated Gafsa. As he rushed to the front, the sight of abandoned American vehicles, his own tanks rolling forward, and the grinning Arabs seemed to stimulate the Desert Fox. He had little stomach for retreat, but once again he was on the attack! For a short period Rommel would appear to be his old self. He would gamble all on a drive to Tébessa.

The battle which has come to be known as Kasserine Pass involved a great deal of surprise and maneuver. The two prongs of the Axis attack—Von Arnim at Faid and Rommel at Gafsa—went through the American positions on the Eastern Dorsal with little difficulty. Two battalions of the 168th Infantry, 34th Division, were lost near Faid—and their commanders with them. Attacks by CCC, a task force of 1st Armored, were disastrous against Von Arnim's 10th and 21st Panzer Divisions. By February 17 Von Arnim and Rommel had penetrated deeply on nearly parallel routes; Rommel occupied the Fériana plain and Von Arnim reached the important communication center at Sbeitla.

At this point Kesselring ordered Von Arnim to send his two panzer divisions over to Rommel. Von Arnim expressed his annoyance by delaying the transfer on purpose. They did, however, arrive. Once more in the center of the stage, with three panzer divisions, Rommel requested permission to drive northwestward through Kasserine Pass to Tébessa. And, he urged, if successful enough, he might even drive to the sea at Bône! But confusion at the highest command levels entered the picture, and an unhappy Rommel was ordered to turn due north toward Le Kef (in Anderson's rear) with the 21st Panzer from Sbeitla and the 10th Panzer through Kasserine Pass. Only the Afrika Korps, the weakest of the three panzer forces, would head toward Tébessa, the goal Rommel wanted to seize.

In the meantime the confused American units had been reinforced by two British brigades from Anderson's First Army, and the 21st Panzer at Sbiba (north of Sbeitla) and the 10th Panzer at Thala were stalled. But Rommel's Afrika Korps at Kasserine had overrun the gallant but bewildered American troops from the 1st Division and CCB, 1st Armored. This battle, the first serious American action, provided the household name for the entire offensive.

By the night of February 21–22 Rommel realized he had gone as far as he could. The Allies had been more humiliated than actually hurt. In terms of ground gained the penetrations had been spectacular—about ninety miles from El Guettar to Kasserine and another thirty miles from Kasserine to Thala, for a total of a hundred and twenty miles (twice as deep as the more famous "Bulge" in late December 1944). But he would

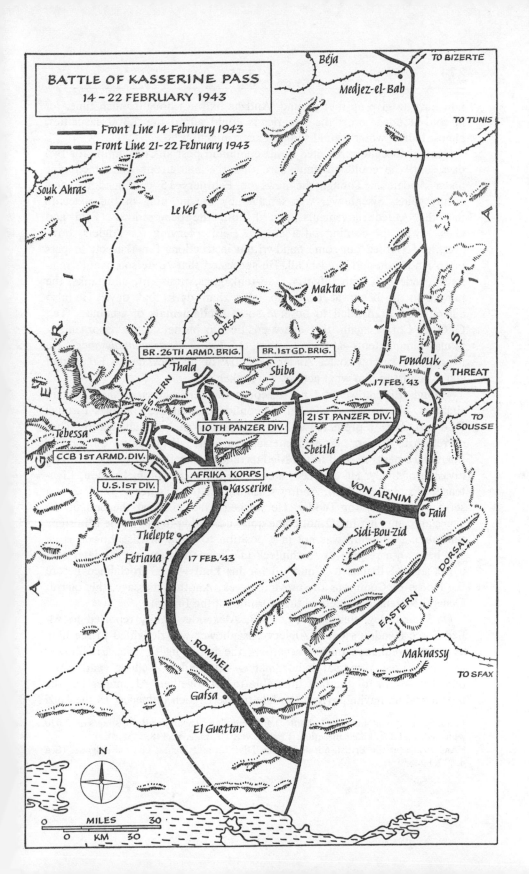

BATTLE OF KASSERINE PASS
14 – 22 FEBRUARY 1943

Front Line 14 February 1943
Front Line 21-22 February 1943

TO BIZERTE

Béja

Medjez-el-Bab

TO TUNIS

Souk Ahras

Le Kef

Maktar

DORSAL

BR. 26TH ARMD. BRIG.

BR. 1ST GD. BRIG.

Fondouk

Thala

Sbiba

THREAT

17 FEB. '43

WESTERN

21ST PANZER DIV.

TO SOUSSE

Tebessa

10TH PANZER DIV.

CCB 1ST ARMD. DIV.

Sbeitla

AFRIKA KORPS

VON ARNIM

U.S. 1ST DIV.

Kasserine

Faid

T U N I S I A

Sidi-Bou-Zid

Thélepte

Fériana

17 FEB. '43

EASTERN

DORSAL

Maknassy

A L G E R I A

ROMMEL

TO SFAX

Gafsa

El Guettar

N

MILES
0   30

KM
0   30

now have to give up that ground. And he had not bought much time, for in cold-blooded terms the Americans could afford the 5,300 casualties, almost half of whom would soon be back in action.[4]

General Eisenhower waited in his command post at Constantine for two days, until he could be quite sure that the battlefront was functioning under Anderson. Though the news on February 15 continued to show enemy gains, Eisenhower was satisfied by the morning of the sixteenth that the Allied movements toward both the penetrations (Faid and Gafsa) were proceeding satisfactorily. Before leaving for Algiers, however, he scribbled out some handwritten instructions for Truscott to pass on to Anderson and Fredendall. He suggested that Anderson should reinforce Fredendall with infantry, anti-tank guns, transport, and tanks, the movement to begin at once, no later than dark that day.[5] He also admonished Fredendall to observe some fundamentals of combat: "Tell C. G. II Corps, again, that every position to be held must be organized to maximum extent—at once—mines, etc. *Emphasize reconnaissance.*" He instructed Truscott to let Anderson know of his message to Fredendall and to report to him what actions were taken.

Though Eisenhower did not discount the seriousness of the Tunisian situation, his messages reflected his confidence that these attacks through Faid and Gafsa represented only an incident in the over-all picture. Thus on return to Algiers he sent a message to Marshall giving an estimate of the replacements needed in the Mediterranean Theater to execute the later invasion of Sicily. He also sent a cable to his successor in London, Lieutenant General Frank M. Andrews, asking for the transfer of Ira Eaker to serve as a deputy for Tedder. He warned Churchill that the end of the Tunisian campaign might not come quite according to the Prime Minister's timetable. (Churchill was not in a position to threaten Eisenhower as he had been with respect to Auchinleck and even Alexander.) He later sent a message of thanks to Churchill for his kind words proclaimed before the House of Commons the previous week. Another message, this one to General Marshall, concerned the rearming of the French.

On Wednesday, February 17, 1943, Alexander finally reported to Allied Force Headquarters in Algiers. Eisenhower was delighted to see him, as he still remained uneasy regarding the battle in Tunisia. Eisenhower and his three principal subordinates—Alexander, Tedder, and Cunningham—were for the first time able to get together. Alexander left the next morning, having arrived too late to exert much influence, as the Nazi

[4] American losses included about 2,460 missing (nearly all prisoners), 2,620 wounded, and 190 killed in action. Eisenhower, *Crusade,* p. 148.
[5] Anderson sent the British 6th Armoured Division and the 1st Guards Brigade. (See p. 272.)

high-water marks had been nearly reached and the necessary Allied forces committed. The bitterly fought action at Kasserine was already under way, and despite the loss of that pass it was apparent that the Axis offensive, now being conducted exclusively by Rommel, would achieve no decisive results.

Looking to the future, Eisenhower's main concern centered around the conduct of the American commanders. The American troops had fought gallantly, though their greenness showed up clearly. This condition would be rectified by further training and experience. The jolt into reality provided by Kasserine would enhance motivation in the future. But for the moment he had somehow to bolster the flagging Fredendall. He had developed serious doubts regarding Fredendall's ability to command in combat, but he still wanted a "second opinion."

*

Major General Ernest N. Harmon, Commanding General, U. S. 2nd Armored Division in Morocco, had been receiving only sketchy news of the Tunisian battle. A tough, bald, stocky man with a small mustache and a gravel voice, Harmon was known as one of the foremost tank officers in the American Army. As a division commander in training he was among the best.

Harmon had a way with troops. With his understanding of their psychology he could calculatedly violate the "book" principles of leadership and substitute his own personal style. "All you men are going to wear that steel helmet," he once growled. "It's no goddam good. You're going to wear it because I say so. I'm going to wear this soft cap; it's more comfortable." And his men, rather than being resentful, laughed and repeated the story with zest.

On February 20, 1943, a telegram arrived in Rabat ordering Harmon to report to General Eisenhower in Algiers. It did not define the term "limited field duty." Harmon's first reaction was only to hope that it didn't mean losing command of his beloved 2nd Armored Division, which he knew would see a lot of combat before the war was over. Harmon and his aide left in the dark and reported to Allied Force Headquarters the next morning.

As Harmon strode into Eisenhower's office in the St. George, he saw immediately that Ike's normal cheerfulness was not much in evidence. Word had come in that American forces had been overrun at Kasserine Pass and Eisenhower was concerned for the safety of II Corps Headquarters at Tébessa and the Youks-les-Bains airfield nearby. He was, he told Harmon, even more perturbed by reports of dissension among American commanders, particularly Fredendall's complaints about Orlando Ward of the 1st Armored. And he had also received unfavorable reports of Fredendall's relations with Anderson.[6]

As they talked, it became evident to Harmon how much responsibility Eisenhower was placing on his own shoulders. He was to go to II Corps, assist in the tactical battle, and then take over command of *either* II Corps or its subordinate 1st Armored. Harmon's characteristic bluntness got the best of him, astonishing even himself. "Well, make up your mind, Ike, I can't do both."

"That's right," Eisenhower answered, "but right now I don't know what is to be done down there. I'm going to send you as deputy corps commander. Your first job is to do the best you can to help Fredendall restore the situation. Then you will report direct to me whether you should relieve Ward or Fredendall."[7]

Harmon, feeling on the spot, left dejectedly. He knew that he was probably best qualified to take command of the 1st Armored, but command of II Corps would be a step up the military ladder. More than that, he knew nothing of the ground and would be walking into a nebulous situation in his first major battle. Eisenhower had put supreme faith—perhaps too much—in Harmon's personal integrity.

At 2:00 A.M. the next morning, Eisenhower and Butcher knocked on the door of Harmon's room. Harmon, exhausted, was tossing in a near-coma. Though disoriented, he finally realized that his two visitors were helping him dress.[8] Delayed until about 3:00 A.M. by an air raid, the small party left Algiers in Eisenhower's sedan for Constantine. Harmon was embarrassed because in his weariness he would often fall asleep while the Allied Commander was talking.

[6] On February 4, ten days before the attack, Eisenhower had written Fredendall a "personal" letter which reflected his worries obliquely:

Truscott has told you something of my concern about a report that had been made to me of your criticism of the British. This is all cleared up, because I . . . have no doubts concerning your loyalty and determination to do your full part in the winning of this war. . . .

One of the things that give me the most concern is the habit of some of our generals in staying too close to their command posts. Please watch this very, very carefully among all your subordinates. . . . Generals are expendable just as is any other item in an army; and moreover, the importance of having the general constantly present in his command post is frequently overemphasized. . . .

I have sent in again a recommendation for your promotion. . . . This is not important, except as it expresses . . . the complete confidence of your superiors up to and including the President. . . .

Eisenhower to Fredendall, February 4, 1943, quoted in Chandler, II, 939–41. Eisenhower sent a copy to General Marshall, who knew Fredendall far better than did he.
[7] Harmon, *Combat Commander*, p. 112.
[8] "I have enjoyed telling my grandchildren that a future President of the United States once laced up their groggy grandfather's combat boots." Ibid., p. 112.

Shortly before dusk the party arrived at Constantine, and Eisenhower took his leave. Harmon and his aide began the hundred-mile trip to Tébessa, witnessing for the first and only time in Harmon's career an American army in rout. Making his way through the dangerous, rear-bound traffic, Harmon arrived at Tébessa about 2:00 A.M. on February 23. In the confusion the revived Harmon experienced difficulty in even finding II Corps. When he finally succeeded, he, like others before him, was shocked by the elaborate installation. Fredendall, sitting groggily at a stove in his dugout, looked up. "We've been waiting for you to arrive. Shall we move the command post?"

Harmon had nothing to go on. He had arrived in utter darkness, with no real idea where he was or where the front lines were. With nothing to go on, he shot from the hip. "No, sir," he replied, "we'll let it stay right here."

"That settles it," mumbled Fredendall. He turned to his operations officer: "We'll keep the command post here."[9]

Fredendall then gave Harmon his instructions as deputy corps commander. He was to take "battlefield command" of the 1st Armored facing the Afrika Korps thirty miles away, about half the distance between their present location and Kasserine Pass. The British 6th Armoured Division, elements of which were now holding Rommel's 10th Panzer at Thala, would also come under him.

Leaving Fredendall, who had drifted again into sleep, Harmon headed for the 1st Armored at Haidra, some twenty miles northeast. There he found General Ward asleep in a slit trench. Harmon hated to assume command from an officer who ranked him by a thousand files in the Regular Army, but Ward, happily, promised to cooperate. After examining the situation, Harmon came up with an uncomplicated formula: "We are going to hold today and counterattack tomorrow. Nobody goes back from here."

Ward promptly issued an order: "All units will be alerted at dawn for movement in any direction except to the rear."[10]

*

From Ward's command post Harmon headed about fifty miles to Thala, where Brigadier Cameron G. C. Nicholson, commander of the British 6th Armoured Division, was holding the German 10th Panzer. Harmon was unshaven and dirty, in contrast to the freshly shaven and crisply uniformed Nicholson, but there was no question as to who was in charge. Harmon's very first action established his authority, when Brigadier Gen-

[9] Ibid., p. 114. Fredendall's symptoms reflected nights without adequate sleep. See *Crusade*, p. 145, for Eisenhower's conversation suggesting counterattack earlier in the evening.
[10] Harmon, p. 116.

eral Stafford L. Irwin, a friend from West Point days, rushed excitedly into the command post. General Anderson, Irwin said, had ordered him to move his 9th Division artillery back to Le Kef, fifty miles to the north. Nicholson's protest was immediate: How would the British tankers react if they saw American artillery pulling out? Harmon agreed, and besides he had nothing to lose. "Ignore those instructions," he told Irwin, "and keep your artillery right here." Irwin and Nicholson were both overjoyed. After the long trip back to Tébessa Harmon told Fredendall that the front was pretty well stabilized. He planned to counterattack the next day.

At daybreak Harmon and his staff, which consisted of five men in a half-track, arrived back at the front. Incoming German artillery was weak, an indication that no serious attack was in the offing. That, Harmon decided, was the signal; soon he was back with Ward planning a counterattack toward Kasserine. It would require a few hours of the short day to prepare, and when the attack jumped off, the enemy had disappeared. The battle of Kasserine Pass was over.

Back in Algiers Harmon went at once to the St. George. Ward, Harmon reported to Eisenhower, was doing well, but Fredendall had been by-passing him, sending orders directly to Robinett, his subordinate, and rendering Ward helpless.

"Well, what do you think of Fredendall?"

"You ought to get rid of him."

"Do you want to take command of the II Corps?"

Harmon hesitated a moment: "No, ethically I can't do that. I've reported to you that my superior is no good. It would look like I had sold him down the river to better my own assignment. My recommendation would be to bring Patton here from Morocco—let him take command of the II Corps. Let me go back to my 2nd Armored. That's the best way out of this mess."

He was right. Harmon could never take Fredendall's job on his own recommendation. On the face of it, Eisenhower probably should not have asked.

*

The battle that ended at Thala, northwest of Kasserine Pass, turned out to be a valuable lesson for Americans of all ranks. Coddled compared with their counterparts of other armies, they had developed an unjustified cockiness after the easy landings in North Africa against short resistance. But this was real war. And the combat soldiers, despite the efforts of their commanders, were psychologically unprepared to face the dangers to which they would be exposed when they met a serious, determined enemy. Moreover, those who had landed in North Africa had been overseas since shortly after Pearl Harbor, and had therefore missed the intensive training (partly based on the Kasserine experience) that would so much better prepare their later comrades for their first moments of combat. The men of II Corps had learned reality the hard way. It would no longer take three days to set out a mine field around a new position.

The Allied Commander also learned, and he thought long and hard. How might he have averted this temporary disaster? For one, at least, he held no regrets: he could have exercised caution and refused to try the desperate gamble to take Tunisia in November 1942. The British and Americans could have remained back on a line where Rommel and Von Arnim could not have caught them off balance. But then why were they there in North Africa? Further, he had no regrets about gambling on defense of the Eastern Dorsal with weak forces; if Montgomery had arrived sooner, possession of the Thélepte and Fériana airfields would have proven invaluable. That decision admittedly had been a mistake, as things turned out, for it entailed extending southward as far as Gafsa. But Eisenhower's gambles were consistent with the philosophies of Marshall and King. "We've seen what happens when commanders sit down and wait for the enemy to attack," King had said in Algiers. "Keep slugging."

Another area in which Eisenhower felt no personal responsibility was that of the failure of the professional intelligence services, a deficiency easily corrected with the arrival of Brigadier Kenneth Strong as new G-2 (Intelligence).

Eisenhower's regrets centered on his handling of command matters. He regretted his delay in directing a unified front under Anderson. For despite his concession to Juin, the French turned out to be unprepared for frontline combat anyway. Anderson had therefore been denied the opportunity to become acquainted with the terrain and with the problems of American troops.

One matter, the command of U. S. II Corps, could be redressed. Based on his discussion with Harmon—and later with Truscott and others—Eisenhower finally decided that Fredendall must be removed. Ethics or no ethics, he could insist that Harmon take the command. But he probably had George Patton in mind from the first, even though Patton was engaged in planning HUSKY.

Eisenhower flew to Tébessa on March 5, 1943, to inform Fredendall of the change, which he couched in terms of a routine assignment; and he would recommend that Fredendall be given command of a training army in the United States. This was, admittedly, kid-glove treatment in the light of all reports on Fredendall's performance, but Eisenhower was conscious that not all the errors in the Tunisian battle could be laid at Fredendall's feet, and Fredendall had been General Marshall's personal selection. Nevertheless, had Eisenhower, at that time, possessed the confidence he would develop during the next year, he might not have been so lenient.[11]

*

The teamwork that General Eisenhower was trying to develop between British and American forces in Tunisia survived the tenure of George S. Patton, Jr., as commander of U. S. II Corps. And the forty days during which Patton held that position saw some Allied successes. But those days did little to further any spirit of cooperation between the two nationalities.

As Patton took command, Eisenhower, reflecting on Fredendall's anti-British attitudes, felt it necessary to send some words of serious advice. Partly he was writing for himself:

I expect you to respond to General Alexander's orders exactly as if they were issued by me. I want no mistake about my thorough belief in unity of command. . . .

You need have no doubt whatsoever about enjoying my fullest confidence. I mention this again because it affects your handling of personnel under you. You must not retain for one instant any man in a responsible position where you have become doubtful of his ability to do his job. . . . This matter frequently calls for more courage than any other thing you will have to do, but I expect you to be perfectly cold-blooded about it.

Patton was not disposed to enjoy receiving such an admonition from an officer seven years his junior in the Regular Army. Moreover, his own dislike of the British probably exceeded Fredendall's, and his animosity was heightened by evidence that they—Alexander in particular—looked disapprovingly on the American performance at Kasserine.

Patton had no doubt about the ability of his American troops to fight as well as or better than anyone, given reasonable training and proper leadership, which he was sent to supply. To prove this point, and to build confidence, he, Patton, would have to be aggressive; he must tout and even exaggerate all American success.

Inevitably, of course, this chauvinism would make him highly critical of any concession that Eisenhower would have to make to the British, but Patton truly believed that he was serving as a balance against the overpowering numbers of British troops engaged, and only by being totally Yankee—as Montgomery was totally British—could he prevent humiliation of his troops.

Surprisingly, Patton developed an instant liking and admiration for

[11] Eisenhower, conversation with author, late 1945.

Alexander, despite the latter's British ways. But he also developed a personal animosity toward Montgomery which he would never lose. The Axis armed forces, particularly the Nazis, were the enemy, the problem; but to Patton the personal adversary would always be personified by Montgomery.

*

If the Americans felt a trauma as a result of the blow they had received from Von Arnim and Rommel, the results of the offensive brought no joy to Rommel either, since he well knew that the German panzers had failed to reach any really significant objectives. And he could see that the troops of the American II Corps had conducted themselves well after Kasserine; they had kept the passes toward Tébessa and Le Kef. Thus when radio intercept picked up Orlando Ward's messages forbidding further withdrawal, Rommel felt the impact. He was in fact personally defeated before he ordered withdrawal on that February 22. Kesselring, personally present in Rommel's operations truck at the time, attempted to persuade Rommel to continue his attack, but Rommel knew that the Americans would hold, and he could no longer afford to ignore Montgomery's build-up on his rear.[12] As he headed south that day, he could hear the depressing sounds of demolitions in Kasserine Pass. His troops were now delaying, not attacking.

Ironically, when Rommel arrived back at Sbeitla he found a telegram from Rome appointing him commander of Army Group Afrika. This appointment, though it pleased him, had come too late. Had it come a few days earlier, he could have ordered Von Arnim's panzers to reinforce the drive toward Tébessa and Le Kef. Then he *might* have given the Americans a sterner, perhaps decisive defeat. But it had not.

The time had now come for Rommel to leave. Physically and mentally he was in a poor state, and his stay in Tunisia was now voluntarily reduced to days. Angry that neither Von Arnim nor the Italians treated his prestigious new appointment with much respect, Rommel set the departure date for early morning, Tuesday, March 9. Having recommended that all forces in southern Tunisia be pulled back to the hills of Enfidaville, Rommel and two aides boarded a plane at Sfax. He flew to Rome, never to return.

*

Alexander's plan for the conduct of last phases of the Tunisian battle was logical—even obvious. Montgomery's Eighth Army, coming from the south, would constitute the cannon ball that would crush Von Arnim's remaining forces; British First Army and U. S. II Corps, conducting an

[12] See Irving, pp. 274, 275, for a version of the Rommel-Kesselring conversations.

aggressive defense on the west, would constitute one side of the barrel, and the Gulf on the east would provide the other. It was not mere sentiment that led Alexander to employ the Eighth Army in this major role. Montgomery's force was strong, with six refitted, battle-hardened divisions plus a separate tank brigade. It was deployed on a front of only some thirty-five miles. Anderson's and Patton's commands, on the other hand, though in total strength about equal to Montgomery's, were spread thinly over two hundred and fifty miles. Thus Alexander planned to halt Patton when he had reoccupied the Eastern Dorsal. Von Arnim's channel of retreat northwest would thus be confined to a small corridor, with Montgomery in hot pursuit.

The major question regarding this whole plan involved the role of Patton's II Corps. After the Kasserine battle the Americans had retaken only the airfields at Thélepte and Fériana and had stopped to build up. Patton would still have to advance another sixty miles to even restore the position as it existed before the Von Arnim–Rommel attacks. But Patton, looking ahead, visualized even more ambitious objectives than Alexander assigned him. Certainly he could retake the Eastern Dorsal, but why stop there? He could drive forward to Gabès, he insisted, and cut off Von Arnim's rear. But Alexander, still concerned about the combat capabilities of American troops, held firm. Patton could maintain an "active defense," he said, but his objectives should be "limited." He would be satisfied for Patton to retake the Eastern Dorsal.

Patton was ready to attack within less than two weeks after having assumed command on March 8. With II Corps now up to strength, he sent the 1st Division to retake Gafsa and continue eastward to El Guettar. North of the 1st Division he sent the 1st Armored toward Maknassy. El Guettar was occupied the first day, and by the end of March the Eastern Dorsal from Faid south was once more in American hands.

General Montgomery's Eighth Army began the attack on the Mareth Line the night of March 20. Resistance turned out to be stronger than expected, however, and his three infantry and two armored divisions were stopped cold. But in the meantime, however, he had sent the New Zealand Corps on a wide, two-hundred-mile end run around Von Arnim's right, hitting his rear area nearly forty miles behind the line. In making this long march the New Zealanders discovered that they were encountering no opposition, so Montgomery, on receiving this word, instantaneously changed his plan, reinforcing the New Zealanders with the 1st British Armoured Division, a move which cracked the Mareth Line. By March 28, a week after the attack began, Montgomery had reached Gabès. With no defense line short of Enfidaville about two hundred miles to the north, Von Arnim withdrew in a swift but orderly manner,

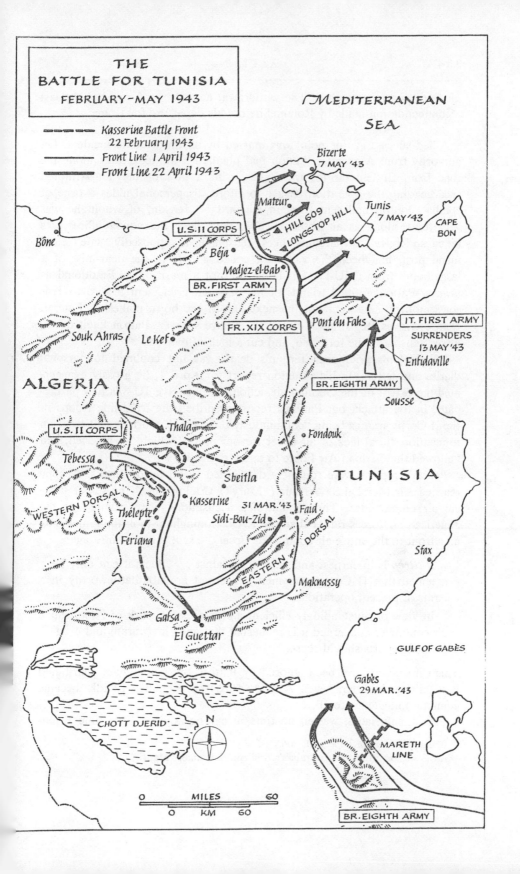

THE
BATTLE FOR TUNISIA
FEBRUARY–MAY 1943

Kasserine Battle Front
22 February 1943
Front Line 1 April 1943
Front Line 22 April 1943

MEDITERRANEAN
SEA

Bizerte
7 MAY '43

Mateur

Tunis
7 MAY '43

CAPE
BON

U.S. II CORPS

HILL 609

LONGSTOP HILL

Béja

Bône

Medjez-el-Bab

BR. FIRST ARMY

FR. XIX CORPS

Pont du Fahs

IT. FIRST ARMY
SURRENDERS
13 MAY '43

Souk Ahras

Le Kef

Enfidaville

BR. EIGHTH ARMY

Sousse

ALGERIA

U.S. II CORPS

Thala

Fondouk

TUNISIA

Tébessa

WESTERN DORSAL

Sbeitla

Kasserine

Thélepte

Sidi-Bou-Zid

31 MAR.'43

Faïd

DORSAL

Sfax

Fériana

EASTERN

Maknassy

Gafsa

El Guettar

GULF OF GABÈS

CHOTT DJERID

N

Gabès
29 MAR.'43

MARETH
LINE

0   MILES   60
0   KM   60

BR. EIGHTH ARMY

his force nearly unscathed. The withdrawal actually conformed to the last recommendation made by Rommel before his departure for Rome.

Allied success at this point was marred by an unfortunate incident. On authority from Alexander, Patton had planned a limited attack along the road from El Guettar toward Gabès, with a unit of the 1st Armored spearheading the operation. Eager to afford his personal aides a taste of combat, Patton had sent Captain Richard N. Jenson, of whom he was very fond, along as an observer. Two days later the young officer was killed under freakish circumstances. Jenson, in a supposedly "safe" command post, had been the victim of concussion from the near-miss of a large bomb from a JU-88. His body had not a mark on it. Emotional as always, Patton notified friends of his personal grief, sent a wire to Jenson's mother, and went out the next day to the boy's makeshift funeral. Before Graves Registration closed the mattress cover, Patton knelt down, kissed Jenson on the forehead, and cut a lock of hair.

But Patton's grief over Jenson's death was not confined to personal diaries and letters. In his situation report for April 1, he grossly exaggerated the extent of the German air action. Only twelve JU-88s had participated in the attack, but Patton's report described the front-line troops in the II Corps area as being "continuously bombed all morning." It went on to mention "total lack of air cover for our units," which, he asserted, had "allowed the German Air Force to operate at will."[13]

Patton's reports were routinely distributed to all headquarters. A copy reached Air Marshal Sir Arthur ("Mary") Coningham,[14] the senior tactical air commander. Though Patton's accusations were pointed at the American air forces rather than the RAF, Coningham took the remarks as an affront to the entire air command. Upset, he sent Patton a message:

> If *sitrep* is in earnest and balanced against . . . facts it can only be assumed that II Corps personnel concerned are not battleworthy in terms of present operations.
>
> In view of outstandingly efficient and successful work of American air command concerned it is requested that such inaccurate and exaggerated reports should cease.

This wire might have been ignored by Patton, but Coningham distributed it to all headquarters, even AFHQ. Thus the exchange rapidly became common knowledge to all.

Patton, infuriated, wasted no time in calling Algiers. This time Eisen-

---

[13] Blumenson, *Patton Papers,* II, 206.
[14] An evolution from the Australian's original nickname, "Maori."

hower also was distressed at what he considered an unnecessary affront to American troops, and he promised that Coningham would immediately send an apology to the troops. Soon Coningham's "apology" came, but it was "altogether inadequate," in Patton's words, as it simply "canceled" the previous message. Eisenhower therefore ordered Coningham to visit Patton at Gafsa to make amends.

Coningham arrived at II Corps Headquarters around noon on April 4. Patton, not certain that he would break bread with the Australian, had eaten lunch early, and he had previously instructed Hugh Gaffey, his chief of staff, to remain while they talked. He refused to shake hands.

In the course of the conversation Patton said that he personally was willing to accept Coningham's apologies but that an oral statement was not good enough for calling 60,000 American soldiers "unbattleworthy." Both men spoke loud and forcefully, but Patton finally gained the upper hand. "If I had said half of what you said," he shouted, "I would now be a colonel and on my way home." Coningham had to agree and promised to send another message retracting his remarks.

Then and only then would Patton shake hands. He took Coningham off to what was for Patton a second lunch. The meeting over, Patton fell ill with pains in his back, an ailment he assuaged by inspecting the front lines for relaxation.

The next day Coningham informed Eisenhower and Alexander of the results of his visit. His disparaging message, he said, had been misinterpreted. The text should be changed from the wording "II Corps personnel" to "few Corps personnel" and went on to dwell on his high regard for American forces. This was a lame apology but Patton, having made his point, accepted it and responded with the generosity of which he was always capable, by accepting partial responsibility for the misunderstanding.

On the bottom of the file copy of the message, however, Patton wrote by hand, "The sentence . . . I put in—though a lie—to save his face. I may need his help some day in another matter."

The Coningham incident having been smoothed over, Tedder consulted Spaatz and the two decided to visit Patton to cement the new cooperative spirit. On April 8, therefore, one week after the Patton report, Tedder, Spaatz, and Kuter arrived at Gafsa. Major General Omar N. Bradley, deputy corps commander, joined. The atmosphere was cordial. Hardly had Tedder finished his assurances of the over-all Allied air superiority, however, than four German FW-190s flew down the street, scattering people and camels alike, passing fifty feet from the window of the command post, and spraying machine gun bullets and dropping small bombs. Plaster fell from the ceiling and the door jammed. Tedder never quite lost his sense of humor. When the noise quieted down, he smiled slightly and said, "I always knew you were a good stage manager, but this takes the cake." Spaatz asked how the hell Patton had managed it.

"I'll be damned if I know," beamed a triumphant Patton, "but if I could find the sonsofbitches who flew those planes, I'd mail each one of them a medal."

The battle for Tunisia was now drawing to a close. Despite the fact that his losses in the withdrawal from Mareth were minimal, Von Arnim now faced superior numbers, with little room for maneuver—and he was pinned down by Allied air superiority. He prepared for his last-ditch stand on a line which included Tunis, Bizerte, and Cape Bon.

In the meantime General Eisenhower made frequent trips to the front, determined to keep his eye closely on the tactical situation without interfering unnecessarily with Alexander's conduct of the battle. Now, on April 14, Eisenhower was forced to assert himself over the objections of Alexander, or at least of his staff. Von Arnim had completed his weeklong withdrawal to the Enfidaville line the day before, and Montgomery's cannon ball had gone up the tube of the barrel according to plan. But the Americans of the II Corps now found themselves stranded, facing Montgomery's rear area with nobody to fight. This situation had been foreseen for some time, and Eisenhower had discussed it with Alexander and even General Marshall by cable.

Before this conference at Constantine, Alexander, with Eisenhower's acquiescence, had planned merely to send the U. S. 1st and 9th Divisions to serve under British command in reducing the remaining Axis bridgehead. This, Eisenhower had concluded, was not enough. The last phase of the battle for Tunisia could not be exclusively a British operation. The participation of the Americans was particularly important at this time because after Kasserine the image of the American troops was still tarnished back in the United States. Eventually the bulk of the war would be borne by the Americans, and it was important that troops presently training back home view the performance of those in Tunisia as a credit. This required American participation in the final victory.

Alexander and his logistics staff still demurred. From a tactical point of view the transfer of the II Corps to the north was unnecessary and inconvenient. Moving a force of 60,000 men with full equipment and vehicles across the overcrowded supply lines of the First Army would cause disruption, and the British V Corps, already in the line, was adequate for the final drive on Bizerte. Moreover—and more serious—Alexander had not yet overcome his doubts regarding the American troops. The implications of Kasserine had been revived only a week earlier in another incident, this time involving the U. S. 34th Division, which had rekindled the anger of the Americans and the suspicions of Alexander.[15]

But Eisenhower now insisted and for once gave Alexander a direct order to move the entire II Corps to the north, where, under its own command, it could drive on Bizerte. The British First and Eighth Armies, with the French XIX Corps, would attack Tunis.[16] The move was successful, and the corps displayed a remarkable professional performance, relieving the British V Corps in only a couple of days. The American command, now under General Bradley, was maturing.

Eisenhower's replacement of Patton with Bradley on April 15 reflected no discredit on Patton's performance. As he so vehemently pointed out to everyone, Patton had been acting as II Corps commander on a temporary basis; his primary role was to plan for the invasion of Sicily (HUSKY) as the future U. S. Seventh Army commander. But Patton had one thing to get off his chest, and he stopped off in Algiers to vent his ire on Eisenhower for exhibiting what he considered an excessively pro-British attitude. Eisenhower took Patton's words in stride, for at least he was talking in private. And to be criticized by each nationality for favoring the other came with his job as Allied Commander.[17]

*

To regard the end of the Tunisian operation as "easy" would be callous. The hardships, privations, and dangers of the front-line soldiers were always there. However, from the viewpoint of Allied unity, no significant further problems occurred. The battle line as finally drawn up consisted of U. S. II Corps (Bradley) on the north; British First Army (Anderson) on the right of the II Corps; French XIX Corps (Koeltz) on Anderson's right; and the British Eighth Army (Montgomery) on the extreme right, its flank resting on the Gulf of Hammamet. Since the Eighth Army was by all odds the largest force—and since Montgomery was attacking along the ideal avenue of approach—Von Arnim had stacked two

[15] The 34th Division had been attached to Lieutenant General Sir John T. Crocker's British IX Corps at Fondouk. It had failed in an attempt to cut off Von Arnim's rear and Crocker had criticized the Americans to the press. Though the furor had been minor, the bad publicity had reached the United States. The incident had brought to the fore the problem of American morale in Tunisia and at home.

[16] Alexander in his *Memoirs* wrote of the II Corps move to the north as if it had been his own idea in the first place. Eisenhower, in *Crusade,* minimizes Alexander's resistance.

[17] In a message to General Marshall regarding the Patton-Coningham incident, Eisenhower philosophized that the built-in animosity between the Americans and British had existed "ever since we had read our little red school history books." Eisenhower to Marshall, April 5, 1943. Quoted in Chandler, II, 1071.

German and three Italian divisions on Montgomery's front. By the end of April, Alexander could see Montgomery was not going to make much progress.

Before the final assault began on May 5, therefore, Alexander secretly moved some of Montgomery's divisions to Anderson's sector, where they would be less heavily opposed. Thus the final morale boosts fell to those who needed it most, British First Army and U. S. II Corps. Even the terrain seemed to balance the burdens—and the headlines—for each had a major obstacle to seize in its respective sector, a terrain feature with a name attractive to the press. In the II Corps sector was Djebel Tehent, which came to be known familiarly as "Hill 609." In the First Army sector the critical objective was called "Longstop Hill." Both were seized at about the same time. Bradley assigned Hill 609 to the previously unfortunate 34th Division, which, fighting under favorable circumstances for the first time, restored its damaged spirits. Bizerte fell to the U. S. 9th Division and the French Corps d'Afrique (part of II Corps) the same day that Tunis fell to the British 6th and 7th Armoured Divisions.

The last Axis units to surrender were the much-maligned Italians, who held out for nearly a week after the fall of Tunis and Bizerte. During the last week of fighting the Allies captured a total of about 275,000 prisoners, a figure exceeding those taken at Stalingrad.

On May 13 the Tunisian Campaign was over. General Eisenhower wrote home that he had a "lighter heart" than "for many a moon." His Allied team had worked well, and the three British commanders whom he referred to as "the three stars of the British Empire" had each become his warm, lifelong friend. The Allied team was molded, if not polished.

*

General Jürgen von Arnim, the highest-ranking prisoner taken by the Allies, was expecting the comradely treatment so often accorded between professional soldiers. He asked to call on General Eisenhower. Kenneth Strong, the G-2 (Intelligence), brought the message. Eisenhower, to whom the war had become a crusade in a real sense, held no such interest. He fixed Strong with a steely look.

"Get all the information that you can out of him," Eisenhower snarled. "But as for his paying a call, the only German generals I'm interested in are the ones we haven't captured yet."

Part Four

CHAPTER XVII

WE CANNOT AFFORD
TO REMAIN IDLE

In the spring of 1943, with the end of the Tunisian campaign in sight, President Franklin Roosevelt had domestic matters as well as the war on his mind. The tough, shrewd, bushy-browed John L. Lewis, president of the United Mine Workers, had called a strike for all organized coal miners. Determined not to allow the nation's resources to be paralyzed, Roosevelt sent an order to Harold Ickes, Secretary of the Interior and Solid Fuels Administrator, to take over all bituminous and anthracite mines that Lewis might shut down. The U.S. flag should be flown at each, he directed, and the U. S. Army would provide security against sabotage.

A couple of days later, on Sunday, May 2, Roosevelt received a message as he was being wheeled to the elevator on the second floor of the White House. On the ground floor he was to broadcast an appeal to the miners. This late word was news of tactical triumph: Lewis had just announced that the miners would return. Not one to be upstaged, Roosevelt went through with his speech as if no word had reached him.

The settlement of the coal strike now freed the President's mind for the upcoming Third Washington Conference with Prime Minister Churchill, which was to be held in a little over a week. Scarcely three months had passed since Roosevelt's return from the Casablanca Conference, but events were moving rapidly; and though it had been agreed that the Allies would follow up a Tunisian victory with an invasion of Sicily (HUSKY), they had addressed nothing beyond that. HUSKY would surely take place only a couple of months hence, and there was no time to lose in coming to some agreement as to the move after that. Thus General Eisenhower, in

Algiers, was thinking in terms of the Sicilian invasion before the Tunisian campaign was over and the top leaders in London and Washington were thinking two jumps ahead, beyond Sicily.[1]

*

The Third Washington Conference (TRIDENT), in May 1943, came about with a minimum of hesitancy and counterproposals. On a trip to Washington in March Foreign Minister Anthony Eden had received the impression that the Americans would welcome a meeting of Churchill, Brooke, Marshall, Hopkins, and Eisenhower in Algiers to decide on the next (post-Sicily) move. On April 11 Churchill sent such a proposal to Roosevelt, who, however, refused to agree to such a dramatic and important meeting in which he would not participate. There the matter stood until Churchill, on April 29, proposed that he once again come with a large party to Washington. Roosevelt accepted on the same day as his radio speech to the coal miners, inviting Churchill once more to stay with him in the White House. Churchill, as always, was all set to go.

Whenever the Prime Minister traveled, the mode of transportation remained unsettled until the last minute. This caused no difficulty because time was not so pressing as it had been a year earlier, and the threat of U-boats was noticeably letting up. (The Battle of the Atlantic is considered to have been "won" as of mid-May.) Besides, the Queen Mary happened to be available.

Churchill preferred the sea and for once used his health to justify this slower mode of travel. The comfortable but undefended flying boats were confined to the northern route, not yet open this early in the summer; and travel at 10,000 feet by unpressurized bomber, Churchill claimed, might bring on a recurrence of the pneumonia he had contracted after returning to London in early February. That settled it: the party would travel on the Queen Mary. Two days after Roosevelt's confirmation Churchill, along with a hundred officers and clerks, left London for the Clyde River. The Atlantic trip would take six days.

Accommodations on the Queen Mary were comfortable. Members of the official party were housed in cabins on the top deck; communications facilities and maps were plentiful. Though the ship would observe strict radio silence, messages would be sent visually from the Queen Mary to accompanying destroyers and then transmitted by radio from a safe distance. The ship carried a strange cargo; it included Churchill's delegation

[1] Ismay has called 1943 the "Conference Year." And so it was. With Casablanca (SYMBOL) in January; Washington (TRIDENT) in May; Quebec (QUADRANT) in August; and Cairo-Teheran (SEXTANT-EUREKA) in November and December, the Anglo-Americans averaged something like a full-scale conference every two and a half months.

and, as well, some 5,000 German prisoners taken in Tunisia. Also stacked away in a remote part of the ship were some vermin-infested materials sealed in airtight compartments.

During the journey the BCOS met daily, sometimes twice. The Prime Minister would usually meet with them in the afternoon. General Wavell, Lord Frederick Leathers (Minister of Transport), and Ismay were aboard, Wavell to advise on Burma. At least one emergency drill was held, at which time the Prime Minister demanded a mounted machine gun for his personal lifeboat. If the ship should go down—the most remote of possibilities—Mr. Churchill would not be taken alive.

On the morning of Tuesday, May 11, the *Queen Mary* docked at Staten Island. The party was met by Harry Hopkins, and a luxurious train whisked them to Washington. On the train they had lunch, which included a "small steak." This, Ismay noted, represented a weekly meat ration for the British. None of them could finish the whole thing.

*

TRIDENT would have been a more harmonious gathering if the participants could have started exactly where the Casablanca Conference had left off. But time had elapsed, sufficient time for both British and Americans to put the Casablanca agreements into effect and for each to evaluate the zeal with which the other had adhered to spirit and letter. In this case the Americans had made almost all the concessions at Casablanca and to some of the British they appeared to be dragging their feet in implementing those points on which they had given way. Alan Brooke, for one, felt the Americans had not done their best, and he personally could do little to force them. The Americans, Brooke recalled, regarded the Casablanca decisions as defeats, and in his view were preparing "a counteroffensive." Brooke knew that the Americans had learned from the thoroughness of British preparations for Casablanca and had determined in the future to be likewise prepared.

The key man, as Brooke saw it, was General Marshall, who possessed enormous power for the allocation of resources and who, when forced to choose between King's Pacific strategy and the British concept of further action in the Mediterranean, still seemed to prefer supporting King. Further involvement in the Mediterranean, to Marshall, would endanger even an eventual ROUNDUP.

Brooke had showed his distress with the American attitude as early as February 25, when he had written: "Am very worried by the way the Americans are failing to live up to our Casablanca agreements. They are entirely breaking down over promises of American divisions to arrive in this country." He was even fearful for the survival of the basic "Europe First" strategy.[2]

After the Prime Minister's train reached Washington the party spent the rest of the day, May 11, settling down and attending a welcoming reception. The first plenary meeting (of six) took place the next day, May 12, at 2:30 P.M. Once again, as a year earlier, the group gathered in President Roosevelt's Oval Study. Not many were present: besides the Prime Minister and President only the BCOS (including Ismay) plus Field Marshal Dill participated; the American side comprised only the Joint Chiefs and Harry Hopkins.[3]

The American JCS were of course used to this office because here they periodically met with the President. But to the British the room had a special meaning, for it evoked memories of a year before, when the word had come in that Tobruk had fallen. Churchill and Brooke recalled vividly how General Marshall had, without hesitation, stripped a couple of American armored divisions to provide three hundred Sherman tanks to the defeated British Eighth Army. When Churchill felt impelled to mention that meeting, however, he met a cold reaction. The Americans, who associated that meeting with the first of their major negotiating defeats, recalled it with irritation. Even President Roosevelt's generous reference to TORCH's having been "set on foot" in this room only reinforced the determination of the American military not to be outdebated again.

Prime Minister Churchill did not at first sense the American stiffening and he opened with a discourse on the benefits to be gained by the fall of Fascist Italy. Such a collapse, he intoned, would cause "a chill of loneliness over the German people, and might be the beginning of their doom." But even if Italy's dropping out of the war should not prove "immediately fatal" to Germany, the results would be great. Turkey would be affected, as she always compared herself with Italy in the Mediterranean. And there might be, Churchill went on, a parallel to 1918 when Germany might have continued the fight on the Meuse or the Rhine except for the defection of Bulgaria, which "brought the whole of the enemy structure crashing to the ground."[4]

Churchill's eloquence failed to move the Americans; it even prompted a sarcastic imitation by Harry Hopkins when he later described the event to a curious absentee.[5] Roosevelt, also, was now noticeably inserting more of

[2] Bryant, *Turn of the Tide*, pp. 492–93.
[3] Lieutenant General Joseph McNarney, Marshall's deputy, substituted for General Arnold, who had suffered a heart attack.
[4] Churchill, IV, 791.
[5] Moran, p. 102.

his own views into the strategic conversations. The President had obviously been communicating far more with the Joint Chiefs of Staff than previously.

Through it all, Alan Brooke, increasingly depressed by the entire scene, bided his time by trying to memorize the peculiar, very personal collection of paraphernalia on the President's desk: a blue lamp, two frames, a bronze bust of Mrs. Roosevelt, a bronze ship's steering wheel clock, four cloth toy donkeys, one tin toy motorcar, one small donkey made of two hazel nuts, a jug of ice water, and other articles. The donkeys for some reason were particularly memorable from the previous June.[6]

The next day the Combined Chiefs of Staff met at 10:30 A.M. Admiral Leahy opened by presenting the American viewpoint, which (1) allowed considerable latitude for the diversion of force in the Pacific and (2) specified that the European war would be finished most quickly by the early establishment of a second front in France. This line was what the pessimistic British Chiefs had been expecting.

A new wrinkle was introduced on Friday, May 14, however. Since an invasion of Burma was now on the agenda, the list of conferees that morning included representatives from the China-Burma-India Theater: Field Marshal Sir Archibald Wavell, Admiral Sir James Somerville, and Air Chief Marshal Sir Richard Peirse. Lieutenant General Joseph W. Stilwell and Major General Claire L. Chennault had come from China to participate for the Americans. Including these strong personalities in negotiations only added to the normal confusion, for not only did the British and American viewpoints differ, but the two Americans, Stilwell and Chennault, also disagreed. The British were generally negative regarding any large attack soon in Burma: the supply problem was just too great. Chennault, however, promised that his 14th U. S. Air Force could do much to bring Japan to her knees—that is, if all the tonnage available for the Far East should be allocated to him. Only Stilwell saw the need for an immediate ground invasion of Burma.

The differences were more than merely logistical. The Americans had felt closely associated with Chiang Kai-shek from the 1930s, when from the Philippines they had watched the Japanese occupying the China coast. American support for Chiang had been strengthened by the public charm of his American-educated wife, whose command of the English language entranced the American press. And the faith the Americans held in the Chinese potential was shared by the President and the military alike. But it was not shared by the British.

[6] Bryant, *Turn of the Tide*, p. 505. Brooke's diary mistakenly refers to July.

Discussion of operations in Burma would have been difficult enough under any circumstances, but they were made doubly so by the personality of Stilwell, theoretically Chennault's superior. Brooke described him as "a strange character . . . one of Marshall's selections . . . a stout-hearted fighter suitable to lead a brigade of Chinese scallywags [though] I could see no [other] qualities in him . . . a Chinese linguist [with] little military knowledge and no strategic ability . . . [whose] worst failing was, however, his deep-rooted hatred of anybody or anything British. It was practically impossible to establish friendly relations with him. . . ."[7]

This harsh evaluation did injustice to Stilwell's generally accepted ability as a troop commander. However, it well portrays Stilwell's personality as seen (rather accurately) by the British. Even Ismay later wrote that Stilwell ". . . was essentially an individualist who was incapable of cooperating with anybody." He hated the British and despised Chiang Kai-shek, but his pet aversion was his own countryman, General Chennault. "They fought like cat and dog from the beginning to the end. . . ."[8]

And Stilwell, on his part, wrote in his oft-quoted diary: "Nobody was interested in the humdrum work of building a ground force but me. Chennault promised to drive the Japs right out of China in six months, so why not give him the stuff to do it? It was the short cut to victory. . . . With Wavell in command, failure was inevitable; he had nothing to offer at any meeting except protestations that the thing was impossible, hopeless, impractical. Churchill even spoke of it as silly. The Limeys all wanted to wait another year. After the Akyab fiasco,[9] the four Jap divisions in Burma had them scared to death."

Stilwell also had views on the political chiefs: that "Churchill has Roosevelt in his pocket. . . . The Limeys are not interested in the war in the Pacific, and with the President hypnotized they are sitting pretty.

"Roosevelt wouldn't let me speak my piece. I interrupted twice, but Churchill kept pulling away from the subject, and it was impossible.

"So everything was thrown to the air offensive. . . . They will do the Japs some damage but at the same time will so weaken the ground effort that it may fail. Then what the hell use is it to knock down a few Jap planes?"[10]

Though Stilwell's judgments were biting, his evaluation of the outcome

7 Ibid., pp. 505–6.
8 Ismay, p. 299. For a thorough and amusing description of the Stilwell-Chennault feud, see Theodore White, *In Search of History*, pp. 138–44.
9 An unsuccessful attempted counteroffensive by Wavell on the west coast of Burma from September 1942 to May 1943.
10 Stilwell, pp. 204–5.

was essentially correct. The bulk of the logistical effort in China would go to the air war directed by Claire Chennault.

With the atmosphere in Washington becoming increasingly acrimonious, it was fortunate that the weekend came. As a year before, Roosevelt and Churchill went their way and the Combined Chiefs went theirs. This time, instead of going to Hyde Park, Roosevelt chose a closer location, a small camp in the Catoctin Mountains of Maryland known as Shangri-La.[11] The drive from Washington required three hours in those days, and the route took the Roosevelt-Churchill-Hopkins party through Frederick, Maryland. There beside the road stood the house of the legendary Barbara Fritchie, immortalized by the poet John Greenleaf Whittier for her defiant gesture during the Confederate invasion of September 1862. Hopkins and Roosevelt, like many Americans, could quote only two lines: " 'Shoot, if you must, this old gray head, but spare your country's flag,' she said." Whereupon Churchill, drawing on his memory of years earlier, proceeded to recite the entire poem. His accuracy may not have been perfect, but none of his hosts could correct him. After spending a pleasant night in the cool air, the three returned to Washington Monday morning.

In the meantime General Marshall was again host for the military delegation, and he took the British to see the original capital of Virginia, restored to resemble its appearance during British colonial rule. Once at Williamsburg it was only natural to make a stop at nearby Yorktown. Ismay, it so happened, had served some years in India, where Lord Cornwallis had regained his reputation after the surrender during the American Revolution. Feigning temporary lapse of memory, Ismay mused, "Let's see, what was the name of that chap that did so badly here?"[12] After a candlelight dinner in the Raleigh Tavern—and with plenty of birds for Brooke to observe—the Combined Chiefs returned to Washington the next day and held a meeting the same Sunday afternoon.

*

On Wednesday, May 19, 1943, Prime Minister Winston Churchill addressed a joint session of Congress for the second time in seventeen months. His former address, just after Pearl Harbor, had been delivered

---

[11] The camp had been named Shangri-La at the time of the Doolittle raid on Tokyo in April of 1942. Since no announcement could be made as to the location from which Doolittle's B-25s had been launched, Roosevelt had simply described it as Shangri-La, the setting of Hilton's *Lost Horizon*. (Actually the planes were launched from a carrier.) The name "Shangri-La" had caught Roosevelt's imagination, and he named the camp after it. Twenty years later President Dwight D. Eisenhower renamed it Camp David, which it remains at least at this writing.

[12] Pogue, II, 203.

in an atmosphere of rage and defiance, so Churchill could be excused for crowing a bit this time. After all, it had been only a week since the Axis surrender in Tunisia:

> For this we have to thank the military intuition of Corporal Hitler. We may notice, as I predicted in the House of Commons three months ago, the touch of the master-hand. The same insensate obstinacy which condemned Field-Marshal von Paulus and his army to destruction at Stalingrad has brought this new catastrophe upon our enemies in Tunisia. . . .
>
> The African excursions of the two Dictators have cost their countries in killed and captured 950,000 soldiers. In addition nearly 2,400,000 gross tons of shipping have been sunk and nearly 8000 aircraft destroyed, both of these figures being exclusive of large numbers of ships and aircraft damaged. There have also been lost to the enemy 6200 guns, 2550 tanks, and 70,000 trucks. . . . Arrived at this milestone in the war, we can say, "One continent redeemed." . . .[13]

Churchill's address, as usual, was well received. It pleased the Congress and it also pleased the President. But Churchill's words were not mere self-congratulation. By dwelling on the huge successes attained as the result of following British strategy, Churchill had strengthened his position in the arguments as to what to do next.

That same day, May 19, constituted the crucial point of the TRIDENT Conference. As at Casablanca, agreement was reached just when all seemed to be lost. The Combined Chiefs met at 10:30 A.M. and then again at 4:30 P.M. and in the latter meeting the atmosphere degenerated to the point that Marshall suggested putting it off the record. The British assented, and the thirty advisers were dismissed. Only the eight principals —four British and four Americans—remained.

Thus freed from the scrutiny of their staffs, the Chiefs finally reached a compromise, which naturally included something for both sides. The Americans were happy to receive assurances of a target date of May 1, 1944, for the cross-Channel invasion, henceforth to be known as OVERLORD. Further, Marshall secured an agreement that seven divisions would be transferred from the Mediterranean to the United Kingdom beginning on November 1, six months away. The Americans, on their part, conceded the possibility of continued operations in the Mediterranean after the fall of Sicily. The wording was vague, allowing for actions "best calculated to eliminate Italy from the war and to contain the greatest

[13] Churchill, IV, 799.

number of German forces." They did not specify at this point what area of the Mediterranean would be the next target; in fact they inserted the caveat that each subsequent move would first have to be approved by themselves, the CCS. Neither Italy nor Sardinia was mentioned by name. By 6:00 P.M. the CCS were at the White House to report to the President and the Prime Minister.

*

Thus ended the formal portion of the Third Washington Conference. The agreement on May 1, 1944, as the target date for OVERLORD appeared to be a fair exchange for leaving a door ajar to further operations in the Mediterranean. Both sides seemed satisfied.

But the troubles were not quite finished, for Churchill now had a whole weekend to rethink the issues and his concessions. He had not, he apparently concluded, driven a hard enough bargain, and on Monday afternoon the Prime Minister began reopening the strategic concepts. To Brooke's horror, the items reopened were confined to those the British had conceded. Two weeks of hard work and tension could now be nullified, and such an action could destroy what trust the Americans still had. And the credibility of the BCOS was at stake also, for the Americans would inevitably believe that they had gone to Churchill behind their backs. Though Brooke was innocent of such chicanery, he knew that Roosevelt would never personally reopen issues already decided without advice from his military, and he feared that the Americans might presume the same of Churchill. But Churchill, on his own, simply desired everything to conform exactly to the positions he had drawn up on the *Queen Mary*.

Just as all seemed ready to fall apart, Harry Hopkins pulled Churchill aside and confidentially told him of the dire consequences of reopening these issues. Churchill listened attentively and decided to retreat, saving face by making changes in matters of rhetoric.

Still the Prime Minister was far from satisfied. The American failure to mention Italy in the agreement rankled, and he began to seek other avenues to get his way. Again Hopkins came forward. President Roosevelt's back was up, he said, and it would take a week to change his mind —and the prospects even then were uncertain.[14] Churchill therefore decided to make a journey to see General Eisenhower in Algiers, as the views of the Allied Commander would obviously carry tremendous weight in Washington. To gainsay any accusation of underhanded intentions, however, Churchill requested Roosevelt to allow General Marshall to accompany him. The Chief of Staff, who had been hoping to visit the Pacific with Admiral King, was disappointed, if only because he needed a rest.

[14] Ibid., p. 810.

But when the request to go with Churchill was brought up, Marshall agreed with a slight wave of the hand.

Though George Marshall, the good soldier, concealed his disappointment, Secretary of War Stimson suffered from no such inhibitions. "To think of picking out the strongest man there is in America," he wrote, "and Marshall is surely that today, the one on whom the fate of the war depends, and then to deprive him in a gamble of a much needed opportunity to recoup his strength . . . and send him off on a difficult and rather dangerous trip across the Atlantic where he is not needed except for Churchill's purposes is, I think, going pretty far."[15]

Henry Stimson was a strong, outspoken man, whose mistrust of the British may have stemmed from his experiences as Secretary of State under Herbert Hoover. But to object to the "dangers" of Marshall's traveling with the Prime Minister was, to use his own words, "going pretty far." Stimson was sincere, but his views either were not expressed to the President or were ignored.

Churchill had long known that Marshall was influential in matters pertaining to strategy in Europe, and he had begun dealing with Marshall on a direct, informal basis as early as the Arcadia Conference just after Pearl Harbor. But Marshall could not fully appreciate the Mediterranean scene from Washington, so the Prime Minister was luring his target to Algiers, where he hoped the "Mediterranean strategy" would look more attractive than when viewed from Washington. Or so Churchill reasoned.

Aside from softening Marshall's resistance toward the Mediterranean, however, Churchill had every reason to want to see Eisenhower. The British and Americans, in Washington, had agreed to conduct operations "best calculated to eliminate Italy from the war and to contain the greatest number of German forces." These vague words represented no decision at all. The vacuum, therefore, placed Eisenhower in a position to interpret their meaning. Thus Eisenhower had by default become the key man in the whole discussion. Churchill also suspected that in General Eisenhower he would have at least a partially sympathetic ear, for Eisenhower, as Allied Commander, would be the man commanding the 1,500,000 men who would lack an objective for a year if action were to cease after Sicily. Churchill knew that no commander would like such an idea.

And Churchill was right: Eisenhower had been giving further operations in the Mediterranean much serious thought. As early as April 19, with Von Arnim's forces cornered in northeast Tunisia, Eisenhower had wired Marshall regarding future action, specifically as to his own next

[15] Stimson diary, May 25, 1943, quoted in Pogue, II, 213.

move should the Sicily campaign turn out to be easy. If the Axis there should collapse suddenly, Eisenhower believed, he should be ready to move instantly to some other worthwhile objectives. This he could do with the forces he had right there on hand.

Eisenhower's message had gone even further, analyzing what these "worthwhile objectives" would be. He favored Italy, though he recognized the objection to assuming the responsibility to provide for large segments of the civilian population. To avoid this, he could confine an invasion to a small area in the south[16] where the large airfields would make it possible to hit Ploesti and central Germany with his bombers. Marshall's answer had *not* been a flat no. Eisenhower, he advised, should be ready for prompt exploitation if HUSKY went well, naming Sardinia, Corsica, or the heel of the boot as possibilities.[17]

Both men were always reluctant to launch a major invasion of Italy, and neither would consider any operation that could interfere with the cross-Channel invasion the next year. However, they recognized that circumstances could practically force further operations in the Mediterranean in 1943. Marshall was not nearly so adamant as he had to pretend to be in the presence of Churchill.

*

On the morning of Wednesday, May 26, 1943, the various members of Churchill's party—Marshall, Brooke, Ismay, and others—were picked up by staff cars and delivered to a flying boat moored on the Potomac. The President and Harry Hopkins accompanied Churchill from the White House, and while final preparations were being made Roosevelt chatted with Brooke, repeating his previous invitation to visit Hyde Park. Brooke was again touched. The party took off at 8:30 A.M.; its first destination was Botwood, Newfoundland.

Once in the air, the Prime Minister pulled out some papers and showed them to General Marshall. In the hectic last days of the meeting Churchill and Roosevelt had worked on several messages to Stalin explaining what had been—or rather what had not been—decided at TRIDENT. Churchill had with him various drafts, not yet agreed, and still in a state of some disarray. Marshall, though weary, took the papers to another section of the airplane and within a couple of hours returned a clean copy. Churchill, a severe critic as an English wordsmith, was struck by the quality of Marshall's version, and he saw a new side of the Chief of Staff, a grasp of the political considerations that Churchill had not previously observed. At Botwood, Churchill cabled Marshall's text back to Roosevelt, who subsequently sent it to Stalin unchanged.

The pause at Botwood was short. The next leg of the journey would

16 Chandler, II, 1096.
17 Ibid., p. 1097.

cover the twenty-seven hundred miles to Gibraltar, and the passengers went to bed almost immediately after take-off. During the night Churchill awoke at the sound of loud noises. He crawled up to the cockpit of the airplane to check on the difficulty. The plane, the pilot answered casually, had been struck by lightning, but all was well. The Prime Minister went back to sleep, unaware that more apprehension had been felt among the crew than they had let on.

By dawn Churchill was as usual in the co-pilot's seat, and by midmorning was poring over accumulated dispatches. A still-weary Marshall, who was reading a book, developed an uncomfortable feeling that once Churchill had finished with his papers he would be back pounding once more on the virtues of a Mediterranean strategy.

Marshall sensed right. As soon as the Prime Minister had finished with his dispatches, he headed for Marshall's seat. Marshall, however, had a plan to avoid discussing strategy, at least until lunch. The book he was reading, loaned to him by Lord Halifax, the British ambassador in Washington, dealt with the dramatic and lengthy impeachment trial of one Warren Hastings, a former governor general of India. As Churchill sat down, therefore, Marshall brought up the matter of the Hastings trial and asked some questions calculated to titillate. Churchill took the bait, and for twenty minutes gave a discourse on the difference between "impeachment" in the United States and the "bill of attainder" in Britain. This he did so clearly that Marshall became interested. Then, when Churchill had finished on this subject, Marshall had another question: the significance of the dramatic flight of Rudolf Hess to Scotland in May 1941. Churchill again held forth.

With lunch approaching, Marshall finally inquired as to Churchill's role in the abdication of King Edward VIII in 1936, this time fearing that he could be touching a raw nerve. Not so: Churchill talked on, covering the various legal and political ramifications, and concluding that the King should have married Mrs. Wallis Simpson arbitrarily and dropped the matter in the lap of Parliament. At about this time came the call to lunch.[18] Churchill had enjoyed the conversation immensely and later glowingly reported his success in convincing Marshall that the "sovereign procedure" of the British Bill of Attainder must be retained.[19]

As the flying boat neared Gibraltar the passengers were uncomfortable to note that no fighter escort had been provided. Furthermore, a couple of strange-looking aircraft, probably Spanish, seemed to be showing interest. Concerns proved groundless, however, and the flying boat landed at 5:00 P.M. As it was late in the day, the party, as usual, stayed overnight in the Convent.

[18] Anecdote from Pogue, III, 215.
[19] Attainder, a power retained by Parliament, involves dishonor and loss of civil rights. It is associated with treason, thus going beyond impeachment.

The next morning, May 28, Marshall and Brooke were conducted around the defenses of the Rock of Gibraltar, and the Churchill-Marshall party then left in the early afternoon on a British Catalina. Because the Mediterranean had been cleared of Axis aircraft, the flight was in no danger, and on arrival at Maison Blanche Airport, Algiers, the party found Eisenhower, Alexander, Cunningham, and Coningham on hand. Eisenhower had planned to stick with his procedure of the previous February and send Churchill and Brooke ahead while he followed with Marshall. This time Churchill would have none of the arrangement and insisted that Eisenhower go along with him. This gesture, whether calculated or not, allowed no time for Eisenhower to talk to Marshall before Churchill could get in his own point of view to Eisenhower. Immediately on arrival the Prime Minister walked over from Cunningham's villa to Eisenhower's a hundred yards away and began pounding again on his thesis that Italy must be the next goal after Sicily.

Eisenhower, as always, was willing to entertain any strategic idea to exploit success so long as it would not divert resources from the cross-Channel invasion the next year. However, he soon became a bit bewildered by Churchill's repetitions, which continued throughout dinner that evening. Having completed his work on Eisenhower, Churchill then seemed to turn back to Marshall, leaving Brooke and Eisenhower together.

The next morning Churchill learned that both Giraud and De Gaulle would soon be present in town. He therefore sent a message to London urging Eden to come to Algiers. In touchy political matters such as this Churchill liked to lean on his Foreign Minister: "He is much better fitted than I am to be best man at the Giraud–De Gaulle wedding." This political aspect of Churchill's visit would be an exclusively British activity, as General Marshall could not—or would not—speak for the President on political matters. Churchill also arranged to meet with General A. J. Georges, a retired French officer now working closely with Giraud, whom Churchill had mentioned to De Gaulle at Casablanca. Georges might prove to be helpful in this difficult period ahead.

The events of that day, May 29, 1943, as reported by Churchill, demonstrate the Prime Minister's attitude regarding Anglo-American relationships. After his meeting with General Georges, Churchill called in Brooke, Tedder, Cunningham, and Alexander for a "British" conference to prepare for facing the Americans that afternoon. Alexander, Cunningham, and Tedder were theoretically Eisenhower's subordinates, who reported, at least by American concepts of command, to him. But to the Prime Minister, they were his own British advisers rather than "Allied" commanders; in conference they were expected to hew to an agreed British position. Not surprisingly, they fell into the line as Churchill desired: Sicily should be followed up in the Mediterranean; OVERLORD the next year should be viewed as a vague distant development, almost a British concession to the Americans.

Churchill's attitude toward Eisenhower's command at this time reveals —though he never said so openly—that he regarded Eisenhower as a sort of constitutional monarch, whose continuing position as Supreme Commander should be a cause for the Americans to be grateful. In a way he had a point, for three quarters of the ground forces in the Mediterranean were British, as were four fifths of the naval forces and half the air forces. Since Alamein the British had lost eight times as many men as the Americans. And yet the British had acceded to the appointment of Eisenhower, an American, as Allied Commander, retaining the "American" complexion of the North African battle!

Churchill banked on an American virtue which he planned to exploit to the fullest—their natural generosity. "If you treat Americans well," he confided, "they always want to treat you better."[20] This was shrewd thinking and not without a certain grudging admiration. But it was British thinking, not Allied, even though the discussions would be focused on "Allied" strategy.

That afternoon the British and Americans met on the porch of Eisenhower's villa with Eisenhower, as host, presiding. Marshall and Bedell Smith flanked him. Churchill sat opposite Eisenhower with Brooke, Alexander, Cunningham, Tedder, and Ismay. The first subject to be addressed was the proposed attack on Pantelleria. A small island with rocky shores, heavy armament, and a garrison of 10,000 Italians, Pantelleria had been described by some as the "Gibraltar of the Eastern Mediterranean." Seizing it could be difficult, but Eisenhower, backed by Cunningham, was insisting that it be assaulted within a couple of weeks. Alexander remained strongly opposed, fearing that the British division scheduled to attack would incur "unthinkable" casualties. Tedder opposed the operation at first, but he had come around to Eisenhower's views as, like Eisenhower, he wanted its airfield. In the light of the short range of British Spitfires and American P-40s[21] it was nearly vital for the invasion of southern Sicily.

Eisenhower's decision to go ahead with the attack fell within his purview as Allied Commander; therefore this portion of the meeting consisted only of a briefing and short discussion. Churchill, perhaps to comfort Alexander or needing to insert at least something, declared his satisfaction.

Then, at Churchill's request, Eisenhower outlined the plan for the inva-

20 Churchill, IV, 817.
21 *Crusade*, p. 165.

sion of Sicily. This tactical matter presented little problem, and all present seemed satisfied with the way supplies were flowing forward. Attention now turned to the real reason for the conference, the next move beyond Sicily. Eisenhower, as Churchill had expected, was less adamant than Marshall. He agreed with Brooke's argument that the Russian Army was the only land force that could do much during 1943 and that the Western Allies should try to divert Germans from the Russian front. Therefore, if capturing Sicily should prove easy, the Allies ought to go directly into Italy, a viewpoint consistent with his previous exchanges with Marshall. Churchill was prone to consider this a "decision" in the light of Eisenhower's flexible instructions from TRIDENT. In turn, therefore, Churchill verified May 1, 1944, as the date for a force of twenty-nine divisions to invade across the Channel. This reaffirmation of Churchill's, of course, was the main point on which both Marshall and Eisenhower insisted and which had already been agreed on in Washington.

Throughout the discussions Marshall remained aloof and non-committal because, as he later revealed, he was simply tired of talking on the subject. Nothing transpired to disrupt his former agreement that definite plans could not be made until the extent of the resistance in Sicily was known. Churchill seemed to believe that Sicily could be cleared by August 15, but Marshall remained non-committal even on that question.

At the end of the meeting Eisenhower declared that the discussion had simplified his own planning problem. He summarized that if Sicily were to succeed within a week, he would at once cross the Strait of Messina into the toe of Italy. If not, he would submit recommendations. To make the alternatives easy he would create two staffs, one to plan for an invasion of Sardinia and one for southern Italy.

The next day was Memorial Day, and General Marshall paid a visit to American combat troops. Since the units were still in Tunisia, Marshall flew to Constantine and then went to visit the 34th Division, staying overnight. While Marshall was gone Churchill spent his time writing a very extensive memorandum for future arguments and at 9:45 P.M. he called Eisenhower to ask if he could walk over for a short visit. He was a little late in arriving and then bent Eisenhower's ear for two hours. Alan Brooke could be forgiven a bit of a chuckle the next day, having undergone the same experience himself many times.

Foreign Minister Anthony Eden appeared for the second meeting, again in Eisenhower's villa, on the afternoon of May 31. For openers the Prime Minister reviewed his previous position, stressing with all his power the advantage of an invasion of southern Italy. "The alternative between southern Italy and Sardinia," he said, "involves the difference between a glorious campaign and a mere convenience." He then followed up with a new offer. So passionately did he desire to see Italy out of the way (and Rome in Allied possession) that he would be willing to commit eight additional British divisions from other parts of the Middle East, bringing the potential number of Commonwealth divisions available for Sicily up to twenty, as contrasted to the nine American. Never mind that the limitations were on shipping and logistics, not troops.

There the positions stood: Churchill for a definite commitment to attack the southern portion of Italy; Marshall hostile but not closed-minded, determined to await developments; Eisenhower less reluctant than Marshall, but also convinced that a final decision would have to come later. As Eisenhower recalled his feelings, "These and other reasons led to an agreement which, in effect, left exploitation of the Sicilian operation to my judgment—but expected me to take advantage of any favorable opportunity to rush into Italy. . . ."[22]

One incident in the course of the later discussions created an uncomfortable misunderstanding. Anthony Eden, in addressing the Turkish situation, remarked that knocking Italy out of the war would go a long way toward bringing the Turks in. So far so good. But he then added that the Turks would become much more friendly "when our troops had reached the Balkan area." Instantly the Prime Minister jumped in to assure the Americans that he was *not* advocating sending an army into the Balkans, either now or in the near future. Eden backed off, but this inadvertent remark gave rise in the minds of the Americans to the belief that Churchill was secretly hoping for a major effort toward Germany through the Balkans.

Churchill has since written that he had no more pleasant memories of the war than of those ten days spent in Algiers and Tunis. And well he might. The Allies had won their first major campaign, capturing some 275,000 Axis troops; and the thinking now was on how to exploit victory rather than how to stave off defeat. The pictures of the meetings of the principals show all looking calm, even smug. The most publicized photo, taken on a balcony of Eisenhower's villa, shows the Prime Minister seated, white suit and cigar, beaming at a map as if about to carve a juicy turkey; Eden, Eisenhower, Brooke, and Marshall are seated around him. And standing just behind, leaning slightly and properly attentive, are Alexander, Cunningham, and Montgomery, apparently engrossed in Churchill's map. Only Tedder spoils the picture by glazing whimsically, pipe in hand, off into space. Confidence oozed from all pores.

The conferees spent the two days following May 31 relaxing, each in his own way. Churchill and Alexander flew to Tunisia, where the Prime

[22] *Crusade,* p. 168.

Minister spoke to thousands of troops in a Roman amphitheater, the acoustics so effective that no loudspeaker was necessary. And the next day Marshall held a memorable press conference. He began by asking for all questions at once, then answered each in detail, turning and facing the individual who had asked. Though he was admittedly dealing with subjects in which he had been immersed for a long time, his memory and assurance astonished the witnesses. And after seeing with his own eyes the vast cages of prisoners taken in the recent campaign, Marshall let down just a touch. Now, he told Ismay, he viewed TORCH "with a less jaundiced eye." This was a lavish statement from George Marshall.

*

To General Eisenhower this conference represented only an interlude in the hectic days of planning for HUSKY. His later writings do not dwell on it. To him the most significant aspect was a conversation he had one day with Brooke. As Eisenhower understood it, Brooke volunteered that he "would be glad to reconsider" the projected cross-Channel assault the next year, even eliminate it. He would favor instead an Allied strategy confined to blockade by air and naval forces and the destruction of German industry.[23] This impression took Eisenhower aback, especially since at this time Brooke was generally expected to command the invasion when it should come. Brooke later insisted that Eisenhower was mistaken; he had never wavered, he wrote, in his support of a cross-Channel invasion, so long as the way were paved previously.[24] This divergence was undoubtedly only a misunderstanding; and whether Brooke actually said what Eisenhower later recalled was unimportant. The fact was that Eisenhower at the time understood Brooke to be having second thoughts on OVERLORD, and this belief colored his attitude toward the CIGS from that time on.

With the easy time over—the visits to troops, the oratory, the swimming in the sea, and the basking in the sight of success in Tunisia—the party met once more for a final meeting on Thursday, June 3. This time, however, the issues were less controversial—at least those present were in agreement. General Montgomery joined the group and expressed confidence in the prospects for HUSKY, of which Eighth Army would comprise the British portion.

The one important substantive matter was the contemplated aerial bombardment of the environs of Rome. Eisenhower was anxious that the railroad yards south of the city be destroyed, as they represented a vulnerable funnel in the supply line from northern to southern Italy. The military merits of this point were indisputable, but all, including Eisenhower, de-

23 Ibid., pp. 167, 168.
24 Bryant, *Turn of the Tide,* p. 520.

sired to preserve the historical and cultural treasures of the Eternal City. A study, however, had established that the yards were some distance from the Vatican and the Forum. Thus it should be possible, by dint of pinpoint daylight bombing, to destroy the railroad yards without danger to the historic and religious treasures. Churchill therefore agreed to recommend approval of the bombing to the War Cabinet. Marshall promised to do the same with President Roosevelt.

The ten-day session ended with a series of mutual congratulations. The trip had been a triumph of good will, although very few new agreements were reached. General Marshall, though largely silent, remained unchanged in his views. And General Eisenhower's authority as the Allied Commander had been much enhanced.

*

Churchill and his party left Algiers for Gibraltar on Friday, June 4, 1943, after a luncheon given for Giraud and De Gaulle. No Americans, not even Eisenhower, were present. Despite a threat of delay in Gibraltar, the Prime Minister reached London on schedule.[25]

Lord Moran, having missed the Algiers episode, was curious as to what had transpired. He found Churchill exuberant, especially over his new relationship with Marshall. He was quite sure, he confided, that he would get his way regarding operations after Sicily. Marshall, he told a skeptical Moran, was ready to accept the British plan. Moran asked why. For a moment Churchill paused and then mused, half to himself, "The merits of the case are surely beyond any question."[26]

[25] Not so fortunate were the prominent movie actor Leslie Howard and thirteen other passengers on a civilian airliner bound from neutral Portugal to London. Nazi agents thought they recognized Churchill as one of the passengers and the plane was shot down. Efforts to assassinate Churchill in his travels were no figment of the Allied imagination.

[26] Moran, p. 109.

CHAPTER XVIII

DE GAULLE TAKES OVER

A t the end of the Tunisian campaign in May 1943 General Henri Honoré Giraud was at the zenith of his power and prestige. He had held the positions of High Commissioner and Commander-in-Chief of the French Armed Forces, North Africa, since the death of Darlan the previous Christmas Eve and had enjoyed a position of mutual respect with the Americans. As head of the Council of the Empire, Giraud had been recognized as cooperating with, not subservient to, the Americans. His apparent lack of future political ambitions made him, to Roosevelt, a "safe" Frenchman to deal with. This position made him admirably suited to negotiate and supervise the rearmament of the 200,000 French troops in Northwest Africa. And, while the performance of French troops in the Tunisian campaign had been disappointing, nobody blamed Giraud—and the fact received little or no attention anyway. The American public knew that one of the sectors on the Tunisian front was the XIX "French" Corps, with a French commander, and that the French Corps d'Afrique had participated with the U. S. II Corps in seizing Bizerte.

Thus Giraud came across to the world as the commander of the rejuvenated French forces which had fought side by side with the British and Americans. And at the victory parade staged in Tunis on May 20, Giraud and Eisenhower stood in full glory as Giraud's troops marched proudly past. (Little notice was given to the small Gaullist contingent, which refused to march with the other French and took its place in a different part of the column.) And then on May 29, in a surprise move, Giraud conferred on Eisenhower the Order of Grand Commander of the Legion of Honor, the highest French military decoration, which legally could be presented only by the French head of state.[1] The significance of the gesture was barely noticed by any but the followers of General de Gaulle, who understandably interpreted it as Giraud's attempt to assume the trappings of supreme power.

During this period Giraud was enjoying the full support not only of Eisenhower but of Roosevelt and Hull as well. Even Churchill believed that the Casablanca encounter had cast De Gaulle in the role of Giraud's subordinate. And Eisenhower, preoccupied with the end of the Tunisian campaign, had kept stalling on a prospective meeting with De Gaulle, much to the latter's annoyance. Giraud, for the time being, seemed far in the forefront as between the two rival French generals.[2]

But even during this period of personal glory certain inexorable political forces were moving to bring about Giraud's downfall. A traditionalist, Giraud's objective in the government of Northwest Africa—and presumably for the future of France as well—was the maintenance of the old establishment, the status quo. Pensions for former government servants were to be respected; and people in authority, unless tainted too severely with the Vichy brush (which Giraud was not), should be kept in position as administrators. But as time went on and economic conditions in North Africa failed to improve under the Giraud regime, the restive population was beginning to turn more and more to the revolutionary doctrines of De Gaulle.

De Gaulle was still in London, but his supporters in North Africa, headed by one René Capitant, editor of the newspaper *Combat,* were actively proclaiming the need for a "new" France, reshaped from top to bottom, the government of which should include leftists whom Giraud would have ignored. And in France the growing resistance movements were looking to De Gaulle, not Giraud, as their future hope and leader.

Giraud's apparent indifference to political matters also played into De Gaulle's hands. Marcel Peyrouton, who had been appointed Governor of Algiers by Eisenhower, with the approval of Secretary of State Hull and

---

[1] Giraud made the matter personal by announcing that he was giving General Eisenhower his own decoration. Eisenhower said that he would wear it only when the French flag flew over Metz.

[2] General Eisenhower, in his communications with Giraud, addressed him as the French authority, couching his requirements as requests:

June 3, 1943

As you know, we are now contemplating another operation. American troops will be under command of General Patton. He has expressed a great desire to have one Moroccan Tabor with him on this enterprise. I think he has a particular organization and commander in mind; but if you could authorize this attachment . . . my staff will . . . arrange the details. I assure you that we would not only be highly honored but greatly assisted in having this group with us.

Quoted in Chandler, II, 1166–67.

the President both, turned out to be a serious mistake. Peyrouton was without doubt an able administrator, but the Americans had failed to appreciate the degree of resentment among the French population which Peyrouton's Vichy past would stir up. De Gaulle's network of propagandists from Brazzaville to Algiers made the most of it. And Giraud had done nothing to protest Peyrouton's appointment. Finally, the Jews of North Africa were becoming disenchanted with Giraud's failure to repeal some of the old French laws, oppressive to them. This group also turned to De Gaulle.[3]

To assist Giraud in his administration of Northwest Africa, President Roosevelt had, on the urging of Hopkins, sent him an adviser, a financier by the name of Jean Monnet. Monnet was an unusual man. His family owed its fortune to the wine industry, but he himself had decided to become a banker and he had become one of the most influential men in Europe. Always active in political affairs, he had helped finance France in World War I and had served as First Deputy Secretary General of the League of Nations in Geneva. The fall of France in 1940 had found Monnet by chance in London, where he understandably remained. But though the De Gaulle movement was spawned and nurtured by the Churchill government in London, Monnet had always remained aloof from public association with the Free French. This refusal had been noted with satisfaction by the Americans, and Monnet, now in Washington, appeared ideal to advise Giraud in the ways of politics.

But Hopkins and Roosevelt had found the wrong man for their purposes. While not a member of the Gaullist entourage, Monnet was no follower of Giraud's either. Monnet looked at any situation only in the context of the interests of France, and when he evaluated Giraud's future usefulness, he soon found the general wanting, lacking any political acumen. "When the general looks at you with those eyes of a porcelain cat," he exclaimed one day to Murphy, "he comprehends nothing!"[4] Nevertheless Monnet played the game for the moment and soon attained the confidence of Giraud and everyone else.

De Gaulle's following continued to grow. René Capitant not only spread anti-Giraud propaganda; he encouraged soldiers of the Free French, most of whom had come westward with Alexander's forces, to desert the British Army and make their way to Algiers, where they could proselytize the soldiers of Giraud's Regular French Forces with promises of more rank and better pay. Not many of Giraud's soldiers were enticed,

[3] The Rabbi of Constantine had appealed to Eisenhower in private that these laws not be abrogated too suddenly for fear of possible bloodshed between Jew and Arab, but the Jewish leaders would never dare make such statements in public. *Crusade*, pp. 128–29.

[4] Murphy, p. 180.

but the large numbers of Free French deserters in Algiers periodically caused General Eisenhower real concern.

What the Allies failed to realize was that De Gaulle was not thinking in terms of this war. He did not, like Giraud, thirst for personal participation in combat for the liberation of France. For by mid-1943, after Stalingrad and the clearing of North Africa, De Gaulle already saw an Anglo-American victory in Europe as inevitable. He was therefore concerned primarily with his own position and with his future role in France. Postwar France would have to be rebuilt and he was the man to do it.

Nearly four months had passed since the ending of the Casablanca Conference. During this time Giraud and De Gaulle had been in contact and were proceeding to implement Giraud's agreement, made at Casablanca, to allow some of De Gaulle's representatives—"liaison officers"—to join the administration in Algiers. Finally, on May 17, 1943, Giraud sent De Gaulle an invitation to come personally, and De Gaulle answered quickly, "With pleasure." Citing the authority of his own National Committee, he proposed that all discussions between him and Giraud be secret, pointed toward forming a nucleus to exercise a "central joint authority" over which the two would preside alternately. He looked forward to "joint collaboration in the service of France."[5] Such matters as his previous demands for the removal of all administrators who had ever served under Vichy—and Giraud's refusal to comply—were swept under the rug for the moment.

De Gaulle arrived at Algiers on Sunday, May 30. Churchill, Marshall, Brooke, and Eisenhower had completed the first plenary meeting of the Algiers visit the day before and the visitors were taking the day off for recreation. Though De Gaulle arrived with no official announcement to the public, he was correctly greeted at Maison Blanche by Giraud: *"Bon jour, Giraud." "Bon jour, De Gaulle."* Giraud then drove De Gaulle to the Germaine Villa, where De Gaulle was to stay, and the newcomer immediately headed down the hill to the Monument des Morts for a special memorial service arranged by his supporters, who distributed leaflets bearing his likeness. The crowds roared support. He returned to the villa, alone and erect, surrounded by motorcycles, and then held a press conference in which he made caustic references to all other French leaders. Giraud, though not mentioned by name, was De Gaulle's obvious target.

The next morning preliminary discussions began for forming the new French Committee of National Liberation (FCNL). Its composition had been negotiated beforehand and supposedly was "balanced." Giraud and De Gaulle, co-chairmen, were to alternate in presiding. Of the other five members, two were roughly identified as Gaullists, though neither had

[5] De Gaulle, "Documents," II, 169, 170.

been original members of the De Gaulle movement.[6] Supposedly supporting Giraud were Jean Monnet and Churchill's friend, General Alphonse
Georges. General Georges Catroux, newly appointed governor of Algeria
in place of Peyrouton, was considered neutral. (Peyrouton had just
resigned.)

The Committee was therefore composed of "men of moderation," and
the line-up looked balanced on the surface. "If De Gaulle should prove
violent or unreasonable," Churchill assured Roosevelt, "he will be in a
minority . . . and possibly completely isolated. The Committee is therefore a body with collective authority with which, in my opinion, we can
safely work."[7]

Even that first meeting, however, had a stormy beginning. Two issues
were at stake: (1) De Gaulle's insistence on the replacement of five top
French officials, including Noguès and Boisson, and (2) control of the
Army. In both instances Giraud held the cards for the day, as such a
committee would naturally be reluctant at the outset to take drastic action
without consulting the British and Americans. Dismissing the administrators who had been serving the Allies through these many months would
be a rash step indeed. Further, the one issue on which General Eisenhower remained adamant was control of the French Army. Eisenhower
insisted on looking to one man for that purpose and that man, in his view,
had to be Giraud. De Gaulle stomped out of the room.

Several days of tension passed while the Anglo-American leaders were
addressing future military strategy at Eisenhower's villa, all except Eisenhower apparently oblivious to Giraud's fears that the 2,000 Gaullist
soldiers at Algiers might quickly try to take over the city.[8] Fortunately,
the critical period passed, and on Thursday, June 3, it appeared that this
FCNL was going to function smoothly.

Churchill, while he had long since despaired of exercising any control
or restraint over De Gaulle, felt that he and Eden together had exerted
considerable influence in bringing about a workable arrangement
(FCNL). Therefore the luncheon he gave for Giraud and De Gaulle just
before departure for London was, to both Brooke and Murphy, a "victory" celebration of De Gaulle's "interposition" in the Algiers administration.[9]

[6] René Massigli and André Philip.
[7] Churchill, Vol. V, *Closing the Ring*, p. 174.
[8] Actually Eisenhower alerted two battleships, a carrier, and certain air units to be
ready in case of an uprising in the city. No American, British, or Regular French
troops were in Algiers, but the chief of police, Admiral Muselier, had a formidable
organization. Muselier was a disenchanted former De Gaulle follower, now
staunchly pro-Giraud. In fact, De Gaulle feared that Muselier might have a warrant
for his own arrest.
[9] Murphy, p. 180.

Hardly were Churchill and his party airborne for London, however, than the delicate arrangement came apart. At 6:00 A.M. on June 7 Robert Murphy was awakened by a telephone call from Giraud's naval aide asking him to rush to French headquarters. This did not seem unusual to Murphy, as he knew that Giraud began his day at 4:30 A.M. On arrival, however, he was startled to be shown several documents that Giraud, on the advice of Monnet, had signed. The provisions included the addition of six more men to the FCNL, bringing the total to thirteen. Though these six newcomers included three theoretical Gaullists and three Giraud supporters, Giraud had unwittingly agreed to a committee which would inevitably drift toward the more liberal De Gaulle. Murphy did his best to explain to Giraud what he had done, but the general seemed indifferent, almost pleased to give up political power. His only interest was to remain as head of the French armed forces.

De Gaulle's long-range advantage was not immediately obvious, however, since the bulk of the Committee could not be expected to instantly rubber-stamp the major surgery he was demanding. Thus on June 10 De Gaulle again walked out of a meeting, this time resigning. Eisenhower, on learning of this development, revived the forlorn hope that his problems with French politics might possibly be over, as Giraud seemed now to be in complete control. But this was a dream. De Gaulle's following in North Africa was such that his removal from the FCNL would cause dissidence, even disorder, throughout the region, and Eisenhower, who dearly desired to devote his entire attention to HUSKY, was back into French politics with both feet.

The next day, June 11, President Roosevelt began to inject himself more into the picture, apparently uninformed as to the potency of De Gaulle's power in North Africa and France. Possibly he plainly refused to admit it. Churchill, having witnessed the tortures of France in 1940, could retain a grudging admiration for De Gaulle even at his worst, but not so Roosevelt. Piqued by De Gaulle's continual defiance, stemming at least from the time of the St. Pierre and Miquelon incident at Christmas 1941, Roosevelt's distaste for the Frenchman bordered on the irrational. This he expressed by insisting that the Anglo-Americans were executing a military occupation.[10]

No Frenchman saw it that way. Perhaps during the very first stages of the Allied landings in November 1942 this supposition may have been realistic, although continued French resistance could have neutralized any Allied capability to fight Rommel and Von Arnim. But now, by early June 1943, French sovereignty in Northwest Africa was becoming every day

[10] On June 5, 1943, Roosevelt cabled Churchill: "I want to give you the thought that North Africa is in last analysis under British-American military rule, and that for this reason Eisenhower can be used on what you and I want." Churchill, V, 173–74.

more real: all of the Anglo-American combat forces were either in Tunisia or preparing for HUSKY. The French had from the start been administering the territory, and the only bargaining weapon the Allies had left was the rate of French rearmament. Even this Anglo-American leverage was resented, and De Gaulle freely referred to it as "blackmail." But Roosevelt seemed blind on that score. Any political or military action, he insisted, would have to be approved by General Eisenhower and therefore ultimately by himself and Churchill, with emphasis on himself.

Thus Eisenhower's elation over the successful reduction of Pantelleria by air and naval action on June 11 was dampened somewhat by the messages he was receiving from Roosevelt on French politics. Three arrived in a single day. One involved the fate of Pierre Boisson, the Governor General of French West Africa, whom De Gaulle was determined to remove,[11] but to whom Roosevelt had promised protection. Roosevelt's message directed Eisenhower to extract assurances from both Giraud and De Gaulle that Boisson would be retained in his position, *without quoting the President in the process.*

Eisenhower sent Murphy to do what he could and the next day reported the results of his efforts. Giraud had assented immediately and De Gaulle, in an amiable frame of mind, had spent some time pleading with Murphy for a better understanding between the United States and himself. He even acknowledged the poor quality of some of his representatives in Washington. But on the question of Boisson, De Gaulle remained firm. Observing that replacing Boisson could not possibly affect Allied military operations, De Gaulle said that, by yielding to Anglo-American "exigence" in any matter involving French sovereignty, he would be violating a matter of principle—and then he would be lost.

In the course of Murphy's meeting, Eisenhower reported, De Gaulle made no mention of his own "retiring" from the FCNL but made it clear that he could never serve as a member of a committee he could not dominate. The last sentence of Eisenhower's message to his political chief was rueful: "The impasse on the question of French military authority continues."[12]

When the Committee met again a couple of days later, Giraud suddenly realized the extent to which he had given up his power by signing Monnet's papers a week earlier. Convinced that he had been betrayed, he now threatened to resign. During Eisenhower's absence on an inspection trip, therefore, Murphy pleaded with Giraud to remain in office and sent a gloomy message to the President (in Eisenhower's name) predicting an

[11] Under the Vichy government, Boisson had easily beaten off the abortive Free French–British effort to take Dakar in September 1940. De Gaulle was not a man to forget humiliation.

[12] Eisenhower to Marshall for Roosevelt, June 12, 1943. Chandler, II, 1189.

inevitable Gaullist takeover. Roosevelt's answer was waiting when Eisenhower returned on June 17, and it was not reassuring. Consistent with Roosevelt's misunderstanding of the French situation, it insisted that Eisenhower make absolutely clear that "we have a military occupation in North and West Africa and therefore no independent civil decision [can] be made without your [Eisenhower's] full approval."[13] Later in the day he cabled again that he might break relations with De Gaulle "in the next few days."[14]

Eisenhower now recognized that he was faced with an emergency, especially with HUSKY only three weeks away. On June 18 he assured the President that "local French difficulties in reaching workable agreements [had] been magnified in certain reports . . . and in the public press." He attributed the present uproar more to "French characteristics" than to any probability that no answer could be reached.[15] He advised the President that he was arranging a meeting between himself, Giraud, and De Gaulle for the next morning to lay down his minimum requirements regarding the French Army (to remain under Giraud). He also assured Roosevelt once more that if De Gaulle should break on that issue he would be placed in an "indefensible position." This command of the French Army was the only issue that he planned to place before the two French officials. He was, he concluded, fully alert to the potentialities of the situation and would never accept any solution which would jeopardize HUSKY.[16]

Eisenhower was more frank in the message he sent Marshall that same day. Here he addressed the question of Boisson, whom he had not mentioned by name in his message to Roosevelt, and pointed out that if the United States and Britain should continue to insist on keeping Boisson as Governor General of French West Africa (a post not important to Allied military operations), De Gaulle would be able to charge the Anglo-Americans with interference in French civil affairs. This, Eisenhower feared, might draw a "sympathetic response" from Frenchmen and create unnecessary disturbances in the area. The issue on which to face De Gaulle, in Eisenhower's opinion, was solely that of military command. He finished by saying that Murphy's telegram to Roosevelt had been more gloomy than justified. It did not appear that De Gaulle actually controlled the FCNL, as he had only four sure votes out of fourteen against six or seven moderate independents, including men like Catroux and Monnet.[17]

At the meeting of June 19 De Gaulle turned out to be every bit as obdurate as expected. He made a point of arriving late and seizing the floor

---

[13] *Foreign Relations of the United States* (*FRUS*), II, *1943*, 152–55.
[14] Chandler, II, 1193, footnote 1.
[15] Eisenhower to Roosevelt, June 18, 1943. Quoted in ibid., p. 1192.
[16] Ibid.
[17] Eisenhower to Marshall, June 18, 1943. Quoted in ibid., pp. 1193–94.

immediately. He confronted Eisenhower, Giraud, and the rest by stating that he had come in his capacity as President of the French Government. Turning to Eisenhower, he said, "If you wish to address a request to me concerning your province, be sure that I am disposed beforehand to give you satisfaction, on condition, of course, that it is compatible with the interest at my charge."

Such a pronouncement might have dismembered another man, but Eisenhower—now well accustomed to French sensibilities—took it in his stride. He held a wry view of the range of French emotions, a view which had been conditioned fifteen years earlier when as a major he had lived in Paris. So he took De Gaulle's posturing philosophically: no emotional outbursts should be surprising, and he simply reported to Marshall that the meeting had produced nothing decisive. He had agreed to put his statements and demands regarding the command of French Armed Forces in writing but had supported General Giraud completely. He asked Marshall to ask the President that nothing be done at home to increase local difficulties until HUSKY was a week old. His message ended by quoting Giraud's assurance that his control of the French Army was as effective as ever.[18] The status quo remained, including Giraud's command of the French armed forces.

Essentially the "local political mess" was settled for the time being, at least so far as it affected the interest of the Americans and British in pursuing the war against the Axis. On June 24, 1943, Pierre Boisson removed that thorn from the side of the Eisenhower-Roosevelt relations by resigning. (He received little mercy from De Gaulle and his Committee; both he and Peyrouton were soon imprisoned.) The FCNL, now dominated by De Gaulle, continued to function, though never fully recognized by either Allied government throughout the war.[19] Giraud remained the commander of the French forces for some time, but having lost his political power, he was helpless when De Gaulle later had him removed to a lesser position and finally retired. By that time, however, British and American forces had moved far beyond Northwest Africa and had lost interest. Thus De Gaulle prevailed and Giraud eventually disappeared from the scene.

Giraud's fall from power, which stemmed largely from his decency and naïveté, constituted a poignant end to the efforts of a man truly dedicated to the winning of the war and the interests of France. Despite his eventual eclipse, Giraud had made a substantial contribution to the Allied cause.

[18] Eisenhower to Marshall, June 19, 1943. Quoted in ibid., pp. 1200–1.
[19] Exchanges of communications between Roosevelt and Churchill showed a difference of opinion, with Churchill desirous of recognizing the Committee in some form less than the government of France. Roosevelt refused to recognize it in any legal manner, although he permitted dealing with it on certain issues.

CHAPTER XIX

THE FALL OF IL DUCE

On Friday afternoon, July 9, 1943, General Dwight Eisenhower
and Admiral Sir Andrew Cunningham sat—and paced—in Cunningham's elaborate office in Valletta, Malta.[1] Unexpected bad
weather in the Mediterranean was making the invasion of Sicily
(HUSKY) more dangerous by the hour. The invasion forces were at sea,
but storms were brewing and winds were rising to forty knots. Eisenhower,
unused to "force numbers" to depict the velocity of winds, could follow
the news primarily by watching Cunningham's face. Eisenhower could,
however, deduce that "Force V" was worse than "Force IV"—and the
numbers kept going up! The landings were scheduled for early the next
morning, 2:35 A.M., July 10; and if the invasion were to be called off,
Eisenhower would have to do it before ten-thirty that evening. To recall
the vast invasion armadas long at sea was almost unthinkable, yet it
might have to be done. When a message came in from General Marshall
asking if the invasion were on or off, Eisenhower's only reaction for the
moment was, "I wish I knew!"

Eisenhower and Cunningham came from widely different backgrounds
—a U. S. Army officer from Kansas and an admiral of the Royal Navy
from Scotland—but then comradeship in war had developed between
them an unusual mutual respect. On June 8, a month earlier, the two had
boarded Cunningham's flagship to take a close look at the effects of the

[1] Cunningham's headquarters was in the Auberge Castile, on a hill at the edge of
town.

Allied bombardment of Pantelleria, the attack on which had been the cause of so much disagreement. It had been an exciting experience for Eisenhower, and not completely without physical risk. On their safe return they had been rewarded three days later when the island surrendered without land invasion. Their judgment vindicated, Eisenhower and Cunningham had shared a triumph. Even the Prime Minister had lost a small wager.[2]

But this situation was no personal adventure; rather it resembled the hours they had endured during the TORCH landings the previous November at Gibraltar. Now, as then, Cunningham's calm, cheerful confidence was contagious; in these moments of anxiety probably no man could provide greater comfort to the Allied Commander than this Scottish admiral.

Though winds continued to rise, the meteorologists who came periodically into Cunningham's office were predicting a drop-off at sundown. By midnight, they believed, the force would reach an acceptable level. Until then the suspense would remain great.

Late that afternoon Eisenhower, Cunningham, and a small group went to a lighthouse on the southeast corner of the small island. They climbed a hill on a point of land above Valletta Harbor to observe the C-47s and glider elements of the British 1st Airborne Division headed toward their destination near Syracuse. The planes and gliders—Cunningham counted sixty-four—were illuminated in the beams of the lighthouse. Eisenhower went off alone for a short while and mumbled a silent prayer for his troops.

The British were committed, and their landings could be effected even in bad weather as they were to land on the lee (eastern) end of the island. By 10:00 P.M. Eisenhower decided that the full invasion had to go ahead; Patton's Seventh U. S. Army should attempt its landing. Accordingly Eisenhower sent a message: "The operation will proceed as scheduled. . . . All of us hope to have good news . . . tomorrow." He then penned a letter to his wife and returned to Cunningham's office.

By the next morning word came in that the landings had proceeded satisfactorily. Cunningham went by destroyer to inspect the American beaches and reported back elated. The entire Allied command breathed a sigh of relief.

*

The island of Sicily is shaped roughly in the form of an isosceles triangle, with one long side, the northern coast, running about a hundred and

[2] Eisenhower, *Crusade*, p. 166.

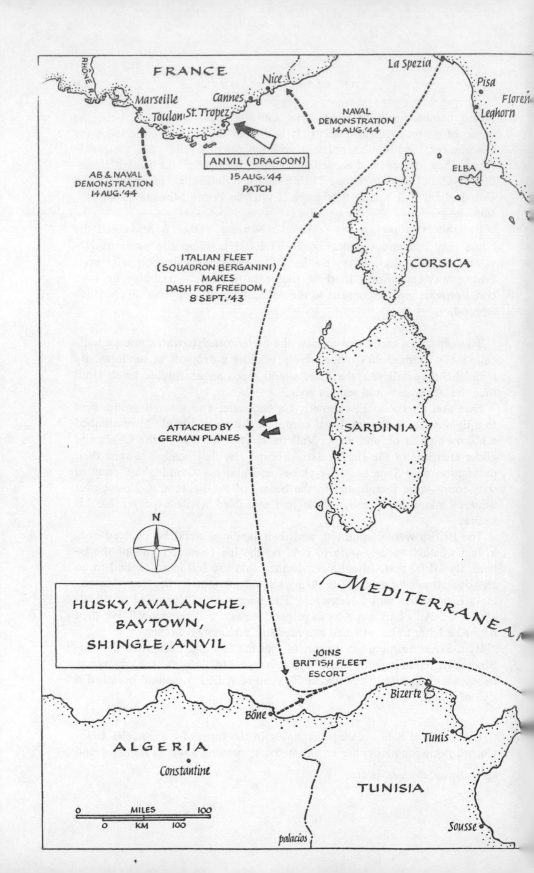

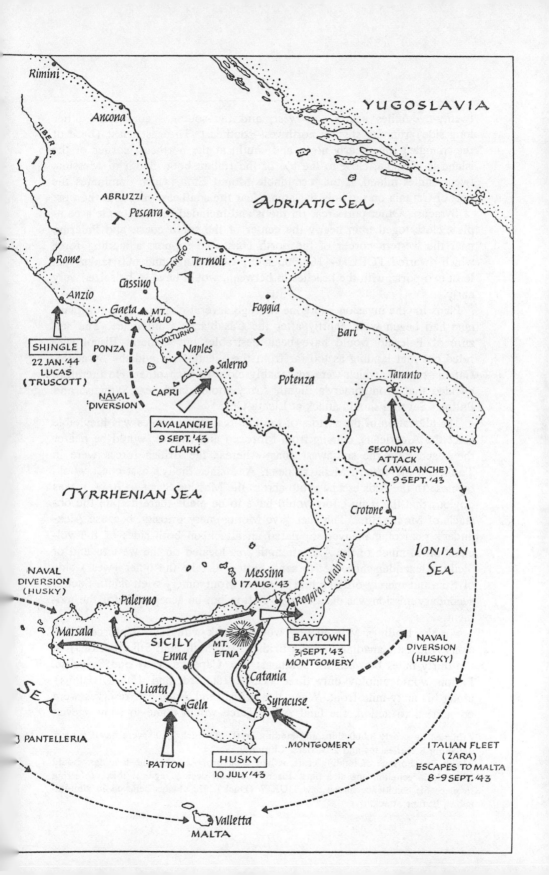

Rimini

TIBER R.

Ancona

YUGOSLAVIA

ABRUZZI

Pescara

ADRIATIC SEA

Rome

Cassino

SANGRO R.

Termoli

Anzio

Gaeta ▲ MT. MAJO

Foggia

VOLTURNO

Bari

SHINGLE
22 JAN. '44
LUCAS
(TRUSCOTT)

PONZA

Naples

Salerno

Potenza

Taranto

NAVAL
DIVERSION

CAPRI

AVALANCHE
9 SEPT. '43
CLARK

SECONDARY
ATTACK
(AVALANCHE)
9 SEPT. '43

TYRRHENIAN SEA

Crotone

IONIAN
SEA

NAVAL
DIVERSION
(HUSKY)

Messina
17 AUG. '43

Reggio-Calabria

Palermo

NAVAL
DIVERSION
(HUSKY)

Marsala

SICILY
Enna

MT.
ETNA

BAYTOWN
3 SEPT. '43
MONTGOMERY

SEA

Licata

Gela

Catania

Syracuse

PANTELLERIA

PATTON

MONTGOMERY

ITALIAN FLEET
(ZARA)
ESCAPES TO MALTA
8-9 SEPT. '43

HUSKY
10 JULY '43

Valletta
MALTA

twenty-five miles nearly east–west; and the southern coast (the other long side) running slightly northwest–southeast. The east coast (base of the triangle) runs nearly north and south; at the northeast corner of the island is Messina, close to the toe of the Italian boot. South of Messina, twenty miles inland, is the formidable Mount Etna, which dominates the port of Catania on the only flat area. Near the southeast corner is the port of Syracuse. Other port areas on the island included the Licata-Gela complex, close together in nearly the center of the south coast, and Palermo near the western corner of the north coast. To support a landing force which dwarfed TORCH—160,000 men, 1,800 guns, and 600 tanks[3]—at least two ports, with the beaches in between, would have to be seized very early.

Plans for the invasion had gone through several changes since the planners had begun work shortly after the Casablanca Conference. The seizure of Palermo would have been desirable, but General Eisenhower ruled out that landing as too far from the Licata-Gela and the Syracuse-Catania regions, which were reasonably close to each other. He therefore decided that Montgomery's Eighth Army should land near Syracuse and Patton's Seventh should attack at Licata-Gela.[4]

The allocation of the sectors of the two respective armies was inevitable since the Americans, coming from Morocco and Bizerte, would be nearer the beaches on the southwest coast whereas the British forces were in Tunis and the eastern Mediterranean. And since Sicily's east coast would be close to the Axis escape route across the Messina Strait to Italy, it was obvious that the main effort would have to be made there despite the obstacle of Mount Etna. This fact gave Montgomery priority, because Alexander's plan of maneuver stipulated an attack on both sides of the volcano. Since much of the Axis strength was located on the western end of Sicily, Alexander chose not to send Patton to take the other (west) side of Etna but merely ordered him to cover Montgomery's left flank. Such a secondary mission was distasteful to Patton but he accepted it for the moment.

For the landings Montgomery would attack with four reinforced divisions (the 1st Canadian and the British 51st, 50th, and 5th Divisions) in the thirty miles between the southeast tip (Cape Passero) and Syracuse. Patton would employ only three (U. S. 1st, 3rd, and 45th Divisions) along his sixty-mile front. When the British and American reserves were committed to action, the final Allied force would come to some eleven

[3] Carried by nearly 3,000 ships and landing craft, of which 1,200 were naval vessels, including 8 battleships and 2 carriers. Churchill, V, 24.
[4] With the shortage of landing craft, it had been proposed that the landings should be made in echelon, one at a time. Eisenhower had decided against this, preferring to place his confidence in the new DUKW (Duck). He always believed in simultaneous, instant attack.

reinforced divisions, six American and five British. For the first time the British and Americans would be fighting on a roughly co-equal basis.

This plan was known to all the newspapermen stationed at Allied Force Headquarters nearly a month before the landings. With nearly two months between the end of the Tunisian Campaign and the assault on Sicily, General Eisenhower had been well aware of the bits and pieces of information that curious newspapermen could put together. If left on their own, these reporters could, by the observation of troop movements, locations of supply depots, and loading of ships, devise a good guess as to the date and size of the attack—and the units involved. In order to scotch such speculation, therefore, Eisenhower had called together a group of flabbergasted reporters on June 12 and outlined the entire plan, including the date. In so doing, he admonished his audience that their responsibility was now as great as his to keep the plans secret. Nobody let him down.

After Eisenhower's first optimistic reports to the Combined Chiefs of Staff on the morning of July 10, good progress continued. Alexander, his deputy and commander of 15 Army Group,[5] reported success. A severe German counterattack by the Hermann Goering Panzer Division threatened the front of the U. S. 1st Division at Gela on the eleventh but was defeated with the help of superior naval gunfire. Licata-Gela and Syracuse were soon safe and functioning as ports. Success was marred only by the tragic loss of twenty-three American air transports from Allied naval fire the same July 11.

In achieving this early success the Allies had been favored by the enemy strength and dispositions. Italian General Alfred Guzzoni's Sixth Army consisted of over 300,000 men, as opposed to 478,000 for the Allies; but his force boasted only five "mobile" divisions. Of these only two, the 15th Panzer Grenadier and the Hermann Goering, were German. And with his eye on Palermo as one of the anticipated landing sites, Guzzoni had positioned three of the five mobile divisions in the extreme western end, with only the 1st Italian and the Hermann Goering Panzer Divisions near the actual Allied landings. Soon, however, Guzzoni rectified his situation by withdrawing from the west and concentrating his forces along Montgomery's front on the east.

By July 14 the situation had developed sufficiently for Alexander to mature his plans for the campaign. Speed was essential, as the Axis was reinforcing its Sicily garrison—the German 29th Panzer Grenadier Division was arriving—but the Catania–Mount Etna position was holding Montgomery to a standstill. Here Alexander could have changed his tacti-

[5] So named by adding the numbers of Eighth and Seventh Armies.

cal plan to send the bulk of Patton's Seventh Army around the north of Mount Etna toward Messina, or he could leave the whole job of taking Catania and Mount Etna in the hands of Montgomery. Alexander chose the second alternative, even in light of the changed enemy dispositions, and in so doing gave Montgomery the all-important north–south Vissini–Enna road, taking it from Patton. A single road does not mean much in rolling country; but in rugged terrain such as Sicily it becomes a life line. Thus by transferring this road from Patton Alexander squeezed the Americans even farther westward. Omar Bradley, commanding II Corps under Patton, was therefore forced to pull his right division (the 45th) from the line and send it westward by way of the rear. This further reduction in the role of the U. S. Seventh Army angered both Patton and Bradley, but the order stood.

As it turned out, with the Axis forces in western Sicily now heading toward the eastern end of the island, Patton's five (later six) divisions soon found themselves mopping up only scattered resistance. And Patton went about his ground-gaining mission with a vengeance. He drove his army northward[6] in a manner Alexander could not have predicted. The 3rd Infantry Division, for example, using the "Truscott trot" (named after their commander, Eisenhower's former deputy), covered the rough hundred miles from Licerta to Palermo in only four days. Meanwhile Montgomery's forces on the east made little progress.

On July 20, with western Sicily cleared, Alexander, with urging from Patton, changed his plan once again. Montgomery retained the responsibility for taking Mount Etna, but the British sector was reduced to allow Patton to attack eastward along the north coast. Only four main roads led to the final objective of Messina; Alexander allocated the Americans two. On the north coast Patton sent the 45th Division (later replaced by the 3rd). With superb coordination by the Navy, the coastal force executed three small amphibious encirclements around blown roads in the precipitous cliffs. Farther inland he sent the 1st (later replaced by the 9th) in a parallel drive, where a tough battle was fought for Troina. In contrast to earlier rapid gains, it now took nearly three weeks for the Seventh Army to go a hundred miles.

On August 17 Truscott's U. S. 3rd Infantry Division entered Messina a few hours before the lead elements of Montgomery's Eighth Army. The campaign was over; Sicily was cleared.

*

The Axis defense had been skillful. By holding the east coast from Syracuse to Messina in force, Guzzoni had prevented any fateful en-

---

[6] The 2nd Armored Division, the 3rd and 45th Infantry Divisions, and the 82nd Airborne Division were new to battle but superbly trained. The 1st and 9th Divisions had fought in Tunisia.

circlement of his forces. The Italians began evacuation on August 3. The three German divisions—the Hermann Goering Panzer and 15th and 29th Panzer Grenadier—constituted the rear guard, withdrawn relatively intact on August 17, 1943, available to fight another day.

The Sicilian Campaign took longer than had been originally hoped and the escape of three fine German divisions was disappointing. But conceding that it was, on the whole, an excellent operation, it might have gone faster had Alexander not underestimated American troops. Had he sent Patton toward Enna and then eastward toward Messina at the outset, the victory might have been more complete. But since the new American divisions were still an unknown quantity to Alexander, it is difficult to blame him for putting the bulk of the burden—that is, the capture of Catania and Mount Etna—on Montgomery's veteran Eighth Army. As it turned out, both armies performed with distinction, although the far greater distance covered by Patton's Seventh Army caused their commander, probably prematurely, to label them "the best group of fighting men in the world."[7]

The Sicilian Campaign featured the first serious rivalry between American and British troops. Up to this time, even in the last weeks of Tunisia, the Americans had been overshadowed. The British Eighth Army had been hailed by the Western press from El Alamein to Tunis, gaining mile upon mile while the green, under-strength Americans sought to find themselves on the rough Eastern Dorsal of Tunisia. The capture of Bizerte on May 7 had helped American morale but had by no means bridged the gap. Now the shoe was on the other foot, with the Americans making the spectacular gains—miles are the only visible yardstick of success to the public—and even seizing the grand prize of Messina before Montgomery, in whose sector it was supposed to be.

This turnabout would normally have been taken in stride by the soldiers themselves—troops demanding the "honor" of shedding blood for prestigious objectives are rare—were it not for the newspaper headlines and radio broadcasts, all emanating from London. Naturally the British Broadcasting Corporation (BBC), the only station the Americans could pick up, tended to emphasize the role of the British at the expense of the Americans. And even more sensitive than the troops themselves, unfortunately, were the American commanders, Patton and Bradley in particular, who tended to exaggerate real and imagined British slights.

At first the British press and radio seemed to view the one-sided ground gaining with some dismay, and toward the end of July General Eisenhower felt it necessary to point out publicly that the Eighth Army was

[7] Bryant, *Turn of the Tide*, p. 572.

facing extremely heavy Axis resistance on the Catania Plain. Later, however, the BBC seemed to adopt a more petulant attitude, and August 6,
the day after Catania finally fell, Harold Macmillan was recording in his
diary:

> . . . the B.B.C. has been guilty of some frightful "gaffes" which
> upset the Americans terribly. They said the other day that the Sev-
> enth Army had "nothing to do except walk through Sicily, eating
> melons and drinking wine." This caused a terrific "shemozzle."[8]

And on August 4 Eisenhower felt the situation serious enough to send
an urgent message to Churchill:

> It is reported to me that a recent broadcast by the B.B.C. stated in
> effect that the Seventh Army was lucky to be in the unoccupied west-
> ern portion of Sicily eating grapes. The facts in the case, as reported
> to me by the head of my Intelligence Division, Brigadier Strong (well
> known to the C.I.G.S.), are that during the early stages of the inva-
> sion the Seventh Army faced at least two-thirds of the German
> strength on the island, that the only serious counter-thrusts made by
> the Germans were directed at the Seventh Army, and that all or at
> least practically all the German tanks were at that time employed in
> the Seventh Army area. . . . I think you can see why the statement
> alleged to have been made by the B.B.C. has very much annoyed the
> Seventh Army. A soldier is apt to class the B.B.C. and the British
> Government as one and the same thing. . . .[9]

Churchill never answered. Instead he passed the message to Robert
Dunnett, of the BBC, who wrote that "the offending program had been
misinterpreted." Dunnett had done all that he could. One is inclined to
think Churchill could have done more.

Other irritations occurred, in which Churchill was quick to criticize
AFHQ rather than Alexander or Montgomery, who periodically gave the
press situation reports which never reached Eisenhower's headquarters.

A certain amount of bickering even went on between Churchill and Eisenhower. The most serious episode involved a complaint from Churchill
to Harry Hopkins in early August regarding a broadcast from AFHQ
which attributed a temporary bombing halt (necessitated because crews
were exhausted) to Allied generosity. Churchill complained that the
broadcast, having political overtones, should have been cleared with London. When Macmillan discovered that the message had been sent out by
British members of Eisenhower's staff, Churchill forgot the matter

8 Macmillan, p. 310.
9 Eisenhower to Churchill, August 4, 1943. Quoted in Chandler, II, 1318, 1319.

quickly. The tensions are significant principally as illustrations of frayed nerves at the time.

The quick initial successes in Sicily practically dictated that the operation be followed up by an invasion of Italy. Even if the campaign dragged on until mid-August—the joint estimate of Eisenhower and Alexander—plenty of time for campaigning would remain before major forces had to be diverted from the Mediterranean to London for OVERLORD. Accordingly, on Saturday, July 17, Eisenhower called Alexander, Cunningham, and Tedder to Algiers to discuss what recommendations Eisenhower would make to the Combined Chiefs of Staff.

Eisenhower intended to make these recommendations the next day. He had already decided to push for an invasion of the mainland of Italy, and the only remaining question—no small one, actually—was whether it should entail only a crossing of the Strait of Messina by Montgomery or include a bolder action, a landing near Naples. A Naples landing at Salerno Bay would be hazardous. The Nazis had significant reinforcement capabilities, and landing craft would, as always, be a limiting factor. Tentatively Eisenhower decided to include the Salerno landing (AVALANCHE), and the Combined Chiefs approved the dual assault in principle a little over a week later. Too many variables, however, would be constantly changing to allow a firm decision in July. The final decision would remain in the balance for six weeks.

As it turned out, political considerations soon seized the spotlight from the military.

*

Before the Allies could mount any invasion of the Italian mainland—in fact only a little over two weeks after the Sicily landings—the government of the Italian dictator Mussolini fell. The event, while a surprise at that moment, was not totally unexpected. The Allies had begun propaganda efforts to topple Il Duce soon after HUSKY was launched, and Eisenhower's directive "to plan such operations . . . as are best calculated to eliminate Italy from the war . . ." left no doubt that Fascist Italy was expected to fall before Nazi Germany.

To accelerate Mussolini's fall, therefore, Roosevelt and Churchill during the first week of July were preparing a joint statement for broadcast to the Italian people. Roosevelt's first draft began by reminding the Italians that the combined armed forces of the United States and Great Britain were carrying the war deep into the Italian territory. It described threats to the Italian soil from the sea and concluded that the sole hope for Italy's survival lay in "honorable capitulation" to the "overwhelming power" of the United Nations.

The most notable aspect of Roosevelt's draft was the fact that it made
no mention of the term "unconditional surrender"; in fact it appeared to
give the Italians great latitude, promising a chance for Italy to "occupy a
respected place in the family of European nations."

This wording was largely satisfactory to Churchill, though he made
some editorial changes to further emphasize the role of Britain.[10] Roosevelt readily agreed to the amendments, and the message was broadcast as
soon as Eisenhower assured the CCS that he was safely ashore in Sicily.

Meanwhile the Italian dictator seemed to be unaware of the rapidly
moving events. He showed no inkling that two concurrent plots, one by
King Victor Emmanuel III and the other by the Fascist Old Guard, were
being hatched for his overthrow. Unsuspectingly, Mussolini and the Chief
of Staff of the Italian Armed Forces, General Vittorio Ambrosio, flew on
July 19, 1943, to meet Hitler at a villa near Rimini, an Adriatic resort in
northern Italy. He was planning to tell Hitler that Italy could no longer
continue in the war, and he was confident that he possessed the authority
to do so.

At Rimini Il Duce found Hitler adamant. Italy, he declared, must be
defended "so that Sicily may become for the enemy what Stalingrad was
for us." The Italians, furthermore, would produce both the manpower and
organization necessary to do so. This rebuff came as a blow to Mussolini,
and despite Mussolini's earlier resolve, he could not bring himself to
stand up and speak his piece. Thus ended a fruitless meeting. Its principal
effect, possibly, was to convince all, even Ambrosio, that Mussolini was
no longer fit to be a leader.

Before Mussolini and Ambrosio left the Rimini meeting, word arrived
of the long-planned Allied air raid being executed at that moment near
Rome. On hearing this, Hitler softened somewhat, but Mussolini left
cheerless. On the way back he flew through a cloud of smoke rising from
hundreds of fires in the Littorio railway station.[11]

Mussolini then visited King Victor Emmanuel, who, frowning and nervous, declared that Sicily was lost. Italy itself could not go on much
longer. The discipline of Italian troops was disintegrating, and the King
was sure the Germans would double-cross them. Mussolini, still in a
dream world, hoped to disengage Italy from the Axis by September 15,

---

[10] He added, for example, the words *"and his deputy General Alexander"* after Eisenhower's name. He also substituted the names "United States and Great Britain" in
place of "the United Nations" in referring to the air armadas.

[11] This was the much-discussed raid on the rail yards south of Rome. Four hundred
heavy bombers dropped 1,000 tons of bombs. Bombing of installations so close to
Rome had been an agonizing decision, but the risk turned out to be justified. The
Pope later rendered a sort of approval.

two months away, and showed little concern two days later when Dino
Grandi, the leader of the Fascist Old Guard, told of his plans to restore
the King as supreme commander of the armed forces. Mussolini now
stood to lose his most important sources of power, the armed forces and
the ruling Fascist Party.

On July 25, the Fascist Grand Council met at the Palazzo Venezia, all
members dressed in their black uniforms. Mussolini's personal bodyguard
had been shunted aside, but still the dictator seemed unaware of what was
transpiring. He defended himself in the ensuing discussions, but Grandi,
in a violent speech, proposed calling upon King Victor Emmanuel
to emerge from obscurity. Soon it became evident that the Grand
Council and the Court had been in contact, with even Mussolini's son-in-
law Ciano supporting Grandi. The debate continued for nine hours, after
which a vote was taken, nineteen members siding with Grandi and seven
with Mussolini. Abruptly Mussolini dismissed all members without the
formalities of the Fascist salute. It was now 2:00 A.M. None of the
members of the Grand Council slept at home that night; the possibility of
assassination made it prudent to be elsewhere.

The following day was Sunday, July 25. Mussolini spent the morning in
his office and visited some sites hit by the bombing six days earlier. He
went to see the King late in the afternoon, expecting the monarch only to
withdraw the command of the Italian armed forces.[12] Even now Mussolini
entered the King's villa apparently without forebodings, despite the reinforcements of surrounding *carabinieri*. The King, dressed formally in his
marshal's uniform, was waiting for him in the doorway. Without waiting
the King said, "My dear Duce, it's no longer any good. Italy has gone to
bits. Army morale is at rockbottom. The soldiers don't want to fight any
more. . . . The Grand Council's vote is terrific—nineteen votes for
Grandi's motion, and among them four holders of the Order of the An-
nunciation! . . . At this moment you are the most hated man in Italy.
You can no longer count on more than one friend. You have one friend
left you, and I am he. That is why I tell you that you need have no fears
for your personal safety, for which I will ensure protection. I have been
thinking that the man for the job now is Marshal Badoglio. . . ."[13]

Mussolini attempted to remonstrate. The people, he said, would consider the war ended if the man who had declared it were to be dismissed.
Stalin, he said, would be the principal beneficiary. But the evening before
had driven home some facts: "I realize the people's hatred," he said. "I
had no difficulty in recognizing it last night in the midst of the Grand
Council. One can't govern for such a long time and impose so many

[12] The King had delegated this position on June 10, 1940, the day that Italy declared
war on Britain and France. Grandi had broken with Mussolini at that time.
[13] Mussolini, *Memoirs*, p. 81.

sacrifices without provoking resentments. . . . In any case I wish good luck to the man who takes the situation in hand."[14]

The meeting was over. At the door the two men shook hands and the King left. As the former Duce went down the few steps toward his car, however, a *carabinieri* captain stopped him and said, "His Majesty has charged me with the protection of your person." Mussolini was motioned toward an ambulance and driven away under heavy guard.

Even at this point Mussolini still thought that these measures were being taken "in order to protect my person." Two days later, on the orders of Marshal Pietro Badoglio, Mussolini was taken for internment on the island of Ponza.

On Monday, July 26, the day after Mussolini's removal, Prime Minister Badoglio went on the air. "The war," he said, "continues. Italy, though cruelly hurt in its invaded provinces, in its destroyed cities, keeps faith to its pledged word." No one in the Western world took Badoglio's pronouncement very seriously.

*

At 11:00 A.M., July 25, 1943, a plane carrying Field Marshal Erwin Rommel sat down on an airfield near Salonika. The day was broiling hot, and Rommel's spirits were low, as he hardly relished the task of inspecting the defenses of Greece. After his evacuation from Tunisia in March, he had spent several weeks convalescing in the hospital and had then reported to Hitler's Wolfsschanze (Wolf's Lair) in East Prussia as a military adviser. Almost at once he began feeling uncomfortable as he felt the jealousy of some, Keitel and Jodl in particular, who far outranked him. He did not stay long, and by July 15 had been sent to a new command, Army Group B, charged with organizing future German resistance in central Italy. This assignment had been canceled three days later, and Rommel was now to organize German forces in Salonika to protect against the Allies in Crete or Greece.

Twelve hours after Rommel's arrival in Salonika the phone rang. On the other end was General Warlimont at the Wolfsschanze, who advised that Rommel's orders had been changed in view of Mussolini's arrest. At Hitler's headquarters once again Rommel found a mass of utter confusion. Nobody knew exactly what had happened. Hitler, however, saw the situation as serious, and, having no confidence in either King Victor Emmanuel or Marshal Badoglio, he was certain that they would soon pull out of the war. Seventy thousand of Germany's finest troops were still in Sicily, vulnerable to entrapment by an Allied landing somewhere up the long coastline.

Hitler's reaction was for immediate, drastic action. First he would have

[14] Ibid.

to withdraw his two German divisions from Sicily as rapidly as transport would allow; then he would send the 3rd Panzer Division into Rome to arrest the conspirators, liberate Mussolini, and even seize the Pope. Hitler's advisers, confused and frightened, dared not disagree. Rommel, however, as an outsider esteemed by Hitler, was in a better position to advocate a more conservative move: quiet build-up of German troops in Italy, ready to take over when the Italians surrendered. This course might leave the Italians unaware of the extent to which the Germans had taken over their territory. Hitler saw the wisdom of Rommel's views and charged him with implementing the quiet occupation of Italy. Thus, two days after his arrival back at Wolfsschanze, Rommel was again headed for Munich, where he placed the 44th and 30th Infantry Divisions in position to secure the passes through the Alps.

By July 29, four days after Mussolini's fall, radio intercepts between Roosevelt and Churchill had confirmed to Hitler that the Italians would defect from the Axis. He therefore ordered Operation ALARICH, the stealthy invasion of Italy, to begin the next day and instructed Rommel to move the 26th Panzer Division to a position just north of Rome. The troops were to be friendly and Rommel was to stay out of sight, still running the operation from Munich. The move proceeded smoothly, and within two weeks Rommel was assembling eight strong divisions near the 26th Panzer. The German occupation of Italy was now a fact.

For Rommel himself the duty in Italy was too sedentary and, carrying a measure of sympathy for the Italians who had served under him, he soon ran afoul of Himmler's SS, many of whom were among the occupying forces. Thus when orders to leave Italy arrived in early November Rommel was happy. He was to inspect the much-publicized but largely ineffective Atlantic Wall and in January 1944 was given command of the coastline of Northwest Europe from the Netherlands to the Loire.

*

Harold Macmillan, Minister of State and British political adviser to General Eisenhower, was under little pressure as July 1943 drew to a close. Free to live where he pleased, he had happily accepted Alexander's invitation to become a member of the general's mess, located near Tunis. Since Macmillan was a guest, not a subordinate, no barrier existed to their developing a strong personal friendship. With this informal relationship, they could make a practice of swimming together in the Mediterranean every morning without any risk to Alexander's dignity before his staff. This they began to do on a regular basis. The Battle of Sicily was going hard and Alexander was busy. But Macmillan's responsibilities as political adviser were for the moment light.

Macmillan was enjoying his stay. And it was good to live among his own countrymen. He enjoyed drawing a parallel between the Greeks and Romans of ancient times and the British and Americans in 1943. In both cases the former possessed the sophistication and the wisdom, the latter the power. Here he was privileged to live among the "Greeks." Physically, the mess was comfortable, located in a large country house where its members came to meals but otherwise attended to their own business —in his case, with the "Romans." Recreation was adequate, the sky cloudless, the sea lovely and dark. Slight breezes blew by day and the nights were cool. What pleased Macmillan most was the fact that, though a great battle was in progress, it was never mentioned in the mess. There the conversation conformed to the practice of educated Englishmen everywhere. A little history was discussed—politics, banter, and philosophy—but no current war. Even when a message would come in for the chief, Alexander would pause so as not to disturb the conversation at hand, whether the subject be the campaigns of Belisarius, Gothic architecture, or pheasant hunting, before excusing himself to open and read it. He would then continue in the original discussion for a few minutes and then, if the message should call for his action, he would unobtrusively retire. Such an atmosphere was made to order for the suave Macmillan, a lover of British understatement.

On Sunday night, July 25, 1943, Macmillan dined with General Mast, the governor of Tunisia, who had worked with the Allies ever since the planning for the November landings. On returning to his quarters Macmillan went to his room to read. A member of the intelligence staff called: Benito Mussolini had been ousted as Premier of Italy. Excited, Macmillan headed down to the mess and to his disappointment found it nearly deserted. He and a fellow member, Captain Lord William Scott, however, found a radio and finally made it work; on the midnight news the BBC confirmed that Mussolini had either resigned or had been dismissed. No details were given.

Macmillan was now in a quandary, wondering whether to wake up General Alexander. He decided, however, that proper manners would forbid such an intrusion as it would infringe on the customs of the mess. So Macmillan went off to bed. The next morning during his usual 7:00 A.M. swim with Alexander, he told of Mussolini's fall. Macmillan's diary commented, "He seemed pleased."[15]

Hardly were the swimmers out of the water when the telephone rang. Macmillan was asked politely but firmly to come at once to General Eisenhower's villa. The Allied Commander had just received the word and was charged up for direct and immediate action, so much so that Macmillan and Murphy had some difficulty in restraining him.

Having committed himself to the invasion of Italy at Messina (Opera-

[15] Macmillan, pp. 303–5. Alexander, of course, had no responsibility in this political arena.

PRIME MINISTER CHURCHILL AT ALGIERS, June 1943. Seated, left to right: Eden, Brooke, Churchill, Marshall, Eisenhower. Standing, left to right: Tedder, Cunningham, Alexander, Montgomery, June 1943. THE IMPERIAL WAR MUSEUM

KING GEORGE VI VISITS ALGIERS, June 1943. U. S. ARMY

MAJOR GENERAL LLOYD R. FREDENDALL (1883–1963) U. S. ARMY

LIEUTENANT GENERAL SIR KENNETH A. N. ANDERSON (1891–1959) U.P.I.

DUKW ("DUCK") LANDS AT SALERNO, September 1943. U. S. ARMY

LANDING CRAFT, INFANTRY. GEORGE RODGER, LIFE MAGAZINE © 1944 TIME INC.

PATTON AND MONTGOMERY,
SICILY, 1943. U. S. ARMY

ALEXANDER AND AIR MARSHAL CONINGHAM.
U.P.I.

EISENHOWER ON H.M.S. *Nelson* TO SIGN ITALIAN SURRENDER, September 1943.
RONALD MORRIS

CHÂTEAU FRONTENAC, QUEBEC. Locale of the First Quebec Conference (QUADRANT), August 1943. U. S. ARMY

THE PRIME MINISTER GREETS PRESIDENT ROOSEVELT, QUEBEC. U. S. ARMY

HENRY L. STIMSON (1867–1950)
© KARSH, OTTAWA, WOODFIN CAMP

THE GENERALISSIMO, PRESIDENT, PRIME MINISTER, AND MADAME CHIANG KAI-SHEK, CAIRO, November 1943. Standing, left to right: Somervell, Stilwell, Arnold, Dill, Mountbatten, Carton de Wiart. U. S. ARMY

BRITISH, CHINESE, AND AMERICAN POLITICAL LEADERS, CAIRO, November 1943. Standing: Anthony Eden (third from left), Ambassador John G. Winant, Macmillan, Dr. Wang Chung-hui, Minister of State R. G. Casey, W. Averell Harriman. U. S. ARMY

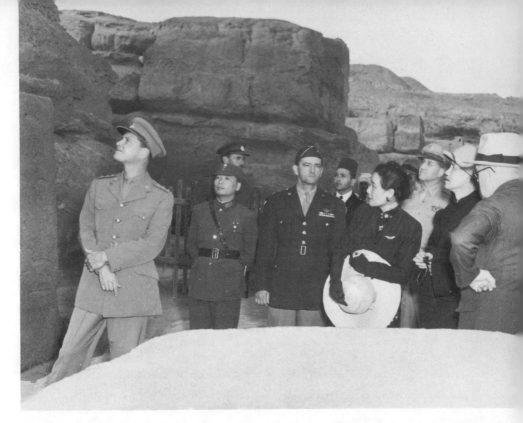

THE GENERALISSIMO AND MADAME AT THE FOOT OF THE SPHINX. Accompanied by Major General Claire Chennault and Major General Ralph Royce, USAAF. U. S. ARMY

BRITISH CAMP AT BASE OF CHEOPS PYRAMID, 1943. U. S. ARMY

BRITISH CHIEFS OF STAFF COMMITTEE, CAIRO, December 1943. Left to right: Ismay, Brooke, Dill, Cunningham. U. S. ARMY

AMERICAN JOINT CHIEFS OF STAFF, CAIRO, December 1943. Left to right: Arnold, Marshall, Captain F. B. Royall, Leahy, King. U. S. ARMY

The "Big Three" at Teheran, November 1943. U. S. Army

Photograph Being Taken of the "Big Three." U. S. Army

Sword Ceremony, Teheran. u.p.i.

Stalin Receives the Sword of Stalingrad, Teheran, November 1943. u. s. army

DINNER OF THE "BIG THREE" AT BRITISH LEGATION, TEHERAN. U. S. ARMY

ANTHONY EDEN LEAVES THE BRITISH LEGATION, TEHERAN. U. S. ARMY

GENERAL MARSHALL VISITS GENERAL MACARTHUR, PORT MORESBY, NEW GUINEA,
December 1943. U. S. ARMY

THE PRESIDENT DECORATES LIEUTENANT
GENERAL MARK W. CLARK, SICILY,
December 1943. U. S. ARMY

PRESIDENT ROOSEVELT AND GENERAL
EISENHOWER ABOARD *The Sacred Cow,*
December 1943. U. S. ARMY

HENRY MAITLAND ("JUMBO") WILSON AND JACOB L. DEVERS. U. S. ARMY

CLARK AND ALEXANDER TAKE PT BOAT TO ANZIO (Operation SHINGLE). Accompanied by Brigadier General (later General) Lyman L. Lemnitzer. U. S. ARMY

The SHAEF (Supreme Headquarters, Allied Expeditionary Force) Team. Left to right: Bradley, Ramsay, Tedder, Eisenhower, Montgomery, Leigh-Mallory, Walter Bedell Smith. U. S. ARMY

Sir Arthur Tedder and Lieutenant General Carl Spaatz. U.P.I.

AMERICAN TROOPS IN ENGLAND,
spring 1944. FRANK SCHERSCHEL,
LIFE MAGAZINE. © 1944 TIME INC.

EISENHOWER, TEDDER, AND MONTGOMERY
OBSERVE TRAINING, spring 1944. U. S. ARMY

AMMUNITION DUMP, spring 1944. BOB LANDRY,
LIFE MAGAZINE. © 1944 TIME INC.

ᴄ Majesty King George VI With His Prime
ᴍɪɴᴄsᴛᴇʀ. WIDE WORLD PHOTOS

De Gaulle and Churchill Visit Eisenhower,
Portsmouth. u. s. army

OK, We'll Go! Eisenhower sends off the U. S. 101st Airborne Division. U. S. ARMY

tion BAYTOWN) and Salerno (Operation AVALANCHE), Eisenhower saw the attitude of the Italian people as important to him. While BAY-TOWN should be little problem, AVALANCHE could well be a touch-and-go proposition. The Bay of Salerno lay barely within the extreme range of Allied fighter aircraft; further, the American Chiefs—Marshall in particular—were insisting that the Mediterranean should receive no reinforcement; indeed they had every intention of going through with the removal of seven divisions from the Mediterranean to the United Kingdom. Thus AVALANCHE, the riskiest operation Eisenhower had yet undertaken, could readily be affected by the immediate political developments in Italy. The Allies sorely needed the help—or at least the neutrality—of the Italian Government, armed forces, and population.

Eisenhower was, therefore, understandably disposed to make exit from the war as easy as possible for the Italians, providing them with what he described as a "white alley," and his instinct was to take action to that end immediately. He would broadcast a proclamation to the Italian people congratulating them on their removal of Mussolini and offering them peace with honor, including repatriation of Italian prisoners of war. To Macmillan and Murphy fell the uncomfortable task of pointing out that he, as a military commander, had no authority to make such a proclamation without the approval of both the British and American governments. Somewhat taken aback by the impact of modern communications on his domain, Eisenhower mumbled, "If we were still in sailing ships, I could deal better with the Italians myself." Nevertheless, he stifled his impulse.

But the matter of a proclamation was minor compared to the possible problem of responding locally to an Italian peace offer, for no political terms or directives from home were on hand. Macmillan knew that the staffs in London and in Washington were working on an elaborate set of surrender terms—some forty proposals in all—but they were not yet completed. In the absence of any directives, therefore, Eisenhower turned to Macmillan and asked him to draft two telegrams, (1) a proposal for the proclamation that Eisenhower wanted to make to the Italian people, and (2) a set of proposed surrender terms. The terms, he said, should be purely military articles which, though they contained no mention of the words "unconditional surrender," would be so stringent as to amount to the same thing.[16] Macmillan finished these messages and Eisenhower sent them to both capitals during the next couple of days.

[16] These terms included immediate cessation of hostile activity, denial to the Germans facilities that might be used against the United Nations, return of prisoners or internees of the United Nations, and immediate transfer of the Italian fleet and aircraft to points designated by the Allied Commander-in-Chief. They reserved to the Allied Commander-in-Chief (Eisenhower) the right to take any measures necessary for the protection of Allied interests.

Eisenhower could do no more for the moment, but Macmillan, who saw the situation much from AFHQ point of view, took it upon himself to rally support in London. He strongly urged the British Government to accept the military terms he had drafted, especially if, as he suspected, the long document currently under negotiation should be too stringent. The signing of a local, interim armistice should not be delayed.

Roosevelt and Churchill both received news of Mussolini's fall the night of Sunday, July 25. Their reactions were quite different. Churchill, predictably, took the news with much the same excitement as Eisenhower. At Chequers with his family and Brooke, Churchill and his group had settled down to watch a film when the word of Mussolini's removal was brought in. Immediately the Prime Minister was on the telephone with Eden for confirmation and then, stimulated, discussed the implications of the event further with Brooke, who congratulated himself on escaping by 1:30 A.M. The next morning Churchill sent a message to Roosevelt urging that the two consult together to decide on immediate joint action. "Hitler," he gloated, "will feel very lonely when Mussolini is down and out." He then busied himself writing a long memorandum for the War Cabinet, a copy of which he sent to Roosevelt.

Roosevelt, on the other hand, received the news at Shangri-La a little earlier in the day because of the six-hour time difference. Judge Sam Rosenman and Robert Sherwood, Roosevelt's two chief writers, were with the President putting the finishing touches on a speech to be delivered Tuesday, a plea to rescue the National Resources Planning Board (NRPB) from abolition by Congress. This Planning Board was, as Sherwood saw it, "very dear to Roosevelt's heart," but in the tenor of the times the very word "plan" was considered a Communist invention by many of the conservative majority on Capitol Hill.[17]

In the late afternoon of this pleasant summer day, Steve Early, the President's press secretary, called from Washington to report the news flash. Roosevelt was somewhat surprised but not particularly excited, possibly because of the poor reputation of Rome Radio as a source of information. While the Office of War Information frantically searched the air waves for further word, Roosevelt, Rosenman, and Sherwood resumed work on the speech, enjoyed a leisurely dinner, sent a low-key message to Churchill,[18] and drove back to Washington. Late in the evening Roosevelt

[17] The House of Representatives at the time comprised 222 Democrats and 209 Republicans. The Senate consisted of 57 Democrats and 38 Republicans. Since some of the Democrats were from the South (generally more conservative than Republicans), Roosevelt was actually faced with an anti–New Deal Congress.

[18] "July 25, 1943. By coincidence I was again at Shangri-la this afternoon when the news from Rome came. . . . It is my thought that we should come as close as possi-

tried to reach Churchill on the telephone. The fact that he, the President, had been kept virtually in the dark for something like five hours seemed to bother him but little.

General Eisenhower's proposals to Washington and London for an immediate proclamation to the Italian people and for approval of his tentative surrender terms soon ran into difficulty. Roosevelt and Churchill agreed on one point: no repetition of a Darlan-type agreement; any negotiations in the field must be based on terms approved by both governments. But aside from that simple, rather theoretical precaution, their respective viewpoints differed. Roosevelt, wedded to his own declaration for "unconditional surrender," reacted publicly with a hard line, harder than Churchill would have preferred. In his speech Tuesday defending the NRPB he injected some words about Italy:

> "Our terms to Italy are still the same as our terms to Germany and Japan—'Unconditional Surrender.'
> "We will have no truck with Fascism in any way, shape or manner. We will permit no vestige of Fascism to remain."

On the other hand Roosevelt seemed to be less cautious than Churchill regarding Eisenhower's proposal for a direct broadcast to the Italian people. And in the next few days Roosevelt's political antennae seemed to soften his hard public line. The significant Italian vote in the United States, anxious to end the war with Italy—especially the bombings—was making itself felt.

Churchill had been inclined from the start toward lenience. In his message to Roosevelt written upon receiving the news of Mussolini's fall, he had specified, "I don't think myself that we should be too particular in dealing with any non-Fascist Government, even if it is not all we should like. Now Mussolini is gone, I would deal with any non-Fascist Italian Government which can deliver the goods."[19] But since the British population, press, and government were so sensitive to the question of ideology, Churchill could not go overboard, especially in public. And there was the possibility of Eisenhower's offering too lenient a political agreement to a King who had long supported Mussolini.

---

ble to unconditional surrender followed by good treatment of the Italian populace. But I think also that the head devil should be surrendered together with his chief partners in crime. In no event should our officers in the field fix on any general terms without your approval and mine." Lash, *Roosevelt and Churchill,* p. 356.

[19] Part of the dichotomy between Roosevelt and Churchill lay in Churchill's belief that constitutional monarchy was the best form of government for European states. Roosevelt felt the opposite. Thus Churchill was far more disposed to retain the House of Savoy and deal with King Victor Emmanuel III. See Sherwood, p. 743.

Churchill therefore telegraphed Eisenhower on July 29: "There are obvious dangers in trying to state armistice terms in an attractive, popular form to the enemy nation. It is far better that all should be cut and dried and that their Government should know our full demands and maximum expectations." He went on to say that Eisenhower's proposed surrender terms would arrive at AFHQ in plenty of time "for any negotiations which you may have to conduct or which we shall be handling."[20]

Churchill would have much preferred for negotiations to be handled through diplomatic channels rather than Allied Force Headquarters. One way might be through the Vatican.[21] But in this he was doomed to disappointment, as the Italians distrusted the Vatican as too penetrated by members of all nationalities to allow secret negotiations.

The Prime Minister was much in error on one other important matter: the amount of help the Italians might give the Allies. Unbeknownst to Churchill, the Germans disarmed the eight Italian combat divisions overnight. And further, Italian troops had lost all will to fight anybody. Eisenhower quickly advised Churchill of these unpleasant facts. As it turned out, Italian efforts to help the Allies would indeed prove feeble.

The flurry of messages that now began to fill the airways between Washington, London, and Algiers was increasing Eisenhower's vexation. Macmillan, on his part, viewed the atmosphere with detachment, humor, and sympathy:

[July 29] was equally hectic but not unsatisfactory in the end.

I spent from 9 to 12 going backwards and forwards between my own office and A.F.H.Q., and conversation with General Eisenhower and Bedell Smith. . . . Poor Eisenhower is getting pretty harassed. Telegrams (private, personal and most immediate) pour in upon him from the following sources:

  (i)   Combined Chiefs of Staff (Washington), his official masters.

 (ii)   General Marshall, Chief of U. S. Army, his immediate superior.

(iii)   The President.

 (iv)   The Secretary of State.

  (v)   Our Prime Minister (direct).

 (vi)   Our Prime Minister (through me).

(vii)   The Foreign Secretary (through me).

---

[20] Churchill, V, 60.
[21] Churchill to Roosevelt, July 29, 1943. Ibid., pp. 60–61.

All these instructions are naturally contradictory and conflicting. So Bedell and I have a sort of parlour game in sorting them out and then sending back replies saying what we think ought to happen. As this rarely, if ever, coincides with any of the courses proposed by (i), (ii), (iii), (iv), (v), (vi), or (vii), lots of fun ensues. But it gets a bit wearing, especially with this heat.[22]

That same day, July 29, Churchill cabled Eisenhower directly in order to make clear his determination that negotiations would be conducted at the political, not the military, level. If Eisenhower were to receive any responsible peace feeler, he wrote, he "would naturally refer it to both governments." Eisenhower answered, also directly. After giving assurance that he would carry out instructions from *both* governments—the "both" was a meaningful word in this situation—he urged that the governments "should give me a general directive on this subject couched in as accurate terms as they can now foresee as applicable. Should such an event as a request for an armistice come about, it may be necessary for me to act with lightning speed. . . .

"I realize clearly that there are many implications and corollaries to the problem that far transcend the military field and my own authority, but I urge that we do not allow ourselves to get in a position where military opportunity may slip out of our fingers and important advantages therefore disappear."[23]

Eisenhower's message may have been the factor that turned the tide. Whether or not it did, action began. The revised text of the proposed proclamation was approved the same day, although with promises a little less generous than Eisenhower had originally proposed, especially with regard to exchanges of prisoners.[24]

The agreement on the specific military terms of an armistice took a little longer than the proclamation, and Churchill was now the driving force. The day after receiving Eisenhower's message the Prime Minister called the War Cabinet out of bed at 1:30 A.M. and kept all members up until four. By the time they were finished an exhausted British Government had produced a draft now come to be known as the "Short Terms." Roosevelt quickly concurred, and Chuchill sent the Short Terms to Eisenhower with the admonition to negotiate with the Badoglio government, should an overture come in, on the basis of that document alone. The Short Terms turned out to be close to Eisenhower's original proposal

[22] Macmillan, p. 308.
[23] Cable No. 5499, Eisenhower to Churchill, dated July 29, 1943. Chandler, II, 1300. Churchill's message is quoted in Chandler but not in his own memoirs.
[24] Churchill, V, 59, 61.

except for an addition which insisted on the immediate return of all 74,000 Allied prisoners in Italian hands.[25]

Thus by the end of July Churchill considered the problem of a sudden Italian surrender taken care of and now began to push for what he called the Instrument of Surrender. This document, which came to be called the "Long Terms," was much more comprehensive and severe than the Short Terms. Churchill was, he admitted, rather puzzled that Roosevelt showed little or no interest in these Long Terms, which he considered only an extension.

At this point Churchill was visualizing a two-stage surrender. If, for example, Eisenhower were called on to negotiate with the Italians, he would be restricted to the Short Terms. After the signing of the Short Terms— and only afterward—he would produce the longer, harsher Long Terms. By that time the Italians would be too helpless to back off.[26]

On August 3 Roosevelt cabled that he seriously doubted whether the Instrument of Surrender should be used at all. The Short Terms, already sent to Eisenhower, should suffice: "Why tie his hands by an instrument that may be oversufficient or insufficient? Why not let him act to meet situations as they arise?" These matters stood pending another upcoming conference between Roosevelt and Churchill.

*

On the night of August 4, 1943, Churchill and a large party departed London on the *Queen Mary* once again. This time they were headed for Quebec, a location proposed by Roosevelt. Roosevelt still refused to go to London, and by this time he had again wearied of entertaining Churchill in Washington. On the trip over, Churchill spoke at length with a young brigadier named Orde Wingate, who had performed remarkable exploits in Ethiopia and the jungles of Burma. Churchill, according to Lord

---

[25] Bryant, *Turn of the Tide,* p. 558.

[26]

Prime Minister to Foreign Secretary   31 July 43
   Many things in life are settled by the two-stage method. For instance, a man is not prevented from saying, "Will you marry me, darling?" because he has not got the marriage contract, drawn up by the family solicitors, in his pocket. Personally I think the terms which Eisenhower may now offer are much more likely to be understood by an envoy, and thus be capable of immediate acceptance, than the legal verbiage of the Instrument of Surrender, and they will look much better if published. If we get emergency terms it means that the Italians will have given themselves up to us, lock, stock, and barrel. There would be nothing improper in our requiring them to hand over the pull-through and other cleaning materials afterwards.

Churchill, V, 64.

Moran, hoped to find in him another Lawrence of Arabia, but when it turned out that Wingate was more eccentric than genius—no Lawrence—Churchill's interest waned. Churchill also composed a twelfth term to be added to the eleven already sent to Eisenhower, this one mentioning the Instrument of Surrender which would follow the signing of the Short Terms.

He arrived in Quebec on Wednesday, August 11, and the next day left for Hyde Park. Meanwhile the Combined Chiefs of Staff met in a relatively leisurely atmosphere, waiting for the two political leaders to join them.

Events in Italy had moved forward, and on August 15 the Allies received what appeared to be a truly substantive peace feeler. It was not the first, to be sure, but it was the only one so far that represented true authority.[27] The approach had been made by one General Giuseppe Castellano, Chief of Staff to the Italian high command, who had arrived in Madrid and made contact on August 15 with Sir Samuel Hoare, the British ambassador. Castellano claimed that he would be representing the Italian military at the highest levels, with authority to act for Badoglio, though he carried no official documentation.[28]

This news was waiting to be discussed when Roosevelt, Churchill, and Hopkins arrived at Quebec from Hyde Park on August 17 (the day of the end of HUSKY). On hand was a message from Eisenhower proposing that he send a staff officer to Lisbon to investigate, not to make promises. That staff officer would be Brigadier Kenneth Strong. If directed *not* to send Strong, Eisenhower urged that the British military attaché in Lisbon secure all the information he could squeeze out of the Italian.

On receipt of this exciting news, Churchill spent most of his time discussing it with Brooke. The following day the Combined Chiefs, who

[27] On July 31 the newly appointed counselor of the Italian legation to Lisbon, one Marchese d'Ajeta, made contact with the British ambassador, Sir Ronald Campbell. D'Ajeta could offer nothing but a plea for the United Nations to save Italy from the Germans.

On August 6 a Signor Berio approached British diplomatic representatives in Tangier, this time mentioning an Italian desire to discuss "armistice terms." Berio's purpose seemed to be to assure the Allies that a meeting that day between the Italians and Ribbentrop and Keitel had no significance.

[28] As a substitute Castellano produced a letter from the British minister at the Vatican, Sir D'Arcy Osborne, testifying that he was genuine. Castellano would obviously have been shot by the Germans had they known what he was up to; therefore he was traveling (at great risk) under an assumed name. He remained inconspicuous by coming as a member of a delegation, on a block visa. The purpose of the delegation —legitimate in other aspects—was to greet the returning ambassador to Chile, with whom the Italians had broken relations. In view of the danger to Castellano's life in Madrid, Hoare arranged for him to go on to Lisbon, less permeated with Nazi agents.

had been in session off and on since their arrival earlier, sent Eisenhower a directive since referred to as the "Quebec Memorandum." Eisenhower was to send two staff officers, one American and one British, to meet with "General C." These representatives would be given no latitude in negotiating and were authorized to say only that "unconditional surrender" would be based on the Short Terms. Political, economical, or financial terms would come later. Though active Italian assistance in fighting the Germans was not expected, these terms could be modified later depending on the aid the Italian Government and people would render the Allies. Prisoners of war should be protected from capture by the Germans and released if necessary. The Italian Government must, at the hour of the armistice, order the Italian fleet to put to sea for Allied ports. Military aircraft should fly to Allied bases. The emissaries were authorized to give no information of Allied plans or dispositions.

The first step in a peace with Italy had been taken.

CHAPTER XX

A CLOSE-RUN THING

Brigadier Kenneth Strong had been Eisenhower's intelligence officer since Kasserine, and during that six months he had won the admiration and respect of his chief and his peers alike. Slim, black-eyed, and pasty, Strong presented an unsoldierly appearance by conventional standards. But his very homeliness worked to his advantage in his position as intelligence officer, the staff position often affectionately referred to as the "spook," and nobody expected him to infringe in other areas. In his own field Strong knew his business and, more important, he felt comfortable with his Yankee comrades. "The best time in a man's life," he once wrote, "is when he gets to like Americans."[1] His discovery was not new. In 1937, as an attaché in Berlin, he had made a point of studying the American psychology and had identified it as basically continental, like the German and the Russian. The American and German high commands, he concluded, had much in common in their military thinking.[2] This realization caused Strong no anguish; he merely noted it and placed it among his other intellectual tools.

*

The Quebec Memorandum arrived at AFHQ at about noon, August 18, and soon thereafter Strong received word to report to Bedell Smith, with whom he would go to Lisbon early that afternoon. Strong was surprised that he, rather than Macmillan, had been selected to represent the British until he learned that one of his tasks would be to obtain detailed information about Italian and German military formations in Italy.

[1] Strong, *Intelligence at the Top,* p. 112.
[2] Ibid., p. 73.

Smith and Strong left Algiers at about 4:00 P.M., carrying with them a copy of the Short Terms and a directive from Eisenhower specifying exactly how the discussion with Castellano should be conducted. They were authorized to make no further commitments beyond the Short Terms; therefore, this would have to be a preliminary meeting. For even the Short Terms themselves, while infinitely preferable to the prospective Long Terms, would still be difficult for the Italians to accept outright.

To avoid being interned in neutral Portugal, Smith and Strong would have to travel as civilians. The matter of appropriate passports became serious, since no American consulates existed in either Algiers or Gibraltar. Smith had an American passport with him, but unfortunately it listed as next of kin "The Adjutant General, U. S. Army," an improbable entry for a civilian. Smith grudgingly acknowledged, therefore, that he would have to travel on a British passport, and Harold Macmillan promptly made arrangements to produce the falsified document.

Bedell Smith, from his haircut to his speech, was unlikely to pass easily as an Englishman and he would be forced to avoid saying anything in public. He also retained an American suspicion of this part of the world not shared by the urbane Strong, who felt very much at home in the Mediterranean area. Having spent the night at Gibraltar, an astonished Strong noticed the next morning that Smith was prepared for any eventuality. Under both armpits and in both hip pockets he had packed small pistols —a total of four—in case of emergency. "If we were cornered," Strong later observed, "I envisaged a desperate gun fight in the best Western manner."[3]

That morning of August 19 the two emissaries left Gibraltar for Lisbon, where they were driven by a member of the American Embassy to the flat of the chargé d'affaires. There they were to remain for the rest of the day. Thus confined to quarters by a young embassy officer, Smith and Strong were unhappy but helpless.

That evening the two were driven to the British Embassy and were conducted to the drawing room. At precisely 10:30 P.M. General Castellano appeared, accompanied by a member of the Italian Foreign Office, a Signor Montanari. The Italians, Strong observed, were somewhat nervous, and each obviously had a precise, preordained role to play. Castellano, a small, dark-eyed Sicilian about fifty years old, was obviously a man of importance. Though he spoke no English, he demonstrated a remarkable grasp of the details when they were translated to him. Montanari, it turned out, had been born of an American mother and educated at Harvard; he acted much like an Anglo-Saxon, but he was obviously very much the junior partner and remained silent and sad, participating

[3] Ibid., p. 145.

only as interpreter, which he did with great accuracy, as Strong, fluent in Italian himself, could detect.

Smith conducted the meeting in a brisk, rather self-important manner; but his accustomed precision left no doubt in anyone's mind exactly what he was saying. He made it clear at the beginning that he and Strong—and not the American and British diplomats—were the only authorized Allied negotiators. The meeting was to be strictly of a military nature between the representatives of the Italian high command and those of General Eisenhower. No political interference was desired.[4] Smith, Strong knew, was in considerable pain, suffering from the stomach ulcers that were to plague him for the rest of his life, but at the end of the meeting Sir Ronald Campbell, the British ambassador, told Strong privately that the talks were the "most brilliantly conducted diplomatic conversations he had ever attended."[5]

From the very beginning it was obvious that Smith and Castellano had come to Lisbon with different sets of instructions. When Smith handed Castellano the Short Terms with a warning that they applied to a military armistice only and must be accepted in toto, Castellano answered at once that there must have been some misunderstanding. He had come, not to ask for an armistice, but to ascertain how Italy could cooperate with the Western Allies in driving the Germans out of his country. The Italian intentions, Castellano said, were simply to do a turnabout and join the Allies. Smith gave Castellano no encouragement, pointing out that the future state of the Italian armed forces would be settled later; the present meeting was being held to discuss terms under which the Allied forces would cease hostilities. Smith then read out the Short Terms slowly, paragraph by paragraph. As Montanari translated, both Italians became increasingly glum.

In due course the conference recessed. Smith and Strong left, allowing the Italians time to relax over a drink—left available by a considerate ambassador—and talk in private. When Smith and Strong reappeared, Castellano requested clarification of each paragraph.[6] This Smith was

---

[4] This was no mere pomp and bluster on Smith's part. Roosevelt and Churchill were insistent that this meeting be free of political commitment.

[5] Bedell Smith was an enigma, even to his close associates. In the American Army he was known for his toughness, ruthlessness, and short temper. But beneath this exterior—which was real when operating in an official capacity—Smith had a loyalty and compassion which showed through. These qualities gained him the warm admiration of many British colleagues, no matter how different in disposition themselves. Eleven years later Smith would be the American Undersecretary of State during the agonizing 1954 talks over Vietnam. The suave Anthony Eden would welcome Smith's arrival at the Geneva Conference with a sense of relief.

[6] It soon became obvious that Castellano was being held back by not only the physical presence of German troops in Italy but also the number of key positions held by Germans in the Italian armed forces.

willing to do; but he emphasized that he had no power to make any concessions. In only one important matter was he able to give Castellano
comfort. The Allies, he promised, would treat King Victor Emmanuel and
his family with all the personal care and deference due to his rank and
position. As with most diplomatic confrontations, the conference eventually became repetitive. But the terms were intricate, and each one
required detailed study. The language barrier slowed the process.

Finally Castellano asked for details of Allied military plans. Smith,
though he would have liked to make some concession to these sincere
men, refused. This withholding entailed more than secrecy, important
though that was, for in fact the Allies lacked the military strength on hand
necessary to give the Italians confidence. Castellano did not know—and
could not know—that Allied top strategy had now made the Mediterranean a secondary theater. Badoglio was contemplating an Allied landing of fifteen divisions; the Allies could deliver three.[7] But despite Smith's
refusal, Castellano gave Strong the details of German and Italian military
dispositions. Strong was happy to note that his information coincided with
that already in the hands of the Allies. At least Castellano was genuine.

As the meeting was about to end, Castellano agreed to take the Short
Terms back to Rome. Then and only then did Smith inform him that the
Italian Government would later receive the Long Terms containing political, economic, and financial requirements. The participants left at 7:00
A.M., after eight and a half hours. Smith and Strong were returned to their
hiding place and left for Algiers that day, August 20. Castellano and Montanari would return to Italy under their prearranged cover. They were to
meet again on August 31, twelve days away, and in the meantime arrangements would be made for direct communication between the Italian
Government and AFHQ.

During this period the Badoglio government in Rome was becoming nervous. Castellano and Montanari suspected that they would be
delayed longer than they had originally planned—and so told Smith,[8] but
Badoglio, out of touch with Castellano, decided to dispatch a second emissary, General Giacomo Zanussi, chief assistant to the Italian Army Chief
of Staff. He and a Signor Lanzi de Trabia arrived in Lisbon on August
26. In order to establish their good faith, the Italian Government this time
sent along Lieutenant General Sir Adrian Carton de Wiart, a British
prisoner since 1941,[9] who was to be turned over to Allied custody.

Despite this gesture, however, Zanussi and De Trabia were greeted with
suspicion. A second mission seemed unnecessary to the Allies, and Castellano, in his meeting with Smith, had cast some doubts on the leanings

[7] Ambrose, *The Supreme Commander*, p. 255.
[8] Eisenhower to Combined Chiefs of Staff, August 20, 1943. Chandler, II, 1349.
[9] Churchill, V, 108.

of Zanussi's chief, General Mario Roatta. The British ambassador, therefore, was instructed to keep Zanussi closeted away, and though his stay in Lisbon overlapped Castellano's by four days, the men never met.

Zanussi, however, soon proved his sincerity. On August 27 the forty-two Long Terms, now agreed, had been sent to Eisenhower and to others, including Ambassador Sir Ronald Campbell in Lisbon. When Sir Ronald showed the terms to Zanussi, he was shocked. It might be possible, he thought, for Italy to negotiate under the Short Terms, but the severe Long Terms could serve as an excuse for the Italian Government to continue the war. He therefore asked that the date for Castellano's next meeting with Smith be delayed from the understood August 31. Badoglio would need more time. Zanussi also warned that German strength in Italy was building up, a matter again confirmed by intelligence sources at AFHQ.

On August 28 General Eisenhower sent the Combined Chiefs of Staff a final argument in favor of using the Short Terms only, emphasizing once more that the Italians might capitulate in the next day or two. In any event, Eisenhower expected Castellano to arrive on the thirty-first, in which case, Eisenhower gave support to the procedure Churchill had been advocating. Castellano could sign the Short Terms and only then be handed the Long Terms. A crooked deal, admittedly, but better than facing the Italians at the outset with the Long Terms.

In conclusion Eisenhower wrote, "The risks attendant on AVA-LANCHE [Salerno landing] . . . will be minimized . . . if we are able to secure Italian assistance just prior to and during the critical period of the actual landing. . . . It is these factors which makes me so very anxious to get something done now."

The next day Eisenhower was rewarded. A message from the Joint Chiefs informed him that President Roosevelt had authorized surrender negotiations on the basis he had proposed.

Zanussi meanwhile arrived in Algiers. But he still had not completely lived down Allied suspicions, principally because he had no way to prove his trustworthiness. Macmillan, for example, who feared the consequences of anyone's disclosing the Long Terms, recommended that Zanussi and De Trabia be kept isolated during their stopover. Possibly trying to size the Italians up, Macmillan visited them, swam with them, and enjoyed their company. But he still noted that they believed their good faith should be "accepted because of their open countenances."[10]

Actually Zanussi continued to be cooperative. After talking with Eisenhower he voluntarily sent De Trabia back to Italy to urge the Italians to believe in the good faith of the Allied governments and accept the Short

[10] Macmillan, p. 317.

Terms. He recommended that he or Castellano remain in Sicily. The Italians needed a permanent contact with Allied Force Headquarters.

*

During all this period General Eisenhower was distressed over a dilemma caused by the recent conduct of General George Patton. On August 17, the day that Messina fell to the U. S. Seventh Army, Eisenhower's joy had been diluted by the news that Patton had disgraced himself by slapping a soldier in a field hospital during the campaign. Patton, on a routine morale-building visit, had become emotional at the sight of the wounded, and when he came across a man without a scratch (but with a high fever) he lost control of himself, berated the victim verbally, and struck him twice with the back of his hand. The man's helmet liner rolled across the floor and out of the tent.

The merits of the case were immaterial. Whether or not the victim was actually a malingerer, Patton's bullying constituted a gross violation of the accepted officer-soldier relationship, and it could never be suppressed since the incident took place in front of fourteen witnesses and was quickly confirmed by two responsible reporters, Merrill Mueller and Demaree Bess, who reported it to Eisenhower in Algiers. Everyone took the side of the abused soldier, and bitterness against Patton was rife throughout the entire Seventh Army.

On learning of this, Eisenhower had taken action immediately, sending Patton a letter of reprimand and ordering him to make apologies to the soldier, the hospital staff, and all the troops in Sicily.[11] On August 22 Patton made personal apologies to those involved, especially the soldier he had abused.

But though he had done everything possible, Eisenhower could not be sure that his actions could save Patton's future as a commander. The answer to that question depended to a large extent on the understanding exhibited by the troops in the field and the public back home. At night Eisenhower scarcely slept, turning over the situation in his mind and seizing at straws of rationalization. One problem, he mused to Butcher, was that he lacked the high-ranking officers necessary to constitute a court-martial if that should be required. Orating to an understanding but baffled naval aide, Eisenhower cited history to illustrate that great military leaders had "practically gone crazy" on the battlefield in their zeal to win a fight. This, he felt, applied to Patton. Eisenhower doubted that the anger of the troops, as reported to him, was as bad as was said, since soldiers respected successful leaders.

Eisenhower may have been misreading the attitudes among the rank and

[11] See Eisenhower to Patton, August 17, 1943. Chandler, II, 1340. Also Eisenhower to Marshall, August 24. Ibid., p. 1353.

file, but right or wrong, he was not indifferent. The crisis eventually stabilized itself as the result of the reprimand, Patton's apologies, and the passage of time. Patton, though not overly repentant, was willing to submit to the conditions. He was thus spared for greater accomplishments.

*

Concern grew daily at Allied Force Headquarters regarding the fate of Castellano. Granted, he was not expected to return to Rome from Lisbon until about August 28, but it was still disconcerting to be left in the dark about his situation. Finally, on August 30, the day before Castellano was supposed to meet Smith, Eisenhower gave up and sent Smith, Strong, Murphy, Macmillan, and Zanussi to Cassibile, Sicily, near Alexander's new headquarters. On arrival they found Alexander concerned by word that the German force in Italy had grown to some nineteen divisions. Since the Allies would have only three to five divisions to land at Salerno, depending on naval and air power to redress the balance, the risk would be high. Italian cooperation was therefore no luxury; it had now become absolutely essential to AVALANCHE.

The next day, August 31, Castellano and Montanari took an Italian plane, as promised, and landed at Cassibile.[12] Thus began the first official Italian meeting with Smith and Strong—the political advisers were still excluded.

Castellano was bringing, he believed, good news. The Italian Government would accept the Short Terms after the Allies had landed in heavy force, at least twelve to fifteen divisions. Smith, therefore, now had to bluff, stating arbitrarily that Badoglio could either (1) take the Short Terms and announce the end of the fighting or (2) continue to be regarded as an enemy. Obviously Smith could never reveal how disastrous it would be for the Allies should the Italians select the second alternative.

Smith could bluff to this extent, but he would not falsely give assurance of large forces to land near Rome. This August 31 meeting, therefore, was disappointingly inconclusive. Castellano agreed to return to Rome and urge the acceptance of the Short Terms, but in so doing he insisted on the condition that the Allies would land "in force" near Rome, no numbers mentioned. To accommodate him, therefore, Smith agreed to urge an airborne landing by the portions of the U. S. 82nd Airborne Division (scheduled for AVALANCHE) to be made at three airfields near Rome. Castellano and Montanari then left.

From Rome, Castellano soon sent a message that the Short Terms were

[12] The clandestine radio link which had been established between AFHQ and Rome told nothing until late afternoon on the thirtieth, when a message came in that Castellano and Montanari would reach Sicily the next day. This word apparently arrived after Eisenhower had decided to send the Zanussi party to Sicily. Strong, pp. 154–55.

acceptable. Based on this, Roosevelt and Churchill sent an optimistic message to Stalin outlining the facts and the difficulties and including the possibility of landing an airborne division near Rome. Eisenhower would sign any armistice on behalf of the Soviets: "We are of course anxious that Italian unconditional surrender be to Soviet as well as to Great Britain and United States."[13]

The optimism was premature. The same day as the Roosevelt-Churchill message, Castellano and Montanari reappeared in Sicily, this time only to discuss plans for the airborne landings near Rome. This was a blow! It was now September 2.

At this point Macmillan, not participating but on hand, proposed a ruse. Alexander, also without a role in the negotiations, might nevertheless strike some fear into the negotiators' hearts. The plan appealed to Bedell Smith, who was ready to try anything; Alexander also agreed. He would personally pay a formal "call" on the Italians.

Alexander spared nothing. He decked himself out in a well-pressed uniform with immaculately cut breeches, highly polished boots, spurs, and gold-peaked cap—and decorations, of course. Since both he and the Italians were housed in the middle of a large, protected enclosure, Alexander and his staff were required to climb the wall in the rear, shake the dust from their uniforms, and mount their vehicles in order to drive pompously through the entrance.

Alexander's confrontation with Castellano and Zanussi was correct but icy: no shaking hands, no exchange of civilities. Alexander, pretending to believe that Castellano and Montanari had returned to sign the armistice, staged a bit of histrionics when they protested. He had reached the end of his patience, he said, and was beginning to doubt their good faith. Feigning cold fury, Alexander threatened to bomb Rome within twenty-four hours if the Italians failed to sign. Stalking out of the tent, with a small detachment of smartly uniformed troops at present arms, Alexander then remounted his vehicle and proceeded around to the rear of the enclosure, where he once again climbed the wall. He sat in Murphy's tent to await the results. Soon the Italians were assuring Smith that they would contact Rome at once to ask for authority to sign the Short Terms.

Late that day Eisenhower, at the little farm he enjoyed just outside of Algiers, received urgent word from Smith that the Short Terms would soon be ready for signing. If Eisenhower could not be there in time, Smith requested authority to sign for him. Eisenhower hesitated. He could make it to Cassibile the next day, he thought, but did he want to? The agreement with the Russians specified that he should sign the surrender personally, but this document was only an armistice, not a surrender. And though he had acceded in the two-step surrender—even recommended it as a desper-

13 Churchill, V, 110. Message sent September 2.

ate move—he still found it distasteful. He wrestled with the problem and then left for Cassibile the next morning.[14]

*

Again the Allies sat in suspense. Communications were poor between Sicily and Rome, and the Italian Government was obviously in a state of turmoil. On the other hand, communications between Sicily, Algiers, London, and Washington were too efficient, for Eisenhower was soon deluged with requests from members of the United Nations asking to witness the signing ceremony. Theoretically it was impossible to turn down these requests, but Macmillan noted that most of them came from Britain and the Commonwealth. He therefore volunteered to pick up the hod and discourage such an "extravaganza" as impossible on the basis of pure logistics. Things would happen too quickly.[15]

*

On the morning of September 3, 1943, as the Allied representatives were awaiting an answer from the Italian Government, Montgomery's two-division assault across the Messina Strait, Operation BAYTOWN, went unopposed. The fact that the Allies had now established themselves on the mainland of Europe was not lost on the Badoglio government.

Shortly after 4:00 P.M., September 3, 1943, the long-awaited word came in from Rome: "General Castellano is authorized by the Italian Government to sign acceptance of the armistice conditions." The message was verified by Sir D'Arcy Osborne in the Vatican, and a little over an hour later the Short Terms were signed in an olive grove at the Cassibile Airfield. General Eisenhower, on hand, decided at the last minute to allow Bedell Smith, as the man who had carried the negotiations, to sign. Having witnessed, Eisenhower departed, leaving to Smith the chore of handing Castellano the Long Terms. The negotiating parties then celebrated the signing, though emotions were a little mixed, with a drink of whiskey from dirty glasses.[16]

For the first time Castellano was then shown the Long Terms with the words "surrender unconditionally" included. Like Zanussi, he protested and expressed doubt whether his government would ever accept them. On his own initiative then, as had Zanussi before him, Castellano volunteered to withhold knowledge of these Long Terms until Badoglio had committed himself.

The timing of the announcement now took on considerable importance. Smith specified that it should be made at 6:30 P.M. on some unspecified

---

14 Butcher, p. 405.
15 One actually did make it through. General Theron of South Africa turned up. However, on learning the circumstances, he happily agreed to stay out of the way. Macmillan, p. 322.
16 Strong, p. 158.

date, designated as "X-Day." The morning after X-Day, it was agreed, the Allies would launch the major invasion of Italy. To identify X-Day, the Italians should listen to the BBC for two specific broadcasts, both of which would refer to Nazi propaganda in the Argentine. On that day Eisenhower and Badoglio would speak simultaneously at 6:30 P.M., and in the morning the Allies would hit the boot of Italy.

That same evening, September 3, Eisenhower cabled the Combined Chiefs of Staff:

> I was present this afternoon while my Chief of Staff signed for me and General Castellano signed for Marshal Badoglio the short term military armistice with Italy.
>
> Formal signature will take place after the announcement of the armistice which as you know is to be timed to fit our operational plans. The present document was absolutely necessary as the basis for definite military planning with the Italian representatives and will be kept secret for the time being. At the final signing to take place later we will arrange to have the highest ranking Italian officials present.
>
> I repeat that today's event must be kept secret or our plans will be ruined.[17]

*

Major General Matthew B. Ridgway, the dynamic commander of the U. S. 82nd Airborne Division, was no shrinking violet. But he was no madman, either, and he was not disposed to sacrifice his elite unit uselessly. Originally the 82nd Airborne had been scheduled as part of the "floating reserve" for AVALANCHE (Salerno) and part of the division had been scheduled to land by sea to protect the left flank. However, since Marshal Badoglio had insisted on an airborne drop as a condition for the Italians to sign the Short Terms, Ridgway had been summoned to Alexander's headquarters in Cassibile on September 2. His task would be to plan airborne landings on three airfields near Rome.[18] Elements of the U. S. 45th Division would replace the 82nd Airborne at Salerno.

The planners worked all through the night of September 2 and the next night as well, as Eisenhower had now tentatively approved the concept of the drop. In the course of this planning, however, Ridgway detected so

---

[17] Chandler, II, 1382, 1383.

[18] One parachute infantry regiment was to land at Cerveteri and Furbara airfields the night of September 8, before the landings at Salerno, and push to Rome. The second regiment would drop on Guidonia, Littoria, and Centocelle airfields. It was assumed that the six Italian divisions near Rome would have the airfields secured before the 82nd Airborne units arrived. Garland and Smythe, *Sicily and the Surrender of Italy,* p. 498.

many questionable assumptions that he finally told Alexander and Smith that such an airborne drop near Rome would be a tragic mistake.[19] He was convinced that the two political advisers, Murphy and Macmillan, were responsible, and he confronted them: they would be in the lead aircraft of this airborne operation. To his surprise neither held any objection. Even Eisenhower approved with a dry "Well, all right! There's nothing in the regulations that says diplomats are not expendable."

But though Ridgway had planted the seeds of doubt, Eisenhower still, as late as September 6, seemed to accept the idea as possible. On that day he cabled to the Combined Chiefs that he had held two days' continuous discussion between officers of his staff and General Castellano and as a result had made adjustments in his plans. No appreciable reinforcement was contemplated for BAYTOWN, and no airborne troops would now be employed in AVALANCHE. The floating reserve for the latter would now consist of a regiment from the 45th Division. In this message, however, Eisenhower said that a "senior officer of the 82nd Airborne Division is now on his way to Rome to settle details."[20]

That "senior American officer" was Brigadier General Maxwell B. Taylor, Division Artillery Commander, 82nd Airborne. Accompanying him on this highly dangerous mission was Colonel William T. Gardner, of the Troop Carrier Command. They departed from Palermo by British PT boat at 2:00 A.M. on Tuesday, September 7, transferring to an Italian corvette which took them to a beach near Gaeta. Here an Italian sedan delivered them to a point where they transferred to a Red Cross ambulance. They wet their uniforms to give the appearance of aviators shot down and rescued from the sea, passing several uninterested German patrols along the Appian Way.

In Rome, the two Americans found accommodations in the Palazzo Caprara agreeable, with a rather elaborate dinner awaiting them, but it seemed that nobody in the Italian Government planned to meet. Taylor and Gardner, aware of the imminence of the invasion—which the Italians were not—had to see someone in authority that evening. Finally they got their point across.

At 9:30 P.M. that September 7, with time running short, Taylor and Gardner met at the palazzo with two high-ranking Italian officers, who notified them that German forces around Rome had now grown to a strength of 12,000 paratroopers, equipped with heavy weapons, including 100 artillery pieces. The 3rd Panzer Grenadier Division now had 24,000 men with 200 tanks. At the same time, the Germans had cut off gasoline

19 Ibid.
20 Eisenhower to Combined Chiefs of Staff, September 6. Chandler, II, 1386. Code name for airborne landing was GIANT TWO.

and munitions from Italian units. The Italian "motorized corps" was now virtually immobile, with ammunition sufficient for only a few hours of combat.

Taylor had been aware that some German build-up had occurred and he knew of the disarming of the Italians; but the crucial piece of news was that the Italians could no longer secure the airfields, nor could they provide supplies for whatever troops were landed. The Italians, primarily interested in saving Rome from destruction, now believed that the only way to do so would be to avoid overt acts against the Germans. Finally, Taylor and Gardner disclosed that the Allied invasion was imminent, and the two Italians realized the urgency of the situation and escorted the two Americans quickly to Badoglio's villa.

Badoglio's view of the situation was pessimistic. He never expected the invasion to come so soon, he said, and therefore he had changed his mind on making a radio broadcast the next night. Taylor bored in. "Do you realize," he asked, "how deeply your government has been committed as the result of the agreements already signed?" Badoglio replied that the situation had changed and that Castellano, in signing, had not known all the facts. Italian troops, he insisted, could not possibly defend Rome from the Germans, and the only effect of an immediate announcement would be German occupation and a Neo-Fascist regime.

Taylor then asked if Badoglio could visualize what an Allied bombardment could do to Rome. Badoglio replied that he hoped the Allies would attack the Germans by bombing rail centers but spare Rome and other Italian population centers. Through it all, Badoglio expressed sympathy for the Allies and hoped that Taylor would explain the new situation in Italy to General Eisenhower.

Taylor refused to be placed in the middle. All he would do, he said, would be to serve as a messenger. At 11:00 P.M., therefore, Badoglio sent a message to Eisenhower canceling his earlier commitments:

> Due to changes in the situation brought about by the disposition and strength of the German forces in the Rome area, it is no longer possible to accept an immediate armistice as this could provoke the occupation of the Capital and the violent assumption of the government by the Germans. Operation GIANT TWO is no longer possible because of lack of forces to guarantee the airfields.

Taylor, as a backup, then sent one of his own by secret radio:

> In view of the statement of Marshal Badoglio as to inability to declare armistice and to guarantee fields GIANT TWO is impossible. Reasons given for change are irreplaceable lack of gasoline and munitions and new German dispositions. Badoglio requests Taylor re-

turn to present government views. Taylor and Gardner awaiting instructions.[21]

At about 2:00 A.M. Taylor and Gardner returned to the Palazzo Capraro and gave both messages to the Italians to be coded and sent. At 8:20 A.M. Taylor sent a third. Later, though he realized that AFHQ had acknowledged Badoglio's, Taylor dispatched a final missive consisting only of the code to call off the airborne drop: SITUATION INNOCU-OUS.[22]

Late in the afternoon Taylor and Gardner, accompanied by an Italian staff officer, returned safely to Amilcar, Tunisia, where Eisenhower awaited them. In Algiers Macmillan and Murphy, ignorant of the hard military facts and giving little weight to the Italian attitude, were disappointed by the cancellation of GIANT TWO, as they felt the Allies had made concrete political commitments. Eisenhower, however, if not relieved, was stoic. He immediately gave orders to recall the 82nd Airborne, part of which was already on its way,[23] and turned his attention to the possibility of Badoglio's backing down on the agreed broadcast to the Italian people.

Badoglio's message backing down on the armistice and recommending cancellation of GIANT TWO had been slow in reaching Eisenhower. Sent to Algiers, it had to be recoded and relayed to Amilcar, where Eisenhower was staying in order to be in close touch with Alexander (AVALANCHE was the next morning). As a result Badoglio's message went directly to Bedell Smith, who dutifully forwarded it not only to Amilcar but also to the Combined Chiefs. With the copy to the CCS he enclosed a message in Eisenhower's name advising on the cancellation of GIANT TWO and asking for advice on proceeding with the armistice announcement.

When Smith's message arrived at Amilcar, Eisenhower displayed the temper he usually succeeded in concealing. His fury at first focused on Smith for asking the advice of the CCS on the scheduled announcement; he wanted no advice from Washington and London. (Smith's hide was saved only by the distance between Amilcar and Algiers.) Soon, however, his rage was turned on Badoglio for having backed off on his previous agreement. As he could not undo Smith's action, therefore, Eisenhower wired to Badoglio:

21 Garland and Smythe, p. 502.
22 Ibid.
23 As it turned out, the cancellation of the airborne drop on Rome was a touch-and-go affair. With the hour approaching for the 82nd to depart, time was too short to encode and decode a message to Ridgway, who was waiting by a radio at Cassibile. Eisenhower therefore sent a staff officer to take the message in person. Sixty-two of the aircraft carrying units of the 82nd Airborne were already circling above Sicily when the message arrived. They returned to their airfields in time.

I intend to broadcast the existence of the armistice at the hour originally planned. If you or any part of your armed forces fail to cooperate as previously agreed I will publish to the world full record of this affair. Today is X-day and I expect you to do your part. . . .

Failure now on your part . . . will have most serious consequences for your country. No future action of yours could then restore any confidence whatever in your good faith and consequently the dissolution of your government and nation would ensue.[24]

Eisenhower then turned to a message to the Combined Chiefs of Staff:

I have just completed a conference with the principal commanders and have determined not to accept the Italian change of attitude. We intend to proceed in accordance with plan for the announcement of the armistice and with subsequent propaganda and other measures.[25]

This message asked no advice. Later in the day, however, a message arrived, presumably in answer to Smith's of that morning, confirming agreement on Eisenhower's refusal to accept Badoglio's back-off.

In the meantime Eisenhower turned on a frightened General Castellano, whom he had ordered down from Tunis, and vented his wrath on that unfortunate person, reading him line by line the message he had sent to Badoglio. He than sent Castellano back to Tunis where facilities would enable him to communicate with Badoglio. Perhaps Castellano could persuade the Prime Minister to change his mind once again. There was now little to do but await word of whether or not Badoglio would go ahead with his announcement at 6:30 P.M. as agreed.

Back in Algiers Murphy and Macmillan missed the excitement going on at Amilcar, but they had a little chore of their own. Because of the leaky security in his organization, General Charles de Gaulle had not been privy to the Italian armistice until 5:00 P.M., an hour and a half before Eisenhower's scheduled announcement. When Murphy and Macmillan informed De Gaulle's Foreign Minister, René Massigli, of the imminent military armistice with Italy, Massigli received this news with mixed emotions. The armistice with Italy was fine, but he regretted that the French Committee had not been informed. Macmillan gave the feeble excuse of "confusion," pleading truthfully that the Anglo-Americans had not even been able to tell the Commonwealth governments.

An hour later the two diplomats were ushered in to see De Gaulle. The

24 Eisenhower to Badoglio, September 8, 1943. Quoted in Chandler, III, 1402, 1403.
25 Eisenhower to Combined Chiefs of Staff and British Chiefs of Staff, September 8, 1943. Quoted in ibid., p. 1404.

general, who could not have been totally unaware that something was transpiring, received the news with some humor, congratulating the Anglo-Saxons on the end of their war with Italy. France, of course, was still at war, as his government was not a party to the armistice. Macmillan let this remark go by but said he hoped that as a soldier De Gaulle would understand the need for secrecy. To this De Gaulle replied, "I am not a soldier."

Macmillan was tempted to ask why De Gaulle dressed himself up "in a peculiar and rather obsolete costume" which surely no one would choose to wear unless it was imposed upon him by military necessity.[26] But he held his tongue.

When 6:30 P.M. arrived, Macmillan and Murphy put Eisenhower's prerecorded broadcast on the air. They then anxiously listened to hear whether Badoglio would confirm as he had agreed. Nothing came. Therefore the two decided on an out-and-out deception. Thanks to Strong's foresight, they had in their possession a complete text of Badoglio's message. With the aid of a fluent Italian reader, they put the message on the air immediately—purportedly from Badoglio himself. A little over an hour later all were relieved when Rome Radio broadcast Badoglio's statement. The Italians had indeed kept their word.[27]

*

Little did the members of Allied Force Headquarters realize, either in Amilcar or Algiers, the difficulties that the King and Badoglio were going through. Their very lives in danger, they fled without baggage to Pescara on the Adriatic. Here the party boarded two Italian corvettes that Eisenhower had permitted them to reserve for their own use. Eventually the King, his family, Badoglio, and key governmental officers reached Brindisi on the Adriatic coast of the Italian heel, where they established a temporary Italian Government.

The Italian surrender was now to all intents and purposes accomplished. Not everyone liked dealing with King Victor Emmanuel and Badoglio, of course, but Churchill's penchant for support of constitutional monarchy (which meant the King) and irrefutable military necessity made this arrangement inevitable.[28] To the elation of the Western Allies,

26 Macmillan, p. 324.
27 Ibid., p. 325.
28 One of those disliking the retention of King Victor Emmanuel and dealing with Badoglio was Harry Hopkins, who wrote in his diary:

I have grave misgivings about both the King and Badoglio. Certainly neither of them, by any stretch of the imagination, can be considered to represent a democratic government.

It is very easy to recognise these people, but it is awfully hard to throw them overboard later.

the King gave the order from aboard ship for the Italian fleet to leave port and to surrender to the Allies at Malta.

The Italian Navy obviously had no stomach for being taken over by the Germans, for when the King's order came all was in readiness. The fleet took to sea in two squadrons on the evening of September 8.

One squadron, under Admiral d'Zara, consisted of two battleships, some cruisers, and some destroyers. It steamed out of Taranto, on the heel of the boot and, aside from sighting some Allied naval vessels, proceeded without incident to Malta. Here in St. Paul's Harbor it anchored, awaiting the rest of the fleet.

Not so lucky was the main body, which was based in La Spezia and Genoa, on the Ligurian Sea north of Corsica. This portion was directly under the Commander-in-Chief, Admiral Bergamini, and it sailed under hazardous conditions, exposed to German air attack from France. Unfortunately, this fleet of three battleships, five cruisers, and five destroyers was detected and attacked as it skirted the west coast of Sardinia. One battleship, the *Roma,* sank in twenty minutes, Admiral Bergamini being among those lost. The Italians at first feared that they had been attacked by the Allies, and they sent a frantic message to Algiers imploring no repetition. They were soon assured that the raid had been executed by the Germans, and no further troubles were encountered.

The Italian fleet—or rather what was left—was met just off Bône, Algeria, by Force H, the main British fleet in the Mediterranean, and then led single file past Bizerte along the channel which had been cleared between Tunis and Sicily. As it passed Bizerte, the British force was greeted from a destroyer by Cunningham and Eisenhower, the latter keeping his presence a secret since this was Cunningham's day. Eisenhower soon left for Amilcar to check on the progress of AVALANCHE, which had been launched the previous morning.

When the British-Italian naval force reached Malta, it sailed into St. Paul's Harbor and joined the squadron from Taranto. The battleship H.M.S. *Warspite,* carrying Cunningham, continued south and anchored in the Grand Harbor of Valletta. Admiral d'Zara, now the senior Italian officer, arrived in Valletta at 4:00 P.M. Cunningham gave his defeated opponent every courtesy, including an honor guard from the *Warspite,* and the surrender ceremonies were duly concluded. The next morning, September 11, 1943, Cunningham sent a message to London: "Be pleased to

I surely don't like the idea that these former enemies can change their minds when they know they are going to get licked and come over to our side and get help in maintaining political power.

Sherwood, p. 744.

inform their lordships that the Italian battle fleet is now anchored under the fortress guns of Malta."[29]

*

By Sunday, September 12, political prisoner Benito Mussolini had been moved to a citadel in the Italian mountains near Abruzzi. That morning ninety SS parachutists under the command of Obersturmbahnführer Otto Skorzeny overwhelmed Mussolini's guard, and Skorzeny, piloting a small Storch, took Il Duce on a hazardous trip to join Hitler in Munich. Mussolini by this time was a grim, pathetic figure, clad in black, with a hat pulled almost over his eyes, in need of a shave, and with a haunted look. At Hitler's insistence, he soon set up an ineffectual Neo-Fascist government on Lake Garda.

*

On September 29, 1943, the formal Italian surrender was signed aboard the H.M.S. *Nelson* in Valletta Harbor. General Eisenhower, unpleasant as he considered the proceedings, turned up and personally affixed his signature to the Long Terms. Marshal Badoglio did likewise. The Long Terms, as Eisenhower had predicted, would not be published until many years after the war. The most stringent provisions were never put into effect.

*

While the political negotiations were going on, General Eisenhower's main concern was Operation AVALANCHE, so much so as to shove politics almost to the back of his mind. For a political situation might be confused and fuzzy, but the defeat of an attempted landing, with Allied forces being driven back into the sea, would deal a tremendous blow to Allied morale—and, just incidentally, to his own future as well. By this stage of the war the two Western democracies were in no mood for any defeats; in fact they were already criticizing the extent of the victories.

Eisenhower would probably have given even less attention to Italian politics had he possessed the forces necessary to ensure certain military victory at Salerno, but he did not. Landing craft, as always, constituted a limitation on the force he could deliver, and this time it had been particularly difficult to plan since the number of craft available could not be determined until the completion of the Sicilian campaign on August 17. Until then the craft would be delivering supplies and reinforcements across the Sicilian beaches.

During this time Eisenhower's relations with his chiefs in London and Washington, principally Churchill and Marshall, were difficult. Churchill,

[29] Butcher, pp. 411–16; Churchill, V, 114–15.

on the one hand, persisted in urging Eisenhower to be as aggressive as possible, questioning why the Allies should "crawl up the leg [of Italy] like a harvest bug from the ankle upwards."[30] Anxious to emphasize the Mediterranean Theater—and Italy in particular—Churchill had sent a message to Eisenhower on July 18 (only the day after Eisenhower's recommendation for the execution of AVALANCHE and BAYTOWN), quoting Smuts to the effect that the next operation should be directed against Rome. "We should attempt only vital blows at this stage of the war," Smuts had written, "and sideshows should be avoided."[31] To this Eisenhower had replied:

> I always find my sentiments in full accord with any suggestion that seeks to avoid nibbling and jabbing in order to leap straight at the vitals of the enemy. I think, however, that no one can long be engaged in this business of modern war and fail to be convinced of the absolute necessity of keeping his shipping, particularly when large amounts of vulnerable vessels are involved, under the protection of his own shore-based fighter craft. . . . If a large invasion force would sail directly to Naples or to the northward without the benefit of a strong fighter cover, it would certainly be asking for trouble.[32]

But while Churchill was urging more aggressiveness in the Italian campaign, Eisenhower found General Marshall, who provided most of the men and matériel, becoming stingy. Eisenhower, as Allied Commander officially reported to the CCS as a body, but Marshall was the hand that fed him. And Marshall, though forced to agree to landings in Italy, was determined to restrict resources allocated for that purpose to those on hand. He would also hold the British to their agreement that, despite the Sicilian victory, those four American and three British divisions would be transferred to the United Kingdom by November 1.

Worse yet, from Eisenhower's viewpoint, was Marshall's determination to employ the heavy bombers based in the United Kingdom against the Luftwaffe even at the expense of taking some risk on AVALANCHE. "The most the Americans would agree to," Alan Brooke complained, "was the temporary loan of three groups of heavy bombers from England to bomb the Rumanian oil fields."[33]

Marshall was not alone in his resolve. On the day after the fall of Mussolini, July 27, Secretary of War Henry L. Stimson arrived in Algiers. He had been in Britain to inspect troops but in London had been drawn

---

[30] Tedder, *With Prejudice,* p. 455.
[31] Chandler, II, 1263ff.
[32] Eisenhower to Churchill, dated July 18. Ibid., p. 1262.
[33] Bryant, *Turn of the Tide,* p. 458. It turned out to be four groups, however.

into lengthy discussions with Churchill which had disturbed him. Interspersed with theoretical professions of support for the cross-Channel invasion the next year, Churchill's mind had kept wandering back to the Mediterranean—to Italy, to the Balkans, and to Turkey—and the discussions had convinced Stimson that Churchill was going to be a problem. The Secretary's purpose in coming to Algiers, with Churchill's hearty support, was to consult General Eisenhower. Talking with Eisenhower, Stimson stressed—as if he needed to—that the Americans had given way in July 1942 by agreeing to TORCH and again at Casablanca in agreeing to HUSKY. Now they were following HUSKY with BAYTOWN and AVALANCHE. The fall of Mussolini made little impression on Stimson, and he was becoming more and more vehemently opposed to the British "circular strategy."

In this Eisenhower was somewhat torn. He had always been a staunch supporter of the cross-Channel invasion since he had first drawn up the plans for ROUNDUP and SLEDGEHAMMER. On the other hand, as Allied Commander in the Mediterranean Theater, he could see great possible gains. But most important, he was conscious that AVALANCHE, which he had been ordered to execute, was a very considerable risk. On a temporary basis, therefore, Eisenhower wanted more forces than Marshall and Stimson were willing to give, so long as nothing was done to add additional risks to OVERLORD the next year. Satisfied, Stimson returned home.

On arrival back in Washington Stimson submitted an informal report to the President and then on August 10 he wrote a formal letter, the thrust of which was that the time had come for the American Government to take the lead in the prosecution of the war. So as to avoid implicating General Marshall in his own opinions, Stimson completed it, signed it, and only then showed it to Marshall. He would, he said, make changes that Marshall violently disagreed with, but short of that he would send the letter forward on his own responsibility. Marshall had no objections but agreed that he should not be associated with the document.

Stimson had now concluded, the letter began, that the Allies could not rationally hope to cross the Channel and come to grips with the German enemy under a British commander. The experiences of Passchendaele and Dunkirk, Stimson believed, had made the British leadership too frightened of land operations on the Continent. They would pay lip service to "ROUNDHAMMER" (Stimson's own code name for OVERLORD), but its successful execution would require more faith and vigor than could reasonably be expected of any British commander. Stimson's second point was that the British really did not believe it necessary to mass the vigor and power of the American and British nations in the north of France. British thinking was that Germany could be beaten by a series of attritions in northern Italy, the eastern Mediterranean, in Greece, the Balkans, and Rumania—"pinprick warfare."

Finally the Secretary put his chief's feet to the fire:

I believe therefore that the time has come for you to decide that your government must assume the responsibility of leadership in this great final movement of the European war which is now confronting us. We cannot afford to begin the most dangerous operation of the war under halfhearted results. Nearly two years ago the British offered us this command. I think that now it should be accepted—if necessary, insisted on.[34]

He wound up his letter by naming General Marshall as the man who most surely could, by his character and skill, furnish the military leadership necessary. The Secretary saw no alternative.

Stimson took the letter by hand to the White House on August 11 and then experienced one of the most satisfactory meetings he ever held with the President. Roosevelt listened with interest as he told about his trip; and after having read his letter said that he had come to the same conclusions himself. When the Joint Chiefs arrived, Stimson stayed for the meeting and later declared that Roosevelt was clearer and more definite than he had been at any other time during the war. The President, he reported, was in favor of going no farther into Italy than Rome—and that only for the purpose of "establishing bases." As a politician, he also recognized that the U.S. force in the United Kingdom should be larger than that of the British by the time the cross-Channel invasion should take place, in order to make the idea of an American commander more palatable. Stimson was elated. "The cross-Channel attack," he wrote, "had now at last become wholly his [Roosevelt's] own."[35] American attention had definitely switched from the Mediterranean to northern Europe nearly a month before AVALANCHE.

*

In late July and early August, while HUSKY was still in progress, General Eisenhower was undergoing a new experience, a refusal of support from General Marshall. Up to this time Marshall had done his best to meet every request Eisenhower had made, but now, with the Mediterranean Theater becoming secondary, he refused a direct Eisenhower request, even a plea.

During the Stimson visit Eisenhower was studying the air support for AVALANCHE. On July 27 and 28 he spent several hours with Air Chief Marshal Sir Arthur Tedder and his deputy, Lieutenant General Carl Spaatz. At that time American heavy bomber strength in the Mediter-

34 Stimson, p. 437.
35 Ibid., p. 439.

ranean consisted of four groups of B-17 Flying Fortresses and two under-strength groups of B-24 Liberators.[36] If that strength could be doubled, they felt, they could disrupt German installations and communications to such an extent as to reduce the risks dramatically. Accordingly Eisenhower cabled the Combined Chiefs outlining the difficulties of AVALANCHE and requesting a temporary loan of four groups of B-17s from the U. S. Eighth Air Force in the United Kingdom. The bombers would remain in the Mediterranean only until September 15.

A copy of Eisenhower's message was sent to Lieutenant General Jacob L. Devers,[37] who, with Ira Eaker, commanding Eighth Air Force, protested strongly. At that moment the Allies were beginning to win the air war over Germany, and this, they argued, was no time to let up the strategic offensive. A transfer of four groups would take only a third of the Eighth Air Force bombers, but it would reduce fighting capability by about half because of aircraft grounded for repair and maintenance.

Marshall decided in favor of Devers and Eaker, though hinting that four medium groups might be provided Eisenhower as a substitute. To Eisenhower the mediums were no substitute but they were better than nothing.

In the meantime, a long-scheduled, high-risk air raid on the Ploesti oil fields in Rumania was to be executed on August 4 by four groups of B-24 Liberators from the Eighth Air Force. The operation was to be based on Tripoli, in Eisenhower's territory, and he felt some responsibility for it. He hoped that the losses would not exceed 20 percent, but when the raid was duly carried out, at least a third of the original 177 bombers failed to report back.[38] A follow-up was ruled out; the raid made favorable headlines, but German oil production was hardly affected. By any yardstick the raid was a failure.

Eisenhower, seeing an opening, now sought to retain those four groups of B-24s—or what was left of them. But two days after the raid the Combined Chiefs rejected his request. Even the loan of the four medium groups was meeting opposition from Devers, and after full consideration Marshall had decided not to recommend their transfer. Eisenhower would have to make do with forces already assigned to the Mediterranean.

Eisenhower was at this time, mid-August, undergoing a spell of frustration. He had gone to the dispensary for a physical checkup (he was up for promotion to colonel in the Regular Army), and the doctors, finding

[36] A bomber group was an extremely elastic unit. The ones in question averaged about thirty-five aircraft each. Letter to author, Major General John W. Huston, Chief, Office of Air Force History, February 14, 1980.
[37] Devers had replaced Lieutenant General Frank Andrews, killed in an air crash, as Commanding General, European Theater of Operations.
[38] Butcher, p. 378.

his blood pressure excessive, had told him to go to bed. That he had done, although in fits and starts; and he could never get his mind off the current situation. Four days later Butcher recorded that he was still in bed as much as possible, responding well to his rest, but exercised over what he thought history would call his "big mistake." He had, he lectured, made an error in being too cautious in the invasion of Sicily. What he should have done, Eisenhower said as he sprang out of bed and paced the floor, was to attack Sicily and Italy on both sides of Messina Strait, the landings to include both Messina (Sicily) and Reggio (Italy). This area would have cut off the two German divisions in Sicily and would have achieved wholesale surrender, saving time, equipment, and especially landing craft. (The first mistake, the inclusion of Casablanca as one of the landing sites for TORCH, had not been Eisenhower's sole decision.) After a questionable rest, Eisenhower was back at a commanders' meeting the next day.

On August 17, the day that Messina fell—and the day before Smith and Strong headed for Lisbon—Eisenhower made one more effort to hold on to the B-24 groups scheduled for transfer back to the United Kingdom. "If our present heavy bombing strength should suffer this [ongoing] reduction," he wrote to Marshall, "we would be skating on very thin ice in AVALANCHE." He concluded by pleading as strongly as possible:

> The hostile bomber strength has been steadily building up in this theater for some days and we simply must get on top of this matter if AVALANCHE is to be a success.[39]

Two days later General Arnold, on Marshall's behalf, again turned down Eisenhower's request. There was nothing to do; the bomber groups would have to be returned, and Eisenhower would go on with AVALANCHE without them.

Tedder, on the other hand, was somewhat more successful in his dealings with the Chief of the British Air Staff, Sir Charles Portal. In a series of heated telegrams Tedder fought against the removal of three Wellington squadrons. The exchanges of messages were reasonable and personal, as Tedder and Portal were friends and contemporaries. Probably because the British put more emphasis on the Mediterranean than did the Americans, Tedder was able to stall off the switch of the Wellingtons, at least until September 15, at which time AVALANCHE was expected to be established.[40]

[39] Eisenhower to Marshall, August 17. Chandler, II, 1339.
[40] ". . . there is a tendency to consider the Italian chicken as being already in the pot, whereas in fact it is not yet hatched. Possibly also a tendency to count too much on the military value of an Italian collapse. If H.M.G. still regard the elimination of

On August 25 Eisenhower received word, not surprising, that the Combined Chiefs at Quebec had confirmed the withdrawal of those seven divisions from the Mediterranean, starting November 1. Eisenhower was now beginning to think that the CCS were stripping his fighting force prematurely, ignoring the rapid build-up of German forces. He was not, however, so concerned about the divisions (of which he had more than he could transport), as his main problem was that of bomber strength and landing craft. But more upset than Eisenhower was Alan Brooke. Five days after the Quebec Conference he was writing in mixed metaphors: "We have now arrived in the Orchard and our next step should be to shake the fruit trees and gather the apples. . . . Success breeds success in these cases and the ball was at our feet."[41]

*

On the evening of Sunday, September 5, 1943, four old friends were engaged in a bridge game in General Eisenhower's Villa Dar el Ouard in Algiers. Of the four, Major General Alfred Gruenther was by all odds the acknowledged expert, in the professional class, having supplemented a lieutenant's pay during the 1930s by refereeing professional tournaments in New York. Gruenther's partner in this game was Dwight Eisenhower, who, though not a professional, was a top-flight amateur. These two made a good combination, for Gruenther had the edge in expertise and Eisenhower had the edge in rank. Their opponents this evening were Lieutenant General Mark W. Clark and Commander Harry C. Butcher, not players in Gruenther's or even Eisenhower's class, but competent enough to make a game.

Little was said of business, although at one point Eisenhower told how he would like to get his hands on Mussolini and try him by court-martial before he hanged him. And Clark, on his part, seemed to have his mind somewhere else. For good reason. When the game was finished, Clark and Gruenther boarded the U.S.S. *Ancon,* their command ship, on route to the Salerno beaches. And Clark would have the next two nights on the

Italy and the establishment of heavy bomber bases in Central Italy as being effective contributions towards defeating Germany, surely we should concentrate on this immediate object." Tedder, p. 462.
41 "When arguing with Marshall I could never get him fully to appreciate the very close connection that existed between the various German fronts. For him they might have been separate wars, a Russian war on one side, a Mediterranean war on another and a cross-Channel one to be started as soon as possible. I have often wondered . . . how different matters might have been if I had had MacArthur instead of Marshall to deal with. . . . I must, however, confess that Winston was no great help. . . . Marshall had a holy fear of Winston's Balkan and Dardanelles ventures, and was always guarding against these dangers even when they did not exist." Bryant, *Turn of the Tide,* pp. 559–60.

water to worry about losing the 82nd Airborne Division from the Salerno landings. Given the uncertainty of the Italian attitude, Clark knew that this, his first battle, would be no pushover.

The next day (three days after the signing of the Short Terms) Eisenhower, his usual optimism restored, sent Marshall his final message:

> Montgomery had no opposition at all getting ashore in the Toe— a week before the attack I told him he wouldn't have any. . . . However, the AVALANCHE operation is a horse of a different color and I am frank to state that there is more than a faint possibility that we may have some hard going. But our commanders and troops are in good heart, and . . . I am determined to hit as hard as I can.[42]

As of 3:30 A.M. on Tuesday, September 9, AVALANCHE was launched according to schedule. Operation GIANT TWO had been called off but at the last minute Eisenhower ordered a seaborne attack on the naval base at Taranto by the British 1st Airborne Division. The convoy delivering the 1st Airborne passed the Italian fleet sailing out of the harbor on the way to surrender. For a while there was some doubt as to whether the Italian ships were out to surrender or to fight, but not a shot was fired.

AVALANCHE, BAYTOWN, and the landing at Taranto were all under the tactical command of General Sir Harold Alexander, whose 15 Army Group had remained intact since the Sicilian campaign. Of the forces subordinate to Alexander, the British troops were all veterans, the two (5th and 1st Canadian) from Montgomery's Eighth Army (BAYTOWN) and the two (46th and 56th) which comprised Lieutenant General Sir Richard McCreery's X British Corps, half of Clark's Fifth U. S. Army (AVALANCHE). The two divisions which comprised U. S. VI Corps, on McCreery's right, were the U. S. 36th and 45th Infantry Divisions, up to strength and well trained. The 45th had seen action in Sicily, the 36th was new. Clark would have like more forces—any commander would—but four divisions were all that could be carried in available landing craft.

In the first landings Clark's men encountered only one German division, the 16th Panzer. Though the high command suspected that Salerno, with fit beaches and within the range of their short-range fighter planes, would be the spot for Allied landings, Kesselring still could not afford to gamble by placing more than one division in any particular area; Allied naval and air superiority made it possible for them to strike anywhere in Italy—and even the Balkans. So Kesselring and Rommel, now with eigh-

---

[42] Eisenhower to Marshall, September 6, 1943. Chandler, II, 1389–90.

teen divisions, had contented themselves by staying in readiness, disarming the Italian Army, and preparing to reinforce their opposition to a major landing in any area—once it was identified. Furthermore, the 16th Panzer Division was a fine unit, and not mauled in Sicily. It would be alert in its defense of the Salerno area.

At the end of the first day of battle, both sides, German and Allied, seemed satisfied. The Germans were happy that the Allies had not pushed their attack more energetically against the single panzer division, but the Allies could feel relief that Clark's Fifth Army was at least ashore, and the push about ten miles inland to the Calore River was fairly easy. But Kesselring was now ready to reinforce around the bridgehead. Soon the Hermann Goering and 15th Panzer Grenadier Divisions, though under strength from the Sicilian operation, were facing McCreery's X Corps, and the 29th Panzer Grenadier Division, having withdrawn easily from Montgomery's front in the south, was facing the U. S. VI Corps.

By the morning of September 12, therefore, Clark's four infantry divisions, reinforced by rangers and two battalions from the 82nd Airborne, were being assaulted by six panzer or panzer grenadier divisions. The situation was becoming increasingly dangerous, and it appeared that the Allies might suffer their first major defeat. Anxiety at Allied Force Headquarters was deepened by the rumor that Clark, concerned that the bridgehead might be split in two, was preparing to disembark on a command ship, even contemplating withdrawal of the entire Allied force.

At this point General Eisenhower had to take drastic action. Alexander was doing all he could on the battlefield, but he needed help. On Monday, September 13, Eisenhower asked the Combined Chiefs for the use of eighteen LSTs known to be en route to India and for the return of the three bomber groups which had been denied him previously. Both requests were granted.[43] Eisenhower also contacted Cunningham, who ordered two battleships to Salerno. And at this critical moment Spaatz volunteered to try a revolutionary gamble; he would use his heavy bombers in direct support of the land operation.

The next morning the whole weight of Allied air power, every plane that could fly, was concentrated on the sensitive spots, and by evening the bridgehead was considered safe. So effective was the new-found support that Bedell Smith suggested creating an entire staff section to keep Washington worried.

On September 16 an element of the British 5th Division, part of Montgomery's Eighth Army, made contact with a U. S. Fifth Army patrol southeast of Salerno Bay. The front was now continuous across the boot;

43 Butcher, p. 416.

Naples would fall on October 1. The Allies would fight a laborious battle in Italy for the rest of the war.

*

On September 23, 1943, General Eisenhower received two messages which were notable for their contrast. One was from Prime Minister Churchill: "I congratulate you on the victorious landing and deployment northward of our armies. As the Duke of Wellington said of the Battle of Waterloo, 'It was a damned close-run thing,' but your policy of running risks has been vindicated."[44] This was gratifying to Eisenhower because Churchill back in July had been urging him to more and more audacious operations.

But Eisenhower's spirits were dampened somewhat by a message from Washington. Marshall and Dill now seemed to feel that Eisenhower's tactics had not been sufficiently aggressive: ". . . at long range it would seem that you give the enemy too much time to prepare and eventually find yourself up against a very stiff resistance."

It grieved Eisenhower to think that Marshall had not given him credit for "cracking the whip." After all, Eisenhower reasoned, he himself had insisted on going through with AVALANCHE despite misgivings and moanings from many of his staff. And Marshall, he felt, had stinted in his support.[45]

In a message the next day, in which he outlined his reasoning in the AVALANCHE and BAYTOWN operations, Eisenhower allowed himself a small riposte:

> As a matter of interest to you I received . . . from the Prime Minister a telegram congratulating me on the success of my "policy of running risks." I feel certain that some of his correspondents in this area look upon me as a gambler.[46]

[44] Wellington has also been quoted as saying "a near-run thing." See p. 47 above.
[45] Butcher, p. 424.
[46] Eisenhower to Marshall, September 24, 1943. Quoted in Chandler, III, 1454.

CHAPTER XXI

THE "LAWYER'S BARGAIN"

Sunday, August 15, 1943, was a bleak day for Britain's foremost soldier, General Sir Alan Brooke. The previous five days had gone well enough, at least better than expected. Brooke had lost none of his distaste for these trips, and he would never become accustomed to the inevitable confrontations with the Americans; but so far the stay at Quebec had been relatively painless. The Prime Minister had left for Hyde Park two days after arrival and the British Chiefs had made use of the weekend to prepare their final positions. On Friday, August 13, the Americans had arrived, and the next day the Combined Chiefs had met. Brooke, as host, had acted as chairman. Nothing substantive had yet been addressed. They had agreed on an agenda and had indulged in only preliminary sparring. There had even been a bit of time for sight-seeing.

Brooke spent that Sunday morning with his British colleagues preparing for the CCS meeting to be held at two-thirty that afternoon. First was to be a lunch with the Prime Minister, who had just returned from Hyde Park. Brooke gave it no thought when notified that Churchill wanted to see him a quarter of an hour before the rest would gather.

When Brooke knocked on Churchill's door, the two men stepped out on the terrace of the Citadel[1] to take in the magnificent view of the St. Lawrence River. Below lay the Plains of Abraham, the field where British General Wolfe and French General Montcalm had both fallen in battle nearby two centuries earlier (1759).

[1] The Château Frontenac, which had been taken over by the Canadian Government, housed the staffs and provided space for the conferences. Roosevelt and Churchill stayed in the Citadel nearby. The Citadel was the summer residence of the governor general.

But history was not on Churchill's mind, for he was preparing himself to undergo the painful experience of telling Brooke that an American, not he, would command OVERLORD. Previously it had been tacitly assumed that any cross-Channel invasion of France, launched from Britain, would be commanded by a British officer, and based on this, Churchill had informally promised Brooke that this most coveted command of the war would be his. But at Hyde Park Churchill and Roosevelt had agreed that OVERLORD should be commanded by an American, which meant that Brooke's great moment would be denied him, not because of his lack of ability but because of his nationality. Hiding his feelings—and confident of Brooke's loyalty—Churchill laid out his reasoning for the change. Brooke was stunned, but Churchill was relieved at his lack of response. Brooke, Churchill observed, "bore the great disappointment with soldierly dignity."[2]

Through the rest of the day Brooke performed his duties as usual. After lunch he chaired a difficult conference with the Americans at a meeting which he described as "painful," and for a while his own personal feelings seemed to slip his mind. Ironically his efforts that day were devoted to securing American approval of an increase in future resources for the Mediterranean. Marshall, who had now become the prospective OVERLORD commander, was refusing to admit any great link between the two separate war theaters and had apparently reached the limits of his patience. He had had enough of British attempts to emphasize the Italian campaign, and he once more threatened to limit U.S. contribution to OVERLORD to one small corps (the same as had been planned for 1942)[3] and reorient the war toward Japan. After three hours the meeting broke up.

That evening Brooke dined alone, as he wanted to be by himself. Years later he would still remember the "dark cloud of despair" that had crossed him that day. He recalled how he had voluntarily turned down the North African command before El Alamein in order to remain with the Prime Minister. Now that the global strategy of the war had been established, completing his mission with Churchill, Brooke felt free to go. But it was too late and Brooke, insensitive to Churchill's own agony at passing the news, misinterpreted his abruptness as a lack of feeling. "He offered me no sympathy," Brooke said later, "no regrets of having had to change his mind, and dealt with the matter as if it were one of minor importance."[4]

[2] Churchill, V, 85.
[3] Bryant, *Turn of the Tide*, p. 578.
[4] Ibid., p. 579.

Allowing personal ambition to affect one's attitude toward such life-and-death matters as military operations is one of the unattractive failings of the professional warrior's psyche. Not all succumbed. In this case Brooke honestly felt himself to be the best-qualified individual.

Intellectually, however, Brooke could take comfort in realizing that American command of OVERLORD was inevitable. Up to this time the burden of battle in the Mediterranean had been sustained predominantly by the British, and even though the Allied Commander had been an American, the proximity of Britain to Hitler's Nazi Europe had caused everyone quite unconsciously to think of the European War as primarily a British enterprise—as the Pacific was considered American. Thus up to this time the hard fact of future American preponderance in OVER-LORD—approximately 80 percent of the eventual invasion force—had been overlooked. Churchill and Roosevelt had become conscious of this future development at about the same time.

Roosevelt's realization had been stimulated by the detailed and forceful letter Stimson had submitted on August 10 (the day Churchill landed in Quebec). Thus, had Churchill failed to offer the OVERLORD command to an American—which he did—Roosevelt would have insisted anyway.

The First Quebec Conference (QUADRANT) was one of the less dramatic of the high-level wartime meetings. In the early stages the CCS were absorbed by the appearance of General Castellano in Madrid. This resulted, as mentioned, in the Quebec Memorandum which the CCS sent to General Eisenhower on August 17. After that the subjects discussed were less pressing: the invasion of northern France, the allocation of landing craft to the Pacific, future operations in Burma, and now, in a new light, the future military operations against the Italian mainland.

But smaller matters also made their way into the conference. One of these was a project which had long been a favorite of Admiral Mountbatten, the conversion of a large iceberg from northern Canada into a two-million-ton aircraft carrier, which he called a HABAKKUK.[5] This carrier would, of course, be unsinkable and could be repaired easily by merely pouring fresh water into any cracks or holes that might develop. As armor plate, Mountbatten's staff had devised a special type of ice called "Pykrete," 95 percent of which was wood pulp. This idea, originally a source of some amusement to the British Chiefs, was now becoming something to contend with, since it had caught the imagination of Churchill. Brooke, who earlier had dismissed it as folly, could no longer ignore it. He was annoyed by Mountbatten's insistence on presenting it to the CCS, and when the admiral approached him (as chairman) just before the meeting of Thursday afternoon, August 19, Brooke burst forth, "The hell with HABAKKUK!"

Brooke then caught himself, a little embarrassed: he was, he realized,

[5] Habakkuk 1:5. Behold ye among the heathen, and regard, and wonder marvellously: for I will work a work in your days, which ye will not believe, though it be told you.

preoccupied by the next confrontation he expected with the Americans. But Mountbatten, undaunted, kept pleading to have his moment in court.

The session that day turned out to be as acrimonious as Brooke had feared, and once again the sixty-odd staff officers were dismissed from the conference room. And, as so often before, the issues became resolved more easily by the unchaperoned Combined Chiefs. Relieved, Brooke was about to declare adjournment when Mountbatten rushed up and asked to present HABAKKUK. Marshall nodded, and a reluctant Brooke gave Mountbatten the floor.

In his element, Mountbatten then explained the properties of Pykrete, and upon his signal some attendants placed two large cubes at the end of the room. The one on the left, Mountbatten pointed out, was of ordinary ice; that on the right was Pykrete. Now, in order to demonstrate the superior protective properties of Pykrete, he would fire a bullet from his revolver into each.

As Mountbatten reached into his pocket, the Combined Chiefs of Staff of the United States and the British Empire rose from their seats and sidled into positions behind him.

Mountbatten's aim was true. The first bullet struck the ordinary ice and, as predicted, showered splinters all over the witnesses. "There," said Mountbatten. "That is just what I told you. Now I shall fire at the block on the right."[6] Again his marksmanship was impeccable, but this time the bullet rebounded from the block and buzzed around the room, nicking the leg of King's trousers[7] and barely missing Portal. Immediately the doors flew open and the staff officers rushed back in. "Good heavens!" one shouted. "They've started shooting now!"

Such incidents of comic relief were, however, few, and Brooke muttered, "Thank God," when the Combined Chiefs submitted their recommendations, which set the target date for OVERLORD at May 1, 1944, provided three conditions were met:

1. There must be a substantial reduction in the strength of the German fighter aircraft in north-west Europe before the assault takes place.

2. There should be not more than twelve mobile German divisions in northern France at the time the operation is launched, and it must not be possible for the Germans to build up more than fifteen divisions in the succeeding two months.

[6] Bryant, *Turn of the Tide*, p. 584.
[7] King and Whitehill, *Fleet Admiral King*, p. 487, attributes the revolver shot to an assistant. Bryant says it was Mountbatten. Some more elaborate accounts picture the ice carried out the door under cover, being mistaken by the staff as a corpse.

3. The problem of beach maintenance of large forces in the tidal waters of the English Channel over a prolonged period must be overcome. To ensure this it is essential that we should be able to construct at least two effective synthetic harbours.[8]

Roosevelt and Churchill then approved the general invasion plan that Lieutenant General Sir Frederick Morgan's staff had been working on since his designation as "Chief of Staff to the [unnamed] Supreme Commander" (COSSAC) the previous January. Churchill added one more caveat in addition to the three stipulations: an increase in landing craft by 25 percent.

Brooke's hope for reinforcing the Mediterranean was, however, accepted only in part. With the Italian surrender negotiations under way, Marshall had accepted an invasion of Italy, but with forces far short of Brooke's expectations. American emphasis on the war against Japan, moreover, was more than the British liked, as the Pacific action was engaging the vast bulk of the United States fleet. Wake, the Gilberts, the Marshalls, Palau, the Carolines, and the eastern half of New Guinea were to be assaulted in 1944. Meanwhile Admiral Mountbatten, named as the new Supreme Commander of the China-Burma-India Theater, would attempt to reopen land communications with China. "I am not really satisfied with the results," Brooke wrote. "We have not really arrived at the best strategy but I suppose that when working with Allies compromises with all their evils become inevitable."[9]

*

Though the question of the OVERLORD commander never appeared on the agenda at Quebec, the selection of General Marshall for the command was generally assumed. Marshall had been the most prominent and tenacious proponent of the cross-Channel assault; and his prestige would assure Churchill that the Americans would now give OVERLORD all priority of resources. Marshall's new assignment seemed so definite after Quebec that Mrs. Marshall felt safe in moving some of their personal furniture from Fort Myer to their home in Leesburg, Virginia, where she would wait out the war.

Roosevelt made no formal announcement. However, he obviously could not keep the decision strictly to himself, so his subordinates had to be notified. Soon the word leaked to the public and spread, probably with some encouragement from Roosevelt himself. And when the word inevitably reached the press, the reaction was far from unanimous. It was, in

[8] Ismay, p. 311.
[9] Bryant, *Turn of the Tide*, p. 586.

fact, criticized severely by commentators of every political persuasion. The protest—"hullabaloo" is the word used by Sherwood—was not directed against Marshall, nor did any other name come up as an alternative. Rather it centered around the unfair treatment that Marshall was supposedly receiving at the hands of Roosevelt. The *Army and Navy Journal,* for example, directly asserted that "powerful influences" would like to eliminate Marshall as Chief of Staff, adding that such action would cause shock to the Army, the Congress, and the nation. The *Army and Navy Register* likewise interpreted such an appointment as simply a means of getting rid of the Chief of Staff.

Other publications went even further. The Cheyenne *Tribune,* a habitual enemy of the Roosevelt administration, laid the prospective move to "Hopkins' slimy hand," implying that Hopkins would like to see Marshall replaced by his own personal friend, Lieutenant General Brehon Somervell, who had worked with him during the days of the WPA. The term "Global WPA" was used to describe the future command setup in Washington for the war.[10]

The blasts from the press inevitably traveled overseas. In Algiers rumors of Marshall's upcoming appointment reached Harry Butcher as early as October 1. Later the word reached enemy intelligence, whereupon Dr. Goebbels' propaganda machinery blasted forth that Marshall had been "fired" and that Roosevelt himself was now assuming the job of Army Chief of Staff, as Hitler had taken personal command of the German Army. This last announcement at least lent some levity to an otherwise uncomfortable situation.

But despite urgings from Churchill (himself under political pressure of a different kind), Roosevelt still refused to commit himself in public.

Roosevelt's silence during this period was no oversight. In fact, he had simply not decided. On the one hand, he was coming to rely more and more upon Marshall, not only for advice but because of the general's personal prestige with the Congress and his ability to handle, as well as any man could, the prima donna MacArthur. These factors would point to keeping Marshall in Washington.

On the other hand, since Roosevelt wanted to do well by Marshall, his sense of history pushed him toward sending him to Europe. Roosevelt was keenly aware that the generals enshrined in military annals were the field commanders. In the First World War, for example, John J. Pershing, not Army Chief of Staff Peyton C. March, had attained prominent public

[10] The three publications are all quoted from Sherwood, which includes a more complete review of press reaction. Sherwood, pp. 759–62.

stature.[11] And Roosevelt's associates were sharply divided. Hopkins and Stimson (who claimed to know Marshall's innermost desires) urged that Marshall get the command he "so much wanted," while the other three member of the JCS—Leahy, King, and Arnold—hated the thought of Marshall's departure. King swore he would fight the change down to the last moment.[12] But though Roosevelt delayed, Churchill felt pressure. At the end of September 1943 he was urging a quick announcement of Marshall's appointment "after the next good news."[13]

Roosevelt then came up with a proposal designed to repudiate any notion that sending Marshall from Washington would be a "demotion." Why not, he asked, create a post that would combine all forces (other than Russian) engaged in fighting Germany? Marshall could be the supercommander, with both the Mediterranean and European Theaters, headed by British generals, reporting to him. When the idea crossed the Atlantic, however, Churchill protested strongly.[14] Such an arrangement would destroy his efforts to maintain equal status between Britain and the United States by keeping the Mediterranean (British) with the same prestige as OVERLORD. Roosevelt's scheme was shelved for the moment, but he kept it in the back of his mind.

If General Marshall should remain in Washington, then who would command OVERLORD? The only alternative even remotely considered was General Eisenhower. There were, to be sure, those who had advocated Eisenhower from the beginning. Admiral King was one. And others, such as Harry Butcher, said early that it would take Eisenhower

[11] This feeling he expressed in a letter to Pershing himself, hospitalized in Walter Reed Hospital. He wanted, Roosevelt wrote, "to make Marshall the Pershing of the Second World War."

[12] Parenthetically, the relationship between King and Marshall may seem incongruous in the light of King's perverse nature and his inherent distrust of Army officers in general. To King, Marshall was an exception; and as Brigadier General Frank McCarthy has observed, King held a certain hero worship for him. Interview, Frank McCarthy, Phoenixville, Pa., October 4, 1968.

[13] The "good news" Churchill visualized was the fall of Rome, which did not occur until June 5, 1944, the day before OVERLORD was actually launched.

[14]

Prime Minister to Field Marshall Dill (Washington) 8 Nov. 43.

You should leave Admiral Leahy in no doubt that we should never be able to agree to the proposal of putting the "Overlord" and Mediterranean Commands under an American Commander-in-Chief. Such an arrangement would not be conformable to the principle of equal status which must be maintained among the great Allies. . . . You may at your discretion impart the above to Mr. Hopkins.

Churchill, V, 305.

six months to learn Marshall's job and it would take Marshall six months to learn Eisenhower's. Butcher was wise in the workings of Washington but he was in no position of influence.

The main disadvantages in considering Eisenhower for OVERLORD were psychological. He was young (fifty-two), junior on the Regular Army List, and in the spotlight only a little over a year. In his favor, he was associated with the cross-Channel concept, and his victories in North Africa and Sicily had been heady stuff for the Allies. And in achieving these victories Eisenhower had built a comradeship between Americans and British unique in the history of warfare. But the warm friendship he had developed with Prime Minister Winston Churchill was, in the eyes of Stimson at least, a mixed blessing.

One difficulty Roosevelt faced in evaluating Eisenhower was the fact that the two men were hardly acquainted, having met for the first time when Eisenhower had been in Operations Division. They had conversed personally only at Casablanca the previous January—and that episode had been brief. Thus Eisenhower was to Roosevelt an unknown factor. There the matter stood as the President and Prime Minister began thinking of another meeting, this time in Cairo and Teheran.

*

The idea to try again for a three-power summit meeting was born remarkably early, considering when it actually transpired. While still en route to Quebec, Churchill sent a message to Stalin again suggesting a meeting, this time at Scapa Flow in northern Scotland. By the time Churchill landed at Quebec, he had received Stalin's usual regrets that, as Russian military commander, he would be unable to travel so far.

During QUADRANT, Roosevelt and Churchill sent a joint acknowledgment. In the meantime Stalin recommended Archangel in northern Russia or Astrakhan at the delta of the Volga. Roosevelt and Churchill, themselves, unwilling to go that far, countered once again with Fairbanks, Alaska. But realizing that this game could go on a long time, they suggested that the respective Foreign Ministers meet to set up an agenda and pave the way for a later top-level conference. As the conferees left Quebec, Stalin's refusal of Fairbanks had come in, agreeing, however, to a Foreign Ministers' meeting.

From Quebec, Churchill went on to Washington for a few days, and before leaving the United States in mid-September he sent Stalin an enthusiastic message. If Soviet Foreign Minister Molotov could be present, he wrote, he would then send Eden. He proposed London as the location and suggested participation by the military, with General Ismay representing him. Churchill hoped that the meeting might be held in early October.

Stalin's answer was immediate. October was fine as the date, but instead of London he proposed Moscow. In the meantime, as a result of separate communications between Stalin and Roosevelt, the former agreed on a three-power "summit" meeting in November or December 1943, the exact timing to remain fluid until the last moment. Stalin added that the battles on the Eastern Front were involving five hundred divisions on each side. Faced with this meet-in-Moscow-or-not-at-all ultimatum, Churchill, with Roosevelt's approval, agreed. He was happy, he added, that the summit meeting might be held between November 15 and December 15.

Stalin's insistence on Moscow as a location for the meeting of the Foreign Ministers caused a great deal of irritation among the British and Americans. Geographically, London was the central point; and Secretary of State Cordell Hull, at seventy-two years of age, was showing signs of frailty. But Stalin gave no excuse for his insistence on Moscow. Hence Moscow was settled on as the location.

This Foreign Ministers Conference would be important, as it would represent the first significant meeting of any high-level members of the Big Three and would therefore serve as a prototype for more important future conferences. But its possibilities for major agreement were limited; and as the time neared, it was obvious that the preoccupation of the three powers were widely divergent. Molotov would be pushing almost solely for a second front, across the Channel, in the coming spring. Eden would be charged with explaining the difficulties of the establishment of this same second front. Hull, personally indifferent toward military matters, would attempt to obtain Soviet agreement on a General Declaration for the Post-War World, a draft of which had been agreed between Roosevelt and Churchill at Quebec. Somewhat to the dismay of some of his entourage, Hull put such great weight on recognizing China as a member of the Big Four that the Secretary seemed almost oblivious of anything else that might be discussed at Moscow.[15]

The lack of a united position between the American and British delegations to the Foreign Ministers Conference came about partly by design, as President Roosevelt was determined that there would be no evidence of an Anglo-American "ganging up." Americans and British would travel to Moscow separately, of course. But when Eden proposed to meet Hull in Cairo on the way, the American Secretary demurred.

*

Anthony Eden left Northolt Airport, near London, the night of Saturday, October 9, 1943, and arrived the next morning in Algiers with a special reason to see General Eisenhower. At this point, the Prime Minister was preoccupied with an invasion of the Dodecanese Islands in the east-

15 Harriman and Abel, *Special Envoy to Churchill and Stalin*, p. 236.

ern Mediterranean, and things were not going well. Rhodes was in German hands—no problem there—but Leros, Cos, and Samos, occupied by small British forces after the departure of the Italians, were in grave danger of attack by the Germans. Churchill's pleas to Roosevelt to help bail out what the Americans considered a strictly Churchill-Wilson[16] project had been abruptly turned down. Roosevelt and Marshall had, in refusing to allocate resources, authorized General Eisenhower to provide temporary, limited support from forces he could spare from Italy. But Eisenhower, facing an emergency on the Italian front, had simply provided some air units on a very temporary basis and had then withdrawn them. Eden and Ismay had been charged with persuading him to be more forthcoming, but they held little hope of doing so.

Eisenhower and Tedder were both in Tunisia when Eden arrived, as they were anxious to get to Italy. Major German reinforcements had arrived and for the moment Kesselring was enjoying a preponderance of strength in a desperate battle. Eisenhower had met with Tedder, Alexander, and Cunningham the day before, and after full consideration had agreed that no forces could be spared.[17] Rather than pursue Eisenhower on a vain mission to Tunisia, Eden gave up. On arrival in Cairo he learned that Cos had fallen to the Germans and, painful as he knew it would be to the Prime Minister, Leros and Samos were doomed.[18] Eden and his party continued on to Teheran.

Two American contingents converged on Algiers five days after the British. W. Averell Harriman, ambassador designate to the Soviet Union, arrived on the evening of October 14 and stayed with Eisenhower in his villa.[19] That evening Cordell Hull and the newly appointed chief of the American Military Mission to Moscow, Major General John R. Deane, also arrived. The next day Harriman and Hull proceeded separately to Teheran and, after only a few moments to shake hands with Eden and Ismay, they completed the journey together in Hull's C-54. Both the British and the American delegations arrived in Moscow on a frosty October 18, where they were met by Foreign Minister Molotov and his deputy,

[16] General Sir Henry Maitland Wilson, C-in-C, Middle East. His British command had little by way of forces.

[17] In later accounts it turned out that opinions were not so unanimous as Eisenhower thought, but his decision was made in that belief. See *Crusade*, pp. 190–91.

[18] In the final, humiliating defeat, 5,000 British troops and several naval vessels were lost. Churchill later described the episode as "the most acute difference I ever had with General Eisenhower." Churchill, V, 224.

[19] At lunch the next day Harriman perturbed his host with news of the uproar in Washington over the OVERLORD command.

Andrei Vishinsky, amid due ceremonies. Soon Hull and Harriman were driving the five miles to Spaso House, the U. S. Embassy Residence,[20] where Harriman would take up his ambassadorial duties and Hull would stay as his guest for the next sixteen days.

Once in Moscow, the conferees lost little time in getting down to business. The night of the Westerners' arrival the three Foreign Ministers met in the Kremlin in a cordial but businesslike atmosphere. All quickly agreed on procedures: foremost was no speechmaking.

The next session was scheduled for the following afternoon. In the meantime, however, both Eden and Molotov stopped in at Spaso House for separate visits with Hull. Eden would have liked to coordinate the British-American positions, but Hull's orders were still to avoid any such efforts. And later, when Molotov dropped by, Hull took pains to assure him that the Americans and British were not there as a team. All three delegations would be equally close.

Plenary sessions after the first evening were held at the Spiridonofka Palace, a relatively agreeable, ornately decorated czarist mansion in the city. Though both logic and protocol dictated that Molotov, as host, should chair the meetings, a certain diplomatic ritual had to be followed. Thus, according to this charade, Molotov feigned appropriate protest when led to the chairman's position but, having thus been honored, he beamed. His delegation seemed equally pleased.

The first order of business was that of the Russian preoccupation, euphemistically entitled "Measures to Shorten the War in Europe." Realistically this involved discussion of Western Allied plans to cross the English Channel the next spring. Molotov presented a paper which came to the point. It urged:

> That the Governments of Great Britain and the United States take in 1943 such urgent measures as will ensure the invasion of Northern France by Anglo-American armies, and, coupled with powerful blows of Soviet troops on the main German forces on the Soviet-German Front, will radically undermine the military-strategical situation of Germany and bring about a decisive shortening of the duration of the war.
>
> In this connection the Soviet Government deem it necessary to ascertain *whether the statement made in early June 1943 by Mr.*

---

[20] Spaso House is located in a congested district on the main ring around Moscow (Chaykovskogo Avenue) near the Moscow River at about two kilometers west of the Kremlin. "Monstrous" was the word Kathleen Harriman used to describe it in her diary.

Churchill and Mr. Roosevelt, to the effect that Anglo-American forces will undertake the invasion of Northern France in the Spring of 1944, remains valid.[21]

The American and British delegations avoided direct reply, promising that their military officers would deal with this question the next day. Shortly thereafter the meeting adjourned.

Eden and Hull opened the next meeting, on October 20, by assuring the Russians that the plans for OVERLORD the next spring remained unchanged. To handle the details of this presentation, however, they called on their respective military representatives. Ismay, speaking first, took about an hour to give sufficient information to leave no doubt as to the firmness of the Allied intent. He then explained the significance of the "conditions" agreed to at Quebec (see pp. 370–71). After Ismay, General Deane presented the American concerns. Molotov and his delegation appeared satisfied.

That night Eden and British Ambassador Sir Archibald Clark Kerr drove to the Kremlin to call on Stalin to discuss some bilateral British-Soviet matters, particularly the Arctic convoys. This meeting, like that of the afternoon, was surprisingly easy. The next day, however, Eden was jolted by a long telegram in which the Prime Minister once again expressed doubts about OVERLORD, or at least the timing of spring 1944. The British agreement to go across the Channel was, Churchill wrote, a "lawyer's bargain." He further asked Eden to investigate what the Soviets would think about operations in the Balkans.

The third formal meeting, on October 21, now turned to political matters and could very well be termed "Cordell Hull's Day," as it afforded him the chance to present his cherished Four-Power Declaration. Hull and Eden had expected resistance from Molotov, but they were now astonished that the Russian expressed no objection "in principle." He was troubled, however, by the thought of including the Chinese as signatories. The Soviet Union, he pointed out, was not at war with Japan, and any move to offend Japan, occupying a good part of China, would constitute a threat to the Soviets. No agreement on this point was reached at first.

During the intermission, however, Hull pressed his point with Molotov and even issued a veiled threat. "Dumping China on her face" would cause terrific repercussions in the Pacific area since Chiang's forces were making a great contribution to the war effort. Such a move might even call for "all sorts of readjustments" by the United States. Molotov claimed to understand Hull's position and during the second portion of the conference he agreed to "leave open" the question.

On this issue Eden's loyalty to the British-American cause was put to

[21] Italics supplied.

the test. The British had never been enthusiastic about considering China as one of the four great powers, as Churchill held little respect for China's potential contributions. Further, Churchill feared that the Chinese position in a postwar world would simply be a "faggot" vote—a rubber stamp for the Americans. But Churchill was finding Roosevelt increasingly firm, and the emotions of the American people were still directed toward the Far East. Therefore, Eden gracefully supported Hull on the matter of Chinese participation.

That day Harriman paid his routine ambassadorial call on Molotov. In the course of this normally meaningless visit Molotov exhibited an avid curiosity regarding American-British relations,[22] asking if their close cooperation in military operations was based on a treaty. Harriman assured him that there was no formal pact, but a clear understanding existed between the two peoples that they would fight the war together in both Europe and the Far East. This, he explained, was made possible only by the close relations between Roosevelt and Churchill. Molotov seemed intrigued but volunteered nothing about Stalin's joining in as a third partner.[23]

If October 21 could be called "Hull's Day," then the next might well be called "Eden's Day." During the formal meeting Eden proposed what turned out to be by all odds the most far-reaching development of the conference, the establishment of the European Advisory Commission (EAC) in London. This commission was to develop recommendations to the respective governments on future questions, particularly how to deal with conquered countries after victory. Its composition would consist of diplomatic representatives from the United States, the Soviet Union, and Britain. Hull had previously been unreceptive to the idea of such a permanent organization, having advocated a series of tri-power meetings to be held from time to time in the various capitals. However, he cheerfully gave way on this point, as did Molotov, whose original proposal for a Military-Political Committee closely resembled the EAC. "Liberated"—in contrast to "conquered"—countries were at first excluded from the EAC's responsibilities.[24]

At this point, with the Soviets having been assured of the cross-Channel invasion, with the acceptance of the Four-Power Declaration, and with the establishment of the EAC, each of the Foreign Ministers had achieved his own primary objective. And though considerable discussion would

[22] This was a somewhat surprising development, as the Soviets had been receiving joint letters from Roosevelt and Churchill after every conference. And after all, both British and Americans were fighting together under a Supreme Commander in the Mediterranean.

[23] Harriman and Abel, p. 240.

[24] The most controversial nation to be considered "liberated" was Austria.

transpire over the next week, the tendency would be to shelve the issues, though certain liberated countries would be referred to the newly established European Advisory Commission.

A fourth matter might well have become a major issue had Hull supported Eden. Even this early in the war the British Foreign Secretary was already concerned over the postwar borders between the Soviet Union and Poland, and he desired to address the problem. To Hull, however, the future of Poland was a "piddling little thing." Hull was interested in broad, general concepts, vague though such concepts might be. Thus the question of the future Polish-Soviet border was, like so many other matters, swept under the rug.

On Saturday, the last day of the first work week, the discussion centered on the postwar treatment of German war criminals. The three ministers easily agreed that any war crimes committed by German officials from this day on—not retroactively—would be tried within the jurisdiction of those countries in which they were committed. This move would serve notice that German proconsuls would be tried, not by the Allies, but by the people on whom they perpetrated their crimes. The top leaders of Nazi Germany were exempted, but the message to the lower-level officials should be clear.

When the discussion turned to the top Nazis, Eden advocated formal trials of all, according to law. At this point Hull interjected, "If I had my way, I would take Hitler and Mussolini and Tojo and their archaccomplices and bring them before a drumhead courtmartial. And at sunrise on the following day there would occur an historic incident."[25] The Soviet delegation broke into cheers and for a minute the normal calm of the conference broke up.

On Monday, October 25, the American and British delegations had been in Moscow a week. Hull therefore approached Molotov regarding the possibility of a meeting with Stalin. He was not sure what the proper form would be in such cases—and he had been cautious to avoid this approach as it might seem to downgrade the Foreign Ministers Conference. To Hull's surprise he was told that Stalin would see him at three that same afternoon. He decided to take Harriman and Charles E. Bohlen along with him.

Stalin's personal office turned out to be a room about thirty feet long, with a desk in one corner and a green baize table on the left. Aside from pictures of Lenin, Marx, and former Russian military leaders, the walls were bare. Stalin came around from behind his desk, quietly shook hands, and motioned his guests toward the table. Molotov and his interpreter joined the group, and Bohlen interpreted for Hull. The pleasantries went

25 Hull, p. 1289.

on for a while, including such unlikely subjects as the planting of wheat, raft logging, and Hull's pleasure at being in Moscow. Then the group got down to the purpose, to discuss where the proposed three-power summit meeting would be held the next month, an issue still far from settled.

To this Stalin had obviously given careful thought. The Russians and British, he pointed out, had occupied Iran back in 1941, and Soviet Army communications between Teheran and the Russian front were excellent. He personally could go that far, but since unusual opportunities still existed to destroy the German war machine, he insisted he could never budge one inch farther.

Teheran was a long way from Basra, Iraq, the location proposed by Roosevelt; but it was neither pride nor prestige that prompted the President's reluctance to go all the way to Teheran. He was concerned primarily about communications with Washington. Congress was in session, and according to the American Constitution a bill passed by Congress would automatically become law if not signed or vetoed by the President within a ten-day period. Legislation could automatically become law without his signature simply because of weather conditions over the mountains. Actually both heads of government had legitimate points. But neither completely understood the other's.

The upshot of the Hull-Stalin meeting was therefore simply an impasse. The location of the three-power summit conference was not to be decided at the Moscow Foreign Ministers Conference.

*

By Tuesday afternoon, October 26, it looked as if the Moscow Conference had settled all that it was going to, but that day a startling message came from Churchill. General Eisenhower had just sent him a message which enclosed a lengthy document, "Review of the Battle Situation in Italy," submitted by Alexander. It warned that the Germans could reinforce more rapidly than the Allies, possibly even seizing the offensive unless Allied forces in Italy were reinforced. To Churchill this bolstering of forces in Italy might mean further delay of OVERLORD.[26]

Obviously this new turn of events had to be reported to Stalin, and Eden secured an appointment for the following evening, Wednesday, October 27. Stalin gave a congenial dinner for Hull and afterward received Eden, Kerr, and Ismay. They brought a Russian translation of Eisenhower's message, which Stalin read aloud to Molotov.[27]

[26] The message was written by Alexander primarily for the use of Eisenhower. Eisenhower's follow-up "Conclusion" was not so pessimistic. See Chandler, III, 1529, and Churchill, V, 289. It was on the basis of this growing emergency in Italy that Eisenhower had declined to allocate forces for the Dodecanese Islands.
[27] Ismay, p. 327.

Once again, to everyone's surprise, Stalin took this news with equanimity, partly due to Eden's deftness. Stalin questioned one point: What did a "postponement" mean? Did it mean for one month or did it mean indefinitely? Eden answered firmly that the postponement would be short, probably only about a month. Stalin said that his own intelligence on German and Allied strengths differed slightly from that cited in this message, but perhaps the Allied figures were accurate. He would let the matter ride.

The next morning, apparently stimulated by Eisenhower's message the night before, Molotov asked Ismay to clarify once again the "conditions" for OVERLORD. How rigid were these conditions? When the Anglo-Americans referred to "twelve German divisions" in northwest France, for example, did this mean that thirteen would rule out the invasion? Quickly Ismay assured him that it did not. Diplomatically overlooking that a Russian "division" was less than one third the size of an American or British, he explained that these "conditions" were flexible and would in all probability be met. Molotov let the matter go and that night the British were elated that Molotov, Vishinsky, and Litvinov attended a dinner at the British Embassy.

Saturday, October 30, saw the last formal session of the Foreign Ministers. Permission having arrived from China, the Four-Power Declaration was signed. After a preamble that bound the powers to continue the war until all their enemies had "laid down their arms on the basis of unconditional surrender," the Declaration went on to provide that the Allies would:

Work together to maintain peace and security, as they had fought together in the war.

Act together "in all matters relating to the surrender and disarmament" of their common enemies.

Take all necessary measures to guard against enemy violations of the surrender terms.

Agree on the necessity of establishing at the earliest practicable date an international organization for the maintenance of world peace and security that would be "open to membership by all nations, large and small."

Consult together when necessary with other members of the United Nations "with a view to joint action on behalf of the community of nations" until the new system of general security was in being.

Confer on a general agreement that would regulate armaments in the postwar period.

Critics have mentioned that the Declaration was easy to come by because it was so general—and indeed Molotov had succeeded in knocking out the word "agreement" whenever "consultation" was mentioned. Nevertheless, Secretary of State Cordell Hull, now at the peak of his career, felt rewarded:

> I was truly thrilled as I saw the signatures affixed. Now there was no longer any doubt that an international organization to keep the peace, by force if necessary, would be set up after the war. . . .
>
> As Soviet newsreel cameramen took motion pictures of the signing of the Four Nation Declaration, I could not help feeling that they were recording an historic event.[28]

28 Hull, p. 1307.

CHAPTER XXII

NO GANGING UP ON STALIN

Agreement on the location for the forthcoming Big Three conference was reached nearly a week after Secretary Hull's return from Moscow. American ambassador Averell Harriman was convinced that the meeting should be held at all costs and feared that the prospect might fall through if both Stalin and Roosevelt remained intransigent as to venue. He therefore intervened by asking General Deane and his staff to check out the topography of Iran in hopes that Teheran would turn out to be less inaccessible than had been assumed. The response was encouraging: previous reports on Teheran weather had been exaggerated, and the records showed that serious delay of scheduled flights between Cairo and Teheran had been exceedingly rare. Harriman thereupon sent a message to Roosevelt urging him to come to Teheran even if he could stay only thirty-six hours. On receiving this word, the President decided to give way, and on November 8, five days before he was scheduled to sail from Norfolk, he wired Stalin:

> You will be glad to know that I have worked out a method so that if I get word that a bill requiring my veto has been passed by the Congress and forwarded to me, I will fly to Tunis to meet it and then return to the Conference. Therefore, I have decided to go to Teheran and this makes me especially happy. . . .

The itinerary was thus set: a meeting of Roosevelt, Churchill, and Chiang would convene in Cairo on November 22 (SEXTANT I); on November 28 Roosevelt and Churchill would meet with Stalin in Teheran

(EUREKA); on December 2 Roosevelt and Churchill would meet again in Cairo (SEXTANT II). Chiang was not welcome in Teheran.

*

In the early morning of November 11, 1943, the American Joint Chiefs boarded Admiral King's flagship the *Dauntless* at the Washington Navy Yard for the sail down the Potomac. By midafternoon they boarded the U.S.S. *Iowa,* America's latest battleship, at Point Lookout in the Chesapeake. The next morning the presidential yacht *Potomac* pulled alongside, and the President, Admiral Leahy, and Harry Hopkins boarded. The battleship then cruised slowly down the bay to Hampton Roads where it would take on the fuel oil necessary for crossing the ocean.[1] By evening Captain John L. McCrea, commanding officer of the *Iowa,* was ready to go. Roosevelt, however, had a superstitious aversion to sailing on a Friday, so departure was delayed until just after midnight, now November 13. Three destroyers served as escort.[2]

The seas were rough, but the 3,800-mile trip was now relatively safe from U-boats. A near-mishap even afforded some amusement. One day out of Norfolk an exhibition of anti-aircraft gunnery was being staged for the benefit of the President, who enjoyed displays of naval muscle. Hardly had it begun when an alarm sounded and a shout came from the bridge: "This ain't no drill!" At that moment the battleship listed from full rudder as the *Iowa* veered away from the oncoming wake of a torpedo, headed right in the *Iowa*'s direction. All anti-aircraft guns were turned on the almost invisible threat. Perhaps one gun scored a hit, for the torpedo exploded harmlessly after passing to the stern of the ship.

As it turned out, this was no Nazi submarine attack; the torpedo had been launched by mistake from one of the escorting destroyers which had apparently been using the *Iowa* as an aiming point for sighting exercises. The unfortunate skipper of the U.S.S. *Porter,* the vessel that had fired at the Navy's newest battleship with the President aboard, blamed the heavy seas for breaking the torpedo loose. Furious and humiliated, Admiral King was about to relieve the officer on the spot and was dissuaded, at least for the moment, by orders from his Commander-in-Chief.

In the course of the week at sea the Joint Chiefs met continually in preparation for the forthcoming conferences. Twice during that time they met with the President in the admiral's cabin, once on November 15 and again on November 19, the last day. This was the first time that the JCS had crossed by ship with the President, free from the day-to-day routine

---

[1] The oil had been off-loaded to allow the *Iowa* to make it up the Chesapeake.
[2] King and Whitehill, pp. 500–1.

of Washington, and the opportunity proved invaluable.[3] And instead of the skeleton staff they had taken to Casablanca, they now brought sixty staff officers loaded with facts and statistics.[4]

The American Chiefs still had their own respective preoccupations, but they were now unified in one respect: their resolve to prevent any further diversionary actions in the eastern Mediterranean. Further, they regarded the first part of the conference at Cairo (SEXTANT I) as a sparring session rather than an attempt to hammer out a solid Anglo-American position to take to Teheran, as Churchill would have liked. On the contrary, the Americans were determined to defer any final decisions until the President had met with Stalin; the Russian point of view must now be brought into play in the formulation of plans.

The two main issues the President discussed with the JCS were (1) plans for the conduct of the war against Germany in 1944 and (2) command arrangements for the direction of Anglo-American forces fighting the Germans. The first entailed broad plans (the what) and the second their implementation (the how).

Operations in three main areas were currently being considered for the near future, 1944:

(1) OVERLORD (insisted on by the Americans and agreed to by the British);

(2) further operations in the eastern Mediterranean, especially to seize Rhodes and to bring Turkey into the war (advocated by the British and violently opposed by the Americans); and

(3) operations to retake Burma to aid Chiang Kai-shek (advocated by the Americans and concurred in halfheartedly by the British).

All three ventures might be considered desirable except that they competed for limited resources. Therefore, at best only two could be carried out during the year.

OVERLORD, currently scheduled for May 1, 1944, was acknowledged as first priority by both British and Americans. Though Churchill chafed over American insistence on a May 1 date, even he gave lip service to its primacy. The problem then resolved itself as to whether an operation in the eastern Mediterranean or one to retake Burma (Operation ANAKIM) could be executed without unacceptable delay or damage to OVERLORD. Sufficient land and air forces would be available to mount all three operations, and the limiting factor would once again lie in the

[3] En route to Casablanca, it will be recalled, the trip had been made by air, the JCS separated from the President.

[4] Matloff, *Strategic Planning for Coalition Warfare: 1943–1944*, p. 344.

shortage of landing craft, those unimpressive second-priority naval vessels so neglected earlier. The same craft, to be sure, could be used in more than one operation if time were allowed for refitting and transfer; thus the Allied forces were in, essentially, a car pool.

Rarely before had the President and the Chiefs of Staff understood each other so well. The military supported the President's desire to bolster Chiang Kai-shek, and the first step, they agreed, should be to seize the Andaman Islands, part of the chain linking the west coast of Burma to the northwest tip of Sumatra. Possession of the Andamans would set the stage for a later landing near Rangoon. And all were firm against any further operations in the eastern Mediterranean.

The second matter, that of the command for all Anglo-American forces fighting Germany, was more confused. Despite Churchill's earlier rejection of a single commander over both OVERLORD and the Mediterranean, the Americans were not yet ready to give up on the idea. Major proposals seldom die with a single rejection. And on no other basis would Leahy, King, and Arnold agree cheerfully to General Marshall's leaving Washington. Marshall supported the concept but advocated offering the position to Sir John Dill (though to no other British officer) as the only way to secure Churchill's concurrence. Roosevelt went along with the idea reluctantly; giving the command to Dill would defeat the reason he had dreamed up the whole half-baked idea in the first place, to justify Marshall's departure from Washington.

Apart from the possibility of a supercommander for the war against Germany was the future command in the Mediterranean. At the moment the Mediterranean was still divided into two theaters, Eisenhower's in the west and Wilson's in the east. Between the two, Eisenhower had nearly all the forces, and though Marshall supported Eisenhower's action with regard to the Dodecanese, he still felt that retention of two commanders in the Mediterranean, each responsible for his own portion, represented unsound organization. If they should be combined, however, Marshall wanted to remove the Fifteenth U. S. Air Force, as a strategic bomber command, from the Mediterranean command and incorporate it, along with British Bomber Command and the U. S. Eighth Air Force in Britain, in a single independent air command. Admiral Leahy advocated holding unification of the Mediterranean, which the British would like, as a bargaining position, to trade for the supercommander concept. Marshall objected. The two issues were separate, he believed, and the establishment of an over-all Mediterranean commander, without strings, would show "good faith." King supported Marshall, and in the end the President agreed.[5]

[5] Pogue, III, 318; Matloff, pp. 339–40.

*

Meanwhile, in Algiers, General Eisenhower remained innocent of all this high-level discussion. Preoccupied with the current crisis in the Italian fighting, he considered the matter of future arrangements an annoyance. True, he was disturbed by Harriman's word of dissension in Washington over the OVERLORD command, but this one opinion was overshadowed by those of Navy Secretary Frank Knox, Colonel Frank McCarthy, and others. Eisenhower tried to ignore all this speculation; his long service in Washington had taught him that rumors in that city were as numerous as the population.

On November 17 Eisenhower greeted Prime Minister Churchill and his party when they arrived aboard H.M.S. *Renown* at Malta. This was the day that Leros, in the Dodecanese Islands, fell to the Germans, and Churchill held Eisenhower partially responsible for this British disaster. Eisenhower's stock with the Prime Minister was probably as low at this time as ever in their long association, but Churchill made no personal issue of the matter, and from his bedside in the spacious San Anton Palace—he was suffering a severe respiratory illness—he brought Eisenhower up to date. To an astonished Eisenhower Churchill confirmed that the appointment of Marshall to OVERLORD was not completely settled. To make matters worse, he said that Eisenhower himself was being rumored as a possible alternative. This was the first that Eisenhower had heard such a thing officially. He could not escape the feeling, he wrote later, that he and his mentor were merely "a couple of pawns in a chess game, each compelled to await the pleasure of the players."[6]

Churchill's confinement in bed provided time for a private, rather intimate conversation. He spoke candidly of his keen disappointment that Brooke would not command OVERLORD and, apparently forgetting Leros, he confided to his friend Ike what he had never indicated to Brooke himself: how deeply worried he, Churchill, had been over Brooke's anguish.[7] And he was generous concerning the possibility of Eisenhower's commanding OVERLORD. Having conceded the command to an American, he said, "It is the President's decision; we British will be glad to accept either you or Marshall."[8]

---

[6] Aside from this disconcerting news, Eisenhower found the atmosphere at Malta unusually pleasant and relaxed. No new operation was looming to foment tension; the crisis on the Italian front was finally coming under control. In what Eisenhower described as a "simple but gracious ceremony" the Prime Minister presented Alexander and him with a service ribbon designed by the King and called the Star of Africa. Only two of its kind would ever be issued, for they bore the numerals "1" and "8," signifying command of both the First and Eighth British Armies.

[7] Eisenhower, Unpublished Manuscript, August 24, 1967, pp. 46–47.

[8] *Crusade*, p. 197.

But Churchill could say nothing of that nature outside his bedroom. That evening, at a dinner with about a dozen people present, he seized the opportunity (speaking louder than usual) to reiterate that Marshall would be appointed. He took a great deal of comfort in that decision, he went on, because "with General Marshall in command we shall have no fear but that the operation shall have an abundance of American power." Then, turning to Eisenhower, he declaimed, "I am sure you will realize, my dear general, that we are quite happy with you. But it would obviously be unfair to us to be foreclosed from both major commands in Europe." Eisenhower replied that he understood.[9]

If Churchill's remarks caused Eisenhower a feeling of uncertainty, it clarified one question: no matter what the future arrangements, he personally was destined soon to depart as Allied Commander in the Mediterranean.

*

After the meeting on Malta Eisenhower returned to Algiers and then continued on to meet the President and his party when the *Iowa* docked at Oran on November 20. The Presidential C-54, the *Sacred Cow,* was on hand, and Eisenhower joined the group for the hop to La Senia Airport at Tunis.

In Tunis Roosevelt was housed in a villa locally known as the "White House," and invited Eisenhower to dinner. General Marshall and Admiral King, billeted in Eisenhower's cottage at nearby La Mersa, were delighted to be excused from the evening's event to relax in peaceful surroundings.

Before joining the President, however, Eisenhower dropped by La Mersa to have a drink with Marshall and King. King, never casual and always outspoken, almost immediately brought up the OVERLORD command. While Marshall sat in obvious embarrassment, King outlined the prospective moves very much as had the Prime Minister. However, unlike Churchill, King was not prepared to accept Marshall's departure from Washington. And he added a new dimension: if Marshall went to London, Eisenhower was to assume the Chief of Staff job in Washington. This Eisenhower believed, was his first word of such a possibility from an American.[10]

King then made a bow in Eisenhower's direction. If all this came to pass, he said, he would afford Ike the same cooperation as he had given to Marshall. And the prospect of Eisenhower's coming as Army Chief of Staff was all that prevented Marshall's departure from being unbearable. Having said that, however, King pressed his main point. "We now have a

[9] Eisenhower, Unpublished Manuscript, August 24, 1967, pp. 41–44.
[10] Ibid., p. 44. Here Eisenhower's memory was faulty. Frank Knox, at least, had mentioned the possibility. See Ambrose, "How Ike Was Chosen," *American History Illustrated,* November 1968.

winning combination," he exclaimed. "Why do we want to make a radical change? Each of us knows his own role; each of us has learned how to work with the others. Why doesn't the President send you [Eisenhower] up to OVERLORD and keep General Marshall in Washington? Marshall is the truly indispensable man of this war: Congress and the public trust him; the President trusts him; his associates in the Combined Staff trust him; and the commanders in the field trust him. Why do we change?"[11] Arnold and a number of others, King insisted, agreed with him.

Obviously King was not looking for an answer; there was none to make. Eisenhower said simply that he would do as he was told. He did, however, tell of his conversation with Churchill on Malta and of the Prime Minister's regrets over Brooke's disappointment. Here Marshall spoke for practically the first time, mentioning Brooke's arguments of the previous June in Algiers, especially his doubts as to the desirability of any land campaign to be conducted in Western Europe. Brooke, the three speculated, must have experienced a change of heart, because he could scarcely have wanted to command an expedition to which he, as a matter of conviction, was flatly opposed.[12] As to his own future, Marshall steadfastly refused to give a hint to anybody as to his own personal desires.

President Roosevelt was comfortable in Tunisia, so much so that he decided to stay an extra day to tour the battlefields with General Eisenhower. Eisenhower, oblivious to the fact that Roosevelt was anticipating a chance to further evaluate him, enjoyed the outing and the opportunity to hear the Commander-in-Chief hold forth. Roosevelt did not disappoint him, telling of the relationship between TORCH and the 1942 congressional elections, the political situation in North Africa (especially as it pertained to his "Vichy policy"), and his views on Darlan, Boisson, and Giraud. He dwelt on the fall of Mussolini and on his personal uneasiness during the Kasserine battle. He admitted to differences with Churchill but at the same time emphasized his admiration. "No one could have a better or sturdier ally than that old Tory!"[13]

Eisenhower made no record of his responses. But what later stuck in his mind most vividly was their discussion of the relationship between the recent battles and those between Rome and Carthage. The battlefield of Zama, for example, where the Romans finished off Carthage in 202 B.C., had never been pinpointed, and speculation on it was intriguing. Both agreed that, since Hannibal had used elephants, the battle must have been fought in the plains, not the mountains.

[11] Ibid., p. 45.
[12] Ibid., pp. 44–46.
[13] Eisenhower, *Crusade,* p. 195.

Pertinent to the present situation, Roosevelt outlined his own dilemma regarding the command of OVERLORD: he was reluctant, he said, to allow General Marshall to leave Washington. But he still realized that the soldiers best remembered in history are the field commanders. He personally would like to give Marshall a chance to establish his place in history as a great general.[14]

The outing was informal, and when Eisenhower excused himself for a moment to inspect some burned-out tanks, the ever present Secret Service insisted that they move on. This encounter was the only time that Roosevelt mentioned the OVERLORD command to Eisenhower before the decision was made.

In spite of all this talk, it never seriously occurred to Eisenhower that he was being considered for command of OVERLORD. However, he was still restless to learn what was going to happen, since Churchill had warned of his own inevitable replacement in the Mediterranean. Leaving a job unfinished would, of course, be a disappointment, but what concerned Eisenhower most was the specter of being transferred back to Washington, even to the post of Chief of Staff. When asked his preference, he would always demur regarding OVERLORD; but he felt free to state his preference to command an Army group under Marshall rather than return to the United States.[15] He had even asked Smith, on a trip to Washington in October, to keep his ears open for this possibility.

And from this time on, Eisenhower realized that every act he took would affect the future Mediterranean commander. He personally was now a lame duck, and he was impatient to go on to whatever else awaited him.

*

As the Cairo-Teheran conferences approached, the mood of the British contingent on Malta was far different from the optimism they had felt when descending on Casablanca in January. For the Americans, they

[14] Sherwood, p. 770, quotes Roosevelt:

"Ike, you and I know who was the Chief of Staff during the last years of the Civil War but practically no one else knows, although the names of the field generals—Grant, of course, and Lee, and Jackson, Sherman, Sheridan and the others—every schoolboy knows them. I hate to think that 50 years from now practically nobody will know who George Marshall was. That is one of the reasons why I want George to have the big Command—he is entitled to establish his place in history as a great General."

Eisenhower's *Crusade in Europe,* written before Sherwood's book, gives the same essence but somewhat more succinctly.

One might quarrel with comparing Halleck's position in the Civil War to that of Marshall; it is also doubtful that every schoolboy knows all the names Roosevelt mentioned. Nevertheless, he made his point.

[15] This attitude is traditional in the Army. It is not frowned upon to agitate to stay in the fighting.

knew, were now united on pushing OVERLORD. At Casablanca the Americans had lacked a purpose, and almost all of the important strategic concessions had been made by them. But ironically, even though those concessions had proven wise, the Americans still resented what had happened, and since they would soon be making the major contribution to the war effort, they would be in a position to force their will. To Alan Brooke it was extremely painful. On arrival at Cairo he wrote:

> I wish our Conference was over. I despair of getting our American friends to have any strategic vision. Their drag on us has seriously affected our Mediterranean strategy and the whole conduct of the war.[16]

By this of course Brooke meant that the Americans failed to appreciate the obvious truth, as he saw it, that the war could be won—or at least vastly shortened—by further extended operations in the Mediterranean.

But if the Chief of the Imperial General Staff was dispirited, the Prime Minister was even more so. After Eisenhower left Malta on November 18, the absence of any Americans now seemed to encourage Churchill to recrimination. He launched into a "long tirade" on "the evils of Americans and of our losses in the Aegean and Dalmatian Coast."[17]

And circumstances added to his annoyance. Rations were short. The San Anton Palace, in the center of the island of Malta (about five miles west of Valletta), is plain but spacious, with ceilings twenty feet high. But the windows of Churchill's suite opened on a village street. The local population, having learned that the great man was there, were mingling noisily in the street, hoping for a glimpse. Churchill appeared once, an angry face stuck out the window, demanding quiet.[18]

But the "evil" Americans, the painful losses on the Dalmatian coast, and the noisy crowds could have been tolerated had Churchill been able to look forward to retaining the co-equal status with Roosevelt that he had previously enjoyed. He "hated having to give up the position of the dominant partner which he held at the start," Brooke observed.[19]

For Churchill was no longer the Colossus of the West, standing alone and glancing over his shoulder at his rescuers behind him. He was now beleaguered, not by his enemies but by those same rescuers who threatened to push him into the background along with the power and prestige of the entire British Empire.

Even Brooke, contemptuous as he sometimes was toward the Americans, now feared that Churchill would react irrationally. He was likely,

[16] Bryant, *Triumph in the West,* p. 74.
[17] Ibid., p. 71.
[18] Letter, Ambassador John I. Getz to author, December 3, 1980.
[19] Bryant, *Triumph in the West,* p. 71.

Brooke feared, to propose all sorts of outlandish schemes simply to annoy his allies. Churchill was capable of "cutting off his nose to spite his face."[20]

On that same November 18, the day after arrival, Churchill received a message from Roosevelt. Nazi agents had become aware of the forthcoming meeting at Cairo, and perhaps the location should be changed to Khartoum. Churchill's first reaction was to switch the meeting to Malta (to the horror of the governor, Lord Gort), but first he sent a message to the *Iowa* describing the elaborate security measures the British had arranged at Cairo. Thousands of anti-aircraft guns would be on station, a secure encampment had been built, and strong interceptor forces would keep the air clear. In the meantime he still prepared to leave on November 19 and that evening the President's agreement came in. After dinner, therefore, the Prime Minister boarded H.M.S. *Renown* once again, this time bound for Alexandria.

The *Renown* made good time covering the nearly thousand miles and on Sunday morning, November 21, the Churchill party docked. From there it was only a short hop to the airfield near the Giza Pyramids and the Prime Minister was soon in the villa of the British ambassador, Sir Hugh Casey, within the Mena compound.

Churchill was met with disagreeable news: Chinese Generalissimo and Madame Chiang Kai-shek, accompanied by Stilwell, Chennault, and four Chinese generals, had arrived a couple of days before. Lord Louis Mountbatten, newly appointed Supreme Commander in Southeast Asia, would normally have been a pleasure to see, but this time even Mountbatten cast a pall, as he was present to discuss unwelcome operations.

Churchill had tried to prevent Chinese participation in SEXTANT I. Though he had been powerless to prevent Roosevelt's inviting Chiang, he had still hoped that the Chinese contingent would not arrive so soon. But here they were, and their premature presence gave Churchill a sense that the Americans were deliberately avoiding direct British-American talks before Teheran. He had been willing to discuss Chinese matters with Roosevelt—but only after the return.[21] However, it became increasingly apparent that the Americans were not the least unhappy to be thus chaperoned.[22]

From their own point of view, Churchill and his associates had every reason to resent Roosevelt's concern over Stalin's viewing the British and

[20] Ibid.
[21] Churchill, V, 318. Churchill was of course correct in his assessment of the American attitude.
[22] Ismay, p. 334.

Americans as "ganging up."[23] For the British had lost none of their feeling that they supplied the brains and experience to the Alliance while the Americans supplied the resources. With that assumption, "ganging up" was exactly the thing to do! And the Americans can be forgiven for feeling otherwise. But it was somewhat unnecessary for the Americans to further offend Churchill by neglect of amenities; the Prime Minister learned of Roosevelt's plans to go to Teheran in the first place only through the British Ambassador to Moscow. Churchill had protested in a message to Roosevelt ten days before.[24]

*

The Americans flew to Cairo from Tunis in four C-54 aircraft. The military arrived the same afternoon as Churchill, and the next morning the President came in aboard the *Sacred Cow*. The Prime Minister was at the airfield to meet him.

During the six days of SEXTANT I only two plenary meetings were held, both in Roosevelt's villa. But Roosevelt took advantage of his presence in Cairo to receive visitors from all directions—Britons, Egyptians, Greeks, Yugoslavs, Russians, and Chinese.[25] The military met every day, the respective national chiefs in the mornings and Combined Chiefs in the afternoons. Their arena, the elaborate Mena House, was small compared to the Anfa Hotel at Casablanca, but its conference rooms were adequate; and the thirty-seven separate villas located inside the enclosure provided living space for all members.

The first of the plenary meetings was held at 11:00 A.M., November 23. Churchill's last surprise was now realized: on arriving at the villa he found Chiang Kai-shek and—whether invited or not nobody knows—Madame. "All hope of persuading Chiang and his wife to go and see the Pyramids and enjoy themselves till we return from Teheran fell to the ground," Churchill groaned, "with the result that Chinese business occupied first instead of last place at Cairo."[26] But welcome or not, the Chinese were objects of great interest. The Generalissimo himself was strange even to most of the Americans, although Madame not only had visited Washington but had been entertained at the White House.[27]

Assessments of the two strangers, especially by the British, were not necessarily friendly. Chiang was observed as small, spare, smooth-faced, and inscrutable. He appeared unsure of himself, prone to take refuge in making demands which systematically grew as each previous one was

[23] Churchill had at least headed off participation of Soviet Foreign Minister Molotov at the first Cairo meeting.
[24] Pogue, III, 298–99. Churchill, V, 318.
[25] Burns, *Roosevelt: The Soldier of Freedom,* p. 403.
[26] Churchill, V, 328.
[27] See Burns, op. cit., pp. 376–77, for her visit to Washington.

granted. Physically he was overshadowed by his wife, who was seen as "lovely" or "plain," depending on the eye of the beholder. Brooke seemed to take an unusual dislike to her, and he later wrote in a catty manner about her "flat Mongolian face." But even Brooke could see that Madame was "well turned out." He admired her black satin dress and her ability to allow a bit of shapely leg to appear periodically from beneath the slit in the side. Churchill found her a "remarkable and charming personality." But far more important than her looks was the fact that her language ability surpassed that of the interpreter. Repeatedly she would correct his version of what the Westerners said (to Chiang) and what Chiang said (in English). All present suspected strongly that she was taking considerable liberties; they also considered her the dominant figure of the two.

This first plenary meeting opened with a briefing on the proposed operations in Southeast Asia, as drawn up at Quebec. Mountbatten, as Supreme Commander, outlined the specific plan, which involved a seven-stage operation to begin in January 1944, currently code-named TARZAN.[28] To supplement this long land campaign, the plan called for an earlier demonstration of British naval strength in the Indian Ocean followed possibly by an amphibious operation against the Andaman Islands (BUCCANEER). These islands were necessary for the next stage, landings near Rangoon.

At this point Chiang spoke up. The reconquest of Burma, he said, depended on the amphibious operation in the south. He showed little interest in the land campaign in the north but considered the landing at Rangoon all-important. The Prime Minister disagreed. The British could make a contribution, he said, by simply controlling the seas. The Burma campaign and the growing British strength in the Indian Ocean (and Bay of Bengal) bore little relationship to each other. The British and Chinese were each prepared to allow the other to bear the burden.

This meeting was brief, and Churchill was glad to pass the Chinese leader off to the Combined Chiefs of Staff.[29]

*

SEXTANT I was possibly the most acrimonious meeting among the Western Allies held during World War II, even though the United States and Britain had been conferring as Allies for nearly two years. A major reason for this paradox was the tendency at each high-level meeting to defer unpleasant decisions to the next. Thus even at this late date many

[28] A British and Indian force was to move along the southwest coast of Burma. At the same time two Chinese forces, one coming from the Ledo Road eastward and another from Yunnan Province westward from China, were to meet at Bhama.

[29] He described the Chinese "story" as "lengthy, complicated, and minor." (V, 328.)

basic divergencies had still not been resolved. Add to this fact the British petulance over the reversal of dominant roles and the tension caused by the prospect of meeting with the formidable Stalin a few days hence. The presence of Chiang and Madame constituted the final irritant.

The antagonism of SEXTANT I burst forth at a CCS meeting during the afternoon of November 23. At 2:30 P.M. Alan Brooke, though chairman, had no idea whether Chiang or his representatives would appear. Nor did even Stilwell, Chiang's chief of staff. Before the meeting Stilwell had received a message from Chiang saying that he himself would come. "Then he wouldn't," Stilwell wrote, "That he would. Christ."[30]

But Stilwell was not trying to run a meeting; Brooke was. In the absence of the Chinese, therefore, Brooke opened the session and drew battle with the Americans. When Marshall proposed the attack on the Andaman Islands (BUCCANEER) as the start of the campaign to take Burma, Brooke moved to postpone the discussion, soon thereafter making a counterproposal to divert the landing craft from BUCCANEER to the Aegean. King, angered by Brooke's supercilious manner, rose from his side of the table. Stilwell, witnessing, was delighted. "Brooke got nasty," Stilwell later wrote, "and King got good and sore. King almost climbed over the table at Brooke. God, he was mad. I wish he had socked him."[31]

There the matter lay, apparently nothing more than the usual clash between King and Brooke, when at three-thirty three Chinese generals entered. Brooke turned and asked them for their views on how to bring about the Japanese defeat. The Anglo-Americans had spent many hours, he reminded them, preparing the plans that they were familiar with. Could they help? A long silence followed. The Combined Chiefs, backed up by sixty or seventy British and American staff officers, then witnessed a dozen or so Chinese staff officers whispering excitedly together. Finally a spokesman arose and said, "We wish to listen to your deliberations." Another silence.

Once again Brooke said the same thing: the "deliberations" had been complete after many hours of work. Could they have the Chinese views? And once again the silence, the whispering, and the answer, "We wish to listen to your deliberations." Finally, Brooke suggested that the Chinese had not been afforded sufficient time to study the plans. If they would like to return in twenty-four hours, he said, he would attach special staff officers to help them. At this suggestion all the Chinese disappeared out the door. Turning to Marshall, Brooke said, "That was a ghastly waste of time."

30 Stilwell, p. 245.
31 Ibid.

"You're telling me!" exclaimed Marshall. Wryly Brooke thought to himself that, since the Americans were responsible for the presence of these people, Marshall might have expressed his regrets in a little more positive manner.[32] He charitably described both meetings of November 23 as "farces."

Perhaps the most significant actions of that long November 23 came in the evening. President Roosevelt, anxious to do his best by the Chinese, invited Chiang and Madame to dinner; Churchill, conscious of Marshall's position among the Americans, invited him to dine alone; Alan Brooke invited the remaining Combined Chiefs for a congenial dinner in which no military subjects—but much history—were discussed. The personal relationships between the British and Americans were, as usual, restored.

The concessions that night were made by President Roosevelt, as he realized that Chiang needed bolstering. Confidence in the ranks of the Chinese Army was ebbing, and even Chiang was coming to realize that American successes in the central Pacific were influencing American planners, now beginning to think of attack against Japan from the Pacific rather than from China. This trend of thought was making Chiang's position less important to the final outcome, but Roosevelt was still anxious to keep him in the war. He therefore desired to give Chiang as much satisfaction as possible and made various promises, mostly vague and postwar: China should be a full member of the Big Four and play a role in the military occupation of Japan (which Chiang declined). Chiang would receive extensive reparations. China's four northeastern provinces, Taiwan, and the Pescadores should be returned. China and the United States, he said vaguely, might sign a postwar security alliance. While taking a strong line against colonialism, Roosevelt even mentioned Hong Kong. The Generalissimo and Madame were amenable to these gratuitous offers, but they appeared not to be overly excited. At one point Chiang suggested that the President discuss the matter of Hong Kong with the British.

When the Generalissimo asked for Chinese membership on the Combined Chiefs of Staff, however, Roosevelt drew the line. During the meeting that day such a proposal had been brought up; the idea of a "United Chiefs of Staff" had met with cool American and frigid British reactions.[33]

Churchill, in his own villa, did his best that evening to win Marshall's support regarding the importance of the Dodecanese Islands, Italy, aid to the partisans of the Balkans, OVERLORD, and air operations. They continued the discussions in the courtyard of Churchill's villa until 2:00 A.M.

[32] Bryant, *Triumph in the West*, pp. 80–81.
[33] Burns, op. cit., p. 404.

Very little resulted; at least Marshall, though impressed by Churchill's rhetoric, was not budged.[34]

The next morning "Vinegar Joe" Stilwell had completed a set of questions which he had been drawing up for the Chinese to offer at the CCS meeting that afternoon. Being specific, they might prevent another meeting like the last. Chiang was not included in the morning plenary session but he was, as before, invited to meet with the CCS after lunch.

The British and Americans met alone at 11:00 A.M., again at Roosevelt's villa. Here came Churchill's opportunity to bring up what he had come to the meeting for, to plead that the word OVERLORD not be spelled with the letters "T-Y-R-A-N-T." Alexander, he argued, should be able to retain for an additional month the sixty-eight LSTs (Landing Ship, Tank) scheduled to move to Britain on December 15. This request brought the Americans to the alert at once, and Churchill's pleas got nowhere. (Churchill's propensity to mention Alexander rather than Eisenhower when referring to the Mediterranean could not have furthered his arguments with the Americans.)

Central to the issue of these landing craft was Churchill's remaining obsession with seizing Rhodes. Marshall, unswayed by his session with the Prime Minister the evening before, stood firm. As time went on, emotions again rose. At one point Churchill grabbed the lapels of his suit and spoke forth. "His Majesty's Government can't have its troops standing idle. Muskets must flame."

"God forbid if I should try to dictate," Marshall retorted, "but not one American soldier is going to die on that goddamned beach."

Everyone else, including Roosevelt, looked shocked, but secretly they appreciated Marshall's speaking for them. Marshall was later happy that Churchill never held this outburst against him.[35]

That noon General Marshall had lunch with Generalissimo and Madame Chiang Kai-shek. Stilwell interpreted, and his irreverence extended even to his friend "George." "He [Marshall] talked a streak during lunch, and afterward G-mo held forth on the plans. Not much hope for [Burma to receive] United States troops. Peanut first said he'd go to meeting and then reneged, telling me to tell them his views."[36] But whether or not anything was accomplished by this exchange, General Marshall at least asked that afternoon that the Combined Chiefs keep Chiang better informed about the naval situation in the Bay of Bengal. Even this mild suggestion was received coolly by Brooke and his colleagues.

[34] Pogue, III, 306.
[35] Marshall interview, November 20, 1956, quoted in Pogue, III, 307.
[36] Stilwell, p. 246. "G-mo," popular abbreviation for "Generalissimo," more widely used than "Peanut."

The Chinese generals turned up again as on the previous day and again were asked to present their questions. This time they had Stilwell's list. Brooke was not pleased by the tenor of what he heard, however, and for good reason; Stilwell's questions, such as a request for the number of British troops anticipated to participate in the future Burma campaign, were discomforting. American participation—or at least the nature of it— was clarified when Marshall laid it on the line that U.S. planes, pilots, and money were to be controlled by Americans, not subject to any demands of Chinese "rights."

From the sidelines Stilwell exulted. Marshall had given a grand speech for the benefit of the Chinese—and incidentally for the "Limeys." Brooke, however, had had enough, and terminated the session by promising that Admiral Mountbatten would be asked to visit Chiang. Stilwell this time was spared the dirty work and left in an unusually elated frame of mind.

Thursday, November 25, was a day of respite from the strain of the previous two days. Americans and British each held their respective Chiefs of Staff meetings in the morning and then went down from Mena House to Roosevelt's villa for the inevitable series of photographs. These pictures came in three different casts of characters. The first included only the four principals (described by Brooke as the "high and mighty"): Roosevelt, Churchill, and Generalissimo and Madame Chiang Kai-shek. A second group included the military; a third group added the civilian advisers and diplomats. The CCS meeting that afternoon was conducted off the record, more relaxed than the others. And when Brooke mentioned the prospect of a month's delay of OVERLORD, he was astonished at the mildness of the American reaction. Perhaps May 1, 1944, was not so sacrosanct after all!

The rest of that day was devoted to festivities. In honor of Thanksgiving, Roosevelt hosted a family dinner which included Churchill, Sarah Churchill, Robert Hopkins, and Elliott and Franklin Roosevelt, Jr. The gaiety was topped off by dance music. Sarah Churchill, the only woman, never sat down, and her father delighted the other guests by dancing with Major General Edwin M. ("Pa") Watson,[37] probably—next to himself— the most corpulent person in the room.

The British and American Chiefs of Staff, now joined by General Eisenhower, had an equally rewarding though less festive gathering. At 6:00 P.M., dinner over, all attended a Thanksgiving service arranged by the Prime Minister at the British cathedral.

But November 26, the last day of SEXTANT I, saw renewal of previous disagreements. The CCS meeting began quietly enough while General

[37] Roosevelt's military aide.

Eisenhower briefed on the situation in Italy and the prospects for the future. If the Italian campaign were pushed, Eisenhower advised, he could reach the line of the Po by early the following year. If it were not, he would have to stop somewhere just to the north of Rome. From either position he could spread out and take some islands in the northern Adriatic, and he was not averse to operations in the Aegean. Eisenhower's views varied from those of the American Chiefs; but his lack of aversion to the Aegean was predicated on stopping the campaign in Italy. Further, his prognostications lay far in the future. Eisenhower was followed by General Wilson, commanding the eastern Mediterranean, who spoke even more enthusiastically, of course, regarding the possibilities in the Aegean.

The flare-up came late—and unexpectedly. Brooke once more suggested canceling BUCCANEER and sending the landing craft thus saved to the Aegean. This time Marshall's reaction was so violent that the room was cleared of staff officers once more. Previously he had seemed somewhat relaxed regarding BUCCANEER—unless it injured OVERLORD. But Marshall now declared that the invasion of the Andaman Islands was non-negotiable and it would definitely be executed unless a contrary decision came from the political level. Actually Marshall's stiff attitude had been brought about by a promise President Roosevelt had privately made to Chiang at dinner two days earlier.[38] Marshall was not free, however, to mention the reason. Thus the final meeting ended on a sour note.

One small episode was yet to be played out. That afternoon of November 26 "Hap" Arnold, accompanied by Stilwell, Chennault, and other Americans, met with Chiang in an unrewarding session. Chiang's concern this day was to ask about the amount of tonnage the Americans could deliver by air to China over "The Hump." Arnold, who already considered the Chinese hopeless, was designated to discuss this matter with him. When Arnold mentioned increasing the tonnage from present levels to 8,000 tons per day, Chiang replied. "I'm not satisfied; I must have 10,000 tons." When Arnold raised the figure to 10,000 tons, Chiang asked for 12,000. After that Arnold had advised the President not to take Chiang's demands too seriously. He could, once organized, deliver even more than Chiang was asking.

And now Chiang took up another complaint, asking that the British, personified by Admiral Mountbatten, be divorced from Chinese operations. Arnold realized—and wondered why Chiang did not—that communications between China and the outside world would be hopeless without the use of facilities in Burma and India, undeniably under Mount-

[38] Roosevelt had also promised eventually to equip ninety Chinese divisions. Pogue, III, 308.

batten's command. It was a sobering experience; even the Americans were now becoming disenchanted with their Chinese ally.

*

Thus SEXTANT I produced no decisions and no agreements. This result was actually satisfactory to the Americans, as they regarded this phase of SEXTANT-EUREKA as preliminary. To the British, however, SEXTANT I was a disappointment. The two nations would not go with a solid front to Stalin. Rather the British were beginning to feel like the odd man of the three.

Churchill and his chiefs had one compensation, however. On November 25 the Americans had submitted their proposal, discussed on the *Iowa,* for the appointment of a European supercommander. The British Chiefs, well prepared, had answered in a long written rebuttal and the Prime Minister had supplemented it with one of his own.

The Americans gave way easily. The British now knew that they would no longer have to fight to retain command of a unified Mediterranean.

Part Five

CHAPTER XXIII

TEHERAN

T eheran (EUREKA), the only military meeting between Stalin, Roosevelt, and Churchill during World War II, was planned on such short notice that the arrangements appeared nearly haphazard. Though the accomplishments of the conference would be great, setting a final course for victory in Europe, success would come about not by following a pre-agreed course of discussion but by the force of one man's personality, Stalin's. Eventually Teheran would set a binding agreement on the date for launching OVERLORD, in coordination with operations on the Russian front, and force Roosevelt to name a supreme commander within days after the meeting adjourned. And yet this supreme war council took place without even a prior agenda. Stalin, the prime mover behind the military agreements, came to Teheran professing to believe that the conference would deal only with political questions. The haste with which the conference had been thrown together was reflected in many aspects, the most obvious being the physical.

*

In the early morning of Saturday, November 27, 1943, the participants of SEXTANT I left Mena and the Cheops Pyramid, heading in various directions. Generalissimo and Madame Chiang Kai-shek returned to China, content with the promise of President Roosevelt that the campaign to retake Burma would soon begin. Stilwell stayed in the Cairo area to await the return of the parties and the reopening of SEXTANT. Eisenhower, on Marshall's orders, took a couple of days to visit Luxor and Jerusalem, returning soon to Algiers. The rest of the group—Roosevelt, Churchill, and their staffs—flew to Teheran over a scenic path which crossed Jerusalem,

Bethlehem, Beersheba, Hebron, Transjordan, and Baghdad. The trip required five hours.

At that time Iran was technically "neutral" territory, but the country was occupied in every sense of the word. The Soviets and British had, in 1941, removed the former Shah, whose pro-German leanings could not be tolerated. Though the Iranian Government had continued to run the country with the Shah's young son on the Peacock Throne, the Russians and British had stationed sizable contingents of troops on Iranian soil "for the duration." And the Americans, on Harriman's recommendation fifteen months earlier, had taken over work on the Persian Gulf–Caspian Sea railroad line. Many American engineer troops were in the vicinity of Teheran, and their main camp, Amirabad, could house the American party.

Though Roosevelt and his aides approached Teheran in high spirits, Churchill and the British remained glum. Churchill's heavy cold and sore throat, which had plagued him since Malta, continued to render him nearly unable to speak. But worse than his physical affliction was Churchill's undiminished resentment at the barren results of SEXTANT I for which, he felt, the Americans were to blame. And as his plane flew over the jagged mountains surrounding Teheran, Churchill was thinking out loud: "I could not justify to the House of Commons the last two months in the Mediterranean. . . . The Germans have been allowed to get their breath after Mussolini's collapse because the Americans want to invade France in six months time. That is no reason why we should throw away these shining, gleaming opportunities in the Mediterranean."[1]

Churchill's mood was worsened when he saw the inadequate measures taken by the Iranian Government to ensure his personal safety between the airfield and the British Legation. His car was open, and the route of travel was guarded only by ceremonial Iranian cavalrymen spaced at fifty-yard intervals. A police car at the front of the cortege signaled the approach of someone important. Fortunately the people, who lined the streets four deep, were friendly and nobody tossed a hand grenade or shot at the motorcade. And the wide street, cut out through an otherwise congested city, allowed the car to move along. Churchill, conscious of his own importance and of the competence of Nazi agents, was therefore relieved to reach the British Legation, where he would now be guarded by a regiment of Indian Sikhs. Roosevelt fared better, at least on the ride from the airport, as the U. S. Secret Service had made their own plans for the trip rather than trust the Iranians. Thus he and his party landed at the Gale Morgbe, an obscure airfield five miles out of the city, and his convoy followed a circuitous route unbothered by cavalrymen to signal his approach to the crowds.

[1] Moran, p. 143.

On arrival at the American Legation, however, Roosevelt found himself faced with a new, more serious security problem. The enclosure was located a couple of miles from the British Legation and the Soviet Embassy[2] and repeated travel between them could well be dangerous. Molotov, soon after Roosevelt's arrival, pointed this danger out to Harry Hopkins. Citing an alleged plot by German agents to kill one of the Big Three, Molotov recommended that Roosevelt move to a large villa located inside the Soviet Embassy compound. The British Legation would be just across the street and, as an added precautionary measure, a cordon of Russians had been placed around the two compounds together. All three, if Roosevelt came, could visit each other on foot with impunity. The building would not be lavish, but it was spacious enough to house him, Hopkins, the Filipino mess boys, and the Secret Service. Roosevelt agreed, but since he was safe for the moment inside the American Legation, he felt it only polite to remain for the first night as the guest of the minister. The next day he moved to the villa in the Russian compound.

Molotov's "plot," which made this move necessary, was viewed with some suspicion by Harriman, Bohlen, and others, for by moving into Soviet territory the President was placing himself under the scrutiny of Stalin; conversation would have to be guarded, as the walls of the villa could very well be loaded with microphones. The British were also sensitive that this arrangement would further separate Roosevelt from Churchill, ruling out their ever meeting in secret. Churchill, however, did not share his staff's anxiety on this particular matter. As a fellow target for assassins, he claimed to be touched by Stalin's concern for the President's safety. Soon even he, however, would realize the psychological effect of this arrangement on the President.

Roosevelt moved from the American Legation into his temporary villa during the early afternoon of Sunday, November 28. It was a beautiful, mild day. Within a few minutes after he arrived, Stalin walked over from the Soviet Embassy. Witnesses were taken aback by his well-tailored tan uniform with the wide red stripes down the sides of the trousers and the gold braid on his military cap. This relatively rich attire—a far cry from his previous plain Bolshevik tunic—was well calculated to put an aristocratic President at ease. Stalin and Roosevelt had never met before, and their words were casual. "I am glad to see you," said Roosevelt. "I have tried for a long time to bring this about." Stalin expressed his pleasure and excused himself with ever so small a dig: he had been preoccupied with military matters.

[2] At that time the British and American Legations were headed by ministers. The Soviets had a full-fledged ambassador and embassy.

The first meeting was only a call, part of the get-acquainted phase of EUREKA. Conversation therefore skimmed over several subjects: the military situation on the Russian front; Chiang Kai-shek; De Gaulle (Stalin rather preferred Pétain, who represented reality); Indochina and the French; the British in India (Roosevelt warned of British sensitivity). Soon it was time for the first plenary meeting.

The formal, politico-military Big Three meeting at Teheran lasted for three days, November 28–30. Following the format which had now become routine between Roosevelt and Churchill, the plenary sessions, one each day, were held in the main conference room of the Soviet Embassy. The first of these plenary sessions took place at 4:00 P.M., Sunday, November 28. It was apparently planned on the spur of the moment, so suddenly, indeed, that Generals Marshall and Arnold received no advance word. Assured that nothing would be transpiring that afternoon, they had left their quarters at Camp Amirabad and were indulging in a tour of the woods around the city when the principals and their staffs sat down for the first time. And Charles Bohlen, who had come from Moscow with Harriman, now found himself filling a vacuum as the President's only interpreter. Working with no agenda, no coherent set of ground rules, and no other note taker, Bohlen would carry the entire burden of interpreter and recorder during the conference.

President Roosevelt, as the only head of state, acted as chairman for all three meetings.[3] At this first one he opened up in a light vein, claiming the distinction of being the youngest member present, welcoming his elders. Churchill, in his turn, dwelt on the historical significance of the occasion: "In our hands we have the future of mankind." Stalin, as host, kept his welcome short, following it quickly with a terse "Now let's get down to business."[4]

Roosevelt spoke first. His presentation was obviously designed for Stalin's consumption, a reminder that another great war was in progress besides the battles on the Eastern Front. The President outlined the status of the Pacific fighting in some detail, emphasizing the gains that the Americans had been making against the Japanese and stressing how much American effort was being put into that area. A million Americans, he pointed out, were involved in the Far East, and vast amounts of resources were devoted to building the ships to make the naval campaign possible. Roosevelt's facts and figures appeared to make an impression on Stalin; he extended his congratulations and regretted only that the Soviet Union could not yet participate against Japan. In this he was sincere. For despite

[3] Stalin was Premier of the Soviet Union; the President was Kalinin.
[4] Bohlen, *Witness to History*, pp. 141–42.

their bravado, the Russians were still nervous about Japanese capabilities for moving against Siberia. Churchill, on his part, had already heard more than he cared to regarding the Pacific.

When discussion of the Pacific ended, Churchill set about to review the current strategic situation in Western Europe. He began by denying any downgrading of OVERLORD as top priority, but he recommended some flexibility in fixing the date of its launching. He would like the three military staffs to review this matter the next morning.

Churchill's lengthy presentation seemed to make Stalin impatient. Clearly he held no interest in Churchill's Mediterranean strategy. Furthermore, he had not, he claimed, come to talk about technical military questions and in fact had brought no military staff. If the British and Americans insisted that the military men get together the next morning, Stalin said that Marshal Voroshilov, sitting at his side, would "do his best." Thus ended what seemed to be a rather bland meeting, but Churchill could already see that Stalin was impervious to his own arguments.

At 7:20 P.M. Churchill crossed the street to his room in the British Legation. Lord Moran, perhaps out of concern for Churchill's mental well-being, asked a preoccupied Prime Minister if anything had gone wrong. Churchill brushed him off: "A bloody lot has gone wrong." And he would say no more.

Brooke, not called on to speak, had taken in the whole meeting with more detachment than Churchill. He had been particularly interested in watching Stalin. "During this meeting . . . ," he later wrote, "I rapidly grew to appreciate that he [Stalin] had a military brain of the very highest calibre. Never once in any of his statements did he make any strategic error, nor did he ever fail to appreciate all the implications of a situation. . . . In this respect he stood out compared with his two colleagues."[5] Brooke was a keen observer, but he would have been keener had he conceded that any viewpoint other than his own could possibly have merit. Thus he faced a problem in reconciling Stalin's "military brain" with the fact that the Russian's views bore no resemblance to those of Churchill and himself. For Stalin had showed no desire to see Turkey enter the war, nor did he see any reason to push the war in Italy. On the contrary, he had agreed with Roosevelt's idea of reducing the forces in Italy by six divisions and landing them in southern France even before OVERLORD.

Since Stalin's ideas had actually been parallel to those of the Americans, Brooke concluded that he was not really serious. "I feel certain," Brooke wrote, "that Stalin saw through these strategical misconceptions, but they mattered to him little, his political and military requirements

[5] Bryant, *Triumph in the West*, p. 90.

could now be best met by the greatest squandering of British and American lives in the French theatre. We were reaching a very dangerous point where his shrewdness, assisted by American short-sightedness, might lead us anywhere."[6]

That evening Roosevelt hosted a steak-and-baked-potato dinner for his colleagues, the meal a monument to the resourcefulness of his mess boys. As always, the President enjoyed mixing his own elaborate pre-dinner cocktails, but his gesture of bountiful hospitality was lost on Stalin. When a compliment was solicited, the Russian said simply that the special martinis were "cold on the stomach." But Stalin talked freely of politics, at first castigating the men of Vichy but soon turning to postwar Germany. Means must be found to prevent her rising again. Stalin spoke softly, without gestures. He punctuated his sentences with diffident phrases such as "it seems to me." But his words were harsh; perhaps Stalin was testing the Allies' reaction.

While dinner was in progress, Roosevelt suddenly became ill and excused himself. The guests were tense until word came out that he was suffering from nothing more than indigestion—probably the kind of stomach upset that commonly afflicts travelers in the region. At that point the conversation increased in intensity, so much so that few remembered afterward that Roosevelt had been missing. Important matters such as the future borders of Poland and the merits of Roosevelt's "unconditional surrender" formula were discussed.[7] Stalin questioned the value of such a pronouncement, but Roosevelt was not present to defend it. The controversial question never became an issue again at Teheran.

The next morning Roosevelt had recovered completely.

As agreed at the plenary meeting on November 28, the military chiefs of the three governments met at 10:30 A.M. on November 29 to discuss OVERLORD. As it turned out, Stalin had been serious regarding Marshal Voroshilov's limited ability to contribute, for he was obviously ill equipped to discuss military subjects. He had been one of the original Bolshevik revolutionaries and had always occupied a top military position in the Soviet hierarchy, but his ineptness as a commander had been established at Leningrad in September of 1941, and his marshal's uniform was now recognized by all who knew as a costume.[8] But Voroshilov was aware of his own limitations and cleverly saved face by asking questions

[6] Ibid., p. 91.
[7] Bohlen, pp. 143–44.
[8] In all likelihood Voroshilov's ineptness caused Stalin no uneasiness, since no military subordinate would be allowed to speak for him anyway.

directed only to preparations going forward for OVERLORD. Example: How many tons of supplies and how many troops had arrived in the United Kingdom? Brooke was unable to interest Voroshilov in the tactical plans for the OVERLORD landings, but Voroshilov knew the key question on Stalin's mind, simple as it was. Suddenly he asked Brooke whether the British attached the same importance to OVERLORD as did Marshall. Brooke, bristling, replied that they did. As a hedge, however, Brooke reviewed the "conditions" laid down at Quebec.[9]

Leahy and Marshall were relatively silent during the Brooke-Voroshilov exchange. Only when Voroshilov compared the forthcoming invasion to the crossing of a wide river (a common Soviet way of denigrating OVERLORD) did Marshall rise: "The difference between a river crossing, however wide, and landing from the ocean," he said pointedly, "is that failure of a river crossing is a reverse while failure of a landing operation from the sea means the almost utter destruction of the landing craft and personnel involved."[10]

Marshall allowed that point to be translated and to sink in. He then continued. "My military education and experience in the First World War has all been based on roads, rivers, and railroads. . . . Prior to the present war I never heard of any landing-craft except a rubber boat. Now I think about little else."[11]

Voroshilov backed off pleasantly: "If you think about it, you will do it."[12] Having caused a stir, Voroshilov seemed content with his military contribution.

Churchill had been able to rationalize Stalin's calling on Roosevelt when the latter first arrived in the Soviet compound the previous afternoon, as he could not logically resent Roosevelt's desire to become acquainted. Churchill had not only met Stalin a little over a year before; the two had spent almost an entire night drinking in an atmosphere of great conviviality. But the next morning Churchill was less understanding when Roosevelt spurned his invitation to lunch. Even when Roosevelt sent Harry Hopkins over to explain Roosevelt's attitude, Churchill was far from satisfied. He had not, after all, seen the President alone since they had been in Teheran. This seemed too consistent with Roosevelt's attitude at Cairo. "It's not like him," Churchill murmured.[13]

But Roosevelt then made matters worse. Having declined lunch with

[9] See p. 370–71.
[10] Pogue, III, 312. Sherwood, p. 783, says that Marshall described the failure of a landing operation as a "catastrophe."
[11] Sherwood, p. 784.
[12] Ibid.
[13] Moran, p. 146.

Churchill, he dined alone with his son Elliott. Then, after a short meeting with his Joint Chiefs, he asked Stalin to come by his villa again. This meant a second conference in two days. At that point Churchill decided to deal with Stalin on his own.

The meeting with Stalin on this day, however, was no mere social call, for Roosevelt had now listed three specific requests to present. One involved arrangements for U.S. bombers in Britain to refuel at Russian air bases after hitting their targets in Germany (the so-called shuttle bombing). Second, Roosevelt desired to begin planning for American use of Siberian bases to bomb Japan after the German defeat. Finally, he proposed to step up the exchange of information on Japan. Stalin readily agreed to the shuttle bombing idea but said that the Far Eastern matters would have to be "studied" in Moscow.

Then, at Roosevelt's suggestion, Stalin agreed to discuss Roosevelt's draft of a peace plan for the postwar world. The President had been thinking about such an organization for a long time. Twenty years before, in fact, while adjusting to being a cripple, he had spent many hours writing up a plan for submission in a contest. The project had given the polio victim a meaningful diversion, and the basic concepts he had developed during those long hours had remained with him. In the course of his life Roosevelt prepared more than one peace plan, all based on the first.[14]

Stalin was more tolerant than enthusiastic in listening to Roosevelt's outline. However, one facet of Roosevelt's plan evoked a reaction, the concept of the "Four Policemen"—U.S.S.R., U.S., U.K., and China—who together would constitute an emergency military enforcing agency. Specifically Stalin balked at the inclusion of China. That country would not be very powerful, Stalin said; and even if it were, European states would resent a Chinese role on the European scene.

Soon Stalin had the conversation back on his own favorite political subject: the future of Germany. The incorrigible Germans would have to be held down in the future by Allied occupation of military strong points. Roosevelt agreed.

*

At 3:30 P.M., just before the scheduled second plenary session, the conferees met in the hallway of the Soviet Embassy to allow Churchill to present to Stalin a ceremonial sword struck, by order of King George VI, in commemoration of the Soviet defense of Stalingrad. The atmosphere was solemn, made even more so by the backdrop of tall, formal Russian guards. Churchill's speech, though brief, was eloquent. Roosevelt, not a participant, witnessed from his wheelchair a few feet away, eyes brimming. Stalin accepted the sword, kissed it, and passed it to Voroshi-

---

[14] The contest for the American Peace Award of $100,000, conducted in 1923 by Edward Bok. Eleanor Roosevelt, *This I Remember,* p. 24. Also Appendix 1.

lov, who dropped it on the floor. The occasion was not marred, however, and the sword was borne out of the hall with great ceremony.

Once inside the conference room, the Big Three began with a review of the morning's military talks. Brooke, Marshall, and Voroshilov had, of course, very little to report, as no decisions had resulted. Stalin seemed uninterested. But at the end he leaned forward and brought the conference to life. "Who," he demanded, "will command OVERLORD?" Sparring and getting acquainted were over. The tone for the rest of the Teheran Conference had been set.

President Roosevelt was responsible for answering Stalin's question, as Churchill had already deferred to him in the matter. At the moment, however, he could not give an answer and he was forced to say that he was still undecided. Until a supreme commander was named, Stalin concluded, he could not believe in the "reality" of the OVERLORD operation.

Churchill apparently failed to realize at first that Stalin was finished with listening to his Mediterranean concepts. Valiantly though vainly he tried once more to paint a picture of a blazing peripheral front extending from the English Channel around Gibraltar to southern France and Turkey. He said that the conference should survey (1) the whole field of the Mediterranean, (2) how to relieve Russia, and (3) how to help OVERLORD.[15]

At this point, Stalin interrupted. "If we are here in order to discuss military matters," he said, ". . . we, the U.S.S.R., consider OVERLORD the most important and decisive." From the Russian point of view, "Turkey, Rhodes, Yugoslavia and even the capture of Rome" were unimportant. He then gave his own version of a directive to the military staffs:

"(1)   In order that Russian help might be given from the East to the execution of OVERLORD, a date should be set and the Operation should not be postponed.

"(2)   If possible, the attack in Southern France should precede OVERLORD by two months, but if that is impossible, then it should be launched simultaneously with or even a little after OVERLORD. . . .

"(3)   The Commander-in-Chief for OVERLORD should be appointed as soon as possible. Until that is done, OVERLORD cannot be considered as really in progress."[16]

Churchill then made even another futile attempt to get Stalin to consider an attack on Rhodes to bring Turkey into the war. Stalin turned on him. He would like, he said, to ask a rather indiscreet question: Did the

[15] Sherwood, p. 788.
[16] Ibid.

British really believe in OVERLORD or were they expressing their approval of it merely as a means of reassuring the Russians? Churchill had to concede defeat, at least to fall back. So he repeated that if the Quebec conditions were met Britain would "hurl . . . every sinew of her strength" across the Channel at the Germans.

At this point Roosevelt, sensing that the atmosphere was becoming tense, suggested adjournment. The Anglo-American Combined Chiefs could meet in the morning to settle the details of OVERLORD.

Before dinner that evening Lord Moran went to Churchill's room to syringe his throat. The Prime Minister was walking up and down, now fully aware of the Soviet-American solidarity he was facing. Since Roosevelt and Stalin were in obvious agreement on the primacy of OVERLORD and were further insisting on a landing in southern France, the back of the conference had been broken. "No more can be done here!" Churchill exclaimed.

But then, as if struck with a new thought, Churchill remembered that he would still see President Inönü of Turkey in Cairo. In this fortuitous circumstance the Prime Minister still saw a ray of hope. Even though the conferees at Teheran had rejected any further adventures in the Mediterranean he might still be able to revive them by inducing Turkey to come into the war.[17]

That evening Stalin hosted a dinner for a small group. He had with him only Molotov; Roosevelt was accompanied by Hopkins and Harriman; Churchill, by Clark Kerr and Eden. Bohlen, V. N. Pavlov, and Major A. H. Birse interpreted. Since the main issues of EUREKA had been settled, the atmosphere was relatively relaxed. However, Stalin appeared to carry over some resentment toward Churchill, stemming perhaps from the latter's anti-Bolshevik past or merely because Stalin regarded Churchill as the enemy of OVERLORD. At any rate, Churchill's weakened condition seemed to bring out the bully in Stalin, and Churchill responded weakly at first. Instead of the pugnacious counterattack he had unleashed a little over a year before, he appeared defensive, even plaintive, and the Russian made the most of his weakness.[18]

The climax of the badgering came when Stalin, apparently testing the limit to which Churchill could be pushed, declared that the entire German military hierarchy should be liquidated after the war. If some fifty to a hundred thousand top Germans were shot, Stalin said, the national capacity for waging war would be eradicated. Churchill took the bait and began

[17] Moran, p. 148.
[18] Bohlen, p. 146. In August of 1942, it will be recalled, Stalin and Churchill had a serious confrontation one evening.

to pace the floor. "The British Parliament and public," he declared, "will never tolerate mass executions . . . they would turn violently against those responsible after the first butchery had taken place. The Soviets must be under no delusion on this point."[19]

Stalin pursued the point, perhaps amused. "Fifty thousand must be shot," he repeated.

Rising in anger, Churchill retorted, "I would rather be taken out into the garden here and now and be shot myself than sully my own and my country's honour by such infamy."[20]

Now Roosevelt, in a feeble attempt to reduce the exchange to a joke, injected a compromise. Not fifty thousand—only forty-nine—should be shot, he said. But this effort, even Eden's fruitless gestures, failed to calm the Prime Minister. His breaking point occurred when the President's son Elliott, whom Stalin had spied in the hall and beckoned in, rose when called on and called the whole matter academic. The Allied armies, he hoped, would "settle the issue" for fifty thousand and hopefully more Nazis.[21]

Churchill could stand it no longer. Being hounded by Stalin was bad enough, but this gratuitous contribution was too much. He shook his finger in young Roosevelt's face and stomped out of the room into the semi-darkness. A moment later he felt Stalin's and Molotov's hands clapped on his shoulders. Stalin was capable of formidable charm, and he was now employing all of it, claiming that he had only been joking. Churchill had no choice but to rejoin the party.[22]

In the meantime the three British military chiefs dined at the billet of the British First Secretary, Adrian Holman. Usually a confident group, they seemed this evening to be exasperated, convinced that there was no point in remaining in Teheran any longer. "It is the first time at a conference," Portal said, "I have felt I was completely wasting my time." Cunningham agreed.

And Brooke, who seemed to have become increasingly bitter since his bad day at Quebec, walked across to Lord Moran, who was also present. He fixed the doctor: "I shall come to you to send me to a lunatic asylum. I cannot stand much more of this."[23] All the members of the BCOS were ready to leave Teheran the next morning.

Later that evening Moran went by the British Legation to check with the Prime Minister. Here he found Ambassador Clark Kerr and Anthony

[19] Churchill, V, 374.
[20] Ibid.
[21] Elliott Roosevelt, *As He Saw It*, p. 190.
[22] Churchill, V, 374.
[23] Moran, pp. 148–49.

Eden wearily reviewing the day's events. Churchill was demanding a
drink. Moran listened as Eden proposed to give the Soviets the entire Italian fleet, brushing over the probable protests of the absent Cunningham
on the basis that "Admirals are a trade union."[24]

When Clark Kerr and Eden left, Moran checked Churchill's pulse and
found it high. He admonished the Prime Minister to slow down on all the
"stuff" he was drinking. Churchill cheerfully refused. But back in the bedroom Churchill's mood changed. "I believe man might destroy man and
wipe out civilization. Europe would be desolate and I may be held responsible. . . . Why do I plague my mind with these things? I never used
to worry about anything. . . . Do you think that my strength will last out
the war? I sometimes think I am nearly spent."

These were Churchill's last words that evening. When Moran asked him
if he wanted the light out, the Prime Minister was already asleep.[25]

Tuesday, November 30, 1943, was formally the last day of the Teheran
conference. On the afternoon before, the political leaders had directed the
American and British Chiefs of Staff, without Voroshilov, to meet and
settle on a specific Y-Day for OVERLORD. They now met at 9:30 A.M.
for that purpose.[26] This time the British Chiefs gave way on all points: a
Y-Day for OVERLORD would be set for some time in May 1944. The
first of May need not be rigidly adhered to, but the invasion must be
scheduled during the month. OVERLORD would be supported by an amphibious operation against southern France, the forces executing it to be
drawn from Italy. The BCOS could never have made these concessions
without the blessing of Churchill. Sometime the previous evening—or
that morning—the Prime Minister had decided to cease resistance.[27]

Late that same morning Churchill visited alone with Stalin. Concerned
that the Russian had received a warped view of Anglo-American relations, he told about Roosevelt's promise to Chiang of BUCCANEER. He
also reviewed his own previous strategic arguments, though he concurred

[24] Ibid., p. 150.
[25] This account comes from Moran, p. 151. The exact timing of the incident leaves
some room for doubt.
[26] The terms Y-Day and D-Day are confusing. Y-Day would be the "official" date
for the launching of OVERLORD, as agreed on between governments. The exact
D-Day would be the first date after Y-Day in which landing conditions were suitable, as determined by the Supreme Commander.
[27] Bohlen heard of a visit by Hopkins to Churchill the night of the twenty-ninth.
Possibly Churchill decided that night not to fight things any more. This would have
occurred between the Stalin dinner and the time that Moran came to see Churchill.
See Bohlen, p. 148. No mention in Sherwood. Adams, *Harry Hopkins,* simply cites
Bohlen.

with Stalin's pressuring Roosevelt to name a supreme commander soon. He further assured Stalin that the rifts between the Americans and British were very narrow. His own position regarding OVERLORD had been misunderstood only because he advocated additional operations in the Mediterranean which he believed would not interfere.

Churchill knew what the CCS had decided on that morning, but he felt he had no right to disclose the May date to Stalin without Roosevelt present. Moreover, the dramatic moment for such announcement, would be at luncheon, when the three would be together in Roosevelt's villa. When the time came, only the three heads of government (and interpreters) were present. Roosevelt allowed Churchill to act as the spokesman, and the Prime Minister announced the date for OVERLORD with as much zest as if it had been his own idea.[28] Stalin seemed greatly pleased. It was a "solemn and direct engagement," he said.

The final plenary session of EUREKA took place at 4:00 P.M., November 30. Nearly thirty people were present in the conference room. The meeting began with a briefing by Brooke on the results of the Combined Chiefs' meeting that morning, which came as no surprise to Stalin as he had been told at lunch. The general conversation then drifted toward the Baltic Sea and the long-standing Russian desire for warm-water ports. However, Stalin would not be sidetracked from what had now become his single purpose. At the first pause he demanded once again, "When will the Commander-in-Chief be named?" As before, Roosevelt hedged. He would need three or four days to consider the matter.

Otherwise this last meeting was so bland that it goes practically unreported. Even Brooke dismissed it all: "The President, PM, and Stalin made pretty speeches." He then added, "One thing is quite clear; the more politicians you put together to settle the prosecution of the war, the longer you postpone its conclusion."[29]

The dinner that evening was held in the British Legation. Churchill claimed the privilege of being host because of (1) his alphabetical standing, (2) his age, and (3) the fact that this was his birthday. The many toasts unavoidable at these dinners, therefore, nearly all included him. Harry Hopkins, for one, analyzed the structure of the British Constitution and the War Cabinet, concluding that both consisted at a given time of

[28] Sherwood, pp. 790–91; Moran, p. 153. Churchill, V, 381, says Roosevelt told Stalin personally.

[29] Bryant, *Triumph in the West*, p. 95. Brooke overlooked the fact that it required the pressure of Stalin to make the Western Allies, as late as the morning of November 30, 1943, decide once and for all when the final blow would be dealt in the West.

what Churchill wanted them to be. While deprecating such obvious flattery, Churchill was pleased.

One minor moment of tension occurred between Stalin and Brooke. Stalin had noticed Brooke's haughty demeanor—he could hardly know that the Americans came in for their full share of it—and wished in a toast that Brooke could be more friendly to the Russians. Brooke, of course, was required to respond. He did, however, take time to allow his famous temper to cool; he then answered diplomatically that Stalin had been deceived. Others around the table sighed with relief when the Marshal admired Brooke's direct answer. That memorable incident, however, was overshadowed by the distress of one hapless waiter who dumped a great cake of ice cream on interpreter V. N. Pavlov while Stalin was speaking. Pavlov never dropped a syllable. The incident of the fallen cake was remembered by many guests after most of the substantive issues of Teheran had been forgotten.

The next morning, December 1, 1943, the British and American military chiefs left, this time bound for Jerusalem where the British, who occupied Palestine, would be able to repay the hospitality rendered earlier by the Americans at Williamsburg. After one day the military would return to Cairo, to arrive simultaneously with the political leaders and staffs. Roosevelt, Stalin, and Churchill stayed over in Teheran another twenty-four hours to confer on long-range political matters. That night, after a final dinner hosted by Stalin, the President left for Camp Amirabad where early in the morning he could visit American troops. He and Churchill left for Cairo at 9:30 A.M., December 2.

Thus ended the Teheran conference. Beside the all-important opportunity for leaders of East and West to become acquainted, it had resulted in the decision to launch OVERLORD during May of 1944. It had also forced Roosevelt to come to a decision in naming the Supreme Commander soon. Disagreement could have been the result; in contrast this single three-way military conference of World War II culminated in an atmosphere of good will and hope. As Robert Sherwood put it, "If there is any supreme peak in Roosevelt's career, I believe it might well be fixed at this moment, at the end of the Teheran Conference. It certainly represented the peak for Harry Hopkins."[30]

*

Roosevelt, Churchill, and the Combined Chiefs all landed at Cairo on the afternoon of Thursday, December 2, and returned to the same lodgings they had occupied some five days earlier. Now began preparations for

[30] Sherwood, p. 799.

the final, rather anticlimactic phase of the SEXTANT-EUREKA conferences, SEXTANT II.

The few days in Teheran had been wearying for both Roosevelt and Churchill, as they had been operating in alien territory under circumstances in which every statement, every innuendo, held significance for delicate relationships. The strain had been particularly severe for Churchill, who had been ill the whole time. Friday, December 3, was therefore left free for relaxation, correspondence, and, in Roosevelt's case, signing bills from home. The two principals met only to dine together that evening. The Combined Chiefs met at 2:30 P.M. that day, but the results were not fruitful, producing little other than British annoyance at the American rush to get away.[31]

On Saturday, December 4, 1943, President Inönü of Turkey arrived at Giza with his small delegation. During the next couple of days he would find himself fending off arguments by Prime Minister Churchill as to why Turkey should enter the war. In this matter the British and Americans again differed. The American Joint Chiefs, in particular, actually feared Turkey's entry, for, as Marshall put it, the need to support her would "burn up our logistics right down the line." But in this case the President did not see fit to meet Churchill head on. Instead he preferred to remain in the background, reasonably certain that Churchill would fail in his efforts. (Stalin had actually said as much at Teheran.)

As it turned out, the Americans had little to worry about. Although President Inönü sat through two meetings—and then had dinner with Churchill Sunday evening—he remained distressed but firm. So unreceptive were the Turks from the moment of arrival that a story grew up: the Turks were wearing hearing devices "that . . . all went out of order . . . whenever mention was made of . . . Turkey's entering the war."[32] Inönü stayed until the President left, but he played little role in the conference.

The matter of BUCCANEER was not so easily resolved. Its final fate, however, was given a shove when Roosevelt and Churchill, on returning to Cairo, found a telegram from Mountbatten raising his previously estimated requirements to levels far higher than any mentioned earlier. Instead of 14,000 men to invade the Andaman Islands Mountbatten was now asking for 50,000.

In the first plenary meeting of SEXTANT II, held that same afternoon of December 4, Churchill was bent on one point: BUCCANEER's abandonment. At the end of the meeting Roosevelt summarized his viewpoint:

[31] So indignant was Brooke that in his diary he accused the Americans of "sharp practice," a strong British term meaning "duplicity." Brooke, like everyone else, was tired and disappointed at the time; on later consideration he recognized that his use of such a term was unfair. Bryant, *Triumph in the West,* p. 106.
[32] Sherwood, p. 799.

(a) Nothing should be done to hinder OVERLORD. (b) Nothing should be done to hinder [the invasion of southern France] "Anvil." (c) By hook or by crook we should scrape up sufficient landing-craft to operate in the Eastern Mediterranean if Turkey came into the war. (d) Admiral Mountbatten should be told to go ahead and do his best [in the Bay of Bengal] with what had already been allocated to him.[33]

Churchill tried to add one exception: (e) Resources might have to be withdrawn from Mountbatten in order to strengthen OVERLORD and ANVIL. The President, however, would have none of this addition. He would not agree to withdraw his support of BUCCANEER. Thus ended a fruitless meeting.

By that evening (December 4), President Roosevelt had made his decision regarding the man to command OVERLORD. He would not permit Marshall to leave Washington, and the only other who could be considered for this gigantic undertaking was Eisenhower. So Eisenhower would be appointed. Exactly why it took the President this long to decide has never been made completely clear. Perhaps he and the JCS still held some hope of creating a "supercommander." Perhaps Roosevelt needed time to think alone. Perhaps he hoped that Marshall would ease the decision by expressing a preference one way or the other. Probably it was a combination of all three.

But even after the President had decided, he could not tell Marshall personally that he was being denied a command that Hopkins, in particular, felt sure he desired. It was always difficult for Roosevelt to give disappointing news to a highly regarded associate. He lacked the gall to treat the matter casually as Churchill had done with Brooke. Roosevelt therefore orchestrated a scenario which he hoped would make Marshall take himself out of consideration. Knowing that Marshall would never ask for anything, Roosevelt hoped that the Chief of Staff might, if apprised of the President's train of thought, volunteer to stay in Washington. He therefore sent Harry Hopkins to Marshall's villa for a talk. Perhaps he could turn the trick.

"The President," Hopkins told the general on arrival, "is in some concern over . . . [your] appointment as Supreme Commander." Marshall, however, simply reiterated to a frustrated Hopkins the position he had always held, that the decision had to be Roosevelt's. Whatever that should be, Marshall said, he would go along wholeheartedly. Hopkins returned to Roosevelt's villa.

[33] Churchill, V, 410.

The President's decision, however, had been final, and the little game between Hopkins and Marshall that evening had been merely an effort to assuage feelings—or Roosevelt's conscience. In fact, the President had already mentioned Eisenhower's appointment to Churchill earlier.

Thus Churchill and Brooke knew more about the future than did Marshall. At dinner, as they plotted strategy to sink BUCCANEER, they also discussed the appointment of Eisenhower to command OVERLORD. Both were content, but Brooke particularly so. Though they had shared in the assumption that Marshall would be appointed, this arrangement made sense. Eisenhower, Brooke observed, was beginning to "find his feet." And Marshall, he mused, had never commanded anything more than a company in the First War.[34] What Brooke did not say was that Eisenhower might be easier for him to deal with than Marshall, who had often been Brooke's direct antagonist.

The next day around lunchtime Roosevelt sent for General Marshall. Having received no word of Marshall's desires regarding OVERLORD, the President realized he must now face his Chief of Staff personally. But he could not give the word directly. As Marshall recalled long after the war:

> "[Mr. Roosevelt] . . . asked me after a great deal of beating about the bush just what I wanted to do. Evidently it was left up to me. Well, having in mind all this business that had occurred in Washington and what Hopkins had told me, I just repeated again in as convincing language as I could that I wanted him to feel free to act in whatever way he felt was to the best interest of the country and to his satisfaction and not in any way to consider my feelings. I would cheerfully go whatever way he wanted me to go and I didn't express any desire one way or the other. . . . Then he evidently assumed that concluded the affair and that I would not command in Europe. Because he said, "Well I didn't feel I could sleep at ease if you were out of Washington."[35]

But at least Marshall was now aware that he would remain in Washington. It could have come as no surprise.

The matter of the OVERLORD commander settled, President Roosevelt was now able to concentrate on the impasse over BUCCANEER. In the morning CCS meeting, Sunday, December 5, the deadlock had continued; the British and Americans had again split, with the American Chiefs, not particularly wedded to BUCCANEER, still supporting the promise

[34] Bryant, *Triumph in the West,* p. 106.
[35] Marshall interview, November 15, 1956, quoted in Pogue, III, 321.

their President had made earlier. The plenary meeting that afternoon saw no outward change, although Mountbatten's request for increased forces was providing Churchill with ammunition. At the end, Churchill asked Roosevelt if together they couldn't ask Mountbatten to settle for a smaller operation, without most of the shipping formerly promised to him. Roosevelt once more refused, but Churchill could see that he was distressed.[36]

That evening Churchill received good news: Roosevelt had finally decided to give in. Apparently in no mood to dwell on the subject, he sent Churchill a terse message, "BUCCANEER is off." Elation immediately hit the British camp. Ismay later wrote, ". . . If anyone had said a harsh, or even a kind, word to me at that moment, I should have burst into tears."[37] And Brooke, who learned only the next morning, was almost equally exultant. "At any rate," he wrote, "we can now concentrate all our resources on the European Theatre."[38]

The Combined Chiefs' meeting and the last plenary meeting, both held on December 6, 1943, consisted almost entirely of compliments. But one small incident made the latter one memorable. At one point President Roosevelt signaled General Marshall that he wanted to send a message. Marshall brought out a yellow lined pad and the President dictated:

> "From the President to Marshal Stalin. The immediate appointment of General Eisenhower to command of OVERLORD operation has been decided upon."

Marshall wrote out Roosevelt's words and passed the pad over for Roosevelt to sign, and the message was sent. The next morning Marshall retrieved the original handwritten draft and added a postscript of his own at the bottom:

> Dear Eisenhower:
> I thought you might like to have this as a memento. . . .

*

The long and distinguished career of George C. Marshall reads as a series of difficult assignments, superbly filled, and always measured in his own eyes against the call of the soldier's duty. Marshall had his flaws, although biographers are challenged to find them. And one may not agree with all his judgments and decisions. But what shortcomings Marshall

---

[36] Churchill, V, 411. As in the SLEDGEHAMMER discussions, the Americans were demanding an operation for which the British would have to supply most of the forces.

[37] Ismay later attributed his emotionalism to the fact that he was coming down with bronchitis. Ismay, p. 342.

[38] Bryant, *Triumph in the West,* p. 109.

may have had, such as his perhaps unnecessary aloofness, all stemmed from his conscious application of his rigid code.

Nowhere does Marshall's adherence to his principle of selflessness show forth more vividly than in his attitude toward the command of OVER-LORD. He may have burned inside for this professional opportunity; he may have yearned to employ the mighty fighting machine he had forged; on the other hand he had to be aware of his own value in Washington and of Eisenhower's successful record as a theater commander. Though Hopkins and Stimson professed to know Marshall's inner thoughts, their claims are not convincing. The Chief of Staff succeeded in remaining to the outside world as non-committal as humanly possible.

A lesser man might have adopted such a posture in public while dropping subtle hints by word, by facial expression, or by body language that might be detected by those anxious to fulfill his personal wishes. In no way did Marshall accommodate them.[39]

Given Marshall's credo of selflessness, one may ask why, when he knew of the President's discomfiture, he still refused to eliminate himself from consideration for the Supreme Command. One word to Harry Hopkins on the evening of December 4 would have saved his Commander-in-Chief considerable anguish. But such an act would also have violated Marshall's code of duty. It was up to the President to make the decision and Marshall would not participate. Removing himself from consideration would in itself be expressing a preference, as would asking for the job. And Marshall's rare consideration in saving the Roosevelt message as a memento for Eisenhower reflects the act of a man at peace in the knowledge that he had behaved completely in accordance with his own set of principles.

*

In Tunisia, twelve hundred miles west of Cairo, General Eisenhower was still in the dark as to his future. As of Monday morning, December 6, Harry Butcher was still assuming that his boss would return to Washington as Chief of Staff. Eisenhower was, in fact, already laying plans to make the trip back to Washington by way of India and the Philippines to see Mountbatten and MacArthur before assuming his new duties. During the day Eisenhower received a telegram from Marshall, which seemed mysterious. The confusion came from Marshall's incorrect assumption that Roosevelt or an aide had sent the word. Eisenhower paid little attention.

[39] "He [Marshall] once said that during the war he saw more of me than of anyone except Mrs. Marshall, and I can testify as to the veracity of this statement. . . ." Letter, McCarthy to author, February 8, 1981.

The next morning, December 7, the President's party landed at Tunis. Eisenhower was out to meet them. Once in the car Roosevelt happily popped his news: "Well, Ike, you'd better start packing, you are going to command OVERLORD."

CHAPTER XXIV

ORGANIZATION FOR OVERLORD

T he second conference at Cairo had afforded President Roosevelt little rest from the strenuous period at Teheran, so he was glad to spend the evening of December 7, 1943, quietly at Carthage. But the next morning he was ready to go. Accompanied by Eisenhower as commander in the Mediterranean, Roosevelt and his small party made the short flight to Malta where, at the Governor's Palace in Valletta, the President paid tribute to the heroism of the garrison and the Maltese population.[1] He was soon off again for Sicily, where he reviewed American troops and decorated Generals Wayne Clark and Bedell Smith.[2] Plans to fly from there to Marrakech that evening had to be canceled because of trouble with the hydraulic system in the *Sacred Cow,* but the plane could make it back to Carthage. Roosevelt stayed in the Maison Blanche for a second night.

During this time the President, finding Eisenhower a congenial compan-

[1] A plaque on the wall of the Governor's Palace bears Roosevelt's words:

In the name of the people of the United States of America I salute the Island of Malta, its people and defenders who in the cause of freedom and justice and decency throughout the world have rendered valorous service far above and beyond the call of duty.

Under repeated fire from the skies, Malta stood alone but unafraid in the center of the sea, one tiny bright flame in the darkness . . . a beacon of hope for the clearer days which have come. . . .

[2] Eisenhower's AFHQ failed to notify General Harold Alexander, who appeared extremely touchy about his authority as military governor of Sicily. He later complained to Eisenhower, who apologized for the unintended slight. Eisenhower had also warned Clark after he had committed a similar oversight.

ion, conversed on a variety of subjects, including his plans for the postwar world. On only one count did he render advice. Speaking like a reformed alcoholic, Roosevelt warned of the pressures and blandishments which Churchill would exert when Eisenhower assumed his duties in London. Roosevelt himself had been slow in learning to withstand the Prime Minister's persuasiveness and, apparently unaware of how much communication Churchill had been maintaining with the Allied Commander, was generous in sharing his own experience. Eisenhower gave no response.

At six-thirty the next morning the *Sacred Cow* was repaired. Roosevelt and his entourage left for Dakar while Eisenhower remained in Tunisia to await the arrival of his next guest, Prime Minister Churchill.

*

Churchill's plane arrived at 9:00 A.M., on Saturday, December 11, having landed at the wrong airport, forcing a sick, worn-out Prime Minister to sit on the step of a deserted building while the plot ascertained why nobody was on hand to meet him. The hop over to El Aouina had taken only a couple of minutes once the error was discovered, however, and soon Churchill was at Villa Maison Blanche. Here he collapsed.

The respiratory ailment which had so plagued Churchill at Malta, Cairo, and Teheran was now developing into pneumonia. At first unwilling to admit the seriousness of his illness, Churchill insisted on supervising Lord Moran, demanding periodic reports as to the number of white cells in his blood. He made the concession of canceling his trip to visit Alexander in Sicily, but in the course of two days he managed to attend a luncheon, a dinner, and two conferences with General Eisenhower. Nevertheless his condition was growing worse, not better.

The talks between Churchill and Eisenhower were relatively brief, dwelling primarily on future assignments of key people when command in the Mediterranean passed from an American to a British officer. Eisenhower, conscious of the magnitude of the OVERLORD task, quite naturally desired to take his most proven and trusted associates with him to London, but Churchill was alert not to denude the Mediterranean of the best talent. To Eisenhower's satisfaction, Churchill agreed that on the British side he could take Tedder, Strong, John Whitely (Eisenhower's planner), and Humphrey Gale (Logistics).[3] As regards the transfer of American officers, however, Eisenhower felt somewhat uncomfortable, since General Marshall would be the assigning authority. And Marshall was en route to Ceylon and Port Moresby, out of touch. Nevertheless Eisenhower felt that he and Marshall would be in general agreement, and he

---

[3] Brooke, it turned out, was not so generous. These transfers later became the subject of a bitter argument between him and Bedell Smith. Smith carried the day, though Brooke complained to Eisenhower about his attitude.

knew that he could count on Marshall's support of any reasonable requests.

The major point of controversy between Churchill and Eisenhower centered around the future of Bedell Smith. The Prime Minister, like nearly all the British, had developed great confidence in Smith and felt that Smith should remain in the Mediterranean as deputy to General Wilson, the probable new Allied Commander. Smith, he felt, could provide continuity when Wilson arrived with his own staff. Eisenhower and Smith, however, had long been a close team, and Eisenhower knew that Smith keenly desired to go with him to OVERLORD. The discussion with Churchill was therefore academic, since Eisenhower had already decided to order Smith to London regardless.[4] He could justify this peremptory action to Marshall later. Finally, however, Eisenhower allowed Smith to remain in Algiers long enough to allow Wilson to get a feel for his new position. Eisenhower would recommend Lieutenant General Jacob L. Devers, currently Commanding General, U. S. Forces in the European Theater, to become Wilson's deputy in Smith's place.

A secondary concern was the timing of the public announcement on the command changes. Roosevelt had originally presumed that some statement would be made soon,[5] but Churchill had not completely ruled out Alexander, rather than Wilson, to command in the Mediterranean. Until Churchill could make up his mind, no announcement could be made, since British prestige dictated that the change in the Mediterranean be made public simultaneously with that for OVERLORD. In order to arrange this, Churchill was prepared to delay for as much as a fortnight. In the meantime Eisenhower would have to behave in public as if he were destined to stay.

These issues settled, Eisenhower returned to his headquarters in Algiers. He had other matters to attend to, the first of which was to consolidate his recommendations to Marshall on U.S. personnel assignments. Then he could indulge a yen to establish his own command post on the continent of Europe before leaving the Mediterranean. The Prime Minister remained behind in Tunis, still prostrate. So serious was his condition that in due course both his daughter Sarah and wife, Clementine, came to nurse him.

*

In Moscow, Ambassador Averell Harriman received instructions to notify Stalin of Eisenhower's selection to command OVERLORD. Harriman was worried over Stalin's reaction, noticing that at Teheran the Soviet

[4] Butcher, p. 456.
[5] He did in fact, send a message from Dakar on the way home requesting that an announcement be delayed until his arrival in the United States. Actually it would take another two weeks.

leader had informally congratulated General Marshall on his new command. Stalin might, Harriman feared, interpret the naming of Eisenhower as a sign that OVERLORD was being downgraded. To Harriman's surprise, however, Stalin accepted the choice with enthusiasm and cabled Roosevelt welcoming the appointment and wishing Eisenhower success.[6] Soviet intelligence had been studying Eisenhower closely, and Stalin, like others, applauded the logic of retaining Marshall in Washington and Eisenhower in the field.

*

On January 22, 1944, President Franklin D. Roosevelt signed Executive Order No. 9417, which established the War Refugee Board, its membership consisting of the Secretary of State, the Secretary of the Treasury, and the Secretary of War. The purpose of the board was to implement the government's new policy of taking "all measures within its power to rescue the victims of enemy oppression . . . in imminent danger of death. . . ." Though the order did not specify any group by name, the "victims" it referred to were primarily the European Jews who, from the days of early September 1939, had been singled out for methodical extermination in accordance with Hitler's so-called "Final Solution."

Evidence of Hitler's intention to exterminate the Jews had been available and convincing. As early as Pearl Harbor, for example, the German novelist Thomas Mann, in London, had been broadcasting reports of mass killings in Europe. The Ambassador of the Polish Government-in-Exile, Jan Ciechanowski, had appealed to the White House, asking that bombing of German cities be linked publicly with Nazi intentions to continue the planned Jewish extermination.[7] And there was the Polish agent Jan Karski, who, in late 1942 and 1943, had personally talked to Eden, H. G. Wells, and Arthur Koestler in London and Hull, Stimson, and Roosevelt himself in Washington. Karski had published articles in the New York *Times,* the New York *Herald Tribune, Collier's,* the *American Mercury,* and the *Jewish Forum.*[8] Still the Allies could not—or would not—understand.

John W. Pehle, of the Treasury Department, was appointed Executive Director of the board. He knew that his staff could accomplish no miracles, for its establishment had come too late. But for the moment he was too busy to ponder. In later years he would wonder why the State Department had prevented private Jewish agencies from using official fa-

[6] Harriman and Abel, p. 285.

[7] See accounts of Rolf Hochhuth, *The Deputy,* and Jan Ciechanowski, *Defeat in Victory,* both quoted in Fiengold, Henry L., *The Politics of Rescue: The Roosevelt Administration and the Holocaust, 1938–1945,* Rutgers University Press, 1970.

[8] Jan Karski, presentation to the International Liberators' Conference, held at the Department of State, Washington, D.C., October 28, 1981.

cilities in Switzerland to report the facts to the American Jewish community. Perhaps, as Elmer Davis of the Office of War Information believed, the public would not believe the enormity of the tragedy. And perhaps State Department officials feared that pressure from an aroused citizenry would embarrass Roosevelt and Churchill in formulating an optimum Allied strategy, particularly as it affected the timing of D-Day. Pehle had no way of knowing.[9]

*

By December 18 Eisenhower was ready to leave for Italy. His message to Marshall was in the encoding room; it would be on hand when the Chief of Staff arrived back in Washington. In the message Eisenhower requested the transfer of Spaatz to London as his chief American airman (under Tedder) in which capacity he would control both the American and British strategic bomber forces.[10] Omar N. Bradley would command the First U. S. Army until an American army group could be established, at which time he would step up to command that army group. Patton should be in England, available to take command of Third Army. Devers and Ira Eaker could be sent to the Mediterranean, Devers to be American Theater commander (and Wilson's deputy) and Eaker to replace Spaatz.

One paragraph of this December 17 message was to affect Anglo-American relations later. In the first stage, Eisenhower believed, all ground forces for the OVERLORD assault should be commanded by a single army group commander, who he assumed would be British. When American strength grew to the point that Bradley should organize the American army group, then he and the British commander would serve co-equally. Alexander, who Eisenhower assumed would be the British officer designated, would continue to command the British army group. But of course the choice of Alexander as the senior British ground commander would be Churchill's decision.[11] In this message Eisenhower made

[9] John W. Pehle, presentation to the International Liberators' Conference, Washington, D.C., October 28, 1981. Letter to author, December 1, 1981.

[10] Eisenhower was presuming that Tedder would command the Allied Expeditionary Air Forces rather than be his deputy. He also presumed that all Strategic Air Forces would come under him.

[11]

At the beginning of the operation and for many weeks following that—in fact up until the time when the ground front becomes so broad as practically to compel the utilization of two separate tactical air forces—there should be a single ground commander. If the British would give him to me, I would like to have Alexander. My conception of his job would be that his eventual assignment would be in command of the British Army Group but that until the time for employment of two complete army groups arrived, he would be my single ground commander. . . . This arrangement to my mind is absolutely necessary

no mention of Bedell Smith, treating his transfer to London as a foregone conclusion.[12]

With these recommendations sent off, Eisenhower flew to Italy. His new headquarters was at Caserta, only thirty-five miles behind the front lines. The building was a stone hunting lodge infested with lice and rats but well protected by a high walled enclosure with hundreds of acres of woods and bridle paths.[13] By this act of establishing this headquarters, Eisenhower had satisfied his desire to express the emotional tie he had developed with his Mediterranean command. His gesture went unnoticed in the rapid rush of events.

Eisenhower remained in Italy until Christmas Day, 1943, visiting naval and air installations at the port of Bari on the Adriatic coast and taking a day out to visit the Isle of Capri. He and his party celebrated Christmas in a bombed-out house called the Ridgway Villa, old Roman coins serving as presents for household staff and guests. On Christmas Eve President Roosevelt's radio announcement of Eisenhower's appointment to OVER-LORD added excitement to the celebration. The broadcast, however, contained one disappointment: instead of Alexander, whom Eisenhower had counted on as his senior British officer, Churchill had elected to appoint Montgomery.[14] Alexander would stay with 15 Army Group in Italy, while Wilson took command, as originally planned, in the Mediterranean. Eisenhower and his staff knew that Montgomery's personality would cause some difficulties in the OVERLORD team, but he was professionally competent. The substitution did not, as Eisenhower thought it over, affect his intention to launch OVERLORD under a single British ground commander.

*

In Carthage Prime Minister Churchill by this time was recovering sufficiently to begin exerting some energy in war planning. Disappointed

---

because of the compelling necessity for complete coordination between tactical air and ground forces. The front is so narrow that the employment of two separate tactical air forces at the beginning is unthinkable. This means one tactical air force man in control, and this means also one ground commander in control. Message, Eisenhower to Marshall, December 17, 1943. Chandler, III, 1605.

[12] Smith received a promotion to lieutenant general within days of arrival in London. It would have been guaranteed had he remained in Algiers.

[13] Eisenhower shot one rat in the bathroom with a Colt .45 pistol. To his disgust, it took him three tries. See Butcher, pp. 460–61.

[14] On December 18 Churchill had cabled Roosevelt: "The War Cabinet desires that Montgomery should command the first expeditionary group of armies. I feel the Cabinet are right, as Montgomery is a public hero and will give confidence among our people, not unshared by yours." Churchill, V, 424–25. Alan Brooke had exerted strong influence.

by the progress of the Italian campaign, he had been casting about for some way to employ Allied air and naval superiority to crack Kesselring's Gustav Line. This position, running straight across the peninsula from Mount Majo on the left (south) to the river Sangro on the right, was being held tenaciously by nine German divisions with two (Hermann Goering and 16th Panzer) in reserve. An enthusiast for amphibious operations from the inception of the Gallipoli operation in World War I, Churchill had resurrected a plan which Eisenhower and Clark had considered previously, a two-division landing at Anzio about thirty miles south of Rome on the Tyrrhenian Sea. This turning of the Gustav Line, Churchill hoped, might cause a general enemy withdrawal. The capture of Rome was still foremost in his mind. (See map on pp. 320–21.)

Churchill code-named this operation SHINGLE. Though Eisenhower and Clark had shelved it six weeks earlier because of landing craft requirements, Eisenhower was no longer in a position to influence a decision on its execution. Churchill was considering January 20, 1944, as the target date, and by that time Eisenhower would be long gone. With Wilson and Alexander in command, Churchill could now pretty much order any operation he desired in that region—so long as the Americans would supply him. A meeting had therefore been set up to plan SHINGLE. Churchill, Wilson, Alexander, Smith, and Tedder would attend, and Eisenhower was invited out of courtesy—but, more important, because he was the future OVERLORD commander.[15] Churchill had a request: Would Eisenhower agree to delaying the transfer of some sixty LSTs scheduled for transfer from the Mediterranean to England? Eisenhower thought it over and decided that he could handle a delay of two weeks, but informally he warned that a mere two-division landing would be risky and not in itself decisive. He saw no certainty that the potential threat it posed to the Germans would cause Kesselring to order a general withdrawal.[16] For Eisenhower the matter was closed, but Churchill con-

[15] Wayne Clark, whose Fifth Army would execute the movement, was not invited, owing to an "oversight."

[16] Eisenhower, Unpublished Manuscript, pp. 55–56:

First I said that due to the shortage of adequate types of sea transport the forces to be sent forward could not be equipped for any aggressive action immediately after the initial landing. There would be a shortage of guns and, of equal importance, of vehicular transportation. Thus, there would be two weak and relatively immobile divisions landed on an exposed and distant shoreline.

I [therefore] thought it possible that no *immediate* advantage would accrue to the Allies as a result of the landing at Anzio. For a while, at least, the fighting . . . would take place in exposed positions in coastal area, not in the inland areas through which ran the Nazi lines of communication.

If this kind of situation should develop I thought the requirements of the ensuing battle might seriously delay the arrival in England of the needed landing craft.

tinued to give SHINGLE close attention while he remained in Carthage and later while occupying the Taylor villa once more at Marrakech.

Back at AFHQ in Algiers, Eisenhower received disconcerting news. Marshall, during his trip, had drawn up a set of American personnel changes which differed somewhat from his own recommendations of December 17. Specifically Marshall believed that Lieutenant General Lesley J. McNair (Commanding General, Army Ground Forces) should be given a position of high responsibility in OVERLORD.[17] Having trained the ground forces under Marshall, McNair would be both capable and deserving. Marshall also questioned assigning Devers and Eaker to the Mediterranean.

Immediately, Eisenhower sent a cable agreeing to keep Devers in the United Kingdom to serve eventually as the other army commander alongside Patton (Devers had expected to be one notch higher at army group) —but under Bradley. McNair, Eisenhower feared, would be handicapped by his progressive deafness, especially in dealing with the British.

Marshall, who had always been generous in giving Eisenhower the people he wanted, did not insist: Devers and Eaker to the Mediterranean; Spaatz and Smith to London (Bradley had been there since Sicily). And in the same message he practically ordered Eisenhower home for a few days: "You will be under terrific strain from now on. I am not interested in the usual rejoinder that you can take it. It is of vast importance that you be fresh mentally and you certainly will not be if you go straight from one great problem to another. Now come on home and see your wife and trust somebody else for twenty minutes in England."[18]

The prospect of a return home altered Eisenhower's previous plans, as he had planned to assist Wilson in effecting a smooth turnover of command. Furthermore, Eisenhower had hoped to make one more visit to say farewell to his troops in Italy. But Marshall was obviously in earnest, so Eisenhower went through the motions of securing the permission of Churchill and left Algiers on New Year's Eve. After a quick stopover visit at Marrakech to see Churchill he would be flying to Washington early the next morning.

I then repeated that I would promptly make the desired recommendations to the Combined Chiefs-of-Staff because of the assurance I would have, as the Commander of OVERLORD, that *except for this short postponement, all troops and equipment destined to go from the Mediterranean would leave as scheduled.* (Italics supplied.)

[17] Early in the war Marshall had organized the U. S. Army into three commands: Army Ground Forces (McNair), Army Air Forces (Arnold), and Army Service Forces (Somervell).

[18] Marshall to Eisenhower, December 29, 1943, quoted in Chandler, III, 1632.

*

General Sir Bernard Law Montgomery, on his way to London from Eighth Army in Italy, arrived at Marrakech at almost the same time as Eisenhower, late on December 31, 1943. The two generals had little time for more than a handshake, however, since Montgomery was staying in the Taylor villa with Churchill; Eisenhower, leaving at 4:45 A.M., was staying elsewhere. However, Montgomery had already visited Eisenhower in Algiers, and Eisenhower, expecting at that time to follow him to London, had asked Monty to act as his personal representative during the short interim. They had discussed the OVERLORD plan, which Eisenhower had already concluded was too weak and too narrow.[19] The conversation had been relatively general, however, and Montgomery had been afforded no chance to study the plan in detail. Eisenhower's "compromise" with Churchill regarding the delay of Bedell Smith's departure had been forgotten, and Smith would be in London to help.

After Churchill had finished conferring with Eisenhower on New Year's Eve, he sent for Montgomery and gave him a copy of the OVERLORD plan, asking for comments. With unusual modesty Montgomery demurred. His exposure to the plan had been cursory, he said, and he had not been able to consult with the air and naval commanders. But Churchill was insistent, and Montgomery could at least use this chore as an excuse to retire early for the evening. Ailing though he was, the Prime Minister was still certain to usher in the New Year.

The next morning Montgomery submitted his general comments, beginning with the obvious: the landing was on too narrow a front and confined to too small an area. Further, it provided inadequate beaches, which the British and Americans would be forced to share. There must be, Montgomery commented, a British sector and an American sector, each with its own port or group of ports. Keenly aware of the sketchiness of his comments, Montgomery attempted to recover his written notes, but Churchill refused to yield them. They would be useful as "future background."

New Year's Day was pleasant, and Montgomery accompanied Churchill for the latter's first outing into the High Atlas Mountains. He left that evening in an American C-54 provided by Eisenhower. Montgomery's own Dakota (British nickname for the C-47, or DC-3) was filled with Moroccan oranges.[20]

---

[19] Both men were quick to point out that this deficiency was not the fault of Lieutenant General Sir Frederick Morgan (COSSAC). Morgan had been planning under certain arbitrary assumptions, which had allocated insufficient men and material.
[20] Montgomery, pp. 190–91.

*

Upon arrival in London Montgomery established his headquarters at St. Paul's School, West Kensington, where he had been a schoolboy many years before.[21] (He noted wryly that this was his first glimpse of the room of the "high master.") Almost immediately he began receiving messages urging him to move his headquarters elsewhere, as the people in the neighborhood feared that the presence of a military headquarters might attract enemy bombers. Montgomery of course refused, and although the area was later bombed, he received no evidence that his presence was responsible. The 21 Army Group remained at St. Paul's until its final move to Portsmouth just before D-Day.

Montgomery, as usual, lost no time in exerting his own personality, approaching the commanders awaiting him in England, both British and American, with the same Christ-cleansing-the-temple attitude he had shown at Eighth Army some eighteen months before. Those who had been too long in the United Kingdom, Montgomery believed—or professed to believe—were lacking in a sense of urgency. Therefore he called a conference of all general officers as early as January 13 to give them the "atmosphere" in which all would work together. He also boasted (without War Office approval) that he was making some changes in the organization of British units. Representatives of the War Office were in the audience and reported what they had heard.

Informed by Brooke of ruffled feathers, Montgomery proposed to lunch with the British Secretary of State for War, Sir James Grigg, to discuss his apparent disregard of established authority. This may have passed as a gesture of humility, but Montgomery had a distinct advantage and he used it. He explained to Grigg how much needed to be done in such a short time. He apologized for the abruptness of his conduct while at the same time justifying it. He asked for trust in his judgment, and if in the future he should again go too fast, he would be perfectly happy to be sent for and again "ticked off."[22] Grigg was defenseless.

But in addition to the job of training his own army group for the future, Montgomery had the temporary task of standing in for the Supreme Commander. And the more he saw of the OVERLORD plan the more he

[21] Montgomery was succeeding General Sir Bernard Paget as Commander-in-Chief, 21 Army Group. Paget had been training the units that would participate in OVERLORD, and it fell to CIGS Sir Alan Brooke to break the news to a fine officer and friend. Things wound up relatively happy for Paget, however. He was eventually appointed to be British Commander-in-Chief, Middle East. The policy of replacing top officers stationed in the United Kingdom with those from the Mediterranean with "sand in their boots" permeated all echelons from Eisenhower's down.

[22] Ibid., p. 196.

disliked it. Only one corps was being used to control the whole front, and the plan called for no landing on the Cotentin Peninsula despite the overriding importance of Cherbourg as a port. He therefore drew up a revised outline plan which called for five or six landing beaches and airborne drops on both the east and west flanks. He called for eight divisions to be on shore by the evening of D-Day and twelve by the evening of the next. The British and American sectors should be distinctly separate, with each sector under a commander of its own nationality.

Montgomery's plan was good, and Eisenhower, fretting back in the United States, was being kept abreast of the changes as they were made. The additional strength in the landing would greatly increase the probability of success. But the revisions created one problem: the shortage of available landing craft would almost certainly dictate cancellation or delay of the landing in southern France, which the political leaders had promised Stalin at Teheran. Thus personal relationships between heads of government would contribute to the complications of military planning.

*

On Sunday evening, January 15, 1944, General Dwight Eisenhower arrived in London by way of Prestwick Airport, Scotland, and was driven to his temporary residence, Hayes Lodge, near Berkeley Square. His two weeks in Washington had been fruitful. He had conferred twice with the President and several times with General Marshall. He had also been allowed time to visit his family—his son at West Point and his mother and brothers out in Manhattan, Kansas—and to spend six days with his wife at White Sulphur Springs, West Virginia. All these movements had been concealed from public knowledge in order to keep the Germans off balance, for radio intercept indicated that Hitler was halfway expecting a winter invasion. Miraculously, Eisenhower's presence in the United States was never discovered until his arrival in London.

Eisenhower had tolerated his stay at home but was relieved to be in Britain, as he was impatient to get on with his job. Back once more in Grosvenor Square, he was happy to find an atmosphere far different from that which had greeted him in June 1942: "Now began again the task of preparing for an invasion, but by comparison with the similar job of a year and a half earlier, order had replaced disorder and certainty and confidence had replaced fear and doubt."[23]

Eisenhower himself had changed with the times. He had aged, he had gained a little weight; but more noticeably, he had gained in confidence and authority. He no longer thought of himself as an expendable young officer with a tough job. Short of major disaster, his position as a top war

[23] *Crusade,* p. 220.

leader was secure. And whereas in June 1942 he had been commander of only the American component of a desperate venture, SLEDGE-HAMMER, he was now Supreme Commander of all Allied Forces engaged in an expedition expected to end the war in Europe.

The first few days in London were busy, as Eisenhower would have to pay some calls, get acquainted with those he would work with, and take care of getting his staff organized and housed properly. Thus Eisenhower spent the first four days going through the formalities of visiting King George VI, U. S. Ambassador John G. Winant, and the British members of the Combined Chiefs of Staff. (CIGS Sir Alan Brooke had in the meantime been promoted to field marshal. Churchill was in the process of returning from Marrakech.) Interspersed with these activities were conferences with his future associates in the Allied Expeditionary Force. Some, such as Omar Bradley, Bedell Smith, and Carl Spaatz, he knew well. Others, such as Air Chief Marshal Sir Trafford Leigh-Mallory (air commander), Admiral Sir Bertram Ramsay (naval commander), and Lieutenant General Sir Frederick Morgan (planner of OVERLORD), he must become better acquainted with.

In this first flush of activity Eisenhower also felt it necessary to make two public appearances. Within thirty-six hours of arrival he met the press. Here, in front of the newsreel cameras, he gave a short, crisp talk, warning the enemy that they would soon realize the power of "aroused democracy." And for once he consented to pose a bit. He spoke through clenched teeth and was photographed gazing at his watch with an expression of cool inexorability, indicating to Allies and Nazis alike that the day of reckoning was not far off. He was described as "exuding confidence." Two days later he addressed the top officers of the Supreme Headquarters staff, one hundred twenty in all, at Grosvenor House.

On one housekeeping matter Eisenhower had made up his mind well before arrival; he would prepare this invasion, not in the middle of London, but out in the countryside. Over the protests of many, who believed that SHAEF (Supreme Headquarters, Allied Expeditionary Force) should be located near Whitehall, the heart of the British Government, Eisenhower insisted on moving it to a schoolhouse in Bushy Park, near Wimbledon. Since the site had been occupied earlier by the headquarters of the U. S. Eighth Air Force, it already had a name: "Widewing." And in order to live near his new place of business, Eisenhower decided to occupy on a regular basis the house in Kingston, Telegraph Cottage, which had been his hideaway during the planning days of TORCH. He would soon have cause for satisfaction in moving the headquarters, for its distance from London engendered a family atmosphere among the SHAEF staff which far transcended any inconvenience in coordinating with London.[24]

By Friday, January 21, the Supreme Commander was ready to hold his first formal meeting with the new Allied team at Norfolk House. This meeting was one of the most important of the war, as it set the stage for OVERLORD early, only six days after Eisenhower's arrival. The basic planning was far advanced, thanks to the assiduous work of Lieutenant General Sir Frederick Morgan and his staff. Morgan had based his work on Eisenhower's directive from the Combined Chiefs, which had instructed him to land on the coast of France and thereafter destroy the German ground forces. The critical paragraph read: "You will enter the Continent of Europe and, in conjunction with the other Allied Nations, undertake operations aimed at the heart of Germany and destruction of her Armed Forces."

To comply with this directive, Morgan, and now Eisenhower, visualized that all of France—and as much of Holland and Belgium as possible—would have to be liberated before the Allied force could make a decisive move into Germany. One reason for this was the need for adequate ports through which to receive supplies from the United States. The amount of supplies to be received was substantial; on the American side alone 48 million tons would eventually be delivered. Therefore the ports of Marseille, Antwerp, Brest, Le Havre, and many others would have to be seized, cleared, and developed.

To reach the point where the Allies could break out and liberate all of France, Morgan and his planners had counted on a large build-up within a so-called Lodgement Area, which they estimated could be reached by ninety days after the landing. This area would be bordered on the north by the Seine River and on the south by the Loire, which together form nearly an island with a gap of only about fifty miles at a point just east of Paris and Orléans. That Lodgement Area would include not only the Normandy beaches but the ports of Cherbourg and Brest as well. After an adequate build-up in this area, according to the logistical planners, operations to free the rest of France could be launched. (See map on p. 456.)

Holding the perimeter of this Lodgement Area would be extremely expensive in Allied troops. Even though one division could occupy a front of many miles along the unfordable Loire, the south flank would have to be at least screened if German troops were to be left roaming in the south of France. For this reason ANVIL, the landing near Marseille, was so important. A drive from that area northward up the Rhône River could link

[24] That was Eisenhower's point of view. Those who enjoyed London in the evenings may have disagreed.

up with Allied forces moving eastward from OVERLORD. That link-up would result in capture or rapid evacuation of all German troops in France.

As the first step toward securing the Lodgement Area Morgan's planners had chosen three landing beaches between Le Havre on the Seine and the base of the Cotentin Peninsula. British forces would logically be on the left, since in their movement toward Germany they could be supplied from Britain via the French and Belgian ports. The Americans, on the right, would eventually swing around to the east, and when they reached the borders of Germany, they would receive much of their supply and reinforcement through Cherbourg, Brest, and eventually (after ANVIL) Marseille.

This scheme of maneuver had long been agreed upon, but the issue now at hand was the size of the landing itself. Eisenhower, Montgomery, and others had agreed that Morgan's plan was too modest and had generally accepted a five-division rather than a three-division assault.

Nevertheless, the adjustments to Morgan's plan had to be formalized. Eisenhower approved the addition of two landing sites in the beachhead area, one of which, at the base of the Cotentin Peninsula, would facilitate the quick seizure of Cherbourg. He also formalized his earlier decision that three airborne divisions would be included in the initial assault, the U. S. 82nd and 101st Airborne Divisions behind the Cotentin beach and the British 6th Airborne over the Orne River, near Caen on the east.[25]

As Eisenhower had realized, even while in the United States, the shortage of landing craft occasioned by this expanded beachhead would have to be dealt with. ANVIL could not be executed concurrently with OVERLORD in early May. In order to save ANVIL, therefore, Eisenhower announced his willingness to accept a month's postponement of OVERLORD, from early May to early June, which would ease the problem of landing craft. Besides, June would provide better weather than May for a concurrent Soviet offensive.

The ground and naval plans thus settled for the moment, Leigh-Mallory, the Allied air commander, described the air battle over the Continent as it had gone up to this time. Happily he reported that operations to destroy the German Air Force (POINTBLANK) had reduced enemy fighter production from an expected 1,500 planes per month to 600. The decisive battle in the air, however, was still to be fought. And while the skies were being cleared of the Luftwaffe, plans would have to be made for the destruction of targets on the ground. Tedder agreed, as did all.

But behind the generally optimistic atmosphere surrounding this meet-

[25] Air Chief Marshal Leigh-Mallory expressed doubts about these drops, but Eisenhower believed them necessary to protect the flanks. He was supported by veteran paratroopers such as Matthew Ridgway, who had commanded the 82nd in Sicily.

ing, Eisenhower picked up an ominous piece of news: word that Prime Minister Churchill had begun to waver in his promise, made on New Year's Eve, to give him direct control of all British air forces. An article in the London *Express* had carried a story to that same effect the day before. Coupled with the impression he had received in Washington that the Pacific and the Mediterranean would be competing with OVERLORD for resources, Eisenhower was faintly troubled.

Two days later he had pulled together the results of the meeting at Norfolk House sufficiently to enable him to cable his changes in OVERLORD to the Combined Chiefs. He told of his willingness to postpone D-Day by a month to provide landing craft for ANVIL and listed his minimum requirements for ships. But he began his message with a paragraph that bordered on a scolding:

> I have now had an opportunity of discussing the OVERLORD plan with my Commanders-in-Chief. We are convinced that in all discussions full weight must be given to the fact that this operation marks the crisis of the European war. Every obstacle must be overcome, every inconvenience suffered and every risk run to ensure that our blow is decisive. We cannot afford to fail.[26]

These words may sound a little pompous coming from a theater commander to the Combined Chiefs. In Eisenhower's mind they were, unhappily, necessary.

But admonitions to the CCS and the glow of predictions were only preludes to hard work. Eisenhower and his subordinates had much to do. And since the OVERLORD community was not completely self-sufficient, its members were forced to draw on and contend with outside authorities. Of these the key figures were Prime Minister Churchill and CIGS Sir Alan Brooke, both close at hand and likewise concerned with every detail. And by force of habit, though certainly not from malice, British officials were inclined to limit the powers of an OVERLORD commander operating from British soil.

"Supreme Commander" is a nebulous term. Although it was used informally in the Mediterranean, it had not been an official title. And no commander is ever completely "supreme." The fact that Eisenhower's position in OVERLORD became so nearly all-powerful was due, not to the original intentions of Churchill and the BCOS, but rather to the force of his own will, and he would accept the blame if he sometimes appeared to border on petulance. For Eisenhower was conscious of the need to fight if he were to retain personal control of all aspects of OVERLORD; the British had given him plenty of warning when he was in the Mediterranean.

[26] Eisenhower to the Combined Chiefs of Staff, January 23, 1944. Quoted in Chandler, III, 1673.

But retain control he was determined to do, for he realized that he was the man on the spot in both senses of the word. It was up to him to make OVERLORD work, and the blame would be his if it should fail. Accordingly he determined to extort from all Allied sources every ship, every key officer, and every aircraft possible. This he did by persuasion, by occasional outbursts, and even by threat. He was sustained by the knowledge that his own prestige had rendered him, as a figure, practically indispensable. He would run the European war, as much as possible, the way he saw fit.

*

Churchill's brain child, Operation SHINGLE, landed at Anzio, south of Rome, on the morning of Saturday, January 22, 1944. At first it met with heady success, and the two assault divisions, the British 1st and the U. S. 3rd, got ashore safely. The backup forces, however, were too weak to allow the lead divisions to move inland and render a decisive blow, and a build-up would be slow because of the lack of a major port in the area. German commander Albert Kesselring, moreover, reacted skillfully. He did not, as Churchill had hoped, withdraw headlong from the Gustav Line; he merely thinned it out. He could, at one time, hold the Gustav Line and use several divisions to threaten the very survival of the Allied force at Anzio. Though unsuccessful in efforts to destroy the beachhead, Kesselring at least rendered it ineffectual. SHINGLE soon became a running sore, where the Allied troops on the low ground were pounded by German artillery on the rim. The lack of a major port meant more than the inability of SHINGLE to deliver a knockout blow; it caused the force to depend for its very survival on resupply across beaches. This meant amphibious landing craft. But the craft feeding SHINGLE were those originally earmarked to transport ANVIL; therefore ANVIL could no longer be launched simultaneously with OVERLORD.

When it became apparent that ANVIL must be delayed or canceled, neither Marshall nor Eisenhower took it lightly, as they both considered it part of OVERLORD. Marshall's insistence on clinging to the concept was even stronger than Eisenhower's, however, for the latter could visualize some benefit to OVERLORD from cancellation or delay. (The landing craft left over might come to Britain if ANVIL were scratched.) Marshall, however, regarded ANVIL in another light. He saw the dispatch of a strong force from Italy to France as a guarantee against Churchill's using those ten divisions later in the Adriatic. Since Eisenhower was tending to agree with the British on at least delaying ANVIL, Marshall sensed his dilemma. In a message of February 7 he said he hoped that Eisenhower was not becoming affected with "localitis."[27] The next day Eisenhower defended himself hotly and Marshall seemed satisfied.

27 Ibid., p. 1708, note 3.

To make matters worse, from Eisenhower's point of view, the American Joint Chiefs, now preoccupied with the operations in the Pacific, refused an invitation to fly to London to discuss the matter. Instead they deputized Eisenhower to represent them. Since his exchange with Marshall over "localitis" was only one day old—this was February 9—Eisenhower's position was more awkward than ever. On the other hand the British, though puzzled by the delegation of so much responsibility to a field commander, were happy. That field commander, in this instance, would have preferred otherwise.

True to his charge to represent the American JCS, Eisenhower did all he could to save ANVIL. On Saturday, February 19, he met with the British Chiefs, proposing to exchange six troop transports from Britain for twenty LSTs and twenty-one large infantry landing craft LCT(L) from ANVIL on the basis that the transports could be used in the mild landing conditions of southern France.[28] The BCOS agreed on the condition that ANVIL be delayed. Eisenhower, pleased, reported the exchange to Washington. The JCS went to Roosevelt, who disapproved the delay in view of his promise to Stalin.[29]

At the same time, however, the BCOS began to back down on even this agreement. With the Americans renewing their insistence on ANVIL, the situation was back where it had been on the seventh of February.

Eisenhower, nearly desperate, then asked if the next twenty-six LSTs earmarked for the Mediterranean could be sent to him. He would soon make them up.[30] "It seems to me that all concerned except ourselves take it for granted that the actual [OVERLORD] assault will be successful and relatively easy. . . . This seems most unfortunate . . . as it would be fatal to underestimate the difficulties of the assault."[31]

On March 26 the impossible seemed to happen. Admiral King consented to divert twenty-six LSTs from the Pacific to the Mediterranean! The JCS, however, added a string, that "some-sizeable operation of the nature of ANVIL is on the books."

The British refused. Alan Brooke angrily called the "condition" a "pointed pistol." But this time American anger at the British rejection was equally strong, and Dill let the BCOS know: "The Americans were shocked and pained to find out . . . how gaily we proposed to accept their legacy while disregarding the terms of the will."[32]

[28] Memo, Eisenhower to British Chiefs, dated February 18, ibid., p. 1732, and Eisenhower to Marshall, February 19, ibid., p. 1735.
[29] ". . . call attention that we are committed to a third power and I do not feel we have any right to abandon this commitment to ANVIL without taking up the matter with that third power." Roosevelt (Leahy) to Eisenhower. Ibid., p. 1745, note 3.
[30] Eisenhower to Marshall, March 3, 1944, ibid., p. 1758.
[31] Eisenhower to the Joint Chiefs, March 9, 1944, ibid., p. 1763.
[32] Matloff, p. 425.

By this time all were tired of the foolishness. On April 3 Churchill met with Eisenhower and Smith over lunch. Eager to reach compromise, they agreed that (1) in the Mediterranean the capture of Rome would remain top priority, and (2) ANVIL would be planned for, with a target date of July 10. This delay meant that landing craft could now be dispatched to the United Kingdom for OVERLORD and returned in time for a later ANVIL. The Americans, including Roosevelt, were now either too weary to resist or had lost interest. Eisenhower would no longer have to plan OVERLORD on quite such a shoestring.[33]

ANVIL (renamed DRAGOON) was finally launched on August 15, long after the original date agreed at Teheran. Churchill was never reconciled to it because it took several divisions from the Mediterranean Theater. But he was on hand to witness when the troops went ashore.

*

In dealing with the issue of ANVIL General Eisenhower had been placed in an embarrassing position, but the stakes in the conflict in no way affected his own powers as Supreme Commander. Not so the control of the heavy bombers, which Eisenhower insisted should lie within his prerogatives. The commands involved were the U. S. Strategic Air Forces, Europe (Spaatz), and the British Bomber Command, under Air Marshal Sir Arthur Harris.[34] Up to that time these two commands had at least theoretically operated under the direction of the Combined Chiefs.

Eisenhower's appointment as Supreme Commander came less than three months after his close squeak at Salerno, an experience that had made him resolve never again to have to negotiate for the forces he needed. And since air power was the factor which made this enterprise possible, and Eisenhower did not intend for others, Churchill and Harris especially, to fritter away a substantial portion of his potential air support in sideshows unrelated directly to ensuring the success of OVERLORD.

Eisenhower, as a ground officer, was not interested in meddling in techniques of the air arm. He had specialists for that. And he could appreciate the sensitivity of the newly emancipated airmen, who had long been

[33] Landing craft available on D-Day were finally:

	LST	LCI (L)	LCT	LCVP
U.S.	168	124	247	1089
BRITAIN	61	121	664	0
Total	229	245	911	1089

Designations are Landing Ship, Tank; Landing Craft, Infantry (Large); Landing Craft, Tank; and Landing Craft, Vehicles and Personnel.

Morison, *The Invasion of France and Germany, 1944–1945.*

[34] U. S. Strategic Air Forces included the Eighth Air Force, based in Britain, and the Fifteenth Air Force, based in the Mediterranean.

kept in a secondary role by the ground officers of the Army. But he could, Eisenhower felt, cope with the pride of the airmen by exercising his over-all control of the strategic air forces through one of their own. And fortunately his deputy, Sir Arthur Tedder, was among the most respected of all the Allied airmen.[35]

After the first meeting of the SHAEF staff at Norfolk House Eisenhowever received the additional word that the Prime Minister was cooling in his support of Eisenhower's unified control of all air forces.[36] However, at that time (January 21) Eisenhower still believed he enjoyed the support of Hap Arnold, based on conversations in Washington.[37] Troubles had already begun even in that quarter, though the extent had not yet been made obvious. The main problem lay in the question of doctrine, the strategic air force advocates insisting on fighting their own war. These "bomber barons" considered themselves a group apart, separated emotionally from even their brothers in the tactical air forces, whose primary job it was to support the Army. To Harris and Spaatz the prospect of even temporarily allowing their bomber forces to be directed by Leigh-Mallory, a "tactical" airman, was unthinkable. The long-range bomber would be "misused," they argued. But emotionally—even more important—they feared that their dearly won autonomy from the tactical ground battle might be discredited.

Personalities complicated the issues. "Bomber" Harris, the autocratic advocate of long-range destruction of Germany, enjoyed tremendous personal support from Churchill. Even when he boasted, early in the game, that he intended to command *all* the air forces (including those of OVERLORD) Harris was never rebuked. Occasionally, Harris had been

[35] Tedder's assignment to Europe had been agreed between Churchill and Eisenhower in Carthage. Eisenhower had at that time visualized Tedder as his air commander, the position he held in the Mediterranean. But since Leigh-Mallory had already been fighting the OVERLORD air battle, the BCOS would not replace him, and Tedder's role was switched from air commander to deputy supreme commander. Churchill's fear that Tedder might be relegated to a meaningless position turned out to be groundless. Tedder, pp. 490, 499, 501. Churchill, V, 424.

[36] "Incidentally, when Beetle visited the Prime Minister at Marrakesh, the PM had reiterated that control of all operational aircraft would go under the Supreme Commander for OVERLORD. . . . Ike feels the PM will go 'all out' for the proper arrangement when the time is opportune." Butcher, p. 476.

[37] In an undated letter Arnold wrote:

"I believe that you . . . expressed [your views] somewhat forcefully to the Prime Minister and that he, at least, had not rejected the desirability of the measure."

Arnold also asked Eisenhower to give him the details and inform him in advance of his request to CCS, so that he (Arnold) could support the proposal.

Eisenhower answered on January 23, 1944. Chandler, III, 1677.

bold enough to ignore the targeting priorities set by the Air Ministry. And he held a personal bitterness: the replacement of Eaker by Spaatz. Eaker had lived in Harris' house and the two had become close friends.

Spaatz, on the other hand, was in a peculiar position, with a strong personal bond to Eisenhower from West Point days and the Mediterranean, but also a disciple of Major General William ("Billy") Mitchell, the patron saint of the independent strategic air forces. (Like others, Spaatz resented the second "A," for Army, in the initials USAAF.) But Spaatz had been flexible enough to volunteer his heavy bombers to hit tactical targets at Salerno, and his loyalty to Eisenhower would transcend his doctrinaire side. In the meantime Spaatz, a gregarious, poker-playing sort, could not understand Leigh-Mallory's reserve, and he mistook it for hostility, which he returned in kind. Spaatz and Harris had doctrine in common, and they buried their differences in insisting they would never serve under Leigh-Mallory. If they were to come under Eisenhower's control, therefore, it would have to be through Tedder, never through the AEF air commander.

The key man in the air question turned out to be Tedder, a member of both the bomber and tactical schools. With no set doctrine to fetter him, Tedder had seriously studied the question of the air role in support of invasion. In the Mediterranean he had recruited the services of an Oxford professor, Solly Zuckerman, who as a medical doctor had at first been interested in analyzing the effects of bombing on the human body. Under Tedder's sponsorship, Zuckerman's studies had expanded to encompass all phases of air targeting, anatomical being only one. Taking into account that the surrender of Pantelleria (before Sicily) had been brought about by bombardment alone (which Zuckerman considered a special case), he had concluded that the most effective way of assisting a contested amphibious landing was to isolate the battlefield by destruction of railroad marshaling yards. Tedder became convinced by Zuckerman's arguments and adopted them as his own. Thus the name "Transportation Plan," a concept which attracted few followers outside of Zuckerman and Tedder in early 1944.

Tedder's new idea caused Harris and Spaatz to band together against the common threat. For this Transportation Plan, as they saw it, would constitute an interference with Harris' desire to hit cities at night with saturation bombing and Spaatz's aim to destroy German oil production.[38]

One phase of the air effort, however—the destruction of the German Air Force (POINTBLANK)—was contested by nobody. Eisenhower, above all, insisted that a considerable portion of the Allied air effort be

[38] Even Spaatz agreed that attacks on petroleum could make no contribution to the safety of OVERLORD in the first stages, as the time was too short.

devoted to this mission, for the destruction of the Luftwaffe was as important to OVERLORD as to the others—even more so.

Despite conflicts of doctrine and personality, optimism about finding a reasonable solution for the air support of OVERLORD continued to prevail. While a scheme was being drawn up, air priorities were directed by a committee comprised of Portal, Harris, Spaatz, Leigh-Mallory, and Tedder, with emphasis on POINTBLANK. Since unresolved questions required compromises, each command was relatively free to concentrate on its own preferred targets. On February 15, however, a confrontation erupted in a meeting called by Leigh-Mallory. Feelings previously hidden came out in the open when both Harris and Spaatz virtually declared war on the Transportation Plan. Two days later Harris wrote a memo saying that Leigh-Mallory's requirements (to execute Tedder's plan) could not be met. Harris felt, he wrote, "compelled to disavow any responsibility for the consequences. . . ."[39]

This turn of events brought Tedder, representing Eisenhower, to send a memorandum to Portal on February 22:

I am afraid that having started as a confirmed optimist I am steadily losing my optimism. . . . The immediate cause . . . is the fact that the examination of plans . . . has shown no signs so far of producing any constructive results. *I am more and more being forced to the unfortunate conclusion that the two strategic forces are determined not to play.* Spaatz has made it abundantly clear that he will not accept orders, or even co-ordination, from Leigh-Mallory, and the only sign of activity from Harris's representatives has been a series of adjustments to the records of their past bombing statistics, with the evident intention of demonstrating that they are quite unequipped and untrained to do anything except mass fire raising on very large targets.[40]

A week later, on February 29, the Prime Minister came out openly opposing Eisenhower's control of the bomber forces. He was not willing, he now declared, to turn over all forces in the United Kingdom to the Supreme Commander of a task force operating from British soil. The whole British Bomber, Fighter, and Coastal Commands had other functions.[41] The British would assist OVERLORD with these three commands, but the Combined Chiefs should retain control. To Churchill sup-

[39] Zuckerman, *From Apes to Warlords,* p. 233.
[40] Tedder to Portal, February 22, 1944, quoted in Tedder, p. 508. Italics supplied.
[41] Churchill did not define these other functions. They included his secret project of building up the Maquis in the South of France, east of the Rhône, possibly as a device to eliminate the need for ANVIL. See Arthur Layton Funk, Manuscript.

port of OVERLORD should be cooperative. There was no need to place everything under SHAEF command.

Eisenhower, as might be expected, found Churchill's attitude unacceptable.[42] He would settle for nothing short of complete operational control of all Bomber Command and the U. S. Strategic Forces. And he had no intention even of submitting his final bombing plan to the Combined Chiefs. The battle lines were drawn.

The crisis in the discussion came during the first week in March. Tedder had just received a report from Zuckerman confirming that Leigh-Mallory's bombing of rail centers had been more effective than senior British officers had admitted. He gave the report to Portal, who, impressed, decided to put the matter to a test. Since the alleged inability of the heavy bomber to hit marshaling yards had stood at the crux of Harris' arguments, Portal ordered Harris to hit the railway center at Trappes, southwest of Paris, on the night of March 6. When the reports of the mission came in, Portal was startled by the success: the important yards were put out of action for an estimated month. Harris was not pleased to learn how good his crews were.

Once again Portal's broad approach exerted itself, and he was willing to admit that Tedder's Transportation Plan had been proven feasible. During the first ten days of March, therefore, Portal and Tedder met almost every day, discussing not only the plan itself but some way to surmount Churchill's reluctance to comply with Eisenhower's demands. Fortunately, Portal now was in a position of unusual influence, having been designated as the representative of the entire Combined Chiefs for this problem. Convinced that the Transportation Plan would work—and that success of the plan went hand in glove with Eisenhower's demand for control—he wrote to Churchill:

> Neither General Eisenhower *nor I* consider that the assignment of strategic bombers for the purpose of executing either plan . . . can be made on the basis of allocating a *proportion of the forces,* or of their effort, to him.[43]

Brooke, recently converted, gave Portal his support.

The Prime Minister finally gave in while pretending not to—by exacting a promise that POINTBLANK would not be downgraded. The CCS, he said, should assign Eisenhower "such uses of the strategic bombers that might be necessary to execute the OVERLORD and POINTBLANK plans, [the CCS] retaining the right to impose additional tasks."[44] Once

42 Tedder, p. 511.
43 Ibid., p. 514. Italics supplied.
44 Ibid.

OVERLORD was firmly established, beyond the possibility of catastrophic disaster, this directive should be reviewed. The arrangement was quite satisfactory to Eisenhower.

By mid-March the CCS formalized Churchill's memorandum and confirmed Eisenhower's control, theoretically effective on their own approval of an over-all air plan. Though that approval would surely come at a meeting on March 25, with Portal acting for the CCS, Eisenhower was impatient:

> The actual air preparatory plan is to be the subject of a formal meeting on this coming Saturday, March 25, between Portal, Spaatz, Harris, Leigh-Mallory, Tedder and myself.
>
> If a satisfactory answer is not reached I am going to take drastic action and inform the Combined Chiefs of Staff that *unless the matter is settled at once I will request relief from this Command.*[45]

No such drastic action was even remotely required, for in the meeting the Transportation Plan was adopted. Eisenhower, having been given the power to direct the strategic air forces, considered the matter settled.[46]

But the difficulties did not quite end there. Possibly in an effort to sabotage a decision that had been made on a military basis, Harris then went to the War Cabinet with a startling estimate of French casualties that would result from the bombing of rail yards: Between 80,000 and 100,000 would be killed. The War Cabinet was gravely concerned when it met on April 3, for civilian casualties in these numbers would hit a raw nerve. The British were anxious for a friendly postwar France, and such a slaughter could rekindle bitterness. The 1940 episode at Mers-el-Kebir could not be repeated.

This new argument promoted new discussion, which Eisenhower could not bring to a conclusion, though he tried. The French people, he pointed out, were now slaves and only a successful OVERLORD could free them. The Transportation Plan, necessary for success, was therefore essential to their very future. Further, he and Tedder severely doubted the estimate submitted by Bomber Command. Casualties could be reduced by sending warnings to the French to stay away from railroad yards. (Perhaps General de Gaulle could make broadcasts to the French.) In this argument

[45] Chandler, III, 1785. See also Eisenhower, *Crusade,* p. 222. Italics supplied.
[46] At this meeting Eisenhower decided on the Transportation Plan over targets to destroy enemy oil production. Exceptions to the decision were soon made, and Professor W. W. Rostow, who was involved, believes that Eisenhower made the decision without having been given all the alternatives. The matter of importance to this story is that Eisenhower now had the authority, regardless of later revisions on specific targets. See Rostow, *Pre-Invasion Bombing Strategy.*

Field Marshal Jan Christiaan Smuts tried to help, advising Churchill that "political considerations must yield to the military arguments."[47]

Still the War Cabinet continued to worry. Finally on April 15 Eisenhower, on his own, ordered Spaatz and Harris to put the Transportation Plan into effect regardless of possible protests from the British Government. The order was obeyed; the Prime Minister and War Cabinet did not dispute his action.

But as the pre-OVERLORD air operations continued, Churchill never ceased to fret, and he badgered Portal with daily memoranda demanding figures on French losses. The reports were favorable. Only a week or so before D-Day only 6,000 civilians had been killed—way short of the 80,000 estimate. Further, the temper of the population was reported rising because of the lack of food, transportation, and electricity—but the French were blaming the Germans.

Finally the War Cabinet drew up a paper for submission to President Roosevelt. In it they balanced an estimated 10,000 French casualties before D-Day against the success of OVERLORD. Roosevelt replied categorically that military considerations must dominate.

> However regrettable the attendant loss of civilian lives is, I am not prepared to impose from this distance any restriction on military action by the responsible commanders that in their opinion might militate against the success of "Overlord" or cause additional loss of life to our Allied forces of invasion.[48]

Churchill was relieved, for the responsibility was now shared equally by the President and him.[49]

And yet only a week before D-Day Churchill was still inquiring of Tedder: "Have you exceeded the 10,000 limit [of French civilian casualties]?"[50]

[47] Tedder, p. 530.
[48] Roosevelt to Churchill, April 11, 1944. Quoted in Churchill, V, 530.
[49] Churchill later wrote:

> The sealing-off of the Normandy battlefield from reinforcement by rail may well have been the greatest direct contribution that the bomber forces could make to "Overlord." The price was paid.

Ibid.
[50] Ibid., p. 715.

CHAPTER XXV

THE APPROACH OF D-DAY

By no means did these controversies regarding ANVIL and the Transportation Plan reflect the over-all atmosphere in SHAEF, the British Government, or the operational units. Rather these issues should be viewed as growing pains, the correction of deficiencies and adjustment of national differences in command concept. And while these wrinkles were being ironed out, the heavy bombardment of the European continent was continuing; 150,000 men per month were flowing from the United States to Britain; and top commanders—Eisenhower, Montgomery, Bradley, Tedder, and others—were spending the bulk of their time out of London. Eisenhower made it a point to inspect every unit scheduled to be available as of D-Day. This meant visits to twenty U.S. and fifteen British (and British-affiliated) divisions. Sometimes an inspection would require an overnight trip by train, particularly to see American units on the Salisbury Plain.

In this activity Montgomery once again proved that he was a master of soldier psychology. His leadership techniques were particularly suited to British soldiers, but he was immensely popular with American troops as well, for he engendered confidence. His cocky assurance might infuriate American commanders, but his reputation for never having met defeat grew among the troops of both nationalities. Obviously Montgomery would take no chances. This characteristic may result in lost opportunities, but the willingness to take "calculated risks" is more admired among generals than among foot soldiers.

*

On February 22, the same day that Tedder was writing his first pessimistic memo to Portal, the British officers who had served in the Mediterranean made a gesture that overwhelmed the normally matter-of-fact

General Eisenhower. At a small dinner at Claridge's, a group of his former comrades presented Eisenhower with a silver salver, a copy of the
kind used at the time of George II. The signatures of John Cunningham,[1]
Tedder, Gale, Strong, Macmillan, and thirteen others, all British, were
inscribed on the back. Andrew Cunningham's warm words left Eisenhower speechless, so much so that the next day he penned the admiral an
apology: "The occasion itself and the sentiment it represented all cli-
maxed by the extraordinary generosity of the language you used in speaking of me, came so nearly overwhelming me that my only recourse was to
keep a very tight hold on myself."[2]

Eisenhower then placed the tray in a London bank, insured it, had it
photostated, and sent the photostat to his wife. When Butcher entered Eisenhower's bedroom the morning after the ceremony, he found the
Supreme Commander polishing a thumbprint from the salver with a
bedsheet.

*

Prime Minister Winston Churchill set aside much of his preoccupation
with Italy when he returned to London from Marrakech in mid-January.
Immediately he set up a weekly committee, over which he himself would
preside, to keep OVERLORD preparations under constant surveillance.
The mechanism itself was already in existence; the Anti-U-boat Warfare
Committee, long established, could now be placed on a two-monthly basis,
since the sea lanes had been clear since the previous May. The facilities
and staff of the committee could serve Churchill's new purpose.

Among the foremost preoccupations of the "Former Naval Person" was
the progress of the artificial harbors which were designed to convert two
of the Normandy beaches into major ports. The concept had originated
with Lord Louis Mountbatten's Combined Operations Headquarters earlier in the war, and its evolution had resulted in a series of exotic
code names such as MULBERRY, GOOSEBERRY, PHOENIX, and
WHALE. The Royal Navy intended to construct one full-scale harbor
(MULBERRY) in the British sector at Arromanches (GOLD Beach)
and one in the American sector at St. Laurent (OMAHA Beach). Each
of these two harbors would include an inner breakwater of sunken ships
(GOOSEBERRY) and an outer breakwater of huge hollow concrete
blocks (PHOENIX), which were to be towed across the Channel and
sunk in place. The remaining three beaches (UTAH, JUNO, SWORD)
were to be provided with one lesser harbor of sunken ships (GOOSE-
BERRY) each. Thus each of the five landing beaches would have some
sort of harbor, two with the major MULBERRY and three with the

---

[1] Admiral Sir John H. D. Cunningham, who succeeded Andrew Cunningham as
naval commander in the Mediterranean.
[2] Chandler, III, 1747–48. See Eisenhower, *Letters to Mamie*, 169–70.

smaller GOOSEBERRY. Twenty-three floating pier units (WHALES) would be distributed among the two MULBERRIES and three independent GOOSEBERRIES. The GOOSEBERRIES, consisting of ships which could come into place under their own power, could be installed almost at once. Construction of the line of PHOENIXES, however, would take about fourteen days. Altogether the Admiralty would use 8,000 yards of block ships consisting of 74 vessels, with the Arromanches MULBERRY eventually developing a capacity of 12,000 tons per day. The Americans would provide nearly half the ships to form the GOOSEBERRIES. The PHOENIXES were conceived and provided completely by the Royal Navy.

Just before one of his sessions with the Weekly Committee Churchill received word that labor for the construction of these harbors was tight; British manpower could not supply the effort. To remedy the shortage he called Eisenhower and asked if the Americans could supply a few engineer units. Eisenhower replied that they could: the units would be available the next day.

"Oh, no, General," Churchill exclaimed. "I just want you to *offer* them, not *send* them!"

The discussion that evening got nowhere at first. Every official claimed that he had scraped the bottom of the barrel. Churchill then turned to Eisenhower and in a rather plaintive voice asked how this shortage would affect operational plans—if so, did he have any ideas? Eisenhower took the cue: the harbors were absolutely essential, he said, and if he must he would volunteer a number of well-trained American engineer battalions.

Churchill turned back to the committee:

"It seems that our Commander-in-Chief is the only one present who can produce a constructive idea. We thank him for his generous offer, especially since its acceptance would interfere with his necessary military program. But, gentlemen, are we to admit that the British Government is so helpless, so unimaginative, so lacking in determination that it cannot, except by calling on our allies, carry out a simple duty that it took upon its own shoulders? I want each person here to make another survey of his organization and expect to meet with you here tomorrow, when we shall produce a solution to this problem, which I refuse to admit is unsolvable."

The next day Churchill called Eisenhower to say that the project was once more on the track.[3]

By no means did the Prime Minister confine himself to matters such as the MULBERRIES, GOOSEBERRIES, WHALES, and PHOENIXES,

[3] Eisenhower, Unpublished Manuscript, pp. 65–67.

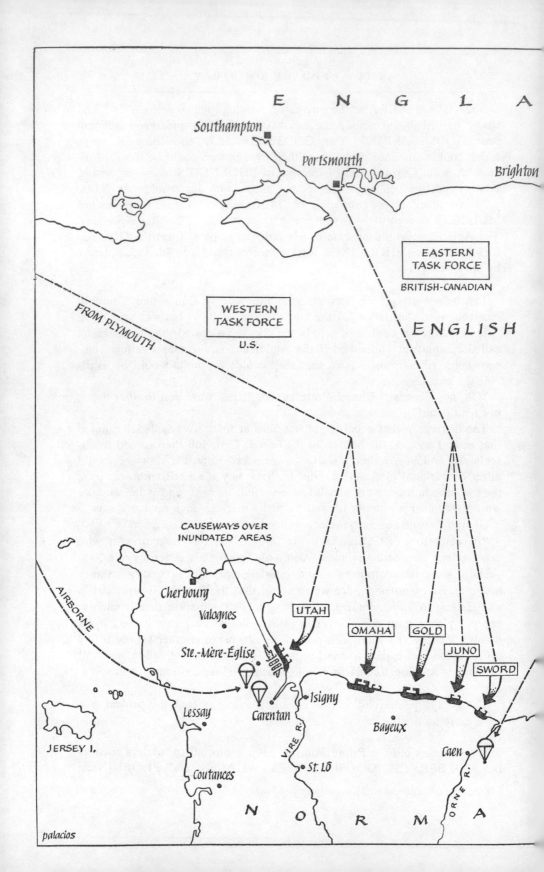

E N G L A

Southampton

Portsmouth

Brighton

EASTERN
TASK FORCE

BRITISH-CANADIAN

FROM PLYMOUTH

WESTERN
TASK FORCE

U.S.

ENGLISH

CAUSEWAYS OVER
INUNDATED AREAS

AIRBORNE

Cherbourg

Valognes

UTAH

Ste.-Mère-Église

OMAHA

GOLD

JUNO

SWORD

Isigny

Lessay

Carentan

Bayeux

JERSEY I.

VIRE R.

Caen

ORNE R.

Coutances

St. Lô

N O R M A

palacios

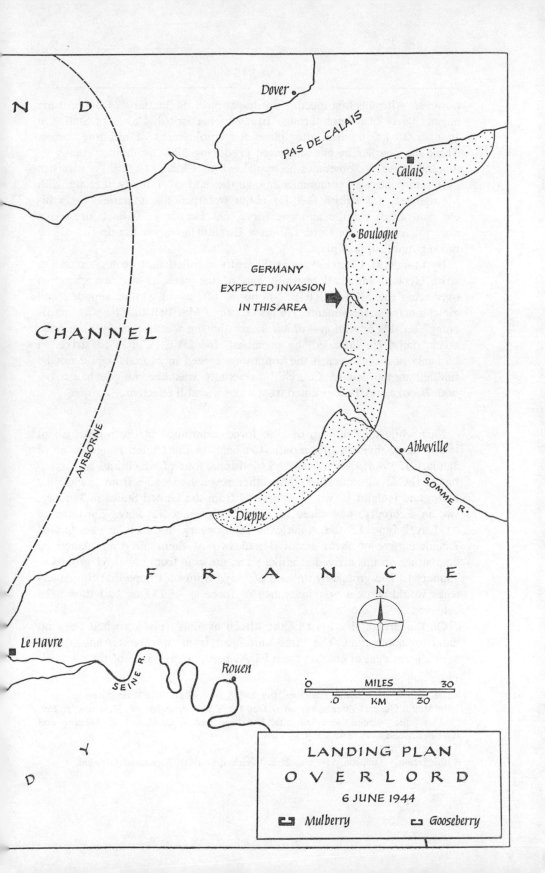

N D

Dover

PAS DE CALAIS

Calais

Boulogne

GERMANY
EXPECTED INVASION
IN THIS AREA

CHANNEL

AIRBORNE

Abbeville

SOMME R.

Dieppe

F R A N C E

N

Le Havre

SEINE R.

Rouen

MILES
0   30
0   30
KM

D   Y

LANDING PLAN
O V E R L O R D
6 JUNE 1944

Mulberry   Gooseberry

however. After his first meeting on that subject on January 24, he sent his normal flurry of memos through Ismay to the British Chiefs of Staff. On January 28 he inquired after plans for employment of airborne forces. Three days earlier he had suggested producing 300 "swimming" tanks by the end of April. Sometimes he by-passed his Chiefs of Staff. As Minister of Defense he was communicating at the end of January directly with Montgomery (as British C-in-C) about waterproofing materials for vehicles and airlift for the airborne force. On February 20 he addressed a note to the First Sea Lord (Andrew Cunningham) on the details of the naval gunfire support plan.

By March 11 Churchill was sufficiently satisfied that he took pains to write General Marshall assuring him of the care he was exercising in overseeing the MULBERRIES, airborne lift, naval gunfire support, and air command arrangements. He also assured Marshall that he was "hardening" on this operation—which meant that he was becoming more optimistic daily. He intended, he promised, for OVERLORD to strike "if humanly possible" even if the conditions agreed in Moscow could not be fulfilled to the letter.[4] Churchill personally was becoming exhausted—both Brooke and Tedder noted it—but he was still effective.

*

Meanwhile the build-up of U.S. forces continued at the rate of about two or three divisions per month. On hand in the United Kingdom as of January 1, 1944, were eleven U.S. divisions, four of which had seen combat in the Mediterranean.[5] (The other seven had come from the United States and Iceland.) Two more arrived from the United States in January, two in February, and three in April. One came in May. Thus, as of "Y-Day," June 1,[6] the Americans had twenty divisions in the United Kingdom, five of them armored and two of them airborne. American combat air groups arrived at a like pace, growing from about 51 groups in January to 102 groups by the end of May.[7] Stimson's hope that the Americans would show a preponderance of force as of D-Day had thus been achieved.

On the British side most of the fifteen available divisions had been on hand for some time. The three units sent from the Mediterranean[8] had seen a great deal of combat from El Alamein on. Because of their experi-

---

[4] Churchill, V, 590.
[5] The 1st and 9th Infantry Divisions, the 2nd Armored, and the 82nd Airborne.
[6] On May 8 General Eisenhower set D-Day for Y plus 4, or June 5. Harrison, p. 269. "Y-Day," the "official" invasion date, had been agreed as May 1 at Teheran and later postponed to June 1. See p. 416 above.
[7] Matloff, p. 407.
[8] 50th Infantry Division, 51st Highland Division, and 7th Armoured Division.

ence, these veteran divisions were all to be used on D-Day or shortly thereafter.

*

On April 7, 1944, a briefing for presentation of plans was held at General Montgomery's headquarters in St. Paul's School. The Prime Minister was present, as well as a succession of speakers—Montgomery, Ramsay, Leigh-Mallory, Bradley, Dempsey—and even the corps commanders summarized the situation in their respective spheres of responsibility. This was, to put it simply, Monty's day and, as the ground commander for the assault, he covered the surface operations with confidence and precision. Fifty-five German divisions, he estimated, would be available in the West on D-Day, and against them the Americans and British, in approximately equal numbers, could put ashore 7⅔ divisions on D-Day, 10⅓ by D plus 1, 14⅔ by D plus 4, and 24 by D plus 20. By three months after D-Day all the 35 Allied divisions presently in Britain would be on the Continent.[9] On the surface this methodical build-up would appear to be risky in view of the German strength in France. The numbers emphasize that the Allies were relying on air supremacy to immobilize German divisions, thus cutting their real effectiveness to a fraction of the fifty-five that showed on the map. No wonder that the Transportation Plan, formally put into effect a week later by General Eisenhower, was so important!

*

Two days after the meeting at St. Paul's, Eisenhower asked Brooke for help on a touchy but urgent issue: censorship of foreign diplomatic communications. Reports of military movements from embassies and legations in London could well, when put together, compromise one of the two major pieces of information Hitler lacked: the timing of the assault. (The other was the place.) Movements to embarkation areas could not be hidden, and if the Germans were to be alerted, the risk of defeat would be greater. Since the matter of censorship was delicate—and since it was the British Government that was going to absorb the protests—Eisenhower elected to approach Churchill and the government through formal channels, the Combined Chiefs. Brooke, as chairman of the British Chiefs of Staff Committee, would be the logical contact.

Brooke took care of the matter, and the War Cabinet finally ruled that foreign diplomatic representatives would no longer be permitted to send or receive uncensored communications; no diplomatic couriers could now leave the United Kingdom. Churchill and the Cabinet, much as they

[9] "Brief Summary of Operation 'OVERLORD' as affecting the Army, given as an address to all General officers of four field armies in LONDON on 7th April, 1944." Personal Papers of DDE, 1916–52.

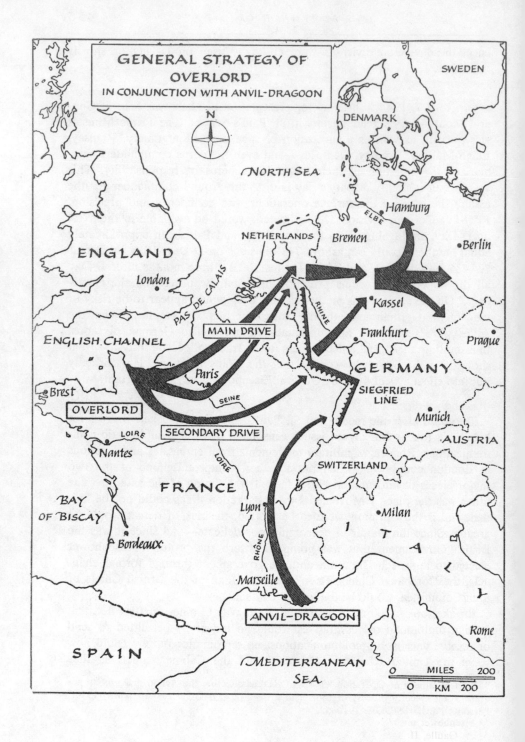

GENERAL STRATEGY OF
OVERLORD
IN CONJUNCTION WITH ANVIL-DRAGOON

N

SWEDEN

DENMARK

NORTH SEA

Hamburg

ENGLAND

NETHERLANDS   Bremen   •Berlin

London

PAS DE CALAIS

ELBE

MAIN DRIVE   •Kassel

ENGLISH CHANNEL

RHINE   Frankfurt   •Prague

Paris   GERMANY

Brest   SEINE   SIEGFRIED
LINE

OVERLORD

SECONDARY DRIVE   •Munich

LOIRE   AUSTRIA

Nantes   SWITZERLAND

LOIRE

BAY
OF BISCAY   FRANCE

Lyon   •Milan

RHÔNE

Bordeaux   I T A L Y

Marseille

ANVIL-DRAGOON   •Rome

SPAIN

MEDITERRANEAN
SEA

MILES   200

KM   200

disliked the procedure, were willing to take their lumps.[10] Churchill notified Roosevelt of the action a week later.

One unexpected consequence of this censorship was the interruption of Allied efforts (particularly Eisenhower's and Churchill's) to secure cooperation from General Charles de Gaulle, still in Algiers, the man they considered the key to future relations with the people of Metropolitan France—in other words, the Resistance. De Gaulle, on learning that his messages to and from London would be censored, retaliated by ceasing all communications with his recently designated liaison officer, General Pierre Koenig. Better no communications, De Gaulle reasoned, than communications subject to the Anglo-Americans. Koenig now had no purpose in being there.

This development constituted a considerable setback to Eisenhower, who later admitted that his role of middle man in French politics was the "most acutely annoying" problem[11] he had to face in planning OVERLORD. The situation was doubly irritating because Eisenhower was, as De Gaulle recognized, the best friend the FCNL had in London. A long time before, Eisenhower had concluded that De Gaulle was the man he would have to deal with in order to marshal the maximum cooperation in the French Resistance. To improve relations, he had visited De Gaulle on December 30, 1943, the day before leaving Algiers, and during the meeting had admitted to poor judgment in his initial opposition to De Gaulle and his committee. As far as he was concerned, Eisenhower said, he would recognize no power in France other than De Gaulle's "in the practical sphere."[12]

But Eisenhower's authority in this area was limited—perhaps he had exceeded it in Algiers—and while in Washington during January he had done his best to persuade the Combined Chiefs and the President of the need to work closely with De Gaulle. His efforts had been blocked when Cordell Hull intervened with some pious "hopes" that the French would "subordinate political activity to the necessity for unity in ejecting and destroying the enemy." The very vagueness of this terminology had nearly negated previous understandings, and nobody in the United States seemed to agree that De Gaulle was the only realistic "vehicle" to deal with.

On arrival in London, even before the first formal SHAEF meeting at Norfolk House, Eisenhower had tried to bring the French political situation into focus back in Washington via a message to General Marshall:

It is essential that immediate crystallization of plans relating to civil affairs in Metropolitan France be accomplished. This requires confer-

10 Chandler, III, 1814. Pogue, *Supreme Command*, p. 163.
11 Eisenhower interview, quoted in Pogue, *Supreme Command*, p. 140.
12 De Gaulle, II, 545.

ences with properly accredited French authorities. I assume, of course, that such authorities will be representatives of the Committee of Liberation. . . .[13]

When President Roosevelt got around to answering this plea some two months later, he relented a little on the tight rein he had been holding, allowing Eisenhower to "consult" with anyone he chose on French civil affairs. If that choice should be the French National Committee, he went on, Eisenhower should require guarantees which together would ensure that the committee would do nothing to entrench itself pending a free choice of the French people.[14]

De Gaulle, on learning of the President's message, particularly as it gave Eisenhower an option as to whom he should consult with, was unimpressed: "Actually, the President's intentions seemed to me on the same order as Alice's Adventures in Wonderland."[15] He likewise observed that the Allies could find "no other troops than those of which I [De Gaulle] was the leader.[16] Nevertheless, De Gaulle was not worried, as he continued to place stock in Eisenhower's previous views. Based on what he construed as Eisenhower's and Churchill's intentions, therefore, De Gaulle had sent Koenig to London, only to have him cut off from all communications almost on arrival.

Churchill and Eisenhower together, therefore, decided they would have to bring De Gaulle to London before D-Day. Churchill would carry the initiative.

*

In the early morning of Friday, April 28, Eisenhower, Tedder, and Bradley arrived in London on Eisenhower's private train. They were returning from a discouraging visit to Slapton Sands, an invasion training beach between Dartmouth and Plymouth on the southern coast of England, where they had observed the practice landing of the U. S. 4th Infantry Division, the unit scheduled to land on UTAH Beach. Happily no enemy air or submarine attacks had attacked the ships involved in the exercise—which had happened before—but otherwise there was little to be encouraged about. The landing had been delayed, and the landing craft and cargoes of floating tanks had been left milling around. The first assault wave of infantry had been launched from transport vessels eight miles out—much too far. While waiting, the crowded and unprotected

[13] Eisenhower to Marshall for CCS, January 19, 1944, quoted in Chandler, III, 1667.
[14] See Ambrose, *The Supreme Commander*, p. 380. Also *FRUS, 1944,* III, 675–76.
[15] De Gaulle, II, 544.
[16] Ibid., p. 545.

amphibious tanks had been easy targets for a determined enemy on shore.[17] Furthermore, Eisenhower had found his closest friend, Major General "Gee" Gerow, commanding U. S. V Corps,[18] showing signs of fatigue, his spirits in need of bolstering.

On the way from the station to Widewing, Eisenhower dropped in at Whitehall to check with the Prime Minister, who needed further reassurances regarding the bombing of the French railroad yards. After a short visit he went on. At Widewing, Eisenhower found a telegram from General Marshall, who had received word through the American press—though Eisenhower had not—that Lieutenant General George S. Patton, Jr., had done it again. After repeatedly promising to be cautious in his public utterances, Patton had spoken at a British service club emphasizing the value of American-British friendship which would become so important because it was the destiny of America, Great Britain, and Russia to "rule the world."

Apparently Patton's supposedly off-the-record remarks had been incorrectly reported and his reference to the Russians had been omitted. When news of the speech reached the United States, the Republican members of Congress had risen in wrath, demanding to know what a general was doing invading politics. Patton was still under a cloud because of the soldier-slapping incident and he had not, since then, done anything to restore his status with the public. Marshall now asked Eisenhower to reconsider whether to retain Patton for command of the Third Army.

Once again Eisenhower seriously pondered Patton's future. He was not so concerned by Patton's statement as by his failure to fulfill a personal promise. In Eisenhower's office, Patton wept and offered to resign his commission. He was ashamed, he said, of the embarrassment he had caused the Supreme Commander.

An ordinary commander would have been finished on the spot, but Patton was a known quantity—an officer imbued by the spirit of mobile warfare, with a rare thirst, a lust, for pursuit. Eisenhower, even now visualizing a rapid sweep across France with Patton in command of Third Army, decided with some trepidation to retain him; he so informed Marshall. Marshall agreed, even though Patton's indiscretion had forced him to withdraw an entire Regular Army promotion list then before Congress.

*

Under the auspices of Supreme Headquarters a final conference was held, again at St. Paul's School, on Monday, May 15. King George VI,

[17] Butcher, pp. 528–29.
[18] Scheduled for OMAHA Beach.

the Prime Minister, Field Marshal Smuts, the British Chiefs of Staff, and all the commanders for OVERLORD were on hand. After Eisenhower opened the proceedings, the King spoke briefly, as did the Prime Minister, who remarked (as he had written to Marshall) that he was "hardening" toward the enterprise.[19]

Churchill's optimism was welcome, as his confidence of success had sometimes been a cause for doubt. Only a week before Churchill had tearfully said to Eisenhower, "I am with you in this thing to the end and, if it fails, we will go down together."[20] And at another time, when Eisenhower foresaw the Allied armies knocking on the border of Germany by the end of 1944, the Prime Minister had said, "General, if by the coming winter you have established yourself with your thirty-six Allied divisions firmly on the Continent, and have the Cherbourg and Brittany peninsulas in your grasp, I will proclaim this operation to the world as one of the most successful of the war. . . . And if, in addition to this, you have secured the port at Le Havre and freed beautiful Paris from the hands of the enemy, I will assert the victory to be the greatest of modern times."[21]

Three days later, on May 18, a Nazi broadcast declared that the invasion would come "any day now."

As suspense grew, Churchill dealt with his anxiety, as after Pearl Harbor and the fall of Mussolini, with stepped-up personal activity. At the meeting of May 15 he noted with shock that, twenty days after the landing, 189,000 vehicles would be landed in France along with the 902,000 personnel, amounting to one vehicle for every 4.77 men. Dismayed, he sent a message to Montgomery and four days later turned up at St. Paul's School. It was all Montgomery could do to prevent the Prime Minister from demanding changes in the loading plans, which were now far too complete to permit revision. Some feelings were involved, and Churchill was particularly annoyed when the story reached the public that Montgomery had threatened to resign.[22]

Tensions among all Allied participants continued to mount. The atmosphere on the streets and in the pubs of London, Bournemouth, and the hamlets of the Salisbury Plain portended that the time was near. German broadcasts—that of May 18 was only one—confirmed that the advanced state of Allied preparations was known to Hitler's intelligence.

[19] Eisenhower was unaware that Churchill had used the same expression, "hardening," in a letter to Marshall on March 11. Churchill, V, 615. *Crusade,* p. 245.
[20] Ehrman, *History of the Second World War,* Vol. V, *Grand Strategy,* pp. 574–75, quoted in Bryant, *Triumph in the West,* p. 203.
[21] Eisenhower, *Crusade,* p. 243. Churchill never contested this quote.
[22] Churchill, V, 616.

Allied counterintelligence was exceedingly sensitive to every small possibility of a leak.

Some frightening incidents occurred. A tense moment came when twelve copies of the OVERLORD order, the most secret information of World War II, blew out the window of the British War Office, scattering among a crowd of pedestrians. Everyone in the office, from top staff officers to clerks, raced down the stairs. Eleven copies were recovered easily, but the twelfth was not, and losing one was as bad as losing all. Two agonizing hours passed. Finally a stranger walked up to the British sentry on the opposite side of the street and handed him the missing copy. The man's identity was never known.

At about this time an American major general committed an indiscretion at a cocktail party by indicating that the Allies would be in France before June 15. It was not a passing comment; he offered to take bets that he was correct. On hearing of this action Eisenhower relieved the offender of his position, stripped him of his rank, and sent him home. The officer, a friend and West Point classmate, pleaded for clemency on the basis of his outstanding service with the air forces. Eisenhower wrote back that his past record was the only thing that kept him from going before court-martial.[23] Fortunately his indiscretion never reached enemy intelligence.

Sometimes innocent matters caused grave concern. One victim was Mr. Leonard Sidney Dawe, a physics teacher from Leatherhead, Surrey, who was noted for the tricky crossword puzzles he published daily in the London *Telegraph*. On his return from walking his dog on Sunday morning, June 3, he was astonished to be greeted by two concerned Scotland Yard men. Politely they began to interrogate. In five puzzles during the previous month a suspicious array of secret words had appeared: NEPTUNE (code name for the naval phase), OMAHA, UTAH (the two American beaches), and MULBERRY. OVERLORD had appeared just the day before. It turned out that the alarmed man was innocent. Some of the puzzles had been made up six months before.[24]

The timing and location of OVERLORD were naturally the counterintelligence matters of paramount importance, as anyone could tell that an invasion was afoot. The exact day of attack, it was hoped, would be concealed by the restrictions on diplomats and by the quarantine of the south of England. But active measures were necessary to protect the location of the landings. Nazi intelligence had correctly narrowed the possibilities to two, the Pas de Calais and Normandy; the Pas de Calais was the more obvious, with the Channel at its narrowest; the terrain firm for tanks; and

---

[23] Chandler, III, 1848.
[24] This story comes from Cornelius Ryan, *The Longest Day*, pp. 46–48.

nearly three hundred miles closer to the German border than Normandy. But the obvious aspect of Calais made Hitler suspicious. He would continue to grant it top priority in defenses but those in Normandy must catch up. In both areas he feverishly constructed obstacles designed to make any landing costly: tetrahedrons, dragon's teeth, underwater mines, and pillboxes.

The vital need now was to keep the Nazis convinced that the landings would be made at Calais.

Allied intelligence was going to great lengths. A dummy headquarters, designated First U. S. Army Group (FUSAG), had been set up in southeast England, and radios in that area produced a volume of traffic on the air equal that produced by any headquarters in the United Kingdom. Persons known to be double agents were fed information about FUSAG and its proximity to Dover. The plan for aerial bombardment—the Transportation Plan—was also slightly modified. And even the assignment of George Patton (whose presence had been noticed by everyone in the United Kingdom) was used to deceive the enemy. Secondary landings might be made elsewhere, the stories went, but the great main effort, under Patton, still waited near Dover. These deception plans were elaborate. But who could tell whether they would be effective?

By May 28, 1944, all detailed plans were finished. Senior commanders were informed of their landing locations. Subordinate commanders were told only that D-Day would be June 5. Troops and sailors were sealed in their ships or at their camps and assembly points. Mail was impounded and private messages forbidden. The entire south of England had been sealed off from the rest of the country. On June 1 the Allied Naval Commander, Admiral Sir Bertram Ramsay, assumed control of operations in the Channel.

There was now no turning back.

CHAPTER XXVI

OK, WE'LL GO

T he south of England was sealed; plans had been made in minute detail: 4,000 ships, 176,000 men, and 20,000 vehicles were ready to go. It now appeared that the only decision left would be the solitary one to be made by the Supreme Commander, the exact date and time. Not many options were available, as only a handful of days a month would meet all the necessary conditions. The tides would have to be low at dawn to permit clearing out of underwater obstacles. Some moonlight would guide the airborne troops, but there should not be too much; a full moon might reveal the mighty fleet as it crossed the Channel. Three days, June 5, 6, and 7, fitted these requirements. After that the next feasible date would be June 19, but a delay until then would be nearly unbearable. Prudence would dictate the fifth of June, the first of the options—which Eisenhower had taken—weather permitting. There was little to do now but wait until the early morning of Sunday, June 4, when Eisenhower would meet with his staff and commanders to confirm whether June 5 would be the actual day.

On Tuesday, May 30, with all seemingly set, Eisenhower was approached by Leigh-Mallory, who had never reconciled himself to the risks accompanying the planned airborne drops at the base of the Cotentin Peninsula. Leigh-Mallory had studied photos of the German defenses: anti-aircraft guns, flooded areas, and anti-glider obstacles in the open fields. (Field Marshal Erwin Rommel, now German commander in northwest Europe, had been thorough.) The losses in the 82nd and 101st Airborne Divisions, Leigh-Mallory feared, might reach a figure of 70 percent in glider strength and 50 percent in the paratroopers. Their tactical power destroyed, the two airborne divisions would have no effect on the battle.

Leigh-Mallory's strong conviction came as a shock to Eisenhower. The air marshal was, after all, an acknowledged expert in tactical air operations and known for his sincerity and his personal courage. If his frightening estimates should prove correct, then Eisenhower would have on his own conscience the destruction of two divisions, not to mention the fate of the attack across UTAH Beach. For the success of the U. S. 4th Division, landing on UTAH Beach, depended on the ability of the airborne divisions to secure the vital causeways that provided exits across the flooded area.

Though Leigh-Mallory's warning had been turned down by Montgomery, the problem was now Eisenhower's alone. Having been in close touch for months with those immediately responsible, particularly Bradley and Ridgway,[1] he now saw no point in asking anyone for further advice. To protect Leigh-Mallory, however, he asked the air marshal to submit his views on paper. If his prediction should turn out to have been correct, Leigh-Mallory would be exonerated. Eisenhower then sat down to review the matter from the beginning:

> If I should cancel the airborne operation, then I had either to cancel the attack on Utah Beach or I would condemn the assaulting forces there to even greater probability of disaster than was predicted for the airborne divisions.
>
> If I should cancel the Utah attack I would so badly disarrange elaborate plans as to diminish chances for success elsewhere and to make later maintenances perhaps impossible. Moreover, in long and calm consideration of the whole great scheme we had agreed that the Utah attack was an essential factor in prospects for success. To abandon it really meant to abandon a plan in which I had held implicit confidence for more than two years.[2]

Satisfied in his mind, Eisenhower telephoned Leigh-Mallory. The operation would go as planned, he said, and he would confirm the call in writing. The decision was final.[3]

The tension was not confined to Leigh-Mallory. Everybody felt it. Even Brooke, only indirectly responsible as a member of the CCS, was worrying as if he were carrying the burden himself:

[1] Major General Matthew B. Ridgway, commander of the 82nd Airborne Division, was considered the senior American airborne expert.
[2] *Crusade*, p. 247.
[3] Leigh-Mallory was the first to express his relief when the operation's success was finally established.

It is very hard to believe that in a few hours the cross-Channel invasion starts. I am very uneasy about the whole operation. At the best it will fall so very far short of the expectation of the bulk of the people, namely all those who know nothing about the difficulties. At the worst it may well be the most ghastly disaster of the whole war. I wish to God it were safely over.[4]

The Prime Minister was no less concerned, and he continued to submerge himself in the details of matters which properly belonged to subordinates. Now he decided that, as Minister of Defense, he could escape the suspense by boarding a cruiser and personally witnessing the gunfire and the landings. He made arrangements directly with Admiral Ramsay and was all set to embark on H.M.S. *Belfast* during the late afternoon before D-Day. Ramsay's conscience, however, got the best of him and he disclosed Churchill's plans to the Supreme Commander.

Eisenhower immediately protested. It was not in the interest of the war effort, he contended, that the Prime Minister should run such unnecessary risks. Perhaps to allow Churchill to cancel his plans without losing face, Eisenhower pointed out that his exposing himself to enemy fire would only add to his own, Eisenhower's, burdens, which were already enormous.

This attitude struck Churchill as presumptuous. He was, after all, Prime Minister, head of one of the governments under whom Eisenhower was serving. In that position, how could he be less "burdened"? And even as Supreme Allied Commander, Eisenhower had no authority to interfere with the composition of one of His Majesty's ships. If Churchill were to be assigned as a crew member of the *Belfast,* Eisenhower would have no say about it. Eisenhower had to agree.

At this point, however, King George VI entered the disagreement. At first he was enthusiastic, as he saw himself participating likewise, but he was soon dissuaded by his advisers. And perhaps with only a touch of unconscious jealousy, the King asserted that, if the Sovereign could not go, then neither could his Prime Minister. Churchill was not persuaded.

Their exchange of viewpoints when they met on June 1 approached a confrontation. It was not right, the King repeated, for Churchill to go if he himself could not—and the admiral did not really want either of them. Churchill retorted that he was going in the exercise of his duties as Minister of Defense. The King then played another card: the Prime Minister had no authority to leave the United Kingdom without his own permission. Churchill's reply: on one of His Majesty's ships one is not out of the United Kingdom. The King returned to Buckingham Palace without having carried the day.

[4] Bryant, *Triumph in the West,* pp. 205–6.

The next day Churchill received a final written plea, signed "Your very sincere friend, George R. I." Having now reached the point where continued resistance would be defiance, Churchill wrote a note which was the model of formality:

> I must defer to Your Majesty's wishes, and indeed commands. It is a great comfort to me to know that they arise from Your Majesty's desire to continue me in your service. Though I regret that I cannot go, I am deeply grateful to Your Majesty for the motives which have guided Your Majesty in respect of
>
> Your Majesty's humble and devoted servant and subject,
>
> WINSTON S. CHURCHILL[5]

*

On the night of June 1 Eisenhower left Widewing for his Advance Command Post at Portsmouth. Here in Southwick House, the home of the Royal Navy War College, elaborate communications had been set up for both him and Montgomery. The main building was impressive and comfortable, with high ceilings, a feeling of space, and comfortable leather seats and couches. Desiring privacy, however, Eisenhower elected to stay with his personal staff about a mile down a dirt road in the woods below, where he could be alone in his trailer. Except for dinner with Montgomery and his commanders the night of June 2—and for the morning and evening meetings—Eisenhower remained isolated.

At 4:00 A.M. Sunday, June 4, Eisenhower climbed into his jeep under a black and starry sky. The vehicle jostled its way up to Southwick House. Already some of the slower-moving naval formations had put to sea.

Now the weather reports, which had begun to be discouraging the previous morning, had become critical. Group Captain J. M. Stagg, the thin, solemn Scot who headed the meteorological team, predicted low clouds, high winds, and formidable wave action. Landing on June 5, the next day, would be exceedingly hazardous. Eisenhower looked around the room and asked each commander for his opinion. Montgomery was in favor of going ahead despite all; Ramsay was neutral. But the two airmen, Tedder and Leigh-Mallory, warned flatly that under these conditions the air forces could not do their job. Regretfully, Eisenhower postponed the invasion for at least a day. The convoys at sea would have to be called back —not easy, but it could be done. The armada would be forced to wait in port for at least a day.

Eisenhower returned to his trailer in the woods. There he spent a fretful day pacing up and down, talking to associates, but expecting no answers.

---

[5] Churchill, V, 623–24. This elaborates considerably on Eisenhower's version, *Crusade*, p. 251.

Merrill ("Red") Mueller, one of the four correspondents assigned to Eisenhower's headquarters, spied him at one point outside his trailer, hands in pockets. Noticing Mueller, Eisenhower beckoned. "Let's take a walk, Red." After Mueller caught up, Eisenhower seemed hardly to notice. For one time this normally aggressive reporter felt it only decent to avoid intruding on his thoughts.[6]

That afternoon of June 4 Churchill and Smuts came to Eisenhower's trailer. They had been by the day before, but this time they brought a third visitor, Charles de Gaulle, who had just arrived in London from Algiers on Churchill's plane—at the Prime Minister's urging and with Roosevelt's reluctant concurrence.

Churchill, Smuts, and Eden had already been conferring with De Gaulle aboard a private train parked nearby, and the atmosphere had almost from the start been acrimonious. Churchill had apologized for the French casualties caused by Allied bombing of rail yards, but De Gaulle's interest lay elsewhere. In particular he was still smarting from the fact that British censorship on diplomatic messages had included his own FNCL. He had, in fact, refused to come to London until assured that he would be free to send encoded messages back to Algiers.

Churchill, like Eisenhower, felt that his ability to deal with De Gaulle was crippled by Roosevelt's adamant attitude toward any recognition of the French Committee.[7] But when De Gaulle insisted that his own authority should have been recognized as far back as the previous September, Churchill retorted angrily. The British and Americans were going to risk the lives of hundreds of thousands of men in liberating France, he said, and if forced to choose between Roosevelt and De Gaulle he would always take the former. At an impasse, Churchill hoped that Eisenhower could do better with *le grand Charlie* than he.[8]

At his camp, Eisenhower, though preoccupied, took pains to treat De Gaulle cordially. With Churchill and Smuts fading into the background, he took De Gaulle into his map van and explained the OVERLORD plan in some detail. De Gaulle was impressed with the Anglo-American "gift for planning"[9] and was unusually diffident when Eisenhower asked his advice on the decision now foremost in his mind. Insisting on the obvious, that the decision was completely Eisenhower's, De Gaulle said that he, personally, would not wait, as the "atmospheric dangers" seemed less than delay for several weeks, which would "prolong the moral tension of

6 Ryan, p. 59.
7 Roosevelt's pique had been brought to a fury when the French National Committee of Liberation (FNCL) had changed its name on May 26 to the "Provisional Government of the French Republic."
8 Churchill, V, 628–30.
9 De Gaulle, II, 558.

the executants [sic] and compromise secrecy."[10] Eisenhower had of course come to the same conclusion, but De Gaulle was glad to be consulted.

Eisenhower had one earnest request, that De Gaulle make a radio broadcast to the French people to be put on the air immediately following Eisenhower's. He showed De Gaulle his text, already recorded. De Gaulle quickly decided that he could not comply, for the text of Eisenhower's talk was manifestly unsatisfactory. First of all De Gaulle disliked France's being part of a list which included Norway, Belgium, Holland, and the Netherlands. But even more he disliked the tone. Whereas Eisenhower's words to the other nations placed himself in the capacity of a military commander, with no reference to their politics, the attitude changed when the text addressed the French, instructing the nation to "carry out orders" and directing everyone to continue to "fulfill his functions." It made no reference to the authority of De Gaulle and his Provisional Government. These aspects sounded to De Gaulle as if the Anglo-Americans were planning to occupy and run France.[11]

If he spoke immediately after Eisenhower, De Gaulle concluded, he would appear to be endorsing this distasteful message, which had undoubtedly been drafted in Washington. Always pragmatic—even his recalcitrance was calculated—De Gaulle simply acknowledged that he could not stop the Anglo-Americans from acting on their miscalculations, but he would not help them either.

The visit was over. De Gaulle returned with Churchill to his train but refused to accompany him and Smuts back to London. He preferred, he declared, to motor back to the city with his French officers.[12]

*

The second scheduled meeting at Southwick House was held at 10:00 P.M., June 4. News of the fall of Rome had come in, a good omen. This time Stagg gave a slight smile and a hope of some twenty-four to forty-eight hours of acceptable weather, which should arrive the next evening. Again Eisenhower listened to all views and then sat by himself, head bowed, hands folded. "It looks as if there's nothing else to do," he mumbled. But though the slow convoys had departed once more, the die was not yet cast.

After a fretful few hours, involving little if any sleep, Eisenhower and his top officers were back at Southwick House again. It was now 4:00 A.M., June 5, 1944. The weather was behaving as Stagg had predicted,

10 Ibid.
11 Ibid., p. 559.
12 De Gaulle later made a broadcast after the landings. It was aired at a time separate from the messages of Eisenhower and the other governments in exile.

cloudy with drizzle and high winds. What would have happened if the invasion had gone ahead under these conditions? But Stagg reiterated his predictions for June 6. To lend confidence, he called attention to this bad weather which he had predicted under clear skies.

Again Eisenhower polled his commanders. Montgomery, as always, was anxious to go. Ramsay was content. Even Tedder and Leigh-Mallory were more hopeful.

Alone, Eisenhower sat in silence. If June 7 should be as bad as June 5—which was likely—the consequence would be an unthinkable delay until June 19. To some of the witnesses Eisenhower sat silent for two minutes; others said four. Eisenhower remembered forty-five seconds. Finally he looked up.

"OK, we'll go."

BIBLIOGRAPHY

CORRESPONDENCE, LETTERS TO AUTHOR

Carter, Lieutenant General Marshall S., USA (Retd.), May 3, 1979, February 22, 1981.

Clark, General Mark Wayne, USA (Retd.), February 17, 1976.

Cook, Captain Charles O., Jr., USN (Retd.), November 20, 1978, October 1, 1978, October 30, 1978, July 19, 1979.

Emerson, William R., Director, Franklin D. Roosevelt Library, Hyde Park, NY, October 9, 1975.

Getz, Ambassador John I., December 3, 1980.

Hamblin, Michael, July 16, 1979.

Harmon, Major General Ernest N., USA (Retd.), June 29, 1978.

Huston, Major General John W., Chief, Office of Air Force History, February 14, 1980.

Lemnitzer, General Lyman L., USA (Retd.), February 26, 1977, March 2, 1979.

McCarthy, Brigadier General Frank, AUS (Retd.), February 13, 1981, February 19, 1981. (*See also* Interviews.)

Murphy, Ambassador Robert, January 21, 1976, February 23, 1976.

Pogue, Dr. Forrest C., April 3, 1979.

Rostow, Professor Walt W., August 7, 1979.

Tyson, Victor E., August 25, 1975, January 6, 1976. (*See also* Interviews.)

Vanderkloot, Robert, October 29, 1976.

MINUTES AND MEMORANDA
NATIONAL ARCHIVES, WASHINGTON, DC
(Chronological order)

ARCADIA *Conference*

Memorandum by the British Chiefs of Staff (*W.W.-1*) *American-British Strategy,* dated 22 Dec 1941.

Notes of Meeting at the White House with the President and the British Prime Minister Presiding, dated 23 Dec 1941, George C. Marshall.

Memorandum by the British Chiefs of Staff (*revised by the U. S. Chiefs of Staff*) *American-British Strategy,* dated 31 December 1941. (ABC4/CS-1.)

QUADRANT *Conference*

JCS 105th Meeting. *Minutes of Meeting Held in Room 2104, Château Frontenac Hotel,* on Monday, 16 August 1943, at 1000.

SEXTANT *Conference*

Minutes of First Plenary Meeting, Held at Villa Kirk, on Tuesday, 23 November 1943 at 1100.

Minutes of Second Plenary Meeting, Held at Villa Kirk, on Wednesday, 24 November 1943 at 1100.

Conferences at St. Paul's School, London

Brief Summary of Operation OVERLORD as affecting the Army, Given as an address to all general officers of the four field armies in LONDON on 7th April, 1944. (Personal Papers of DDE 1916–52, Box 75, "Montgomery.")

Address given by General Montgomery to the general officers of the four field armies on 15 May 1944. (Personal Papers of DDE 1916–52, Box 75.)

INTERVIEWS
(including numerous informal conversations)

Blumenson, Martin (telephone), 1978, numerous visits.

Bohlen, Charles E., October 29, 1973, 4:00 P.M., Georgetown, Washington, DC.

Carter, Marshall S., April 25–26, 1981, Colorado Springs, CO.

Eisenhower, Dwight D., circa fall, 1945, Frankfurt, Germany, numerous conversations.

Eisenhower, Milton, numerous visits, Baltimore, MD.

Funk, Arthur Layton, University of Florida, Gainesville, FL, numerous visits, March–June 1976.

Gruenther, Alfred M., Washington, DC, December 24, 1978.

Harriman, W. Averell, September 30, 1975, Georgetown, Washington, DC.

McCarthy, Frank, Phoenixville, PA, October 4, 1968, numerous visits and correspondence.

Tyson, Captain Victor E., U. S. Merchant Marine Academy, Kings Point, NY, August 19, 1975. Subsequent correspondence.

BOOKS

Adams, Henry H. *Harry Hopkins: A Biography.* New York: G. P. Putnam's Sons, 1977.

Alexander, Field Marshal, Earl of Tunis, *The Alexander Memoirs: 1940–1945,* edited by John North. London: Cassell & Co., 1962.

Ambrose, Stephen E. *The Supreme Commander: The War Years of General Dwight D. Eisenhower.* Garden City, New York: Doubleday & Co., 1970.

————., with Immerman, Richard H. *Ike's Spies: Eisenhower and the Espionage Establishment.* Garden City, New York: Doubleday & Co., 1981.

Armstrong, Anne. *Unconditional Surrender.* New Brunswick, New Jersey: Rutgers University Press, 1961.

Army Times Editors. *D-Day: The Greatest Invasion.* New York: G. P. Putnam's Sons, 1969.

Arnold, Henry H. *Global Mission.* New York: Harper & Brothers, 1949.

Ayer, Frederick J., Jr. *Before the Colors Fade: Portrait of a Soldier, George S. Patton, Jr.* Boston: Houghton Mifflin, 1964.

Beesly, Patrick. *Very Special Intelligence.* New York: Doubleday & Co., 1978 (first published in Great Britain by Hamish Hamilton, Ltd., 1977).

Bellush, Bernard. *He Walked Alone: A Biography of John Gilbert Winant.* The Hague, Paris: Mouton & Co., N.V., Publishers, 1968.

Bishop, Jim. *FDR's Last Year*. New York: William Morrow & Co., 1974.

Blumenson, Martin. *Kasserine Pass*. Boston: Houghton Mifflin Co., 1967.

──────. *The Patton Papers: 1940–1945*. Boston: Houghton Mifflin Co., 1974.

Bohlen, Charles E. *Witness to History, 1929–1969*. New York: W. W. Norton & Co., 1973.

Bradley, Omar N. *A Soldier's Story*. New York: Henry Holt & Co., 1951.

Brown, Anthony Cave. *Bodyguard of Lies*. New York: Harper & Row, 1975.

Bryant, Arthur. *Triumph in the West: Based on the Diaries and Autobiographical Notes of Field Marshal the Viscount Alanbrooke*. St. James Place, London: Collins Clear Type Press, 1959.

──────. *The Turn of the Tide: A History of the War Years Based on the Diaries of Field Marshal Lord Alanbrooke, Chief of the Imperial General Staff*. Garden City, New York: Doubleday & Co., 1957.

Burns, James MacGregor. *Roosevelt: The Lion and the Fox*. New York: Harcourt Brace & World, 1956.

──────. *Roosevelt: The Soldier of Freedom, 1940–1945*. New York: Harcourt Brace Jovanovich, 1970.

Butcher, Captain Harry C., USNR. *My Three Years With Eisenhower: The Personal Diary of Captain Harry C. Butcher, USNR, Naval Aide to General Eisenhower, 1942–1945*. New York: Simon & Schuster, 1946.

Campbell, James. *The Bombing of Nuremberg*. Garden City, New York: Doubleday & Co., 1974.

Chalfont, Alun. *Montgomery of Alamein*. Paterson, New Jersey: Atheneum, 1976.

Chandler, Alfred E., Jr., ed. *The Papers of Dwight David Eisenhower: The War Years*, Vols. I, II, and III. Baltimore and London: Johns Hopkins Press, 1970.

Churchill, Winston S. *The Second World War*. Boston: Houghton Mifflin Co., 1948–53. Vol. II, *Their Finest Hour*, 1949; Vol. III, *The Grand Alliance*, 1950; Vol. IV, *The Hinge of Fate*, 1950; Vol. V, *Closing the Ring*, 1951.

──────. *Memoirs of the Second World War* (abridgment), abridgment by Denis Kelly. New York: Bonanza Books, A Division of Crown Publishers, 1978.

Clark, Mark W. *Calculated Risk*. New York: Harper & Brothers, 1950.

Coffey, Thomas M. *Decision Over Schweinfurt: The U. S. Air Force Battle for Daylight Bombing*. New York: David McKay Co., 1977.

Cooper, Sir Alfred Duff (Viscount Norwich). *Old Men Forget.* New York: E. P. Dutton & Co., 1954.

Crozier, Brian. *De Gaulle.* New York: Charles Scribner's Sons, 1973.

Davis, Kenneth S. *Experience of War: The United States in World War II.* Garden City, New York: Doubleday & Co., 1965.

————. *Soldier of Democracy: A Biography of Dwight Eisenhower.* New York: Doubleday, Doran & Co., 1945.

Deane, John R. *The Strange Alliance.* New York: Viking Press, 1947.

De Gaulle, Charles. *The Complete War Memoirs of Charles de Gaulle.* New York: Simon & Schuster, 1964. Vol. II, *Unity, 1942–1944,* translated by Richard Howard.

Edwards, Kenneth. *Operation Neptune.* London: Collins, 1946.

Ehrman, John. *History of the Second World War.* London: Her Majesty's Stationery Office, 1956. Vol. V, *Grand Strategy.*

Eisenhower, Dwight D. *At Ease: Stories I Tell to Friends.* Garden City, New York: Doubleday & Co., 1967.

————. *Crusade in Europe.* Garden City, New York: Doubleday & Co., 1948.

————. *Letters to Mamie,* edited and with commentary by John S. D. Eisenhower. Garden City, New York: Doubleday & Co., 1978.

Eisenhower Foundation. *D-Day: The Normandy Invasion in Retrospect,* Foreword by Omar N. Bradley. Lawrence, Kansas: University Press of Kansas, 1971.

Eisenhower, John S. D. *The Bitter Woods.* New York: G. P. Putnam's Sons, 1969.

————. *Strictly Personal.* Garden City, New York: Doubleday & Co., 1974.

Eisenhower, Milton S. *The President Is Calling.* Garden City, New York: Doubleday & Co., 1974.

Esposito, Colonel Vincent J. ed. *The West Point Atlas of American Wars.* New York: Frederick A. Praeger, 1959.

Essame, H. *Patton: A Study in Command.* New York: Charles Scribner's Sons, 1974.

Farago, Ladislas. *Patton: Ordeal and Triumph.* New York: Ivan Obolensky, 1964.

Feis, Herbert. *Churchill-Roosevelt-Stalin: The War They Waged and the Peace They Sought.* Princeton, New Jersey: Princeton University Press, 1957.

Fields, Alonzo. *My 21 Years in the White House.* New York: Coward-McCann, 1960.

Funk, Arthur Layton. *Charles de Gaulle, The Crucial Years: 1943–1944*. Norman, Oklahoma: University of Oklahoma Press, 1959.

———. *The Politics of TORCH*. Lawrence, Kansas: University Press of Kansas, 1974.

Garland, Albert N., and Smythe, Howard. *Sicily and the Surrender of Italy*. Washington, D.C.: Office of the Chief of Military History, Department of the Army, 1965.

Grigg, John. *1943—The Victory That Never Was*. New York: Hill & Wang, A Division of Farrar, Straus & Giroux, 1980.

Guingand, Major General Sir Francis de. *Generals At War*. London: Hodder & Stoughton, 1964.

Gunther, John. *D-Day: What Preceded It; What Followed*. New York and London: Harper & Brothers, 1943, 1944.

———. *Eisenhower: The Man and the Symbol*. New York: Harper & Brothers, 1951, 1952.

———. *Roosevelt in Retrospect: A Profile in History*. New York: Harper & Brothers, 1950.

Hancock, William K. *Smuts: The Fields of Force*. Cambridge: Cambridge University Press, 1968.

Harmon, Ernest. *Combat Commander*. Englewood Cliffs, New Jersey: Prentice-Hall, 1970.

Harriman, W. Averell, and Abel, Elie. *Special Envoy to Churchill and Stalin: 1941–1946*. New York: Random House, 1975.

Harris, Sir Arthur. *Bomber Offensive*. New York: Macmillan Co., 1947.

Harrison, Gordon A. *Cross-Channel Attack*. Washington, D.C.: Office of the Chief of Military History, Department of the Army, 1951.

Hein, Al, narrator. *D-Day, The Invasion of Europe*. New York: American Heritage Publishing Co., 1962.

Horrocks, Brian. *Corps Commander*. New York: Charles Scribner's Sons, 1978.

———. *Escape to Action: An Autobiography*. New York: St. Martin's Press, 1960.

Hull, Cordell. *The Memoirs of Cordell Hull,* Vol. II. New York: Macmillan Co., 1948.

Hunt, Frazier. *The Untold Story of Douglas MacArthur*. New York: Devin-Adair Co., 1954.

Irving, David John Caldwell. *The Trail of the Fox*. New York: E. P. Dutton & Co., 1977.

Ismay, General Hastings, Lord. *The Memoirs of General Lord Ismay*. New York: Viking Press, 1960.

Jablonski, Edward. *A Pictorial History of the World War II Years*. Garden City, New York: Doubleday & Co., 1977.

Jackson, W. G. F. *The Battle for North Africa: 1940–1943*. New York: Mason Charter, 1975.

Jenkins, John Gilbert. *Chequers: A History of the Prime Minister's Buckinghamshire Home*. Oxford, London, Edinburgh, New York, Toronto, Sydney, Paris, Braunschweig: Pergamon Press, 1967.

King, Ernest J., and Whitehill, Walter Muir. *Fleet Admiral King: A Naval Record*. New York: W. W. Norton & Co., 1952.

Kraus, René. *Old Master: The Life of Jan Christiaan Smuts*. New York: E. P. Dutton & Co., 1944.

Lash, Joseph P. *Eleanor and Franklin: The Story of Their Relationship Based on Eleanor Roosevelt's Private Papers*. New York: W. W. Norton & Co., 1971.

————. *Roosevelt and Churchill, 1939–1941: The Partnership That Saved the West*. New York: W. W. Norton & Co., 1976.

Leahy, Fleet Admiral William D. *I Was There: The Personal Story of the Chief of Staff to Presidents Roosevelt and Truman Based on His Notes and Diaries Made at the Time*. New York, London, Toronto: Whittlesey House, McGraw-Hill Book Co., 1950.

Lewin, Ronald. *Montgomery as Military Commander*. New York: Stein & Day, 1971.

Lewis, William Roger. *Imperialism At Bay: The United States and the Decolonization of the British Empire, 1941–1945*. New York: Oxford University Press, 1948.

Loewenheim, Francis L., Langley, Harold D., and Jonas, Manfred, eds. *Roosevelt and Churchill: Their Secret Wartime Correspondence*. New York: Saturday Review Press/E. P. Dutton & Co., 1975.

Longmate, Norman. *The G.I.'s*. New York: Charles Scribner's Sons, 1976.

Lyon, Peter. *Eisenhower: Portrait of the Hero*. Boston, Toronto: Little, Brown & Co., 1974.

MacArthur, Douglas. *Reminiscences*. New York: McGraw-Hill Book Co., 1964.

McCann, Kevin. *Man from Abilene*. Garden City, New York: Doubleday & Co., 1952.

MacDonald, Charles B. *The Mighty Endeavor*. New York: Oxford University Press, 1969.

McKeough, Michael, and Lockridge, Richard. *Sergeant Mickey and General Ike*. New York: G. P. Putnam's Sons, 1946.

Macmillan, Harold. *The Blast of War, 1939–1945*. New York: Harper & Row, 1968.

Maisky, Ivan. *Memoirs of a Soviet Ambassador, The War: 1939–1943,* translated from the Russian by Andrew Rothstein. New York: Charles Scribner's Sons, 1968.

Manchester, William. *American Caesar: Douglas, MacArthur, 1880–1964*. Boston and Toronto: Little, Brown & Co., 1978.

Marshall, Katherine Tupper. *Together: Annals of an Army Wife*. New York, Atlanta: Tupper & Love, 1946.

Matloff, Maurice. *Strategic Planning for Coalition Warfare: 1943–1944*. Washington, D.C.: Office of the Chief of Military History, Department of the Army, 1959.

————, and Snell, Edwin M. *Strategic Planning for Coalition Warfare: 1941–1942*. Washington, D.C.: Office of the Chief of Military History, Department of the Army, 1953.

Mellor, William Bancroft. *Patton: Fighting Man*. New York: G. P. Putnam's Sons, 1946.

Middlebrooke, Martin. *Convoy*. New York: William Morrow & Co., 1977.

————. *The Nuremberg Raid*. New York: William Morrow & Co., 1974.

Monnet, Jean. *Jean Monnet Memoirs,* translated by Richard Mayne. New York: Doubleday & Co., 1978.

Montgomery of Alamein, Viscount Bernard Law. *The Memoirs of Field Marshal The Viscount Montgomery of Alamein, K.G.* Cleveland and New York: World Publishing Co., 1958.

Moran, Lord (Sir Charles Wilson). *Churchill: The Struggle for Survival, 1940–1965, Taken from the Diaries of Lord Moran*. Boston: Houghton Mifflin Co., 1966.

Morgan, Lieutenant General Sir Frederick, K.C.B. *Overture to Overlord*. Garden City, New York: Doubleday & Co., 1950.

Morison, Samuel Eliot. *The History of the United States Naval Operations in World War II*. Boston: Little, Brown & Co., 1947–57. Vol. XI, *The Invasion of France and Germany, 1944–1945*.

Murphy, Robert. *Diplomat Among Warriors*. Garden City, New York: Doubleday & Co., 1964.

Mussolini, Benito. *Memoirs, 1942–1943,* translated by Frances Lobb, edited by Raymond Kalbansky. London: Weidenfeld & Nicolson, 1949.

Neal, Steve. *The Eisenhowers: Reluctant Dynasty*. Garden City, New York: Doubleday & Co., 1978.

Nelson, James, ed. *General Eisenhower on the Military Churchill: A Conversation with Alistair Cooke.* New York: W. W. Norton & Co., 1970.

Nicolson, Nigel. *Alex: The Life of Field Marshal Earl Alexander of Tunis.* London, Weidenfeld & Nicolson, 1973.

Panter-Downes, Mollie. *London War Notes.* New York: Farrar, Straus & Giroux, 1971.

Pendar, Kenneth. *Adventure in Diplomacy: Our French Dilemma.* New York: Dodd, Mead & Co., 1945.

Perkins, Frances. *The Roosevelt I Knew.* New York: Viking Press, 1946.

Pogue, Forrest C. *George C. Marshall.* New York: Viking Press, 1963–73. Vol. I (with the editorial assistance of Gordon Harrison), *Education of a General: 1880–1939;* Vol. II, *Ordeal and Hope: 1939–1942;* Vol. III, *Organizer of Victory: 1943–1945.*

———. *The Supreme Command.* Washington, D.C.: Office of the Chief of Military History, Department of the Army, 1954.

Reilly, Michael F. *Reilly of the White House,* as told to William J. Slocum. New York: Simon & Schuster, 1947.

Roosevelt, Eleanor. *This I Remember.* New York: Harper & Brothers, 1949.

Roosevelt, Elliott. *As He Saw It.* New York: Duell, Sloan & Pearce, 1946.

———, and Brough, James. *A Rendezvous With Destiny: The Roosevelts of the White House.* New York: Dell Publishing Co., 1975.

Rostow, Walt W. *Pre-Invasion Bombing Strategy.* Austin: University of Texas Press, 1981.

Rust, Kenn C. *The 9th Air Force in World War II.* Fallbrook, California: Aero Publications, 1977.

Ryan, Cornelius. *The Longest Day.* New York: Simon & Schuster, 1975.

Schofield, B. B. (Vice-Admiral, Royal Navy). *Operation Neptune.* Annapolis, Maryland: Naval Institute Press, 1977.

Shankland, Peter, and Hunter, Anthony. *Malta Convoy.* William Collins Publishers, 1961.

Sherwood, Robert E. *Roosevelt and Hopkins: An Intimate History.* New York: Harper & Brothers, 1950.

Smith, Walter Bedell. *Eisenhower's Six Great Decisions.* New York, London, Toronto: Longmans, Green & Co., 1956.

Smuts, J. C. *Jan Christiaan Smuts.* New York: William Morrow & Co., 1952.

Stagg, Group Captain J. M. *Forecast for Overlord.* New York: W. W. Norton & Co., 1971.

Stevenson, William. *A Man Called Intrepid.* New York: Harcourt Brace Jovanovich, 1976.

Stilwell, Joseph W. *The Stilwell Papers,* edited by Theodore White. New York: William Sloane Associates, 1948.

Stimson, Henry L., and Bundy, McGeorge. *On Active Service in Peace and War.* New York: Harper & Brothers, 1948.

Strawson, John. *The Battle for North Africa.* New York: Charles Scribner's Sons, 1969.

Strong, Major General Sir Kenneth. *Intelligence at the Top: The Recollections of a British Intelligence Officer.* Garden City, New York: A Giniger Book published in association with Doubleday & Co., 1969.

Summersby, Kay. *Eisenhower Was My Boss.* New York: Prentice-Hall, 1948.

Tedder, Lord (Sir Arthur William Tedder). *With Prejudice.* Boston, Toronto: Little, Brown & Co., 1966.

Thompson, R. W. *Churchill and the Montgomery Myth.* Philadelphia and New York: J. B. Lippincott Co., 1967.

————. *D-Day: Spearhead of Invasion.* New York: Ballantine Books, a Division of Random House, 1968.

Toland, John. *But Not in Shame: The Six Months After Pearl Harbor.* New York: Random House, 1961.

————. *The Rising Sun: The Decline and Fall of the Japanese Empire, 1936–1945.* New York: Random House, 1970.

Tompkins, Peter. *The Murder of Admiral Darlan: A Study in Conspiracy.* New York: Simon & Schuster, 1965.

Truscott, Lucian K., Jr. *Command Missions.* New York: E. P. Dutton & Co., 1954.

Tuchman, Barbara. *Stilwell and the American Experience in China, 1911–1945.* New York: Macmillan Co., 1970.

Tully, Grace. *F.D.R.—My Boss.* New York: Charles Scribner's Sons, 1949.

Wainwright, General Jonathan M. *General Wainwright's Story,* edited by Robert Considine. Garden City, New York: Doubleday & Co., 1946.

Wedemeyer, Albert C. *Wedemeyer Reports!* New York: Henry Holt & Co., 1958.

White, Theodore H. *In Search of History: A Personal Adventure.* New York, Hagerstown, San Francisco, London: Harper & Row, 1978.

Willkie, Wendell L. *One World.* New York: Simon & Schuster, 1943.

Winant, John Gilbert. *Letter from Grosvenor Square: An Account of a Stewardship.* Boston: Houghton Mifflin Co., 1947.

Winterbotham, F. W. *The Ultra Secret*. New York: Harper & Row, 1974.
Zuckerman, Solly. *From Apes to Warlords*. New York, Hagerstown, San Francisco, London: Harper & Row, 1978.

BOOKS ALSO REFERRED TO

Catton, Bruce C. *The Warlords of Washington*. New York: Harcourt, Brace & Co., 1948.

Krock, Arthur. *Memoirs, Sixty Years on the Firing Line*. New York: Funk & Wagnalls, 1968.

Mason, Philippe. *De Gaulle*. New York: Ballantine Books, 1972.

Mauriac, François. *De Gaulle*. Garden City, New York: Doubleday & Co., 1966.

Montague, Ewen. *The Man Who Never Was*. Philadelphia and New York: J. B. Lippincott Co., 1954.

Puryear, Edgar F., Jr. *Nineteen Stars*. Washington, D.C.: Coiner, 1971.

Ryan, Cornelius. *The Last Battle*. New York: Simon & Schuster, 1966.

Schoenbrun, David. *The Three Lives of Charles de Gaulle: A Biography*. New York: Atheneum, 1965.

Toland, John. *The Last 100 Days*. New York: Random House, 1966.

Truman, Harry S. *Memoirs*. Garden City, New York: Doubleday & Co., 1955. Vol. I, *Years of Decision*.

GOVERNMENT DOCUMENTS

Department of State, *Foreign Relations of the United States: Diplomatic Papers*. (All volumes in Washington, D.C.: U. S. Government Printing Office.) Vol. II, *1943;* Vol. III, *1944*.

Eisenhower, Dwight D. *Report by the Supreme Commander to the Combined Chiefs of Staff on the Operations in Europe of the Allied Expeditionary Force, 6 June 1944–8 May 1945*. Washington, D.C.: U. S. Government Printing Office, 1946.

UNPUBLISHED MATERIALS

Eisenhower, Dwight D. Manuscript, dated August 24, 1967.
———. Personal Papers, 1916–1952.

Funk, Arthur Layton. Manuscript, "Churchill, Eisenhower and the French Resistance," circa June 20, 1979.

Stoler, Mark Alan. "The Politics of the Second Front: American Military Planning and Diplomacy, 1941–44." Ph.D. dissertation, University of Wisconsin, 1971.

NEWSPAPERS

Anderson, David, New York *Times,* November 11, 1942 (article dated November 10, 1942, appeared November 11, 1942, saying that Darlan was "in Allied hands in Algiers").

Hurd, Charles, New York *Times,* December 9, 1941 (re: losses at Pearl Harbor).

The Times [London], November 11, 1942 (re: Churchill's "First Minister" speech).

MAGAZINES

Ambrose, Stephen E. "How Ike Was Chosen," *American History Illustrated,* November 1968.

Byrd, Martha H. "Six Minutes to Victory: The Battle of Midway," *American History Illustrated,* May 1975.

Churchill, Winston. "Victory in Africa: We Mean to Hold Our Own," *Vital Speeches of the Day,* November 15, 1942.

Lay, Lieutenant Colonel Beirne, Jr. "I Saw Regensberg Destroyed," *Saturday Evening Post*, November 3, 1943.

Storr, Anthony. "Winston Churchill's Black Dog," *Esquire,* January 1969.

INDEX

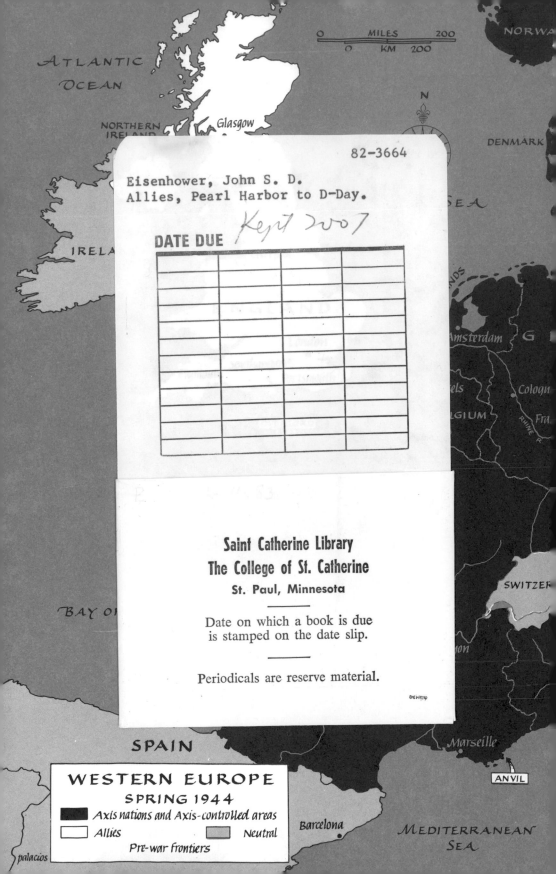